# WHEELER AND GOLDHOR'S PRACTICAL ADMINISTRATION OF PUBLIC LIBRARIES

*Wheeler and Goldhor's*

# PRACTICAL

# ADMINISTRATION

# OF PUBLIC

# LIBRARIES

COMPLETELY REVISED BY *Carlton Rochell*

**HARPER & ROW, PUBLISHERS,** New York
*Cambridge, Hagerstown, Philadelphia, San Francisco,*
*London, Mexico City, São Paulo, Sydney*

1817

*Designer: Sidney Feinberg*

Library of Congress Cataloging in Publication Data

Wheeler, Joseph Lewis, 1884–
    Wheeler and Goldhor's Practical administration of
public libraries.
    Bibliography: p.
    Includes index.
    1. Public libraries—Administration. I. Goldhor,
Herber, 1917–    joint author. II. Rochell, Carlton.
III. Title. IV. Title: Practical administration
of public libraries.
Z678.W5    1980    025.1    79–3401
ISBN 0–06–13601–4

81 82 83 84 10 9 8 7 6 5 4 3 2 1

For her encouragement, understanding, and patience,
this book is dedicated
to
Rebecca R. Rochell
Washington Square, January 1980

# Contents

# Contents

PART **III**
**Administration of Support Services**

# Acknowledgments

---

I am indebted most directly to Meredith Bloss, Hoyt Galvin, and Nancy Kranich, who read and reread various draft sections and contributed substantively to this revision. In addition, I am thankful to Kathryn Kazan and Nancy Hernandez, whose great assistance kept me organized throughout the task. I also acknowledge my editor at Harper & Row, Hal Grove, for his forbearing, sensitive, and unselfish support.

I was fortunate to have Joe Wheeler as a friend and mentor during my first years as a public library administrator. This revision was undertaken in his memory and I hope I have done him justice.

# Introduction to the Revised Edition

The wisdom and guidance of the first edition of *Practical Administration of Public Libraries* by Joseph L. Wheeler and Herbert Goldhor (New York: Harper & Row, 1962) has influenced countless students and practitioners for nearly two decades. It is hoped that this revision will continue that quality and tradition of practical service. This new edition has retained as much as possible of the basic content and character of the first edition. In order to take into account the many changes in the theory and management of public library services over the two decades, however, many chapters have been rewritten. The order of addressing the various topics has been modified so that the book moves from the general and theoretical to the more practical and specific aspects of administration.

Part I of this edition covers general administrative topics. In the early chapters, public library goals and priorities are outlined and a practical plan of action is presented—one that will meet the information needs of local citizens. These chapters have been almost entirely rewritten to reflect present thinking in the library community. The original chapter on administrative viewpoint has been substantially revised as well, bringing together material on general policy with practical techniques such as participative management. All aspects of personnel administration have been combined into a single revised chapter that includes the increasingly significant topic of collective bargaining. The chapters on organization and on finance and budgeting have incorporated new material on the planning process and current budgeting techniques.

Part II of this book focuses on services to the public. Materials selection and collection maintenance are treated here as components of the various public services: adult, young adult, children, reference and information, audiovisual, and branch. Also added to this section is material on serving the adult independent learner and on the information and referral function. The chapters on children's services and work with schools have been combined, as have those on publicity and community awareness. The chapter on nonprint materials incorporates a considerable amount of new content related to audiovisual services, taking into account the many changes that have taken place in recent years. In the last chapter of Part II, the extensive growth and development of public library systems and networks in recent years are discussed at considerable length. The importance of this section must not be underestimated, since interlibrary cooperation presents a substantial challenge and opportunity for the future success of the public library movement.

Part III of the book deals with support services. Order work and cataloging, binding and mending, and circulation control have been combined here into one chapter on technical services. In addition, this chapter incorporates substantial new materials on automation from an administrative and planning perspective. Also in this part, trends in the planning for remodeling and construction of library buildings have been introduced. Finally, recent efforts to analyze public library performance in user-oriented terms have been highlighted in the closing chapter on measurement and evaluation.

Since the publication of the first edition of this book, a multitude of trends and events have reshaped the delivery of public library services. This new edition highlights many of these developments of the last two decades and how they have influenced the administrative structure of public libraries. By press time, other forces were already determining new directions for the library's future. With a full agenda set for the 1980s that incorporates recommendations by the delegates to the first White House Conference on Library and Information Services, the next decade promises to be even more turbulent for libraries than the previous two. In order to implement the twenty-nine resolutions adopted by the conferees, public libraries will need to face such challenges as the elimination of illiteracy; the expansion of cooperative programs; the guarantee of full, free, and equal access to library resources for all; and the growth of information and referral services. Should public libraries fail to modify their goals and priorities to suit the demands of an age characterized by accelerated changes in information, technology and practices—changes that will undoubtedly be highlighted in a future edition of this book—the very survival of the public library as an institution will be jeopardized.

# Excerpts from the Introduction to the First Edition

This book is intended as a guide to management principles and their practical application in public libraries. It incorporates changing viewpoints and methods from a wide range of library situations, including those found in more than a hundred surveys and consulting projects. . . .

The book is addressed not only to library heads and their staffs, but to trustees, public officials—such as mayors, city managers, councilmen, and appropriating groups—and to laymen, all of whom need to understand what public libraries are supposed to accomplish and how they are managed and operated. It is intended also for library school instruction and in-service training.

Much of it applies to college and other types of library service, cutting across compartments and gulfs that set different types of library service too far apart. In their fundamentals all libraries partake of the same general purpose and the same principles and problems. . . .

The book is written also for department heads, first assistants, the heads of 4,000 branch libraries, and for all others having administrative or supervisory responsibilities. A majority of library school graduates find themselves within four or five years, if not immediately, in administrative or supervisory positions, but with little practical preparation. Whether administrators are born or made, it seems reasonable that they could do a still better administrative job by considering the condensed published experience of others.

After working and talking with hundreds of alert and ambitious assistants in many libraries, one must conclude that none gets the fullest satisfaction from his work unless he understands the principles of administration. If he has reasoned out why certain things are done as they are and how they might perhaps be done better, he can play a more enjoyable and rewarding part in the development of his own library. Conversely, this understanding may encourage some head librarians to share their administrative problems and decisions and the execution thereof with their colleagues more easily and fully.

Undoubtedly the small local public libraries will eventually combine into large systems to their administrative advantage. But it seems hardly logical that only this road can lead to administrative improvement, or that bigness will necessarily assure excellent administration, with expensive administrative specialists to be drawn on. The majority of libraries will at best continue independently for some years. Hundreds of existing branches of city systems are by no means as well managed as they could be, and as yet there has been little discussion of bringing the great proliferation of school libraries into larger systems except in the larger cities. No matter how large or small the library, and whether it be public, college, school or special library, it seems realistic to focus attention and study on developing administrative skills by all those whose present responsibility is to administer—the librarians, department and branch heads, and the numerous persons called on to instruct and guide the work of others.

The lessons from public, business, and industrial management make it clear that administrative skills can and should be developed now and every day on every level, including students and young assistants, most of them college graduates, eager to get their teeth into something more substantial than the ABCs of the administrative aspects of the profession in which they expect to spend some years, if not to carve a career. Some present teaching encourages the outdated assumption that there is a gulf fixed between the chief librarian and the beginner, assistant, clerical worker, page, or janitor, or between the trained and the untrained. This book rests on the conviction that books, reading and study are increasingly important, that library service is a fascinating and socially useful endeavor, to be shared equally by a whole circle of colleagues, each able with encouragement to cultivate the ability to see, to understand, and to participate.

JOSEPH L. WHEELER, *Benson, Vermont*
HERBERT GOLDHOR, *Urbana, Illinois*

*January 5, 1962*

# PART I

## PLANNING, MANAGEMENT, PERSONNEL, FINANCE, ORGANIZATION

# 1 Goals, Objectives, and Functions of the Public Library

## Some Citizen Views

"That is the library's purpose: to provide a good collection of good books. The library is a place where people for whatever reason can go and get books and take them home and read them and bring them back. It is as simple as that. . . . The libraries should do well what they are supposed to be doing. And they should try to do a better job of what they are charged with doing."[1]

"I think the public libraries are searching to try to feel where they function. . . . It's not only the libraries; it's outside the libraries. People who talk about libraries, or who fund libraries, or who are developing legislation for libraries; to some extent they want the libraries to be all things to all people. . . . My basic need is to get to information that I know has either been written and published, or recorded by some other means: the body of knowledge that mankind has produced."[2]

"The library planner views the public library as an institution that should achieve publicly desirable goals and should be planned so as to achieve these goals with a maximum number of desirable consequences, a minimum number of undesirable ones, and at the lowest possible cost. . . . Public libraries will have to be planned for the kinds of people in the particular service area. In middle-class neighborhoods, the contemporary library is desirable, with its emphasis on child, student, and nonfiction readers. . . . These people can accept the middle-class aura that surrounds the public library. In low-income areas, which are increasingly important in the changing metropolis, this middle-class library is unsatisfactory. Here a library is needed that invites rather than rejects the poorly educated person, with book stock, staff, and catalogue system that are designed to help him read. It should be geared to two types of readers: the small number who are already motivated . . .

3

and, more important, the much larger number of people who would like to read but are afraid or scornful of the ethos of the middle-class library. There is a third group of potential users here, adults who cannot read well but would like to learn. The library should teach these people or work with adult education agencies that could teach reading."[3]

## The Public Library Defined

To consider administration of the public library, it would be well to define it. Most works on the public library describe it in terms of goals, functions, services provided. Some are eloquent appeals for understanding the proper role of reading, others are dedicated to the proposition that library use will result in various kinds of individual and community benefits. The 1966 publication on standards of the American Library Association declares that "the public library provides materials and services. . . ." The standards statement is "a tool to be used rather than a statement of what a public library should be. Each library will differ from its neighbor, just as each community is different from all others."[4]

While it is true that there are differences among the more than 8,000 public libraries in the United States, there are certain common elements or components. The following definition is offered as a baseline, to incorporate those common elements.

The public library is an agency of local government: town, village, city, county, school district, and library district (and one state, Hawaii).

The public library, of whatever size or complexity, is composed of three basic elements:

1. A collection of books and other materials, printed and nonprinted. These materials are sometimes called resources.

2. Space for display and storage of materials and resources, for people to use and consult the collection, and for supportive operational and administrative requirements.

3. Personnel to select, organize, and maintain the collection, to administer and supervise its use, to help people in use of the collection, and to interpret the library's contents and relate them to individual need.

These are the basic elements of public library service. Differences among them will be found in size, complexity, emphasis, quality, specialization, and purpose.

Common elements in the operational procedures, the way the public library service works, are:

1. Free and open access to all regardless of residence. Even though the public library service is provided and paid for by a local political unit, anyone may walk into any public library anywhere in the country and, without

identification or even proof of need, consult the materials displayed on the open shelves and receive answers to requests for information. Borrowing books for use outside the library is limited to residents, but others may usually borrow under various kinds of reciprocal or fee arrangements.

2. Educational and social purposes constitute a major thread in the fabric of public library development. This is significant because it serves as the major justification for public support: the betterment of the individual and hence of the entire community.

The brief definition of what the public library is may therefore be expanded and stated in different terms. The public library is a community's agency for display, storage, and retrieval of information that will be in the individual or general interest. It is maintained as a municipal or publicly supported facility on the assumption that the diffusion of knowledge among the people will enhance the quality of life in the community. It is a basic tenet of democracy that for people to govern themselves and each other, they need to have information. A community that has a strong, active, and aggressive public library and information service, responsive to people's needs, will be a better place in which to live for all citizens, it is assumed, whether they use the library or not. Facts, information, ideas, flowing into the community through the individual interests, curiosity, and intellectual inquiries of some people will have a generally beneficial effect upon the decisions that are made affecting the welfare of all citizens.

## Functions

Public library statements of function have been prolific over the years. The most recent official statement by the Public Library Association, a division of the American Library Association, was adopted by the Public Library Association in January 1979.

The statement begins by describing four major social needs "demanding a new institution." The four needs listed are: runaway social change, exponential increase in the record, total egalitarianism, and depletion of natural resources. Under the heading "Needed Response" the statement sets forth that:

If one were to invent an information agency to respond to the social needs of today, that new agency would need to perform the following services:

1. Provide access to the human records of the past—factual, imaginative, scientific, and humanistic—partly through its own collections and partly through an effective network linking all collections in the region, state, nation, and the world.

2. Organize this human record so that access can be made to it from a myriad of directions allowing not only the facts but also the wisdom in the record to be retrieved. The agency would facilitate cross connections within the record, among many disciplines, literary forms, and periods of history.

3. Collect, translate, and organize the human record on all intellectual levels in many packages, print and nonprint.

4. Conduct a vigorous program of dissemination dramatizing the relevance of the record of past and present human experience to resolving today's problems. The program would include public information about what is available, guidance to individuals in its use, and group activities designed to foster interpersonal dialogue.

5. Develop, in cooperation with other information agencies and libraries, a responsible policy for preserving and erasing portions of humankind's voluminous current record as described in the section dealing with the exponential increase of records. The agency would negotiate consensus about criteria for judging between materials which are significant or representative and those which are trivial or redundant.

6. Take leadership in defining a new statement of professional ethics and in creating new structures to protect intellectual freedom in the light of the responsibility to preserve or erase.

7. Take a leadership role in coordinating the acquisition policies of other libraries and information agencies, because no one agency can preserve all significant and representative materials in all forms at all levels.

8. Having developed policies for shared acquisition, assume leadership in creating and maintaining an effective network so that all citizens would have easy access to any record, no matter where stored.

9. Not only select, collect, organize, and preserve the human record, but also become expert in using flexible procedures for allowing citizens to inform themselves uniquely.

10. Package and present the human record to allow easy access for people previously excluded by lack of education, lack of language facility, ethnic or cultural backgrounds, age, physical or mental handicaps, and apathy.

To accomplish all of the above, the agency would need to be accountable to the total community rather than to some specific segment or constituency. It would need to be a public agency, publicly supported and publicly controlled, because its responsibilities would be of central social importance. It would need to be a flexible agency, able to respond to as yet undefined social needs which may emerge in a changing world.

The agency described in the preceding ten categories does not yet exist. The awesome responsibilities described could not, and should not, be vested in only one type of library, or indeed in librarianship alone. Nevertheless, libraries in general are the agency to which American society has assigned primary responsibility to identify, select, organize, retrieve, disseminate, and make totally accessible the record of human thought. Libraries collectively must be the agency described above.

The specific role of the public library in responding to the broad needs of society grows out of its existence as a public agency, with broad tax support and the responsibility to serve the total community rather than a specific clientele. For the user with specialized information needs, the public library must continue to act as a point of entry into the national network of libraries and information resources. For individuals or groups in their life roles, the public library must continue to act as a popularizer, making the human record accessible, alerting people to it, and stimulating its use. As the one type of library accountable to the total community, the public library of the future must play a strong coordinative role, leading all libraries in their response to today's new social needs.[5]

One hundred twenty-seven years earlier, in 1852, at the beginning of the public library movement in this country, the Reverend John Burt Wight of Wayland, Massachusetts, wrote a statement as part of the proposed draft of the Massachusetts library law, which remains as a clear and succinct summary of the role and function of the public library.

### Proposed Massachusetts Law (House Document No. 124)

To authorize, encourage, and ensure the formation, increase and perpetuation of Public Libraries, in the several cities and towns of this Commonwealth for the use and benefit of all their respective inhabitants.

*Whereas,* A universal diffusion of knowledge among the people must be highly conducive to the preservation of their freedom, a greater equalization of their social advantages, their industrial success, and their physical, intellectual and moral advancement and elevation; and

*Whereas,* It is requisite to such a diffusion of knowledge, that while sufficient means of a good early education shall be furnished to all the children in the Common Schools, ample and increasing sources of useful and interesting information should be provided for the whole people in the subsequent and much more capable and valuable periods of life; and

*Whereas,* There is no way in which this can be done so effectually, conveniently and economically as by the formation, increase and perpetuation of Public Libraries, in the several cities and towns of this Commonwealth, for the use and benefit of all their respective inhabitants: . . .[6]

Statements of function have been enunciated from time to time by the American Library Association:[7]

#### FUNCTIONS OF THE PUBLIC LIBRARY

The modern public library collects the printed and audiovisual materials needed to conduct the individual and group life of its constituency. It organizes and makes accessible its resources to be convenient and easy to use. It interprets and guides the use of materials to enable as many people as possible to apply in their daily lives the record of what is known. Collection; organization and distribution; interpretation and guidance—lack of any one of these results in sub-standard library service.

In essence, the public library provides materials and services. The other topics discussed in this document—personnel, physical facilities, etc.—have to do with the necessary means of achieving adequacy in these functions.

#### MATERIALS

The books and other resources of the library constitute the road by which each individual can escape from his limitations; thus selection of needed materials is a basic function of the public library. In making its choices from the vast array of available material, the public library must be guided not only by the demands of those who use the library constantly; it must also be aware of unspoken needs within the community if it is to serve effectively as an open door to "the wisdom and experience of all mankind."

Its materials are provided:

To facilitate informal self-education of all people in the community
To enrich and further develop the subjects on which individuals are undertaking formal education
To meet the informational needs of all
To support the educational, civic, and cultural activities of groups and organizations
To encourage wholesome recreation and constructive use of leisure time.

Provision of materials means more than occasional availability. It means a supply sufficient to make the library a dependable source for most people most of the time. In addition to books, the public library selects and provides pamphlets, documents, and other nonbook sources in printed form, and films, tapes, discs, and other nonprint stores of knowledge and opinion.

SERVICES

Providing materials is only the first step. The second basic function—that which differentiates a library from a mere collection of books and other materials—is service, encompassing:

The organization of material to make it easily accessible to potential users
Lending procedures to ensure that materials may be used at the time and place desired by the public
Guidance to assist the user to find what he wishes, either in the material immediately at hand or in whatever library may possess it
A program of public information to make its resources not only available but eagerly sought by its community.

In the last analysis, service, collections of books, the staff, and the physical environment recommended in this statement of standards have meaning only as they reach all the people.

During the 1950s and 1960s some public librarians began to think about a return to people-oriented services, thinking that perhaps the public library had grown somewhat remote from its origins and potential clientele. The general social unrest of that time, and the concerns about and dissatisfactions with established institutions and agencies, were reflected in soul-searching among the official library organizations. For example, in 1965 the Public Library Association adopted the following statement written by the committee's chairman, Meredith Bloss, who was then city librarian of the New Haven, Connecticut, Free Public Library, where the library-neighborhood-center concept of service had been introduced in 1964:

### The Public Library's Responsibility for Service
### to the Functionally Illiterate

The public library's responsibility for service to people who are unable to read well enough to function satisfactorily as workers, as citizens, or as members of the community, is clearly an extension of the library's long-held educational goals.

The public library is an activity of government. Our government is self-government, that is, by the people. It is based on the premise that enough of the people will know enough, enough of the time to govern each other.

This condition of knowing will not come about by chance. It is the responsibility of those directing the government's educational agencies, of which the public library is one, to work aggressively and creatively to increase the opportunities for people of limited reading ability to reduce their ignorance and to include them among those who are reading. . . .

To reach and serve the functionally illiterate, public libraries may need to think of what Herbert Gans has called "user-oriented" facilities, that would be more permissive, that would have materials not found in traditional libraries, and that would be less formidable, perhaps smaller, and closer to people. . . .

The new neighborhood service outlet . . . would be less formal. . . . It would have books and reading matter especially at lower or easier reading levels. It would use all the arts and techniques of communication, at whatever degree of complexity or simplicity is needed. Neighborhood advisory groups of local residents would advise and consult on needs, hours of service, programs.

This responsibility for service to undereducated persons grows from recognition of the public library's major social role as change-agent: to select, organize, provide, and stimulate use of materials for communication and learning.[8]

During the 1960s, largely through the availability of federal funds through the various antipoverty programs, there was a considerable increase in the number and variety of library service programs for the disadvantaged. A *Comprehensive Annotated Bibliography* cited 260 articles appearing in the library press and elsewhere during the period 1964–1968.[9]

A National Book Committee study noted that most antipoverty services were additions to the library's regular program, and observed that "one fact stands out: while a great variety of approaches and experiments are being pursued, New Haven, Connecticut, is the only city in which library-sponsored, library-administered multi-media neighborhood centers exist as an integral part of the regular municipal library system."[10]

### The Value and Formulation of Goals

In serving its community, a library should study and formulate what it should or should not attempt. With specific objectives it can plan its immediate and long-range program. Goals determine daily decisions and make book selection more effective. They influence the internal organization, the selection and assignment of staff members, and the quality and kind of service. They determine the extent of public support and establish criteria by which results may be measured.

Goals should derive from many sources: from the librarian's knowledge of present trends and problems in society; from an awareness of what goes on, nationally, in education and in cultural and intellectual fields; from national and local library leaders who have the background of discussion, debate, observation and experience. The staff members who are in constant contact with library users should participate in drawing up library goals.

The statement of goals should be realistic and possible to achieve. The statement needs periodic review in the light of results achieved and of changes in the local situation. It should be compared with current developments elsewhere but not distorted by temporary fads. It should be comprehensive but aimed at a coherent concept of the library's purpose and not diffused in scattered questions, problems, or ideals.

*Goals* lead to objectives. Goals deal with the larger aim: what the library hopes to accomplish. *Objectives* are specific statements that describe what is to be done with what resources. Objectives are realistic and attainable and capable of measurement either in narrative terms, degrees of satisfaction, or in statistics. In some planning statements, the terms *goals* and *objectives* are used interchangeably. It is important to make a distinction.

*Activities* are specific operations or events undertaken or sponsored by the library to advance toward objectives. *Procedures* are operational details for activities. *Standards* are officially adopted or widely accepted measures by which to evaluate results; they may be derived from reliable data, or they may be rule-of-thumb dicta based on trial and experience.

## The Background of Present Goals

One can hardly understand and appreciate the philosophy and prevailing goals of a profession without knowing what led up to them. Libraries stemmed from the ideal of improving society, a purpose or goal widely accepted. The ideal goes back to a national belief, prevalent since colonial days, in human progress. Many books deal with this viewpoint, sometimes called "social Darwinism in American thought." Franklin and Washington and their colleagues in organizing our government held this concept, characteristic of their time, of the indefinite perfectibility of man and his institutions, the beliefs that man could determine the main line of his progress, that institutions existed to further progress, and that education was one of the principal means.

This continuing, altruistic American conviction underlies social legislation and other public effort to ameliorate living conditions in the face of indifference and compromise. Under the influence of this conviction, librarians assume that the library is a potent factor in forwarding education and economic and social progress.

One goal remains constant: *to provide and service materials for enlarging the mind and dispelling prejudice and ignorance.* "This implies the necessity of making access to the truth easy and rapid for anyone who seeks it. For the overwhelming majority, the quickest and easiest access to the world's best thought is through the public library."[11] This means very recent facts and ideas as well as the wisdom of the ages; the library *must be current as well as retrospective.*

### Goals Statements in Practice

In his landmark report on the Chicago Public Library in 1969, Dr. Lowell Martin introduced the chapter on goals and principles with these words: "Two concepts underlie this report on the Chicago Public Library: excellence and innovation. In this age of particular dependence on information and knowledge the Library must have the capacity to help Chicago capitalize on its opportunities and solve its problems. Then the agency must find new ways to make its resources widely available and used."

Listed are "the six social goals which should inspire and guide the agency in the next ten to twenty years." Each is followed by explanation and amplification. The six goals are:

1. The Chicago Public Library is to open opportunity for self-development for people at whatever their stage of education and culture. 2. . . . is to bring people and resources together, closing the gap between the individual and the record of knowledge. 3. . . . is to bring information on contemporary living into the lives of people. 4. . . . is to enter into the community and cultural life of the City, serving as a local center through its branch libraries and as a metropolitan center in its central activities. 5. . . . is to add to and supplement the formal education programs of schools and colleges, by supplying materials for students that cannot be adequately and conveniently provided by the institutions of formal learning. 6. . . . is to provide specialized resources to sustain the life of a great city.[12]

It is clear that different terms may be used by different planners to describe what is essentially the same idea: the job that the library is to do for the community being served. What is called a goal in Chicago is called a "role statement" in some places: what role this library should play in this environment, serving this population. An example is the role statement of the Baltimore (Maryland) County Public Library:[13] "To make readily available to the greatest possible number of County residents, the most wanted library materials of all kinds, and to serve as a point of access for any needed information."

Another example of a library goal, from outside the library profession: "To present library services that, to the extent possible, provide the greatest satisfaction to citizens, including timely, helpful, and readily available services that are attractive, accessible, and convenient."[14]

These succinct statements leave some questions in respect to the often stated goal or purpose of library service as an agency of continuing education.

In 1975 the Council on Library Resources published a report of an inquiry into the management of fourteen library systems in ten large American cities, and the part that goals and objectives setting played in this management.[15] The investigator, Larry Earl Bone, found, among other things, that the terms *goals* and *objectives* were being used interchangeably or were reversed in many libraries. He noted that some libraries follow in general the Blasingame and Lynch[16] definition of goal as a "large on-going ambition which may never be achieved or which will only be achieved in the very long-run" and their definition of objectives as "more immediate aims . . . anything from a short-term aim to a multi-year aim, short of the overall goals." It may be noted in passing that goals and objectives, in budgeting terms, are defined with greater distinction and precision, as will be discussed in Chapter 7, on budgeting and finance.

Bone's summary and conclusions were that:

The goals and objectives setting process seems clearly to be an activity whose time has come in many libraries. . . .

The business world for some time has made goals and objectives an essential part of progressive management. Because public libraries have come to such a process late, and because many such efforts are in their initial stages, it is too soon to assess the overall impact of goals and objectives setting as a management technique in large public libraries.

Library literature before 1970 has little documentation to guide libraries interested in undertaking such a process. Recently there have been more reports and articles on what has been done in particular libraries. Norman Crum's *Library Goals and Objectives: Literature Review,* published in 1973 as an ERIC report, provides a useful survey of the literature on the subject.[17]

. . . Basic steps that should be followed in the setting of objectives within a library include:

1. State mission.
2. Write set of guiding principles.
3. Identify and articulate *real* objectives.
4. Be specific, distinctive, and brief.
5. Use commonly understood terms.
6. Develop meaningful measures of expected accomplishments.
7. Make goals and objectives challenging.
8. Get involvement.
9. Determine objectives for all library levels.
10. Balance set of goals and objectives.
11. Establish order of priority.
12. Produce draft, discuss and then redraft.
13. Agree, recommend and obtain approval.
14. Publish and publicize.
15. Put objectives to practical use.
16. Review and re-examine periodically.
17. Modify as necessary.

Have the large public libraries which have engaged in a goal and objective setting activity totally embraced this process? There seems to be no question that in general consciousness is being raised to the need for meaningful goals and objectives. . . . Some libraries have become most aware, and some still have not. . . . Unless there is complete commitment to such an approach, usually from the top management of a library, the process may turn out to be an exercise in futility.

. . . Goals and objectives are judged not by their mere statement but by the degree to which they affect an institution's operation and its ongoing activities, and whether in the final analysis they are successfully implemented. . . .

No matter how admirable the statement may be—whether it be called goals or objectives—it must include action plans. It must include, or at least be followed by, a concrete blueprint which shows how and when the goals or objectives will be achieved.

. . . Librarians continue to resist priority setting, sometimes quite defensively, in spite of the exhortations to do so from such diverse camps as management experts, the National Advisory Commission on Libraries, *A Strategy for Public Library Change,* and prominent library leaders. . . . Management experts counsel that "no business can do everything. Even if it has money, it has to set priorities. The worst thing is to try to do a little bit of everything. This makes sure that nothing is being accomplished. It is better to pick the wrong priority than none at all." . . . Lowell Martin pinpoints the problem [of failure to set priorities]:

". . . The public library seeks to do almost everything. In practice it provides a wide range of services, each to only a fragmentary extent, and each utilized by a very small portion of the population. . . . This eclectic policy was tolerable—perhaps even best—in a period when the vitalizing values of the society were not being questioned and when more public money could be expected as the years went by. However, the policy has to be reconsidered when both intellectual leaders and government officials are asking why we maintain each public agency and how much support it should get."

Public librarians should not wait for *others* to ask why the public library should be maintained. They should ask this question and answer it. If public librarianship has come of age, it must make priority selection a way of life. This selection of priorities may turn out to be the most difficult part of the whole goal and objectives setting process, and may in the final analysis be the best test of the effectiveness of the process.[18]

### Research Needs

Among topics and problems that now concern library readers are:

1. Stepped up efforts by libraries and library organizations to extend the financial base of public libraries through increased funding at local, state, and federal levels. Special action to change federal priorities and new management approaches to finance used by business, industry, and government should be explored.

2. A more active role for the library in the community as an intellectual powerhouse and rallying point, making it a vital force that meets the needs

of all the people. Development and use of creative outreach undertakings, independent learning programs, and special information services are new steps in this direction.

3. Better communication between the library and the community through an improved public relations program that goes beyond exhibits, posters, booklists, and newspaper columns. Professional public relations people should be employed where possible.

4. Improved preparation for librarians and paraprofessionals in library schools and elsewhere to serve the library's new readers and assume active leadership roles in reaching out to neglected community groups.

5. Sustained testing, development, and evaluation of regional, state, and national library networks with their possibilities for union catalogs and lists, cooperative development, sharing and storing of resources, centralized processing, and sharing computer centers.

6. New studies on the relationships between school and public libraries, including further experimentation with joint school–library ventures.

7. Fresh appraisals of book selection, taking into consideration possible conflicts between standard selection aids and what people in the community actually want to read. The difficulty large libraries have in maintaining a collection with balance when time forces them to resort to blanket orders and mass purchasing.

8. The need to develop more effective means to measure library use.

9. Continued attention to advances in automation and technology, non-print materials, and CATV with its potential for telecommunication and programming.

10. Further involvement of the American library community in international library planning.

### The Primacy of Print

By 1976, citizens of the United States were borrowing more than 900 million books a year from their public libraries, not to mention what they borrowed from school, college, and other libraries. On the basis of population in the areas served, this amounted to 4.2 books per capita in 1950. In 1960 the total figure was 550 million.

Even more impressive, national book sales amounted to an estimated $4.14 billion in 1977, compared with $2.2 billion in 1967. The popular demand for paperback books grows fastest of all; sales are now at the rate of $4 million a day and include an increasing proportion of nonfiction and quality fiction.

People consider book service to be the public library's province and books its reason for existence. Books, reading, and study afford opportunities for improvement and relaxation and sources of information not obtainable through radio and television. Some books have profoundly influenced the destiny of nations. They have deeply affected the lives of countless individuals. In the present concern for national progress and production, public libraries are a prolific source for objectives, ideas, and facts to help the intelligent public in its enterprises. They deserve far more recognition and financial support than they have so far received. Although enrollment in schools at all levels is now declining, libraries have been directly affected and encouraged by the tremendous increases over the past several decades: grade school, from 31 million in 1960 to 34 million in 1970; high school, from 9 million in 1960 to 14 million in 1970; and college, from 3 million in 1960 to 6 million in 1970. M.A. degrees climbed from 78,000 in 1960 to 208,000 in 1970; doctorate degrees from 9,800 in 1960 to 29,800 in 1970. In 1970, 37 million people were enrolled in federally aided vocational programs in home economics, trade, industry, and agriculture, and in 1975, over 17 million people were participating in adult education classes.

### The Usefulness of Books

1. Libraries are extending their sources of information with the addition of nonprint materials; however, books are still the primary source of information.

2. With their extended and thoughtful interpretations of life, books offer the most complete means to grasp the enormity of the human soul. Few films, television programs, or radio programs carry the impact of *Hamlet, The Grapes of Wrath,* or *The Gulag Archipelago.* Certainly, a good film or a musical production based on a book and a textual explanation and evaluation of it can be a combination more rewarding than either alone. To this end, libraries are creating programs that combine books and films, video and audio cassettes, programmed learning materials, and discs.

3. No other medium can let the demands of the content, rather than some outside consideration, dictate the length of the presentation. Thus, to deal with an idea of any scope and with the intensity it deserves, only the book will serve. Most subjects, descriptions, and characterizations can be handled adequately only by having time enough and material enough to do them justice. The reader is the one to decide how slowly or how fast to go, how much skimming and how much intensive repetition to indulge in, and when and for how long to put the mind to the matter.

4. Only the book, or print, can eliminate the distraction of the personality of the actor or the broadcaster and the awareness of commercialized or group pressure. Though occasional exceptions are highly encouraging, to anyone who reads with enjoyment and attention these extraneous influences are distracting, exasperating, and often intolerable.

5. Only print makes it practicable for the ordinary citizen to turn back to what was seen, read, or heard even a few days ago and to find it, in order to follow up some idea, question, objective that has been sticking in

the mind as worth pursuing. Programed learning materials, which enable the reader to check on his progress, are a logical extension of this concept.

6. Only books and print meet the need of one who wishes to inquire, think, and act on a chosen subject, for one's own reasons and in one's own way, instead of being influenced or controlled by group thinking and objectives. Often it is only in books that one can examine all sides of a subject.

7. Only the book, among major communication media, encourages the highly desirable habit of quiet, relaxed thinking and reflection. The rising demand for mental skills and the burgeoning of knowledge put heavy pressure on schoolchildren. If children are to be eager learners and thinkers, adults must set an example. Reading parents raise reading children. Thus libraries should be not only places of learning but also places of delight.

### Objective: To Serve Individuals

A good library works closely with all community organizations. The library director and other staff members will serve on committees, take charge of community activities that are generally related to the library's mission, and otherwise be a part of the community life. They will also take the initiative in encouraging various community organizations in constructive programs, as a phase of adult education. But the library administrator cannot overlook or neglect the continuing obligation to the individuals who already come and those who can be encouraged to come to the library seeking services. The library should attract and serve a greater proportion of the population than is reached in most communities, enabling them to use library materials for reading and study. Many of these prospective patrons belong to organizations only vaguely aware of what the library can give them.

Librarianship involves great challenges. The purpose is to supply "the right book to the right reader at the right time." The extraordinarily intimate and delicate transactions involved in reader's advisory work should be guided by a clear understanding of why and how individuals are affected by what they read. This idea of paying attention to the individual is in sharp contrast to the mass transfer of information and impressions over TV and radio. Thomas Finletter has stated:

When I think of ten million passive spectators, all watching one man on a television screen, all listening at the same time to one persuasive voice, I am a little frightened. . . . The thinker-for-himself comes, stubborn and alone, to wring his own meanings and fill his own needs. . . . The public library seeks not to enforce the one idea upon the many, but to open to each individual user the unnumbered wealth of intellectual resources from which he can serve not another's ends, but his own.[19]

It should be a major objective for the public library to recognize and aid individuals as such, even though they are most easily reached through a group. Libraries should give constant stimulation to adults to read for information, for cultural self-development, for citizenship, for recreation. The public library shares this objective with the school and college library. It therefore needs to have a keen interest in and understanding of methods and problems in teaching reading, and in the humanities, as part of its own background for service.

## Notes

1. Meredith Bloss, Paper on the future of library services, 1979 (unpublished).
2. Ibid.
3. Herbert J. Gans, in Ralph W. Conant, ed., *The Public Library and the City* (Cambridge, Mass.: M.I.T. Press, 1965), pp. 67, 71.
4. American Library Association, *Minimum Standards for Public Library Systems* (Chicago: American Library Association, 1967), pp. 8, 14.
5. American Library Association, *The Public Library Mission Statement and Its Imperatives for Service* (Chicago: American Library Association, 1979), pp. 1–4, 6–8.
6. Jesse H. Shera, *Foundations of the Public Library* (Chicago: University of Chicago Press, 1949), chart following p. 192.
7. American Library Association, *Minimum Standards for Public Library Systems,* pp. 8–9.
8. Peter Hiatt and Henry T. Drennan, eds., *Public Library Services for the Functionally Illiterate* (Chicago: Public Library Association, 1967), pp. 9–10.
9. Carla J. Stoffle, "Public Library Service to the Disadvantaged," *Library Journal,* Jan. 15–Feb. 1, 1969.
10. National Book Committee, *Neighborhood Library Centers and Services* (New York: National Book Committee, 1967), p. 4.
11. Gerald W. Johnson, "Role of the Public Library," in American Library Association, *Introduction to Public Library Service* (Chicago: American Library Association, 1956).
12. Lowell A. Martin, *Library Response to Urban Change: A Study of the Chicago Public Library* (Chicago: American Library Association, 1969), pp. 14–17.
13. Vernon E. Palmour and Marcia C. Bellassai, *To Satisfy Demand: A Study Plan for Public Library Service in Baltimore County* (Arlington, Va.: Public Research Institute, 1977).
14. Harry P. Hatry and others, *How Effective Are Your Community Services?* (Washington, D.C.: The Urban Institute and the International City Management Association, 1977), p. 67.
15. Larry Earl Bone, "The Goals and Objectives Experience: A Report to the Council on Library Resources, 1975." (Available from Council on Library Resources, Washington, D.C.)
16. Ralph U. Blasingame and Mary Jo Lynch, "Design for Diversity: Alternatives to Standards for Public Libraries," *PLA Newsletter* 13 (June 1974): 16.
17. Norman J. Crum, "Library Goals and Objectives: Literature Review" (Washington, D.C.: ERIC Clearinghouse on Library and Information Sciences, 1973).
18. Lowell A. Martin, "Standards for Public Libraries," *Library Trends* 21 (October 1972): 176.
19. Thomas Finletter, in Benjamin Elkin, "Are We Trying to Do Too Much?" *Illinois Libraries* 42 (March 1960): 192–93.

# 2 A Program to Serve the Whole Community

The public library has long been dedicated to the concept of "service to all." From an administrative point of view, this may be taken to mean service to all who elect to use the facilities and resources that are provided under the program, according to the goals, objectives, and priorities that have been worked out and adopted. If the library's operational service plan has been developed in collaboration with a wide representation of the community, and if it has been organized to respond to manifest needs of citizens, one may assume that the correlation between the library program and the community will be positive. But this state of affairs will more properly flow from a realistic than an idealized view. There has been and probably still is an opinion held by many public librarians that reading (and consulting other library resources) is a desirable end in itself and that if more people could only be motivated to read more, the library would indeed be successful. This attitude results from fuzzy goals, and is attested to by the fact that the only measure of performance uniformly employed by public libraries is the count of books borrowed for home use. If the public library's mission or goal is educational or social, the total number of books borrowed has meaning in relation to that goal only if it may be assumed that social good always or usually results from the process of reading or consulting resources. But reading is a means, not an end in itself.

On the other hand it may be argued that if the library's resources and materials have been selected with judgment and discretion, with an appropriate concern for quality and authority of content and presentation, then it must follow that the measure of the numbers of these books read, or at least borrowed with probable intent to read, is an indicator of the library performance. This is obviously the understood if not stated premise underlying the use of circulation figures as a performance measure. In brief, if the library is one of excellence, however defined, its use may be assumed to have some social good. But these are all big "ifs" and may or may not apply with equal force in all public libraries. There is the possible suspicion that once circulation is accepted as a measure, it tends to become a goal, if only to aid in securing operational funds. Therefore it becomes tempting to build the library collections to a greater extent on books that will be borrowed to reflect the current popular taste of the widest possible borrowership. This is the operational policy of the mass media, but they lay no claim to social purpose or good. The question of the quality of the collection, or of its major characteristics, will be dealt with in more detail in the chapter on materials and resources.

What it comes down to is that the methods for evaluating results of library performance in terms of avowed goals and ideals have apparently yet to be discovered.

But planning for a program for the whole community can begin. There are several bases that can be established and considered in the planning process. The first that might be consulted is the subject of the information needs of people. Some work has been done in this field, and public library planners could begin to use the results of this research with profit.

### The Process of Planning

Planning a program for the whole community will involve questions of who is to do the planning, and the steps that are to be taken. The planning group or team may include different people in different libraries, but there are some who should certainly be involved: the library director and in larger libraries key members of the administrative staff; some line members of the staff, preferably selected by the rank and file; the trustees; elected or appointed public officials; and representatives from the community being served. This latter component is critical to a satisfactory planning process. Great care should be exercised to assure that there is articulate, concerned, and critical representation, not just some library users who will agree with everything proposed by the library director. The state conferences on planning for the 1979 White House Conference on Library and Information Services found out that the citizen delegates, perhaps somewhat to the surprise of the "library-related" delegates, had some new and different ideas about what libraries ought to be and do.

Whether the library director should serve as the executive of the planning team will depend upon the local situation. In any event the library members will do well to serve as resource persons and to listen more than speak, perhaps to point out alternatives and suggest possible results of certain courses of action. They should view themselves as the technical experts; they may assist in the formation of policy but should not make a policy and ask for citizen support.

However constituted, the group that will be doing the planning will be referred to in the succeeding discussion as the planning team.

The steps that are to be taken, the planning process, should be carefully considered. It should be clearly understood that the process, if it is to be at all successful, will require, first, that *all* the necessary steps be taken and completed; and second, that a fair amount of time and effort will be required by all participants—that the planning process is not just a matter of a few meetings with people sharing their opinions on what ought to happen, writing up a report, and calling it quits.

Finally, there should be a definite consensus among the members of the planning team and among staff, trustees, and public bodies in the background who are concerned but not participating that (a) conclusions and recommendations are to flow from the data and that (b) the conclusions will be put into practice. The planning effort should be substantive, serious, and imbued with commitment. Also, the planning process, once completed for the first time in an orderly fashion, will then be continued as results of the process are evaluated and as new data and conditions become available.

The words used to describe the steps in the planning process may differ depending upon which expert sources are consulted, but the following are suggested as basic to the total process:

1. Assess community and library environment.
2. Determine the role of public library in the community.
3. Evaluate current library resources and services.
4. Establish goals, objectives, and priorities.
5. Prepare and describe plans for action; activities to be carried out to meet and fulfill objectives.
6. Prepare performance measures of objective fulfillment.

When the results of the planning process have been adopted and placed into operation, there will be continuing measurement, evaluation, and observation to see what is working well and what is not. The succeeding phases of the planning process will deal with the changes necessary as a result of the evaluation process.

*Step One: Assessing Community and Library Environment*

This will include demographic, economic, cultural, and other data—the usual elements in a community analysis.*

The analysis of the library environment should properly include a careful study of other library facilities and services available to the community being analyzed. As Meredith Bloss has pointed out in a recent article, the public library does not exist in isolation in most communities but is one of many public sources of books and information. He suggests:

---

* There are several excellent manuals on this phase of the process: Ruth Warncke, *Studying the Community: Basis for Building Library Service* (1960); American Library Association, *Studying the Community;* Priscilla Gotsick, *Community Survey for Assessment of Community Information and Service* (1976); and the works of Roger Greer on community analysis.

[the] field theory of library planning . . . based on the thought that what one library has and does in a particular community (whether that community is one of place or of interest), or does not have and does not do, will have an effect upon all other libraries serving that community. Therefore, when one begins to think about planning . . . for any one of the units in the array of libraries, one would need to look to the others first to see where they are, what they are doing now, and what they plan to do, both as to program, and as to space.[1]

Planners for the public library service, as the umbrella agency, may well need to take the initiative in this approach on a community-wide basis.

Library planners usually begin the needs assessment, if undertaken at all, with a study of library and information needs, forgetting or overlooking the simple fact that these needs, even if precisely defined, should be viewed in the context of human needs in general.

A statement by Ricking and Booth contains cogent remarks about the relationship of human needs, and their assessment, to the library service program.[2]

### NEEDS ASSESSMENT

Central purposes, goals, objectives, if they are to have any meaning, must arise in direct response to need. In 1954, Abraham Maslow formulated a theory of motivation based upon the following hierarchy of needs:

I. Physiological needs
   Food, water, sleep, shelter, sex
II. Safety needs
   Security, stability, protection; freedom from fear, anxiety, and chaos
III. Social needs
   a. Belongingness
   b. Love for others
IV. Esteem needs
   a. Strength, achievement, adequacy, mastery, competence, confidence in face of the world, freedom, independence
   b. Reputation, prestige, status, fame, glory, dominance, recognition, attention, importance, dignity, appreciation
V. Self-Actualization
   "What a man can be, he must be.
   To become everything that one is capable of becoming."[3]

These needs are related to each other in what Maslow calls "a hierarchy of prepotency." A person who is lacking food, safety, love, and esteem, will hunger for food more strongly than for anything else. But once a need is fairly well satisfied, the next higher need emerges. "The organism is dominated and its behavior organized only by unsatisfied needs."[4]

The Maslowian hierarchy poses important questions for the library in terms of where in the hierarchy we can accommodate the need for information, education, desires to know, to understand, and to explain. What do we know about informational needs in different societies, e.g., technologically advanced vs. emerging? What do we know about information needs of different socio-economic groups or rural vs. urban communities? In librarianship, we are just beginning to ask these questions; we have few, if any, answers. To understand the process and role of librarianship, we must begin to devote greater effort to examining and reexamining societal needs as to the fountainhead for the services and materials of the library. Needs must be studied first, and only then—in response to needs—can and should library services and resources be provided.

If an assessment of needs clearly indicates that all or part of the central purposes, goals, objectives, programs, and resources of a given library currently accepted or in use are not needed, then those purposes, goals, objectives, programs, and resources should change. Too many agencies are out of date, out of phase, and out of touch with the real needs of their client constituencies. As needs change, central purposes must change, as must all steps in the systems sequence.

In all too many library situations, we tend to start with existing services and resources and ask how we can restructure societal needs to fit what we currently provide as products, services, or other output. If society does not use what we provide, or support what we propose, the fault is assumed to be with society and not with us. This is probably a common error of maturing or mature agencies which have failed to make recurring assessments of the needs for which they were created.

Harriett L. Robbins, Director of Evaluation of the former Evaluation Center of Ohio State University, suggests a framework for describing the needs derived from an existing situation. These statements appear in a letter to a state library officer, and while they were written in specific response and reaction to a long-range plan for library service in a specific state, they have application in suggesting in a more general way, means of connecting objectives with goals, and goals with the needs from which they derive:

1. What are the needs of the people of———which can and should be served by a———library system?
2. What is the extent of the needs, i.e., who are the relevant populations involved? Where are they? And how many people are involved?
3. Can the problem be dealt with within the existing institutional framework, and if not, what changes need to be made to adequately serve these populations? And finally,
4. How critical is each identified need? In other words, what is the cost of meeting the need compared to the cost of ignoring it? . . . The point is that a clear statement of how much change is necessary is crucial to sound planning.[5]

In a letter to another state library officer, Robbins raised the following questions:

1. What is the source of these objectives (goals, targets)? What do these objectives represent? In other words, where did these objectives come from? Are they the result of meaningful assessment of the needs of the people of———, or are they the policy decisions of a small group of individuals?
2. What are the priorities of your objectives? Are some more important than others, and if so, why (e.g., a particular objective has strong legislative support, etc.)? Can you identify the most critical objectives (i.e., the ones which address the most pressing needs)?
3. What do these objectives mean in light of your present situation? For example,

are the programs which you specify as targets presently ongoing, in preparation, or still at the planning stage?

4. What are the temporal aspects of your plan? Are certain objectives to be sequenced or are all to be pursued at the same time?

5. How will you know when an objective has been realized?

6. How will you monitor the plan's success over time? Can you specify certain benchmarks and/or timetables which you would consider to be successful implementation?[6]

## STAFF AND COMMUNITY INVOLVEMENT

Ralph Conant points out the very real need for libraries to involve representatives from government, industry, business, and the professions, as well as all levels of the community, in making an assessment of societal needs. A serious concern with major problems can create a new image for the profession and involve the community in a vital understanding of what libraries can mean to the entire society.[7]

Barbara Conroy reinforces the concept of a community involvement in assessing and establishing goals:

> The survival of the public library, as such, is presently in jeopardy. As a social institution, its function is to provide for the informational needs within its community. Presently, it is often found wanting in meeting this function. As a service agency, it is responsible to its clients. In the most dormant instances, its performance of this function is being ignored or by-passed. In the most alive instances, libraries and librarians are being asked to look to new roles and new patterns of service in the community.
>
> In theory, the library's clients include the entire spectrum of individuals and groups in the community. In actual practice . . . utilization of library services is often selective, due to the method by which library services are delivered or due to the lack of community awareness of or responsiveness to the services offered. . . . Access to information, having it and using it, is a strong element of power for individuals and groups. . . . The realization that having information is vital to what people want and need to do is a growing one. That realization translates into alternative means of getting information if public library services do not meet those needs. Some of the current alternatives include hotlines, government information centers, business reference services, etc. However they get it, citizens need information with which to make decisions in meeting their personal, career and civic responsibilities. . . .
>
> Most fundamentally, successful outreach programs are done by the librarian *with* the community, not by the librarian *for* the community. In this changing world, librarians need to . . . develop the necessary abilities and attitudes for outreach librarianship. Libraries need to build policies and programs which are closely related to community needs and which incorporate community involvement in new ways. The community needs to change in relation to the library by actively being involved in the planning and use of library services.[8]

The demographic information about the community will be available from various sources: city or town planning office or planning consultant; federal census data; state and local school planning and statistical reports; utility companies; Chamber of Commerce and Manufacturers' Association reports. The library planning team will be fortunate indeed if the community has recently developed a well-researched town or city master plan, which will include much of the required data.

The latest census and special reports may show income per family, the percentage of the fourteen- to eighteen-year-old groups in school, the median number of school years completed, and the percentage of the population that has completed high school or more. These figures are seldom up to date and they do not cover communities of less than 25,000. It is difficult to get data coordinating current population counts, current incomes, and current educational backgrounds; all constantly change and are not reported simultaneously. Fairly realistic current estimates on income per family and population for cities over 10,000 are found in the current edition of *Survey of Buying Power.*[9]

The information on the library environment will probably be somewhat more difficult to obtain. Some libraries issue annual reports, but these may be inconsistent as to what data are included. The state library extension agency usually collects statistics for public libraries; those data will be useful if a regional analysis is undertaken. This aspect of planning will be discussed in more detail in the chapter on library systems. Personal interviews will doubtless be required to find out about future plans of other book and information agencies, unless the community is fortunate enough to have in place a library council that is already collecting that kind of information.

A second phase of step one will be concerned with determining the information needs of the population to be served. In a very real sense, this will be an exercise in the elusive. The Goals, Guidelines and Standards Committee of the Public Library Association in a 1977 Mission Statement has defined information as including "all knowledge, ideas, facts, and imaginative works of the mind which have been communicated, recorded, published, and/or distributed formally or informally in any format."[10]

In a 1979 document, *The Public Library Mission Statement and Its Imperatives for Service,* the committee adds another element to the definition: "Information includes not only the sum total of recorded human experience—factual, imaginative, scientific, and humanistic—*but also* the unrecorded experience which is available only from human resources to which library users may be referred" (italics added).[11]

Joseph Becker, writing on information as a national resource in a 1978 brochure prepared for the delegates to the White House conference on Library and Information Services in 1979, began with a disclaimer and ended with a definition:

It is somewhat hazardous to attempt an overall characterization of information because information is so pervasive. It is of concern to everyone and it touches all aspects of our lives. We must, however, try to define the concept so that we have a common framework for discussions. . . .

Information can be defined as the messages of human experience. In this context an information message can be seen from two perspectives—from the point of view of its content and from the point of view of its processing.

The intellectual essence of an information message is its content. Process refers to the means we use to produce, publish, communicate, organize, store, retrieve, and otherwise transfer information messages.

We should be careful to distinguish information from knowledge. Knowledge derives from the process people use to understand and analyze information. A knowledgeable person is one who learns to fit substantive pieces of information into a pattern of thought that leads to intelligent action. Wisdom, on the other hand, is different still. A wise person is someone who applies knowledge successfully and has the ability to discern inner qualities and relationships. The real worth of information lies in its utilization. . . . When information is viewed as the main ingredient of knowledge, its value as a national asset becomes apparent immediately. Recognition of the worth of information and of its potential power to solve national problems has prompted many countries to approach information almost as if it were a national resource.

In a 1978 survey of the information needs of Californians, citizens were asked to recall questions that arose during their everyday situations. Among information needs: "What's going on, how will things turn out? What are my options, what's the best choice to make, the best thing to do? What do I really want, what are my priorities? When or where can I do something? Can I get some information about the situation, what information can I get? Am I alone, is anyone listening, is anyone aware, does anyone else agree with me?" There were eleven other kinds of questions, in similar vein.

Information is, as Becker suggested, a complex matter. Webster's third edition gives a total of thirteen definitions, including two with specific legal applications. As an example of the use of one definition, "the communication or reception of knowledge or intelligence," the dictionary says that "the function of a library is information."

A narrower concept is expressed in "Public Library Information and Referral Service," edited by Clara Stanton Jones which states: "Information (as in information and referral) means information to meet human needs." This concept has been described in other publications as "coping information"—the facts that people need in order to cope with the increasing complexity of existence. This was the idea behind the study and proposal in 1966, by Alfred J. Kahn and osmers, for a system of neighborhood information centers for New York City, modeled after the successful British Citizens Advice Bureaus. It was a central notion in *Neighborhood Library Centers and Services, a study by the National Book Committee for the Office of Economic Opportunity,* published by the Committee in 1967.

There is a growing body of literature on the information needs of the people. Some suggested titles are cited in the reading list for this chapter in the Appendix, and the planning team will want to keep abreast of current works as they are published.

In order for the planning team to draw conclusions from Step One in the planning process, they will have to talk about the data they have gathered in Step One and the relationship of the data to goals, objectives, and action plans. Experts have testified that there are positive correlations between socioeconomic characteristics of the population and library and information needs.

### Step Two: Defining the Role of the Library

After the completion of Step One, in which facts about the community and library environment have been gathered and analyzed, the team will consider and define the role to be played by this particular library in this particular community. This is as critical as each of the other steps in the planning process and must be completed before subsequent steps can be taken. It will form the basis for goals, objectives, and plans for action. Should the library try to be a little of everything for everyone, as is so often the case? Should the library concentrate on those segments of the population that have access to no other information and library services? What are to be the emphases in collections, services, and other aspects of the service role?

The role statement may simply be a written statement of the library's present operating philosophy, or it may be revised if it is seen to be irrelevant to the population and environment. In any case, the role statement, as indicated in Chapter 1, is to be clear and specific.

### Step Three: Evaluating Current Library Resources and Services

This will include various kinds of data to be collected:

1. Current library statistics and reports on inputs and outcomes or results: expenditures for staff, library materials, other operating expenses.
2. Number and kind of staff, including qualifications and experience.
3. Description and analysis of service facilities, including square feet of space for reader services, book and materials display and storage, administrative and technical services, and qualitative appraisal of these facilities.
4. Size and evaluation of collections: print and nonprint.
5. Number of registered borrowers.
6. Uses: circulation of materials; reference questions received and number successfully and unsuccessfully answered; numbers and kinds of programs and activities offered, and attendance and participation; number of in-library users; nonborrowing users; attendance; any other service counts available.

These data should cover a period of at least five years, if possible.

A second kind of data to be gathered for Step Three is staff evaluation of the library. This can be undertaken before the planning process is started. It does not require a major effort, but it must be conducted with both care and adequate preparation so that the staff will feel comfortable about participation. Each staff member will be invited to participate. This survey may be carried out along various lines, but questions that might be covered would include:

1. Staff evaluation of library policies, procedures, and services.
2. Evaluation of effort and productivity of oneself and of other staff members and/or the administration.
3. Philosophy of library service (of the staff member).
4. Views about library strengths and weaknesses.
5. Attitudes about priorities; what should the library place highest on the agenda in the action plan?
6. Degree of satisfaction with working conditions, salaries, benefits.
7. Suggestions for improvements in the library service program.

The third kind of data to be gathered is the citizen and user survey. There are several models for this activity. Some user surveys are conducted by volunteer groups: Friends of the Library, League of Women Voters. These surveys may be taken of segments of the population: students, in-library users, sample of the general population. The purpose is to get some sense of how the community thinks about present library services.

The Public Library Association in 1977 engaged a professional research firm to prepare a manual on the planning process for public libraries, and this document was in draft form in 1978. It was being field-tested in several libraries around the country during 1978 and 1979. Publication by the American Library Association is scheduled for 1980. It will include detailed instructions and forms for undertaking the various steps in the planning process.

*Step Four: Establishing Goals, Objectives, and Priorities*

This phase of the planning process has been dealt with at some length in Chapter 1 and will again be considered in the light of the budgeting process in Chapter 7. The goal setting is very important. There should be a clearly understood distinction between goals and objectives. The goals may have to be stated, discussed and revised, and then restated before a satisfactory conclusion can be reached. The same will be true of the objectives. Once these statements have been completed satisfactorily, it will be possible to decide on priorities: which of the objectives can be achieved with the financial and human resources available in a specified time period.

*Step Five: Plans for Action*

Plans for action will be influenced, even within the priorities that have been set, by funding contingencies, which are not predictable in any public organization. Therefore the plans may need to be drafted with various levels of funding in mind. Plans for action will include for consideration the library's present activities: story hours for children, film programs, home lending of books for children and adults, and reference services are obvious examples. Opening an additional branch outlet, reducing the number of branches, adding a bookmobile, adding an information and referral service, and adding or increasing services to target populations are random examples of other action plans that may emerge from the planning process up to this point. Programs or action plans will be discussed in further detail in the chapters on services to children, services to adults, reference, and information.

*Step Six: Performance Measures for Meeting Objectives*

This step may well be the most difficult for the planning team to complete. Clearly, the performance measures employed will need to relate to the degree of achievement of the particular objectives that have been adopted for the particular library. Some research has been undertaken in recent years in an attempt to find more useful measurement indicators than the mix of input, output, and census figures that are normally used in most libraries. Doubtless some common denominators can be employed. In any event, it is certain that more emphasis will be placed on outcomes, effectiveness, and satisfaction than on census figures (number of volumes held and added) and upon input (number of dollars expended) unless it can be shown that there is a direct and predictable correlation between this kind of information and user satisfaction.

In 1970 the Public Library Association launched a research project to develop a new methodology for measuring service capabilities. The project was carried out by the Bureau of Library and Information Sciences Research at Rutgers University. The report, *The Measurement and Effectiveness of Public Library Service Study,* published in 1973, observed that present library statistics collected at the federal, state, and local levels did not respond to evaluation needs, and that librarians were expressing a desire for more information related directly to the user. The report concluded with a suggested methodology in response to that desire, and noted that

the primary purpose of this study was to develop meaningful indicators of performance which could be used by library administrators to assess the effectiveness of their operations. . . . In developing the measurement criteria, we tried to keep the user in focus at all times. . . . The criteria are based on three services common to all public libraries and reflect those areas basic to user needs: collection, facilities, and staff assistance.

Six performance measures were proposed for use:

1. Description of collection, with samples designed to obtain probability of satisfaction in obtaining recently published books and periodicals and in the total collection.

2. Building usage: description of users, time spent, and degree of satisfaction.

3. Circulation: in-library, outside library, and types of items lent and returned.

4. Patterns of reference usage: by time of day, by type of question, by source relationship, and by disposition (answered, referred, not answered).

5. Facilities usage: seating, photocopier, meeting room, microfilm reader and printer, record player.

6. Public service personnel (employees who have contact with the users) by age, length of employment in the library, average number of hours per week at public service and at other duties, highest degree earned, and scheduling by hour.

The report concluded:

The methodology developed is appropriate to the overall objective of the study. Selected data which measures various aspects of the public library program can be collected with minimal assistance at the local library level. The data themselves do discriminate the performance of one public library from that of another. The data come much closer than present library statistics to meeting the demands of both the librarian and the patron for "user-oriented" indicators which are necessary if the public library is going to reflect accurately the variety of activities that it is undertaking.[12]

The Rutgers performance measures, it is reported, are being used in a growing number of libraries around the country. In 1976 the instructional manual for the Rutgers approach, developed during the research phase and field testing, was published.[13]

The Public Library Association planning process manual, expected to be published in 1980 by the American Library Association, will reportedly present a new set of performance measures that will be based in part on the Rutgers indicators and on other sources. The performance measures that have been developed for libraries generally will at the very least serve as models for the local library planning team, and many of the measures may be employed without modification, to the extent that they apply to the local goals and objectives.

In summary, in order to have in place a total program for the total community, a thorough, broad-based, intensive planning process will have been carried through to completion. The process may require six months, a year, or two years and a considerable degree of concentration, effort, and willingness to face and consider the facts as they are developed. But once the planning is accomplished, a much more satisfactory and successful library program can probably be presented. Critics of the public library point to the lack of planning, the operational crises, the failure to establish priorities. A careful plan should overcome that criticism and lay the base for adequate fiscal support.

In a 1976 article on public library standards, it was noted that "a public library is tested by effectiveness, i.e., is only effective to the extent that it works; yields a usable product to the individuals and in a collective sense to the community for which it is designed. . . . The public library is now to stand on the premise of social utility and all activities must be planned with that goal in mind.[14]

## Presenting the Library's Program

Program statements are scarce indeed. A few programs are incorporated in survey reports, but there are few subsequent statements from the libraries as to which survey recommendations have been approved and carried out. A library with a definite two- or five- or ten-year plan, prepared by staff and trustees and well publicized, will make far more headway than libraries that simply run along. This may be reinforced by developing a plan for wide distribution of the program outline in the community. In the Atlanta, Georgia, Public Library, of which Carlton C. Rochell was director from 1968–1976, an updated plan was released to the media describing library plans for its objectives for service through facilities, personnel, and materials. This not only let the people know where their library stood but also served as a good vehicle for political action, because the press invariably took a position in support of the library's goals.

A modified program budget was used in the library and accepted by the City of Atlanta. It outlined specific program undertakings and clearly related personnel, materials, facilities, and other factors to the planned results.

### Notes

1. Meredith Bloss, "The Field/Performance Theory of Library Space Planning," in LJ Special Report no. 1, *Library Space Planning* (New York: *Library Journal,* 1976), pp. 52–54.
2. Myrl Ricking and Robert E. Booth, *Personnel Utilization in Libraries* (Chicago: American Library Association, 1974), pp. 8–12.
3. Abraham Maslow. *Motivation and Personality* (New York: Harper, 1954); summarized from rev. ed. (New York: Harper & Row, 1970), pp. 35–38.
4. Ibid., p. 38.
5. David D. Thompson, ed., *Planning and Evaluation for Statewide Library Development: New Directions* (Columbus: Ohio State University Faculty of Educational Development, 1972), p. 254.
6. Ibid., pp. 265–66.
7. Dr. Ralph W. Conant, Speech presented before the American Library Association Conference, Las Vegas, Nev. June 24, 1973.
8. *Leadership for Change: A Report of the Outreach Leadership Network, New England Center for Continuing Education* (Durham: University of New Hampshire, 1972), pp. 4–6.
9. Sales and Marketing Management, *Survey of Buying Power* (New York: Bill Brothers Publication, annual).
10. "A Mission Statement for Public Libraries—Guidelines for Public Library Service," part I, *American Libraries,* December 1977.
11. *The Public Library Statement and Its Imperatives for Service* (American Library Association, 1979).
12. Ernest R. DeProspo, Ellen Altman, and Kenneth E. Beasley, *Performance Measures for Public Libraries* (Chicago: American Library Association, 1973).
13. Ellen Altman, Ernest R. DeProspo, Philip M. Clark, and Ellen Connor Clark, *A Data Gathering and Instruction Manual for Performance Measures in Public Libraries* (Chicago: Celadon Press, 1976).
14. Meredith Bloss, "Standards for Public Library Service—Quo Vadis?" *Library Journal,* June 1, 1976, p. 1262.

# 3 The Library Board

Most public libraries in the United States are governed by boards composed of lay trustees. Members are sometimes appointed by the mayor or other chief elected official; sometimes they are elected, and in many towns and cities, especially in New England, library boards of trustees may be self-perpetuating bodies. Community representation is the declared intent of board membership, and this laudable goal will vary with the circumstances of selection. In a few cities, the place of the library board has been taken by the city or county manager, to whom the library director reports. Roles and functions of library boards vary considerably, from administrative to advisory. In their 1967 study of public libraries in the U.S., Nelson Associates cites the declining influence of library boards.

## Trends in Library Government

Early in the life of the public library movement, the local institutions were governed by voluntary boards of trustees who were to provide continuity of direction, a channel for the receipt of endowments and insulation from corrupt local governments. The boards were supposed to represent the public interest but they were dominated by the middle class to the exclusion of labor and agriculture. Boards also established the library policy but many were involved in operating matters, too. As librarians became more professional, they resisted incursions into their authority by trustees. Had the boards been able to meet the librarians' financial needs, their influence might have been sustained. But increasingly, libraries have traded their complete independence for the ongoing financial support of local governments. Many librarians believe the public library must be an active part of the political process if it is to flourish. They argue that the interests of the public library would be even better served if it were fully incorporated into city government or mandated as is free public schooling. As the library's ties with local and state governments grow stronger, the library boards tend to become advisory in character. They may continue, however, to protect the library from the dangers of censorship, promote the library in its pursuit of funds and provide the citizenry with a voice in governing their own institutions.[1]

There is an increasing trend toward less fiscal autonomy for library boards. Until recently most boards had the right to determine the expenditure of library funds, whether they came from a special levy or from the general fund. Board authority in this respect has steadily been eroded, as the professional management of cities and towns has increased. Preparation and administration of the library budget is controlled more and more by the same authority that is responsible for other municipal services. Boards, of course, usually retain control of trust and gift funds, where these exist.[2]

## Board Functions and Responsibilities

The board of trustees, whatever its name, is legally the library itself. The various state laws, municipal ordinances, charters, or constitutions create the board of trustees as the responsible body to hold and administer library property and funds to formulate policies and guide the direction of library affairs. Trustees appoint and set the salary of the chief librarian, or library director,* usually in consultation with the governing authority of the city or county. Authority is delegated by the trustees to the chief librarians to manage and operate the library. The library director officially is the board's agent, holding office at its pleasure and carrying out such policies and instructions as it sanctions. The board cannot relinquish or evade its final responsibilities for everything that pertains to the library, its purposes, policies, functions, organization, services, funds, its governmental and public relations, its expenditures and costs, its standing in public estimation, and its growth.

The reasons why boards must take their assignments seriously and be courageous, able citizens and why there is need for board–librarian cooperation become evident when one scrutinizes a board's duties:

1. To make certain that the library prepares a satisfactory plan with goals, objectives, priorities, programs and activities, and performance measures and evaluation procedures; and to participate in the drafting and continual review of the plan.

2. To assure the general efficiency and progress of the library.

3. To maintain good relations with local governments and secure the interest of the library in the overall governmental organization and financial structure and in local planning and improvements.

* There is no unanimity concerning the job title of the public library's executive officer. In early days, the title was simply "the librarian" and that is still used in many libraries, but confusion arises, because there will be in most libraries nowadays more than one librarian. A sample of one hundred public libraries of all sizes in four states in various parts of the country taken in 1979 revealed that a little more than half use the title "library director," somewhat less than half still use the title "librarian," and a few use the title "head librarian," "city librarian," or "chief librarian." The chief of the Chicago Public Library is now called the "library commissioner." In this book, the executive is titled "library director" or simply "director," but this is not a recommendation. References to the director will obviously be applied in the local situation to whoever holds the job, by whatever title.

4. To weigh financial needs in relation to goals and objectives and to see that these needs are convincingly presented to the public and to the appropriating authorities.

5. To understand the functions of a library director, to find and appoint a competent one, giving that employee a free hand in administrative matters, and to evaluate the leadership, lend support, and help overcome weaknesses, if any become evident.

6. To consider, formulate, and decide on policies, as initiated and presented by the library director.

7. To understand the functions and qualifications of the staff at its different levels, supporting the library director in finding and appointing a staff of high quality and in securing an adequate salary scale.

8. To keep in touch with the organization and activities of the library and to measure results in services, costs, and reader satisfaction.

9. To enlarge public and official understanding of the library and its purposes, problems, and progress.

10. To understand, question, and advise on matters that affect public relations, such as services to readers, finances, operating costs, and staff welfare, and to place on record its decisions on such matters.

### A Working Partnership

Paid to be concerned with all these matters, the director shares responsibility with the board. In some instances the board has the greater responsibility and makes the major decisions; in others the director does. In small-town libraries with part-time or insufficiently trained directors, the board naturally plays a larger part in decisions and details than it does in a large city organization with a professional staff. Actually, what is "policy" and what is "administration" is a policy question itself, and the board has to decide it; but it should be clarified each time the board appoints a new director. With responsibility must go authority; therefore lines of demarcation are needed. The logical place to define these boundaries is the bylaws of the board. The director foresees needs and policies, marshaling facts and opinions pro and con, presenting recommendations so that the trustees can decide whether to support them. The director will then either carry out the decisions reached, or obtain further information if required in order for the trustees to reach a satisfactory conclusion—one that is satisfactory to the board and to all concerned.

The director keeps in close touch with the board president and committee chairmen, goes over problems and agenda with them, gets to know the trustees individually, and sees that they visit library departments and branches and become acquainted with operations and staff. In this way and other ways, each new trustee and indeed the whole board are educated as to what the library is all about.

The board has an obligation to question the director and to request data to support ideas and recommendations presented to it. These can be refined and strengthened through discussion with committees of the staff. Trustees with a wide range of experience and attitudes should serve as the director's sounding board while allowing full administrative freedom. The board should never interfere with the routine or in the details of management. Having chosen a competent head it should expect the head to exercise the initiative, do the work, and assume the responsibility for it. In this matter of a clear division of functions, everything depends on the choice of a competent director. The selection of this official is therefore the most important library board function.

When either trustees or director feel antagonism growing up between them, frank discussion to compose their differences is profitable. Unless the board intends an ultimatum or dismissal, it should review mistakes or shortcomings of the director in a manner that will allow them to be rectified. The board should hear the director's version of the situation and accept criticism regarding viewpoints, actions, and failures of the board.

In brief, the respective roles of the trustees and the library director may be summarized as follows:

THE BOARD

Is entrusted with the library on behalf of the owners;

Determines the character and quality of the service and program;

Decides whether the library is to be great rather than mediocre, either by supporting the director or by leadership;

May provide the continuity;

Judges collectively; selects and reviews alternatives; knows what is going on; takes time to find out; prepares, explains, and defends the budget;

Stands up against censorship attacks and ensures that book selection practices do not render the library vulnerable to censorship.

THE DIRECTOR

Prepares the choices, assembles the facts, makes a recommendation, abides by the decision;

Looks ahead and prepares plans;

Keeps the trustees informed; establishes priorities;

Prepares and reviews a workable program.

## Qualifications of Trustees

Good board members are selected not for trade, profession, or religion but for capacity for leadership, for their belief that reading and study are vital, for their willingness to work, and for their commitment to protect the library against political and public pressure.

Library trustees should not be chosen because they are wealthy or influential or are owed a political debt. The board should be democratic, whether elected or appointed, and should represent all segments of its community.

### Age and Tenure Factors

The marked conservatism of library boards is often aggravated by too-great average age and too-long term in office.

Two conclusions emerge, in line with trends in school and public administration:

1. Except to represent a percentage of the community who are in the age group, seldom should persons older than seventy be offered or accept a library trusteeship; on reaching this age, unless within two or three years of the expiration of a term of not over five or six years, they should give up their membership to younger people.

2. Trustees should not serve longer than six or eight years, even on self-perpetuating boards. This change should be incorporated in state laws or board bylaws, of which each new trustee would be informed and to which he or she would agree before appointment. Many people consider a five-year term, specified in the bylaws, an efficient limit, with reappointments made only after a one-year interval.

### The Board in Action

In undertaking to manage their affairs for greatest results, trustees should focus on the obligations of their position rather than on its prestige. They should avoid delaying actions by uninterested members who cannot make up their minds; act strongly to represent the library's interests to municipal government; and eliminate ineffective service and employees.

A well-managed board of trustees holds frequent, well-attended, regular meetings. The larger the board, the less frequent are its scheduled meetings, and the harder it is to get a quorum; this is a great injustice to the library, for the director must keep many things dangling. A board of five is more efficient than of seven, seven are better than nine, and more than nine makes a board unwieldy. Large boards should take steps to reduce their size.

Boards of incorporated libraries, like nearly all municipal library boards, should have regular monthly meetings, with definite bylaws. The bylaws should be revised or reconsidered regularly, since library purposes and methods continually change, though many libraries and boards seem oblivious of this fact.

### Committees of the Board

There are standing committees of some sort in most boards, especially finance, personnel, buildings, and executive committees. Some rarely meet, some discuss routine matters as well as policies, some actually manage certain phases of the library. Theoretical advantages to this division of assignments are (a) each trustee's burden will be lessened; (b) each trustee will become well informed on certain problems of the library's operation; and (c) each trustee will feel more definite responsibility for something and therefore be more likely to give valuable assistance. The danger of standing committees is that trustees who familiarize themselves with details of personnel, buildings, and services are often tempted to perform functions that actually belong to the director.

There may be some virtue in giving up standing committees in favor of special committees to study special problems as they arise. A finance committee may be essential for a library having large endowment funds. And despite pros and cons, many directors depend substantially on the executive committee—a small working group of three or four, whatever its name, as counselors and confidants to whom they may turn for discussion of problems.

The president or chairperson of the board should be the member to whom the library director looks for major guidance, and the president should in turn be available for that guidance and to interpret board policies as required in the day-to-day operation. This is a major function of the board's presiding officer, and if he or she cannot spend a reasonable amount of time and effort performing that task, the leadership position should be declined. Being president is not solely a matter of prestige; there is a definite responsibility involved. This is not to say that the president is to run the library, but regular though brief conferences with the director between board meetings will help immensely to keep affairs running smoothly. In preparation for these conferences the director should have a brief, tight list of questions or issues that may be of concern; should describe problems that may be developing; and should discuss in outline form matters on which a policy recommendation may be in the making. The director must always remember that the president is a citizen volunteer and must not therefore impose upon the time of that individual. The director ought not to expect the president to make administrative decisions or to listen to complaints about "how difficult things are."

Liaison with, or conference with, other trustees by the library director should only be with the full knowledge and approval of the presiding officer. It is not necessary for the president to sit in on all such conferences or meetings—that is for the president to decide—but the president is in charge and must be aware of and responsible for what is going on. Sometimes an aggressive trustee, perhaps with extra time and energy to spare, will take a leadership position in respect to library operations. It will be up to the president to turn that potential contribution into constructive channels.

### At Board Meetings

In carrying on its meetings, the board needs (1) an adequate set of bylaws, which should distinguish between the functions of the director and the board; (2) a definite order of business, which should be listed in the bylaws; and (3) an itemized agenda or docket of current business to be considered. Unprepared-for meetings waste time and discourage efficient members from coming.

Usually the director prepares the docket, arranged according to the board's regular order of business, and goes over items in advance with the president, so that the latter can estimate the time for each topic and can decide how many topics to include. The docket includes a few lines of explanatory summary. The director also has pertinent data on hand as each item comes up. Each trustee should receive a copy of the docket in advance, as well as minutes of the previous meeting. The financial statement will itemize receipts and expenditures as budgeted under six or eight major headings for the year, then for the current month, then for the portion of the year to date, and finally will give the balance on hand to finish the fiscal year.

The director is present at board meetings in nearly all libraries, in the majority of libraries acting as secretary or assistant secretary. Even in a small library the director can hardly operate the library without attending and taking part in board meetings. If the director does not attend board meetings there must be either a misconception on the part of the board of their duties or such a lack of confidence in the director that replacement is in order.

Board meetings should generally be open to the public. Stimulated by passage of the federal government's "Sunshine Law" (P.L. 94-409 [1976]), which requires open meetings, many state and local governments have enacted similar legislation. Since the legislation requires open meetings of public boards, the local library boards should take these statutes into consideration when scheduling both regular board meetings and committee meetings. Most such laws have a provision for executive sessions if sensitive personnel matters are being discussed.

### The Board and Legal Problems

Trustees logically concern themselves also with legal questions. Often they are aided by skilled services given by public-spirited lawyers on the board or in the community, or by the city attorney. Ladenson (see reading list) has a compilation of library laws from all the states. Most state library commissions furnish a summary of state library laws. Still not available is a case book or substantial discussion of the many legal problems that have actually faced libraries. Such questions may arise in acquiring sites, erecting buildings, contracting for services, contracting to join with other library units, handling personnel matters, damages of various sorts, titles to property and rights to funds, interpretation or changes of wills, and the like.

### The Board and Disclosure Laws

Six years after the Watergate scandals forced Richard Nixon to resign the presidency, Congress appears ready to enact legislation designed to prevent future occurrences of similar events. Bills which have passed and others under discussion would require certain public officials to disclose their financial holdings. Some states have already passed such laws. In California, a new law specifies that chief administrative officers, mayors, council members, and other officials of counties and cities make annual reports pertaining to investments, sources of income, property, debts, and loans. Such laws are designed to ensure ethical practices and avoid conflicts of interest. In certain cases they have caused executives to refuse board appointments.

### The Board and Finances

Finance is an ever-present subject facing the trustees, calling for a sound sense of appraisal of needs, courage to ask and sometimes to demand fair support, and resourcefulness to see that the library cause prevails in the competition among publicly supported activities. Library finances are probably discussed by boards far more than anything else. Sometimes much of this is on details, which should be delegated to the treasurer, director, clerical assistant, or business manager, so that the trustees can work on debatable or unusual items.

In practically all libraries the director either is solely responsible for the preparation of the budget or shares the responsibility with the board and/or city agency. More details of budget preparation are discussed in Chapter 7, on Finances. Trustees should be aware of the municipal government's general financial problems, such as the present total tax rate versus first-line new municipal obligations. They are responsible for library personnel, and through them the outcome of reader demands. The obligation of the director and the staff to press for what the public asks in service is just as great as is the trustees' obligation to question and analyze it. And their mutual obligation in this respect is proportionally as great for a five-person as for a two-hundred-person staff.

The board's clear duty is to secure fair appropriations despite objections put forth by the city, often the same city urged by powerful zealots to provide for new cultural enterprises of less value to the public. Many boards, not relishing the struggle with city hall, try to avoid seeking substantial budget increases. Worse yet, some trustees have been appointed by mayors, city managers, and councils with the definite purpose of assuring that the board will not ask officials for more money.

### The Board and Personnel

Next to finances, in time consumed in board meetings and committees, is the subject of library personnel. We have cited the opinion that the most important of all trustee functions is the selection of a competent director, when a vacancy occurs. This requires time, attention, and serious effort.

### Choosing a Library Director

In the search for a director these steps should be taken:

1. Prepare a timetable, in consultation with the outgoing director. Where the vacancy is occurring because of retirement, the opening date is usually predictable some months in advance. In other cases, the leaving director should give at least two to three months' notice. The selection process can be expected to take at least six to nine months, hence it may be necessary to operate with an acting director for a time. The preparatory steps will require perhaps a month; the times required for other steps are listed. The process cannot be rushed; it is an important step, as has been noted, and will have impact on the library's success or lack of it, perhaps for years to come. A wrong or unwise choice can of course be rectified, but only at some cost and trauma to all concerned. It is better to take the steps in order and see that they are well carried out, with due deliberation.

2. Review the duties and responsibilities of the position with the present incumbent, as these have been outlined in the job description (see Chapter 5). This may require a month to complete satisfactorily.

3. Arrange for staff participation in the setting of criteria and qualifications and in the interview of candidates leading to final selection. This essential element in participatory management will prove to be of invaluable assistance. The staff participation process may be drawn up by the director in consultation with key staff members. A good procedure would be to invite suggestions and comments on criteria from all staff members, either verbally or in writing; and then preparation of a consensus on qualifications; and selection by the staff of an advisory committee. This committee should meet early with the board or the board committee that is to screen and interview candidates. The staff committee should be told that their advice and counsel will be listened to and considered seriously but that their role is advisory and that final selection responsibility must rest with the board. It would be advisable throughout the process to maintain communication between the staff committee and the board committee, so that the staff understands what is going on, and how and why decisions have been reached, as they are made.

The staff committee will not need to participate in the candidate screening process, but they should be afforded an opportunity to interview the candidates that are selected for interview. This step can go forward concurrently with Steps One and Two.

4. The board, or its committee, will prepare a clearly stated set of criteria and qualifications, taking into account the recommendations of the incumbent director, the staff consensus, and possibly the Friends of the Library or other citizens' or user groups having an interest. One month should be allowed for this step.

5. Securing candidates will be done by advertisement in accordance with

applicable affirmative action plans, as outlined in Chapter 5, on Personnel. Advertisements may be supplemented by letters and telephone calls to other library directors whose opinion would be of assistance and to the state library agency. A deadline for receipt of applications should be set. National library periodicals require 30 to 45 days from receipt of copy. The local affirmative-action plan may suggest or require advertisements in the minority press. Advertisements may well need to run over a period of a month or six weeks in order to assure adequate coverage. The deadline for receipt of applications will be at least two months from the appearance of the initial advertisement. Therefore the advertising and receipt of applications process will consume around four and a half to five months. The advertising schedule should be arranged so that the initial notice will appear in all selected media at approximately the same time.

6. The board will have appointed a selection or screening committee to review applications received, secure references as required, and decide upon three to six candidates to be interviewed. It may be better to select more rather than fewer, as one or more may withdraw in favor of another appointment or for other reasons, during the process. The entire body of applications after screening may be divided into groups: "to be interviewed," "possible for interview if no candidate found in the group to be interviewed," and "not to be considered." The selection committee will want to work out its own procedure for arriving at consensus, and this will require skill and diplomacy on the part of the chairperson. Needless to say, the president will be an ex-officio member. This step may require at least one month, depending upon the time that committee members have to put into it. Clearly it should be done as quickly as possible.

7. Secure references for candidates to be interviewed, and invite candidates for interview. These two actions can go forward concurrently. Either the library director (incumbent) can secure the references and arrange for the interviews, or this can be done by the selection committee chairperson. Telephone inquiries are often made, and these may not necessarily be limited to the names that the candidate has listed on the application. The step may take two weeks to a month. Some points about this step may be added.

All applications and screening should remain in the committee's hands without interference from other trustees until the committee's recommendations are ready.

While grades and credentials from library schools are of major significance, the evaluations from school placement officers cannot always be taken at face value, nor can recommendations from friendly colleagues. Frank and detailed statements from former employers and from dispassionate observers—that is, other outstanding librarians—as to specific qualities and accomplishments, are more useful.

It is not necessarily true that a good director will wish only to settle down into a secure berth; the chief interest is or ought to be to develop a library to a high point of efficiency, then tackle a large one, or one where conditions are more favorable; sometimes a change may be made with no salary increase, though this is infrequent and not to be counted on.

8. Interviewing selected candidates should go forward within as brief a period as possible, in fairness to all candidates. If it can be done within a few days, so much the better, but candidates may not be able to appear as desired because of other commitments. The staff advisory committee should interview all candidates being interviewed by the board selection committee but at a separate time and location—that is, not with the board committee. Both committees will have done well to have given some thought to questions they will ask and to the interview process: what they are looking for, evidences of competence, and so forth. The incumbent director may or may not be present at the interviews but should not exercise a vote or an opinion unless asked.

The views of the staff advisory committee should be heard by the board committee as soon as possible after the interview, perhaps on the same day. The board committee will decide whether to share their views and conclusions with the staff, but this should not be done until a final set of recommendations has been made to the entire board.

9. As quickly as possible after all interviews have been completed, the selection committee should arrive at a consensus, placing the candidates in rank order. When this has been accomplished, the recommendations should be laid before the entire board, and when consensus is reached, the selection committee chairperson or the board president will make the offer to the selected candidate preferably by telephone, with written confirmation to follow. The candidate will be asked to accept or decline, and if there is acceptance, a starting date will be agreed upon. In point of fact, this item will properly have been discussed during the interview, and confirmed in the offer and acceptance. Obviously if the first choice declines, the committee will go down the list. Time is of the essence once a choice has been made, in fairness to all, and to allow the appointee to give notice and make arrangements for moving.

Finally, in the selection of a new director, it should be emphasized that hunting for bargains is decidedly unprofitable; so is offering a poor salary. Hesitating to offer and advertise as high a salary as possible generally slows down the selecting process.

### General Personnel

With library budgets and salary funds so difficult to attain, and positions too few to cover the services of so many libraries, trustees and director should realize that each position means a substantial piece of work to be done to serve the public, and is to be filled only by the most competent person available and not simply within the present library staff. Some libraries constantly improve themselves by wide, intensive search among the profession for outstanding people, especially to fill positions of leadership. These matters are covered in the personnel chapters later. They are mentioned here to make clear that employment in the library is something more than job holding, and that little consideration should be given to pressure from influential officials and citizens in favor of some person who does not have what it takes to make the library stronger than it was before. There is increasing mobility among librarians, and the trustees' task is to hold the good ones.

In personnel matters, the board should evaluate and make decisions in cooperation and consultation with the director. If staff members are encouraged or permitted to bring their troubles to the board, or to individual members of it, a dangerous situation results that may lead to conflicts, confusion and poor morale. Yet often the board has to act as a court of last resort in controversial situations. Where the director by poor management of personnel matters, by some arbitrary decision or order, or by continued failure to secure fair salaries and other benefits for the staff shows weakness as an administrator, the individual employee or some committee has an obvious right to bring the situation to the attention of the full board. The intention and facts should first be submitted to the director. Due process dictates that, failing satisfaction, the matter will then go to a committee of the board. Any subterfuge or concealment by either director or board, as to all the facts that both should know, will be unfortunate.

Such vital matters as salary scales, hours of employment, pensions, and benefits are normally analyzed and the facts put into shape for board consideration by the director, preferably aided by a committee from the staff. Pros and cons of the problem and of staff attitudes will thus be well understood before decisions are made.

Decisions on many personnel matters, however, are no longer in many cities dependent on the board. Salaries and other benefits for library staffs are determined by what personnel in county or municipal departments are receiving. If, for example, a secretary in the Personnel Department of the town gets a 7 percent increase, so does the secretary in the library. This rule includes department heads and even in most cases the library director.

Today in most libraries appointments are made on the recommendation of the director. Even if the larger library has a personnel officer, the director usually deals with professional appointments. The board, which commonly holds the legal authority to appoint, delegates the actual choice and judgment to the director, who is in the best position to know the needs and is expected to evaluate candidates carefully, presenting the formal recommendations with evidence for the board to consider for approval or disapproval. Often the board or a committee wishes to interview one or two candidates for important administrative posts.

A real handicap for trustees is insufficient knowledge of the detailed work of the departments. They can get some idea by seeing in operation the reference and informational services and the classifying and cataloging of books and services to children, and can realize the essential, detailed and specialized training and experience required.

## The Board and Book Selection

Often by statute, the board is officially responsible for book selection; it may have a book committee and should adopt a materials selection policy. Only in small libraries, however, does the board give substantial attention to the usual run of book selection; the more they delegate this to the library staff, the better for all concerned. In large libraries even the director no longer attempts to decide on the majority of titles chosen. In medium-sized and small libraries the director takes most of the responsibility, drawing on book-and-reader knowledge of the staff.

Voluminous writings have discussed the duty of the library to have controversial material on all timely subjects, to follow the liberal rather than authoritarian trends in the community, and to avoid and withstand censorship. When questions and criticism come directly to the board members, they will report them to the director, for a review and recommendation. This should be a well-balanced overall view of the principles involved, the criticisms against the book, and sound specific reasons why it should or should not be accepted. In a sense the director is interpreter and defender for the mass of actual library users who join neither side in controversies of this sort, but have strong views and should have chief consideration in the decision. Harm will be done to the library if the director takes a doctrinaire attitude, whether liberal or conservative, courageous or timid, or fails to see that the inevitable publicity is well handled. Many directors who handled their part sensibly and courageously have been overruled by trustees stampeded into bad decisions; trustees have been more inclined than their directors to give way to pressure groups, even when general public opinion is against these groups.

A citizen should not consider a position on a library board, where trustees must work closely with librarians, unless the member can concur with the tenets on intellectual freedom outlined in the American Library Association's Library Bill of Rights, formulated on the U.S. Constitution's concept of freedom. Trustees should be aware of the history of the ALA's commitment to intellectual freedom. A comprehensive account of the association's documents and policies as well as essays by library leaders on this subject are contained in the Association's *Intellectual Freedom Manual.*

## Public Relations of the Library Board

Though public relations is a vital trustee interest, few directors suggest the part each trustee can play. Regrettably, some librarians and trustees fear and distrust public opinion about administrative, financial, and policy aspects of the library. The suggestion that board meetings be reported in the local paper has been passed off by many boards as "too hot to handle"; they echo Alexander Hamilton's "The People, Sir, is a Great Beast." It is a democratic principle that public opinion should be recognized. The community can be made enthusiastically favorable to the library, if it so deserves. True, it is more comfortable for boards and directors to run things all by themselves. If library boards regard participation in library affairs by staff, by readers, by citizen groups such as Friends of the Library as an infringement of their rights, then of course democratic administration must fail; the community is not deluded into considering that such a library is a democratic institution.

Some specific suggestions for trustees are: speeches on library topics at public meetings and forums, especially on finance, salary, and policy matters and on building and extension programs; board studies, with librarian or staff committee, on library equipment, building problems, matters involving additional funds, and library salary levels and scales; planned solicitation of gifts, of special or notable materials, or of funds to buy them; contacts, in consultation with the director, with organizations or leaders with whom trustees are acquainted, for furthering library relations with these outside channels.

## The Board's Evaluative Function

The obligation to perform at least a superficial self-evaluation seems obvious. Unless the board understands the factors, can weigh pros and cons, has some basis of comparison, it is in poor position to know what sort of a library it is running. Its lack of information about its own library may be startling, and dismaying to the director and staff it employs.

Here are some suggestions for gaining background and perspective with which to judge and weigh recommendations made to and by a board:

1. Set aside some time in which to go through the library carefully, with the director or a qualified colleague to explain the organization and the work of each assistant in a smaller library or at least the leaders in a larger one, and to learn what each department or branch is doing to build its collections and services. Showing trustees the process of answering a reference question while the reader awaits the result often proves the first revelation of what a library does.

2. Read *Minimum Standards for Public Library Systems, 1966,* published by the ALA, and the 1980 *Guidelines.* Trustees should also look at issues of *The Public Library Trustee,* a monthly newsletter prepared by the ALA that deals with special trustee problems.

3. Visit a few selected well-regarded libraries of similar size or a little larger; attend trustees' sessions at state and regional library conferences; dis-

cuss matters with other trustees; and analyze reports and statistics from similar communities.

4. Raise questions at board meetings and request reports by the director on major questions of development and on details of operation. The board may consider a subject so specialized or technical or expensive that it will appoint a temporary committee to inquire further into costs and benefits.

Criteria by various surveyors of public library situations indicate that a common factor in the good or poor status of a library is the board's constant interest in (a) what the public is getting for its money; (b) what the staff is paid for its talents; (c) whether the library is moving ahead or standing still in its total circulation, its adult nonfiction circulation, its children's services, and the volume and quality of its reference service; (d) the degree to which the library is looked upon by the community and by individual citizens as a constant daily impetus to constructive thinking and activity and to good citizenship, measurable in part by the attention given the library in local or nearby newspapers; and (e) the community's concern with knowledge, which the board has a basic responsibility to promote.

*A Trusteeship Test*

Trustees who wish to undertake some self-evaluation of their effectiveness might find the following brief test a useful exercise:

Score yourself. Directions:
> Circle appropriate number.
> Total your score.
> See rating (page 46).

1. Have you attended every Library Board meeting since becoming a trustee?
> Every meeting   −6        Occasionally   −1
> Missed some   −2

2. How many library system, state library meetings, and library workshops have you attended in the last six months?
> Six or more   −6        One or more   −1
> Three or more   −3        None   −0

3. How many meetings have you attended as a representative of the library in the last year in your community?
> Six or more   −6        One or more   −1
> Three or more   −3        None   −0

4. Have you visited your local library and talked with staff other than the head librarian in the last sixty days?
> Three times or more   −5        Once   −1
> Twice   −2                No visits   −0

5. Have you visited other libraries in the last six months?
Five or more  —6      One or more  —3      No visits  —0
6. Have you reviewed the library's objectives in the last year?
Yes  —1      No  —0
7. Have you taken steps to increase library revenues?
Yes  —1      No  —0
8. Have you encouraged the expanding services of the library?
Yes  —1      No  —0
9. Have you been engaged in public relations activities for the library in the last six months?
Yes  —1      No  —0
10. Have you read your state library law?
Yes  —1      No  —0

**Rating:**

| | | |
|---|---|---|
| 34 to 25 | Excellent | If you have time, consider joining and helping in state, regional, and national trustee associations. |
| 24 to 15 | Very Good | Can you help others? |
| 14 to 10 | Good | Good start. |
| 9 to 5 | Fair | Consider resigning or take more interest. |
| 4 to 0 | Poor | You should resign from the board. |

## The Trustees' Legislative Role

State Senator Lucy T. Hammer, speaking to Connecticut public library trustees, placed the responsibility for increasing state aid squarely upon the trustees. At a trustees' meeting, she was asked to speak on the question "How do public library trustees relate to the legislature?"

I can answer the question very simply. The trustee deals with the General Assembly not at all. What do libraries mean to the state legislator? The answer, professional librarians: the state library committee and its librarians, and the librarians of the larger libraries. The Education Committee of the General Assembly is dealing with an enclave: libraries are run by librarians; needs of libraries are presented by the professionals; legislation is drawn up by the professionals; it follows that professional librarians speak for library interests.

The problem with this is that the librarian speaks in the light of his own professional interest; it is the same with nurses, doctors, teachers, lawyers. The professional presents his case in terms of what is good for libraries, how to improve libraries, and this always comes out as more money for libraries.

The professional library people do not see libraries in the context of the whole community of the larger society.

I fault trustees for the image that is presented. They are supposed to make policy and direct the progress of the library establishment, and perhaps they do, but whatever waves they make in doing this don't wash over into the outside world, and certainly do not reach the General Assembly.

The trustees should be the bridge between the professional and the town and state governments. Government officials are understandably suspicious of professionals advocating their professional cause. How does the General Assembly know whether this is what the public wants? Whether it fits into the economic structure of the town or state?

Is it too much to ask, for the trustees to be the bridge? Trustees, like town and state officials, are lay citizens. They speak the same language; they are personally concerned with the same things: first, taxes, and second, making books and the records of history and education and culture available to the public. Both public officials and trustees want results they can see and understand, such as many people using the libraries, a balanced and reasonable budget, and a tangible return for the dollars spent. They want to hear from the people themselves that the library is a valuable and appreciated asset.

I can assume that the library trustees want these things, but I think they do not do enough to bring them about. And they have to do what has to be done, themselves. They cannot leave it to others to do.

The trustees should be able to look at a funding plan and judge whether it is reasonable and practical. If it is not reasonable and practical to the citizens and trustees, it will not be to the General Assembly.

When you need state money, and this is a perennial problem, talk to legislators before supporting a plan, and even before making the plan, if this is possible. When you, as trustees, make a plan for the state to share in the cost of local library service, make your plan simple, make it *defensible,* and I emphasize that, and make the amount of money reasonable. There is no virtue in asking for an unreasonably high sum to support an indefensible plan, on the premise that you will get something.

We need factual, sensible, taxpayer-type answers to the questions: *Why* do libraries need increased funds? It has to be more than: "they need more funds because someone says so." Is it for salaries, for books, for maintenance? Is it because of inflation? Are there more people using libraries? Is there a public demand for more services? If so, what services?[3]

Ms. Hammer states not only a strong case for a more active trustee public role, but defines in practical terms the line between trustees and directors as to public responsibility.

In general a strong, articulate, dynamic director will engender similar qualities in the trustees. By contrast a weak, ineffectual director will invite indifference, or administrative interference, or both, by the trustees. A wise board of trustees will know that a weak manager should be replaced by a strong manager. Trying to deal with both policy and administration will only prolong trustee frustration. It will not substitute for a competent executive.

## Notes

1. *Public Libraries in the United States: Trends, Problems, and Recommendations* (New York: Nelson Associates, 1967), p. 21.
2. Roberta Bowler, ed., *Local Public Library Administration* (Chicago: International City Manager's Association, 1964), p. 57.
3. Lucy T. Hammer, "How Public Library Trustees Relate to the Legislature," *Connecticut Libraries* 15 (January 1973): 23–25.

# 4  Administrative Policies and Techniques

When one visits any going concern—store, school, manufacturing plant—the question is inevitable: "Who is in charge? Who is running things?" Someone makes the broad decisions, assumes the leadership, bears the responsibility, and provides the overall thinking to keep the organization running, to tie people, ideas, operations together at the top. In a library this administrative function rests with the library director, but it is to an extent shared by other staff members.

Planning and direction are basic to all enterprises. Consider for a moment the complex and varied information on personal finance, taxes, investments, insurance, and law that each of us needs to conduct our own lives. Even in a small library, where one person has to do everything, an administrative viewpoint is essential.

### What Administration Includes

Administration means essentially getting the job done. It involves

Comprehending purposes, needs, and opportunities;

Planning, defining problems, making decisions, finding ways and means, managing and following through;

Organizing, or recognizing and defining, then putting together in sound and simple relationship the component elements or divisions of the operation as a whole, then of its smaller parts—departments and individual jobs;

Selection and administration of personnel: the understanding, choosing, and appreciation of people and their development;

Assigning work according to abilities, with judgment and consideration in fitting them together;

Defining responsibilities and lines of authority;

Giving instructions;

Supervision;

Guidance of staff and seeing that each does the work with distinction; also includes development of employees as individuals, giving them both opportunity and recognition;

Scrutinizing and evaluating, and measuring results, in terms of reader satisfaction, with attention to costs.

Administration is further involved with the government connections of the library, partly through the board of trustees; its relations with other municipal departments and officials; the financial structure of the library and the sources for securing adequate funds, their budgeting and use; public relations—that is, keeping the entire community aware of library purposes, problems, services, and accomplishments—and being aware of what the community thinks of its library.

## Leadership

Four administrative aspects of librarianship deserve special attention: (1) *organization,* (2) *supervision,* (3) *measurement* of activities, methods, and services for efficiency, reader satisfaction, and economical operation, and (4) *promotion* of library use.

An effective leader—one who can take charge of a piece of work, a department, an activity, or a library—is vital to any successful operation. An important element in the administrator's capacity to exercise power and authority, even when such power and authority are intrinsic to the position, lies in one's technical and professional expertise. When subordinates doubt their supervisor's skill and knowledge, the supervisor loses authority and must fall back on sanctions. Finally, leadership ability depends on skill in selecting able people and working with them.

## Some Recent Administrative Approaches

The study of administration, or management, is fairly new. An early approach called Management focused on the organization, its goals, structure, technology, policies, and procedures. It was an autocratic, task-oriented style. This traditional viewpoint later gave way to a field labeled Human Relations, which stressed people. This approach was acceptable to many because it was thought to be democratic. It was also felt that once man's physical and social needs were met, he would be satisfied with his job and produce more.

When subsequent studies showed that job satisfaction led more to apathy than to harder work, Human Relations began to lose its popularity. Today it has been replaced by a new field called Organizational Behavior, which merges a concern for both people and organizations.

Organizational Behavior, for which scholars and practictioners are attempting to develop management principles that will work in public institutions as well as in business, has given rise to many schools of thought. Some of its advocates believe that Human Relations failed because it didn't do enough. They argue that people want more from their work than financial rewards, job security, and humane treatment. In addition to this recognition of physical and social needs, they say workers desire fulfillment from their jobs. Therefore, administrators should consider not only how to supervise their personnel but also how to redesign jobs, make decisions, and set up controls so that people can realize their potential and gain a sense of accomplishment from their work.

## Participative Management

An Organizational Behavior approach that has received much attention is Participative Management. It holds that people will perform best when given an opportunity to participate in the decisions that affect them and their work. It emphasizes the committee process; for example, decisions on hierarchy and job descriptions are made by a consensus of peers.

Like Human Relations, Participative Management urges participation and involvement to encourage feelings of self-worth and to secure cooperation. The new style is different in that it sees participative practices as a way of bringing more talent and greater commitment to bear on important decisions, thus capitalizing on human resources untapped by traditional procedures. Such programs as job enrichment, management by objectives, and self-controlled work teams have evolved from this movement. Most important, this concept of human needs restores performance as a legitimate management interest.

In 1970 Maurice Marchant examined the effects of Rensis Likert's participative management theory on the administration of twenty-two university libraries. He reported that group decision making has two major advantages over decision making imposed unilaterally by management: the superior quality of the decisions and their greater acceptance by the group.[1]

Any enterprise, it is thought by many, will be more productive if the work, the ideas, and the status of each worker are treated with respect. In addition to salaries and job security, workers desire humane treatment, recognition, and self-fulfillment opportunities. Participation in management is important to morale. Participation can be particularly effective in libraries as a source of ideas and as a management method. If carried out realistically, it can be a powerful and constructive influence on the staff. Participation in planning encourages cooperation. If this method is to work, however, the trustees and the director must be open-minded, objective, and receptive to the ideas of others. Participation falls flat, down the line, unless all those in charge believe in it and promote it. Some directors may shun ideas from their colleagues or fear the thought that others on the staff might have valuable ideas or resourcefulness in working out new approaches. The fact is that the forward movement of the library can have no other effect than reflect credit on the director, who would thus do well to use the human resources available and permit them to flourish.

This does not mean that the staff is to run the library or force the director to follow a particular course of action. Good participation is a matter of integrating the ideas and viewpoints of the staff in ways that will promote the library's welfare. The director and department heads are in charge; they are paid for leadership, judgment, decisions, and results. The director or department head who intends to use participative management will first study carefully how to do it well and will then approach the process in a gradual, natural, unheralded manner. The administrative personnel will not ask for staff participation unless there is clear and definite intention to consider seriously the results and to discuss reasons when something is proposed that will not work out. It is not, clearly, a matter of a majority vote on policies and procedures, although voting may sometimes be useful as a way of ensuring that less articulate members have a voice. But basically what is being sought is a consensus, the "sense of the group" on the particular issue or problem.

Of course there will be constructive disagreement, and sometimes there will be agreement to disagree, and some conflict. The director is not in a popularity contest but is there to run the library and to take charge of the operations. The interest of all is to have a productive and useful library program. In essence, participation means establishing a climate in which the staff members can have a voice in the matters that affect them, can know what is going on, can understand reasons for decisions that are made.

## Communicating Library Information to the Staff

Participation starts by acquainting each employee with the library's activities and progress, and with his job and status. A history of the library should be compiled and made available to each staff member. Committees, conferences, and staff meetings should be held frequently. Unless the staff is familiar with the details of new rules and procedures and with the stages of planning, the organization cannot act effectively to obtain its objectives.

## Help from a Few or All?

Many libraries make awards to employees for suggesting ideas that lead to improvements and savings. A few metropolitan libraries have consistent suggestion systems. Some libraries frequently ask everyone to write a suggestion and send it to the department head or director in a sealed envelope; they offer a prize each month and a substantial reward and public recognition each year for the most usable and important ones. All suggestions are acknowledged, appreciated, and considered; the originator personally gets some indication of the outcome of the idea. Suggestions should not disappear into a void.

These staff suggestions may bear on detailed routines and methods in one's own department or work, on improving personal relations with individual readers, on policies, on projects for bettering the library and its service, or on matters of organization and administration.

Staff committees can put suggestions into shape, take them up with heads concerned, and relate the outcome to the ones who put forward the suggestions. If the decision is negative, the reasons behind the decision should be explained.

A staff quickly measures administrative cordiality to new ideas. Does the director or department head have an open door but a closed mind? Confidence and enthusiasm mount when it is discovered that the chief is interested in details, knows what is going on, appreciates suggestions, and does something about them. The director should protect staff members from any resentment that their suggestions might cause and should train department heads to value the suggestions of assistants even though the suggestions may be critical of their departments.

### Recognition and Job Fulfillment

Psychologists and specialists in industrial relations are well aware that morale springs in part from favorable comment on good work. A few large libraries send personal letters of welcome and goodbye; some give a cash award or honorable mention for special accomplishments or good work. They praise clerical and mechanical work such as mending, binding, and typing, as well as book lists, cataloging, reference work, and book selection. Staff recognition has to be handled with care and tact. It should not be neglected even in the small library; a few words of commendation take only a moment.

### Staff Meetings

Staff members may easily misunderstand library affairs—financing, control exercised by board, director and department head, and individual responsibility. A good staff manual is important. So is the well-planned meeting of the whole staff—that is, of all who can be released at one time, as is usual in probably three-fourths of libraries. Even a small staff can hardly have good communication without planned staff meetings. Some library buildings are so arranged that meetings are held first thing in the morning, in or within view of the circulation room; the few readers who arrive early can be taken care of while discussion proceeds.

Time for staff meetings can be justified by a carefully planned program, with preliminary assigned work, items thoroughly prepared, questions formulated, and data gathered. The meeting should have a good leader to guide and encourage discussion, keep to the point, restrain the loquacious, encourage new assistants who may have fresh and often worthwhile viewpoints, summarize what the meeting accomplished, and follow up on policy matters.

A good staff meeting means well-guided discussion of administrative problems; staff problems, salary, and other matters of status; and problems and policies of the library itself. Summaries of debatable questions with reports on what other libraries are doing about them and recommendations from staff committees lend substance and variety. What does the staff wish to know about or to complain about? Specifics, including unwelcome facts and ideas, are better than generalities.

The director in a few minutes can talk about problems and policies, such as the budget, the history of present situations that are misunderstood, hopes for the library. The director will not dominate the meeting, may attend for only part of the time, and will not evade matters of individual personal concern to the assistants. Many staff meetings are planned, chaired, and run by a staff committee, but they may need guidance.

### Committees

Staff committees can be an excellent device for furthering the common good of staff and library. Efficient committees can examine the pros and cons of problems, often producing valuable ideas for consideration. But the committee function should be only advisory, to help the head make up his or her mind, not to decide. Even on a small staff, directors and department heads can draw valuable counsel from a few colleagues who can approach problems practically, with thoughts on public opinion, staff reactions, and better service. Two or three with good judgment, and the courage to disagree with the chief, can help formulate ideas and decisions.

### Staff Organizations and Unionism

Any staff of more than twenty-five will benefit from an organization guided by the staff itself, to accomplish purposes affecting staff status and welfare. Some directors and trustees resent this idea on the ground that they have already thought of all the benefits the staff should expect. Their per capita budgets and salary scales usually belie this. A staff association is justified even when its clear objective is to agitate courageously and create pressure to compel its own library officials to wake up and remedy bad conditions. It should go beyond routine activities—for example, committees on social affairs, on staff gifts and sick visits, on welcoming new recruits, and expressions of sentiment on crucial issues. It should make salary surveys, handle loan funds, and encourage frank expression of staff opinion.

Since the early 1960s, unions in libraries and, indeed, unions in all levels of government have expanded at an unprecedented rate. This growth has been accompanied by demonstrations of militancy similar to those associated with the organization drives of workers in the mass production industries in the 1930s, reflecting a radical change in the historically docile attitude of civil service employees toward their public employer.

The result has altered public service employee–management relations from established unilateral determination of working conditions by the public employer to patterns of bilateralism dominating in the private sector. The determination of working conditions in public employment by legislation or administrative action is being rapidly replaced by collective bargaining between employee organizations and the employer.

The appearance of public collective bargaining, especially in municipal employment, has begun to direct attention to the increasing independence of bureaucracy in public affairs. It is hard to distinguish between working conditions, a subject now within the scope of collective bargaining, and decisions on issues of public policy, which are the constitutional prerogative of administrative and legislative authorities tracing their powers to the people. In a sense this is a public phase of the perpetual conflict in industry over management and union rights. More and more in public service, matters previously limited to official discretion are being written into union contracts.

Many differ on the significance of these trends. Some see in them the collapse of the "barriers between the bureaucracies and the people" and the democratization of public administration. Others fear a breakdown of responsible representative government and the surrender of public authority to private groups that have no legal responsibility to the people but can curtail vital services by strikes.[2]

A further discussion of the practical aspects and application of collective bargaining will be found in Chapter 5, "Personnel Policies and Procedures."

### Getting Things Done Through Others

Administration is largely a matter of getting results through the efforts of many: trustees, public officials, community groups and leaders, and especially staff members. This process involves personal relationships. A summary of ideas from many successful business and industrial leaders may be useful:[3]

1. Motivate staff members positively toward acceptance of ideas rather than using a "hard sell" approach.
2. Understand the attitudes and motives of each staff member.
3. Be a good listener.
4. Criticize constructively.
5. Criticize in private.
6. Commend in public.
7. Be considerate and courteous.

8. Do not take credit for oneself that belongs to another.

9. Overbearing domination throws a wet blanket on all hands and breeds yes men.

10. Show interest in and appreciation of the other person. Be human.

11. Wishes made known by suggestions get better results than commands.

12. In making requests or giving instructions, explain the reasons; people like to know not only what they're doing, but why.

13. The head sets the staff's style and attitudes. Consistency is reassuring.

14. Make it evident that you have confidence in assistants and expect them to do their best; they tend to perform accordingly.

15. Admit errors in actions and ideas.

16. People carry out best their own ideas, feeling a personal responsibility to prove them workable.

17. Care in what one says and in how one says it will avoid misunderstanding and hurt feelings, even in seemingly chance remarks.

### Change

Books on management emphasize change as fundamental to the progress of any institution or business; this appears to be especially true in libraries. They are prone to cling to old ideas and methods, overlooking the saying "When we're through changing, we're through." Joeckel's 1935 assessment is true today:

Perhaps more than any other function of local government, the free public library of today is intimately linked by tradition, by custom, and even by law, with its historic backgrounds. . . .While libraries have been increasingly liberal in the development of their services to users, the various authorities responsible for their management have been immensely conservative in their reluctance to alter the traditional forms of library organization.[4]

Discussion with the boards of more than a hundred libraries about organization, finances, functions, services, and administrative problems, as well as about library building plans and exterior designs, has revealed that on all these aspects of library affairs librarians and trustees have almost invariably been, as Joeckel says, intensely self-satisfied and conservative. They resist change. They permit months and years to elapse before they get up courage and ambition to act.

Willingness to change does not mean a compulsion to alter everything. It means challenging and reevaluating the status quo from fresh viewpoints.

Change cannot be constructive without knowledge of the past. A librarian must have a sense of history to grasp the significance of his or her own library or department. It is helpful to look at such histories as Whitehall's *History of the Boston Public Library,* Harry Lydenberg's *History of the New York Public Library,* David Mearns' story of the Library of Congress, *Up to Now,* or the new *Dallas Public Library* by Larry Grove. A new director or department head should study what predecessors have done before altering policies and programs. Santayana said, "They who forget the past are in turn themselves forgotten." A new head can prepare by scanning recent department or library reports and other records, at least the recent ones; by talking to those who know the story; and by looking through the library press clips. This will further relationships with the staff, the trustees, and the community.

## Administrative Development

Since so many join the profession because of their enjoyment of books and their belief in the power of books and reading as a social force, or because they like working constructively with the great variety of people who use or work in libraries, few librarians prepare for executive and administrative work. Good library administrators are in short supply, not because administrative ability cannot be developed but because few have prepared themselves.

Many able library assistants have declined better-paying positions as administrators because they have lacked self-confidence. Most college and library school graduates, with two or three years of job experience, should be able to take such responsibility, provided they develop administrative thinking. While library workers are busy as assistants they can observe and absorb administrative methods and try to understand the background against which decisions are made.

In business and industry as well as in library service, there are many good books on administration and management, theories of leadership, and executive ability.

As one writer on this subject said:

There seems to be a widespread belief that executive skill is a God-given attribute. It is something that you have or you haven't. . . . There are a limited number of essential executive qualities which are doubtless in the nature of a birthright. . . . But between those individuals who have these few qualities in great measure, and those who do not have them at all, there lies the much larger number of individuals gifted in moderate degree. These are the persons whose progress may suffer because of the notion that executive technique is a matter of a sixth sense, an intuitive faculty which defies explanation, a "hunch" which always tells the right thing to do at the right time. These people tend to close their minds to their problem.[5]

## The Bibliophile as Administrator

A scholar may have great administrative ability. The best librarians are those who combine these two interests. Numerous cases demonstrate that scholarly interests can go with high administrative ability in other fields, as in the case of Benjamin Franklin—that successful businessman, colonel of militia, commissioner to the Indians, scientist, writer, diplomat, and raconteur who founded the first public library in this country. In his *Autobiography* Franklin wrote:

This library afforded me the means of improvement by constant study, for which I set apart an hour or two each day, and thus repair'd in some degree the loss of the learned education my father once intended me. Reading was the only amusement I allow'd myself. I spent no time in taverns, games, or frolicks of any kind; and my industry in my business continu'd as indefatigable as it was necessary.

As role models go, Ben serves our purpose!

## Summary

Administration, or management, of a public library differs little in principle or practice from the management of other public or private organizations, except as to the substance of the services offered and the content of the products delivered. The prudent library director, and the department heads, as well as those seeking to be in a position to take charge, would do well to study the literature of management and especially of public administration. Where the opportunity offers, courses in management, supervision, and administration may be taken. A general book on all aspects of public library administration can do no more than touch the high spots of the subject. Readers will wish to investigate particular areas and subjects in specialized works, of which some are listed in the references for further reading in the Appendix.

This chapter has attempted to show that management, to be successful, requires the application of information, knowledge, and techniques that the average librarian will probably not have acquired in the normal educational program. Participative management is worth particular attention. Libraries have not been in the forefront of the modern labor relations movement, but events have required that serious and careful study be given to a rational approach to the problems. In most public libraries, well over 70 percent of the cost is for human resources. This is a significant investment.

## Notes

1. Maurice Peterson Marchant, *The Effects of the Decision Making Process and Related Organizational Factors on Alternative Measures of Performance in University Libraries* (Ann Arbor: University of Michigan, 1970), p. 3. See also Rensis Likert, *New Patterns of Management* (New York: McGraw-Hill, 1961).
2. Carl Heyel, ed., *The Encyclopedia of Management* (Van Nostrand Reinhold, 1973).
3. These points are based in part on "30 Rules for Getting Things Done Through People," *Modern Industry* 16, Nov. 15, 1948, pp. 67–68ff. By kind permission of *Dun's Review* and *Modern Industry.*
4. Carleton B. Joeckel, *Government of the American Public Library* (Chicago: University of Chicago Press, 1935), p. 1.
5. Erwin H. Schell, *Technique of Executive Control,* 8th ed. (New York: McGraw-Hill, 1957), p. 8.

# 5    Personnel Policies and Procedures

### The Library Director

Recruitment and selection of the library director has been covered in some detail in Chapter 3, under duties and responsibilities of the library board. As also noted in that chapter, for consistency in this work, the job title of the library's chief administrator will be *library director*.

*Functions of the Director*

The director will handle the administrative functions outlined in Chapter 4: formulating overall objectives and policies; determining the organizational framework; making major decisions, including those on personnel; supervising the middle-management heads, so that they carry out well the responsibilities delegated to them; balancing and coordinating all workers and activities into a smoothly operating whole; and evaluating the results.

There should be a detailed, specific job description for the position of library director. If there is not one in force, it should be written by the incumbent director and reviewed for clarity and content with key administrative aides, then with the personnel committee of the board of trustees, and finally with the entire board. It will be useful to staff, board, and community to know what the director's responsibilities and duties are, but the job description should be broad enough to allow the director the necessary latitude for planning and administration. The language in each local situation will vary, but following are some suggested points that might be included:

1. Directing an educational institution whose influence reaches potentially into every home, organization, and workplace, and into the lives of old and young, making service and materials available to people.

2. Envisioning community needs; developing connections with its industrial, business, labor, civic, social, recreational, cultural, and religious groups to see that the library serves them all, giving them reference and audiovisual

materials, assistance in planning programs, and space for meetings.

3. Cooperating with the schools and other agencies in matters of mutual concern.

4. Working with the trustees to ensure that they discharge their responsibilities and promote public support for the library, especially when pressure for public funds should be exerted.

5. Coordinating operations with municipal leaders, either directly or through the trustees.

6. Scrutinizing expenditures for buildings, equipment, books, materials, and salaries to be certain that the public receives a full return for its money.

7. Operating a distribution system of materials, ideas, and information aimed at reaching large numbers of people.

8. Organizing the units of service and the staff; laying out and dividing their activities; delegating and clarifying responsibilities and authority; and modifying the organization when change requires it.

9. Securing able employees—department heads, professional and clerical assistants, pages, and building employees.

10. Developing the initiative, skills, and ability of staff members; securing adequate and fair compensation for work they render the library.

11. Supervising the administrative methods of each department, and the routines of its work, encouraging department heads to see that records and processes are simplified and arranged to eliminate unessential paperwork, waste, and delay and seeing that no staff member regularly performs work that a less highly paid member can do as well.

12. Observing the service given the public at each department and distribution point, and arranging for recurrent tests and checks on it, to be certain that it is as complete and prompt as possible.

13. Drawing upon the best information and judgment within and without the community to select a stock of books and materials adequate to the needs of the community and appropriate to the constant changes in public demand; developing within the staff a thorough knowledge of books and their value.

14. Ensuring that the library discovers and serves the individual citizen, old and young, including people who are not yet library users.

15. Keeping the public informed and strengthening public relations through constant, resourceful, and varied forms of publicity on the work of the library as an institution, its services and materials, policies, and problems.

16. Developing oneself through constant examination of personal viewpoints and methods through professional and general reading and by individual research in some field.

17. Combating inertia in the community and library, working for sound, constructive change, finding ways to overcome public indifference to social problems, while refraining from "library evangelism," thus preventing the

library, through any representative, from becoming a symbol for any controversial attitude.

## The Staff's Influence on the Director

The director's immediate concern is with the staff. The staff as a group inevitably and rightly influences administrative thinking. The director should report to the staff the decisions of the trustees on current problems. In several large libraries trustee actions are reported in the staff bulletin. Conversely, staff attitudes should be reported to the board. A good director, at least in smaller libraries, will work on public service points at times to give workers scheduled there a chance to attend staff meetings; by so doing the director can also get a firsthand view of the services to readers and make administrative thinking more realistic.

## The Users' Influence on the Director

Though the director works inside library walls, he or she cannot forget the population served, the present library users, who represent—with responses to library services, regulations, and publicity—a judgment on the library's progress and therefore on the director's work. Suggestions and criticisms should be welcomed. The extent to which the director encourages the flow of user reaction and takes advantage of it in planning is a factor in good or poor administration.

## Influence of Nonusers on the Director

The people who do not use the library, and the various groups and organizations hardly aware of the library, offer channels for wider service. Since some of them, at least occasionally, bring pressure to bear, the director should be familiar with their characteristics and their reactions to the library's service. Their very status as nonusers is of concern.

Library planning has to move outward from the library's walls toward the community it should serve. The director's endeavors should not be slanted toward any one subject field, activity of the library, particular viewpoint, or element of the population. The library's neutrality is vital to the service of all interests.

## The Director's Relations with Local Government

The director's attitudes toward the community government and politics are certain to influence and be influenced by those of trustees and staff. Ignorance of current local situations does not build library progress. And it is important to add that the public library should serve as a local government reference library. In recent years, particular attention has been given to a growing library–municipality relationship.

In a democracy, schools and libraries thrive on public participation and criticism, and the director has to be prepared for this, believe in it, and not run away from it. Politicians are interested in getting in and staying in office. The director should evaluate which of the library's purposes, plans, and services coincide with those of city officials. He or she can then call their attention to recent reports and articles, such as are indexed in *Public Affairs Information Service,* on current problems of concern to the city.

The director and trustees should support planning that will improve civic centers, mass transit, parking, and housing. Officials who guide progress in these directions are not charged with the responsibility to see that reading and library service are made more effective in the local community—that is the function of the library board and library director. The library is important enough to have its own place in the sun, and library officers will see that along with other worthy civic objectives the library's welfare is in the forefront and does not trail behind.

A public library is not a private enterprise, it is a unit of government. As such, it is "in politics," and cannot dissociate itself. Too many librarians have tried to secrete themselves in remote library corners so as to forestall political attention or involvement. . . . In so doing many have retreated into negativism away from needed positive action.[1]

The question is how to cooperate and be friendly without compromising principles and how to deal with pressure contrary to the welfare of the library and its users. The library's steady program of public relations will help the community to understand and respect what the library is trying to do.

## Influences on the Director from the World of Ideas

The library is the connector between local citizens and the world of intellectual activity, the flow of ideas as reported in print and developments in education, in the cultural fields, and in social, civic, and economic affairs. The director and colleagues will be aware of what is going on outside their walls and translate it into library service. But above this is what many consider a fundamental goal: to manage the library so as to raise the intellectual level and activity of the community.

## The Director's Daily Work

The smaller the library and the fewer the workers, the greater the variety of work for each and the greater the proportion of routine detail the director must handle, with less opportunity for important administrative work such as planning, outside contacts, and promotion. There are decisions on policy activities, methods, and rules to be made; conferences with trustees; reports from staff; interviews with department and branch heads and assistants; personnel interviews with candidates for employment; interviews with readers in regard to services, gift materials, suggestions; interviews with outsiders on internal matters, new shelving or equipment, and supplies; correspondence.

There must be professional reading—new books and periodical articles on library work, education, and administrative methods—and participation in professional organizations.

*Aids to Maximizing the Director's Time*

1. Place the director's office away from the main entrance.
2. Have the office well lighted and quiet.
3. Use the intercom.
4. Perform work that needs concentration without interruption in the quieter hours, perhaps before 10:30 A.M. If necessary have a "retreat," to escape interruptions.
5. Eliminate unnecessary work, and delegate. Answer as few letters as possible; route most of them to staff. Routine letters may often be answered by forms or by a few words to the typist with the original letter, instead of by dictating.
6. The secretary or assistant should receive many incoming phone calls and give the message in shorter form to the director or send some of them to the department where the questions can be better answered.
7. In staff conferences, list the subjects to be taken up; see that those who were to have data ready are prepared; invite only those directly concerned, the fewer the better and quicker; start and stop on time; keep discussion to the point; adjourn when all the essential points have been taken up and the discussion begins to meander; assign followups to specific people; dictate a brief summary of decisions.

## The Business Office Head

In a large library, fiscal routine, purchasing, and office work belong in the library's business office. A competent head for this office work is a justifiable budget item and can relieve the director of time-consuming routine work, carry out specialized studies on methods and costs, contribute useful ideas to the budget process, and discharge certain personnel matters. Final decisions on the budget, on expenditures, and on business policies are the ultimate responsibility of the director.

## The Assistant Director

Serving as an assistant director is valuable and satisfying training, especially if one's chief is creative and efficient. If the director is also a scholar, an educator, and a leader, the assistant director can serve a long term with enjoyment. If the chief is self-seeking, inefficient, or uninspired, life will be tough enough to stiffen the assistant's character, and he or she will observe administrative methods as they are and reflect on how they might have been, gathering experience for a future move.

No adequate study seems available on the functions of this important position. The status of a "Man or Woman Friday" to the director is more frankly expressed by the title *assistant to the librarian,* and in such a case the job description or the letters and discussion before the appointment is made should make it clear that what is wanted is someone to do detail work and draft reports and studies on administrative matters. This is an important position, but not the position of an assistant director.

Most applicants for the assistant director's position expect to be what the term implies—a sharer of the director's administrative work, in which certain administrative functions will be delegated, with authority to make decisions. The two people work closely together, often in adjoining rooms. The assistant director is generally less experienced than the director, or if more experienced perhaps has been passed over because of the absence of qualities required for a director's job. The matter of authority, and of the degree to which the director should intervene, make suggestions, or take the matter out of the assistant director's hands, is a delicate one, involving the self-respect and flexibility of both.

An assistant director or an assistant to the director should not be called on for duties that a competent secretary could perform. The assistant director should be a formulator of ideas and is often assigned or delegated such duties as:

1. Personnel work, recruiting, interviews, recommendations. Depending on the size of the library and trustee functions, the assistant director may appoint directly to clerical and custodial posts and may screen professionals before interviews with the director. On many administrative matters even the director has to get trustee approval before acting; the assistant director need not feel aggrieved if he or she cannot be completely responsible.

2. Study of problems, including the gathering of data; research and formulation of recommendations.

3. General supervision of one of the major aspects of the library, such as the adult circulation and reference departments of a larger library, or all the book selection and preparatory processes, or all the branch and extension work, or the central library's public departments. This means not merely operating a department, but relieving the director of part of the administrative and supervisory work—that is, reducing the span of control. Several department heads may report to the assistant instead of to the director. Large libraries have two or more assistant directors, each handling large segments of the librarian's work.

4. More frequently the assistant director serves also as a department head. In one sense this is an economy device, but it may be sensible in libraries

up to about the 75,000 population class, which will not be justified in paying a full-time assistant director's salary. Partly because of these variations in administrative work and in ability of performance, the assistant director's salary suffers from conflicting viewpoints. It seems fair that it should be close to that of the director.

5. The assistant director is in charge of the library in the absence of the director; represents the director at meetings and in various connections inside and outside; confers with the chief on matters of policy and gives thought to the director's problems and points of view; notifies the director of developments affecting morale, public opinion, and individual staff problems; initiates and suggests ideas that will help in any aspect of the work; prepares reports based on data gathered and on changes in methods, new services, and proposals; acts as liaison between staff and director to whatever degree the director wishes or permits; and presents to all concerned a strict unanimity with the director. He or she may be in fact an assistant, but in viewpoint, purpose and sympathies, a loyal lieutenant. When mutual respect and loyalty evaporate, the assistant should seek another post.

The head of a smaller library, moving up to be first assistant, needs to know definitely the position's scope and authority and will judge how one will get along in daily contacts with the new chief. It is seldom wise to accept a position based on hopes of succeeding to the directorship; too many unforeseen factors make succession an unhappy gamble, open to embarrassments and frustrations.

In smaller libraries someone long on the staff often serves as first assistant, to be called on when the chief is absent and to serve in that place in various capacities. The director will make clear the scope of authority the assistant will have when in charge. Clearly, emergencies will require decisions to be made and action to be taken.

A sensible director should help an able first assistant develop administrative ability as fully and as rapidly as possible. No director ever profited by holding someone back. A good director should find great satisfaction in developing and encouraging department heads and assistant directors to go out to larger positions and salaries.

Under almost any assignment, a good assistant can serve as a bridge between the director and the departments. As a discreet, considerate additional supervisor and observer of the whole internal working of the library, the assistant can be a substantial help to all concerned. The word *assist* is the key word in both titles: assistant director and assistant to the director.

## The Department Head

*Note:* This and the following section, on supervision, form a pair, and apply equally to the branch librarian. Though frequent reference is made to public service departments, most of the materials in these two sections applies in nonpublic departments, which are of equal importance.

The department head provides the leadership that develops an effective staff and service for some unit. The head helps to select and evaluate its personnel and assigns the work among assistants, supervising and improving the performance of each. The head encourages good work and corrects short-comings, thus fostering high morale not only within the department but within the whole library; encourages assistants to increase their knowledge of books and stimulates them to participate in professional activities; and, of course, is constantly aware of the quality of service given by each assistant. The head considers methods in use elsewhere and finds ways to improve, and he or she serves as liaison between the director and the departmental staff.

A newly appointed department head from another library finds a new group of colleagues and a new institution with its own traditions, policies, resources, organization, and style. Whether promoted from within or appointed from outside, the new head will do well to have scheduled, wide-ranging talks with every member of the departmental staff, giving them an opportunity to say what they have to say. The new head should have some thoughtful questions in mind, to direct the conversation but not to dominate it. The climate should permit the staff members to feel at ease in expressing themselves. The department head's job at this stage is mainly to ask and listen, leaving discussion of plans and proposals for a later time, after all have been heard from and any changes or different courses of action have been duly considered.

### Departmental Objectives

The department's objectives will logically be an extension and refinement of the library's objectives and larger goals. Whether a "department" is large or small, it benefits by a simple written statement of its objectives, outlining its scope and its relationship to the library as a whole and to any similar department or enterprise in the community. The departmental policy state-ment or manual should also define its autonomy. To what extent, for example, may the department head and its members make decisions on choice of personnel and assignment of work, on outgoing correspondence, which repre-sents the library regardless of who signs it, or on selection of materials? To what extent is each worker to be supervised by the department head? Similarly, to what extent may the department head make decisions, take the initiative, or represent the department in the community? Some of these points are hard to define in writing, but there should be a clear understanding of the department's policies among those concerned.

Some of the main points to be considered in promoting or appointing a department head:

1. The vacancy should be posted within the library first to give all qualified employees an opportunity to apply within a stated period. Qualifications and requirements will have been stated in writing and will have become a matter of record, as will the job description for the vacancy. All applications should be given serious consideration, with interviews and conferences to determine the applicant's suitability. Seniority is not necessarily to be a major consideration; an employee ought not to feel a right to promotion solely because of years of service on the job. The department head assignment will require leadership ability, either potential or already demonstrated on the job.

2. If a promotion can be made of a present staff member, that should go forward, and others who have applied should be advised of their standing in the competition. There is less apt to be ill feeling if everyone concerned knows what is going on and why and how decisions are made.

3. If in the judgment of the director and whoever else on the staff is involved in personnel choices, there are no qualified local candidates, the search will go outside, in accord with staff selection procedures as outlined later in this chapter.

4. The director, or immediate supervisor of the department head, will state, clarify, and discuss in conference as well as in writing the department head's scope of authority and responsibility and will clear up any questions the new appointee may have about duties, working conditions, and so forth.

The department head has a right to share in selection and appointment of departmental staff, even if the library has a personnel officer. The head will advise and assist the director, assistant director, or personnel officer in the specifications for the job, suggest candidates and methods to locate the best ones, share in interviewing the candidates, and make recommendations to the director.

A good director wishes to be advised on the progress of the departmental staff, services, and community contacts but not to hear about everything that happens. Yet a library will not flourish when the director simply gives general instructions to department heads, turns them loose, and expects that everything will run well because the department heads have adequate training and experience. The director must supervise department heads. This involves a relationship in which each understands how far each is to go.

Just when is the director's attention needed on a department situation? A director in a city of 150,000 was constantly appealed to for an additional assistant by the conscientious, trained circulation head, who seemed almost overwhelmed by management problems. After acceding against his own judgment to the necessity of getting one, the director learned that the circulation head was resigning to accept a larger position elsewhere. The successor, although not professionally trained, had the gift of efficient organization and sought economy. Without prompting, or intimating that the former head was not a good manager, the new head surprised the director a month later by reporting simplified routines and reassigned work, thereby giving as efficient service to readers with five as with seven assistants, a striking example of good department management. Should not the director have taken a closer look, challenged the recommendation of the department head, and insisted on having the department tightened up?

The department head is actually a key person in library staff participation, both upward and downward, participating with the director in library planning and encouraging departmental staff to participate in planning.

Some qualities that help a department head to develop:

1. An open and questioning mind as to present methods and what can be done to improve services to readers.

2. Imagination and initiative to see what is going on with each assistant, what can be done, and how to do it.

3. Courage to try, even if one makes a mistake; little progress is made without some risk and some errors.

4. Readiness to disagree tactfully with one's assistants, one's fellow department heads, and one's superiors.

5. Awareness of progress in other departments, other libraries, and other professions and application of good ideas to one's own department, encouraging one's assistants to do the same.

6. Firmness in sticking to ideas that have been worked out and agreed on; seeing that assistants do well the work assigned them. A staff does not respect a department head who vacillates under pressure or is afraid to be frank in insisting on good results. Many department heads, as well as directors, are too easily satisfied with mediocre performance.

7. Equal treatment in dealing with colleagues. Great exception is taken when one assistant gets all the interesting assignments and another gets all the drudgery, or it is discovered that the department head has made some confidential arrangement with one that is not shared by the others. If such assignments are properly based on comparative background and ability, the problem is to explain why assignments are fair and to do this so that the aggrieved one does not feel let down or unappreciated.

8. Consistency. It does not mean refusal to change when new facts have changed a situation. It does mean refraining from snap judgments and giving hasty instructions that have to be undone or evaded. It does mean thinking things through, with staff participation, and being able to make careful decisions and then to follow steadily along the course set.

## Supervision in the Library

While effective supervision is primarily a major responsibility of each department head and branch librarian, there are many small libraries where the director is the sole supervisor. Other libraries are large enough to have assistant directors and assistant department heads delegated to supervise their respective groups. Frequently, an assistant with a flair for it is sensibly assigned to supervise the work of special groups such as pages or a "task force" for a temporary project.

The goal of supervision is to direct and guide employees so that the objectives of the library are attained. It is a continuous process. Good supervision depends on keeping alert to what each worker is doing. Supervision does not imply a critical attitude. It combines an awareness of what is being done with teaching and development.

Personnel reports and employee rating are devices for development. This evaluation is logically done by a supervisor who has been trained to weigh personal qualities and degrees of job efficiency.[2] Libraries should use rating sheets or records, and supervisors should be frank and honest in recording a worker's shortcomings. This record is of great value and should be regularly filled out by any supervisor with more than three or four assistants. However, the rating sheet conference should not be the first time an assistant knows where he or she stands. Service rating has been called a tool of supervision because, if conscientiously utilized, it brings worker and supervisor closer together to talk over the job, its problems, and the quality of work, and, most important, it results in improvement.

Clearly, the director or a delegated assistant should supervise department heads and branch librarians, who in turn, with their first assistants, should supervise their groups of workers. Supervision is best entrusted to those who are capable teachers. The inexperienced seldom make good supervisors. Selection and training of supervisors is one of the director's critical tasks.

## The Teaching Process

A good instructor lists things to be done and lays out in advance the needed tools, samples, and accessories. Training should be carried out directly on the service "firing line," with instructor and learner working as a team, asking and answering questions, noticing and correcting errors. Often, regular performers of a routine are the best instructors, especially if they are first given some suggestions on teaching beginners. If it can be done, it is desirable to have the leaving person teach the replacement. The method of letting the beginner learn by doing is a lengthy and costly method compared to that of carefully planned instruction.

TRAINING SUGGESTIONS

1. Break down the task into instructional units, preferably in the same sequence as the job details but sometimes with easier tasks first. Put the trainee at ease. Most new workers fear doing something wrong and need close guidance and reassurance at the start. Everyone makes mistakes. Be sure a mistake is worth correcting, and don't get excited about it. Give correc-

tions in a quiet and impersonal way, as suggestions, not within the hearing of others. Do not make an issue of small details. Lead the learner to see how the task may be interesting. Help build a healthy attitude.

2. Explain the fundamentals of the work, outline its purpose, and tell how it relates to the preceding and following processes. Good instructions should be clear and concise. Trainees should repeat the instructions and ask questions, until they are sure they understand what is wanted and how to do it.

3. Fit the instruction to the individual. Some people are detail-minded, others focus on ideas. If a procedure suggested by the trainee will not work as well as the one being taught, explain why this particular method is desirable. Written job instructions are highly useful even though some workers do not comprehend textual information, at least until they see it demonstrated. Explanation may have to be repeated verbally. For manual routines, such as typing a sample card or a pasting operation, it may save time to demonstrate it slowly and to explain each step and how it fits into the sequence. Tell what to expect before you do it. Focus attention on the important part of the operation and have the trainees repeat it until they feel that they have mastered it. Completed examples and forms, models, pictures, or rough drawings on the blackboard can supplement written and verbal instruction.

4. Next, ask a trainee to try the task; one can learn a job only by doing it. This tryout should come as soon as possible after instruction or demonstration. Wrong habits can be prevented by correcting errors immediately.

The supervisor's job is to teach how, and to stimulate the learner's active personal interest, by encouraging questions, by paying attention to the trainee's ideas, and by telling him or her what is being accomplished that is useful to the library.

### Group Dynamics and Training

When the organization is large enough to merit formal classes it is helpful to keep in mind certain principles of group behavior. A successful group, one that is both highly cohesive and highly productive, has several characteristics. First, the objectives of the group are clear and shared by its members. Usually, the personal objectives of the members are identical or compatible with the group's objectives. Another important characteristic of the successful group is the clarity of the roles played by the members of the group, including the role of the supervisor. Each member of the group understands his or her role and that role is recognized by other members of the group. It is vital to the cohesiveness of the group that its members hold many of the same values and agree to be governed by certain norms regarding procedure, including how decisions are to be made and implemented. In addition, membership in a successful group is clear cut and members are heterogeneous.

Membership criteria are relevant to the group's objectives, values, and norms. However, diversity in skills, experience, and interests encourages the fulfillment of differing roles within the group and promotes flexibility. Finally, a successful group has open channels of communication. No one withholds relevant information, including ideas or feelings.[3]

A supervisor should seek to provide a structure that will promote conditions favorable to the development of a successful group. The structure is important because it affects and facilitates behavior.*[4]

*Training Supervisors*

Presumably, supervisors are appointed because they have demonstrated leadership, self-confidence, organizational ability, an understanding of people, and a superior knowledge of methods and books. All these abilities improve by training.

Most public libraries have fewer than a dozen people responsible for supervision. Like many supervisors in small organizations in other fields they can obtain substantial help by reading books and articles on the subject; some libraries maintain a file of such material for staff use. They can attend lectures on supervision at a nearby college, business firm, factory, or school. In addition, training programs are offered by organizations and local government. Perhaps they can induce an instructor to study the library's operations and focus some instruction on library situations. It seems logical also to look to state commissions and regional headquarters to organize and sponsor such courses by experienced instructors.

When a library has ten or twelve supervisors, it should organize a course for them and for their understudies. The waste, frustration, and poor morale resulting from inadequate supervision justify remedial action. The outline for a series of lessons with discussion should grow out of the expressed needs of department heads, supervisors, and assistants; the topics will then reflect actual situations. To obtain ideas for topical coverage, present the idea of training to the group and ask for suggestions. Problem cases can be cited for discussion without embarrassing anyone by identifying the persons concerned. If the instructor is skillful, the total result will be substantial, even in the face of lack of interest or imagination and the listener's failure to translate ideas into terms of actual situations.

Training for library workers, and therefore for their supervisors, can be broken down into several special aspects:

* Further information on these aspects of supervision and supervision in general can be found in the books listed at the end of the chapter, which include two references widely used in university business courses—*Personnel Administration* by Paul Pigors and Charles A. Myers and *Perspectives on Personnel Human Resource Management* by Herbert Hereman and Donald Schwab. *Bringing Women into Management* by Francine Gordon and Myra Strober deals with an increasingly important area in a comprehensive way.

*Types of Training by Level of Personnel*

Administrative and supervisory; professional, such as book selecting and advising, reference, children's; paraprofessional; secretarial; clerical, such as circulation routines, filing and typing; page work; maintenance; and part-time clerical workers.

*Types of Training by Library Objectives*

Orientation training in library and departmental objectives; clerical and handwork routine methods and skills; job relations and personal relations; public service attitudes (for example, in circulation and reference service); public relations; work simplification; specialized subject matter (for subject and special materials departments); and combined selections from the foregoing aimed to upgrade personnel.

*Training Based on Identified Needs for Library Improvement*

Needs of the new employee; renewing interest and morale of older employees; work backlog (for example, new books in the catalogue department); high costs of operation; awareness of unsatisfactory service to readers; evidence of improper attitudes; high absenteeism and turnover (using analysis of exit and other interviews to discover causes); excessive errors and carelessness; changes in procedures of performing the job or keeping records; new position description requirements; employee rating methods; new ideas from supervisors and other employees and from committees or groups; and special project setups, new and temporary.

*Methods of Training "On the Job"*

Demonstration and drill; slow-motion analysis of error and waste; training by supervisor; rotating assignments for stimulating variety; internships, especially for administrative and professional workers; analysis of periodic rating interviews to find strong points and to suggest improvements in weak features; study periods and carefully selected materials; investigation of job methods to encourage assistants to suggest improvements; practice assignments according to special interests and abilities.

*Methods of Training "Off the Job"*

These methods are often overlooked in planning a training program, but they can contribute greatly: informal conference-discussion that follows an outline; selected readings (several libraries maintain a file of current material, arranged by administrative subject, for staff study); academic courses if available nearby (for subject and book knowledge to enrich the job in public departments); simulated situations with role playing (for personal relations, assistant-reader contacts, and so on); staff meetings to discuss topics related to the job training; field trips to other libraries and to nearby operations that parallel the library job; professional meetings, for broader viewpoints and morale; and assignment to similar specialized work in another library when no training is available locally.

*Training Materials*

Little appropriate material is available for small libraries, but large libraries can use already available training devices, such as filmstrips, TV (possibly through a local school hookup with the Bell telephone system), and videocassette films on management techniques and on library service. These are available for a larger library to rent or borrow. Some of the largest producers are McGraw-Hill, Westinghouse, and the National Audiovisual Center in Washington, D.C. Library Training Consultants, located in Maryland, offers training kits for self-instruction.[5] Other materials include bulletins or transcripts of training sessions; exhibits (for example, display of notable work so the public can see it); charts and diagrams (for example, a flow chart of the library's catalogue and circulation departments; textbooks and handbooks from other libraries or from nonlibrary sources containing chapters or passages pertinent to the local situation; examinations and tests of work; and special studies and reports.

*The Personnel Manual*

The best training tool is an up-to-date manual. A committee of the American Library Association prepared in 1977 an excellent brief outline that covers the content to be included in the local library's personnel manual. The publication notes that preparation of the manual is a job for a standing committee of the staff and that the manual is to be designed for all members of the staff, not just management. The manual should cover every aspect of employment that affects the individual staff member. It may be added that a clear, readable, understandable, up-to-date personnel manual for the particular library is an essential element in the personnel process. The ALA publication also includes in the appendix ALA policies relating to libraries. The publication should be in the office library of the director and in that of the personnel officer, if there is one. It is a practical working tool and guide.[6]

## Staff Selection and Appointment

The process for recruitment, selection, and appointment of staff will necessarily vary among public libraries, depending on several factors: civil service, collective bargaining, an affirmative action plan, and a centralized municipal personnel department in addition to or as part of civil service. Also, the process will depend on the statutory role of the board of trustees in the personnel process, the amount of delegation from trustees to library director or other administrative personnel, and the role of other boards and departments in the local government (for example, city manager or fiscal authority). With the trend toward incorporating the library into the regular municipal structure, it is increasingly rare for the local public library to have complete autonomy in the personnel process.

In any event, the first task for the library director, or whoever is in charge of personnel work, is to draw up a clear and specific statement of the personnel selection and appointment process, if this has not already been done. If it has been done, care should be taken to revise it and keep it up to date as changes occur. The statement of the procedure should be a part of the library's staff manual and of the personnel handbook, so that all can be aware of how vacancies are filled. The statement will also be a part of the trustees' manual or handbook, and will of course have been prepared with the cooperation and consultation of the board, or its personnel committee, and will have been approved by the board.

Needless to say, once the process has been established, it should be followed to the letter, without deviation. If there is a need for revision or correction in the process, that correction should be incorporated in the written procedure before the changes are put into practice and should be communicated to all concerned.

### Recruitment

Again, the process will depend upon local conditions. If the public library positions are under civil service, obviously the recruitment will have been done by that office. The library administration can, however, engage in recruiting as required and appropriate, by finding good applicants and encouraging them to apply and go through the civil service process. Depending on the job market, the library may receive applications by mail or in person. All applications as received should be acknowledged and screened. Those meeting the qualifications should be filed for future reference or referred to the civil service department, as appropriate.

It may be noted that the posting process within the library will invite and receive applications for transfer within grade as well as for promotion. The recruitment process will include an announcement of the vacancy, of the desired qualifications, and of the salary offered. The form that the public announcement should take has recently been affected by the passage of federal legislation prohibiting race and sex discrimination in employment. Title VII of the Civil Rights Act of 1964, as amended by the Equal Employment Opportunity Act of 1972, is a wide-ranging law that forbids in job advertisements references to sex- or race-related seniority lists, distinctions between married and unmarried people, and so forth.[7] Advertisements should give prospective applicants enough information so that they can decide whether they are qualified for the vacancy and interested in it.

For nonprofessionals and custodians there are local channels of recruitment, such as private and public employment agencies, local high schools and colleges, and newspaper advertisements.

In order to secure an outstanding person, the library might ask: What do we have to offer and to whom will we appeal? Obviously, salary is important; a higher-than-average salary will bring better results.

New library school graduates are more likely to apply for a position in a library of above-average reputation where they are assured fully professional duties, stimulating and challenging assignments, a chance to grow and develop on the job, and well-developed in-service training. A library that offers some or all of these things would stress the facts in recruitment letters, publicity, and interviews. Is it possible that there are good candidates in the neighborhood?

The "recruitment net" includes sending carefully prepared notices to library schools. Promising candidates often attend state and national library meetings and may be contacted and interviewed on these occasions.

### Older Workers and the Disabled

Like most employers, librarians are reluctant to consider "over forty-five" workers for clerical and subprofessional positions, for fear they may be set in their work ways, slow, intolerant with colleagues, not open-minded in taking instructions, and unhappy in a new field. Several studies indicate, however, that they have as much ability and dependability as younger people. Such findings helped spark a law passed in 1978 that extended the legal age for retirement to 70. In any good-sized town there may be such a person, who may not apply for a position but would accept appointment if encouraged.

Disabled workers too should be considered as a possible source of help. Widespread experience with them has demonstrated convincingly that a disabled or handicapped person is usually able to work satisfactorily at a job that does not involve the disability and that such a worker is more conscientious and dependable than others.

### Part-Time Workers

Most library supervisors prefer one full-time employee to two part-time. The latter require more instruction, they have outside interests (a family or schoolwork), and their irregular schedule offers many chances for tardiness or absence. Almost every public library, however, uses part-time student assistants to shelve books and do other jobs at the peak hours after school and in the evenings, and all college libraries depend on them heavily. Use of part-time employees in public libraries, under appropriate circumstances, would allow many college-trained parents to work part-time.

## Volunteers

There are two schools of thought concerning the use of volunteers in carrying on the work of the public library. Some administrators and boards tend to frown on the practice, because it may have a negative impact on the library's securing adequate funding from the appropriating authority. The library will be told: "Let the volunteers do the work!" It is true that the situation is complicated by the fact that many school libraries are staffed wholly or in part by volunteers, and so are many smaller public libraries, for that matter. It is also argued by those opposing the practice that volunteers are not reliable as to hours of work and performance, and thus tend to undermine the work record of regular paid employees.

On the other hand, there are many tasks in the library service program that can be done capably by volunteers, without threat to the library's budget or to paid staff. These include many kinds of work that may be over and above the regular program and that would probably not get done without volunteers: books taken to shut-ins, special program activities, reading instruction and tutoring for both children and adults, user surveys, public relations programs, inventory of materials in the collection, and specialized book selection advice, particularly in foreign languages. These and many other jobs are currently being done successfully by volunteers in many libraries.

There should be a specific and definite policy governing the use of volunteers: jobs that are not and cannot in the normal course be done by regular staff. And a regular staff member should have clear-cut responsibility for receiving applications and training and scheduling those who volunteer. There will be a positive by-product as well, in that the corps of volunteers can become an active community source of support for the library. Sometimes the volunteer program is associated with or sponsored by the Friends of the Library, and this appears to be a satisfactory arrangement. In any case, the use of volunteers has more pluses than minuses, if well managed.

## Long-Range Recruiting

More and more chief librarians are recognizing the need for long-range recruitment. This means in part paying more attention to the selection of high school and college students who may work only part-time or in summers for the public library. Some of them are interested in librarianship as a career, to begin with; others might be induced to consider it. Those interested should be given more varied assignments, assisted to complete their education, and encouraged to return to the library after library school. Supervisors should see that each promising student worker has a dynamic experienced worker assigned to be guide, mentor, and encourager while the student is working in the library.

If recruiting literature is prepared by the library, it would be well to stress opportunities for satisfying service by meeting human needs in the community; the creative aspects of building and maintaining a relevant collection of resource materials; the personal satisfaction to be obtained from reference, information, and readers' advisory work; and the possibilities for management positions, depending on growth and ability.

## Selecting the Appointee

The process of selecting the one best-qualified person should be carefully thought out and planned, not left to last-minute decisions. The selection process should be reviewed and evaluated from time to time and, if necessary, revised. The steps taken should be based on three main considerations: (1) the library needs staff members of the best possible quality of mind and personality, in each type and level of service; (2) the only basis of consideration should be the merit of the candidates, and no discrimination or preference should be allowed on grounds unrelated to qualities needed for successful performance; and (3) the selection process should operate as swiftly and inexpensively as is consistent with getting the needed results. Pigors and Myers offer sound, practical advice on the various steps in the process of identifying, selecting, and appointing employees.[8]

It cannot be overlooked that selection of a new staff member is a two-way process. The library is looking for the best possible employee. To the administrator this means that potential candidates, especially the best ones, must be persuaded to apply by being given reasonably complete information on the library, the professional opportunity of the position in question, working conditions, chances for promotion, and so forth. It means also that the selection process must be rightly timed, as in the case of library school students, and not be so inconvenient, complicated, or long-drawn-out as to frustrate the applicants or cool their enthusiasm.

Choice of candidates is based on: (1) the application blank, letters of reference, and a transcript of school and college grades; (2) an interview; (3) the results of tests given by the library; and (4) a probationary period. These may all be evaluated by one person or, preferably, a small committee. For clerical and custodial positions, at least two persons should review the evidence on each applicant and agree on the choice. The immediate supervisor of the position to be filled and the personnel officer, director, or other such person with a system-wide point of view should share in decisions for appointment. For professional positions or upper-level positions of any kind, it is well to have a selection committee to interview, review, and submit the top three candidates with justification for their selection.

*The Application Blank*

It should be legible, easily comprehended, short, and simple. It should not ask for information available in other ways—for example, a list of courses taken in college or library school—or not needed until the appointment is made (such as social security number). In line with equal employment legislation, it should not request information on sex, race, age, religion, marital status, or national origin.[9]

Most libraries have an application blank readily available, designed for all positions, though larger libraries may prefer special forms for custodians, pages, clerical assistants, etc. The selection of a new employee begins on receipt of a completed application blank. If delivered in person, it should be checked while the applicant is present to see that all data are there and correct. The applicant should be told of the personnel policies of the library and the salary for the position. If there is a vacancy or if the applicant is unusually well qualified, an interview should be conducted at once by someone able to make a prompt decision or recommendation. Applications need not be kept more than six months; by that time many are unavailable anyway. All promising professional applicants should be told to renew their applications at a given date if they are still interested.

Three or four years after graduation, candidates' academic records are less important than their work records. Library schools vary in the completeness of the information they supply on their graduates; they vary even more, but not so obviously, in the standards they use (consciously or unconsciously) in rating students.

*Letters of Reference*

Letters of reference are peculiarly subject to misuse. Perhaps their main value is as negative checks. Letters of reference carried by the candidate or of which he has been sent a copy are almost completely worthless. Many libraries send to the reference supplied by the applicant a prepared form that requires a minimum of writing. If the reference lives in the same city, it is better to telephone, ask frank questions, get oral answers to the questions on the form, and put down the answers so they will not be misinterpreted or forgotten. One seldom gets the whole truth about a candidate from his character references. Previous employers tend to give a too-favorable report, or a present employer may be anxious not to lose the applicant.

*The Interview with Applicants*

It is a good rule to hire no employee without an interview.[10] In an employment interview, the applicant inevitably feels under considerable stress. The interviewer should plan interviews so that stress and embarrassment are minimized. Persons who regularly need to interview persons for employment will study one or more of the many good books available on the subject. Here are some principles for the interviewer:

Decide in advance what is to be achieved in the interview. Interviewing is not the best method to ascertain the candidate's general intelligence or technical competence. An employment interview should serve one main and two minor purposes—to allow the interviewer to observe the appearance, manner, personality, attitudes, and reactions of the interviewee; and incidentally, to fill out the details in the paper record and to give additional information about the community, the library, and the job in question. The interviewer needs to have a clear idea of the kind of person desired. If the interview is considered as a sort of oral examination, then the applicant is bound to be under stress, and his or her manner and behavior will not be as they are under ordinary circumstances.

Using the paper record of the applicant as a point of departure, the interviewer seeks to get the candidate to talk about himself or herself. It is probably not wise to make extensive notes, which might make him or her self-conscious, especially at the beginning of the interview, but some record of the interview, however brief, should be made immediately afterward.

Having two or more persons talk to the same applicant helps to stabilize the results, especially if they sit in on the same interview. This has the danger of increasing the stress on the applicant, but it has the advantage of allowing independent observations of the same behavior. It permits closer observation of the candidate by sharing the job of conducting the interview, and one interviewer's questions may stimulate the others and the candidate to helpful discussion. The interviewers should record their opinions and discuss them as soon after the interview as possible. The interview is so universal a method of selection and is so easy to improve—within limits—that every librarian is under obligation to ensure these improvements in the process of staff selection. The personal factor is obviously important in library work; for practical results the best available way to assess it is by interviewing.

### Certification

Certification of librarians is no substitute for tests or examinations. Typically an appropriate certificate is issued simply on the basis of academic achievement and years of experience. It does not represent an attempt to look into individual aptitudes and abilities. Whatever examination is offered is an alternative for those who have not gone to college or library school—unlike the examinations in law and accounting, for example, which are required of all and establish a minimum level of demonstrated competence. Even if library certification were always based on such an examination, it would not fill the individual library's need for a means of selecting the one best person. On the other hand, certification is sometimes a positive handicap if the library is unable to consider for employment anyone except those who hold certificates of that particular state. In any case, library certification laws typically have no enforcement provisions. Typically, the qualification statement calls for the candidate to have graduated from a master's program of a library school that has been accredited by the ALA.

*Probationary Period*

A probationary period plays an integral part in the selection process, if it is properly used. No matter how much attention is given to the prior steps in the selection process, they supply only presumptive evidence as to the candidate's job performance. The actual work performance during the probationary period is the acid test, even though only one candidate at a time can be given this test for any one position. The costs to both the library and the candidate who fails this last test are high. New employees whose work during the probationary period is of borderline quality are so often given the benefit of the doubt that most probationers (and their colleagues) take it for granted that they will be retained. For letting these mediocre workers continue, the library pays dearly for years to come. Most public libraries of any size have problem staff members who should never have been allowed to pass their probation. If all reasonable efforts at improvement and adjustment fail, the library and its patrons have priority rights, and the individual and the institution should call it quits.

Though the probationary period is an expensive test, it is the most valid. If it is used as a final test of a new employee's permanent appointment, then it follows that he or she should be so informed before accepting employment and beginning work. The official statement of employment should specify that there is a probationary period, how long it is, and that future employment is conditional on successful completion of the probation. For proper evaluation of a new employee's work, the probationary period should not be less than six months for a nonprofessional staff member or a year for a professional librarian. A library handicaps itself if it waives the probationary period when negotiating or making an appointment, as long as the standards are reasonable.

A report must be made every three months during the probationary period by the immediate supervisor, discussed with the employee, and signed by the supervisor and employee. If the employee takes exception to the rating, or does not understand it, the rating conference is the time and place to clear it up. The employee will, of course, have been apprised upon probationary appointment that probation is a part of the selection process and that termination may be made at any time during the probationary period without prejudice if work performance is considered unsatisfactory by the employing authority. The employee should have the right of appeal in case of disagreement over the fairness of the rating, to the director of the library or to the board of trustees, as the final authority in other than civil service situations. It should be noted that procedures in the local library will clearly depend on regulations and procedures in force in the town or municipal government and on the extent to which these apply to the library.

The probationary appointment should not become permanent automatically; if the employee's work record is satisfactory, the immediate supervisor should so certify in writing and make a recommendation for permanent appointment, and the employee should be notified both in writing and in conference that the action is being taken. Permanent appointment usually means tenure and no future termination except for cause. The supervisor must be aware of the importance of the action, so that a borderline or questionable performance is not approved. After the appointment is made permanent, it is too late.

During the probationary period, the employee should be encouraged to report difficulties and to secure advice and assistance in solving them. An unfavorable report should lead to constructive criticism and advice; one negative report is probably not enough to warrant abrupt dismissal unless the performance clearly cannot be improved. The employee should respond to the evaluation in the service rating interview. Sometimes, assignment to another job, under another supervisor, will be appropriate in the event of a personality conflict.

During the probationary period the library will see that the employee is assigned to work that will permit a maximum contribution and will provide adequate and effective supervision and instruction in the work to be done.

*Appointment and Placement*

The process of employee selection leads to a letter or notice of appointment. Public libraries under some boards of school trustees use a contract; if the library is under civil service, the civil service commission may send the appointee an official notification of employment. A person appointed to a library position, whether temporary or permanent, full-time or part-time, should be so notified in writing, with the terms of employment, the name of the immediate supervisor, and the date on which to start work. Ordinarily this notice should be sent out before the new staff member begins work; if official action by the trustees is necessary to make the appointment legal, the letter may not be sent until after the date of that action. Usually it is not necessary to have the employee accept the appointment in writing, though that may be wise in the case of new professional librarians or other higher-level personnel who live in other cities. Their appointments should in any case be submitted to the board well in advance of the effective date of employment.

Position classification will require that the duties and responsibilities of the position being filled will have been clearly defined and stated. The candidate will be considered for a classified position in the library, not necessarily for a specific assignment except in the case of a higher-level supervisory job or coordinating position. The employer will retain the right to assign and transfer.

## Orientation

Orientation of a new employee is a frequent form of in-service training and includes at least three parts—the details of the work environment, the library history and organization, and everything the employee needs to know about how to do the assigned work. The personnel manual or handbook will be handed out and discussed if necessary. The personnel director or other person in charge of personnel records and operations will explain benefits, time records, vacation, and sick leave allowances and will also obtain additional information necessary to complete the employee's file upon appointment.

Wherever possible, if there are several new employees being appointed within a relatively brief period, a formal course of orientation can be arranged, with the library director leading off with history and organization of the library and the philosophy of service. All department heads and supervisors will be on the schedule with talks and discussion; it may also be appropriate to bring in city officials, such as personnel officers, the mayor or someone from that office, budget personnel, and so forth. If there is only one person to be oriented at a time, it is still wise to have a formal, well-organized, and written schedule of orientation, so that all important points will have been covered. Otherwise, the new employee may complain, and justifiably so, that he or she was not told of important information because one supervisor assumed that someone else had given the information, or that the employee "would know enough to ask." These are not valid assumptions.

In addition to the personnel manual or handbook, the well-organized library will have a staff or procedures manual that will describe all the processes and activities in detail, from book acquisition and processing, to circulation, reference, readers' advisory work, and so forth. This is an essential element of the library's successful operation, requiring a fair amount of careful attention but immensely saving of time and energy in the long run.

## Personnel Records and Files

Some libraries use a checklist for each new employee's orientation training, to see that all the instruction is given; when completed it is placed in the employee's personnel folder. In time this folder will contain such other records as the original application blank, the probationary period service ratings, a copy of the letter of appointment, application for membership in the retirement system, hospital insurance, social security number, sick leave taken, promotions, and salary increases.

The individual employee's personnel folder is the central and official repository of the original documents. It is easy to design a 5-by-8-inch card form that will summarize the pertinent information, and such a card file is a valuable working tool for the librarian or the personnel officer.

The payroll must also be based on the personnel folders, if the record of salary changes is officially kept by name of employee. Large libraries use a personnel action form to record any new or changed information on a given employee; this form is then routed to those who need to see it before it is filed in the employee's folder. Personnel folders naturally tend to grow in bulk through the years. They should therefore be reviewed periodically, out-of-date papers destroyed, and information for previous years summarized. When an employee leaves the library, the folder should go into the inactive file; and after ten years it should be reviewed, the essential information perhaps microfilmed, and the papers destroyed.

### Personnel Administration

Personnel matters in libraries having around 50 or fewer employees will undoubtedly be the responsibility of the head librarian or library director, with the technical assistance of the secretary or business office. In staffs of around 50 to 100, the personnel administration may be handled by either the director or the assistant director, depending on the library's organizational chart. Authorities differ, but it seems clear that somewhere from 75 to 125 employees is the point at which a full-time personnel officer may be justified as a wise investment. These are only rough guidelines, of course. Much will depend on the local situation: the degree of autonomy of the particular library in regard to personnel selection and appointment. The library that is partly or wholly under a centralized civil service system will obviously encounter a different set of conditions than the library that is more or less autonomous.

The only general point that can be made is that no matter what the local conditions are, or the size of the library staff, it is imperative that the responsibility for personnel administration be clearly defined and established: who is to do what, why, when, and how. This should be a matter of record, as previously noted in the chapter on the library board. The duties of the board, the library director, and the assistant library director in regard to personnel administration and related matters have been discussed in sections above.

When the library staff is large enough to warrant the employment of a personnel officer, different conditions pertain. Even if there is a municipal personnel office, a library personnel office will undoubtedly be required in order to work with that office and to serve as the library director's liaison. The personnel officer will probably be a staff rather than a line officer— that is, actual responsibility for most appointments will rest with the director, and/or assistant director and library board. The personnel officer will handle paper work of recruitment, selection, interviewing, appointment, and the other details discussed above in this chapter—also orientation and in-service training. Where there is a collective bargaining unit in place, the personnel officer will have some duties in connection with that situation. (See also the section on library unions later in this chapter.)

A full-time personnel officer need not be a librarian, although a library background will be useful. The chief qualifications are judgment and professional training in personnel work. It is not a specialty that can be acquired by osmosis; one must have studied and worked at it. Personnel work has exacting demands and requirements; to be useful the personnel officer must have the requisite skill and knowledge and must have demonstrated performance in this area, or at least should show evidence that this will be the case.

The work and authority of the personnel officer are delegated by the library director. The personnel officer may handle many personnel problems, receive and discuss complaints, and deal with minor issues between employees and supervisors, but major problems will be discussed with the library director, or the assistant director if assigned. Within limitations, the personnel officer might have authority to approve certain kinds or classes of appointments. The personnel officer will be likely to participate in the interviewing of all or most candidates and may well screen applications as they are received.

### Civil Service

It is probably academic to discuss the pros and cons of civil service. In most cases, it is presumed, the library will not adopt a civil service system independently or autonomously; the system will have been placed in effect as a part of the municipal government. Civil service brings limitations, and these may be considered, although if the system is there, the library is not going to be able to do anything other than work with it and be aware of the limitations: (1) Usually, or often, civil service may restrict the geographical area from which selection may be made. (2) Tests of competence and training are of dubious validity, especially for trained librarians. (3) It takes a long time to hold an examination, score the papers, and certify candidates. (4) Most entry positions are filled on the basis of written examinations graded on two or three decimal places. (5) There is no scientifically supportable evidence that these examinations are related to subsequent job performance. (6) Once a ranked list of examination scores is established, management must choose one of the top three names on the list despite the special qualifications, knowledge, experience, aptitude, or training of other applicants on the list. (7) After the staff member has spent six months on the job, he or she is virtually guaranteed the job for life, unless the supervisor files a special report urging that the employee be discharged or at least that the granting of tenure be deferred; few supervisors take such action. (8) The staff member, after obtaining tenure, can be fired only on charges of flagrant dishonesty or incompetence. (9) An employee is drained of ability and dedication, while given little opportunity for advanced training, personal development, career planning, mid-career job change, or an enriched job that encompasses evolving interests; no manager wants this. (10) Promotions are generally limited to employees who occupy the next lower position within the same department; qualified staff members in other departments of the library are discriminated against, as are applicants from outside the library. (11) Promotions are made primarily through written examinations, with no consideration for good performance.[11]

For these reasons, many library administrators prefer to have all staff exempt from civil service or, if this is not possible, then at least the professional grades.

On the other hand, civil service commissions have pioneered in the practice of position classification, salary schedules, service ratings, formal probationary periods, and other desirable personnel practices. Non–civil service libraries can also use these procedures. Sometimes, it must be said, the failure of the library to put its personnel policies and procedures on a rational basis makes it very difficult to withstand the introduction of civil service by the government.

### Position Classification

Whether there is civil service or not, and whether required by the city, town, county, or other government, all but the smallest libraries will do well to have a written statement of the number and kinds of positions in the library, their assigned duties and responsibilities, and their required qualifications. This is known as position or job classification. It is worth noting that it is the job, not the employee, that is classified.

In broad outline this consists of three main steps: (1) job analysis or the recording of the duties of all existing positions; (2) comparison and grouping of resultant job descriptions into more or less homogeneous classes of positions; and (3) writing of specifications for each such class in order to state its particular attributes and to distinguish it from others.

*Job Analysis*

Job analysis is done by a position description questionnaire. Each employee is asked to fill out a questionnaire, after some explanation of it and of the total project and after a chance to keep a work diary for a week at least. If the position is a new one or is otherwise vacant, the immediate supervisor answers the questionnaire. Precision in stating one's duties (and in regard to such factors as extent of review by others, responsibility for error, and scope of freedom for exercise of discretion) is not easy, as anyone can testify who has ever filled out a position-description questionnaire. The resulting statement should be reviewed by the employee's immediate supervisor to secure comments and opinions without changing the individual employee's words. One of the desirable by-products of job analysis is the clarification of people's ideas as to what they are or are not supposed to be doing. The complete position-description questionnaire is a concise statement of the duties and responsibilities of the employee in question.

### Classes, Grades, and Services

Once the position description questionnaires are all completed and reviewed, they are read and reread by some one person—the personnel officer in the large public library or the director in the small or medium-sized library. This person makes a series of judgments as to the ways in which the various positions, described by the questionnaires, relate to one another. For one thing the questionnaires can be grouped by main type of work performed—namely, professional, library aides, and custodial, in most libraries. These are called services and are vertical groupings in the schematic representation of the resultant position classification plan.

The horizontal division in any one service consists of those positions considered to have duties sufficiently similar in level of difficulty and responsibility to justify being grouped together in the same class and treated alike for personnel purposes. One criterion for deciding when to put two positions in the same class is the applicability of the same tests of fitness for selection or promotion. A position is assigned to a class according to actual duties and not according to the qualifications of the person who happens to be performing those duties. If a registered nurse is serving as a typist, to pick an absurd example, the position is grouped with other typists' positions; similarly a position consisting of clerical duties but performed by a library school graduate should be grouped with other clerical positions and not with the professional positions. All classes of positions, in different services, that consist of duties of approximately the same level of difficulty and responsibility are in the same grade.

### Class Specifications

The third step of position classification is a written statement describing the attributes of each class of positions. Class specifications are from a half to a full page per class, consisting of the class title, the distinguishing characteristics of the work assigned to the class, examples of specific duties, and the qualifications necessary for successful performance of the work. List only personal traits peculiarly important to positions in this class, and state the necessary qualifications in terms of the knowledges and skills clearly needed for successful performance rather than in terms of levels of academic achievement alone. Class specifications are of little value in themselves, save to assign properly a new or revised position, but are useful and desirable in other personnel processes (such as selection, promotion, salary administration, transfer).

*Class Specification for Senior Librarian (Example)*
Distinguishing characteristics of work: supervision over other employees; responsibility for the service of a branch or other agency; constant dealings with readers, the contents of books, and library tools and methods.

Some specific duties: supervising and training assistants, answering reference questions, selecting books for purchase, recommending changes in policies.

Qualifications needed: background, poise, and ability to supervise other staff members and to deal effectively with patrons, as demonstrated by successful professional experience; subject knowledge of books and library techniques; successful completion of an undergraduate college program of study and a master's degree from a graduate library school accredited by the ALA.

The rules for the administration of the position classification plan should include definitions of terms, provision for the reclassification of individual positions and for resurveys of all positions (every five years or so), an explanation of the class specifications, and the procedure for the classification of a new position. A number of individual and corporate consultants will for a fee prepare a position classification plan for a library. The personnel office of the governmental unit under which the library operates will provide guidance and assistance, and the librarian who does it will learn more and appreciate its value and limitations better than in any other way. Though the grouping of position description questionnaires and the writing of class specifications are necessarily done by one person (or at most a small committee), the results should be conveyed to all the employees of the library before the position classification plan is officially adopted by the trustees. The usual procedure is to make available the proposed class specifications and to certify to each employee the class, grade, and service to which his position is being assigned. Within a certain time period, the employee may ask for a review of the allocation of the position. In addition, the plan in its entirety should be reviewed by the director and the department heads. After submission to the trustees and upon their adoption it becomes effective.

This in brief is the process of library job evaluation. The value of a position classification plan is that it enables the director to deal intelligently with relatively few groups of homogeneous positions. A position classification plan rests on individual judgments at certain crucial points and cannot be absolutely impartial and accurate. It needs, therefore, to be kept reasonably flexible, so that errors may be corrected and changes in the service program of the library will not be hampered by it. Job evaluation does not guarantee good personnel administration, but it does provide a good base for most other aspects of personnel work. Position classification, for example, is necessary for a sound salary plan.

*Class Titles—Professional (Example)*

|  |  |
|---|---|
| Junior Librarian | college degree, no experience |
| Librarian I | MLS degree, no experience |
| Librarian II | MLS degree, 3 yrs. experience |
| Librarian III | MLS degree, 5 yrs. experience |
| Librarian IV | MLS degree, 7 yrs. experience |

More classes may be added as required. The number of years of experience required may vary locally. In some cases, the phrase "or equivalent in experience and training" is used after the words "MLS degree." This enables the appointment or promotion of persons with unusual aptitudes or skills, for example in outreach activities, but raises the problem of determining equivalency. If the equivalency requirement is used, it would be advisable to have a specific statement that would describe exactly how equivalency is to be determined: number of years of satisfactory or above-average performance, supplemented by written work or achievement; or relevant courses completed short of the MLS degree.

Class title and job assignment or working title will not necessarily be the same—for example, a Librarian III may serve as a branch librarian, as head of a small department, or as a senior reference assistant. A Librarian IV may be a department head or a coordinator of adult or children's services.

Class titles in the clerical and custodial positions will usually correspond to those in other similar municipal positions, except for the positions unique to the library—for example, Library Page, Library Assistant, Library Technical Assistant. There may be additional levels within each of these classes—for example, Library Technical I, II, and III—to describe work of increasing complexity.*

## Salaries

A public library seeking to recruit and retain outstanding employees has to pay salaries commensurate with those of other libraries, of positions in the new information fields, and of other employers.

Library salaries have always been low, largely because trustees and administrators failed to win public recognition of the value of library service, and partly because of the predominance of women employees. The standardization of library employees with other government workers and the rise of collective bargaining have improved both benefits and salaries for library personnel. Yet, in most cities salaries for librarians are not up to the salaries paid to schoolteachers, school librarians, and members of many other professions with comparable education and experience. Librarians are doing little better

---

* Other detailed examples of such class titles are listed in Kathleen B. Stebbins, *Personnel Administration in Public Libraries.* This detailed and helpful volume is listed among the general references for this chapter in the Appendix and will be found of practical application as an extension of the brief information given here.

in many instances than production workers in manufacturing industries, who earned as much as $240 per week in 1977.[12] Moreover, since most libraries fail to advance salaries for the middle and top ranks in even the same relative amounts as for starting salaries, experienced employees find themselves earning little more than newcomers and with hardly any range of possible increase.

The director should work out a sound salary plan and insist on its adoption by the trustees and city officials, with periodic revision of the schedule in keeping with current conditions. A salary plan includes (1) a salary range (a minimum salary, a maximum salary, and designated intermediate steps for each grade of position as defined in the library's position classification plan); and (2) a set of rules for the application and operation of this salary schedule.[13] Such a salary plan is to be preferred to a secret payroll and the resulting favoritism in paying different salaries for essentially the same work. The many thorny technical problems should be resolved in consultation with the whole staff or with staff representatives, preferably helped by an experienced personnel officer.

Should the maximum salary of one grade be less or more than the minimum of the next higher grade, and by how much? Usually the former is preferred, so that the promotion from one grade to another will mean an increase in salary. But in the higher grades of service where promotions will be few, and wherever the total salary range of a given grade is limited, an overlap in the salaries paid for positions in two adjoining grades is inevitable. The use of merit increases and cost-of-living adjustments have worked to the advantage of librarians, who, in years past, often were left out of citywide salary adjustments. How much difference should there be in the pay scale for different grades of positions? This depends on human judgment and competition for certain types of skills. One good method is to establish a fair salary range for one or two key classes—for example, junior professional librarian, and then work up and down the scale. It also depends on the number and amount of increments, and on whether salaries for different grades overlap.

*Rules for the Salary Plan*

To apply such a salary schedule, a set of rules should be drawn up in consultation with other staff members, be submitted to the board and city officials, and upon their approval be published. Besides definitions of terms, it should provide for periodic review of the salary schedule, for new appointments at the minimum salary of the grade in question (with exceptions permitted in unusual cases), and for the treatment of individuals whose present salary does not fall exactly into the salary steps of the new schedule. An important factor to incorporate into the plan is the basis on which salary increments will be granted, either automatically (as is generally true of teachers) or on the recommendation of the librarian as the result of service ratings or other judgments of individual efficiency. Any plan should recognize that some employees are better than others. Unfortunately, classified service, union pressure, and bureaucracy tend to force automatic increments. This discourages excellence and lowers the library's efficiency and morale. In addition, longevity pay and the requirement of continued academic study every five years or so to qualify for further increases should be included in the rules.

A salary schedule should be reviewed annually, preferably as part of a long-term (five-year) plan, just before the next year's budget is decided. First, every present position and its performance need scrutiny, to assure that every dollar is well spent; it will often be possible by work simplification to divert the time of present higher-paid persons to more profitable effort. Obviously, when a city raises the salaries of all governmental employees, the trustees should see to it that the library employees are included, as they surely will be in any across-the-board cuts.

Sources of data on salaries paid by other public libraries include the latest study of the national scene,[14] the annual statistics issues of many state library bulletins, and the annual survey of salaries received by library school graduates.[15] A survey of salaries paid throughout the community to persons in various standard positions may have been made by the local chamber of commerce or manufacturers' association or by the state government.

A salary schedule may be improved by raising the minimum on one or more grades or raising the maximum, increasing the number or size of increments, adding a cost-of-living bonus or longevity step increases, and so on. There are ways to increase average salaries without directly changing the salary schedule—for example, reclassifying positions from one grade to another, providing for automatic movement from one grade to another (as of junior librarians), reducing the work week (though this can only match what is generally accepted locally), or adding fringe benefits (as increased travel funds). But surveys indicate that real take-home pay needs to be increased absolutely and relatively, now and in the future, to keep up with inflation and to compete with salaries of other occupations.

## Working Conditions

### Tenure

Formal guarantee of tenure or of employment beyond the probationary period is common for teachers. Under civil service, removal can only be done as provided by the rules, usually for cause.

A basic desire of people at work is to be assured of continued employment and to be protected from personal favoritism or caprice, politics, or other factors unrelated to merit. Several librarians have been dismissed for carrying out the principles of the Library Bill of Rights. To deal with this and other arbitrary dismissals, the ALA has established a Staff Committee on Mediation,

Arbitration and Inquiry. It investigates the actions of boards and administrators for bias, the violation of First Amendment freedoms, and other instances of unfair or illegal treatment.[16]

## Fringe Benefits

These normally will include: paid vacation and sick leave, hospital and medical insurance, and paid holidays. They are usually stated specifically for all classes of positions. Local practice will vary as to amounts. Sometimes professional employees may receive a longer vacation period than clerical and custodial staff. According to a survey in 1975, eighteen days a year was considered standard for librarians, and the same was frequently allowed for other library positions as well.[17] Leaves of absence for stated periods without pay for educational or medical reasons are usually allowed; an example of the latter is pregnancy leave. Leave for jury duty is customary; the employer may continue the regular salary and allow the employee to turn in jury duty payment. There is usually a plan for leave with pay for a few days from time to time to attend professional meetings; this privilege should be rotated among staff members, but it is an excellent plan to have the staff active in library associations; visits and conferences with other librarians will usually prove profitable. It is a good practice to suggest that those attending professional meetings make a verbal or written report, or both, to the director and staff so that information gained can be shared. This also serves to remind those attending that this is a part of their work assignment and not just a few days off with pay. Increasingly, travel and other expenses are paid. Some libraries also offer some paid time, and sometimes the cost of tuition and textbooks, for employees in any grade to attend courses that are germane to the employee's work and advancement.

## Retirement

Today most employees are assured of retirement income, and most public libraries have provisions for employee retirement income. In any library without reasonably adequate retirement benefits, the trustees and director should press for a change.

A majority of all public library employees are covered by a state or local retirement system, and many of these systems incorporate federal social security benefits. Still to be desired are interstate agreements to make it possible to transfer pension and retirement credits from state to state, such as is available for many college and university librarians under a retirement and insurance plan designed for educators, the TIAA/CREF system.

Age seventy is the new legal age for compulsory retirement. Reduced social security benefits are available at age sixty-two, and most state and local governmental retirement systems allow similar early retirement benefits schedules. Evidence indicates that loss or retention of ability is not measured always by chronological age. Some libraries require annual physical examinations above some determined age.

But on the average, people do begin to lose vigor in their sixties, and some become more conservative and less willing to experiment. Since older people tend to hold higher-level positions, their failure to retire blocks promotion of younger staff members and may reduce the effectiveness of the library in solving new problems. Furthermore, the usual public library retirement system makes it impossible for an employee within ten or fifteen years of retirement to consider taking another job because of losing the benefit of the employer's contributions to the retirement fund. Provision can be made to continue the services of extra-valuable nonexecutive persons, on a year-to-year basis, perhaps for less than full time or in a less exacting position.

*Professional Development*

Offering career development opportunities to employees on matters of direct practical concern with their work, on paid time and without cost to them, has become a standard practice in many public libraries. Developmental activities could include committee assignments, membership in professional associations, visits to other libraries, writing and publishing, research and sabbatical leave, continuing education, attendance at workshops, seminars and institutes, and, at mid-career levels, consultant work. Today many libraries in larger cities arrange for library schools to give library science courses by extension, and have arranged for local educational institutions to develop courses for paraprofessionals. Special on-the-job training programs are being expanded in many metropolitan libraries for this important new category of staff members.[18]

## Service Ratings

A service rating is the periodic assessment by a supervisor, in a prescribed fashion, of an employee's job performance and efficiency, with comments on potential ability. Unless an effective system is worked out, or if ratings are not made at all, superficial, subjective, and possibly biased opinions will be used by supervisors in judging a new employee's work, deciding whether a staff member is to be promoted, or recommending an employee for a merit increase. The problem is not whether but how to rate work performance fairly. Most people want to know where they stand with their supervisors. Many methods and forms have been developed,[19] including the ALA "Personnel Service Rating Report."[20]

Service ratings are not such valid measures of performance that important decisions should be made solely upon them. Their chief value lies in their use for counseling individual employees, letting them know where they stand,

and helping them to improve; they can also be used as an important guide in the probationary period, as noted above, and annually for other employees. Discussion by all who make ratings will help reduce differences of individual supervisors. Any service rating plan should require that the rating report be shown to and discussed with the employee. Supervisors must learn to make objective ratings. The worker can benefit only by discussing the work with the supervisor. The interview should not stress weaknesses and limitations—it should be a constructive stock taking, with suggested ways to improve. Both parties will feel encouraged when a series of interviews shows progress and successful adjustment. From these counseling interviews the wise supervisor can learn much about each assistant and much about his or her own effectiveness as a supervisor.

*Grievance Procedure*

The purpose of the grievance procedure is to assure that all employees are treated fairly and equitably and that the work of the library may be carried out in an orderly way. The library has the right to expect that the employee will follow orders. Should a dispute arise, the employee is expected to carry out the assignment without delay and file a grievance in accordance with the procedure. The procedure is intended to provide a means for resolving differences at the lowest possible level; the employee should feel at ease about informally discussing any dissatisfaction with the immediate supervisor. That is the first step in the procedure. The supervisor will investigate and respond within a stated period—for example, three days. Most complaints should be resolved at this step.

If the employee is not satisfied with the answer at this stage, the grievance should be written and directed to the library director by letter or prescribed form. The grievance statement should be specific and should state relief sought. The library director should respond in writing within a stated period (three to five days for example). The director will need to consult with the supervisor and perhaps informally also with the employee to obtain additional facts or insights.

If the decision of the library director is not satisfactory to the employee, an appeal to the board of trustees (personnel committee) or municipal officer designated is expected, as the local situation prescribes.

The course of action is described as an example. The procedure to be taken by each library will vary depending upon local conditions. Employees under a collective bargaining agreement will undoubtedly have a detailed grievance procedure as part of that agreement. In general, it must be emphasized that the rights of the employer and the employee must be stated in the procedure; that the employee's right to file a grievance must be taken seriously and treated with respect; but that the employer has the right to direct the work force. Clearly, grievances can be reduced by a well-written and clear personnel manual in the hands of all staff members, so that all know their rights, privileges, and responsibilities. The grievance procedure should be a part of that manual.

## Sick Leave Records

The record of paid sick leave taken by staff members provides an indication of morale and of job satisfaction; often there are comparable figures on sick leave available for local government offices or business firms. Any library can compare its own sick leave rates in one year with the same data for other years, and get an indication as to whether its performance in this respect is improving or declining. The Public Library of Columbus and Franklin County (Ohio) has monthly computer printouts of the vacation and sick leave record for each staff member. The Director of Personnel gives summary reports to the director and board on sick leave abuse.

## Exit Interviews

A practical way of evaluating personnel administration, and the administration of the library, is through an exit interview by the librarian or personnel officer with every person leaving the employ of the library.[21] If the employee is encouraged to speak freely of his work experiences, much of value can be learned about trouble spots in the library's personnel program. Exit interviews serve other purposes too, such as a routine review of necessary steps in effecting the separation, giving the employee a last chance to ask questions and make suggestions, providing some official and personal recognition of his or her leaving the library's employ, and perhaps even persuading him or her not to leave.

## Library Unions

The strong move toward collective bargaining by library employees took place during the social ferment of the 1960s, although there were unions in libraries as long ago as World War I. In the 1930s and 1940s there were local unions in the public libraries of Cleveland, Milwaukee, Chicago, Minneapolis, New York City, Detroit, and Butte, Montana. In recent years, unions have been organized in other metropolitan areas—Newark, Boston, Wayne County (Michigan), Philadelphia, Seattle, San Francisco, and Los Angeles—and in some small communities as well: Oshkosh, Wisconsin; New Haven and Enfield, Connecticut; Berkeley, California; and Bloomfield and Morris County, New Jersey. There is apparently no up-to-date, complete list of all libraries with unions. In Youngstown and Mahoning counties, Ohio, and Buffalo and Erie counties, New York, the existing staff associations were recognized as the bargaining agent. In most of the other libraries, the union was organized by the American Federation of State, County and Municipal Employees, or the Service Employees International Union. AFSCME indicates that there are 18 thousand library employees on membership rolls, and this is but one of several unions with library units.

The current wave of organizing has these characteristics: (a) a collective bargaining contract, (b) all employees subject to the unionization process, (c) "all libraries large and small and from all regions (except the South) are susceptible to union organization," (d) "the unionization of library employees is firmly established."[22]

Biblo concludes that cost-benefit analysis seems not to have been applied to the matter of unionization in any sector and states that library administrators perhaps view unionization as something thrust upon them. (The point is not made, but is perhaps implied, that administrators might look into the matter of cost-benefit, as a concern of mutual interest.) In any event, the cost to the individual is clear. According to a sample taken in 1976, union dues range from $7.50 a month per employee to one-fifth to three-quarters of 1 percent of the employee's monthly salary.[23]

Schlachter, in the same work, advances reasons for the slow development of collective bargaining in libraries:

> Librarians have had a long and fairly consistent history of bargaining individually and emphasizing professional society membership. . . . Librarians remain relatively unorganized. In large part, librarians have shied away from union activity because they question its compatibility with their standards of professionalism. . . . This concern has focused on several major areas: the appropriateness of collective bargaining, the professionalism of union membership, the success of unions in organizing professionals, the split which unions can cause among professionals within the same organization, the problem of striking, the ability of unions to understand professional as well as economic needs, and the value of unions compared to quasi-unions.
>
> . . . There was a general feeling among Pennsylvania librarians that collective bargaining by that group would not be condemned by public sentiment as being unprofessional. . . . The concern appears not to be whether librarians are interested in collective bargaining, but . . . under the auspices of which organization it should take place.

IS UNION MEMBERSHIP UNPROFESSIONAL?

Milton J. Ferguson, addressing an ALA conference, warned, "When, if ever, unionism comes into the library, then we will lower our standards, our morale, our self-respect and our appeal to those we serve. . . . [Unionization] is flatly opposed to the principles which have made American librarianship a useful and proud service.". . .

But the times and the conditions change. Groups of all kinds, in all levels of society, organize to bargain; librarians, and library employees, come to see that professionalism can be tolerant of unionization.[24]

The library employer has been, and still is in most cases, the negotiator with the municipal employer on behalf of the individual. When this works out satisfactorily, the thrust toward collective bargaining is muted. But Schlachter concludes: "Within the library field, many factors are operating in concert to increase the likelihood that librarians will affiliate with unions. Employment concentration, economic imbalance, limited job advancement, job insecurity, union interest, and societal tolerance all contribute to an increasingly favorable climate for collective bargaining."[25]

Moss holds that the introduction of a union in the library has a significant impact upon management:

Collective bargaining implies bilateral decision-making. Union and management discuss terms and conditions of employment, and they must agree to the same conditions. The union voice in bargaining is as strong as that of management. A union refusal is just as final as a management refusal; either party has the power of veto over any proposal.

Management is typically more comfortable in a unilateral decision-making posture. It is much easier to direct someone what to do then to sell him on the merits of the case. It is comfortable to know that once a decision has been made, one has the authority to implement it. With the advent of the unions and collective bargaining, however, management can no longer follow the typical textbook approach to decision-making about the determination of terms and conditions of employment. The union wants to assist with decisions even though no assistance has been sought.

. . . The problem then, is management's understandable unwillingness to surrender historical rights and to bargain bilaterally.[26]

But bargaining does not mean surrender of management rights.

Management rights clauses are present in both private and public employment. Executive Order 11491 provides that all agreements shall state that the responsibility of management officials for a government activity requires them to retain the right, in accordance with applicable laws and regulations, to: (1) direct its employees; (2) hire, promote, transfer, assign and retain employees in positions within the agency and to suspend, demote, discharge, or take other disciplinary action against employees; (3) relieve employees from duties because of lack of work or for other legitimate reasons; (4) maintain the efficiency of the government operations entrusted to them; (5) determine the methods, means and personnel for conducting such operations; and (6) take any necessary action to carry out the mission of the agency in situations of emergency. In a bargaining situation, management must be prepared to present its demands; the union always presents its demands. Management may wish to have work practices changed or policies implemented that may be subject to bargaining. . . . Collective bargaining is a two-way street, with management having as much right to make demands as the union. Management should take a positive position in asserting its demands.

. . . Decisions about the inclusiveness of a bargaining unit—the group of employees to be represented by one union under one contract—can be crucial.

Essentially, a bargaining unit should be limited to those groups which have a community of interest in decisions concerning their employment. For example, many laws, including the National Labor Relations Act, forbid the grouping of professionals with nonprofessionals unless the professionals vote for inclusion.

In summary, an increase in public-employee union membership is forecast and

the scope of bargaining in the public sector will continue to widen in future years. . . .

The need for more expertise and training in employee relations must be stressed. Management must develop skills in labor relations if other leadership efforts are going to be effective in daily operating situations. If reasonable union–management harmony is to prevail, means of reducing the effects of the adversary relationship must be found. It is not possible to generalize on how this can be accomplished. The key is in the attitude of the parties toward each other—a condition which varies from one agency to another. This condition can be as simple or as complex as good interpersonal relations.[27]

During the period 1966–1975, there were fifteen job actions in public libraries in the United States, according to sources consulted. These took place in Chicago (two actions); Brooklyn (three actions); New Orleans; Queensborough, New York (two actions); Contra Costa County, California (strike August 22–September 2, 1968); New York City; San Francisco (strike, three days); Berkeley, California (strike); Youngstown and Mahoning County, Ohio; Ramapo-Catskill Library System, New York; Stanislaus County, California (strike).[28]

Unionization unquestionably introduces a whole new element into the administrative process. One may ponder why employees of a public organization, where there is no profit motive but only a need to render needed services, should have to organize in order to obtain what they feel is due them in fair and equitable working conditions. In short, there would appear at first glance to be no reason for the public employer to exploit the workers.

Upon reflection, it must be observed that the public employer is a body of elected officials, often without much experience in either government or management, and therefore perhaps not even as enlightened as to labor relations as many sectors or private business and industry. Keeping taxes low is of more concern to the official wishing to be reelected than treating the workers fairly. Therefore the library administration may reflect that unionization is probably more of an action against the public employer than against the library heads and trustees, unless of course the library has fiscal autonomy, in which case the administration has a different situation indeed.

Labor relations is not a subject for amateurs. If the staff elects to be represented by a bargaining unit, the administration must respond in a rational manner. Usually, the collective bargaining unit in the library will be a part of a larger group: the other employees of the government of which the library is a part. In this case, the technical assistance and negotiation for the library as employer will be handled by others in the government. Even so, the library director, trustees, and others in the administrative group will be well advised to be closely in touch with the negotiating process. They should be informed, when negotiations are begun, of the demands of the bargaining unit, and of the employer's (city's) counterdemands and counterproposals. The library officials may have some demands or concerns of their own to voice. The union demands may have serious impact upon hours of work and a number of other factors bearing upon the library's ability to operate. The library's needs and concerns in respect to the bargaining unit's demands should be made clearly and specifically as soon as possible, and the library director and trustee should keep in touch with the negotiations as they proceed. Once the contract or agreement has been reached, the decisions have been made for the life of the agreement. The library has no recourse but to follow its terms.

If the library trustees and director are to negotiate with the bargaining unit, apart from a larger unit of government, they will do well to seek expert advice and counsel. The library director cannot be expected to be an expert in this area.

One of the issues to be considered is whether all employees will be required to join, if the majority vote to enter a bargaining unit. Union policy, of course, prefers the closed shop (in which every employee must either join the union or pay an amount equivalent to union dues), since otherwise non-members pay no dues but receive the benefits. Nonetheless, the employees who have voted in the election not to join may retain some feelings about having to participate in and pay dues to an organization not of their own choosing.

In summary, the library union brings another power structure into the hierarchy. Whether this is beneficial to the library will depend on many factors, not all of which the library's administrative group can control. Improvement in working conditions should enhance the library's operational potential. The unionization process can provide the means for an orderly and structured response to any conflicts that may have occurred or that may be incipient.

The library trustees and director will need to become informed and to use their opportunities to see that the union functions in the library's interest, to the best of their ability.

Robert H. Rohlf, director of the Hennepin County (Minnesota) Public Library and 1979 vice-president and president-elect of the Public Library Association, commented in an annual review article in 1977 that

unionization became an issue in many libraries, and library unions were asking for, and in some cases receiving, an expanding role in library decision making. . . . The increasing militancy of library unions seems to indicate a trend and library administrators must learn to cope with unions and deal positively and effectively with them. The militant library unions stood in contrast to semi-passive staff associations which have been prominent in the history of libraries in the United States.[29]

## Notes

1. Morris Greene, "The Library in the Game of Politics," *Wilson Library Bulletin* 38 (March 1964): 539.

2. Lewis R. Benton, *Supervision and Management* (New York: McGraw-Hill, 1972), p. 349.

3. Clovis R. Shepherd, "Features of the Successful Group," in Harold J. Leavitt and Louis R. Pondy, *Readings in Managerial Psychology* (Chicago: University of Chicago Press, 1973), pp. 441–44.

4. David A. Nadler and Michael L. Tushman, *Readings on Managerial Behavior* (New York: Columbia University Press, 1976), p. 136.

5. Paul Wasserman and Marlene A. Palmer, *Training and Development Organizations Directory* (Detroit: Gale Research, 1978). This extremely useful guide gives details about the growing number of organizations that offer training for managerial personnel and tells the fields in which such courses and workshops are conducted.

6. *The Personnel Manual: An Outline for Libraries* (Chicago: American Library Association, 1977).

7. Michelle Rudy, "Equity and Governance Patterns," *Library Trends* 27 (Fall 1977): 185. This article comprises an excellent summary of recent developments in the field and their impact on library administration. See also Public Services Laboratory, Georgetown University, *What Achieves Affirmative Action in Cities?* (Washington, D.C.: National Science Foundation, 1975), pp. 1–47.

8. Paul Pigors and Charles A. Myers, *Personnel Administration* (New York: McGraw-Hill, 1977), pp. 251–57.

9. See Clemm C. Kessler III and George J. Gibbs, "Getting the Most from Application Blanks and References," *Personnel* 52 (January–February 1975): 53–62. See also Kathleen B. Stebbins, *Personnel Administration in Libraries* (New York: Scarecrow), pp. 165–94.

10. A survey in 1957 of 852 companies with several million employees, in 65 different industries, showed that 99 percent required an interview before an applicant would be hired. See William R. Spriegel and Virgil A. James, "Trends in Recruitment and Selection Practices," *Personnel* 35 (November–December 1958): 44–45.

11. E. S. Savas and Sigmund G. Ginsburg, "The Civil Service: A Meritless System?" *The Public Interest* 32 (Summer 1973): 70–85.

12. U.S., Department of Labor, Bureau of Labor Statistics, *Monthly Labor Review* 101 (March 1978): 77.

13. David W. Belcher, *Wage and Salary Administration* (Englewood Cliffs, N.J.: Prentice-Hall, 1955).

14. U.S., Department of Labor, Bureau of Labor Statistics, *Library Manpower: A study of Demand and Supply* (Washington, D.C.: Government Printing Office, 1975).

15. Carlyle J. Frarey and Carol L. Learmont, "Placements and Salaries 1974: Promise or Illusion?" *Library Journal* (Oct. 1, 1975): 1767–74 (reprinted in *The Bowker Annual of Library and Book Trade Information, 1976* [New York: R. R. Bowker, 1976], pp. 281–97).

16. Ruth R. Frame et al., "SMAI Case Report," *American Libraries* 7 (October 1976): 574–577. Also, "Security of Employment in Libraries: A Statement of Policy of the American Library Association," *American Libraries* 7 (July–August 1976): 449.

17. "Vacation Time and Benefits: How Your Library Rates," *American Libraries* 6 (July–August 1975): 407.

18. Billy R. Wilkerson, "Staff for Metropolitan Library Service," *Library Trends* 23 (October 1974): 266.

19. Such as recording critical and characteristic incidents in the daily work of an employee; see John C. Flanagan and Robert K. Burns, "The Employee Performance Record: A New Appraisal and Development Tool," *Harvard Business Review* 33 (September–October 1955): 95–102.

20. Reprinted in Appendix IV, American Library Association Board on Personnel Administration, *Personnel Organization and Procedure* (Chicago: American Library Association), pp. 54–58, and also in Kathleen B. Stebbins, *Personnel Administration in Public Libraries,* revised by Foster E. Mohrhardt, 2d ed. (New York, 1966), pp. 203–52. Includes also several other rating forms from libraries.

21. U.S., Civil Service Commission, *Exit Interviews in the U.S. Civil Service Commission,* 1956.

22. Herbert Biblo, "Librarians and Trade Unionism: A Prologue," in "Employee Organizations and Collective Bargaining in Libraries," Margaret A. Chaplan, ed., *Library Trends* 25 (October 1976): 2.

23. Marilyn Oberg and others, "Unionization: Costs and Benefits to the Individual and Library," in "Employee Organizations and Collective Bargaining in Libraries," Margaret A. Chaplan, ed., *Library Trends* 25 (October 1976): 440–41.

24. Gail Ann Schlachter, "Professionalism vs. Unionism," in "Employee Organizations and Collective Bargaining in Libraries," Margaret A. Chaplan, ed., *Library Trends* 25 (October 1976): 451–53.

25. Ibid., p. 458.

26. Carol E. Moss, "Bargaining's Effect on Library Management and Operation," in "Employee Organizations and Collective Bargaining in Libraries," Margaret A. Chaplan, ed., *Library Trends* 25 (October 1976): 504.

27. Ibid., pp. 504–5, 513.

28. Appendix A, "Chronology of Job Actions, 1966–75," in "Employee Organizations and Collective Bargaining in Libraries," Margaret A. Chaplan, ed., *Library Trends* 25 (October 1976): 517–21.

29. Robert H. Rohlf, "Management, Library" in *The ALA Yearbook 1977 Edition* (Chicago: American Library Association, 1977), p. 201.

# 6 Public Library Organization

Organization is the design of the personnel structure of the library, the grouping of the positions that will best carry out the library's planned role, objectives, and activities. Two general statements may be made: If the planning process proposed in Chapter 2 has been carried out, the library's organization will be based on the results of that process and will be modified as the planning process continues in response to changing needs and conditions. In short, the organization should result from the plan. The second general statement is that given the wide range of size and complexity of public libraries, from those serving a few thousand persons to the large urban or county or regional systems serving several million people, there is no one master organizational chart that can be laid down for all to follow.

If a public library were to be organized anew, it might or might not follow the traditional lines now in force in most libraries. The fact is that most libraries have added departments and units and branches as the population grew without ever taking a hard look at the organization to see what was happening. This reappraisal most often will occur, if at all, when the library runs out of space. Then it becomes imperative to consider what is going on and see whether the organization fits the current and probable future needs. Sometimes it is the rigidity of the library building that fixes the organization: the library has to fit the organization into the rooms available. This is of course unfortunate, and usually wasteful of costly human resources, both staff and public. This is another sound argument for functional library space; it is cheaper in the long run, given the cost of maintaining services, to have the space that is needed and to have it in an efficient arrangement.

The library need not wait for a space survey to force an examination of the organization to take place. Again, it is necessary to reemphasize the major importance of the planning process. When the library's role, goals, objectives, and action plan have been decided on, the library organization can be modified or revised as necessary.

## Logical Arrangement of Activities

Bearing upon the development of the library operational plan, some organizational principles, used in business and public administration, are pertinent. First is to identify and define the various major functions and activities, grouping those that should be related. One may begin by listing activities, working up to a fairly complete schedule, arranged by groups rather than alphabetically. This compels some order of priority. To the visually minded a diagram may clarify ideas and decisions as one goes along.

A second principle is that everything undergoes healthy change as time passes. Flexibility to meet new situations has to be built into the framework.

The third principle is the value of simplicity, which fosters economy. When developments in public service seem to demand a change in emphasis, or a new service or activity, it is a temptation to create a special department, unit, or position, but enlargement of the organizational framework adds costs for materials and personnel, and creating new activities is not a sign of progress unless existing activities are highly efficient and are meeting the needs.

### Grouping

One possible grouping of functions: selection and acquisition of materials; cataloging and other preparation of materials for use, and the circulation routines; adult reader services. Services for young adults (high school age); the services for children; the branches or branch system, if any, along with bookmobiles and other distributing points; and the administrative overhead, including management, clerical, fiscal records, statistics, and building care constitute further divisions. Adult reader services can be broken down into three aspects: (1) the promotion and guidance of book borrowing; (2) the reference and informational services; (3) programming and materials (for example, films).

These groups of activities represent a series that can be arranged into a logical organization because each has a distinctive character sufficiently different from the others so that its responsibility, guidance, and promotion can well be assigned to some individual and each is sufficient in volume of service or activity to justify a separate group of workers.

Frequently library organization diagrams show the seven major groups of activities listed above divided into two larger categories: (1) services to the public, and (2) support services.

### Defining Scope and Authority

A written description of each group of departments and positions and their scope should be brief and simple, clearly defining jurisdiction and authority: just where decisions are to be made and who is to be directly responsible, initiate, give instructions, supervise, and measure results. Overlappings and possible conflicts need to be foreseen, explained, and settled in the statement. A diagram can show lines of responsibility.

Another principle is to place authority and decision making as close as possible to the point of action. This encourages each executive to develop assistants and to initiate and recommend action. Avoid adding levels of authority—that is, keep to a "flat structure" instead of a "steep structure." These middle levels lengthen the "chain of command" and often delay, and sometimes block, suggestions and communication up and down. More personalities have to be dealt with, and they do not always facilitate things enough to repay the costs.

### *Organization: Urwick's Ten Principles*

The following principles are part of Lyndall F. Urwick's "Notes on the Theory of Organization," prepared originally in connection with Col. Urwick's address in an American Management Association unit dealing with organization building.

1. Principle of the Objective. Every organization and every part of every organization must be an expression of the purpose of the undertaking concerned or it is meaningless and therefore redundant. You cannot organize in a vacuum; you must organize *for* something.

2. Principle of Specialization. The activities of every member of any organized group should be confined, as far as possible, to the performance of a single function.

3. Principle of Coordination. The purpose of organizing per se, as distinguished from the purpose of the undertaking, is to facilitate coordination, unity of effort.

4. Principle of Authority. In every organized group the supreme authority must rest somewhere. There should be a clear line of authority from the supreme authority to every individual in the group.

5. Principle of Responsibility. The responsibility of the superior for the acts of his subordinate is absolute.

6. Principle of Definition. The content of each position, the duties involved, the authority and responsibility contemplated, and the relationships with other positions should be clearly defined in writing and published to all concerned.

7. Principle of Correspondence. In every position, the responsibility and the authority should correspond.

8. The Span of Control. No person should supervise more than five, or at the most, six, direct subordinates whose work interlocks.

The key word here is *interlocks*. Where there is no interlocking, the span of control can be greater. That is especially true of employees reporting to the lowest level of supervision. The span of control and the number of supervisory levels are interrelated. The smaller the span, the greater the number of levels. If the span of executive control is 5, and 20 workers report to the lowest level of supervision, then a division head or department head with two levels of executives under him or her can head an organization of 500 rank-and-file employees. With another executive level, the working level would be increased to 2,500.

9. Principles of Balance. It is essential that the various units of an organization should be kept in balance.

10. Principle of Continuity. Reorganization is a continuous process; in every undertaking specific provision should be made for it.[1]

*Span of Control and Delegation*

Mercer and Koester point out factors affecting time available for supervision: degree of dispersal of activities under supervision, degree of decentralization, of operation responsibility, and impact of planning and decisions on the budget. They also point out that since there is probably a 25 percent loss in true communications between each tier, it stands to reason that if there are four tiers between the manager and the lowest skill level under that supervisor's leadership, the communication at the lowest level will be just about zero.[2]

Therefore, it would appear that the number of people reporting directly to the library director, and to others in the supervisory cadre, will effectively depend on several variables that must be determined locally. Obviously, the director who is willing to delegate much of the day-to-day operating responsibility will have time to see that those responsibilities are carried out.

It is clear that any supervisor, from the director on down, must see and be seen in every department, room, and activity under that supervisor's span of control at frequent and regular intervals. Firsthand observation is much better than secondhand or thirdhand verbal reports. And it is good for the staff to see the director, whose tour of visitation should include not only those units within his or her span of control but all other units as well.

*Line and Staff*

These terms describe two types of position within the same organization. A staff position is an advisory position without authority. It provides ideas, facts, and information to the line position. The line position is a decision-making one. In a small library, one in a staff position may be assigned to gather data that will help the librarian in the line position make a decision. In a large library someone in a staff position may head a personnel office or the public relations office, yet still may have no authority. The person in the line position, usually the librarian, has the authority that flows through department heads and supervisors down to assistants. Without this authority an organization would lose its unity and be unable to operate efficiently and effectively to meet its goals.

## Coordinating

Many larger libraries have "staff" coordinators within each of three major age groups—children, young people, and adults—to tie together the book selection, services, and viewpoints between the staffs at all branches with those at central, thereby giving each the benefit of the experience and knowledge of all. This is accomplished by staff meetings, committees, the issuing of a continuous flow of instructional releases and booklists, and especially by frequent visits to all service points by the coordinators and their assistants.

Coordination of these and similar overall functions, such as personnel or publicity, may be delegated to the director's first assistant in systems not large enough to afford age-group or functional coordinators or "staff" officers. If the regular department heads are effective supervisors, special coordinators are needed only in large systems.

## Proportioning Services and Staff

Proportioning has to start with total staff and salary budget available. Median figures from a 1968 U.S. Office of Education survey of 180 public libraries with varying budgets and different regions indicate that large and medium libraries have one staff member per 2,200 population and small libraries have one staff member per 2,600 population. The survey also shows that there are five staff members for every one professional in large libraries and six staff members for every one professional in medium and small libraries. Large libraries have one professional per 12,000 population, medium libraries one professional per 14,000 population, and small libraries one professional per 16,000 population.[3]

## Organization Diagrams

A diagram will show everyone how the library operates. It needs to indicate the major functions or departments and possibly some secondary activities, all in their logical relationship, and with the lines of authority from top to bottom, especially the division of responsibility between chief and assistant librarian, or upper assistant, as to which other persons or departments they supervise.

The diagram will serve in many ways to inform staff, trustees, applicants, city officials, Friends of the Library, and interested members of the community what the library is doing, what the various services and functions are, and how they relate to one another.

Organization charts usually consist of the various service units or departments and functions displayed on a single page, if possible, so that all can be studied at one glance. The various units and functions are enclosed in boxes, with solid lines showing line authority and dotted lines showing staff relationships. The chart may list in brief the duties of the particular office, department, or function, the name of the person in charge, and the number of staff assigned to that unit. It should be identified and dated. The chart will necessarily have to be revised at least annually, but the information it conveys will be worth the effort.

As noted above and repeated many times in this book, the organization chart for the local library must flow from the action plan for that library, but a sample can be shown. This is not a model to be followed, even for format; it should be adapted locally as required. There is no rule of thumb as to when an organization chart becomes useful, but it would seem that when the staff grows to around four or five it would be a good time to begin. The chart shown below is not for any particular size of library.

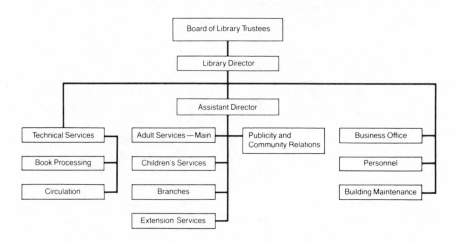

It will be noted that this chart shows a combination of positions, functions, and activities. The individual boxes will include brief information to describe what work is done, the name of the person in charge, and the staff assigned— for example, five librarians, two library assistants, and so on. In a relatively small library it might be possible to list all positions and names.

If the organization chart cannot contain all of the positions, the director may wish to consider an annual "positions list," showing names, positions, and current salary for each position, unit by unit or office by office. This will enable supervisors to be clear about number of positions assigned and will also provide a handy source of projected cost analysis for each unit. The positions list will be based on line budget information and cannot reflect actual costs when a position is vacant, for example, or when it is filled at a rate that is higher than budgeted.

If the organization chart includes the number of authorized positions and the job classification of those positions, it then serves the additional function of serving as a manning chart (or table of organization as it is called in the military). The positions list is simply an extension of the manning chart, showing actual names and allocated salaries for each position on the manning chart.

These three papers: the organization chart, the line-by-line personnel budget, and the positions list, which is the personnel budget rearranged by organization chart, constitute the basic organizational document for the library.

The preparation of this organization document, in two or three parts, is first connected to the budget estimate and then to the budget allocation. The question is: How many and what kinds of staff will be required to carry out the planned services? This will form the basis of the budget estimate. The number and kinds of staff actually allocated will form the basis for the organizational structure for the budget year. The estimate and the allocation may not be identical. As will be discussed in Chapter 7, on finance and budgeting, there should be correlation between needs, performance, and estimate. Support services—book acquisition, processing, circulation, building maintenance, business office operations—are subject to some rough guidelines as to staff needs. These are more or less production departments, with somewhat predictable and measurable outputs. These will be discussed in more detail in the chapters on these functions later in the book. Public services are not production departments. A certain quantifiable output cannot be predicted or measured in terms of staff requirements. The so-called "standard" previously employed of one staff member per 2,500 or 3,000 in the population to be served was not based on documented evidence but was more or less an average of experience in so-called exemplary libraries.

It comes back again to the library role in the community—the goals and then the measurable objectives. These must be clarified, stated, understood. Very little research in job analysis for public libraries has been carried out. A substantial beginning—that is, the groundwork for research—was laid with the Illinois Library Task Analysis Project. The report of this study, *Personnel Utilization in Libraries,* contains a systemic approach to the utilization of personnel in performing library tasks. The data are too specialized and detailed for summary here; the report, by Myrl Ricking and Robert E. Booth, is listed in the reading list for this chapter in the Appendix as well as in the Notes for this chapter. The report was prepared under the direction of a committee of librarians, who note in the introduction:

The greatest use (of this report) will probably be in small to medium-sized public and college libraries. . . . This is not merely because the research upon which it is based was conducted in small to medium-sized libraries, but perhaps more because libraries of this size often do not have the personnel resources to perform the type of analysis that this study provides. This does not deny its usefulness to libraries of any size.[4]

The small library, of perhaps less than fifteen persons or so in full-time equivalents, will undoubtedly be organized around the two basic functions of public services and support services. Public services may be divided into services to adults and services to children and young people, but some or all of the staff may work in either of these age-level services as circumstances require. In fact, the head librarian, and doubtless others as well, may also work part-time in support services: book selection or processing, but preferably not in building maintenance. The fact, however, that staff may work in one or more "boxes" in the organization chart does not obviate the need or utility of the chart. It should in fact show approximately the amount or percentage of the time spent by dual-function personnel in the various functions.

In larger, main urban libraries, Henington reports, "there is a universal acceptance . . . of subject departmentalization as a device for effectively bringing the patron and the material together. The development of departmentalization in public libraries into three major activities divisions—public services, technical services, and administrative services—came early in American library history." Departments in turn were developed "by function (circulation and reference), by clientele age (adult and children), by type of work (acquisitions and cataloging), and by administrative need (business office and building maintenance)." In recent years, the new media, regional responsibilities, effective management, economic strain, the use of the library as an information center have all indicated the need for new patterns of organization.

Although the basic concept of subject departments places all materials on the subject in one place "to assure the widest possible information resource," most large urban libraries segregate audiovisual materials because of special storage and display requirements, mechanical and technical problems, and the fact that selection of audiovisual materials requires different kinds of knowledge than does the selection of printed matter. Some larger libraries "have treated microforms as a storage method." The Houston Public Library plans to put microforms in subject departments with other material. Periodicals are usually placed in the subject department. "Documents are handled in a widely divergent manner." Some libraries put them with the subject, others put them in a separate section.

"There has been an increasing trend toward fewer and larger departments" in order better to serve the user, decrease book selection overlap and reference materials duplication, reduce staff requirements, and reduce the number of subject department catalogues needed. The Enoch Pratt Free Library, where Joseph Wheeler introduced departmentalization, had six subject departments in 1933; the 1965 reorganization plan reorganized these into three. However, according to the American Library Directory, 1978, the Enoch Pratt Library has five subject departments: business, science and technology, fine arts, humanities, and social science and history; other departments listed are: general information, Maryland, popular library, and young adult collection. "There is no absolute agreement as to subject departmentalization," but "there seems to be consensus . . . [on] science and technology, art and music, literature and language, history and biography, philosophy and religion, and sociology and education." Business and economics are combined with science and technology.

There is wide variance as to what should be in the popular library, for the "patron with a general need"; it is "frequently referred to as a branch library within a large specialized library." The popular library at Dallas has the fiction collection; Pratt has fiction and popular books; San Francisco has mostly paperbacks.

In eight urban main libraries queried in 1971, the number of departments were as follows: six in Brooklyn, Cincinnati, Seattle, and San Francisco; seven in Dallas, Enoch Pratt (Baltimore), and Queensborough; and thirteen in the District of Columbia. Dallas moved slightly away from the traditional subject grouping with a new title, the community living department: sociology, law, philosophy, religion, recreation, and sports. Dallas, Pratt, District of Columbia, Queensborough, and San Francisco had popular libraries. There were general reference departments in Dallas and Pratt.

These are departments for adults. According to Henington there is currently a great deal of concern with service to children in main buildings in large cities where emphasis . . . is shifting to serious, scholarly and in-depth research.

As to the administrative framework, most libraries have a conventional approach: director, assistant director, and age-level coordination. This creates span-of-control problems, and some libraries have a chief of the main library, or a director of public service. The age-level coordinators are responsible for materials selection.

The extensive growth of main library telephone reference service has caused a heavy burden. . . . [To reduce use of costly professional staff] libraries are increasingly [staffing this service with] college graduates [which] siphon off simple repetitive questions leaving the serious in-depth research questions to . . . subject librarians.

The concept of public library departmentalization has been effectively tried in a number of variations through the years and has been accepted as the best way to handle large volumes of material and growing requests in greater depth in a better way. The main library is not, as many seem to mistakenly consider it, a large branch library. It is the chief center for information resources within a community or a region, with services principally for the specialist.[5]

### Examples of Large Library Organizations

Denver Public Library: (1976) population served 532,700. Total staff full-time: 410. Total operating expense: $6,206,542 ($11.65 per capita). Salary expense: $4,451,957. Percent for salaries: 72 percent. Ratio of staff to population: 1 per 1,299. Organization: library commission, librarian. Reporting to the librarian are:

1. Director of Administrative Services—
   Responsible for:
   a. Methods analyst
   b. Buildings department
   c. Accounting Office
   d. Circulation and Registration Division
   e. Personnel Office
2. Director of Public Services and Assistant Librarian—
   Responsible for:
   a. Coordination of adult services
   b. Coordination of young adult services
   c. Coordination of children's services
   d. Subject departments
      Art and Music
      Literature and History
      Science and Engineering
      Sociology and Business
   e. Five Regional libraries each with one, two or three branch libraries
   f. Extension Services office
      (Bookmobiles and interlibrary loan)
   g. Health and Hospital Medical Library
3. Director of Technical Services
4. Director of Community Services (who is also an assistant librarian)
   Responsible for:
   a. Public Information Office
   b. Group Services
   c. Great Books Program
   d. Community Aides
   e. DPL Friends
   f. DPL Foundation
5. Western History Department
6. Special Collections
7. Book Selection Center
8. Conservation Library Center

Spans of Control:

Librarian (8)
Director of Administrative Services (5)
Director of Public Services and Assistant Librarian (14)
Director of Technical Services (3)
Director of Community Services and Assistant Librarian (6)

Dallas: 1977–78 population, 879,200. Total full-time staff: 455. Total operating expense: $7,952,035 ($9.04 per capita). Salary expense: $5,537,398. Percent for salaries: 70 percent. Ratio of staff to population: 1 per 1,932.

Spans of control—six report to the director of libraries: two associate directors, for public services and management services; personnel department; cooperative program coordinator; an administrative assistant; and the head of public relations. The public services director has charge of seven: materials coordinator, community education coordinator, media specialist, adult coordinator, youth coordinator, central chief, and branch chief. The associate director for management services has four reporting: systems analyst, technical services chief, business office manager, and circulation chief. Building maintenance is under the business office manager.

### Organizations, Medium-Sized Libraries

There follow four examples of libraries in the 75,000–150,000 population range, showing number of departments. These have been selected at random from American Library Directory, 1978.

1. Decatur, Illinois. Population served: 90,397. Staff: 45 (1 per 2,009). Operating expense: $1,011,929 ($11.85 per capita). Salaries: $503,342 (47 percent of total expense). Organization (lines of authority not available): director, interlibrary loan and reference, adult services, children's services, young adult and media, technical services. One branch.

2. Brockton, Massachusetts. Population served: 101,000. Staff: 33 (1 per 3,060). Operating expense: $625,749 ($6.20 per capita). Salaries: $415,139 (66 percent of total). Organization: Director, adult and reference, children's, technical services, community services, young adult and rare books, bookmobile coordinator. Five branches.

3. Camden, New Jersey. Population served: 102,551. Staff: 40 (1 per 2,564). Operating expense: $395,557 ($3.86 per capita). Salaries: $280,222 (71 percent of total). Organization: director, assistant director and cataloging, reference, technical services and acquisitions, community services, children's. Four branches.

4. Fullerton, California. Population served: 92,900. Staff: 60 (1 per 1,548). Operating expense: $1,110,784 ($11.96 per capita). Salaries: $710,262 (64 percent of total). Organization: Director, adult materials, children's, young adult, media, technical services and acquisition, cataloging, reference and special collections, community services, branch coordinator, bookmobile coordinator. One branch, one bookmobile.

It should be noted that the above data for four medium-sized libraries is drawn from a directory and may not therefore reflect actual departments or units in all cases but only names of staff for directory purposes. The sample may, however, show the similarities and the differences in organization among libraries. Another random sample drawn from the same directory for a number of libraries showed that all have someone in charge of children's services; adult services and reference are sometimes combined and sometimes are separate units. Technical services normally include acquisition, cataloging, and book preparation.

A thorough study of organizational structures and patterns would undoubtedly be a useful piece of research. Superficial observation would lead one to the conclusion that organizational patterns in local libraries may be as much fortuitous as anything, based perhaps on abilities of staff and other local factors. This may not be a justifiable observation. In any event, it seems clear that a model or ideal structure can hardly be laid down.

## Organizational Policies

Stueart and Eastlick stress the importance of clearly enunciated policies on organization:

> In order to maintain consistency and continuity, written organizational policies should be prepared as the organizational structure is established. Of course, any changes in the structure will require changes in the policy statements. . . .
>
> A policy may be defined as a statement that guides present and future action. It is a general statement that guides the action of employees in the decision-making process. It is true that policy has a restrictive effect on the decisions employees may make. But such policies assure compliance with the organizational structure which has been created to achieve goals and objectives.
>
> A policy is a public statement. It is available to all employees and is discussed with them to assure understanding. Employees should not have to try to identify organizational policy from the action or occasional statements of the manager.
>
> Organizational policies should include the following:
>
> 1. Statements identifying the laws that authorize the establishment of the library. . . .
>
> 2. Statements describing the departmentation that has been established as the organizational structure. The tasks and responsibilities of each unit—the large organizational unit as well as each sub-unit—must be defined. . . .
>
> 3. Statements describing the resources of the organizational unit. In libraries it is possible to list the classification numbers for which a department is responsible or to identify the types of resources to be housed in that unit. For example, a fine arts department may be responsible for all books in the Dewey Classification 700. That department is responsible for the selection of all titles and for the replacement, duplication, and weeding of these resources. . . .

The purpose of such organizational policy statements is not to limit the creativity of the staff but rather to assure consistency in the operation of the organizational structure. Such policy statements also provide an excellent method of communicating to the employees the responsibility of each organizational unit other than the one to which they are assigned.[6]

It appears that most public libraries are organized along traditional and historical lines: combinations of age-level and functional or activities groupings.

## The Matrix

In *Library Management,* Stueart and Eastlick introduce the reader to newer ways of looking at organizations:

Some libraries are developing packages of information for specific community groups. In order to have representative resources and services from all organizational units of the library, it is necessary to create a matrix, a lateral slice across autonomous units. For example, the matrix might consist of the organizational unit responsible for services to the disadvantaged. The creation of a matrix structure might be temporary. But it is very important that the administrators of the autonomous units affected understand what is happening and cooperate with the endeavor. Without this understanding and cooperation, it is possible that the organizational principle of unity of command might be violated.

Regardless of new methods of illustrating organizational structure and new patterns of organization, the basic concept of the hierarchical structure is expected to remain. Managers will still be assigned responsibility and the authority to fulfill that responsibility. Possibly new criteria for structuring the organization will emerge. Drucker suggests four criteria for organizational structure:

1. Result-producing activities—activities which produce measurable results which can be related . . . to the results and performance of the entire enterprise.
2. Support activities—[activities]—which while . . . essential do not produce direct results.
3. Hygiene and housekeeping activities—activities which are truly ancillary.
4. Top-management activities— . . . activities that are the conscience of an organization. The conscience function of giving vision, of setting standards, and of auditing performance against these standards is basically a top-management function.

New trends, such as "management by objectives" and "participative management" are not changes in the basic concept of organization. Rather, they represent the "humanistic school's" approach to management.[7]

## Summary

The purpose of the organization of the library is to carry out the library's role in the community, to enable it to do the job that is required in the most efficient and successful manner. The organization should follow the library's action plan. Essential elements include: logical arrangement of activities, defining scope and authority, and determining span of control and degree of delegation. The organization will best be shown in graphic form, on a diagram or chart, showing lines of authority and responsibilities. The line item budget and a positions list or manning chart complete the organizational document for the library.

As the public library's role, goals, objectives, priorities and plans become clearer and more definitive, perhaps a scientific approach to library organization could be undertaken. At the present stage of development, library organization appears to be empirical.

In subsequent chapters, the present broad and traditional organizational pattern is treated in detail: by age-level and by functional groupings. Local libraries will adapt the information and suggestions to local needs and situations.

## Notes

1. Lyndall F. Urwick, "Notes on the Theory of Organization" in Carl Heyl, ed., *Encyclopedia of Management* (New York: Van Nostrand Reinhold, 1973), pp. 658–59.
2. James L. Mercer and Edwin H. Koester, *Public Management Systems* (New York: American Management Association, 1978), p. 49.
3. Ernest DeProspo, *Performance Measures for Public Libraries* (Chicago: Public Library Association, 1973), p. 60.
4. Myrl Ricking and Robert E. Booth, *Personnel Utilization in Libraries: A Systems Approach* (Chicago: American Library Association, 1974), p. ix.
5. David M. Henington, "The Developing Patterns of Main Library Organization," *Library Trends* 20 (1972): 640–653.
6. Robert D. Stueart and John Taylor Eastlick, *Library Management* (Littleton, Colo.: Libraries Unlimited, 1977), pp. 57–58.
7. Ibid., p. 69.

# 7 Budgeting and Finance

Whether the public library is operated as a private association or corporation in the public interest, or as a department of a governmental unit, there are certain principles, policies, and practices that must be applied in the general area of budgeting and finance. As the public contribution toward the cost of quasi-public libraries tends to increase over the years, the governmental interest in participation in and control of the library's operation also rises. Actually, the view held by many boards of trustees, and even some library directors, that the public library ought to be separate and aloof from the government, is fallacious. The public library is of, by, and for the people and therefore should be in the thick of the fray when it comes to the scramble for public revenues, just as it should deliver a product that will justify taxpayer support. In short, the public library should always be a unit of the government that supports it.

The cost of public library service is a variable, depending on many factors both local and national. In steadier times, the American Library Association could recommend a cost per capita, but this stance has been abandoned in the face of rising inflation and, more significant, the realistic need to design the local public library service program to respond to the needs and desires of the community being served. The library staff and director may be guided in planning by the annual costs reported by libraries of similar size and purpose, to the extent that these costs can be determined. State library agencies usually collect and often publish data about costs, and the local library director can extract and manipulate this information to suit local needs. From a budgeting and cost planning standpoint, it is often useful to be able to compare local costs with those of other jurisdictions, to see whether the local requirements are above or below the average. Municipal appropriating authorities usually feel more comfortable about the library's budget estimate of need if they can see that it is not too far out of line with what is happening elsewhere.

One recent writer states that an annual allocation of $15 per capita for public library service is needed to meet the needs of users at both ends of the clientele spectrum—from the highly educated specialist to the culturally disadvantaged and isolated.[1] This figure may fluctuate from library to library depending upon the needs of a particular community, if new recommendations of the Public Library Association are followed. The "mission statement" also speaks to funding in the following terms:

The local public library can no longer meet the needs of its local constituency solely with local resources or local funding. The needs of people in whatever support area cannot be met by the resources of any one type of library or libraries. Within the context of these realities, new patterns of funding and governance for the public library must be implemented with state and federal legislation. Among the changes mandated are:

Alternatives to the property tax as a major source of support for public libraries and a more realistic distribution of funding from local, state, and federal levels.

*Alternatives to the single municipality* as the parent base of public library governance and support.[2]

Whatever the support factor, the library budget will still come to a very small percentage of the local government budget and will compare very unfavorably with the per-pupil cost of public education, even though one of the avowed and agreed upon purposes of the public library service program is to continue and extend on a lifelong basis the education of the individual and to supplement and complement the educational process in the community. More will be noted about this later under methods for obtaining local and other support. In a 1974 survey the National Center for Education Statistics found, as shown in Table 1, that over 40 percent of all public libraries were supported by a per capita expenditure of less than $3. More than two-thirds of all public libraries were sustained on a per capita expenditure of less than $5.

The same survey indicates "that library services, in terms of amount and trends in expenditures, are in an inferior and deteriorating position,

**Table 1.** Number and Percentage of Public Libraries by Total Expenditures per Person in Population of Area Served, 1974

|  | Number of Libraries | Percentage |
|---|---|---|
| Less than $1 | 691 | 8.3 |
| $ 1–2.99 | 2,694 | 32.5 |
| 3–4.99 | 2,273 | 27.4 |
| 5–6.99 | 1,004 | 12.1 |
| 7–8.99 | 617 | 7.4 |
| 9–11.99 | 435 | 5.2 |
| 12–14.99 | 218 | 2.6 |
| More than $15 | 375 | 4.5 |
|  | 8,307 | 100.0 |

*Adapted from preliminary analysis of 1974 survey data made available by NCES.*

**Table 2.** Comparison of Expenditures for Selected State and Local Government Functions, 1974, 1972, and 1967 (in millions)

| | 1974† | 1972 | 1967 | Average Annual Rate of Change 1972–1974 | Average Annual Rate of Change 1967–1972 |
|---|---|---|---|---|---|
| Total General Expenditure | $198,959 | $168,549 | $93,350 | 8.65% | 12.54% |
| Public libraries* | 968 | 816 | 518 | 8.92 | 9.51 |
| Local schools | 53,059 | 46,671 | 27,590 | 6.62 | 11.09 |
| Health and hospitals | 15,495 | 13,023 | 6,640 | 9.08 | 14.42 |
| Police | 7,289 | 6,005 | 3,049 | 10.17 | 14.52 |
| Local parks and recreation | 2,951 | 2,318 | 1,291 | 12.83 | 12.42 |
| Total Excluding Local Schools | $145,900 | $121,878 | $65,760 | 9.41% | 13.13%‡ |

* It should be noted that the total expenditure for public libraries using Census of Government data differs from totals developed from the state survey performed as a part of this study. The variation can be explained by differences in reporting nomenclature and any sampling procedures related to Census figures. The data series are internally consistent and can be used separately for analysis and interpretation.

† 1975 data available to date to be included in this table indicate continuation of the pattern under inflationary impact. Public library expenditures for 1975 were $1.12 billion—up 15.6 percent over 1974, but still lower than increases for other services.

‡ Total general expenditures includes categories not shown on chart.

Adapted from U.S., Department of Commerce, Bureau of the Census, *Governmental Finances in 1973–74*; *Census of Governments, 1967*, vol. 4, no. 5: *Compendium of Government Finances*; and *Census of Governments, 1972*, vol. 4, no. 5: *Compendium of Government Finances*.

compared with other related and contrasting state and local government services." For five state and local government functions—public libraries, local schools, health and hospitals, police, and local parks and recreation—the survey shows that public library expenditures are the lowest of the five services and represent only about 0.5 percent of total expenditures for the group. See Table 2.[3]

Why is public library support so poor in comparison with other municipal services? The answers are complex, and to a considerable extent perhaps not entirely known, or at least provable. Libraries are accepted as "good" if not too costly, but the service is beginning to be costly indeed, along with all other public services. Tax money will be allocated to those services that people consider important. The public library's clientele is composed of individuals; there is no organized lobby to speak out for a better level of service. Indifference of taxpayers to the library may be laid in part to their lack of understanding of the programs and services and the fact that they take the library for granted. It may also be due to the fact that in many cases the library's service program is not really relevant, or at least is not perceived by the people as relevant to the information needs of the general public.

The fact is that some public libraries are supported at a higher rate than others, and this is not always in accord with the tax base available. It would be interesting and very significant to examine on a research level the differences in support from town to town, or city to city, and to attempt to isolate the reasons for these differences. In the absence of solid data, one may assume from experience that some of the factors bringing about increased support, transcending comparative ability, are (1) determined efforts by library officers to keep library services and needs continuously before the public and the appropriating boards; (2) the initiative, resourcefulness and persistence of the director and trustees in pressing for funds; (3) the personal attitude of municipal officers toward the library, the board, or the director; and (4) the rating that the library has in the public mind as to its efficiency and economy. The attitude of the public and the officials toward the library will depend to a large measure on whether the library is seen as aggressive, positive, certain of its mission and purpose, and conscientious and able. One may conclude that the library with a lively, vital, relevant service that responds to the manifest needs of the citizens being served will fare well at the budget table.

### Trends in Tax Revenue

All public libraries have ties with the local government but there are a variety of structural and financial differences. Some are administered as departments of the local government. Most are under control of independent library boards. Others are part of the local school system and some are parts of independent library districts.

Whatever the structural arrangement, however, the traditional means of financing library service has been from local government revenues.[4]

Even a cursory analysis of census data reveals that local revenues have not kept pace with local demands. The property tax was the chief source of most governmental revenue until the beginning of the twentieth century. As late as 1902, just over one-half of all governmental tax revenue was raised locally from the property tax, while the federal government raised 37.4 percent and the states 11.4 percent.[5] With the advent of the income tax, this balance changed. By 1976 the income tax yielded 57.2 percent of the total revenue and property tax only 15.9 percent. Sales and similar taxes produced 21.3 percent of the revenue.[6] Also in that year, local government collected only 17.8 percent of the total revenue and the states 24.1 percent, while the federal government raised 58.1 percent of the total revenue.[7]

### Sources of Library Revenue

Typically, the local public library is supported almost entirely from local tax levies or appropriations. In recent years, there has been an increase of support for local libraries from state funds, from an average of 10.8 percent to 12.9 percent between 1972 and 1974, but this varies widely from state to state. Federal funds, flowing through the state library agencies, also reach local libraries to a limited extent, either via flat grants, special-purpose grants, or in-kind services administered by the state library agencies to local libraries.

At the municipal level, public fiscal officers tend to oppose special levies for individual departments, although some states permit a certain percentage or millage for library support; some libraries have won such votes. But the almost universal procedure is for the library to prepare an estimate of operating and capital fund needs for the next fiscal year, justify the estimate in the most detailed way, and negotiate with the appropriate authorities through the local budget process. Throughout this process, the library trustees and library director and staff will do well to keep the authorities informed about library services and programs and also to make citizens fully aware of what the library is doing for them and for the community. One rule applies: elected officials listen to the voice of the voters; they will support a program that people want and of which they can be proud. They want to be able to produce successful municipal services. It is the job of the library director, staff, and trustees to deliver successful programs that people need and want.

It will little avail the prudent library director to look at national averages or norms or funding patterns in other states or cities unless there is something there that can be turned to advantage in the local situation. Fundamentally, the library director, staff, and trustees should know all that there is to know about how money is raised and voted upon in their own municipality. And they will also do well to keep an eye out for promising developments on the state and federal levels and to lend a positive voice wherever and whenever it is appropriate.

## Gift and Trust Funds

There are various schools of thought concerning the wisdom of seeking out private sources and bequests for library operations. Many libraries were established with bequests, and often these are maintained as trust accounts, from which the income is used to supplement the public revenue or to meet special needs. Some administrators take the view that looking for gift and endowment funds will impair the library's effectiveness in securing adequate tax support. There is an inherent danger, without question, in looking at public library services as objects of charity, so to speak. If the public library is a municipal necessity, it may be argued, then the cost should be borne from publicly voted funds. On the other hand, many excellent and special services have been made available through the generosity of private citizens over the years. It may be considered a good rule for the library to be quite candid and practical in this area, suiting local policy to local climate. In brief, put it on the line with the appropriating officials: if we are able to get up a certain proportion of the operating or capital cost from outside sources, may we expect that we will not be penalized at the budget sessions for the balance of the fiscal needs? Clearly, if this course is followed, it will be important to tell what the outside money is to be used for and how long it will last.

A chapter on library financing must emphasize continuous publicity to keep the public, and local officials, aware of library performance. What is the actual return to the citizen? How many dollars a year would it cost the average family to buy the books they borrow from their public library, to say nothing of the professional assistance rendered, the programs and activities offered, and the study and consultative space provided.

Finally, it will be important for the library to report that it is constantly seeking economies (it must back this by finding, practicing, and reporting such economies as those listed below); that the public is always demanding service the library cannot possibly afford; and that even if the library is well supported by public funds, donors have a right to provide substantial gifts and endowments without jeopardizing public support, especially when these gifts funds are to be used for special materials and services beyond the ordinary pattern the library has been following.

Public libraries, like public schools, should be adequately supported by public funds. But libraries are neglecting programs to secure gift and endowment funds for special purposes, just as state universities do, for example. A continuous program could include: soliciting gift book funds and money for special purchases; finding individuals and organizations willing to give money each year to build collections in their special field of interest; persuading a few discerning persons to contribute salary portions to get or keep outstanding staff members, on whom a high level of service depends; and identifying special items of equipment or service that might appeal to certain individuals.

A library owes it to donors not to divert funds from intended purposes, and it has an obligation to call for expert advice on investing funds safely at maximum return, instead of letting them "rust in the bank" at some nominal interest. A library can honor the memory of benefactors by occasional exhibits and by enthusiastic news stories of what a gift has meant to the community. It can report the wise efforts of committees and individuals responsible for careful investment and the generous interest returns from gift funds. The public likes to know about such examples of good citizenship, which encourage other gifts.

Very active Friends of the Library in such cities as New York, Columbus, Ohio, Philadelphia, and Atlanta, among others, are not only raising funds from private sources but, more important, are becoming very effective lobbying groups for the library's financial needs before city councils and state legislatures.

## Budgeting

*Budget Proportions*

In the past, some library directors and experts have called attention to the proportion within the budget estimate for books and other materials, for salaries, and for other expenses. It has been recommended that about 70 percent should be the proportion for personnel costs, about 20 percent for materials, and the balance for other expense. There appears to have been no other basis for these recommendations than the average expenses of a number of public libraries of varying sizes and situations. Clearly, since the library's business is the exchange of information contained in books and other materials, the collections must be maintained and kept up to date. Similarly, an adequate staff must be on hand. But the local situations contain many variables: number of buildings and service outlets, hours of service, level and adequacy of service, adequacy of other library facilities in the area being served, age and condition of buildings, and others.

Furthermore, with increased attention being given to management by objectives and to zero-based budgeting and other refinements, it seems evident that the rational budget estimate will flow from the local need and situation rather than from national, regional, or state averages based on the experience of other libraries. One point might be made about proportions for estimating: the cost for building operations might well be shown as a separate category. This is particularly true in cases where the library is housed in an inefficient old building.

*Budget Preparation*

Almost universally the budget estimate is prepared under the direction and close supervision of the library director. It is without doubt one of the most important tasks that the director has to perform and is a job that should be given close attention. The director will have to explain and defend the estimate: first before the library board and then before the town or city manager or the appropriating authority. In addition, the director should seek out opportunities to explain the budget estimate to the Friends of the Library, advocates from the media, and any other citizen and user groups that have an interest in the library's welfare. The time to do all of this is during the estimate preparation, prior to submission and final action. After the budget has been adopted for the fiscal year, the die is cast and there is usually very little opportunity for supplemental allocation, except in the case of dire and provable emergency.

In putting together the estimate for operating costs, the library director will work closely with the entire staff. Preparation of the budget estimate is an excellent arena for participative management, since the decision will have an important effect on the fortunes of each staff member and on the well-being of the library in the year to come. Department heads and other line staff should be encouraged to solicit the views of all staff on the needs and concerns they have. The budget estimate process should be explained to the staff carefully and systematically, and there should be attention given to the library's stated objectives. The nub question is: What funds will be needed in order to perform the services to the public that they have a right to expect from their public library? In this process, it is important for the director and the staff to divest themselves of the notion that the budget estimate is a kind of letter to Santa Claus, a request for "what I want because I want it." The estimate is a business proposition.

*Timetable for Budget Estimate Preparation*

Preparation of the estimate for the succeeding year should begin with the hearings on the budget request for the current year. The director, or someone on the staff, should take careful notes during the hearing process, listing questions that were asked and objections voiced. What were the soft spots? What seemed to strike a responsive chord? What were reasons for failure, for success? During the spending year, careful records of expenditures should be maintained, on a line-by-line basis. Certain line items, such as utilities, fuel, service contracts, and so forth, will be more or less fixed and predictable. In some municipalities, the fiscal unit will have guidelines established for estimates in these areas, including inflationary factors where applicable. The same will doubtless be true of salaries, in many cases. The prudent director and staff will try to space out their requests for additional funding in particular areas or for special projects. It is usually unrealistic to go in with a request for a 50 percent increase in total funding, when experience in the local situation will show that such an increase is an unreasonable expectation.

In another view of the timetable, in reverse order, the usual steps:

1. At least a month before the legal or customary date for presenting the budget to town, city, or county officials for consideration, the trustees should have a finished draft to study and discuss, to permit alterations or complete redrafting.

2. Several weeks previous to that the trustees' finance committee or chosen member will go over all budget details with the librarian, to help shape things up.

3. Before that, the librarian and board need to discuss the next budget in a preliminary way as to policies and major additions, and to make a rough estimate of the total. Salaries are the chief item: "The board considers our salary schedule in advance; once this is decided, the rest goes through more easily." This is where a careful one-year or five-year plan shows its value, especially as to needed personnel; this avoids drastic requests and is a simplified form of program budgeting (to be discussed on page 125).

4. Having set a date for this preliminary shape-up, set a date at least a month previous to item 3 for all pertinent data to be assembled, studied and put into rough shape.

5. Notify heads and colleagues far enough before that so they can study and prepare their departmental estimates of needs. Give careful instructions for itemizing their portion of the budget, warnings about economy, and details about what facts are needed.

6. First, determine whether the budget forms and sequence of items used the previous year are to be followed, or whether essential changes will be made in presentation. It is good policy, whether required or not, to use regular local government budget forms and procedures. The library can then say that its budget is as systematic and revealing as that of other departments, that its cards are on the table.

In larger libraries the financial officer, or some staff member of judgment and discretion, will sit in during the preparatory states, to raise questions, assemble the revised items, see that they are in proper sequence, and draw up the budget sheets to hand to the trustees. It is a good practice, in respect to the trustees, to present first a summary of proposed increases and adjustments. This summary, or budget proposal, can be discussed by the board prior to preparation of the final estimate. In fact, the final estimate should then be based on staff recommendations that have been approved by the board. It is absolutely imperative that staff, once consulted, are kept informed about outcomes. If a staff member makes a proposal for an item to be included, and it is the judgment of the director, or the trustees, or both, that the request cannot be included, the staff member must receive an adequate explanation. In smaller libraries, a board member, usually the treasurer but sometimes the president or chairman of the finance committee, generally consults with the library director to go over all the requests and to put the estimate into shape for the entire board.

The fiscal role of the library board will vary from place to place. In some cases the board will have a fair amount of autonomy; in others the role is chiefly advisory, with more and more control being exercised by municipal finance officers.

### Public Budgeting Methods

When faced with the need to allocate scarce fiscal resources in order to carry out specific library tasks or programs, the library must prepare a budget that indicates the source and amount of funds available and how they will be expended. A variety of formats can be employed when preparing the budget, each of which emphasizes a different aspect of the management process. For example, the line-item budget will serve primarily as a monitoring instrument for fiscal control, the performance budget will focus on the efficiency considerations of resource distribution, and the program and zero-base budgets will emphasize the effectiveness of resource allocation in relation to the organization's objectives.

The line-item or object-account budget lists estimated costs by type and quantity for a period, usually the fiscal year. Personnel expenses are usually listed by job titles or classifications, which are subdivided under various functions: public services, technical services, administration, and building maintenance would be examples. Nonpersonal estimated expenditures are listed also by object, under functions or broad objects: books, supplies, utilities, and so forth, in greater or lesser detail as required by the local fiscal authority. The purpose of the line-item budget is control of expenditures to ensure that allocations are used for the purposes intended and to allow the authorities to keep an eye on fiscal resources. The line-item budget tends to encourage management to balance the budget—that is, to use all funds allocated whether actually needed or not, because of the anticipated negative impact leftover funds would have on succeeding requests. The line-item budget is basically an incremental budget, in that managers usually project estimated needs in terms of an increment or increase of a certain amount or percentage over preceding estimates. The approach does not enhance long-range planning and does not relate to measurable results in many cases. Duplication of effort within the library program can be difficult to find. The line-item budget approach is still used in many jurisdictions but is increasingly being replaced by other methods.

The line-item approach does not lend itself to a rational management system. Therefore, certain steps in order must be taken, as noted in earlier sections of this book, or management methods, for example. The library's goals are to be established. There are to be measurable objectives for each goal. There are to be performance criteria: what is satisfactory accomplishment of each objective? There will be measures of performance and then a plan by which the objectives are to be met. This plan of action should include a statement of the methods by which measures will be made.

Finally, the plan is put into effect; the measurements are made and analyzed; efficiency is determined and reported; and changes and improvements are suggested as required. Upon review, it is seen that cost of operation will be a criterion for every objective. The line-item budget clearly does not lay out cost information in a way that can be related to either the activities or the objectives of the library; performance and program budgeting have been developed to meet these requirements respectively.

*Performance Budgeting*

Some of the limitations of line-item budgeting were addressed in the 1950s through the development of the performance budget. This type of budget focuses on the activities of an organization, measuring costs at various levels of each activity. The budget document will show the funds allocated for a particular activity in a specific department, provide a description and quantitative measure of each task, and project an average cost for carrying out the task.

The data compiled by this type of budget yield rough estimates of the relative costs of activities and can be used to indicate operational efficiency over a period of years. These costs, however, are average costs of operation, which do not reflect the incremental costs that may be incurred if a department alters its level of activity. Also, while performance budgets serve to link expenditures and results and, thus, provide valuable implementation and evaluation information, they are of limited value as control or planning tools. They do not list line-item expenses, nor do they look beyond activities to the goals they are supposed to achieve. Nevertheless, for purposes of productivity, performance budgets offer helpful assistance to public organizations.

*Program Budgeting*

Program budgeting was introduced into the federal defense department in 1961. Having determined its success in that department President Johnson ordered its adoption by all federal departments in 1965. It is known as the Planning-Programming-Budgeting System (PPBS). It did not ultimately succeed in the federal government because it was held out as a solution for more than it could deliver, and its use was abandoned in 1971. Some applications and various versions and modifications will be found in some public organizations, and it would be prudent to have a brief overview of the system's essential characteristics or elements.

1. *Program* comprises interdependent, related services that operating together are expected to respond to a major public need or goal. The program, as used for budgeting, should have a limited scope, have little overlap with other programs, be oriented toward output, and have results that can be measured. Examples: public services to children, to young adults, and to adults; technical services; circulation control; building maintenance; administration; and publicity and public or community relations. These are examples only; local applications will vary.

2. *Goals* are broad general statements describing outcomes or conditions that when achieved satisfy major public needs. There are many statements of goals in the literature and in library policies, although many of them are really statements of objectives, or desired activities. In the PPBS context, a goal example for children's services might be to instill in the children of the target area a love and appreciation for good reading, or to carry out activities that will increase the ability of children to use library information resources for daily living as adults. However, these examples, while perhaps pertinent, also point up the difficulty of stating goals for what is essentially an intangible municipal service. Results, other than general feelings of satisfaction among the citizenry, especially the parents, are practically impossible to measure. In the area of services to adults, the extent to which the library is meeting information needs is measurable. More has been noted about these concepts in Chapter 2.

3. *Need.* A statement of the problem that the program is intended to alleviate.

4. *Objectives* are specific statements that describe what is intended to be done, with what resources, and when. Objectives should be realistic and attainable and should move toward the satisfaction of a goal or goals. Again, it should be emphasized that there is a clear distinction, in PPBS terms, between goals and objectives.

5. *Program element* is a subdivision of a program, with its own list of specific objectives.

6. *General program description* explains the activities of the program or program element, providing the budget review authority with a clear understanding, in lay terms, so that they will know what activities and what changes, if any, are planned.

7. *Measures of performance* are to describe the extent to which objectives have been met. They are divided into measures of effectiveness, of efficiency, and of work performed.

As has been noted, most public organizations still use line-item and incremental budgeting, although there are various levels of attempt to incorporate some degree of program and/or performance budgeting. Upon reflection it can be concluded that it is not very effective to have a mixed system. PPBS is complex, technical, and sophisticated. It will require three to five years of hard work, analysis, instruction, and attitude changing to become effective.

## Zero-Base Budgeting

This fairly recent method requires that every estimated cost be justified every year as if it were a new program. Agencies are required to explain and justify not only increased estimates but the continuation of current programs. Zero-based budgeting does not necessarily follow from PPBS, but the latter does provide the data that would be used for the analysis required.

Originated in private industry in the late 1960s, zero-based budgeting has since been adopted by several states which followed the lead of the State of Georgia during the term of Governor Carter who then introduced it into the federal government when he became president. Though the utility of this method has not yet been fully assessed, the growing number of applications warrants a cursory description of this budgeting process. Essentially, the main characteristics of zero-based budgeting as outlined by advocates are: (1) Scrutiny of old or existing activities as closely as new or proposed ones. (2) Identification of decision units within the agency. The decision unit is the lowest unit in the organization for which a budget can be developed. It can be an organizational unit, or it can be a program, line item, cost center, or appropriation item. Lines of service are discrete, from minimum upward. (3) Formulation of decision packages, from an estimating standpoint. A decision package contains: Objective, with statement about how to be achieved; resources required; cost-benefit analysis; measures of achievement; alternatives as to levels of expenditures and methods of providing services; organizational data; unit priority. (4) Ranking of decision packages by priority and reallocation of resources from low to high priority. (5) Allowance for budget reduction or expansion in a planned, rational manner.

The implementation process for zero-base budgeting is clearly not to be undertaken without a fair amount of training and instruction. It is doubtful, for example, whether an individual library, as a municipal department, could put it into effect independently of the public organization; or for that matter whether there would be any advantage. If the library is autonomous in fiscal matters, it could be considered and applied, but again only with expert advice and assistance.

## Five-Year Budgeting

Whether required by the appropriating authority or not, the library might look into the advantages of a five-year budgeting program. This will provide both public administrators and policymakers with a very effective tool for matching program needs with revenue sources in time to allow searching for the new revenues, if needed. Too often, it seems, the budgeting process—estimating, justifying, explaining, and defending—is viewed by the operating department as a tug of war approaching the traumatic, with each side seeking to outwit the other. There are doubtless jurisdictions in which this is somewhat the case. But regardless of the climate in which the particular library finds itself, it is probably true that in the long run a rational approach should yield better results than an irrational one.

The primary objective of a five-year operating budget is to put library goals and objectives into cost estimates for the services to be provided. This process will require that the library think ahead, rather than on a year-to-year basis.

### Summary Budget Process

1. Preparation, justification, explanation, and defense of the library's expenditure estimates offer a signal opportunity for participative management in a critical area of library operations.

2. Whether required in the local setting or not, a rational approach along program-performance lines is to be preferred over the traditional line-item approach, which provides for short-range fiscal control with built-in rigidity.

3. Responsible and professional library cost estimating requires describing programs, stating goals, defining objectives, and installing measures of performance. Some additional detail on these matters has been set forth in Chapter 2. While a great deal has been written, especially in recent years, about budgeting for public bodies, there is no one system that the enterprising library director can take off the shelf and apply without extensive study and perhaps modification and alteration to meet local conditions.

4. There is a clear division of duty in regard to the budget. The library director and staff are to prepare the estimates after due research, effort, and reference to public expressions of need and interest. The trustees are to review the staff work and question it as thoroughly as needed.

The eminent author, editorialist, and friend of libraries Gerald W. Johnson wrote:

Wherever you see a librarian himself forced to make a passionate plea for funds, you may set it down that in that community . . . there exists an imbalance of function. The library may be working reasonably well, but the public is not discharging its reasonable duty. Of course, suspicion always arises that both are weak; for where the library is a vital force, the public is usually pretty much alive to its worth.[8]

## Legislation and Finances

During the fifties and sixties the public library was considerably changed by the impact of federal aid, through the Federal Library Services Act of June, 1956, and its five-year renewal from July, 1961. In 1961, federal funds of $7 million were matched by more than $9 million in state funds and about $4 million in local funds, a total of $20 million annually. Library service was extended to new areas, basic reference collections were strengthened, and general services were improved. Many small-town libraries became part of a growing number of regional systems. The design of library buildings improved and the number increased. In all aspects of librarianship research was undertaken, new programs and new units of service were started, and new clienteles were identified. Many of these activities resulted from grants from the Council on Library Resources and the U.S. Office of Education.

The seventies, marked by economic problems, produced a leveling off in funding for public libraries. The Library Services and Construction Act and Higher Education Act funds were frozen at the 1974 level, while prices of books, periodicals, government documents, and postal and TWX services kept rising.

In 1975, however, libraries did score a significant breakthrough in the fight for federal funding. ALA lobbying forced the Department of Housing and Urban Development to put both main libraries (in small cities) and neighborhood branches (in larger cities) clearly in contention for funding under the Housing and Community Development Act. Libraries also won major funding from the Comprehensive Employment and Training Act (CETA) to bolster shrinking staffs.

There were signs, too, that state, county, and municipal governments were growing more receptive to Revenue Sharing. Even so, losses in tax revenues forced many cities to cut back. For example, in New York City in 1975 public libraries sustained an initial $6.2 million slash in their operating budget.

Yet the economic recession of the period created one high note: a circulation boom—something that enabled some public libraries to win substantial boosts in funding. This increased reliance on public libraries might explain why many communities have still voted for libraries even through this difficult financial period.

In 1979, senators Jacob Javits of New York and Edward Kennedy of Massachusetts introduced a major new piece of federal legislation proposing increased federal aid for libraries; if passed it could have a very favorable effect upon funding for public libraries. The bill calls for the establishment of a national agency to coordinate library cooperation; direct federal aid to the nation's public libraries; new federal assistance to help public libraries better serve the economically and educationally disadvantaged; and federal support for training public library personnel. The intent of the "National Library Act," Senator Javits noted, was to provide "a focal point for debating the key issues for proposed new legislation in connection with the White House Conference on Libraries and Information Services in November, 1979." By the summer of 1980 the study bill had been extensively revised and improved.

The bill was initiated at the behest of the Urban Libraries Council, an organization composed of trustees and library directors of about 100 public libraries serving populations of 100,000 and more; and the National Citizens Emergency Committee to Save Our Public Libraries, headed by an eminent New York City lawyer and author and former United States district attorney, Whitney North Seymour, Jr. He was described as the prime mover behind the drive to get the National Library Act written and introduced.

The act in draft form called for federal aid to go directly to public libraries for operating expenses, bypassing the state library agencies, which under Library Services and Construction Act (LSCA) legislation has the authority to disburse funds under state plans. This has usually meant that the funds have gone for innovative or demonstration projects. Continuation has been left up to local or state governments. The proposed new act would put the federal government directly into the funding of basic, local public library programs. The act also called for funding for public library construction, authorized under the LSCA but not funded in recent years.

### State Aid to Public Libraries

Public library development is an integral part of the states' mandate to provide public educational services, and state subsidy systems for public libraries and local public schools should be more closely related. This is one of the basic conclusions in a 1977 study for the Urban Libraries Council.

The study urges a concerted nationwide effort to increase state fiscal support for the public library in closer conformity with state public education aid systems. Unified support for all sectors of the library community at local, state, and national levels is needed and must be addressed by state legislators, local and national elected officials, political organizations, and public interest groups. Leadership should be generic to each state, and each state should address the problem in terms of its own internal organizational and funding patterns. In this effort, a major and visible emphasis should be on achieving a better balance in the intergovernmental funding of public libraries.

Active support of local government officials and tax groups should be sought. Librarians, local and state library boards, commissions, and advisory boards should deliberately seek to establish closer planning, operating relationships and joint service agreements with public education groups, officials, and institutions. A major objective is to expand the use of public library services as part of lifelong learning.

According to the level of state support, public libraries are an undervalued resource. In 1975 local government provided 82 percent, state government 13 percent, and the federal government 5 percent of public library support. In contrast, the pattern of support for local schools is 44 percent from the states, 48 percent from local government, and 8 percent from the federal government.

On a national basis, the per capita state aid for education is $146, compared with 68 cents for public libraries. Moreover, there is an extremely wide variation in per capita library aid among the states, ranging from 6 cents (Colorado) to $1.65 (New York). Among the states in 1975, state library support ranged from 2 percent in California to more than 36 percent in Kentucky and Georgia. By comparison, state support for schools was a much more consistent and higher percentage of expenditures. It is possible to measure the capacity and effort that characterize each state's fiscal situation and to rank their public library aid effort in relation to their fiscal ability to assume additional costs. Many states, particularly those in the Northeast, rank relatively high in their current expenditure effort and relatively low in their capacity to assume additional costs.[9]

## Notes

1. Virginia Mathews, *Libraries for Today and Tomorrow* (Garden City, New York: Doubleday, 1976).
2. American Library Association, *The Public Library Mission Statement and Its Imperatives for Service* (Chicago: ALA, 1979), p. 11.
3. Government Studies and Systems, Inc., *Evaluation of the Effectiveness of Federal Funding of Public Libraries,* A Study Prepared for the National Commission on Libraries and Information Science (Philadelphia: Government Studies and Systems, 1976), p. 11.
4. Ibid., p. 15.
5. *Public Libraries in the United States: Trends, Problems, and Recommendations* (New York: Nelson Associates, 1967), p. 21.
6. U.S., Department of Commerce, Bureau of the Census, *Statistical Abstract, 1978,* p. 291.
7. U.S., Department of Commerce, Bureau of the Census, *1977 Census of Governments: Compendium of Government Finances,* 4:25.
8. *Minimum Standards for Public Library Systems* (Chicago: American Library Association, 1967), p. 5.
9. Government Studies and Systems, Inc., *Improving State Aid to Public Libraries,* Report prepared for the Urban Libraries Council (Washington, D.C.: National Commission on Libraries and Information Science, 1977), pp. 56–60.

# PART II

## ADMINISTRATION
## OF SERVICES
## TO THE PUBLIC

Part I dealt with the fundamentals of planning, the administrative point of view and methods, personnel policies and procedures, organization, and budgeting and finance. We come now to services to the public, which are the library's reason for being.

As noted in the chapter on organization and in various other sections of Part I, a particular library's organizational structure will differ from those of others, depending on a number of variables. The chapters that follow describing the public services are not intended to establish a norm or set of recommendations for organization, but to provide a body of information concerning current and probable future trends in the various areas of public service.

These follow the more or less traditional divisions of services by age level, by function, and by type of material. Not every library will have the departments or divisions described. Some will have fewer departments and some will have more. Some will have different combinations than those described. There is a separate chapter on audiovisual materials, but some libraries will incorporate those materials into subject departments. Reference service at the adult level may be combined with other services to adults, particularly in smaller to medium-sized libraries. Services to young adults may be combined with services to adults, or with services to the children, or not considered as a specialty, as in many libraries.

## Attitudes Affecting Public Services

The public library is created and organized to give the fullest service possible to the greatest number of citizens, in the belief that the worth of a book is in its use and that books and people should be brought together. In introducing this series of chapters on the management of the library's public service departments, four general viewpoints are pertinent for the entire staff to share: a sense of purpose, a substantial knowledge of books and other sources of information, a desire to serve, and a willingness to please.

*A Sense of Purpose*

Chapters 1 and 2 discussed library objectives and functions and outlined a program for serving the whole community. To some people such topics appear theoretical, difficult, or unimportant. But no public library achieves success unless both the board and the staff have a clear sense of purpose, keyed to the spirit and needs of the times. This sense of purpose is at its strongest when knitted into the fabric of the organization through staff experience and discussion based on observation of other libraries, on reading, and on close attention to each user's success in finding maximum service.

The library's overall purpose will be meaningful only if the employee can see how the job relates to that purpose. The difference between the man who was cutting stone and the one who was helping to build a great cathedral can be paralleled in libraries.

*A Knowledge of Books*

Staff assigned to help people use the library's collections will need to know books, how to find them and how to find out *about* them. Knowledge of books means an ever-growing acquaintance with titles and their authors, bibliographical history, library call numbers and physical locations, but especially the contents of materials and their value, use, and degree of popularity with users. This requires reading many books—in part or in whole—and reading about books. Those who lack a real interest in books, the habit of reading, and the vision and conviction that books can be important aids to citizens, may well ask themselves whether they are in the right occupation.

Some perception of the intellectual content of books marks the professional from the technician, the more effective from the less effective, and the subject literature specialist from the generalist, because it enables the librarian to compare materials on the same subject. Every librarian needs to have this knowledge. Such knowledge has its roots in a librarian's formal education, but it must be updated by continual reading, by in-service training, by book discussion, and by the authorization to read important books and journals on library time. Knowledge of books helps the library staff do a good job in selecting new titles for purchase, in cataloging and classification, in compiling book lists, in handling group activity programs, and in serving individual readers.

*A Desire to Serve*

Seventy-five years ago, individual librarians labored in a wilderness of new problems and public indifference, but with determination they prevailed. If public libraries were supported by users' fees and there were direct competition for those fees, each public service staff member would have to act as though salary depended on the quality of service rendered and thus on the number of repeat customers developed. Users should feel that the assistant is interested, concerned, and anxious to see that they get what they want. These impressions and attitudes, and the quality of service received, make up the users' image of the library.

The library director can promote the desire to serve by the development of a formal policy statement on public service, by appropriate in-service training, by appointing and promoting persons imbued with the spirit of service, by systematic observation, by being assured that supervision is good in each department and branch, by soliciting the comments and reactions of staff members and patrons, and, most of all, by a positive attitude toward the public.

*A Willingness to Please*

Willingness to please encompasses a whole list of specifics, from courtesy to attractive furniture and surroundings. Simple courtesy includes good telephone manners, a pleasant greeting, remembering a patron's name and reading tastes, and the willingness to stop a routine job or conversation with a colleague to serve a patron. An assistant should check to be sure that a patron is served when referred from one desk or department to another and should never seem bored when explaining how to use the card catalogue or other tool. All these are factors of great moment to readers. Courtesy is invaluable and costs nothing.

Good grooming and a neat appearance are highly compatible with good education, cultural enthusiasm, and knowledge of books and are desirable at the library's service points. Best of all is the friendly, outgoing personality— a prime consideration in recruitment and appointment of public service staff. What happens when a staff member meets and serves a patron is the acid test of a library's service program and of its whole administration.

# 8   Adult Services

When they were first established, lending books was the only public service function of public libraries. Reference work came later, and subject departments followed, as libraries grew larger and more complex. The primary lending function accounts for the fact that libraries retained the circulation department as part of the organization. Some libraries now refer to it as the adult services department. This, despite the obvious fact that the reference and information function, and other service departments as well, provide services to adults. The Detroit Public Library at one time called the lending collection of books the home reading department, but this term appears not to have been continued nor to have been picked up by other libraries. Despite the obvious misnomer, *adult services* in this chapter will refer to the administration, provisions, and use of the circulating collection of books for adults, in both main library and branches. The discussion will be limited to the librarian functions in the context of the adult services department, which are defined as selecting the materials, assisting users of the collection for educational, informational, or recreational purposes, and otherwise carrying out the goals and objectives of the library.

The reference function is closely associated with the adult services function as here defined and may in fact in many libraries be actually combined with it. Adult services also includes audiovisual learning devices, readers' advisory services, independent learning programs, and group activities for adults.

Routines associated with the lending and return of books and other materials, registration of borrowers, and care and maintenance of shelves and storage facilities are in a sense services to the public, or rather for the public, but they will be treated here as part of the support services. Circulation routines and procedures, including the registration of borrowers, are essentially management and technical matters, associated with inventory or stock control. They do not require librarianship skills and knowledge, which are properly extended on the intellectual content of the library. As circulation and borrower routines become mechanized, and merged with the materials-processing activity at the initial input level, these routines will become one integrated activity, proceeding from and employing the same bibliographic data base and probably using much of the same automated equipment. This will be discussed at greater length in Chapter 18, on technical services.

For this chapter on adult service, it is repeated that the functions and activities described are those to be performed by librarians and such supporting clerical and technical staff as may be required to enable them to carry out the assigned role, objectives, and action plan. As noted before, this is not to suggest an adult services department for every library, or for any library, but to discuss the general adult services *function* as it seems to be viewed on an overall basis in libraries. More specialized aspects of the services to adults are described in succeeding chapters: reference and information, subject departments, and others.

The library planning team and the administrative group may take the information contained here and apply it to their own library organization in any suitable way, as dictated by their particular needs and conditions.

### Adult Services Defined

Material in these paragraphs is drawn substantially from two articles by Margaret E. Monroe, whose thinking and writing about adult services has had a profound influence on the development of adult services. Specific sources are cited in footnotes.

Adult services in its entirety builds programs of service to users around four major functions: (1) information and bibliographic services, (2) guidance and advisory services, (3) orientation and instruction in library resources and their use, and (4) stimulation of the library's public (user and nonuser) to intensified use of the library's resources and services.[1]

Dr. Monroe observes that there is a

lack of agreement within the library profession as to the goals of adult services, except at the vaguest and most general level of formulation. . . . Measurable objectives have not been possible to conceive since adult services have been activated by the user rather than the library, which maintains a "readiness-to-serve attitude.". . . Because adult services have traditionally been viewed as activities performed when users demand them, they have lacked a sense of intensive purpose or precise objective.

If the services of the library are to be measured in terms of impact on society, then they must be designed with the social problem or the social need clearly in mind. Problem-oriented service design has been emerging in adult services from the time of *Minimum Standards for Public Library Systems,* 1966, in which a new principle for service was enunciated: "The library system serves individuals and groups with special needs." Martin elaborated this concept as a central thesis in his study of the Chicago Public Library as he envisioned the large public library system as "a congeries of special libraries adapted to the distinct groups and interests that character-ize the diverse urban population." The needs and problems of these special groups were to have important influence on the direction of library service. . . .

Principles that provide a basis for analyzing the purposes for which an adult service is appropriate have not been clearly formulated nor agreed upon. New York Public Library's circulation department initiated a service policy manual in the early 1960s, but found the task formidable and difficult of consensus; such a manual of understandings is almost essential to . . . a broad program of adult services. Again, national standards might be assumed an appropriate place for statement of these principles, and the revision of standards now in progress may provide greater clarity of principles of service forms and their interaction in an adult service program.[2]

Ralph Beals (1943) defined the public library's role in adult education/adult serv-ices as the "infusion of authentic information into the thinking and decision-making of the community."[3] This is, indeed, the objective of the new "neighborhood informa-tion centers." Proper evaluation of these community services, often housed in "commu-nity action centers," requires analysis of the total environment within which the information service operates. Major elements in provision of community information that depart radically from traditional reference service and that incorporate an adult services rationale include:

1. Close cooperation with community agencies, both in terms of receiving clients and referring them, and in terms of regular flow of information on which the library and the agencies base their services.

2. Active program of stimulating the use of the service in the neighborhood, with the library seeking out residents in need of information and bringing them to a level of readiness to use the information in an effective style, and adapting the form of information to user needs.

3. Organization of a neighborhood advisory committee, which shares in policy development and guidance of growth of the program.

4. Recruiting, training, and supervising volunteers and part-time and full-time paraprofessionals from the community who serve as frontline service personnel in provision of information.[4]

## Scope of Adult Services

In central libraries of cities with 50,000 to 100,000 population, the reference department is often broadened in scope and purpose to include advisory services and the other professional aspects of adult services. A separate adult services department is a possibility that would be too small and too much a duplicate of the reference department (in its concern with the whole adult nonfiction collection) to be economical or efficient. On the other hand, a department that combines reference work and advisory services will inevitably emphasize one function at the expense of the other; subject specialization by the professional staff would help, or the designation of an adult services librarian.

In a library serving over 100,000 people, the situation is often complicated by the presence of additional adult services that have been added one at a time as separate departments. In libraries of this size there is a strong trend toward the organization of subject departments that combine circulating and reference books or advisory services and reference service. These functions can be combined in special subject fields because the staff does not have to attempt to cover the whole range of knowledge. There may also be a popular library, with both fiction and nonfiction, designed for the general browser. Less desirable is the combination of this agency with the general information department, under the name of a general service department or adult service department, because of the double liability of a wide subject scope (and a much larger book collection than in the case of a library serving from 50,000 to 100,000) and of multiple functions. In larger libraries with well-developed subject departments, one person is often appointed to supervise the popular library and another to coordinate and develop advisory services throughout the system. Staff should be chosen for educational background, wide acquaintance with books, specialized training, and interest in people. The head and first assistant should also have administrative ability. They must be able to train the professional and clerical staff to develop adult awareness of the library as an educational resource. The head should work part-time in direct service to patrons. Even in the largest libraries this firsthand experience is vital to understanding what goes on, and to planning and decision making. All department personnel—professional and nonprofessional—should be able to meet people easily, to make them feel comfortable and at ease, and to handle their requests courteously and expeditiously.

*Facilities*

Facilities for the book collection require ample shelf space for all materials on hand and expected in the near future. Many libraries place newer materials near the entrance, or a collection of popular books on a range of open-faced bookcases. A-frames, display troughs and racks, tables and chairs, slanting shelves, and other devices are useful for special groups of books, for periodicals, and for spotlighting and encouraging the inspection of new materials. It is well to provide a variety of study chairs at tables and some informal seating, to meet the conditions in which different people find it comfortable to read.

The professional staff should be seated at conspicuous desks in the public areas, preferably with a nearby, quiet, enclosed space in which special advisory services can be conducted. If at all possible, the desks for the adult services librarians should be in the open and near the books, so that patrons may see them and be encouraged to consult them. If the adult services and reference functions are close together or combined in one department, there might be two separate desks—appropriately labeled—to allow patrons readily to apply for two different types of service.

## Needs Assessment for Adult Services

Much is made in library planning discussions of the needs assessment process; the implication is that in order to know what library users will want to know about, it will be necessary to go out and ask them. This seems somewhat puzzling, on the face of it. One may speculate that the average adult, if asked, "What are your information needs?," would either look bewildered or would respond, "Well, it depends; they will vary from time to time; I have many needs." Can services really be improved by asking *them* what they are going to ask *us?*

The fact is that librarians who live in the real world, who read the daily press and weekly newsmagazines and listen to and watch the electronic media, and who listen to people as they express their concerns, will know without research what are and will be people's general and specific needs for information. As these words are being written, the topics uppermost in people's minds are national leadership, energy, inflation, the environment, and the threat or promise of nuclear power, crime, war or peace . . . to name but a few of the weightier problems. At a more mundane level, people need information for coping: consumer questions, reducing energy consumption in the home, medical and health concerns, housing, jobs and careers, and many more of similarly practical import. These needs are visible; they are present; they are pressing. It is not necessary to conduct a survey to find out about them, or to wait until people come into the library to ask about them.

A second reliable source for assessing the information needs of adult users of the library is the publishing output. Publishers have presumably a tangible sense of what is needed and wanted by the population; they are in it for tangible reasons. Therefore, the library's role—a role with which one may assume most if not all adult users would agree—is to acquire as much as possible, as quickly as possible, of the publishing output, especially those titles that would illuminate current concerns. The library collection must reflect not only the current view, but also the prospective.

The Reverend Mr. Wight in Massachusetts a century and a half ago, in words cited in Chapter 1, spoke of the public library as an agency for the "diffusion of knowledge." Ralph Beals a couple of decades ago spoke of the "infusion of authentic knowledge." The two phrases are not so very different. They certainly do imply a positive, aggressive stance in which the library does something, goes forward, decides what probably will be needed in the way of materials in response to people's needs, and sees to it that these materials are gotten and put to active use. This is not the passive, insipid library role implied in some public library statements of purpose, which undertake simply to "satisfy demand."

Monroe offers us a persuasive example where a library reacted appropriately to a community crisis:

The Detroit Public Library responded to the Detroit race riots of 1943 with an impressive exhibit of "The Races of Mankind" which thousands of Detroiters viewed in solemnity during the month following the riots. The community task force approach to library service to a learning society is a concept which incorporates the responsibility of the public library for bringing its resources skillfully to bear on decision making in the community at the right time and in the right way for impact.[5]

## Materials of the Adult Collection

Selecting the book titles and other materials that make up the adult services department or function of the library is a prime opportunity and challenge of the librarians assigned to the service. The opportunity is to create a collection that will anticipate the needs of the community; the challenge is to balance selections against funds available for purchase. Basically the selection decisions made by staff must flow from the library plan, the goals, objectives, priorities that have been agreed upon and adopted for the particular library. The plan should inevitably be followed by a written book selection policy, in sufficient detail to guide librarians who are responsible for selection. It is not enough to say that the library will buy all books that are well reviewed, or those that are in greatest demand.

Materials selection is a creative process; new materials selected will relate not only to user needs but to the materials already held as well. The collection of a public library is not an archive but a collection for use, and the retention or replacement of older materials still of value is as important as selecting from the current crop of publishing output. All adult services librarians ought to have a role in materials selection; it may be more efficient in some ways to have selection done by a committee or by one or two department heads, but the public service librarians have a daily contact with user needs. Further, they should have an opportunity to share in the creative process of building the library, which in a sense *is* its collections. This process will require both instruction and guidance by an experienced staff member of good judgment in books and other materials. The adult services staff stand in relation to the adult community as the book and materials people, advisers, and counselors stand in relation to the materials the individual might want for a particular purpose. To provide both continuity and cohesive purpose, therefore, the selection process must be guided by intelligent supervision and a written policy statement.

In the Atlanta, Milwaukee, and New Haven public libraries, adult services librarians are assigned subject selection categories, such as biography, history and travel, social sciences, and business and economics. In some of the larger subjects, two or more librarians may work as a team, with the less experienced ones working under the guidance of the senior member. In Atlanta the plan worked best in conjunction with a full-time collection management officer. When the plan was instituted in Milwaukee in the 1950s, the subject selectors then moved into the cataloging process and cataloged the books they had selected. The New Haven library has had the subject selector method in effect for twenty years. From time to time, the library director will ask the staff whether it should be retained, and the uniform staff reaction has always been favorable to keeping it in effect. The staff agreed that they felt comfortable about having a part in the creation of the library and that it was a major benefit of the job.

The selector, in order to create a good collection of materials in relation to library objectives, will need to do more than read reviews of the currently popular titles, unless it is the library's avowed mission to maintain a collection of only those materials. The sometimes critical city librarian of a large Midwestern public library used to complain that he thought the book selectors followed an "oyster" theory of book selection: they sat still and gathered in whatever grains of sand happened to float by in order to create the pearl of the library. He thought that this might be all right for making pearls in the ocean, but the selector who was going to have materials on hand that would be relevant to daily needs of people would have to exercise some alertness and ingenuity in digging out the needed materials, rather than waiting until they "floated by" in the reviewing media.

A further thought about materials selections is that the increase in the availability of paperbacks, and the tremendous rise in the use of television and radio for leisure-time entertainment, may well relieve the local library of the need to buy heavily, or even at all, in interest areas that are well covered commercially. The library's selection policy might well be to concentrate on obtaining, and retaining, the materials that are not easily available to the general public or that are not apt to be retained in the home library.

*Objectives of Book Selection*

The public library enables people to have access to a larger collection of materials than they would have if they were limited to their own books. A general public library serving a heterogeneous population has a wide range of possible choices and a minimum of reliable guidance for those choices.

Book selection should proceed not by chance or the personal interest of individual staff members but by written objectives and policies. These should be based on the best thinking of staff and trustees and on such policy decisions as total size; distribution between adult and juvenile books, fiction, and nonfiction; relative emphasis on promptness of acquiring new books and of discarding old ones; and types of materials to be included and not included.

The library that is interested in the serious needs of adult readers will have relatively more subject periodicals, reference books, and adult nonfiction books and fewer adult novels. Decisions on such basic matters are influenced by the special strengths and ready public accessibility of the collections in other libraries. Interlibrary loan and acquisition programs are being developed through the establishment of national, regional, and statewide networks. These make the collections of various libraries more accessible to the public and eliminate needless duplication of resources. One of the most powerful informational networks is the OCLC, Inc., which at present has eight hundred members and an experimental interlibrary loan element. Another is the Research Libraries Information Network. A significant step toward a working national network is the recent transmission of MARC records from the Library of Congress data base to that of the Research Libraries Information Network, thereby providing an on-line cataloging system for members. Meanwhile, plans for a national resource center for periodicals is moving forward as Title II-D of the Higher Education Act.

A statement of objectives for a public library book collection should deal with the types of materials to be included and *not* included. Generally, most public libraries do not purchase rare books, books used as texts in local schools, medical texts, or law books. This should not discourage getting textbooks of high quality, which many adult readers prefer. Large libraries have state statutes and the best standard texts on at least the major aspects of the law. For printed and nonbook materials there should be a statement as to what is acceptable as a gift or what will be purchased—for example, among the categories of magazines, newspapers, pamphlets, flat pictures, photographs, prints, maps, and clippings. Manuscripts should be accepted in the typical library only if they deal with local history.

*Policies of Book Selection*

After decisions are made on objectives and inclusiveness of the collection, book selection policies should be written, reviewed by the staff, and approved by the board. Such policy statements guide the day-by-day decision of those who select materials. Their usefulness will be increased by the extent to which they provide specific guidance for selection in all main subject areas, including such issues as controversial political questions, sex, and ephemeral recreational fiction.

The public library seeks to have books on all sides of a controversial issue. There are citizens who oppose this. They believe the public library should not circulate books critical of the economic and political system of this country. They fear such books will weaken readers' support of this country's system of private property and democratic government. Not only is this precisely the stand taken by dictatorships with regard to their public libraries, but it is contrary to the guarantees of freedom in our own Constitution.

Libraries are increasingly subjected to pressure from censors. When censorship has been attempted, however, librarians generally have maintained their dedication to intellectual freedom and have stood firm.[6]

More difficulty is likely to arise with books dealing frankly with sex than with those concerning political issues. A policy statement should be worked out on the subject. Everyone draws the line at some point as to what is objectionable. The public library should draw it at that point of greatest freedom combined with creative value, which is supported by at least a substantial minority of the community. In time this will become the position of the majority. Court decisions have established the rule that a book should be judged in its entirety and not by passages taken out of context, and by its likely effect on an average adult and not on a susceptible young person. Sex frankness in a novel by itself is no recommendation, naturally. To be acquired by a public library, the book should be well written and possess a reasonable degree of artistic integrity. Many librarians devoted to freedom of opinion, especially on social and economic issues, and reluctant to see any form of censorship, are still concerned with the frank treatment of sex in current materials. Nevertheless, if such materials possess artistic integrity and are in demand, librarians must provide them. A new morality in the country, indeed in the world, has brought wide public acceptance of frank treatment of subjects previously ignored.

The book selection policy should set some minimum level of quality for acceptable titles, and a quantity limit as to the proportion of the book budget to be spent on adult fiction.

The policy statement, tested by experience, should be written in terms of the local situation and not merely copied from that of other libraries or from some general pronouncement. It should contain as much detail as necessary; the more general the statement the less helpful it will be in screening titles for purchase. The existence of an established, published policy—well thought out, available to staff and public, and operating satisfactorily—will help to deter attempts at censorship, and provide a systematic procedure for hearing complaints and for reviewing individual titles.

## Budgeting for Adult Materials

There appears to have been very little research on the principles of budgeting for various elements of the adult collections. At the top, inflationary pressures on fixed costs of operation often result in less money left overall in the library budget for materials, that being the one variable item unless staff is reduced or units of service are closed. It is imperative that several steps be taken to ensure the maximum utility of available funds: (1) securing maximum discounts from jobbers; (2) getting new books promptly and getting them on the shelves promptly (it is estimated that the value of many new books declines rapidly after the first year of publication; turnover, usage, and return on investment depend on having books available at peak demand); (3) encouraging gifts; (4) using paperbacks when feasible, especially for titles of topical short-term interest; and (5) engaging in cooperative acquisitions programs with other libraries in the community and the region.

Some libraries lease currently popular books, both fiction and nonfiction, from commercial jobbers. These books come to the library processed and shelf-ready and may be retained for stated periods and returned to the jobber or purchased at a discount. They are rented to borrowers, or lent free along with the library's owned stock. Whether this practice is economically feasible is for the local library to determine.

As libraries move toward, or are required to adopt, program budgeting in some form rather than incremental budgeting, the materials budget will have to be evaluated in terms of goals, objectives, and both short-term and long-term priorities. In short, the library director will be prudent to see where the acquisitions policy is headed, not only for next year but for five or ten years down the stretch. The materials budget should be developed along cost-benefit lines. Quality and purpose in selection can be better assessed if measures are devised to determine the frequency of use of the collections.[7]

## *Level of Budgets for Materials*

Standards enunciated by the American Library Association in the past specified certain stated numbers of books, titles, and proportions of the library budget, as well as dollar amounts, for book and materials budgets. The current stance of the Public Library Association is that "it is no longer appropriate for a committee of public library leaders to propose a single set of standards which would be valid for all public libraries."[8]

After the annual budget for adult services materials is known, the next decision concerns the allotment of available funds by categories, by agencies, and by time, with a monthly statement on the status of the funds.

The allotment by branches and departments needs annual review and adjustment. No formula can be offered for distribution of funds by agency. To distribute book funds according to circulation totals puts a premium on recreational fiction and bestsellers and penalizes informational reading and study. Attempts to combine data on adult nonfiction circulation, reference questions, and other factors, as a guide to book fund allotments, have not produced a satisfactory solution. Allotments are a matter of policy, objectives, and emphasis, to be decided by the librarian and professional staff. A reserve fund should be kept for special needs. Allotments are often made for special types of materials, such as encyclopedias, periodicals, or replacements. Agency expenditures may be limited also to a monthly or quarterly percentage of the year's funds to keep expenditures running evenly, although they may be adjusted for special circumstances.

## *Materials Selection Tools*

Library school graduates and experienced librarians will have had instruction in the tools best employed for book and materials selection, and experienced librarians will have added to that body of knowledge their own views about the applicable media. A few of the best-known and most-used will be mentioned, but the selecting staff will be advised to analyze the available selection and reviewing media periodically, and work with those that best meet their own needs and situation. *Kirkus Reviews* is prompt, working from galley proofs. The notes are candid and usually objective; they were originally designed for bookstores but are used by public libraries as well. The *Library Journal* has brief and usually excellent notes on several thousand titles a year, written by practicing librarians and arranged by large subject categories. These are available in the regular issues and separately on cards, which facilitate distribution to individual selectors. There is also an annual cumulation with an author-title index. The 1978 volume had reviews of 5,800 adult trade books of general interest selected by the Book Review staff. The *ALA Booklist* contains critical reviews of books for the smaller library and reference books. These notes are written by staff in the *Booklist* office. Another ALA publication is *Choice,* which contains reviews of books for college libraries, written by members of college faculties in appropriate subject fields. *Choice* is a useful medium for larger libraries. The daily and weekly press and the monthly literary and newsmagazines are additional sources of guidance and information.

"PW Forecasts" in *Publishers' Weekly,* the book trade magazine for bookstores and libraries, is a useful guide to titles that are expected to be in demand. Listings are from one and a half to two months before publication date; headings are: fiction, mysteries, science fiction, and nonfiction for hardcovers; and nonfiction and fiction originals and reprints. Entries are arranged by date of publication. A sample issue contained notices of eighteen fiction titles, thirty-seven nonfiction titles, and seventeen paperbacks. This is a very useful source for the library that wishes to order probable demand-type books ahead of the demand.

A basic resource for selection, acquisition, and cataloging and classification is the Bowker trade bibliography series, the *Weekly Record:* "a conscientious listing of current American publications" (with some exclusions that are noted), arranged alphabetically by author; the monthly *American Book Publishing Record,* with the same entries as in the *Weekly Record* rearranged by Dewey Decimal Classification; and the *Annual* BPR cumulation. There are author and title indexes in the monthly and annual volumes. These are very useful tools for checking a library's holdings in a particular subject field.

Many other current and retrospective book selection aids are listed in *Building Library Collections,* by Carter and others.[9]

## Weeding and Evaluating the Collection

As book selection is continuous, so should be weeding the collection of outdated and wornout materials. Definite standards and policies should be formulated. In most public libraries it is better to have a small collection of currently useful materials than a large but less useful one. It costs money to house books; many libraries crying for book-space additions would do better to discard outdated books and use interlibrary loans.

In many subjects books are quickly outdated and should be discarded even sooner. Generally, the use of library material drops off rapidly the older it becomes. However, there are certain books that despite their age exhibit a high level of use.

The installation of automated circulation control systems will improve the opportunities for a more rational and scientific approach to evaluative maintenance of the collection. The system can be programmed to produce use counts by subject, title, user reserves, or whatever other use data are desired from the computer. This should eliminate the guesswork in book selection and in evaluation and weeding.

The professional staff should participate in weeding according to subject competence and interests, with the goal of reevaluating all books about once every five years—whether to repair or replace by a new edition of a new copy, dispose of duplicates or get new copies of standards, reclassify, or withdraw. Most weeding programs are based on identification of least-used materials in collections. A study carried out at Newcastle University Library has suggested that volumes that have not been borrowed for twelve years should be removed.

Preliminary weeding, according to definite standards of age, frequency of recent circulation, or listing in the *Standard Catalog for Public Libraries* or other such bibliography, can be done by experienced nonprofessional personnel, especially in branch libraries, for review later by the supervisor. The judgment of experienced staff members who work directly with books is remarkably accurate in estimating circulations and reference value.

The guidelines for weeding should be laid down in the book selection policy, indicating those subject fields to have greater emphasis. Nonbook materials should likewise be reviewed at intervals for possible discard.

## Program Planning in Adult Services

*Services to Age Groups*

1. College students, during four years or more of higher education. Perhaps their required reading is being handled effectively, but for their personal specialized potential needs the librarian can make stimulating suggestions and may have as much influence as a good professor in encouraging students to follow up on their curiosity in new fields.

2. The new adults, including the seventeen- to twenty-one-year-olds, just out of school and college, getting started in new jobs and homes, with related new interests and responsibilities. Many are responsive to citizenship duties,

are keen and critical on current events and local civic, school, and social questions, and are interested in indoor and outdoor hobbies and recreations and in mind-broadening subjects.

3. The great population of more mature years, perhaps from thirty to sixty-five, more settled, less frequently moving, slower to take up new interests.

4. The group over sixty-five, often lacking objectives for happy and useful retirement and feeling useless and unwanted. New planning, new methods, new funds, new studies of this audience might lead to accelerating the reading ability and enjoyment potential of the younger adult and middle-age groups to develop new interests, so that before retirement they might find meaningful and rewarding hobbies or avocations that involve reading.

*Planning to Reach Subject Interest Categories*

The interests of most citizens center on a few major subjects such as:

*Home and Family:* house, garden, furnishing, decoration, family living and financing, babies and child care, school and development of young people.

*Citizenship:* social, political, municipal problems in the community, state, nation, and world. Increased awareness by the average citizen of problems abroad should lead to increased citizenship efforts by the library. Developments closer to home—such as energy shortages, inflation, environmental problems, and transportation—call for up-to-date information to arrive at conclusions. On many current problems books are too long and too late. Current news stories, magazine articles, and public affairs pamphlets encourage adults to study, discuss, understand, and register opinions on today's affairs.

*Cultural:* Librarians can promote new enthusiasm for the humanities. Funds are available through The National Endowment for the Humanities to develop resources in history, travel, literature, philosophy, psychology, and some of the social sciences. Libraries are developing their collections in these fields, adding subject specialists to their staffs, introducing new programs, and sponsoring creative programs.

*Religious:* Recent reawakening of interest in religion and the churches suggests that librarians could be more aware of current religious trends. Clergymen need to know about library materials for sermon preparation and pastoral work. A public library can distribute annual committee-selected lists of books for Protestant, Catholic, and Jewish readers.

*Recreational:* Libraries can provide information on indoor and outdoor recreations—for example, motorboating and water sports. A good approach is through sports clubs and equipment dealers. There are also the indoor leisure hobbies—shop work, handicrafts, and collecting, such as stamps and natural-history specimens.

*Local History:* Few other subject interests have grown so rapidly in popularity in recent years as has local history, and many citizens can be attracted to study and know some aspect of their local background.

*Working Through Organizations*

Libraries have made great progress in group contacts, stimulated by the adult education movement, including film forums, discussion programs, and more recently information and referral services and adult independent learner projects.

How much time and salary can the library afford to spend on contacting, how far shall it go in this group service, and in what ways? The distribution of library publicity through organizations is a major element in increasing book use. Contacts for this important purpose, such as form letters, require comparatively little time or expense but considerable care in wording. The followup on each has to be planned to consume the least possible time.

*Use Surveys*

Use surveys aim to discover the relevant characteristics of the people who use the library, the types of books they use, their satisfaction with those books and with the services of the library, the degree to which their needs for books and library service have been so met, and the existence of needs not recognized or not met. Berelson's *The Library Public*,[10] issued as a volume in the Public Library Inquiry, summarizes all known readership studies from 1930 to 1947 and offers valuable ideas for adult services librarians. Other important surveys include the Bundy study, *Metropolitan Library Users*,[11] and the 1970 Bonser and Wentworth *Study of Adult Information Needs in Indiana*.[12] To help public libraries give better service, many more new and different studies are needed, by trained researchers and properly equipped research organizations working on a national scale. As practical measures at the local level, every library should keep an account of circulation, attendance at library events, and requests for service. These statistics should include counts by percentage of community registered as borrowers. Some of the purposes of this book are to encourage librarians actively to promote and publicize reading and information seeking as a desirable habit for every intelligent citizen, and to show them how to do it. Use surveys may help by refining the measurement of results, but the needs and opportunities are already so obvious as to jar any librarian's complacency. What is needed in the 1980s is resolution and action to improve and increase services to the millions of American adults who are not now using them.

## Adult Independent Study

Adult independent study in public libraries is sometimes defined to encompass many of the activities, described earlier in this chapter, that seek to meet the needs of the independent learner. In addition to the delivery of books and materials, independent study work deals with the intellectual content of these items and offers specific guidance services for the learner. The adult services department seems to be the agency likely to be most concerned with such activities in small libraries.

Seymour describes the role of the public library in independent learning. He emphasizes that many innovative programs offered by institutions of higher learning have been developed without sufficient library services. Such programs for earning credit as proficiency examinations, extended degree programs, and correspondence courses are finding a ready market among working adults and are creating new opportunities for public libraries.

The Commission on Non-Traditional study urges that the public library respond to this new clientele. Seymour agrees by concluding that this clientele must rely primarily on the public library for learning services and materials.[13]

There are four positions that the public library may take as a learning center for independent study. (1) The most conservative sees the library as the provider of materials as requested by those who participate in programs offered on Sunrise Semester, for example, or the individually designed study programs under the College Level Entrance Program (CLEP). (2) A somewhat more liberal library position would be for the library to collaborate actively with institutions offering independent study programs. This would require the library to have staff with information and skills for such work; to become the community's source of information about independent study opportunities; and to have materials for use in independent study programs. (3) Even more liberal is the library as an independent community learning center. This approach would include the conservative roles of provision of materials and might also include the collaborative role, but the library would develop programs on its own; would house a rich collection of learning materials (multimedia packages, films, recordings, and videotapes or cassettes) and would provide guidance in selection of subjects, study programs, and materials. (4) In the most nontraditional role the library would identify the significant community problems and would establish a community task force to work toward solution of those problems in a community task force style. This role goes further than the use of the term independent study as it is now understood, but Monroe tells us that

it falls clearly within the library's adult education role as envisioned by Ralph A. Beals in 1943. Beals, then an adult educator and only later a librarian and director of the New York Public Library, defined the public library's role in adult education as the "infusion of authentic knowledge into the thinking and decision-making process."

Public libraries of modest size as well as large ones with specialized staff can develop a learning-center role for independent study. Determination of the role which the library can afford to play, a decision on the special public that will be served in independent study, a search for the appropriate academic institutions with which to build a collaborative program, and a judicious choice of the specific areas in which the public library might play an independent role—these decisions, made and embodied in a plan for action, are feasible for even the smallest library.[14]

The terms "learning society" and "lifelong learning" were coined by a UNESCO Commission headed by Edgar Faure; the report published in 1972 was harshly critical of the world view that the only education is institutionalized and the only way to transmit knowledge is by the stand-up lecture. This postsecondary educational revolution implies for public libraries an opportunity to devise, execute, and operate new delivery systems for all forms of materials and information. The librarian will need to go far beyond the limits defined by ordinary roles today and become an effective knowledge broker, utilizing the resources of all libraries and interacting with other learning facilities and agencies. Rochell points out:

A proper response for the urban public library will include these components:

1. An information system and referral system on education options.
2. A resource bank of print and nonprint materials.
3. A network of adjunct counseling and guidance personnel.
4. A system of linkages to other components of education delivery including: (a) testing and evaluation, (b) credit evaluation, and (c) assessment.

What about the cost of all this? Is the proper direction of the public library to support formal and informal education? The fact is that the public library is already, knowingly or unknowingly, the major resource both for extended degree learners and for individuals who have used the books in the library, even without a formal, structured program, to advance their education. Society numbers countless individuals, particularly among the leaders, who got their education from the books in the public library. For persons who may need or want a more structured approach to independent learning, the picture becomes clearer. It is estimated that upwards of 3 million people are taking some form of test for credit (GED, CLEP, CPEP, USAFI, and the like) each year. Couple this with the fact that most of them learn about such programs by accident and have to turn somewhere for intelligent assistance. If there are 100 million persons who are involved in learning, *or want to be,* and if the fact is accepted that a system of support from the public library removes the barriers to learning, then the public library has a serious obligation. An estimate of cost for a library serving a city of a half million persons would be for start-up about $800,000. This would involve planning and training of present staff; development of files for information and referral on educational options, and negotiating agreements on collaborative services; development of computer programs; and acquisition of hardware and printed materials not available in most public libraries. The annual operating cost would run to $300,000 to $400,000 for ten additional staff members, computer costs, additional acquisitions of new and replacement materials, and other. According to Rochell:

If this appears to be more than the library feels the service to be worth, let it be quickly understood that the bulk of the cost, particularly for nonprint resources, is for materials and staff that ought to be placed in the public library anyhow, regardless of the mantle used to justify them. The information and referral program builds on services being developed in public libraries and moves one step closer to the library's position as "Community Information Center."[15]

## Services to Target Groups

Library services to disadvantaged adults has become a primary concern of many public libraries during the past twenty years. As noted in an earlier chapter, the Public Library Association in 1965 adopted a policy statement calling for a new and more aggressive approach to serving the functionally illiterate. Numerous studies and reports have been cited concerning proposals and work actually being accomplished in many libraries.

Claire Lipsman in a 1972 study used the case study method to establish a set of criteria against which individual library programs of service to the disadvantaged may be measured and to elaborate a procedure and tools for the use of the criteria. Lipsman structured a case study style, using interviews with library staff, users and nonusers, and community agencies, that nevertheless derived some of the benefits of survey research through its consistent application of questions around a few themes for inquiry. Generalizable findings, therefore, may be said to have emerged from the study of fifteen public library systems serving the disadvantaged.

With skillful use of discriminant analysis of data on users and nonusers, Lipsman broke open some of the stereotypes about library users to show that they differ significantly from nonusers in their upward-mobility orientation, their knowledge of community affairs and resources, and their responsiveness to ideas from many sources in addition to print, and that these elements were more important statistically in distinguishing them from nonusers than the traditional and ever-present data showing income and educational level differences. Such analysis of users and nonusers enables library service objectives to be somewhat more realistically determined. Assessment of service program objectives is one area that Lipsman stresses. She proposes a second approach to evaluation of objectives: the measurement of the gap in perception of library program objectives between library staff, board, agencies, and neighborhood.

The criteria established for measuring effectiveness of program service to the disadvantaged are complex, nonstatistical, and qualitative: (1) community involvement and support of the programs; (2) community assignment of status and significance to the activity; (3) user involvement in some form of activity in relation to the use of the service, or at least as "receivers" of programs that have audiovisual sensory as well as print stimuli present; (4) competent staff for planning strategies for management and leadership, programming, knowledge of materials, and interpersonal relations; and (5) autonomy for the project staff within the library's organization.

Lipsman's study approached the total environment of service to the disadvantaged, observed the full situation, developed criteria for success, and created tools and adapted procedures for their application in assessment of such programs.[16]

Many libraries have organized a variety of programs and services for the economically disadvantaged, and there is a body of detailed literature available on the subject. The service will be discussed in the chapter on branch libraries, since it cuts across all age levels. This is not to say that disadvantaged persons are to be served only at branch libraries, but concentrated and specialized efforts might stem from there.

*Group Services*

The adult activities of libraries that are most often found, are most easily and economically performed, and are most natural additions to their other operations consist of book-related services to groups already organized and functioning, such as service clubs, local chapters of professional and trade associations, PTAs, civic and social welfare groups, and hobby groups. These ready-made possibilities for services can take many forms, such as displaying materials at group meetings appropriate to the group's interests, the preparation of book lists for the special programs of the group and distribution of the programs to the members, the loan of films, slides, and videocassettes to a group, advice to program chairpeople on topics for meetings, setting up a reserve shelf for materials expected to be used in continuing programs, talks on books or on library service to club members and others, and the offer of meeting rooms free of charge.

*Special Programs*

The activities and programs sponsored or cosponsored by public libraries are so varied that no dominant pattern or theme of any permanence has yet emerged. In part this is because public libraries operate on the frontiers of adult learning. Yet, independent study may develop a method of library adult education that will be so eminently successful that it will deserve to become a standard pattern or technique. In the past, the book discussion group was near to such a technique.

Public libraries present discussion groups, book talks, exhibits, individual lectures and series of lectures, poetry and play readings, public film showings and concerts, forums or institutes of some magnitude, and even formal courses, cosponsored by academic institutions or using funds given for that purpose. These now serve as elements in more comprehensive adult independent activities such as the Denver Public Library *Time Alive!* program. The essence of librarianship is the unit combination of the individual user and library materials. Anything that contributes to the number of such combinations, or to the success with which users and materials are matched, is desirable and worthwhile.

## National Endowment for the Humanities

While included as a part of the chapter on adult services, the information that follows will apply to other age-level groups of the library's program. Over the past four years, the National Endowment for the Humanities (NEH) has awarded U.S. public libraries more than $2.3 million in grants ranging from $5,000 to $300,000. The NEH stresses innovation and getting humanists off the campuses and into the libraries. To help local libraries learn how to develop NEH projects, the Southwestern Library Association, with a grant of $120,000 from NEH, put together a learning kit. It was done by librarians working with academic humanists. Examples of funded projects include public television documentaries on Mississippi and Alabama writers; a Prince Georges County, Maryland, discussion effort based on the public television series *The Adams Chronicles;* and a radio publicity campaign to convey information about the nonbook holdings of the Toledo–Lucas County Public Library on the history of northwestern Ohio. The Denver Public Library's well-known *Time Alive!* project, consisting of sixty-five learning units, was funded for several years by NEH. The Oklahoma department of libraries has received one of the largest grants to date for a statewide project that is designed to reach every library in the state, on the theme of the multicultural heritage of Oklahoma.[17]

## Some Views on Services to Adults

The library has three choices. The time-honored goal of "service to all" is not realistic; it is too broad and vague to be capable of any meaning in an increasingly heterogeneous society with a variety of specific and visible needs. This choice, of library as cultural ornament, with a publicly announced goal such as "to open opportunities for self-development for people at whatever their stage of education and culture," will "make the constituency feel warm and secure, and give them an emotional bond with the past and present cultures. This possible future (of the public library) is unlikely. . . . It is doubted that library professionals would ever accept it consciously."

A second choice is

to deny service to the richer, increasingly larger elements of the aggregate, who can afford to satisfy more of their information knowledge requirements through commercial sources. Limit all service to those who cannot afford commercial services. . . . This goal would require considerable promotion among the richer elements of society, since they would be asked to tax themselves for the major share of the library's support.

A third choice would be for the library to provide a very narrow range of special information/knowledge services for everyone, serving the constituency in one or two ways that are least adequately covered elsewhere. Examples: Information for daily living, materials that deal only with historical, philosophical, and literary matters, space and materials for study, a distribution center for documents on demand, a center for "accidental" discovery of new media items (that would not be generally available but that might open up new thoughts and ideas), experimental poetry, films, fiction, and documents.

Unless the library adopts a limited set of goals, instead of trying to satisfy every library-related need, "it will relegate itself to the role of cultural ornament against its will."[18]

The adoption of narrower, "differentiated" goals in contrast to the "demand-oriented service to all" concept has repeatedly been advocated by Lowell A. Martin in articles and library studies. He has proposed that adult services consist of: (1) A *complete information system* that would gather raw data as well as printed and nonprinted materials; that would pay equal attention to very current, even daily, information as well as background and historical intelligence; that would organize and repackage information for distinct user groups; and that would disseminate information rather than wait for the inquirer to seek it out. (2) A *media clinic,* stimulating, guiding, projecting the use of media by individuals and groups. (3) New groups of staff to include information specialists and media advisory specialists; and three administrative groupings: designation of the central library as a state and regional specialized resource center, an information and intelligence center using present facilities and other outlets to be developed, and a media clinic using existing facilities and mass communication channels. (4) Development of multimedia orientation to both collections and services. (5) Deliberate and substantial phasing down of the current-interest supply function; progressive elimination of balanced subject collections in branches (the branch cannot be a miniature replica of the main library); and reduction in duplicate provision of popular current-interest publications throughout the system.

Dr. Martin observes that "this re-direction of adult services will be seen by some as the provision of information beyond its present boundaries in public libraries; by others as simply an intensification of readers' services always provided by responsive librarians." But he concludes:

At least two essential ingredients are not customary in present practice even if they may not be entirely new: adoption of explicitly educational objectives (and by inference the rejection of others) and provision of total information and advisory services (rather than maintaining auxiliary services seeking to find a niche in wider informational and educational structures).[19]

During the early part of the 1970s the standards committee of the Public Library Association, charged with revising and bringing up to date the public library standards that were promulgated in 1966, faced up to the fact that consensus on goals and guidelines would have to be worked out before useful standards could be drafted. There would have to be a generally agreed-upon idea about what library services are. Task forces composed of representative librarians from various parts of the country came to agreement in 1973 on goals and guidelines for the three age-level groupings of public library services. Some highlights of the statement on adult services:

People need a variety of resources in order to flourish culturally, socially, physically, financially, politically, and spiritually. The quality of life is related to the excellence and availability of such resources. Among those resources is information. The word "information" as used here includes not only facts and data, but also ideas and the products of man's creative endeavors.

The public library must ascertain and analyze its community's resources so that it may better fulfill its particular responsibility as an informational resource service agency. Communities will require a system providing coordinated access to the information resources within the community. Coordinated access means that from whatever point an individual enters the community's configuration of resource agencies meeting human needs, that person will be efficiently directed to the appropriate service agency. The public library should develop and maintain a coordinated *access* system or improve an existing system. The public library, as a basic community informational resource center, with its one-to-one service pattern, can and should serve as the core of a reliable information *delivery* system.

*Active and reliable agents* are needed in the community to channel people to the sources. The public library should, as part of the community access-and-delivery system, *gather materials,* both print and nonprint, on all subjects of interest to the community. People also need access to information that has never been published and never will be published, such as the names and addresses of groups in the community or the names and addresses of experts willing to share their skills. This information changes rapidly and is often difficult to find at any particular time. The public library, therefore, should collect these raw data in response to the needs of a particular community and should make sure that these data are accurate and up to date at all times.

An innovative and comprehensive *public relations* program, designed to reach maximum numbers of individuals, groups, and agencies, should be provided. The library will be constantly aware of the need to develop new ways to present its services and resources (e.g., programs, cable TV, etc.).

In order to meet fully the needs of people as expressed in this document, public libraries should recruit, train, and retain *staff members who are people-oriented.* Continued analysis and evaluation of the relationship of library programs to user and nonuser needs should be undertaken. In order to achieve constant revitalization, self-surveys and other measurement devices and advanced research techniques should be employed.[20]

## Notes

1. Margaret E. Monroe, "Evaluation of Public Services for Adults," *Library Trends* 44 (January 1974): 337.

2. Ibid., 338–39.
3. Ralph A. Beals, "The Public Library as an Agency for General Education," in *The Library in General Education: Forty-Second Yearbook of the National Society for the Study of Education, Part II* (Chicago: University of Chicago, 1943), pp. 99–112.
4. Margaret E. Monroe, op. cit., 353–54.
5. Margaret E. Monroe, "A Conceptual Framework for the Public Library: A Community Learning Center for Independent Study," *Library Quarterly* 46 (January 1976): 58.
6. For a historical perspective on intellectual freedom see Ralph McCoy's *Freedom of the Press: An Annotated Bibliography* (Carbondale, Ill.: Southern Illinois University Press, 1968). A continuing selective bibliography is to be found in the *Newsletter on Intellectual Freedom*, issued by the ALA. Librarians should also be familiar with the ALA's *The Library Bill of Rights*. An account of the ALA's involvement with this issue—charting the rise of the Freedom to Read Foundation, the Intellectual Freedom Committee, and the Intellectual Freedom Foundation—can be found in David K. Berninghausen, "The Librarian's Commitment to the Library Bill of Rights," *Library Trends* 19 (July 1970): 19–37. An account of more recent ALA activities related to intellectual freedom is covered in Berninghausen's "Intellectual Freedom in Librarianship: Advances and Retreats," in Michael Harris, ed., *Advances in Librarianship*, vol. 9 (New York: Academic Press, 1979).
7. Stephen Ford, *The Acquisition of Library Materials* (Chicago: American Library Association, 1973).
8. "A Mission Statement for Public Libraries," *American Libraries* 8 (December 1977): 615.
9. Mary Duncan Carter, Wallace John Bonk, and Rose Mary Magrill, *Building Library Collections*, 4th ed. (Metuchen, N.J.: Scarecrow Press, 1974).
10. Bernard Berelson, *The Library's Public* (New York: Columbia University Press, 1949).
11. Mary Lee Bundy, *Metropolitan Public Library Users: A Report of a Survey of Adult Library Use in the Maryland-Baltimore-Washington Metropolitan Area* (College Park, Md.: University of Maryland, School of Library and Information Science, 1968).
12. Charles F. Bonser and Jack R. Wentworth, *A Study of Adult Information Needs in Indiana*, Indiana Library Students no. 3 (Bloomington, In.: Indiana State Library, 1970).
13. Whitney North Seymour, Jr., and Elizabeth N. Layne, *For the People: Fighting for Public Libraries* (New York: Doubleday, 1979), pp. 42–44.
14. Margaret E. Monroe, op. cit., pp. 56–57, 61.
15. Carlton C. Rochell, *Without Walls/Without Barriers, The Public Library and the Learning Society* (A Report Made Possible by a Council on Library Resources Grant, 1975).
16. Claire K. Lipsman, *The Disadvantaged and Library Effectiveness* (Chicago: American Library Association, 1972), pp. 11–30, 31–43, 45–46, 60–64.
17. Carlton C. Rochell, "Libraries and the Humanities, NEH on the Move," *Library Journal* 104 (April 1, 1979): 796–800.
18. Thomas Childers, "Community and Library: Some Possible Futures," *Library Journal* 96 (September 15, 1971): 2728–30.
19. Lowell A. Martin, *Adults and the Pratt Library: A Question of the Quality of Life* (Baltimore, Md.: Enoch Pratt Free Library, 1974), p. 76.
20. Public Library Association, "Community Library Services—Working Papers on Goals and Guidelines," *School Library Journal* 20 (September 1973). A progress report to the Public Library Association from the Task Forces of its Standards Committee.

# 9 Reference Services

This chapter is not a condensed manual of reference work. It considers the administrative aspects of planning and organizing reference service to make it more effective.

## The Reference Function

Reference is the term employed by librarians to describe the library's informational role. It applies to the materials of the collection used for this purpose and to the assistance rendered by public service staff in helping people meet their information needs. It may be that the term "reference" will be supplanted by the actual use of information as the functional description in libraries, particularly if more libraries pick up on the "information and referral" function now being carried out in a few large libraries, and discussed later in this chapter.

## The Current Status of Reference Service

There has been a dramatic, nationwide growth of interest in specialized information, an accelerated demand for facts in an age of facts—in science and industry and in all other fields. The result is the development of a new industry based on the production and distribution of knowledge. About 50 percent of the labor force is involved in the information industry, and the industry is growing at about 10 percent a year.

As early, major conduits for information in this country, libraries are natural partners in this burgeoning information process along with educational institutions, research and development firms, and organizations engaged in publishing, computer services, and data communications.

Competition between these agencies for users and the importance placed on immediate access to information has led to an increase in the variety and quality of information products, systems, and services. The most important recent development for libraries has been on-line references services. Such services, which made impressive progress in the early 1970s, can now be found in thousands of special libraries, academic libraries, public libraries, and technical information centers in the United States and other countries.

There is some difference of opinion among librarians on whether libraries should charge fees for information and referral services. While cost has always been a deterrent to reference automation use in libraries, opposition to fees appears to be growing. Some librarians feel fees would benefit the few who could pay, thus depriving the many. The California Library Association recently voted against charging fees. The vote was based on at least two concerns: (1) they could not square charging taxpayers for information gleaned from data banks built with tax funds, and (2) they felt fees would obstruct the free flow of information.

We are entering a new era, compelled by the public's enlarged demand for information in a more competitive and specialized age, and the library will have to undertake more dynamic programs to publicize and promote adult reference services.

Thomas Galvin has made some cogent comments on the present and possible future of reference services. These are summarized:

Libraries, or information centers, have yet to realize their potential in meeting the informational needs of even a small portion of their several clienteles. There is probably no clear consensus among librarians as to what the optimum level of information service is or ought to be. The problem is characterized by several factors: the exponential growth in the volume of knowledge records; a very significant growth and improvement in the whole apparatus of bibliographical control; and the development of new aids to the storage, analysis, and retrieval of recorded information. The computer has made available to librarians an arsenal of aids hardly even dreamed of a few years ago. A few specialized clienteles are getting the benefits of the new technology, but the general public is not. The quality and quantity of information services rendered by the public library has not improved in relation to the tools available.

In short, the technology—the whole array of tools and resources—has "developed more rapidly than has our capacity or our *will* to make the most effective use of it, except in the form of specialized services to limited client groups. [There is] a failure of vision on the part of librarians." Among the reasons, some are perhaps partly financial, although library administrators may not have planned and budgeted for a more sophisticated level of information service. Another reason is that "many libraries are still materials-centered rather than client-centered organizations." The library is described in terms of its contents rather than its clientele. There is a notable gap between professed goals and the product. Goals set forth the ideal of service for all: "The right of every adult to a library which seeks to understand both his needs and wants and which uses every possible means to satisfy them." That kind of goal in itself forms an obstacle to a higher level of reference service. Since resources are limited, libraries attempt to provide a little service for everyone, rather than to try to offer a higher level of information delivery to any. "The minimum level of service that has been chosen has become the operational norm. This militates against experimentation and innovation."

The problem with the use of the term *reference,* in the process of information transfer, "is partly that it suggests 'referral' of the client to source materials. This implies a process that is essentially static . . . that is considered satisfactorily rendered when some compendium of data has been placed in the hands of the inquirer, or that client has been pointed towards the card catalog."

There should be a distinction between providing bibliographical access to a knowledge record (which is often the chief concern of librarians) and the physical access that is important to the clients.

Beyond this . . . there is often a distinction between recorded data and useful information, and the objective of information service must be to transform the former into the latter . . . unless data has been reformulated into useful information, the information transfer process has been aborted short of completion. . . . Librarians will have to become equally concerned about all three levels of access to recorded knowledge— bibliographical access, physical access, and intellectual access.[1]

## Recent Developments Influencing the Reference Concept

In the last few years, partly prompted by municipal officers intent on performance figures, some libraries have kept elaborate statistics of their operations, and committees have been asked to define categories of reference help to readers. No satisfactory definitions have evolved because there is too much overlapping—that is, many questions do not fall exactly in any one category. A recent study sponsored by the Public Library Association and conducted by the Bureau of Library and Information Science Research at Rutgers University settled on these two categories: source-related and directional. Source-related questions were defined as those requiring use of library materials.

It is questionable whether any set of definitions can encompass all that should be involved in department objectives: planning, materials, services, statistics, and building plans. A reference department is less a separate collection in a separate room than a specially trained staff utilizing the entire library collection. Although the reference function may be administratively a part of the adult services function in small and medium-sized libraries, reference work is a specialized occupation.

To satisfy user needs adequately there must be: (a) a specially selected staff who wish to serve in the information-finding capacity; and (b) an extensive training of these chosen people both as to knowledge of materials and of tools and substantial experience and skill in their use. Having everyone attempt to know and serve all subjects in all capacities, whether for a community of 25,000 or of 250,000, cannot give user satisfaction such as can be given where some of the trained staff are made responsible for concentrating on this specialized intensive service.

In summary, the reference function includes, in addition to information searching, (1) the bibliographic aspect (the use of, and in large libraries, the preparation of indexes and bibliographies, including selected lists); (2) the teaching aspect (instruction given by the librarians to people of all ages in the use of books and libraries, as discussed in Chapter 15); (3) the promotional aspect; and (4) the internal development and improvement aspect.

### Definitions

Any definition of reference work and reference questions is greatly influenced by changes in library objectives during the last few years, as we shall presently note. Reference service may be defined as the librarian's aid in bringing together the inquirer and the printed materials he needs for whatever purpose—the informational, educational, recreational—in other words, the librarian's skilled guidance in choosing or tracking down the best book, books, or nonprint material for a specific piece of information or for a specific purpose. This excludes directional work—such as telling someone where the *Readers' Guide* is—but includes all inquiries in which the librarian actually assists the reader by recommending the best sources for certain types of material, or the best titles, by guiding and aiding in the use of reference books, by finding a specific fact, or by gathering suitable material on a certain topic or for a certain purpose. In brief, reference work is a request that requires the professional aid of the assistant and the use of book knowledge and of knowledge of other sources of information in aiding the reader.

A reference book, as generally understood, is a book to be consulted for some definite information rather than for consecutive reading. The facts are usually brought together from a vast number of sources and arranged for convenient and rapid use. Reference tools serve the inquirer in two ways. They may supply the information directly, as in encyclopedias, dictionaries, directories, almanacs, and similar works, or they may point the way to the place where the information is found, the function of the many ingenious bibliographies and indexes now available.

Reference work is also defined as the direct personal aid within a library to people in search of information for whatever purpose, and also various library activities especially aimed at making information as easily available as possible.

A reference question and the services entailed cannot be limited to materials used only within the building or those considered strictly "Reference" and so marked. Several large libraries maintain files of duplicate unbound issues of periodicals and lend those for reference use outside the building, as well as volumes from duplicate sets of encyclopedias.

## Organization and Development of the Reference Department

The three major aspects of a public service department are materials, staff, and reader services. To what point need these elements grow in order to justify a separate department for reference service? The sequence would be for the reference service to be performed (1) along with other services, at the general user service desk in the small library; (2) at one section of the general service desk, designated by an "Information" sign and with reference tools close by; (3) at a reference desk with someone especially assigned to be responsible for this important service; and (4) in a reference department with its own area and facilities to give the most complete service possible. The number of reference workers would increase appropriately in these stages of development.

### In the Small Library

Without a special department or desk, the small village is obligated to give reference service, occasionally drawing on the nearest regional, state, or other large library for help. The library in the city with less than 15,000 population (about seven employees) can render considerable reference service if its staff is alert enough to encourage it. Post a sign reading "Information" or "Reference Questions" over the most convenient portion of the general service desk. Make the person best qualified by education and reading interest responsible for handling reference questions, calling on others with interests in special subjects. Have the staff get acquainted with a score of the most essential quick reference tools. Subscribe to *Abridged Readers' Guide* at least, and to a score of the periodicals indexed therein. Keep the unbound files for five or six years. The public can be encouraged to ask questions. The staff should know the services and collections at state, regional, and nearby libraries and how to request help promptly through the routines of interlibrary loans. State libraries and central systems libraries are now providing reference training as well as access to central reference collections and WATS and teletype services to assist the small library in its reference work. This trend toward multitype interlibrary cooperation appears to be growing.

### The Special Reference Center

Libraries with populations of 15,000 to 25,000 and upward (with staffs of eight to twelve) should maintain a reference service center. Services develop faster and more soundly at an efficient reference service center, with needed facilities closer at hand, than when nothing special is done. Almost always the reference center has less space than the reference librarian wishes, and priorities of location need study. The following should be included:

1. The reference desk for a trained person, even if scheduled for only half time. In a town of 15,000 or more, one person should give full time to reference work. In a staff of ten, for 20,000 population, the library can justify one full-time and one half-time worker to cover a sixty-hour schedule.

2. Two or three hundred ready reference books shelved near the desk, including the most-used dictionaries, almanacs, encyclopedias, yearbooks, indexes, such as *Readers' Guide* and the cumulated *National Geographic Magazine* index, three or four most-used phone books and city directories, the latest world atlas, and a current U.S. road atlas.

3. A reference workroom. Smaller libraries are fortunate to have even one well-located workroom for circulation, reference, cataloging and preparation activities. New buildings for cities as small as 25,000 should provide a separate reference work space.

4. The public catalog, located most conveniently for staff and users, including borrowers of circulating books. The reference desk and its users should be as near the catalog as possible. Both the reference and the circulation desks should be near the main entrance to the adult reading area.

5. A consulting stand or table close at hand for periodical indexes and encyclopedias used jointly by readers and staff. The larger the library, the more these tools are used. A double-faced stand, with consulting surface and shelves underneath, takes less floor space than a table, which permits no shelving. Most use of printed indexes is for a few moments only, and the encyclopedias can be taken to a reading table. Chairs at the index station obstruct traffic, and tempt students to do their work here, thus interfering with other users.

6. Files of recent unbound magazines. Recent issues of *Time, Newsweek,* and other newsmagazines essential for questions on current events and people in the news should be close by—perhaps a year's file for the twenty most-used titles, with a five-year file shelved not more than forty or fifty feet away. Smaller libraries seldom bind their magazines but keep them in neat piles on bottom or top shelves. Many libraries ask readers to contribute personal copies as extras for circulation and replacement.

7. Pamphlet files. Even the village library needs free and inexpensive pamphlet material, and a four-drawer filing case to hold it. Pamphlets are often more useful and up to date than expensive books and are especially helpful on school reference questions.

## The Larger Reference Area or Room

For cities of more than 30,000 population, a separate area or room should be assigned for reference service, though increasingly the general adult reading space is left in a large undivided whole, with one service center for adult services and another close by for reference. This permits readers to be as close as possible to both adult services and reference materials. The facilities outlined in the preceding paragraphs will all be essential here.

The typical reference room, closed in by walls, or in an area set off by glass or bookcase screens, can be efficient within itself if its entrance is visible from and convenient to the main adult entrance and the card catalogue is close by. It needs a one- or two-station public service desk with an adequate workroom and the most-used materials within eight or ten feet of the desk, supplemented by 2,000 or 3,000 additional reference books and periodicals on double-faced bookcases fairly near the desk. The department staff should study and determine the most convenient locations for individual reference works. One library serving 150,000 population has "R" books shelved in five different locations or zones, according to frequency of use. Such an arrangement calls for a diagram or explanatory statement. In some recent buildings both the reference room and adult services are well placed in the same large general area, separated by bookcases and perhaps with a Plexiglass screen above them to reduce the noise.

For libraries in cities of 200,000 or more, an enclosed reference room may be desirable, but increasingly the equivalent space is set off only by bookcases. The new St. Pancras Public Library in the Land on Borough of Camden (England) divides its Reference Library by bookshelves in ranges at right angles to the walls and down both sides; everything is open and flexible. The whole idea of such a series of large service spaces is in direct contrast with the great reading reference halls at the top of the main New York Public Library building, or Bates Hall at Boston, or those at Michigan, Illinois, and Northwestern universities. These monumental, ornate, discreet rooms which are grand in scale but allowing no flexibility will probably not be planned in any future building. Different needs can be met by setting up bookcases as divider screens, scattering library tables among the stacks, and providing plenty of secluded study carrels and lounge furniture for informal seating. Special arrangements should be made for typing, photocopying, group study, microfilm reading, and the use of audiovisual equipment.

## Departmental Relationships

*Reference–Circulation Relationships*

The natural joint use of the adult nonfiction circulation materials for both reference and adult services makes it essential to place both service desks near the main entrance to the adult reading room, so that both staff and readers can use the collection. This does not mean interfiling reference books with circulating books, though it will often be profitable to shelve reference copies of many books with circulating copies so that readers will find a copy in. The answer depends partly on the distance the reference staff must go to get the book and partly on the value of the book as a reference source. Assuming a sizable collection of the most-used reference tools close to the reference desk, the same reasons call for having at least the most current portion of the adult nonfiction as close as possible to the reference desk.

This is true both for a general collection in the smaller library and for subject departments in large libraries. Most library buildings were planned before the public became even nearly as information-oriented as it is today, and before librarians themselves came to realize that circulating books of nonfiction are often the best source for answering reference questions.

It is common practice in small libraries to assign one or two qualified people as catalogers in the mornings and as reference librarians in the afternoons. There is much to be said, even in large libraries, for regular interchange of professional workers. It provides greater understanding, new ideas, and broader viewpoints that benefit the library. But the investment in special skills for these two types of work, even though they have much in common, may not always make it profitable to carry out this interchange.

## Relations with Neighboring Libraries

It is essential to understand specifically the procedures and materials of college, special, and other libraries in the vicinity, for the reader's benefit. Private citizens, also, are often willing to lend their books to public library patrons when demands run beyond the library's resources. Some libraries use teletype and quick delivery service to and from still larger libraries in the vicinity as a substantial source of needed material.

### Regional Reference Service

The inadequacy of reference materials and service in libraries deserves serious consideration in planning and organizing both local reference programs and the large county or regional library systems. Even if local reference service is good, help should come from a stronger, larger centralized system; this is especially effective in an industrialized metropolitan area. These services would include subject specialization, union catalogues and bibliographies, more, better, and faster interlibrary loans, and film and photoprint service. In fact, next to cooperative cataloging, the regional reference center is the chief motivation for many current regional systems. The state library agencies in response to a program proposed by the National Commission on Libraries and Information Science are encouraging the development of intra- and interstate multitype cooperatives to develop reference functions. These networks give users access to bibliographical files or data banks and reduce costs of service, because libraries will not have to duplicate materials already owned by another library. For example, libraries in Wyoming, Utah, Colorado, South Dakota, Kansas, and Iowa now have access to the data banks of the Denver-based Bibliographic Center for Research. And Illinois recently created an interlibrary cooperation coordinator position in each of its eighteen systems, an arrangement that will greatly facilitate the exchange of materials in that network.

## Reference Staffing

Professional reference workers need well-rounded education and training, supported by a rich cultural background of reading, especially in history, biography, science, social science, and national and world affairs. Intellectual curiosity, keen interest in what is going on in the world and in the community, and the instincts of a detective increase the zest for reference work. Many reference librarians have the vision and imagination to fit the ideas and facts they encounter, titles of books, and statistical and news items into the department's flow of inquiries and help to readers.

The department head should have adequate help in this vital field. The following minimum staff is justified. For libraries with fewer than five on the staff, one-eighth of the total staff time should be devoted to adult reference service. That is, in a staff of four, one trained worker should give at least half time; out of a staff of five to nine, one trained full-time reference worker plus enough time from another to cover a sixty-hour week. For staffs of ten to eighty, one-eighth of the total staff time should be assigned to reference. For staffs of eighty or more, one-seventh of the staff should be assigned to adult reference duty in general reference, subject departments, and branches. This includes professional and clerical workers but not those involved in the ordering, preparation, or checking-in of periodicals and documents or other activities belonging elsewhere; however, some libraries have a clerical worker check these in the reference department.

In libraries large enough to have a clerical worker seated next to the trained reference worker at the service desk, the former may be asked to bring specific books or take readers to specific shelves or materials. Inquiries should not be presented to inexperienced people and fed upward to those qualified to help. This is a disservice and inconvenience to readers, partly because the inexperienced have no idea where the question *should* lead, as to materials needed. This participation by untrained workers is hazardous, but there are always some clerical or untrained but educated workers keenly interested in what is going on; they can make themselves very valuable and after a year or so can take over simple questions.

### Departmental Objectives and Planning

The department head's activities are: (1) planning and leading; (2) supervising and training the staff; (3) reaching and serving as many readers as possible; (4) dividing and assigning the department's routine duties; (5) dividing the selection and checking of materials among those best qualified; (6) compiling indexes and bibliographies and cooperating in union catalogs; (7) preparing statistics and department reports (as few, brief, and specific as possible); (8) preparing personnel reports and budget requests; and (9) promotion for the services. All these need to be programmed and assigned, with everyone informed about what goes on.

*Training*

A reference staff can hardly maintain a high level of self-development without study stimulated by group discussion. Reference in-training should aim at improving reference service techniques and developing fuller knowledge of new and older materials as well as broader knowledge of the subjects that predominate in reference requests.

Topics for discussion meetings of the reference staff or by groups of two or three include local periodical holdings, the recording of statistics, how to instruct new workers on special activities, how to prepare publicity items, how much time to spend on a reference question, when to find the answer and when to show the reader how to find it, how much help to give writers and teachers who ask for it, what resources exist in other departments, exchange of assistants with other libraries, and coaching understudies.

In libraries of any size and in library school, assistants should have practice sessions and demonstrations on how to draw out sufficient expression of the reader's inquiry so it can be understood, how to utilize the special knowledge of each assistant, and how to evaluate the importance of and therefore the time given to individual questions, to best use staff time.

## Building the Collections

Use of the terms *collections* and *materials* signifies the awareness of librarians that books meet only a part of reference needs, though books form the backbone. Checking Sheehy's *Guide to Reference Books* and its supplements, Shores' *Basic Reference Sources,* and new reference titles annotated in *Library Journal, Wilson Library Bulletin, Reference Services Review, Booklist,* and other sources will indicate what reference items are available. Bibliographies are expensive and often neglected in all except large public libraries. A union list of bibliographies possessed by local or nearby libraries may be a large undertaking, but libraries of over 50,000 population with an alert staff will use it. To supplement the card catalog of a library's own holdings, a library of 40,000 population and upward should have at least the *Subject Index to Books in Print* and the *Cumulative Book Index* for identifying titles that may be borrowed by interloan, if they cannot be bought. The extent and efficiency of interlibrary lending and borrowing is a good criterion of the department's usefulness to its community.

## Periodicals

Next to books in importance are periodicals, for both reading and reference help. Since their number is increasing constantly and the quality of individual magazines changes, there should be an annual review of a library's magazine subscriptions. Inclusion of a title in a standard index of periodicals is a major consideration, since that greatly increases its usefulness.

Periodical subscriptions are best handled by blanket order through one or another of several leading agencies. Many valuable periodicals are available free, such as house organs of business and industrial firms. Small public libraries usually bind only those likely to be needed often or over a long period of time, including (in libraries of over 10,000 population) most of those indexed in *Abridged Reader's Guide*. Unbound back issues of magazines are often preferred because they can be lent. A useful device is a collection of duplicate unbound back issues or microfilm files of ten or twelve magazines most often used for reference—*Time*, for example—for replacement and for circulation; gift copies, two or three days old, can be solicited.

## Newspapers

Most public libraries receive and keep all local general newspapers, important papers of nearby larger cities, and a few of regional and national importance, at least the *New York Times*, which is indexed, the *Christian Science Monitor*, and the *Wall Street Journal*.

Modern newspaper stock usually crumbles after twenty-five years. Small libraries should try to get the state library to film local papers as the chief source for local history. In large cities, the solution is to microfilm the papers, thus saving space, eliminating mutilation, and lessening loss by fire or theft (rolls of film have been stolen), since the master negative is usually kept elsewhere. The negative can be used to print full-size copies of individual articles, and microfilm reading machines produce a readable copy of what is seen on the screen. (A discussion of microfilm services follows on page 174). Often the publisher of the local paper may be persuaded to give microfilm print to the library. If not, the library should arrange to help finance its microfilming; if prints can be sold to the publisher and to other libraries, this may cost no more than it would to bind. It is unusual for a newspaper to publish any index. Many public libraries, especially those with several branches, have a staff member scan an extra copy of each day's issue and clip articles for the local history collection or the vertical files; several copies can be processed at one time and sent out for branch filing.

*Local History*

Every public library has an obligation to collect materials on the history of its own locale. These materials sometimes are integrated with the main book collection, especially if a museum or local history society has most of the nonprint items. But in many instances the public library has the major collection, perhaps the only files of local history, especially of more recent years, including not only books, newspapers, pamphlets, maps, pictures, posters, and other print, but also letters, diaries, typewritten manuscripts, official archives of local societies and institutions, oral history, and other records. These tend to become a separately organized collection and to attract gifts of additional materials as they grow and are used. Embarking on this path requires administrative decisions, financial support, and a program of constant publicity and solicitation of materials. But it can lead to an ever more valuable and unique collection, perhaps aided by local volunteer enthusiasts.

*Pamphlets and the Vertical File*

A vertical file in a public library means a collection of pamphlets, clippings, magazine article reprints or tear sheets, and perhaps maps and pictures. Generally these are too thin to stand by themselves and must be kept in folders in standard file drawers, arranged alphabetically by subject. They are available for loan, have a relatively short useful life, and are of value especially for school assignments. The file should be weeded regularly, and a flow of the best current materials should be maintained.

More and better pamphlets are being published today than ever before. Many sources of information about them are available. Often they are free or so inexpensive that it costs less to order a number of copies than to spend time and money deciding how many to get separately in each case. Just as it is desirable to obtain all needed copies of a vertical file item at one time, so it is to be preferred that all copies be processed centrally and distributed to branches, subject-headed and ready for use. Thicker and more expensive pamphlets are treated as books for selection purposes, and many are cataloged and bound. Others may stand on the shelves alone or in pamphlet boxes or Princeton files. But the vertical file is the favorite method.

*Maps, Pictures, Catalogs, and Music*

Maps are sometimes included in a vertical file. The larger public libraries have separate collections of maps, including state road maps, road atlases, the U.S. Topographic Survey sheets, and picture maps. Many are available free or at small cost. The Cello-Clip device—heavy punched tabs mounted at the upper corners of the map and then hanging it from two or three heavy rods, somewhat like an inverted vertical file—is an efficient inexpensive way to handle sheet maps. The public is increasingly map-minded, and a library should have a battery of up-to-date loose maps as well as bound atlases.

Similarly, flat pictures, preferably mounted on cardboard, are valuable. Art prints and informational pictures on a wide variety of subjects can be purchased or clipped from magazines or gift books not otherwise needed. If desired, they may be mounted by using the Seal electric press, which bonds them to a poster board, making them more useful to artists, teachers, students, and children. Most libraries keep clipped pictures simply in folders or envelopes. Some large libraries have hundreds of thousands of items, but every public library should have at least some.

Every library of over 10,000 population needs a collection of current catalogs of major colleges and universities in the region, and a score of those most famous nationally. Some of these are available free; usually they must be requested individually each year. A commercial microfilm service of college catalogs can now be purchased. Though costly, the service can save many hours of work in soliciting the numerous bulletins of schools that are issued annually. There are also mail order and other catalogs. Sheet music is a type of material that only a large public library can be expected to collect. Musical scores and libretti for established operas and for well-known songs should be available in many more libraries in hardcover books. Music in the form of phonograph records is available in most libraries. The selection of both language, literary, and musical records and tapes and films should be the special responsibility of those staff members who service their use. These items should be covered by the selection policy statement of the library.

*Government Documents*

Many documents are of prime importance in answering readers' questions. Libraries that are depositories of government publications receive automatically one free copy of all titles in requested series. The disadvantage to this arrangement is that such libraries are required to keep the publications received on depository privilege for a certain period of time. Nondepository libraries can often secure free copies of new publications from issuing agencies or from their congressmen, as can depository libraries that want extra copies or separate items in series not originally requested. Federal government publications cost little when purchased, and paperwork on orders to the Government Printing Office may be cut by buying coupons to be sent with later orders.

The *Monthly Catalog of U.S. Government Publications* is the current comprehensive listing of these materials, and it is a formidable task merely to review each issue. There are also the subject price lists of the Government Printing Office, the biweekly free list of *Selected United States Government Publications* (probably the best service for smaller libraries), and the lists of publications of the various individual agencies, as well as listings in library magazines like *Booklist.* No one of these sources can be relied on for all the items useful to public libraries. Even depository libraries have this problem, since they receive automatically only those series they have requested and agreed to keep, and often other individual titles are desired. Other tools and listings are available, and each library must work out its own pattern of selection and procurement. Unquestionably public libraries receive and use too few federal publications and have not found short cuts to publicize and use them.

The Superintendent of Documents does not require or recommend any one method of arranging government documents. Most depository libraries shelve them in a separate collection arranged according to the GPO classification number, which appears in the *Monthly Catalog,* and depend on the author, title, and subject indexes of the *Monthly Catalog,* which has begun to use machine readable (MARC) tapes and LC subject headings. Nondepository libraries often catalog federal government publications or put them in the vertical file, depending on their size and importance. Many depository libraries catalog and classify important documents too, such as decennial census reports and the *Statistical Abstract,* and regularly secure extra copies of them.

Some larger libraries file such federal periodicals as *Monthly Labor Review* with the regular magazines and put many other items in the vertical files. Selected hardcover books or thick paper-covered items and important bulletin series, such as *Office of Education Bulletins,* are often cataloged and placed on the regular shelves. All other items could remain in a special documents collection, arranged by the Superintendent of Document's code number. Those items treated specially are then so indicated on the cards of the check-in file. Federal documents will never be extensively utilized until there is a monthly or quarterly subject index, of the same practical character as the Wilson indexes, to the detailed contents of at least the most generally useful half of its current publications. Until then few libraries can afford the time required to find the material on a given subject, except as suggested above.

Unlike federal documents, state government publications are not well listed, indexed, or distributed. The Library of Congress's *Monthly Checklist of State Publications* lists many, and many states issue a frequent compilation of new publications. Local government publications are even more elusive, but every public library should maintain a file of them. The publication and distribution of United Nations documents are well organized, but relatively few are essential except in very large libraries. Libraries can popularize document use by making them more available, by displays, and by publicizing them in the newspapers. Federal publications in depository as well as nondepository libraries may be lent for home use. Some libraries sell GPO coupons to patrons who wish to purchase their own copies of documents. Others sell directly copies of particularly useful documents.

*Microform*

Microform is found in most libraries today. There are several reasons for its popularity and use. First, it is a simple method of storing in a limited area. It permits the acquisition of materials, such as out-of-print books and magazines, that would be difficult to obtain or too expensive to purchase in their original form. It means that on-demand materials are always available and cannot be stolen or checked out of the library. Finally, with the aid of printout devices, pages can be copied, thus avoiding time consuming note taking.

Microform does have some drawbacks. Because it must be used in conjunction with a mechanical reader, and few patrons have such devices at home, the material must be used in the library. A few libraries (New York University being one) lend portable readers for home use. Reading material on microform may also strain the eyes. Equally important, despite its general acceptance, both users and librarians given a choice feel it is a poor substitute for the original.

There are various forms of microform. The most popular is microfilm. This stores materials at reduction rates ranging from 15:1 to 20:1 on reels of film. The microcard, an extension of this system, uses a 3-by-5 card. A typical card can hold as many as eighty pages of a document, magazine, or newspaper. It is opaque and utilizes a different reader. A newer form, microfiche, also uses cards, but the cards are made of microfilm, mounted in apertures. In the past few years micropublication has significantly increased reduction ratios.

Thousands of books and other publications are available in microform. Libraries of 100,000 population and over should have a microfilm copy of the *New York Times* and one of a local paper. Before the microfilm of the *Times* is purchased, the *Index* should be bought; it is a key to dates not only for items in the *Times* but also for items in other newspapers as well. One of the most useful on-line data bases now available to libraries is the *New York Times* data base, which indexes up-to-the-minute information from the *Times* and dozens of other sources. Larger libraries have this service in use. Some publishers of esoteric newspapers, reports, magazines, and books never issue their publications in anything but microform.

Two important guides to the field are Allen Veaner's *The Evaluation of Micropublications* and *Microforms in Libraries,* edited by Albert Diaz. The annual *International Microfilm Source Book* lists important services and pieces of equipment related to micrographics. Journals in the area include *Microform Review* and *Journal of Micrographics,* among others.

## Special Indexes

Locally prepared reference indexes augment the value of a library's holdings. However, the extent to which indexing should be carried out is a moot question. With the world overindexed and wired together, many feel it is less and less desirable to develop and maintain local indexes. An exception to this rule may be an index to a key area newspaper that is not indexed by the company or sufficiently analyzed by Newsbank. Other reference librarians with a zeal for "facts on file" think additional special indexes are indispensable for reader satisfaction, such as indexes to parties and games, legislative bills of the current session, local organizations of all kinds, saints treated in collective biographies, consumer product ratings, popular song hits, popular piano and choral music, movies and their sources under various titles, articles in magazines not covered by Wilson indexes, and mystery stories. This partial list of time-consuming projects suggests (1) the need for careful investigation to avoid duplicating what has already been done, perhaps locally; (2) the possibility of having volunteers produce many of these highly useful indexes; and (3) the desirability of having some indexes duplicated or published for national use. Many, like Lovell and Hall's widely useful *Index to Handicrafts,* are started in volunteered time.

One will not overlook local human resources for special information—people well informed on stamps, science, products, foreign countries, local and national history—generally they are glad to help.

## The User's Questions

Meredith Bloss, New Haven City librarian, retired, states that "the reference librarian is the middleman between the reader and the right book," for "it has been estimated that fully 95 percent of a library's users do not know exactly what they want or where it can be found when they enter a library." This applies to many researchers and college professors.

It is of administrative importance that the reference staff learn to conserve time by learning good questioning techniques—how to discover in detail just what the particular piece of information is that the reader needs and why, thus eliminating much useless searching for often unhelpful material. This questioning has to be patient, friendly, unassuming, and not too persistent. By explaining why one is trying to delimit the search to fit the particular case, the staff member will find that the reader is often willing to explain his need much further.

*Helping College Students*

Since college libraries are generally open as many hours as the local public library, some public libraries may be justified in ruling that college students will get only limited public library reference service. Reading assignments often require the use of every copy of a book available anywhere. The college library's funds may be meager—its staff may consist of inexperienced student assistants. In such instances reference service ought to be given by the public library, whose trustees in turn have a right to enlist local public opinion in insisting that the college build up its library, assemble a trained reference staff, and serve its own students. This is a policy matter that should not be allowed to drift. Committees composed of members of the public library staff, its trustees, and the local college personnel should analyze the problem, weigh the factors of public and college reaction, and make needed decisions.

*Contest Questions*

Many reference departments curtail reference service when high prizes in contests are offered, difficult questions are asked, and high-pressure publicity impels crowds of searchers to abuse and steal valuable reference books. Complete refusal to give service creates misunderstanding and bad public relations, partly because a library may not have already publicized and explained its normal and perhaps excellent reference services, and the public does not realize the problems involved. Other devices used are (1) a fifteen-minute time limit for any book in demand: (2) putting all the relevant books into glassed or screened cases and giving them out only on signed receipts; (3) concentrating users in one area so that one person can oversee all contestants and prevent mutilations or thefts.

*Telephone Service*

The attitude that "if people can't take the trouble to come here for help, let them get along without it" is hardly realistic today. There is a widespread public habit of calling up for help. Some libraries advertise, "You are as close to the library as your phone," and answer so many questions each month that restrictions are needed to curb abuses. A number of large libraries, such as the one in Atlanta, now have special telephone reference service desks and staffs. The Atlanta Public Library secured a telephone number with the last four digits spelling INFO. But in some libraries no school or college student's reference questions are answered over the phone, no telephone question may involve more than fifteen minutes, no quiz or contest questions are permitted, and deferring answers is increasingly used to relieve the pressure and to give the staff more time to do adequate searching. In the course of time telephone service is bound to increase greatly.

## The Reference Attitude

This section is concluded with a summary of seven qualities desirable for every reference librarian: (1) literacy, the ability to comprehend easily and to receive communication; (2) imagination and resourcefulness; (3) enthusiasm; (4) persistence; (5) a sense of media, which makes the good reference librarian a true "master of materials"; (6) humility, so that one doesn't consider it a personal affront if the information cannot be found in the library's collection (and is indefatigable in trying to locate it somewhere else); and (7) "love for serving people, or that spirit of service which we hope motivates all librarians."

## Publicity for Reference Service

"The average person learns from experience, the wise person learns from the experience of others" is an old proverb that can be used for promoting reference service. The average citizen may not have enough intellectual curiosity to find out what others have done or written about the problem. Thus, the department's planning must include finding effective ways to inform all the major population groups that the library can serve them with the information they need as individuals. Unfortunately, recent surveys of adult library use show that the library is not reaching out to the wide sector of population.

The conviction that reference service has hardly scratched the consciousness of the community means that the reference department should publicize reference tools, services, and questions at least as well and as persistently, for instance, as children's services. The department head cannot depend on the publicity officer to initiate the publicity. The reference librarians are the ones to see that reference publicity is greatly multiplied. Every reference assistant needs to think about publicity day after day, making outlines for new stories and other suggestions.

## User Surveys

An example of a reference use survey carried out in a medium-sized region was the one by the Southern Connecticut Library Council in 1972. Eighteen public libraries took part in the study. Major findings were that nonresident use of reference services in the different libraries ranged from 1.4 percent to 49.1 percent; that students and teachers constituted 50.8 percent of the reference clientele; that in-person reference use was 76 percent and telephone inquiries 23 percent of the total and that Monday afternoon was the busiest time of the week. The majority were subject searches and simple, quickly answerable "ready reference" questions; the most popular subjects were history and biography. The card catalogue and the nonfiction circulating collection were the most heavily used materials. The report recommended the establishment of a backup reference service during the busiest hours and compensation for those libraries serving a large proportion of nonresidents.

One of the items on the survey worksheet was titled "results of inquiry," in terms of user satisfaction. The survey found that during the four weeks of inquiry 75.3 percent of the inquiries were satisfied and that 12.5 percent were "partly satisfied." The number of unsatisfied queries was extrapolated to roughly 13,500 for the year in the region of about 400,000 population.[2]

## Measuring Reference Service

*Statistics*

We have noted the increasing pressures on librarians to keep statistical records of reference services, along with statistics of many other activities. In general, there is a conflict between the desire for self-measurement as an administrative service to gain efficiency and economy and the wish to avoid every possible sort of statistical record and paperwork as factor number one in economy. Individual reference librarians and committees have written scores of articles and reports on this problem and as yet no recommendations emerge that are generally satisfying.

It does seem useful that if the total number of reference questions is divided into the total of expenditures for salaries in the reference services, then we get at least a rough cost figure per unit. We do not suggest including costs of material, because of complexities and the time costs for accounting. Most small libraries and a few large city libraries keep no reference statistics, for three fairly good reasons: their cost, the problems of defining categories, and the difficulty in recording them faithfully. The inconsistent bases, definitions, and reportings possible, with the best of intentions, show up especially in comparing annual statistics from the subject departments or branches of individual large libraries. No one can explain their striking contrasts, or the zigzag curves that follow changes in agency heads.

The ALA is currently in search of a solution and plans a study on reference service measurement.[3] The field badly needs a set of standards and codified definitions for the gathering of statistics on reference service.

Meanwhile, the counting of reference questions is still a popular device for measuring reference services. A recent edition of *Public Library Abstracts* reported that 50 percent of sixty-six public library reports abstracted included data on the number of reference questions.[4] Of course, many of the annual reports cited went beyond numbers and described the questions by source, subject, or time expended. Yet, the enumeration of reference questions still seems to be the most common method of measuring service.

One new trend focuses on analyzing reference personnel. Kenneth Beasley has suggested that the number of employees who perform reference services may be the best measure of reference service effort.[5] Charles Bunge looked at the relationship between professional training and the efficiency of reference service effort.[6] Using multiple correlation techniques, David Cravens arrived at five measures of predicting the ability of reference personnel to perform certain information retrieval tasks.[7]

In line with the views of Thomas Galvin, cited earlier in this chapter, about the need for a new concept of the information/reference function, it may well be that libraries ought to consider tallying the *results* obtained on a client basis, rather than counting the number of queries received. How many transfers of information were successfully completed in client-satisfaction terms? Could degrees of completion or satisfaction be recorded? Could the degrees of complexity be measured and tallied? Could types of information transfer be counted? There are challenging opportunities for research and development in this area. Doubtless if the public library were in the information-for-private-profit business, accountability of this nature would have to be undertaken.

If the present method of measurement is continued, a day-by-day score, and in the opinion of many reference workers a list of the questions, should be kept as carefully as possible. The question list is valuable for department staff analysis and discussions to improve service. But frequent careful samplings of both figures and questions—that is, for a week every month or every two months—may well suffice for a fair annual estimate.

If a library reports output, the reference department may find five categories for reference questions developed by Cornell University Libraries helpful: (1) informational and directional questions, (2) reference questions (questions requiring less than fifteen minutes and two or more kinds of sources), (3) search questions (questions requiring from fifteen minutes to an hour, and three or more kinds of sources), (4) problem questions (taking over an hour), and (5) bibliography questions (original compilation requiring at least one hour).[8]

## Costs

Until most libraries keep reference statistics on a common basis, there can be no valid comparative figures of accomplishment or of reference service costs, though both are desirable to stimulate progress. A recent study at the Beverly Hills Public Library estimated reference and guidance costs by dividing the annual costs of the services by the number of people using the service. The study showed an estimated cost of 82 cents per visit.[9] One cannot weigh the significance or validity of such a figure without knowing, for example, what proportion of them came from school pupils. The idea of obtaining an exact unit cost by counting all the fringe and overhead costs involved may occur to those who believe that it pays to spend a dollar of salary time to discover a hidden dime of cost. Statistics and cost figures of reference service should be kept on the simplest and most economical basis possible and not so elaborated that overbusy assistants are diverted from attending to their patrons.

### Evaluation of the Department

Reference service is so greatly a matter of variables and intangibles that attempts to evaluate the department and its operations are rather baffling. A practical, effective test of a reference department is a two- or three-day self-survey of what happens to each patron. "What luck?" is a good heading for a reader questionnaire to ascertain (1) whether the request grew out of school or college assignments or out of the reader's daily job, and in what manner; (2) whether the patron got what he or she came for; and (3) if not, why not, with several possible reasons to be checked. Such an inquiry of all patrons for two or three days every two or three years will reveal many specific inadequacies and reader frustrations that can be remedied. It seems strange that this device is not used in most libraries. Forty years ago a New Zealand librarian wrote: "The demand which is not followed up, the request for which something less than exactly what the reader wants is supplied, the contact which is not made, the enquirer who is kept waiting until he gives up—these are the things which should keep us awake at night."[10] This concern is primary in the thinking and planning of the reference head, who must go further and do something about it; so must the head librarian.

## Information and Referral Services

Although public libraries have for some years provided some degree of information about community services, both for groups and individuals, there has been in the past few years an increased effort to provide a more comprehensive and specialized service. This has generally come to be known as "information and referral," but the term "has differing connotations and denotations, depending on one's background, understanding, and purpose."

In Turick's report on the Neighborhood Information Center we are told that

> Until the early 1970s, information and referral services had been provided primarily by social service agencies with planning, administration, and direct service being performed by social workers and their assistants.
>
> The first national focus for information and referral services in public libraries was provided by the University of Illinois Allerton Institute, "Libraries and Neighborhood Information Centers," held in October, 1971. In 1972, the Neighborhood Information Centers (NIC) Project, the first intercity public library consortium research/ demonstration project ever federally funded in this area, began planning information

and referral services for two neighborhood information centers within two branch libraries in each of the public libraries of Atlanta, Cleveland, Detroit, Houston, and Queens Borough (N.Y.). . . . In 1977 the Public Library Association board of directors approved information and referral as one of six major priority areas of public library concern.[11]

In another article Turick cautions that social workers and others question the entry of public libraries into information and referral because the service

represents *a range of discrete service offerings*—information, referral, follow up, advice, steering, counselling, diagnosis, and advocacy. Social workers will usually take the position that the complete range of services should be made available to all consumers of I and R services.

But librarians consider information and referral as an access service which functions to link those in need with accurate information concerning currently available services. Providing general and directional information which links the individual with a service which will meet his/her need and resolve his/her problem is an acceptable reference service function. Compilation of community information resource files and directories, indexed, catalogued, and freely available as part of public library reference service cannot be faulted.

Librarians can and do provide information "only" and the information and referral (linking) service. The individual who requires advice, counselling, or diagnosis will be referred by the librarian to the professional at the appropriate agency who can help.

Follow up, which is defined as an essential component of information and referral service by social workers and social service organizations, may be included as a component of the library's information and referral service, or it may be limited or non-existent.

The difference in concepts and services thus becomes a difference in *definitions* of information and referral. The purpose remains constant: active linkage between individual and service provider.

Defining its role in relationship to definitions of information and referral is essential to the effective planning for the library's information and referral services.[12]

*Title XX Funding*

Some libraries, and other community agencies, have received federal funding under Title XX of the Social Security Act, for partial funding of information and referral services. The Wake County Information and Referral Center has flourished in the Raleigh (North Carolina) Public Library since December, 1971. It is separate from the reference department. Title XX funding was received for 1977–1978, and the center's director (librarian), Carol H. Reilly, feels that funding will be continued.

Ms. Reilly has some reservations about Title XX funding. For one thing, the regulations prohibit outreach; Title XX employees must wait until clients come in. "I consider outreach one form of public awareness activities. . . . I can go a little further than the rest of the staff. . . . My whole salary is paid by the city government." She continues,

Otherwise I have found very few Title XX requirements and restrictions to be against my philosophy of I & R service. Staff provide information to people of all ages and socioeconomic levels on a broad variety of questions: educational, financial, employment, housing, recreational and health subjects. If an applicant can manage to put together a proposal after reading 25 pages of instructions, then he or she can probably live with the requirements.[13]

### The Neighborhood Information Centers Project, 1972–1975

This federally funded consortium of five major public libraries was administered first by the Cleveland Public Library and in the third year by the Houston Public Library. Turick, who wrote up the evaluation of this project, concluded that: "Each of the five libraries met and completed the original project objectives; each then extended or did not extend services on a system basis according to prevailing local conditions."

Further, according to Turick: "The Detroit Public Library, which had been committed to the development of information and referral services on a system basis prior to project inception became the outstanding library model for total system development in the urban city." The dedicated administrative commitment of Clara Stanton Jones, the director, influenced the planning, development, and continuance of the Detroit TIP (The Information Place).[14]

In furtherance of her belief in I & R service as a proper public library activity, Ms. Jones has edited "a guide for libraries planning to introduce information and referral service, or for anyone interested in its philosophy." She proposes that:

Information and referral service in public libraries merits serious consideration as an important expansion of reference service that satisfies common, everyday information needs. In the evolution of library practice I & R has emerged as a logical response to a demonstrated need for nonbook information about community resources. Where it has been given serious trial in public libraries, the introduction of community information service has been welcomed and greatly used by the public. First, it has let people know that helpful resources exist, and second, it has provided a reliable starting point in any search for information on practical needs—relief from wandering through the bureaucratic maze.[15]

She takes the view that information and referral service is a logical function of public libraries because by its very nature it requires the skills with which librarians are singularly trained and equipped—the ability to collect and organize data so that it can be retrieved successfully upon demand, and a long tradition of willingness to serve the individual at his or her own level of readiness. She says, "Only librarians can do it right!"

The applicability of I & R service to medium-sized and small library communities is of special importance [continues Ms. Jones]. The central community information file would be the only file needed in a small town. In a large city, telephone calls far outnumber "walk-in" I & R service, but in a small community with fewer telephones, shorter distances and more intimate personal contacts, "walk-in" service may be used more. The operation should be adapted to the local need. . . .

The effective practice of information and referral service in public libraries will bring about increased involvement with other professions. The library is entering I & R as a cooperative and complementary participant and should work toward establishing itself as the general information base and equal partner undergirding the various specialized I & R agencies. . . . I & R is not a specialty within libraries, and it is a mistake to employ it in this manner.[16]

The public library can become the community's *comprehensive* information center. The center will have to work with more than published records and data in the collection, and will have to develop a community information file to meet the coping questions that people have.

It is as reasonable to supply answers to these questions from the community information file as it is to search traditional sources to identify a literary quotation, verify spelling or birthdates or look up a patent number. I & R in practice proves to be *expanded reference work.* . . .

There is an obvious need for some institution to be responsible for supplying information that will guide the public through the maze of government and private service agencies spawned by our complex society. Not knowing where to start in their search for information or direct assistance, all too commonly people are shunted around from one waiting line or telephone number to another. Many become too discouraged to continue what seems like a futile pursuit. . . .

. . . The community information file is simply one new reference tool to be used in conjunction with other reference books and materials by whoever happens to wait on a patron. No one librarian should be better qualified than another to use such a tool.[17]

But, Ms. Jones points out, librarians will have to move from the present concept of reader assistance to information guidance.

Expanding reference techniques beyond the traditional practice of offering only in-house materials transforms reader assistance into information guidance. On a larger scale, it transforms a public library into the community's comprehensive information center.[18]

Evaluating the future prospects of I & R programs in public libraries, Dr. Thomas Childers summarizes in his document on the five-city demonstration some conclusions which might be universal in application and based not only on the findings from those projects but on all the others that have spun off and carried on since the I & R development began:

1. The public will respond to public library I & R service in great numbers if the right situation exists. Detroit, where the library is processing about 100,000 inquiries a year, is the clearest example of such success.

2. I & R service can attract substantial "new" audiences to the public library. Moreover, I & R can service affluent middle-class citizens as well as the disadvantaged.

3. Funding authorities may find I & R an attractive way to spend public money. This might be especially true to the extent that the I & R service has a large clientele drawn from library users and nonusers alike.

The public library can indeed be a natural site for I & R services, and will succeed if it follows the path of administrative commitment, training, good publicity, community involvement and responsiveness to people's needs.[19]

Major R. Owens has written and spoken in support of the idea of the public library as optimum information agency, particularly with respect to meeting the needs of inner-city residents who do not in general respond positively to the traditional library services. He wrote:

The present period of fiscal and administrative conservatism is such that most localities will probably choose to utilize their public library system to provide information services. Unless it insists on playing the role of the defiant dodo, the library profession will continue to be the primary body of people determining the scope, shape and thoroughness of information services throughout the country.

The library is the optimum choice for the provision of information services to inner-city communities. Very practical facts of funding, public administration and politics support this conclusion. Some of the factors which must be considered are:

1. Public library systems already exist in most cities. They have linkages with a local tax and budgeting system, and they have an accepted administrative structure.

2. Because of their established place in the system, both private and government funding sources are more likely to view their financing more favorably.

3. No special start-up and no capital construction costs are needed to initiate or to expand information services. All new funds made available may be utilized for materials and personal services.

4. Branch libraries which already exist within the inner-city provide a convenient dissemination and distribution network.

5. The basic administrative and technical services systems developed by the library profession have functioned successfully and would have to be replicated at considerable cost by any alternative system.

6. Alternative systems will find it difficult to survive and sustain themselves in a situation characterized by uncertain, spotty and haphazard financing.

For the public library, nearly everything is in place except the most vital ingredient. To expand and fully embrace the provision of information services as a priority responsibility and duty, the public library needs a new understanding of its mission. As long ago as 1924, William S. Learned, in *The American Public Library and the Diffusion of Knowledge,* clearly and forcefully stated that part of the mission, part of the justification for the existence of the public library was the provision of practical information to the public. Clearly, there is nothing new and revolutionary in the call for libraries to provide information power to the people.[20]

Advocacy seems to be a thorny problem, from which librarians shy away, and rightfully so. And social workers take the view that information and referral without advocacy fail to fulfill the total need. Owens deals with that. "Information is automatically advocacy. . . . When the citizens acquire this changed perception of what adequate information services can do for them, they will have arrived at a point of full understanding of information power."[21]

Kochen states that the public library "has the potential to serve as a kind of citizen forum."[22] Donohue writes:

The provision of comprehensive information services remains a valid function for the public library. The public library, more than any other agency, is suited to the task. While many kinds of agencies distribute information, the public library is unique in our society in combining the following features:

1. Its primary function is to provide information and informational materials.
2. It exists to serve the entire community.
3. Its subject scope is virtually unlimited.
4. Its operators are specialists in document and information handling as such.
5. It is in principle impartial, being dedicated to the interests of society as a whole, rather than of a particular element of society.
6. While generally supported by public funds, its customary form of governance provides some measure of freedom from direct or partisan political control.[23]

## Information Needs

There have been in recent years a number of studies of the information needs of adult citizens. Brenda Dervin has carried out a substantial body of research in this field, and the results have been published. She identifies nineteen "major categories in the information-needs content-analysis scheme," ranging from neighborhood to public affairs, political and miscellaneous. She discusses the application of the scheme to existing information sources, and she writes:

The clearest generalization that emerges from this discussion is that huge gaps exist in the knowledge base relating to average citizens and their information needs. The list of unanswered questions is overwhelming. Two main conclusions emerge very clearly, however.

The first is that the frequently cited concept of information has received very little systematic attention, either from practitioners or researchers. . . .

Second, to deal effectively with the information needs of citizens will require a more interactive, or system, orientation. Most previous research has placed the onus of information seeking (and failure to obtain satisfying results) on the citizen, and yet this study suggests that the onus should be placed on the information keepers as well.[24]

## Summary of Information and Referral Services

There are strong advocates for the service in public libraries. The assessment of citizen needs corresponds very little to the subject organization in most libraries. Libraries are materials-centered; the materials are collected, arranged, and displayed for use; the client must adjust his search to the arrangement. The library tends to view the ideal as associated with "high" culture and the literate society. The everyday citizen's needs for survival information may not be seen as entirely within the purview of most public libraries. Public libraries responding to this need might find that their usefulness in the local situation would be enhanced, and hence they might be able to make a more substantial and practical contribution.

This discussion has not touched at all on the larger subject of information as an industry, as exemplified by the interests of the American Society for Information Science, for example, dealing with the information needs of science, industry, business, engineering, and many other private and public enterprises. About all that the public library director and staff can do in this area, at least in small to medium-sized libraries, would be to have a general awareness of developments as reported in the ASIS annual reviews.[25]

## Notes

1. Thomas Galvin, "The Education of the New Reference Librarian, *Library Journal* 100 (Apr. 15, 1975): 727–30.
2. Mary Lynn Vickers, *Regional Reference Survey Report* (North Branford, Conn.: Southern Connecticut Library Council, 1973), ERIC Report ED 088 457 IR 000 288.
3. American Library Association, *The ALA Yearbook, 1977* (Chicago: American Library Association, 1977), p. 278.
4. Herbert Goldhor, ed., *Public Library Abstracts, 1971: Abstracts of Statistics in American Public Library Annual Reports* (Springfield, Ill.: Illinois State Library, 1973).
5. Kenneth E. Beasley, *A Statistical Reporting System for Local Public Libraries,* monograph no. 3 (University Park, Pa.: Pennsylvania State Library, 1964), p. 21.
6. Charles A. Bunge, "Professional Education and Reference Efficiency" (Ph.D. diss., University of Illinois, 1967).
7. David W. Cravens, "Predicting Performance of Information Specialists," *Journal of the American Society for Information Science* 22 (January–February 1971): 5–11.
8. Caroline E. Hieber, "Measuring Reference Service: A Look at the Cornell University Libraries Reference Question Recording System," *Bookmark* 31 (January–February 1972): 79–81.
9. Joseph P. Newhouse and Arthur J. Alexander, *An Economic Analysis of Public Library Services* (Lexington, Mass.: Lexington Books, 1972), pp. 70–71.
10. Edith J. Carnell, "Try at the Library," *Proceedings of the New Zealand Library Association* 13 (1941): 27–29.
11. Dorothy Ann Turick, "The Neighborhood Information Center," *RQ* 12 (Summer 1973).
12. Dorothy Ann Turick, *Community Information Services in Libraries,* Library Journal Special Report no. 5 (New York, 1977), p. 16.
13. Ibid., pp. 38–41.
14. Ibid., pp. 42–43.
15. Clara Stanton Jones, ed., *Public Library Information and Referral Service* (Syracuse, N.Y.: Gaylord Professional Publications, 1978), p. 17.
16. Ibid., pp. 21–22.
17. Ibid., p. 26.
18. Ibid., pp. 27–28.
19. Ibid., p. 165.

20. Major R. Owens, "Information Power for Inner-City Communities," *Southeastern Librarian* (Fall 1975): 13–14. See also Owens, "Local Leadership, Politics and Public Support," in Jones, op. cit., pp. 126–38.
21. Ibid., p. 16.
22. Manfred Kochen and Joseph C. Donohue, eds., *Information for the Community* (Chicago: American Library Association, 1976), p. 16.
23. Ibid., pp. 92–93.
24. Ibid., pp. 24–25, 35.
25. Martha E. Williams, ed., *Annual Review of Information Science and Technology,* vol. 13 (White Plains, N.Y.: Knowledge Industry Publications, 1978). See also vols. 1–12 for earlier reviews.

# 10 Subject Departments

The trend in large central libraries to departmentalize adult services into large subject fields reflects an increasing public need for more specialized information and the national development in research. Because individual citizens have to formulate their more specialized ideas and plans as efficiently as possible before putting their projects under way, they require specialized library service in which circulating and reference books, reports, documents, pamphlets, and periodicals on related subjects are brought together into coherent major subject groupings. This calls for librarians who can concentrate on the materials, reader needs, and library techniques in their special field.

## Growth of the Subject Department Idea

The first subject department seems to have been set in operation in 1900 by William E. Foster in the central building of the Providence Public Library. The executives, designers, and employees in the silverware, jewelry, textile, and machine tool industries in that city called for a constant flow of information about new research, artwork, designs, and inventions. The librarian was alert enough to supply it. On the third floor of the then new building, he created an Art Department and an Industrial Department, with a readers' service desk between them. This pairing of two departments reflected the locally predominant art-in-industry and machine tool occupations. It seems to have been the first recognition that a library's informational organization should be based on the community's character. The public libraries of Minneapolis and the District of Columbia shortly afterward created subject departments. The slightly earlier subject departments in the Newberry Library and in the reference department of the New York Public Library, both strictly reference libraries, were entirely different in organization and operation from the type of combined circulating and reference department considered here. The later history of subject departmentation is told by Warren,[1] who suggested that the added expense for subject departmentation was hardly justified in cities of less than half a million people. Even then this view might well have been questioned, and factors that in some libraries had created unprofitable costs, such as placing separate rooms on several floors and at some distance apart, have been recognized and overcome.

It is significant that subject departmentation in public libraries started about the same time and developed about as rapidly as the special libraries movement, which resulted in libraries in business and industrial corporations. Subject departments serve in the public library as "special libraries" for the community at large. Many special libraries use also the resources of the public library and vice versa.

A study by Vainstein in 1960 showed public libraries in sixty-seven American and five Canadian cities operating a separate department to serve local business and industrial interests. In a few cases these were operated as branches in separate buildings because the main library was not well located.[2] More than half of these seventy-two departments combined "business and industry," or "business, technology and science," though a few were labeled "business and economics." Departmental labels should be short; and they seldom completely describe the coverage, but in cities of 100,000 to 500,000 the combination of business, economics, trades, industry, technology, and science—that is, the 500s and 600s of the decimal classification—seems to be a favorite pattern. It evidently works well and avoids whatever extra cost results from splitting these in two, despite the fact that there are three or four distinct clienteles to be served. In larger cities the fields of business and economics are sufficiently large and distinct from science and technology, and have so large a clientele, as to warrant their separation for more specialized service.

A 1942 table showed art and music first in department frequency, with 6 in the 10–24 staff group and 19 in the 25–74 staff group, technology 4 and 7, business 4 and 7, and local history 6.[3] Even if technology and business were combined, as is frequently done, art and music had by 1942 become the leading subjects for a combined department of their own, with technology and business close seconds.

In cities of a quarter million or more, it is not uncommon to find complete subject departmentation. The major fields of knowledge are divided into six to ten large groups. Within each group the materials have close subject relationships, and service is given to large and fairly distinct categories of readers by reference workers either trained in or specializing in the subject area.

Obviously, readers do not confine themselves to particular subjects; their personal interests are constantly changing and often have nothing to do with their vocational, social, or cultural boundaries. Consequently they may use several or all departments. The organization and arrangement of these departments present many problems. Some are discussed below, but there may never be a single pattern to meet all situations; building plans and structure greatly influence local decisions.

## Pros and Cons

There is much to be said in favor of subject departmentation, but there is a tendency to see it as more separative, complicated, and costly than need be. The English librarian McClellan said, "Distinct departments become in effect separate libraries within a library. The scale of resources required . . ." would "deter any but the largest systems."[4] But just how large need a library be? And why do departments need to seem like separate libraries? The answer is suggested above when we discussed the split-off of one or two subjects in several cities of less than 100,000 population. Probably all these libraries would say that the cost is justified and the results are gratifying. Since 1930 nearly all the libraries built in cities of over 100,000 have at least one or two subject departments. Those opened since 1950 in cities of over 150,000 usually have three or more.

### Effect on Service and Morale

An advantage, easily observable in action, is that all this greater background knowledge about subjects and materials—the bibliographical techniques and numerous other resources—are focused intensively on the reader. As discussed in the previous chapter, good layout calls for placing the departmental service point, with its workroom, at the entrance of the department to assure that every reader will pass the service staff and have full opportunity to request help. This concentration of attention on the reader characterizes some general reference rooms of the older type, but it does not provide the special interest in and knowledge of the subject *materials* found in subject departments.

A higher proportion of staff time can be focused on reader service. The administrative function takes less time because most of the staff is professional and carries on a homogeneous group of duties that have to do almost entirely with readers and their materials in a restricted field. Circulation routines should be carried on centrally for the building. Clerical helpers should do all that can be delegated by the specialists, just as in any general reference department. A library that builds up a staff of competent subject specialists gains the high regard of its community.

### Greater Costs

It is clear that larger payrolls are involved. Each subject department usually has an added head and at least two or three trained professionals. Ervin J. Gaines has suggested that central libraries tend to be overstaffed with professionals in subject departments. To cut costs he recommends that paraprofessionals be trained to take on some functions of the professionals: "It is costly to retain professionals on tap at reference desks at all times."[5]

It is also costly to duplicate titles, but a number of titles would seem logically to belong in two or more departments.

## Other Difficulties

That average borrowers do not require specialized information has an element of truth. But this is largely due to their unawareness that they could get help on their special undertakings. There are two problems: the difficulties of classifying books that may be of interest to several departments and the handling of questions that cut across several departments. These difficulties were greatest in libraries, such as Cleveland and Los Angeles, where the departments were separated around the outside of a building and on two or three floors, causing excessive loss of reader and staff time. This is partly a matter of building plans. But the spread and complexity of reader demands involve difficult problems in all library situations, including those resulting from reader interest grouping.

Other shortcomings, the validity of which are dependent on local organization and building plans, are:

1. The tendency of a department staff to confine its interest and knowledge so narrowly to its own subject field that it knows too little of the others, assumes a self-sufficient attitude, and fails to use related materials in other departments. This shortsightedness, possible under any form of organization, can be largely overcome by proper coordination, constant alertness, reminders, and carefully prepared schedules of subject analysis and breakdown.

2. The tendency to shunt readers from one department to another, a fault in libraries where the departments are scattered, with no strategic central clearing point for readers, and do not provide enough attention to followup to see how the reader fares. This weakness is not entirely inherent in subject departmentation but in building plan, management, and supervision. And it is just as much a problem when readers have to visit a reference room, a circulating stack or room, a periodical room, and a document room to get materials on a subject.

3. The tendency to undue variation of departments in policies and quality of service, which is due in turn to lack of coordination of activities. This results in a greater number of department heads, who are harder to organize into a working cabinet than a smaller, higher-paid group with closer affiliations.[6] Departments cannot be allowed to operate in their own peculiar way. They must be tied together, guided, and aimed toward a common objective, through coordination, supervision, and cooperation.

## Balance of Advantage

Assuming the St. Louis, Boston, and Los Angeles libraries "as fair representatives of their types of organization," a 1947 study found

The subject-departmental type is the one best adapted to securing adequate and efficient service for the large public library. The functional type . . . St. Louis . . . appears inadequate to supply the needs of so large a city, while the mixed type of organization . . . Boston . . . though more nearly adequate to its task, is very expensive. . . . Only the subject-departmental . . . proved to be capable of providing for a large expansion of reference service at a low cost.[7]

## Organization by Subjects

In a city nearing a population of 80,000 or 90,000, the librarian and trustees need to consider whether to justify added cost for what many regard as their most significant service to the community. A well-administered, community-focused technical and business department, for example, may have a stimulating influence on local industry and trade. If its services could be measured for dollar value to each patron, it could be proved in many cities that the benefit far exceeds the cost.

### Specialized Knowledge Centers

It is the trained mind and special knowledge underlying subject departmentation that make it so useful to readers. The idea can be diagramed as the field of knowledge arranged in its logical sequence by whatever classification the library uses, with a specially informed staff at service desks where the materials center on a few large major headings. Space near each service center is provided for a sufficient number of readers; separate rooms are not essential. Modern buildings are increasingly laid out as large general spaces. This permits a close relationship of subject departments created at the start, as well as a possible subsequent redivision of space without changing the building structure or breaking the logical sequence of materials.

### Keeping the Materials in Natural Sequence

If subject departments are thought of primarily as special-service points or reader areas, within the library's normally arranged total resources, we arrive at the crux of the matter and can reduce costs to salaries and minimum equipment. True, because periodicals and vertical file material play an increasing part in the type of service given, more racks and file cases must be bought. But if, by thus bringing all the subject materials together, the volume of more substantial and convenient service is greater than that of other arrangements, then subject departmenting is hardly a disadvantage.

### Building Plan Influences Separation

If a subject department is created in an existing building, immediately a series of practical difficulties arise. Nearly all buildings before 1940 were

The Simplicity of Subject Departmentation

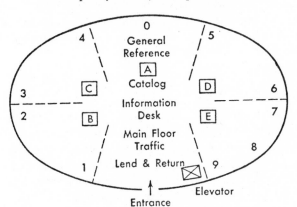

It is not necessary to separate subjects into their own walled rooms, scattered over the architect's plans. Consider the special service points as set up at strategic subject centers, A–E, in the complete circle of knowledge as shown here, arranged in the library's normal classification sequence, 1–10. By keeping traffic to other floors close to the entrance, main-floor traffic is limited to those using main-floor departments. The catalog and overall information desk are close to the center. The general reference department, the keystone, is at the rear center. The subject entrances and service desks are close together to save everyone's time. If the space can be found, nothing need be disrupted when needs and funds justify an additional subject service point. And if a full-time staff is not available, the situation is about as it had previously been.

influenced by restrictive traditional architectural patterns and library organization. Getting the book, the reader, and the service space together on the main floor may seem impossible. Experience shows that "art and music" can be detached from the circle of knowledge with least penalty, but this requires assurance that adequate personnel will be available to staff the department in its isolation on another level.

Physical separation from the rest of the adult collection involves (1) inconvenience and extra steps for staff and readers hour after hour—a costly penalty; (2) probable duplication of the card catalog for this portion of the collection; (3) the handicap of confusion for all concerned because most subjects are tied to others, scattered over the building; and (4) the necessity for inside telephones and other devices for quick interdepartmental communication.

*Special Service Without Special Room*

The idea of staff specialization without departments may well deserve consideration, especially by large libraries with no early hope of a modern, open-plan building. The idea has received little attention in public library practice, perhaps because of the continued neglect and understaffing of all forms of reference and reader advisory service. Borrowing a social worker term the best solution may be to "case load" the librarians for public library service. In college libraries today the practice is common with bibliographers serving faculty groups in a client relationship.

### The Separate Department

Undoubtedly the public would be better served by more subject departmentalization. Libraries could well study the rearrangement of the main floor to accommodate one or two subject departments. This would entail putting parts of the book stock closer to reader space, or vice versa, even at the cost of considerable structural change. A frequent possibility is the major extension of the old building to the sidewalk with the new space completely open and connected effectively to the old, with devices to overcome difference in levels. In planning a new building, it is easier to relate subject departments properly.

### Coordination

The dangers from isolation arising from concentrating in one subject area can be reduced by listing overlapping subjects and developing staff awareness of the need to keep posted on the work of other departments. Frequent meetings to discuss common aims and problems are helpful. Careful supervision and tying together by an executive will coordinate behind-the-scenes departments, the branches, various reader groups, and public relations.

## Function of General Reference Among Subject Departments

If all the fields of knowledge are broken up into six or eight divisions, there is still general material that can best serve the reader at a central clearance point, a general reference or general service department. General reference is not primarily to answer easy, quick questions in all fields. Each subject department has its own flow of such questions, which often develop into intensive search, and general reference also has its quota of difficult, long-search questions, particularly in the field of national and general bibliography. Numerous libraries find it profitable to have a general information desk, supplied with dictionary and *World Almanac,* to handle questions, including many telephone inquiries, that obviously can be answered in a minute or two with little search and at the point where most questions are usually presented by readers. The amount and variety of this general reference work is surprising indeed, especially its servicing of general and national bibliographies. Several large-city libraries with six or eight busy subject departments find that the general reference room is as busy as any of the special departments. To cope with the increasing volume of telephone inquiries, some libraries, notably the Atlanta Public Library, have set up telephone information centers in the general reference room, thus freeing the reference staff to give walk-in patrons more individual attention.

The more frequent situation, with only two or three subject departments, leaves the "general" department with the bulk of reader service. Some major subjects, such as history, biography, and travel cut across current events or economic and social problems. Thus, there has been some tendency recently to leave these more closely interrelated major subjects, as well as the general and collective materials, in a general service department. In several recent buildings a reference center is set up near the general reference books and the adult circulating books in the 800s, 900s, part of the 300s, and the 000s. Such a large general service operation appears to have been dictated in several cases by inadequacy of main-floor space and budget limitations.

Whether to departmentalize political science and sociology; education, philosophy, and religion; history, biography, and travel; and literature as four more departments involves not only costs of staffing and overhead but an understanding of the cross ramifications between some of these subjects and the difficulties of laying them out in the building. A study of reader questions and how they are handled in general and in special departments, such as technology, and the degree of reader satisfaction, in keeping with the constantly increasing specialization of the times, would seem to give the benefit of the argument to creating from five to eight subject departments in cities of 500,000 and upward. A general reference department will still be needed.

### The Subject Department Head's Work

Here we stress the development of (1) the special collections; (2) the special knowledges and abilities of the staff; and (3) the penetration of the department's special services into more and more of the subject-activity centers of the community.

*Developing Staff Knowledge*

The head of a subject department has to stimulate the development of his staff's background knowledge in the special subject field. Increasingly, he (1) appoints assistants with strong subject specialties who have a second master's degree;[8] (2) sees that they are allowed to remain in the subject department where their knowledge is of greatest help, and not rotated in other departments for mental exercise or "career development" by the chief librarian, who may not realize the penalty to readers when the accumulated special knowledge of an assistant is lost; and (3) frees them from rigid schedules and routine clerical work, so that they can produce more effectively.[9]

The subject specialist normally begins with considerable knowledge of at least one segment of the subject field. He extends his knowledge to make it fit the user needs of his department. His knowledge must include as well the scope, purpose, and value of many individual books.[10, 11]

### Community Contacts

The subject department head, and his subject specialists, should be encouraged to develop outside contacts. Art librarians should meet local museum directors; music librarians should visit with conductors of the symphony orchestra; business librarians should sit down with corporate directors. Through such interaction, librarians learn about the interests of their clients. This interaction is vital to the functioning of the library.[12]

### Drawing on Outside Information Sources

The subject department should draw upon the resources of other libraries by using (1) interlibrary loan; (2) union lists; (3) descriptive guides to other libraries' special collections; and (4) photocopies, instead of borrowing the material itself.

## The Three Most Common Departments

With the exception of Marian C. Manley's *Business Information: How to Find and Use It* (New York: Harper, 1955, 265 p.) on business departments, there seems to be no detailed manual for any subject department. Several brief general descriptions appear in library periodicals, but nothing about their management.

### Art and Music

Art and music because of their popularity are the most frequently found subject departments. Art received more attention in earlier years, whereas today music has taken the lead because of the influences of radio, TV, and musical recordings. Most librarians feel more competent in one or the other than in both, but the cost of a staff to operate two separate departments makes it practical to combine art and music in one department, sometimes labeled fine arts. These subjects can be separated from the general library collections with less penalty than can any other major subjects. They are often placed on the second or third floor without great inconvenience, if there is an elevator.

Before organizing an art and music department, one must consider whether or not it is to be allied with tapes, pictures, prints, slides, and other audiovisual materials. The current trend is to group all materials on a certain topic together to provide a strong information center. In this way a researcher on the art of Alexander Calder or the music of John Cage will be able to look at all materials on the subject in one place. Ideally, one would find the literature on art near reproductions of art, and the literature on music within easy reach of scores, recordings, and tapes.

Of eleven large urban libraries surveyed, nine have art and music departments. The placement of recordings, pictures, prints, tapes, and other audiovisual materials in these libraries varied. Some had audiovisual materials combined with the books in the art and music department; others treated them as a separate form and put them in a different location. Storage and care factors appear to have had an impact on these decisions.

William J. Dane points out that since art books "are truly expensive," there is a rising interest among public libraries in cooperative acquisitions and availability of these books. One might add that the same could apply to films, and in fact many libraries do participate in cooperative systems for films only.

Dane adds:

The use of videotape as both a document and as art work is in the embryonic stage in public library collections, but it seems that this new medium will be found more and more in public library collections. Videotape is valuable as an archive of the opinions and creations of living artists and musicians. They may freely and openly discuss their lives and works as there is a minimum of burdensome equipment and special lighting connected with videotape; spontaneity comes easily in such natural surroundings. There is a fascination in watching George Segal create a sculptured figure or listening to Roy Lichtenstein discuss his technique while painting. Tapes come in relatively small reels which are simple to operate and may be viewed privately on a television monitor. Many artists have been searching for methods of avoiding the exclusive decorator object and some artists are making works which are video art and which can be quickly reproduced in unlimited copies.

Of particular interest to the administrator is Dane's comment that "slides, photographs, and videotapes have acquired new importance in art collections, for visual documentation is essential to assuring the permanence of the work of art." The artwork may disappear but the documentation endures; this is especially important in the case of vernacular art. Standards for documentation and procedures and a base for centralized cataloging and cooperative projects are pressing concerns of art libraries. The three major obstacles slowing the development of visual media collections in public libraries are the usual ones: shortage of space, lack of equipment, and insufficient funds.[13]

*Business and Industry*

If this heading were "Business and Economics,"it would more clearly define the narrow scope of what many consider the most important subject field a library should develop; for many communities, business or manufacturing is the chief source of livelihood. The public library in a city of 500,000 is generally justified in creating a separate department to serve business, financial, and office work clientele.

Here again, as an economy, some cities of over 500,000 and most smaller ones from 100,000 up have considered they are carrying specialization far enough if they combine business, industry, technology, and science into a department concerned with practical, everyday working subjects. A good short label is difficult to choose, but these four subjects are all so related that in the light of recent library progress it may be held that any city of 100,000, and any industrialized city of 90,000 or even 80,000, can hardly escape the need to give special service in this area, assuming that it has a strong general reference service.

Required materials and equipment include 8,000 to 10,000 books on open shelves alongside thirty to fifty reader seats, a departmental catalogue if the service desk is over 75 feet from the main catalogue, display racks for 150 to 200 periodical titles, and ten to twenty four-tray vertical file cases. These are just a start for a department that is almost certain to bring heavy response, if the staff is capable and the potential clientele is made to realize the valuable help that awaits inquiries. Publicity plays a large part in developing service to business and technical workers.

## Local History and Genealogy

Many libraries have some collection of local materials, though often no one department or person is directly responsible for their care, servicing, and development. Increased leisure and promotion by historical societies have stimulated interest in local history to the point that most main libraries need to consider special service in a separate room or department.

Before deciding on space, personnel, and coverage, one must look into the library's relations with any local history society; this may be largely a prestige group more interested in museums or in genealogy than in a working informational library. Duplication of materials and activities is likely, but cannot the library and the society cooperate? Whoever heads the library's local history department should discover and stimulate local enthusiasts to prepare and write scholarly materials as well as popularizations for local papers and for young people.

Housing a local historical society in the library building is not undertaken lightly. The future should be safeguarded by a clear understanding that the society's printed materials are to be available to everyone according to the library's schedule, and that the society is to finance the salary of a competent (not merely a deserving) person who works under library regulations—someone to collect materials, stimulate their use, and develop a reference service. Not many historical societies located outside the state capitals realize they can promote their cause through cooperation with the local library. For this reason the library generally must go ahead on its own.

Many public libraries collect and preserve printed and manuscript materials about their areas, including maps, reports, biographical sketches, newspapers, posters, notices, clippings, publications of societies, and photographs (thousands having historical significance can be gathered if properly labeled, simply by asking the owners to lend the negatives). Public libraries are collecting additional information on tape as the oral history movement gains momentum.[14] Moss offers some practical guidelines in this field.[15] Much can be done by volunteer enthusiasts, including Friends of the Library, and by the stimulation of exhibits and publicity, with recognition to donors and helpers. Many family records full of vital information are destroyed every year, when door-to-door solicitation would bring them to the library. The state library or commission can lead in encouraging local libraries through statewide cooperative indexing and union catalogs, as in Illinois.

Organization for local history service involves a high degree of resourcefulness and ability to ask for help, as well as supervision and encouragement of helpers. Branch libraries can gather neighborhood materials. This can be done by volunteers. Invariably a library that collects and attempts to sort and prepare this material is swamped with details; the head needs to break down the various aspects of the work—discovering, requesting, receiving, acknowledging (with carbons of "thank-you" records filed chronologically as a sort of accession book that becomes very useful), cataloging, indexing, publicizing, preparing exhibits, answering questions, and encouraging the preparation of needed articles and leaflets on local subjects.

Anything more than superficial service in the field of genealogy involves expensive material and trained assistance. Only a few large and hardly any small libraries attempt it. They cannot afford it, and most taxpayers resent costly activity that benefits only a few. Instead they refer it to state libraries or state historical libraries, which can handle competent genealogical searching on a large scale and capitalize on the investment.[16] Some libraries have a printed explanation as to why they cannot afford to attempt this kind of intensive search. In other libraries a time fee is charged, or inquirers are referred to a list of competent local genealogists who charge a fee. Local history departments frequently include genealogies of those few families that have played an outstanding part in community development.

### Other Subject Departments

We forgo discussing further special departments because the patterns of division are so differently worked out. With so much of the population in school and college, education is a subject that needs special service. But in the last few years it has usually been combined either with the 300s, sociology, or with the 100s and 200s. Social, economic, local, and world problems play a large part in American thinking at present. A large department for these subjects has seemed to some librarians in the 300,000-to-500,000 population group to be a practical compromise between too many and too few departments, who instead round out the circle with another large department called "The Humanities" but comprising only the 800s and 900s.[17]

A quick random sample of libraries serving populations of 100,000 and more, as listed in the 1978 American Library Directory, shows a considerable variety in the approach to subject departments. Other than the three most frequent ones mentioned above, combinations included literature and history, literature and philosophy, literature and language, history and social science, history and biography, and travel, world affairs, and social science. The problem of handling recreation, which Dewey placed with fine arts, is not clarified in the libraries sampled. One library specifically included it: fine arts and recreation. Obviously, recreation has little to do with fine arts and might be better put into a popular library.

The fact is that subject departmentation and user interests often do not run along parallel paths. Classification of all knowledge into various compartments is all very well for the classifier, and it has to be done in order to bring order out of the mass of print and to facilitate retrieval. But classification is an abstraction, whereas the real-life needs of people are not. There is no ready answer to the dilemma. Subject interest groups—topical approaches to the materials cutting across classification lines—serve browsers but provide problems to users seeking particular books that should be in a particular spot on the shelf. There is much work to be done in this area. Perhaps the growth of automation will yield a satisfactory response to needs of browser, researcher, and user looking for various kinds of information, which will not now be found in one place in the classification.

## Notes

1. Althea Warren, "Departmental Organization of a Public Library by Subject," in Carleton B. Joeckel, ed., *Current Issues in Library Administration* (Chicago: University of Chicago Press, 1939), pp. 110–34.
2. Rose Vainstein, "What's New in Public Library Service to Business," *Library Journal* 85 (Mar. 1, 1960): 913–18. Also, "Public Library Service to Business," *Library Journal* 84 (May 1, 1959): 1402–06.
3. Errett W. and John McDiarmid, *The Administration of the American Public Library* (Chicago: American Library Association, 1943), p. 121. Chapters 5 and 6 discuss subject departments at length.
4. Archibald W. McClellan, "Organization of a Public Library for Subject Specialization," *Library Association Record* 57 (August 1955): 296–303.
5. Ervin J. Gaines, "The Personnel Needed for Tomorrow's Main Libraries," *Library Trends* 20 (April 1972): 744.
6. A detailed list of difficulties is quoted from Warren, op. cit., with comment, in McDiarmids, op. cit., pp. 75–85. Also in John L. Gardner, "Some Thoughts on Subject Departmentalization in a Large Public Library," *Library Association Record* 57 (July 1955): 254–60.
7. Rose B. Phelps, "The Effect of Organization Patterns on the Adequacy and Efficiency of Reference Service in the Large American Public Library," *Library Quarterly* 17 (October 1947): 281–95.

8. Billy R. Wilkinson, "Staff for Library Service," *Library Trends* 23 (October 1974): 259. See also Robert D. Stuart, *An Area Specialist Bibliographer: An Inquiry into His Role* (Metuchen, N.J.: The Scarecrow Press, 1972).

9. Gaines, op. cit., p. 745.

10. Hester R. Hoffman, ed., *The Reader's Adviser and Bookman's Manual*, 9th ed. (New York: R. R. Bowker, 1960). Major revisions and new sections make this essential in looking at the literature of any subject field. Excellent annotations and details. Some earlier editions were referred to as *Bessie Graham's Bookman's Manual.*

11. *Subject Guide to Books in Print* (New York: R. R. Bowker, published annually). This invaluable quick index, with nearly half a million entries in the latest issue, supplements headings in the local card catalog even for books a library may have, as well as for many items it may borrow by library interloan.

12. Gaines, op. cit., p. 748. See also Thomas J. Michalak, "Library Services to the Graduate Community: The Role of the Subject Specialist Librarian," *College and Research Libraries* 37 (May 1976): 257–65.

13. William J. Dane, "Organizational Patterns in Public Libraries," *Library Trends* 23 (January 1975): 330, 342–43.

14. "Oral History Programs Report Steady Progress," *Library Journal* 99 (Jan. 1, 1974): 15.

15. William W. Moss, *Oral History Program Manual* (New York: Praeger, 1974).

16. Marian McFadden, "Skeletons in the Closet—A Cooperative Venture," *Library Journal* 81 (Jan. 1, 1956): 50–52. Describes arrangement to combine the Indianapolis Public Library's endowed genealogy collection with that at the state library. See also two other articles in this issue.

17. Lee Ash, ed., *Subject Collections: A Guide to Special Collections in American Libraries*, 4th ed. rev. and enl. (New York: R. R. Bowker, 1975). Arranged by detailed subject with 3,000 additions and major data about each of 20,000 collections. Invaluable for information seeking and interlibrary loans. This remains the priority work.

# 11 Young Adult Services

The library's service to the intermediate or young adult group is considered here—directly after the major adult public service departments—as an extension of adult work to a slightly lower age level rather than as an upward extension of children's materials and viewpoints. We note first some social conditions that pose a national challenge and the public library's response to these;[1] second, the organization and resources of young adult work and how it is managed; third, the range of services given; and fourth, the relationships of young adult work to other units of the library and to outside agencies.

## Challenge and Response

### Challenge

In our American schools children typically attend elementary school from their sixth to their fourteenth year, and from fourteen to eighteen they are in high school. Nearly all libraries issue an adult borrower's card at fourteen and consider as an adult anyone who has completed eighth grade or is older than fourteen. In fact, many libraries issue one card to all now. Young people do not make an easy adjustment from children's room to adult departments, just as they do not make an easy adjustment from childhood to adulthood. Adolescence is a crucial period in the development of the human being, a time characterized by competing needs. For example, there is the need to prepare for coming adult responsibilities. At the same time a need exists to experiment with varying lifestyles, to discover self. In addition, there is the need for challenging experiences that will provide opportunities for development.

Today, with America's commitment to mass education, nearly 98.9 percent of twelve- to fifteen-year-olds, 94 percent of sixteen-year-olds, 86.2 percent of seventeen-year-olds, and 55 percent of eighteen-year-olds were enrolled in school in October, 1971, according to the 1970 census. Recent high school graduation rates are also high. These and other factors create greater demands on books and library service—for example, the use of multiple sources instead of the single textbook, and the broadening curriculum to provide more vocational courses, more science, and other subjects for the talented. There are new problems of growing up, sex, exploring the world of adult activities, choosing a life work, getting a first job, the restless search for action, excitement, and entertainment. Adolescence is the stage when people struggle to understand themselves and their relations to others and the world about them. Like all other people, young adults wish to be recognized as individuals and to be allowed opportunities for creativity and growth.

According to the 1972 U.S. Office of Education National Panel on High Schools and Adolescent Education, contemporary young adults are more able to take advantage of such opportunities than their predecessors. Adolescents in the United States today are maturing more rapidly both physically and emotionally. Improvements in nutrition, parental and medical care, and housing have led to a physical maturation two and a half to three and a half years ahead of that experienced by their forebears born a hundred years ago. The panel points out that this increased physical capacity allows adolescents to participate in many activities on a par with adults. And many do exercise this capacity in areas that are approved (such as athletics) as well as in areas that are discouraged (for instance, sexual activity and drugs). Exposure to experiences once encountered at a later age by earlier generations has resulted in a certain emotional sophistication.

The books sought by young people now deal with adult subjects. Proms and dances used to be popular high school social activities. Such activities now appeal mainly to junior students. The many children being born to teenagers reflect a sophistication of experience, as does their participation in activities involved in preserving the quality of life on the planet. The panel reports that major concerns of youth, as measured by public opinion polls, include crime, violence, and ecology. It concludes, "Perhaps most significant is the fact that today's adolescents have proclaimed their own culture— a youth culture or counterculture—which they see as largely separate from and superior to that of adults. While one may question the extent of its reality, the self-conscious character of this culture is evidence of increased experiential maturity."[2]

*Response*

Public libraries are attempting to respond to these challenges of adolescence. While young adult library service can be traced back to before World War I, a major landmark was the opening of the Robert Louis Stevenson Room at Cleveland in 1925, and a rapid spread of such facilities came after World War II. Today hundreds of libraries provide organized special services for the fourteen-to-eighteen-year-old group.

Service to young adults has been increasingly related to their school needs and to their maturational needs. Some libraries are attempting to meet the needs of out-of-school youth. The Denver Public Library has set up a "Catch-up Center," a reading improvement program. In particular, service has focused on the needs of disadvantaged young people. Stimulated by the 1966 ALA work, "Guidelines for Library Service to Disadvantaged Youth," much has been accomplished in programming, media and paperbacks, outreach, and cooperation with community agencies. Adolescents are determining the shape many programs are taking, and the result often has little to do with books. Many young people and librarians see libraries as communication centers where information and ideas can be exchanged in dynamic ways. Surprisingly, many programs for the disadvantaged young adult are similar in content and format to those produced for the advantaged young adult. Some common concerns are drugs, self-defense, cars, legal rights, astrology, sex education, sports, black history, folk music, fashion, and adolescent psychology. A series on drugs at Maryland's Prince George's County Memorial Library included talks on drug legislation and addiction and a showing of films on drugs. The Boston Public Library invited black teenagers to an evening of soul sound called, "Come hear your sisters sing the music of today."[3]

Most public libraries have all they can do, in serving young adults, to meet their needs as students and to provide them with recreational and general interest materials. In this aspect of young adult service alone, the traffic and the problems are overwhelming. The majority of high schools have inadequate school libraries. Most school libraries are open only half an hour after closing, and not at all at night, on weekends, or during school holidays; the factor of school bus transit poses great difficulties in changing school library hours. Few have the range of materials to be found in even the average public library. Under the circumstances, high school students can be expected to be regular users of the local public library, and in fact they often come in such numbers as to constitute a problem. The justification for public library service to high school students, even in providing them with curriculum-related materials, is simply that they too are part of the total clientele of the public library and their library service needs are not being adequately met.

## A Philosophy of Library Service for Young Adults

In 1973 the Public Library Association published goals and guidelines for community library service, by age levels. The statement on young adult services was prepared by a task force of thirteen librarians selected from all parts of the country. Excerpts follow:

This paper represents a philosophy of library service for young adults. Libraries dealing with young adults should be alert and responsive to young people's needs, constitutional rights, and their roles as taxpayers and consumers.

What follows is an attempt to make explicit the background philosophy of the library's role in relating the total community resources to young people's needs. Both the philosophy and suggestions for its implementation were determined by investigation, collective experience, research, and testimony taken from young adults themselves.

1. Young adults are entitled to open and equal access to all materials and services—regardless of cost, location, or format—and the right to a confidential client–librarian relationship, a nonjudgmental attitude, respect, and participation in the decision-making process of the library.

Discrimination because of age is as deplorable as discrimination because of race, sex, or class. . . . No library has the right to prevent a young adult from reading, seeing, or hearing anything of his or her choice.

A single type of borrower's card should suffice for all age groups, permitting borrowing of all materials.

Young adults should be extended the use of films, recordings, audiovisual (including videotape) equipment, or anything else available to other users, regardless of cost or fragility.

All services—whether a reserve system, interlibrary loan, or help in translating letters—should be available to young adults. The quality of service should be uniformly high, without regard to the age of the client or staff judgment as to the seriousness of a request.

Young adults are entitled to assurance that information about materials used or questions asked will not be divulged to any third party.

Since young adults do make up a sizable portion of real and potential library users, they should be consulted along with other age groups in relation to library service planning.

Young adults should be eligible to, and should, serve on library boards. They would thus be able to advocate the interests of a group neglected in most communities.

Youth councils should be established in order to increase young adult participation in the development of library services to meet the needs of young people. . . .

2. Young adults should have full access to materials in order to permit individual decisions to be made with a full understanding of options and alternatives. . . .

This often requires the creation and updating of informational tools, such as directories of community resources—institutional and human—annotated lists of recommended media, and the repackaging of information that synthesizes information found in both formal and informal sources. . . .

Young adult specialists should recognize that school-assignment-originated information needs may also be expressions of legitimate personal needs. . . .

3. The special needs and interests and the uniqueness of young adults must be recognized in library services and materials.

Materials of special interest to young adults should be selected by young adult specialists, with some systematic input from young adults, regardless of where the materials will be housed; e.g., the young adult specialists should be involved with film, periodical, records selection, as well as book selection. . . .

Areas [should] be provided that take into account the needs of young adults.

The location and design of these areas, as well as alternatives to conventional library furniture, require careful planning in order to integrate them within the total framework of library services. Talking, typing, and listening are some of the activities that need to be accommodated. . . .

A variety of attractive and frequently changed displays should be provided to help young adults discover library resources of surprising interest.

The atmosphere of the library and the accessibility and attitude of library staff members should enable young adults to find sympathetic adult listeners.

4. Libraries should develop a knowledge of and act as liaisons with other agencies providing information services. The library should identify gaps in community services for young adults and advocate improvement of those services through agencies, governmental offices, etc. . . .

Specialized services to which young adults need access, such as career guidance centers, other types of libraries, family counseling services, schools, and crisis intervention centers, are available in many communities.[4]

## Organization and Resources

### Organization

Experience in young adult work has pointed up a few principles but as yet no one pattern applicable to all communities. Service to young adults should be organized in connection with the adult departments and not with the children's department. Because these young people are close to adulthood and are moving away from childhood views and ways and interests, young adult librarians should relate their point of view and background of service to those of adults. To meet their needs, the adult circulation and reference departments are indispensable. They also involve the upper level of children's materials, the usual run of adult resources, specialized materials such as films, and many of the special techniques or functions, such as group discussion leadership, adult services, and especially reference service. Young adult services should be designed to introduce students of high school age to the library's adult facilities. It is not necessary or desirable that work with young adults be closely tied to or completely identified with any one adult department or be separated and isolated. For organizational and administrative purposes, the young adult librarian is often assigned to the adult department, or to the popular library if there is one. The New York Public Library, with numerous branches, has a young adult specialist in most branches and a coordinator of services for young adults, who stimulates, supervises, and ties together the citywide service.

### Location

Service to young adults has to have an operating center somewhere in the building. Its core is a trained mind and a service desk. Its organizational place is influenced by its physical locus, and this is often dictated by the building plan. The minimum arrangement is a corner of the adult reading room or a section of shelves, in the midst of adult materials and services. Many large city libraries have a separate room for young adults (though in recent buildings this idea is unusual), or a fairly large area of the general adult reading room with a separate staff and desk. A few very large libraries have tried having a separate building, but to give the services needed this demands a large duplication of nonfiction and reference books and trained reference staff. Teenagers wish neither to be isolated nor to be refused access to the regular adult facilities. They do not like to be considered a special or problem group. Some librarians feel that even a separate young adult room segregates its patrons.

## Staff

A major factor in the success of young adult work is the personality, technical competence, and ability of its head and staff. Young adults are likely to turn away from unattractive, unresponsive, and unprepared staff members. Those who work with young people need a genuine liking for them and a sincere desire to treat them as adults without expecting them always to react as adults. These staff attitudes cannot be easily developed. They are more likely to be found in younger assistants with fresh and open minds, who can learn to invite, receive, and refrain from comment on young people's opinions, thoughts, and reactions.

Technical competence means a knowledge of library tools and methods of operation and of the books written for teenagers, the psychology of adolescence, and modern high school curriculum and teaching methods.

Most public libraries do well to have one fully qualified librarian assigned full-time to young adult work, but desirably every branch should have a young adult librarian as well as a children's librarian and an adult services librarian, the latter concentrating on reference and advisory help. Often the one full-time young adult person has nonprofessional assistants assigned, training and supervising them and helping them build their knowledge of books. He or she will develop the program of work with young adults, initiate new programs and projects, build up the Y.A. collection, as supplementing the adult collection, and maintain constructive relations with other departments, with the high school libraries, and with any available student advisory group.

## Materials

Novels or nonfiction written expressly for the tastes and interests of young people of high school age have developed mostly since about 1940. Many adult books and some children's books will continue close to the hearts of young adults, but there are more good books each year, neither juvenile nor adult in their maturity level, in their values, in their depth of detail, and in their subject matter; these speak to the condition of young people with greater insight and to greater purpose than ever before. Careful selection, based on high standards, is needed.[5]

The Y.A. area should include new and old titles, adult as well as juvenile, in all main subject fields and especially fiction, for reference work and for lending. There should also be available career and vocational guidance materials, several hundred college and university catalogues or microforms of them, currently useful pamphlets, an array of consequential magazines, records near a record player with earphones, audio cassettes, and access to the library's files of bound or microfilmed periodicals, newspapers, and video materials. Reader interest classification encourages individual browsing and general reading. Plastic book jackets, interesting displays, bright colors, comfortable furniture, and an air of informality and of relaxed discipline will go far to provide the desirable setting.

## Services to the Individual Reader

The major purpose is to attract the young adult to books thought to be useful and relevant in enriching life, developing personality, increasing knowledge, or giving worthy objectives and incentives. Most young adults like some guidance, but they need even more to be helped to develop their own standards and judgment in order to become self-reliant. Indirect methods of stimulation and guidance include book lists, book displays and exhibits, book talks, book reviews written by young people themselves and published or given over the radio or television, book discussion groups, and activity clubs. Other possible devices include high school book fairs, participation in vocational guidance programs, film showings, library tours, visits of public library personnel to high school classes and assemblies, and activity programs with guest authors or other celebrities. Publicity can reach eighth-grade classes in the spring just before they graduate, when psychologically they are most ready for "growing up" to the young adult room.

### Reference Work

Answering information questions of high school students involves two major policies. To what extent shall the public library offer this service to students from schools with their own libraries? If given by the public library, should it be a function of the special young adult room or of the general adult reference department? Whatever the theoretical considerations, the fact is that for very practical reasons the public library is giving more and more school-connected service. High school students are as legitimate patrons of the public library as any other group of people who may or may not have their own special system of libraries.

In the small or branch library nearly all usable space is in one public room, with one public service desk or at most only one adult service desk. There is heavy pressure from other patrons and other work. The result in many libraries and in the average branch is the familiar one of too small a staff and too few trained people trying to do too many things and attempting under these circumstances to give reference service that requires special knowledge and skills.

The penalty for attempting reference service in a separate young adult room is not only the duplication of materials but also the duplication of the skill and salary of the trained librarian absorbed in reference work with no time for personal counseling on out-of-school reading. We suggest a Quiet Adult Room, screened off from the noise of high school groups, as a device to protect the interest of adults who complain of noise and confusion. A compromise is to duplicate in another room some of the most-used reference books and thus provide almost self-service to the many students who can look up answers to their own questions and thus relieve some pressure in the reference department. On the other hand, if a library can afford the services of a trained Y.A. librarian, there are three good reasons for diverting high school students' reference questions to that person. This service provides a natural transition to the encouragement of individually motivated reading; the young adult librarian needs to know the current assignments and curricular needs of the students properly to select books or to arrange programs; and in most cases the adult reference desk is too busy with older adults to do justice to the high school students. But in any case the public librarian does not write the essay, review the grammar, advise on the outline of a composition, or direct a study hall.

### Curriculum-Related Services

The needs of high school students today for library materials and library service are rapidly expanding and have to be met by the provision of more and better materials and of new and different facilities, and by more and better publicity, both in their school libraries and their public libraries. The public library should build on this situation and develop its services, within the limits of available resources, so as to increase its influence in the lives and reading of such students.

### Adolescent Interests

The young adult librarian needs to be aware of and to understand the concerns of young people as they mature. Besides the study of current literature of the psychological and sociological aspects of youth, this involves a definite objective: a close personal relationship with as many individual young people as possible, trying to learn from them before attempting to advise them. Young people often need and welcome the calm advice and indirect assistance of an adult who is not a parent and not a teacher. The librarian's role as informal counselor is an aspect of library service under development and exploration.[6] Maturational topics include boy–girl relationships, choosing a life's work, drugs, grooming, preparing for and getting into college, and hobbies and other nonschool activities. While the library is only one of several sources of information for the modern teenager, the voluntary, self-chosen, and ever-present assistance available in a well-stocked and well-managed library with a tactful and effective staff is a major and much appreciated asset to the young adult. Books often provide the best help for solving personal problems, even when a community has other organized facilities.

The facts of life are often far easier learned through books at the right age level, especially for the shy youngster, than in any other way. How to maintain one's own standard of conduct in the face of group opinion and other aspects of character development are often well revealed through books, suggested by carefully prepared book lists, book talks, young people's book discussion groups, film showings, and other such indirect guidance devices. Before they are out of the teens, many young people are married or engaged, or seriously contemplating marriage; as a result, the library needs some of the many good books now available for young people on this subject.

The young adult room is the logical place for the best up-to-date information on choosing an occupation, for this is the age group likely to use it most. Pamphlets constitute the best of this literature, when organized for self-service and allowed to circulate. Novels may convey the spirit of different occupations, which is as important to the young person trying to decide on a career as the more factual information of nonfiction books on careers.

About half of all high school graduates do *not* plan to go to college.[7] For them, getting a job, civil service examinations, military service regulations and opportunities, how to handle oneself in an employment interview, and other aspects of everyday work life are pressing concerns. Books can be of great help, provided the staff knows and cares enough to have the materials ready and publicizes them. Teenagers need this help to bridge the gap from school to work; they are at a disadvantage because they often know little about the kinds of jobs open or about their own skills. About 20 percent of sixteen- to nineteen-year-olds in the labor force are unemployed.[8]

Those who go to college will also have problems and questions, as on college entrance examinations, the choice of college, scholarships and other means of financing one's way, and preparing for college life. Printed materials are always needed in these areas. The public library administers no aptitude tests, but the young adult librarian should know where they can be taken and should know of local training agencies, technical schools, guidance services, and so forth. If public libraries begin to organize and staff themselves to give greater attention to the problems and information requests of individual readers—which many consider a current need for development if libraries are to serve their major function—it is likely that the better libraries will provide selected materials to back up trained counselor help for the thousands in the seventeen-to-twenty-five-year-old group who don't know where to turn for intelligent, objective guidance in their jobs, their leisure activities, and their life planning; the right book or magazine article can often be "prescribed" successfully.

The world of personal hobbies, sports, and other out-of-school activities of young people is one in which books are always useful. The hobby of reading may stem from encouraging personal libraries and book buying by high-school-age students, by means of paperbacks and book club titles and by prizes or certificates redeemable in books at a local store. In these and other ways, the public library can see that books play a major part in the lives of busy young adults today.

## Working with Other Agencies

### With Other Units of the Library

Young adult work in public libraries must draw on and contribute to the activities of other library departments, other institutions outside the library, and the young people themselves. It needs to be correlated with the children's department, from which its patrons are just graduating, and the special purpose departments, which young adults will have occasion to use, such as the reference department and audiovisual services. The young adult librarian has the obligation to contribute, from his or her special competence, to the progress of the other agencies, to cooperate with them on projects of mutual concern, and to draw from them what their specialization enables them to contribute to the welfare and progress of Y.A. work. Established procedures and fields of interest may have to be modified to provide for the handling of young adult material, services, and programs, and staff members need to be so reminded.

### With Agencies Outside the Library

The young adult librarian has a special relationship with the high schools, their teachers, and their school libraries. The school and the public library are natural allies; they have a common interest in developing worthwhile reading habits. The public library's program—however worthy—is one of many that are urged on the schools for emphasis and integration in the crowded curriculum. The public library staff must take the initiative to become familiar with the curriculum and teaching methods of the local schools and to work for cooperative projects. Some high school librarians resent the intrusions of the public library into their sphere of activity, but cooperative efforts are increasing. A recent survey in Suffolk County, New York, showed that joint services range from class visits by public librarians to book exchanges, supplemental purchasing, and library displays of student work.[9] In many cities a joint committee of appropriate administrators, teachers, and librarians discuss matters of mutual concern, resolve differences and difficulties and provide a means of communication. There could be periodic meetings of high school and young adult librarians to exchange information and to smooth operating relationships. A policy statement should be prepared spelling out the services that the high school libraries and the public library offer to teachers and students and how they supplement each other.

### With the Young People Themselves

Adolescents have their own lifestyle, which conforms to the standards of their own group. A student advisory board or youth council, given a forum to transmit opinions from its peers, should not be an empty gesture; it can tap the tremendous energy and enthusiasm of young people on matters in which they are truly interested. It should be consulted on policies affecting the library's Y.A. program, especially on those affecting the services of the young adult room. It can suggest appropriate and needed activities, select student book reports for publication by the library, produce TV or radio programs, create films, or conduct a survey of high school library users. High school students tend to commit themselves to programs that they have had a share in shaping and in conducting. In turn, the members of the student advisory board should receive recognition for their efforts, such as a newspaper story at the time of their appointment or on what they are accomplishing and a thank-you letter from the librarian when they conclude their work.

Young adult workers find their activities tremendously challenging as a way to bring books into the lives of young people, and the future of Y.A. service is full of promise.

### Notes

1. Margaret Mead, *Culture and Commitment: A Study of the Information Gap* (Garden City, N.Y.: Doubleday, 1970). An interesting background work.
2. National Panel on High School and Adolescent Education, *The Education of Adolescents* (Washington, D.C.: Government Printing Office, 1976), pp. 20–21.
3. Jane Manthorne, "Provisions and Programs for Disadvantaged Youth," *Library Trends* 20 (October 1971).
4. Public Library Association, "Community Library Services—Working Papers on Goals and Guidelines," *School Library Journal* 20 (September 1973): 7.
5. Richard Peck, "Communicating with a New Generation: A Challenge to Writers and Teachers," *Illinois Libraries* 57 (May 1975).

6. Sara Fine, "The Librarian as Youth Counselor," *Drexel Library Quarterly* 14 (January 1978). This article distills the latest thinking on the subject by psychologists.
7. National Center for Education Statistics, *Digest of Education Statistics* (Washington, D.C.: Government Printing Office, 1976), p. 62.
8. National Center for Education Statistics, *The Condition of Education* (Washington, D.C.: Government Printing Office, 1978), p. 14.
9. "Suffolk County, N.Y., Surveys School–Public Library Co-op," *Library Journal* 98 (Apr. 15, 1973): 1333.

# 12 Children's Services

From the administrative point of view, library service to children represents a solid potential for maximum return on investment, given favorable conditions and a reasonable and well-planned effort. Children between the ages of five and fourteen constitute about 18 percent of the nation's population. There are more than 33 million children enrolled in kindergarten through grade eight. The children in every community are in a prime state to be recipients of what the library has to offer: discovery of the world about them, near and far. They are full of questions: what will happen to me? what is this? what is that? what is going on? what happened before I got here? It is the age of genuine and undiminished curiosity, to which books and other media of communication and information, if provided with the skill of the practiced and dedicated children's worker, can make a useful response.

The children's room in the public library is free and open, unrestricted by the necessary rigidity of the classroom and media center. The children's librarian has a triple clientele: the child in his or her quest for enlightenment above and beyond the curriculum, or in extension of it; the parents who wish to have the best for their children; and the dedicated and interested teachers who look to the public library for materials that are complementary to their classroom teaching. There is a genuine interest on the part of most taxpayers, or at least of taxpaying parents, to have their children get a good start in life, with minds that will be trained to prepare them for the vicissitudes of life ahead. "I want my child to have a better start in life than I had" is a frequently heard comment.

The potential use of the children's services therefore may well run considerably over the 18 percent of the population that children comprise. Children in an inquisitive and learning mode are, or can become, much greater consumers of the library product than adults, who are more preoccupied with making a living or who may feel that they have learned about all they need to know.

Children are not a captive audience, but they have substantial needs for books and information.

A great body of literature about children's work in public libraries has been written by librarians and observers since the beginnings between 1890 and 1900.

## History and Purpose

Seymour and Layne write:

> The highly successful relationship between librarians and children goes back nearly a hundred years. In essence, it is a relationship initiated by the children themselves. They more or less elbowed their way into public libraries, which, with rare exception, had been thought of in the early days as centers of adult learning. Explains Harriet Long in *Rich the Treasure,* a book about public-library service to children, "In some instances [the children] were allowed to come in on Sunday afternoons, or a corridor or alcove was set aside for their use, so that they would not annoy the adults. These corridors and alcoves became rooms as children demanded more space." The 1890s saw the opening of children's rooms in major libraries across the nation. By the time of the great burst of branch-library building at the turn of the century (stimulated by the gifts of Andrew Carnegie), space set aside for children was accepted as a necessity.[1]

In the 1940s, Robert Leigh in the *Public Library Inquiry* wrote:

> Public library service to children is an impressive achievement. Library schools and libraries have developed children's librarians of great skill and personal effectiveness—not only are the children's librarians expert but also in the community they are recognized as such. These children's rooms and children's librarians have been the classic success in the public library.[2]

Dr. Lowell Martin, nationally known library educator, administrator and student of library theory and practice, described the public library work with children in the following cogent paragraph:

> The notable success in the public library has been children's service. This did not develop from observing which children came to the library and then determining what they wanted to read. On the contrary, a purpose was first established, that of introducing children to the best of literature for their age level. Staff members dedicated to this purpose and trained for this group were then hired, appropriate reading materials were acquired, and methods of stimulating and guiding reading were adopted. The children's collections were made up more of what patrons requested. Selection for children was done not by the standard of popularity but of quality. In time the children's librarians themselves have come to influence what constitute the most popular juvenile titles. Methods also have been fashioned to the purpose, with the story hour one of the distinctive educational devices contributed by the public library. It is interesting to note the response to this program, particularly because it was not based on reader demand alone. Conceivably, the high standard of children's services

of the public library might have been ignored for reasons no more complex than that children prefer to play in the street or sit before the television set than to read what some remote adults called librarians consider to be "good books." Many a noble program that ought to get response has shriveled up before public indifference. Yet public libraries today have a decidedly larger portion of the children than of adults as regular readers. The program, though developed years ago, still has full vitality. It works in the slum as well as in the suburb. And in the public mind it is thought of as one of the most natural and significant activities of the public library.[3]

## Goals and Guidelines

A fourteen-member task force of the Public Library Association—composed of children's librarians, children's work supervisors, library directors, branch service heads, a library educator, and a trustee—in 1973 prepared a working paper on children's services. In the preface to the report, the task force noted that it was "concerned with developing patterns of service that will best meet the needs of children. This is not a plan for public library service; rather it is a proposal for total community library service that requires planning by public libraries, schools, and any other community agencies concerned with children." Excerpts from the statement follow.

Libraries, together with other community agencies, should provide and ensure access by all children to information services that include a diversity of media, both print and nonprint; stimulate interest in reading and the use of all types of media; and provide opportunities to develop and use communication skills that will enhance the enjoyment of life. . . .

GUIDELINES [excerpts]

1. *Services:* To provide the highest quality service for each child, the library should:
Identify specific informational and recreational needs of children and select media to meet these needs.
Assure equal access to all the media and services of the library for all users, regardless of age, mental ability, physical handicaps, social characteristics, economic status, ethnic origin, or religion.
Assure the availability of full library service for every child within his own environment. Full library services consist of:

Media . . . and reference materials, with staff guidance available when desired
Programs and activities for individuals and groups
Interlibrary loan service
Referral service to other community, state, or national agencies
Innovative services and programs designed to involve the nonuser

Work with agencies, parents, and other individuals concerned with children, plan with them for meeting the varied needs of children, and interpret the library's services and media in such a way that these will be used to the fullest extent possible. . . .
Maintain a diversified public relations program to inform children and adults

concerned with the needs of children of the variety and availability of library services.

2. *Media:* To assure that children will have access to media (print and nonprint), to stimulate intellectual, creative responses, and to satisfy needs for information on a variety of subjects, the library should:

Establish, adopt, and continually revise a media selection policy that reflects the changing interests and needs of contemporary children, the plurality of viewpoints in society, and the diversity of people in the community. . . .

3. *Staff:* To ensure optimum of effectiveness in anticipating and fulfilling the objectives of service to children, the library should:

Employ professional staff to direct the service to children. Emphasis in professional education should be on the knowledge of library materials and the ability to relate them to the needs of children of various backgrounds and characteristics. Staff attitudes should be flexible, open, and friendly and should reflect an understanding of and respect for children. . . .

4. *Management:* To assure children the best possible library service, management efforts should be directed toward providing a framework for quality library service at all levels, and atmosphere and incentives that call forth the enthusiasm, commitment, and creativity of each staff member. Management should:

[Ensure that] members of the community, including children, . . . be involved in the planning process.

Implement interdepartmental planning, programming, budgeting, and the use of modern technology. . . .

Provide for participation in management by staff members at all levels. . . .

Ensure systematic and continuous evaluation of children's services. . . .[4]

A recent goals statement was written by a professor in the faculty of Library Science at the University of Toronto. She noted that

when libraries first opened their doors to children at around the turn of the century, there was reasonable consensus about what the library was supposed to do for children. Its first task was to provide educational books. Fiction was considered a frill to be discouraged. One great fear was that too much reading of library books might take children's minds off their schoolwork. The major requirements for children's books in libraries were that they must be both educational and morally unimpeachable.

The public library was viewed as a continuation of school more often than a supplement to it. Since the vast majority of children left school by the time they were fourteen years old, children's services were often designed to serve those young people who had no further access to formal education. Children's libraries served children in their last few years of school, after they had been taught to read. The library was supposed to begin a process of lifelong education by developing in children a habit of reading good literature.

Children's services at that time were much easier to evaluate, because libraries served a narrower age span of children in a comparatively homogeneous society. The library's goals were limited, and few people questioned their value. The library stood alone as the only social agency providing children with books, since most schoolwork was based on textbooks and encouraged little outside reading for classes.

GOALS MULTIPLIED

The goals advocated for children's library services today have grown from those comparatively simple beginnings. For example, the public library is often expected to:

Prepare preschool children for their school experiences by introducing them to books and other media;

Provide cultural experiences, such as drama, concerts, and film shows, for children;

Help children adjust to the community in which they live, especially minority children and immigrant children, by providing materials and programs that will keep them in touch with their homelands and introduce them to [their countries'] customs;

Prepare children for living in a multicultural society by providing materials and programs on various ethnic groups;

Help children adjust socially and psychologically to the demands of growing up— and this includes children with physical, mental, and psychological handicaps that present severe problems;

Compensate for deficiencies in homes and schools by providing services for children from homes without books, and for children whom the schools have not taught to read adequately;

Provide programs and materials that will compete with television for the children's interest;

Provide entertainment and a meeting place for children who have few other social outlets—especially during school holidays;

Provide supplementary material for school projects, at times when the school libraries are unavailable;

Provide a variety of materials and services that in one way or another will enrich children's lives (these may include toys, games, pets, craft classes, hobby clubs— the list is limited only by the librarians' imagination); and

Develop in children a lifelong love of reading—this is an old goal that has not been discarded.[5]

## Organization

It is safe to say that service to children is a universal component of the American public library. The work may be carried out in smaller libraries by a librarian or staff member who will also take care of the library needs of other members of the community, but there will be a collection of children's books. In the larger libraries, the children's department is a specialty, with a separate staff and quarters. It is said that children's services have developed proportionately more in the large cities than in small ones. Where the library has a staff of only three or four, it may well be the professional head of the library who gives special attention to children. With six or seven on the staff, and when the head and one assistant are professionally trained, the latter is generally assigned to attend to children's service, even though some time must be given to other work. The assistant becomes the "children's librarian." The others have to take a hand, and in-service instruction in children's books and service becomes one of the major jobs of the children's librarian. Typically the first specialization has been children's work. In most libraries of under 15,000 population the children's work is handled from one circulation desk and suffers from having all the staff undertake to give advice on children's books. A three-part major principle of managing children's service is (1) to assign the best-qualified person to be responsible for it; (2) to encourage this person to be developing constantly knowledge of children's books and understanding of children and how to serve them; and (3) to reduce the random attempts to serve children by other staff members who are less qualified.

As branch libraries increased, they usually included provision for service to children; the main problem was how to relate the branch children's librarians to the person in charge of the children's room at the central library, because usually that person was thought of as in general charge of children's work throughout the library. The most frequent answer has been to make the branch children's librarian administratively responsible to the branch librarian and to give the chief children's librarian some degree of technical supervision over the work done with children in the branches. The chief children's librarian is thus a line officer with regard to the central library children's room and possibly the central library services to grade schools, and a staff officer with regard to the branches in advising them on the selection of children's books, in arranging in-service training for children's librarians, in planning and promoting children's library programs and activities, and so forth. In most libraries large enough to have branches, the pattern of organization does not emphasize the unity and integration of children's work. This may be inevitable, but at least the results can be improved (1) by clearly assigning to the chief children's librarian the responsibility to advise the library administrator on the overall development of children's work in the system; and (2) by seeing that as time passes the head of children's work gives more and more leadership to all the aspects of children's work, including that at each branch.

### The Children's Librarian's Job

Whether in a large or a small library, the person in charge of service to children has to break down the job into the respective parts, and see that (1) each part is effectively assigned; and (2) each person is supervised, encouraged, and developed and work and knowledge are improved. Such components include policies and budgets; staffing, training, and supervising; methods for handling the work; selecting and placing the books; improving reference service; helping parents, instructing groups in the use of books and libraries; making exhibits and lists; storytelling; extending service through clubs, contests, and vacation projects and other projects; promoting and cooperating with outside contacts; and compiling statistics and reporting. This formidable and absorbing range of duties makes children's work challenging.

### Staffing

For years good children's librarians—those who know children's literature, child psychology, and school curriculum, and teaching methods—have been at a premium. Dedicated people trained in these fields naturally give better satisfaction in this exacting work than do any others. In seeking their services, public libraries are in competition with school libraries, where salaries are often higher and the work year is shorter. School librarians are usually required to have the same academic preparation as teachers, while this is desirable but not necessary for children's librarians. But many young people considering librarianship as a career find it easy to get the necessary credits in education and thus qualify for employment in two main types of libraries, with the big pull toward school librarianship.

A final factor that holds down recruitment and retention is the lack of promotional opportunities. Every large library should provide at least a few advanced positions where children's librarians can continue their special interests. It is unusual for the branch children's librarian to be promoted to be the branch librarian and even less frequent for a children's librarian to become library director. This situation has to be rectified if children's librarians are to remain in children's work.

There are many cases where the services of one trained children's librarian could be shared by two or three small libraries if each of them cannot afford a full-time trained children's worker. Certainly any branch or separate library lending 75,000 or more books a year needs a professional children's librarian. It is necessary to pay a large enough salary to secure as director of children's work a person able to plan, organize, coordinate, and supervise all the children's workers in the system. This person should be consulted in the choice of all those assigned to children's work and should direct their in-service training.

### Book Selecting

Knowledge and skill in selecting and servicing children's books, magazines, films, and records are basic to this work, though there is the hard core of standard titles time-tested and sure to be enjoyed.[6] Even these appear in ever new and different editions. The great problem is the rapid increase in number and variety of current titles, many of great value for their own sake and for their usefulness in the school curriculum. Selection for purchase and knowledgeable recommendations to readers require critical appreciation of what is desirable. Book evaluation meetings help in selecting new books and provide valuable in-service training too. Formulation and periodic review of a statement of children's book selection principles has training value beyond its own purpose, for it raises knotty questions about textbooks, condensations of classics, comics, romances, and the like.

Few libraries have a collection of children's books as good as they should have. The number of good children's books increases continually, as do their prices; the absorptive capacity of children for books is never saturated, and the books wear out and become outdated very quickly. Films, records, slides, filmstrips, maps, and pictures ought also to be available. Reference books are even more imperative, ever higher in price, and brought up to date ever more frequently. It is well to schedule replacement purchases of the two best young people's encyclopedias and to buy by plan. Replacement of older titles has to be continuous, absorbing from 10 percent to 20 percent of book funds. Readers and primers for young children are now increasingly recognized as desirable, and so are the picture books beloved by children too young to read at all. Children's books get hard wear, and children are influenced by their attractiveness.

There are enough differences between the use of adult books and of children's books so that major decisions or changes contemplated by catalogers should have the advice of the head children's librarian. Broader rather than narrower classification and sometimes different classification than the adult titles on the same subject are often desirable. Reader interest classification is often used, at least in part, if only to save staff members from having repeatedly to find another horse story for young readers. Descriptive cataloging details need to be minimized with shorter, simpler, and some different subject headings. Indicating the school grade level for which books are considered most nearly appropriate helps in selecting books for an individual child. But with such labeling children may be unwilling to explore books of a higher grade level or embarrassed to use those below their present grade. Furthermore, the higher the grade level, the more difficult it is to assign each book to one grade only. A reasonable solution is to use only broad groupings, such as primary, intermediate, and upper grades, and to use a well-concealed code.

Major book-reviewing publications for children's books in use by children's librarians include the following:

*Booklist,* published by the American Library Association; reviews written by *Booklist* staff; about 1,400 books were reviewed in a recent year.

*Kirkus Services,* issued by a commercial firm; reviews by staff members; about 250 reviews a year.

*Publishers Weekly* (PW Forecasts); notes by staff members; about 500 a year.

*School Library Journal* (R. R. Bowker Co.); reviews by practicing librarians; about 2,000 a year.

*Horn Book,* about 400 titles a year; and the *New York Times Sunday Book Review,* about 350 a year.

In addition, book selectors will refer to current and retrospective bibliographies on special subjects, ethnic backgrounds, and various other aids to selection. One book selector may rely more on one tool than another. The rush to supply bestsellers is not so great with children's books as with adult books. Children are less apt to read reviews, although more discriminating parents may do so. But there is a good reason to select and acquire new books with all deliberate speed because press runs tend to be smaller in difficult times and titles will go out of stock more quickly.

The makeup of the children's book collection differs in another substantial way from the adult collection, in that the clientele has a briefer age span. For instance, the child will use picture books for perhaps only three or four years before going on to the next stage in the collection. Other four- and five-year-olds coming along every year find that all the picture books are new to them. The same is true of children in the upper age ranges: the books they find are new as far as they are concerned, although it is necessary to update the collection in certain subjects. The point, however, is that a fair amount of attention and money must be given to replacement of standard and useful titles, to the extent that these remain in print and stock. And since it has been estimated that libraries account for about 80 percent of the sales of children's books, the selection decisions of children's librarians have a definite impact on what titles remain in stock or are reprinted.

## Standards in Materials Selection for Children

There is a continuing concern about standards of the makeup of the materials in the public library's collection for children. In brief, the issue may be described in some ways as similar to that which plagues selectors of adult materials: demand versus quality—whether to give the children what they will read or to build the collection to a standard of educational and cultural purpose. There are those who hold that if the children want to read "Dick and Jane" and the "Bobbsey Twins" (typical of mass appeal type books), then why not cater to that wish? After all, it is a *public* library, isn't it? Therefore give the public what they want. What right does the children's librarian have to dictate the reading tastes of the people? Another facet of this argument is advanced by some who are, rightfully, concerned about the reading needs of the economically and culturally disadvantaged, and who hold that the reading level and standards of the public library materials collections should be lowered to meet the ability level of these children. It is a pervasive theory but less than valid. One may reflect that a few centuries ago books were reserved solely for the higher classes. Now books and other cultural advantages are available to all who elect to use, view, visit. It would, it seems, be something of a tragic mistake if, just when the masses of people are getting to the point in history where they can enjoy the advantages of a cultural environment, one were to say: "This is really too good for you; you can't understand it, so we who know best will have to bring it down to your level." That is the philosophy of the mass media, and they practice it very successfully, but the public library is not meant to compete with the mass media, nor can it.

Finally, as has been noted in the opening chapter, the public library is by statute and tradition supported by the public, in the public interest, for educational, social, and cultural purposes. This certainly applies to children's work even more than it does to adult services, for it is during the first years that the mold of the life to come is cast.

Sheila Egoff, professor in the school of librarianship, University of British Columbia, Vancouver, has written an eloquent argument concerning the dangers of accepting mediocrity as a standard in children's book selection. She deals with the various reasons that have lately been advanced for "giving the readers what they want" advanced by the pressure that comes "from the left" in these times.

It calls itself, in library circles at least, "social responsibility" and the reasoning is not without some validity. It goes this way. Our society has disadvantaged groups. They are in a desperate situation that will call for desperate remedies, in matters of reading as well as in economics. Worry therefore not about the maintenance of standards, but find something, anything, that will bring them inside the library: cartoon movies, rock concerts, and "easy books."

Adding that she sympathizes with this point of view and noting that the tastes of middle-class librarians may not be appropriate for the needs of slum children, she expresses her concern about "the strong element of condescension which I see implied in this attitude when it equates 'easy' with 'inferior.' What the disadvantaged don't need surely is disadvantaged materials." She continues:

I will admit that finding books that have both simplicity and substance is no small task. And this, of course, is *exactly* the virtue of mediocrity—if you can persuade yourself that almost any book will do, you avoid the labor of selection. This is *exactly* why I am suspicious of this philosophy. Hesiod, back in the eighth century B.C., recognized the problem: "Badness you can get easily, in quantity; the road is smooth and it lies close by. But in front of excellence the immortal gods have put sweat, and long and steep is the way to it, and rough at first. But when you come to the top, then it is easy, even though it is hard."

It takes hard training to be able to run a mile, to weld metal, to split the atom, to write *Crime and Punishment,* to read the Bible. Once the skills are mastered, then the results seem effortless. Working on skills should in no way preclude the effort to reach a goal of excellence, nor should the method of reaching it preclude the exercise of excellence. . . .

My main question is: "Does it matter what children read as long as they do read?" The answers are curiously mixed. Many people would balk at deliberately giving a child a poor book; others would balk at a controversial book. Relatively few, I fear, worry about giving a child something which is simply less than the best.

"If that won't do no good, that won't do no harm." Reading something is better than reading nothing.

Put in that way, such an approach is hard to controvert. But why put it that way? The choice is not really between something and nothing but between various kinds of something—between something so-so and something wow! . . .

. . . The role of literature is to help develop the individual and it takes a good book to do this. A poor book takes a child and puts him back a step or two; a mediocre book takes a child and leaves him where he is. A good book promotes an awareness of the possibilities of life, the universality of life, the awakening of response.

. . . What do we do when we deliberately provide the mediocre? . . . First, we underestimate children. And we should remember that slow learners and poor readers may be just as interested in *ideas* as quick readers. As a matter of fact, they may have more original ideas and minds because they haven't been clobbered by mediocre ideas picked up in mediocre books. . . .

Second, the mediocre rarely gets challenged by adults. If children are constantly presented with mediocre books, how will they know a *good* book when they run into one? . . .

Thirdly, the mediocre builds laziness into children. At an age when they are best prepared for challenge it is unjust to deny it to them. Is it because some of us adults don't want to disturb ourselves with challenges that we find it easier to direct children away from them?

To the argument that good books are often dull, Ms. Egoff replies heatedly that that simply isn't so and cites several examples in support. She adds that

not every "good" children's book appeals to every child . . . but the small percentage of children's books that have something to say to a child and say it well would run into several thousands. Surely they are enough for any childhood. . . .

. . . I would suggest that we teachers and librarians . . . take our cue from Matthew Arnold: "I am bound by my own definition of criticism: a disinterested endeavour to learn and propagate the best that is known and thought in the world."[7]

The child and the parent, visiting the children's room, have a right to expect that the books and other materials displayed there have been selected with care and judgment and taste, as the best of their kind.

Carl Carmer wrote of his bout with pneumonia as an eight-year-old in upper New York State. His mother read to him, but she soon exhausted the town's supply of books. Carmer wrote that when he was recovered enough to leave the house, but not enough to play baseball, his mother's friend, Mrs. Cole, called to him and ushered him into her library. "My children have grown up," she said, "and there is no one to enjoy these books any more. I don't see well enough and Mr. Cole reads new books. Come to this room as often as you like. I'm not going to tell you what to read here. Find out for yourself."

Carmer reported that even after he could return to play, he spent hours in the Cole library. The first book he read was *The Original Travels of Baron Munchausen.* Then he met the Robinsons—Swiss Family and Horseshoe—finding an equal though dissimilar joy in each, and on to others. "Rebellious by nature, I know that had Mrs. Cole told me that reading any of these books would be good for me, I would not have read it. My reading seemed to me entirely haphazard, but in reality it was highly selective. The library had been accumulated by people of taste."[8]

### Individual Guidance

Given access to a collection of books of even reasonable adequacy, children will use it more heavily than will any other group of readers. They go through certain well-defined stages of growth and development and corresponding phases of reading interests. Trained and experienced professional librarians consider it essential to be informed on children's literature, types of motivation, and methods of personal guidance. As a result they can match an appropriate book to a particular child's needs and predict his or her success and satisfaction in any particular reading experience, in a far higher percentage of cases than adult service librarians can do with their patrons.

Although some children's librarians may disagree, as they may view a major mission of the work in terms of instilling the love of good reading, making readers out of nonreaders, and similar laudable goals, it may be said that reading is not an end in itself. Learning to read is an objective, but the child reads as a means of finding out what he or she wants to know, satisfying curiosity, developing and expanding interests. The children's librarian may well wish to consider individual guidance as the practice of finding where the child's interest lies and suggesting books, a film, picture, or other media that will respond to that interest. This might be more useful to the child, in the long run, than simply meeting the requirement for a good book to read. It is granted that in the give and take of the children's room on a busy afternoon, such individual guidance may not be possible.

But this is one of the major differences between the school library, or media center, where the prescribed curriculum is dominating in most cases, and the public library, where free inquiry is more apt to occur. Both approaches are vitally needed; the child, it is true, needs to acquire basic knowledge and information in a somewhat structured fashion or mode, but this can be complemented in the children's library and, in the home, with books borrowed by parents. For the father and mother ought to have a part in the education of their children as well, and not leave it all up to the paid professionals.

### Reference Service

The burgeoning of reference service for children stems largely from the enrichment of the elementary school curriculum, the assigning of projects that require independent study and thinking, the increase and greater variety of substantial out-of-school interests, and the greater availability of more good juvenile nonfiction books than ever. Evidently it stems also from teaching children the use of books and libraries as early as the first grade. Schools and public libraries alike, in many cities, teach elementary school children the use of common reference books, the school library, the public library children's room, the card catalog, the periodical indexes, and so on. Such instruction *needs* to recur at each main stage, so as to be useful and meaningful to the students at that stage of their development, and *not* for the next stage or for the rest of their lives. It also greatly stimulates reference use of books by readers.

Three facts stand out: (1) reference help is one of the public library's prime obligations to children; (2) it needs more administrative attention, especially money for more reference materials and reference staff; and (3) preparation for it has to be planned and continuously active to outbalance the turnover and the shortcoming of people who have not been trained in library school attempting to give reference service.

### Story Hours

The best-known device to stimulate children to read and to explore the world of books is the story hour, popular with nearly every child up to the fifth grade. Some libraries offer story-hour programs on television and radio and as a part of staff members' visits to school classrooms. Libraries also find a ready reception for preschool story hours for children from age three to five. Upper-grade children are more interested in craft clubs; in creative writing, drama, and art experiences; in student library assistant groups; and in other participation programs.

Such activities are examples of the dynamic drive to open up new areas and types of service to ever more groups of patrons. As library service to children has become better developed and understood, children's librarians have been working with children too young to be in school and with school-age children in their out-of-school time. Service to adults by children's librarians is another such area. In recent years, collections of adult books and related services for parents, such as advice on books to buy for children, have become a regular activity. Servicing children's books for teacher use is of long standing in children's departments of public libraries, but books on teaching are part of the services to adults and involve the use of adult reference books—for example, the *Education Index*. In some libraries, scout leaders, Sunday school teachers, and other adults who work with children find that both the adult and juvenile materials they need have been brought together in the children's room. In other cases, the librarians are reluctant to detach any segment of the adult collection, because it is best serviced by the staff that specializes in adult informational tools and materials. Increased emphasis is now given to exceptional children, including the gifted, for whom extra reading is one of the most easily managed and resultful enrichments and encouragements for talented children.

## Some Current Problems and Long-Term Trends

Children's service is concerned with at least five main problem issues—the theory of library habit, the rise of the school library, the appeal of the mass media to children, the effect of long-term trends in child education and psychology, and the relationship between objectives and performance.

### The Theory of the Library Habit

Librarians have long held the theory that if children are attracted to the public library early and induced to use it regularly they will continue to use the library when they become adults, at least more so than they would otherwise, by virtue of having formed the habit. There is no evidence in support of this theory, and some that discredits it; and an alternative theory can be proposed, which makes fewer assumptions.

If the library habit theory were valid, it should have produced greater results; it should have resulted in more than the general good will of the adult public for its library—there should be twice as much adult reading from library materials. But adult registration and adult use of public libraries are still relatively limited, and more of adult reading needs are being met by enormous sales of paperbacks and magazines. Adult use seems to be more nearly a result of formal education and of economic conditions than of early exposure to books and libraries. Public library use is at its lowest point, in the case of most people, in the late teens and early twenties, just after they have left school and just after their exposure to books and libraries. Yet, a greater potential of interest in reading is found in this group—more than in older groups, where age and increased responsibilities may limit recourse to reading as a means of securing information or indulging in recreation or self-education.[9]

While it is always possible that better techniques of library service to children will be more successful in producing lifelong library patrons, it is also possible that an alternative theory is more nearly valid—that any group of potential readers will use books and libraries to the extent to which those services are available to them, are brought to their attention, and are performed so as to meet their present major life needs and wants effectively. It follows that library service should be available to every major group of potential patrons for its own sake and for what it will do and mean for them in their present stage of development. Public library service to children is good for its own sake, and public library service to adults is better when it too is developed in the light of successful approaches to major adult life needs.

## The Challenge of the School Library

The theory of the "library habit" led public libraries early in this century to an extensive development of service to schools. At that time this was a positive good. Generally the service was in the form of classroom groups of circulating books; seldom did it give the increasingly necessary reference service called for by the teachers. School progress, changes in teaching methods and curricula, which favored the use of multiple sources, and new technology combined to make school library service an even larger and more expensive portion of the total service given by the public library until it outbalanced other services.

Through the years, however, the more progressive schools have recognized the value of school library service, established their own libraries, and taken over the functions that the local public library had been attempting to cover in the school. In the last couple of decades, in city after city, the public library has withdrawn from providing school library service on its own. The obvious suggestion of joint financing of the service by both schools and libraries has been tried repeatedly, but this raises administrative, budgetary, and even political difficulties. In their increasing need for the school library as a learning laboratory and media center, the schools have preferred to establish their own libraries if they are going to have to pay even as much as half the total cost. From the viewpoint of individual service to pupils and teachers as well as administratively, the best results are likely to be achieved by media centers administered and financed by the school system, and completely integrated into the structure and functioning of the school itself.[10]

## Children and the Mass Media

The school library and the public library, in its service to children, accept the same basic standards and criteria. In direct competition are the mass media with their tremendous appeal—comics, television, radio, motion pictures, and popular magazines, with enormous financial resources on which to draw, and activated by keen financial and commercial rivalries. Their techniques and methods usually have no necessary connection with nor do they often claim to serve the educational or character-building activities of children. It is not that all reading of hardcover books by children is good and worthwhile, or that none of the mass media ever have anything worthwhile for children. Rather it is that the public library is an antidote to the threat of mass thought control. While publishing in the United States has moved farther away from censorship, broadcasting has increasingly come under government control.[11]

Therefore, it is possible for a library to grow and to flourish in the face of the appeal to children of the mass media. It can also use the mass media for its own ends. Thus radio and television programs have been arranged and produced by many libraries, and with good results; and library use of a good book is often stimulated by local showing of the film made from it, especially when promoted by library advertising of the fact. Technical progress and aggressive advertising have forced libraries to compete with these strong rivals for the time and attention of children in out-of-school hours. Improving the appearance of children's rooms and children's books and simplifying registration and circulation procedures are only forerunners to library promotion that will attract more children as library users and assure them of really interesting but high-quality reading.

There are periodic campaigns to raise the level of content and to eliminate objectionable features in the mass media. Children's librarians would be well advised to consider before they participate in such well-meant but controversial enterprises. But they can introduce a positive note and attempt to get more attention given to the availability of good books in or out of libraries, to the public discussion of what constitutes good reading and of how it can be provided all children, and to those movies and TV programs that are constructive and free from objectionable elements. There is no attempt implied here to gloss over the defects of the mass media in their impact on children, and the worst offenses are indeed shocking. We do not know how or to what extent children make a reasonable adjustment to the mass media over a period of years, but there is evidence that a strong connection exists between children's viewing of television violence and subsequent aggressiveness.[12] A fairly compelling case that all television is harmful because of the passivity it encourages is developed by Marie Wynn in *The Plug-In Drug* (New York: Viking Press, 1977).

## The Trend in Education and Psychology

The present emphasis on research in education and child psychology augurs well for libraries, and the planning by children's librarians needs to take note of the educational changes being made. Current literature on the teaching of reading is stimulating; studies discuss main trends. Among them are the widespread definite attempts to improve teaching methods, to tighten up on the typical curriculum, to require more home study, to do better for gifted children, to give renewed attention to the humanities, to improve the teaching and habit of reading, to encourage independent reading, and, by using multiple sources instead of a single text, to teach ethics and character building without crossing over into religion and theology.

The children's librarian needs to know about developments in the schools, in the curriculum, in teaching methods, and in what current research and thinking say about normal child development. Every children's librarian is in effect an amateur child psychologist, and sustained interest in the schools and in child development makes the librarian's work more effective.

## The Relationship Between Objectives and Performance

In an analytical speech to librarians in 1977, F. William Summers quoted Philip Ennis, Peggy Sullivan, and Pauline Winnick by way of introducing his thesis that children's library services are "well-defined but undocumented and unmeasured." Ennis, he noted, once referred to what he called "the library faith"—the "unanalyzed belief that reading makes you good and that reading good books makes you even better. It seems to me that the children's services of public libraries have been both blessed and cursed by a substantial oversubscription to the library faith."[13] He continues:

Peggy Sullivan has commented, "It may be that good children's or elementary school librarians are so engrossed in their real work that they have neither the inclination nor the competence to chronicle or analyze their efforts."[14] Pauline Winnick has stated that children's services along with other types of library services suffer "from the lag to define objectives, provide current statistics and standards that can be used to measure performance levels, and answer to the community in terms of the social value of their services."[15]

Summers has seven positive suggestions for children's librarians, and these will be of interest to public library administrators as well:

1. Spend less time and effort being concerned about "being unappreciated and misunderstood. . . . It is never someone else's fault that your problems and programs are misunderstood."

2. Develop a means of measuring the outcome of children's services. Begin with anecdotal data about people or groups who benefit, but move on to more structured and carefully designed measures of the outcome.

3. Bring pressure to bear on state library agencies to do something significant about programming in children's services. This is "a sorry record. There are only 18 states in which the position title clearly indicates a primary responsibility for youth services."

4. Look at the local position of children's coordinator and "make a realistic determination, not blinded by the past, of what is needed."

5. Schools and public libraries are faced with the same kinds of demands for accountability and might jointly find measures of successful performance in both agencies.

6. "Be assertive about the quantitative measures . . . most children's departments perform very well on a unit-cost basis. . . . Measure the high-volume operations such as circulation, in order to justify the low-volume, qualitative functions such as story hours and film showings and be prepared to indicate why the higher cost of these is worthwhile."

7. "Be as specific and realistic as you can about what you need and

what you expect from library schools. . . . There is no reason that a program of specialization in children's services cannot be developed."[16]

The future of public library service to children lies not in the mass distribution of books but in the exploitation of its unique aspects—the voluntary nature of each child's reading, the acceptance of each child at his or her present level, the ready availability of many different titles and forms of print and nonprint materials, the ability to give richer and more complete reference service to all. The crucial element is a skilled and imaginative librarian to test and establish how books and library service can help normal children, the gifted and the leaders, and the disadvantaged, those in need of remedial reading, the children who suffer from psychological strains, and the many other categories in which children find themselves.

## Desirable Public Library–Public School Relationships

Three basic principles underlie public library–public school relationships. If these principles are not understood and accepted by both parties, the relationship is likely to be unsatisfactory to one or the other, and less effective than it might be.[17]

The first principle is that every school should have its own school library or media center, controlled and financed by the school system.[18] Library service is important for children, as an integral part of the teaching resources and educational program of every high and grade school. Modern methods of teaching emphasize multiple sources of information and the encouragement of independent thinking, weaving the use of library materials into every possible unit of teaching. The school librarian or media specialist should be qualified by experience and education, both as a librarian and as a teacher, to know the teacher's point of view, to have a teacher's status in the school, to be a part of the teaching team, and specifically to put library materials to work in each teacher's class assignments. There has been a considerable increase in the number of elementary school libraries. This repeats the pattern followed by the high schools; most high schools today have their own school library, largely because of the requirements of the regional accrediting associations and the state departments of education. The process was also speeded up by an infusion of federal funds. The National Defense Education Act of 1958 provided funds for the purchase of certain materials. School libraries were able to extend their collections further with the passage of the Elementary and Secondary Education Act of 1965.

The second main principle is that the public library should seek to encourage the development and improvement of school libraries and to cooperate with them. It was commendable and desirable when public libraries extended their services to the schools,[19] but school officials have recognized the need for having school libraries, and it is no longer desirable or practical for the public library to manage or finance them. Many school librarians claim, with some justification, that continuance of public library service to schools—that is, in the form of branches or classroom collections—has held back the development of school libraries.[20]

Public library relationships to schools could range from the one extreme of public library operation of school libraries, with all expenses paid by the school system, to the other extreme of complete and total separation of and no communication between the two library systems. Neither extreme is actually to be found, nor would either be desirable. The four arrangements most frequently found are (1) the operation of school libraries by the public library with a sharing of expenses; (2) the operation by the public library of branch libraries in school buildings; (3) the placing of classroom collections (in grade schools particularly), financed and deposited by the public library; and (4) the informal cooperation and the many types of services rendered by public libraries to schools that have libraries of their own.

The third main principle is that, to whatever extent the school system is unable or unwilling to provide adequate library service to its own students, then the public library has the obligation to serve the pupils as fully as it can. In the late 1960s the public library became involved in volunteer reading programs for the disadvantaged. Small library units, circulation and study centers, were set up in storefront buildings. Book collections were based on the interests of neighborhood ethnic and racial groups. Exhibits were chosen to reflect the special qualities of their culture. Film/book series, clubs, writing groups, and Sesame Street parties were organized. In cities that have school libraries, the public library continues to be called on for materials that no individual school library can supply, or because the public library has additional copies, or because the school closes before the pupils have enough chance to use the library. The public library has a responsibility to provide at least some degree of service for every large group of potential patrons in its service area, and from a fourth to a third of the local population is in school. But that responsibility is reduced by the extent to which any main part of the provision of library service to a segment of the community is assumed by others (for example, by a special library, a college).

In brief, the experts state the main factors:

1. Materials and services in media centers and public libraries are similar but they serve different functions. Books and materials in the media center reflect the curriculum; in the children's department of the public library the collection has broader scope and emphasizes out-of-school interests. Both will have, or should have, qualified librarians; increasingly the librarians in schools, or media specialists, are required to have training and experience in teaching methods and acquaintance with the curriculum. Librarians in the public library stress knowing the children's books and relating them to

the particular child's need. On the other hand, the school librarian may have an opportunity to be closer to the children, as Henne points out, and should be able to understand them better.[21]

2. In larger cities, it becomes impossible without considerable cost to have the variety and extent of materials and staff in every school media center that the large branches of the public library, and the central library, will necessarily have in order to serve the larger population. Therefore, the students are bound to gravitate toward the larger resources. Even if the media center has a good collection and staff, the disparity will inevitably exist, in back files of periodicals, in reference materials, and in older and standard books. On the other hand, the school library achieves greater density of use than the public library. The per capita cost of school library service is usually higher than the per capita cost of public libraries, but there are no comparative unit costs. For one reason, there is no consensus on what constitutes a unit of service.

3. The major problem with the media center and its use by the students it is intended to serve is a logistical one. In many situations, practically all children are brought in by school bus; they must leave a few minutes after the close of classes. The media centers normally have hours that are more or less coincidental with the class day. If the student can't get his or her library work done during the class day, it becomes routine to go to the public library in the evening. Even if the media center is kept open after class hours, and in the evening, questions of custodial care and librarian schedules arise. As to the high school students, they need books for adults, found in the public library, in higher volume and with increasing intensity.[22]

There is the undocumented impression that good school libraries tend to increase the usage of the public libraries. But the problem remains far from solved, and as taxpayer concerns and budget managers' interest in accountability rises, there will inevitably be pressure to bring a management approach to the problem of school library–public library relationships. It will not be enough to say that both are needed: the school library when the student is there in school and the public library when the student is out of school. Taxpayers look at public library children's rooms that are serving preschool children and some parents during the school hours and then are jammed with children after school, and they also look at school libraries that remain out of use after school hours and during vacations and holidays; they begin to wonder whether the present system is the best one. There could be much more joint planning and effort than takes place now, and more citizen interest as well.

The question of duplication is probably not as great as it seems to the casual observer. The major cost in both media center and children's room is for staff. Unless it can be demonstrated that both staffs are less than fully occupied for their workdays, then merging the two facilities in some way would not result in staff savings; the savings might occur in the provision of space and materials.

More than a decade ago, the State of New York's *Report of the Commissioner of Education's Committee on Library Development, 1970,* recommended that all library services to children in New York be transferred to elementary school media centers. The report had been prepared by a committee appointed in 1967 that was charged with reviewing the eighty recommendations that had been made in a 1967 evaluation of the New York State Library System. The media center proposal provoked a considerable amount of discussion and controversy.[23] Experimentation with new patterns of organization and administration was expressed by the Regents of the University of the State of New York. In answer to the report of the Commissioner of Education's Committee on Library Development in 1970, they recommended appropriation of state funds for research and new pilot projects, since school libraries in the state had been urged to assume major responsibilities for all library services to children.[24] So far, this exploration has not been made possible.

Despite the amount of tax money involved, few communities have explored the possibilities of cooperative action between local school and public libraries. One study was "The Philadelphia Project" by John Benford.[25] This study began with a survey to determine student needs for materials and patterns of student library use. An "action library" was then established, based on the findings and the joint recommendations of public and school librarians. The result is to be a learning resource center divorced from traditional administrative structures.

In any case, the conviction has been strengthened in recent years that reading is the key to the whole educational process, that it helps to develop ability to think and encourages individual effort and purpose. The two systems of libraries should work together for the good of the students they both serve.

### Public Library Operation of School Libraries by Contract

Of the four main types of relationships between public libraries and schools, two are not recommended. One of these is the operation of school libraries by the public library, on the basis of a contract with the school system and a sharing of expenses.[26] This arrangement would seem to guarantee close coordination of school library agencies and the public library. Actually, schoolteachers and officials increasingly feel that the public library does not understand, especially as to curriculum content, and cannot meet the ever greater needs of current school use of supplementary materials. The public library representative in the school is seldom looked upon as a real faculty member, and psychological barriers about loyalties and different schedules and salaries make it difficult to integrate library services fully with classroom objectives and routines. This arrangement continues mostly in those cities where school authorities are more interested in having the public library meet some of the service costs than they are in having really good school library service.

## Public Library Branches in School Buildings

The other type of arrangement not recommended is the housing of a public library branch in a school building. In theory all the neighboring community as well as the personnel of the school will use it. Supposedly it saves the cost of a branch building, and eliminates duplication of juvenile library facilities. Necessarily the public library pays at least part and usually the major part of the expenses, especially for personnel and books.

Many cities have discontinued schoolhouse branches, because they have proved ineffective either as branches or as school libraries. A well-located school is off the main pedestrian arteries, whereas a public library branch belongs in the center of neighborhood pedestrian traffic. The result is that it is used less than it should be even by pupils attending other schools in the general vicinity and hardly at all by adults.[27] Administrative difficulties arise with regard to heating, access to the library room, pressure for classroom space with an "outsider" occupying it, and so on. The more schoolhouse branches, the more the public library budget is dissipated among small, weak libraries, and the higher the unit costs of service. Although there are a few cases where unusual location or relationships make the idea workable, neither a school library nor a public library can adequately take the place of the other; both are needed in the important and ever more complex task of bringing books and other materials, and related services, to all citizens and to all schoolchildren.

## Public Library Services to Schools Lacking School Libraries

Where the school has no library, many public libraries feel an obligation to provide a partial substitute, in the form of classroom sets of books, bookmobile stops, and classroom visits. Some public librarians frankly admit that this is a mass production method to increase their circulation figures; some superintendents admit that this justifies them in not budgeting for real school libraries. Both should be aware that these services are a poor substitute for a good school library; both should work toward the withdrawal of the public library's services inside the school.

Some public libraries assemble their classroom sets of books from a separate school collection, others from the regular stock of children's books. Some lend books only for recreational reading, others lend any sort. Some require teachers to select their own books and to transport them to and from the library; others will select books for the teachers and provide transportation. Some use a relatively short loan period, do not permit the books to be lent again to the children for home use, and hold the teacher responsible for all loss or damage; others use a relatively long loan period, permit and encourage more than one loan of the books to the children, and exempt the teacher from responsibility if the children who so borrow the books are registered with the public library.

In general, it would seem that if this service is provided, it might as well be provided on as liberal a basis as possible. A circulation count or even an estimate of books re-lent from the classroom to individual children should not be required, or if it is it should be reported separately from the rest of the library's circulation. It is spurious circulation, involving no direct service or even contact between the library and the patron; when the schools develop their own libraries, there will be a great drop in the public library's circulation. Figures of this type of circulation, especially when estimated, are often in error or are inflated by estimating informal loans that children make among themselves or by encouraging teachers to accept more books than are needed. The Atlanta Public Library discontinued its block loans to schools in 1970. A consequent drop in circulation was overcome within three years.

Daily across the nation, whole classes rush out to the public library's bookmobile, the children returning books and hastily choosing and borrowing what they can find. The cramped physical quarters, the lack of time for browsing, the slight opportunity for reading guidance or informational help make most school librarians and many public librarians realize that while such crowd service is better than nothing—for example, in rural areas—it is decidedly no substitute for a school library or for borrowing from the public library or branch. It does bring to the students a considerably larger and more varied collection of books than they are likely to get from a classroom set, and children's eager acceptance of this service is shown by the great circulations that bookmobiles typically achieve at school stops. The public library is tempted to give ever more of the bookmobile's scheduled time and ever more of its shelf space to meet the endless demands of schoolchildren; it thereby often neglects the other important types of bookmobile stops and services.

## In Cooperation with School Libraries

To be most successful, cooperative action requires an agreement between the school system and the public library on the responsibilities each will assume. In large cities so much is involved that the public library should have a coordinator of its own services to local public and nonpublic school pupils. It also calls for a channel of communication—desirably a joint committee of one or more school librarians, the city school library supervisor, the superintendent of schools, the chief librarian of the public library, and the public library personnel in charge of work with schools, with children, and with young adults. It should meet regularly to discuss and explore any aspect of the mutual relationship. The committee members will get to know one another and one another's problems, ways of functioning, resources, and needs. Impending changes in each other's situation should be discussed.

Areas of cooperation may include:

1. Supplementing the school libraries' book collection by short-term loans of groups of books or by putting books on special reserve in the public library.

2. Selecting, retaining, and binding magazines by both libraries to provide as well as possible for the anticipated needs of the students, and with a joint list of magazines in both groups of libraries.

3. Joint meetings of appropriate personnel for book selection purposes.

4. Consideration of one another's resources in the preparation of book lists.

5. Cooperation in such special projects as National Library Week or Children's Book Week.

6. Provision of professional books for teachers.

7. Joint purchasing of books, rebinding service, and cooperative cataloging.

The public library benefits indirectly to the degree that the school library can improve the service it gives its students; the better the school library, the better prepared are the students to use the public library.[28] It also benefits directly, for teachers and school librarian can be better persuaded to forward copies of reading lists used, details of homework assignments, and notes of other school activities likely to bring students into the public library. In addition, the public library can often arrange to buy supplies at special school discounts, since schools typically buy larger quantities of many office supplies. The schools' print shop can print public library materials to be used in and with the schools, and the schools' transport system and its larger film collection may be made available to the public library.

Weech noted that

cooperation between school and public libraries has been a major concern for years. There have been innumerable articles, books, workshops and conferences on the subject. Edna B. Berg annotated forty-five articles ... in major journals from 1970 to 1973. Well over fifty books and articles have been published on the subject since the Berg bibliography. Many of the articles are descriptions of ongoing cooperative projects between school and public libraries.[29]

In order to find out more about how much cooperation currently was going on in one state, and also to see what librarians thought would be desirable kinds of cooperative activity, Weech surveyed 360 public libraries and media centers in Iowa in 1978. She found a considerable gap between what librarians considered as desirably cooperative activities and what was actually happening.

**Table 3.** Cooperative Activities Between School and Public Libraries

| Cooperative Activities Checked as Desirable | Percentages | Currently Involved |
|---|---|---|
| Planning of peak research paper periods | 55 | 4.5 |
| Joint book selection meetings | 50 | 1.3 |
| Joint publicity efforts | 46 | 3.0 |
| Coordinated acquisition of some materials | 45 | 2.6 |
| Joint catalog of holdings | 44 | 0.4 |
| Joint summer reading programs | 44 | 3.5 |
| Shared storytelling/book talks | 42 | 3.0 |
| Use of school library materials in school library during summer | 29 | 3.0 |
| Shared film rentals | 27 | 3.5 |
| Joint bindery bid | 23 | 1.3 |
| Joint materials ordering | 21 | 0 |
| Joint cataloging technical processing | 21 | 0 |

*Note:* Percentages total more than 100 because more than one activity could be checked.

A brief summary of the data assembled from the questionnaires appears in Table 3.

While the study by Ms. Weech was limited to one state, and to 230 usable responses, the results may be considered with some interest. The fact that "planning of peak research paper periods" was checked as a desirable cooperative activity by more than half of the respondents is significant: it reflects the traditional battle between teachers who assign students to use library materials without finding whether the materials are there, and the media specialists and public librarians who are faced with the onslaught that has been going on for years. (It is doubtful that any amount of cooperative activity between school and public librarians can resolve this problem.) The cooperative activity must take place between the planners of the curriculum and the teachers making the assignments on the one hand and the media specialists on the other.

But more significant, perhaps, is the fact that several cooperative activities were checked as "desirable" but very little "current involvement" was checked. Weech concluded that "one might attempt to determine if the comparatively low percentage of perceived desirability of cooperative activities can be explained by the minimal extent of current involvement in cooperation. . . . More in-depth analysis of the attitudes toward, and barriers to, cooperation could yield answers to these and other questions."[30]

## Relationships with Other Than Public Schools

Most American communities of appreciable size have one or more nonpublic schools—for example, parochial and private elementary and secondary schools, and business or trade schools. There are also the junior or senior colleges, state university extension centers, and other institutions of higher education. In general, the same pattern of principles for a desirable relationship with the public library holds true of these as of the public schools. The public library will give the best service possible to the students and will serve the students with materials the school library does not have.

In the case of most private schools, it is likely that the public library will have to initiate action to offer services. Some church schools will insist on controlling the selection of books offered their students; this in itself is not unreasonable, but on the other hand the public library should not purchase materials of a particular religious group solely for the use of its schools.

There should be particularly close ties between the public library and any college library in its service area, partly because of the heavy use that the college students can be expected to make of the public library, and partly because many college libraries have collections especially strong in some subjects; this generally makes it easy and appropriate to agree on fields of specialization to avoid duplication.

It may be natural but it is unfortunate that public library personnel overlook the similar aims and close relations so essential between school and public libraries. A public library assistant can give far better service to school pupils, even those served by a school library, by scanning a summary of the local curriculum and some of the guides to handling school reference work, which as we have noted is bound to increase in both types of libraries.

### Notes

1. Whitney North Seymour, Jr., and Elizabeth N. Layne, *For the People: Fighting for Public Libraries* (New York: Doubleday, 1979), pp. 22–23.
2. Robert Leigh, *The Public Library in the United States* (New York: Columbia University Press, 1950).
3. Lowell A. Martin, *Baltimore Reaches Out: Library Service to the Disadvantaged* (Baltimore, Md.: Enoch Pratt Free Library, 1967), pp. 17–18. Also see Sara Innis Fenwick, "Library Service to Children and Young People," *Library Trends* 25 (July 1976).
4. Public Library Association, "Community Library Services—Working Papers on Goals and Guidelines," *School Library Journal* 20 (September 1973): 7.
5. Adele M. Fasick, "Research and Measurement in Library Services to Children," *Top of the News* (Summer 1979): 354–55.
6. Several good books describe and evaluate the standard titles of children's literature—e.g., Cornelia Meigs, et al., *A Critical History of Children's Literature* (New York: Macmillan, 1969). See also R. Gordon Kelly, "American Children's Literature: An Historiographical Review," *American Literary Realism* 6 (September 1973): 89–107; Carolyn Field, ed., *Subject Collections in Children's Literature: A Guide to 500 Special Juvenile Collections in the United States and Canada, 1969* (New York: R. R. Bowker, 1969), and Virginia Haviland, *Children's Literature: A Guide to Reference Sources* (Washington, D.C.: Library of Congress, 1966).
7. Sheila Egoff, "If That Don't Do No Good, That Won't Do No Harm: The Uses and Dangers of Mediocrity in Children's Reading," in *Issues in Children's Book Selection* (New York: R. R. Bowker, 1973); pp. 5–7, 10.

8. Carl Carmen in *Good Reading* (New York: Mentor Books, 1956), Foreword.

9. A. W. McClellan, *The Reader, the Library and the Book* (London: Clive Bingley, 1973).

10. Mary S. Gaver, "Effectiveness of Centralized School Library Service in Elementary Schools (Phase 1)," *Library Quarterly* 31 (July 1, 1961): 245–56. On six out of eight measures, school libraries were superior to classroom sets and central collections.

11. Daniel J. Boorstein, "Libraries in the Age of Broadcasting," in *The Bowker Annual of Library and Trade Book Information,* 22d ed. (New York: R. R. Bowker, 1977).

12. Douglass Cater and Stephen Strickland, *TV Violence and the Child* (New York: Russell Sage Foundation, 1977), p. 54.

13. F. William Summers, "What You Want the Future to Be . . . Children's Services and Library Administration," *School Library Journal* (October 1977): 80.

14. Peggy Sullivan, "Library Service to Children: Celebration and Survival," *Horn Book* 52 (June 1976): 253.

15. Pauline Winnick, "Evaluation of Public Library Services to Children," *Library Trends* 22 (January 1974): 361–76.

16. Summers, op. cit., 81–82.

17. On the general theme of school and public library relationships, see D. Philip Baker, *School and Public Library Media Programs for Children and Young Adults* (Syracuse, N.Y.: Gaylord Professional Publications, 1977); Sara Innis Fenwick, "Library Service to Children and Young People," *Library Trends* 25 (July 1976): 329–60; and Ester R. Dyer, "New Perspective on Cooperation in Library Services to Children," *School Media Quarterly* 5 (Summer 1977): 261–72.

18. For standards of excellence see American Association of School Librarians, et al., *Media Programs: District and School* (Chicago: American Library Association, 1975). This statement and the earlier *Standards for School Media Programs* (Chicago: American Library Association, 1969) reflect the metamorphosis of many school libraries to media centers.

19. Frances Henne and Frances L. Spain, "The School and the Public Library," *Annals of the American Academy of Political and Social Science* 302 (November 1955): 52–59.

20. Helen R. Sattley, "Children Come First," *Library Journal* 77 (Apr. 15, 1952): 670–74. Also, Carolyn I. Whitenack, "Historical Development of the Elementary School Library," *Illinois Libraries* 38 (June 1956): 143–49.

21. Frances Henne, "The Basic Need in Library Service for Youth," *Library Quarterly* 25 (January 1955): 37–46.

22. See Elfrieda McCauley, "Budgeting for School Media Services," *School Media Quarterly* 4 (Winter 1976): 126–34, and Patricia Freeman, *Pathfinder: An Operational Guide for the School Librarian* (New York: Harper & Row, 1975).

23. J. Gordon Burke, "Where Will All the Children Go?" *American Libraries,* vol. 2, no. 1 (January 1971): 56–61, and no. 6 (June 1971): 601–3. Summaries and comments on the recommendations. Also reprinted in J. Gordon Burke and Gerald R. Shielfs, eds., *Children's Library Service: School or Public?* (Metuchen, N.J.: Scarecrow Press, 1974).

25. John Q. Benford, "The Philadelphia Project," *Library Journal* 96 (June 15, 1971): 2041–47.

24. New York State Education Department, "Library Service: A Statement of Policy and Proposed Action by the Regents of the University of the State of New York," *Position Paper* no. 8 (Albany: State Education Department, 1970), p. 20.

26. Ruth M. White, ed., *Public Library Policies—General and Specific, Public Library Reporter* no. 9 (Chicago: American Library Association, 1960), pp. 80–86.

27. Annual studies of the use of five public branches in elementary school buildings in Evansville, Indiana, from 1955 to 1957, showed an average of 5 percent of all circulation was to nonschool personnel, while of four other branches in library-owned buildings, an average of 44 percent of total circulation was to people other than teachers and students of the nearest public elementary school. A sixth school building branch, open two evenings and on Saturdays and closed during 40 percent of the school hours, had an average circulation

of 35 percent to other than the teachers and students in its schoolhouse. See Evansville Public Library, *Staff News Bulletin* (Apr. 15, 1955): 43–44; (June 1, 1956): 49; (Apr. 1, 1957): 49.

28. See Ruth A. Davies, *The School Library Media Center: A Force for Educational Excellence,* 2d ed. (New York: R. R. Bowker, 1974).

29. Terry L. Weech, "School and Public Library Cooperation—What We Would Like to Do, What We Do," *Public Libraries* 18 (Summer 1979): 33–34.

30. Ibid., 34.

# 13 Branch and Extension Work

There are three main stages in the history of the American public library. From 1850 to 1890, the concern was with mechanics of organization, acquisition of books, catalogs and classification systems, housing, and procedures for lending books. From about 1890 to 1925, the emphasis was on making books more readily available, by removing barriers between readers and books, by making book use more convenient to ever more groups of people, and by building branches—this long before the idea of branch banks or department stores. Recently, the focus of attention has been on motivating and guiding readers in their use of books and libraries. It is not that each phase replaced the other but rather that each was added to the earlier emphases. Thus the efforts to make books readily available through branch libraries and other means have increased over the years and may not yet have reached their peak.

Some of these methods have not proved successful or efficient and have either disappeared from the scene or now have only a special and limited role. These include delivery stations, home stations, industrial deposits, home delivery routes, and public library collections of books in hospitals and other institutions. Later, others came upon the scene with greater promise, notably the bookmobile. But for seventy-five years the use of branch libraries has been the backbone of public libraries' extension efforts. Branches will be discussed first as constituting a system and then in terms of the operation of an individual branch.[1,2,3] Bookmobiles will be taken up next, and finally a few other distributing agencies.

## The Branch System

### The Importance of Branches

In any city of appreciable size, the main public library building is likely to be of imposing size and at a prominent location, with a large book collection and many diverse services. For these and similar reasons, it is often taken as the expression of the whole of the public library. The branch libraries on the other hand are scattered, each in a relatively small building or occupying only part of a building designed for some other use, and with a relatively small book stock and limited services. It is in the nature of a branch that it will not be as complete or self-sufficient as the main library, or offer services as extensive or varied. But if a branch is well justified, it has a great importance of its own. In cities with several well-managed branches, their circulation will exceed that of the main library. The larger the population served, the more branches and the greater is their proportion of total circulation, ranging from about 45 percent in cities of 100,000 to above 80 percent in the case of libraries serving a million or more. The automobile has made access to branches easy enough so that they no longer need to be so near each other. If branches are fewer each can be larger, and with parking difficult at most central libraries, branches play a larger part than ever in the citywide service pattern.

A branch public library is usually defined as an agency in its own building or rooms, with a substantial and permanent book stock, with paid staff members, and open to the public on a regular schedule of hours. For many years the attempt was made to draw a distinction between a branch and a subbranch, the latter usually being smaller, with fewer books and smaller staff. Because quantitative limits were never established for either type and because the long-term trend is toward larger regional branches,[4] subbranches will not be considered here separately from small branches. The first modern branch public library is generally considered to have been opened in Boston around 1870, and by 1890 the trend to branches was well established. It was aided by the program of Carnegie building grants from 1895 to 1917, which provided branches as well as central libraries. By 1962 the *American Library Directory*[5] for that year reported 5,770 public libraries with 4,028 branches. Its 1978 issue[6] listed 8,455 public libraries, 1,152 of which had 5,963 branches in city, county, and regional systems.

Despite the undoubted and growing importance of branch libraries, this aspect of public library administration poses more problems and offers less satisfactory answers in practice than almost any other. This stems from lack of clarity about the proper function of branches and about the relationships of branches to one another and to the central library. Two main theories of branch library function have competed with each other. One envisages a branch library as a smaller-scale public library, offering reference and other special services, as does the central library. The other assumes that branch libraries should be mainly agencies for the circulation of popular books at the neighborhood level. Both theories are valid, since they apply to different types of agencies, but there should be far fewer of the small, weak distributing branches and many more of the large, stronger branches that can give information service to adults and young people. In short, we need to distinguish between a book-distributing branch and a library service branch. If one recognizes the difference in their function, many administrative problems are more easily resolved.

A library serving from 25,000 to 50,000 population may need some book-distributing agencies such as bookmobile stops or deposit stations, but not a branch. A city of 50,000 to 75,000 may be justified in investing capital building costs and a segment of its annual budget to operate a distributing branch but cannot afford trained librarians to help people find the materials they come to get. With almost universal ownership of automobiles, not more than one such branch is needed for this population, though in exceptional cities with high economic and educational background two or three branches may do well. Yet is that the most economical and efficient setup? The question should be carefully considered whether a city of this size would not do better to wait until it can finance a large service branch that will go far beyond simply housing and lending books. As now operated, very few of the book-distributing branches include or circulate more than a modicum of adult nonfiction. A library serving 100,000 population may need one and sometimes two service branch libraries in addition to its main library and the minor distributing agencies.

*Desirable Features of Service Branch Libraries*

When branch libraries are conceived of as library service agencies, it is apparent that a minimum size is necessary, just as is true of independent libraries attempting to give the wide range of service that modern public libraries render.

A branch is justified only when an objective survey shows that it will be assured a minimum annual circulation of 75,000 and desirably 100,000 books (of which 45 percent to 50 percent will be adult circulation) and that at least 10,000 adult informational questions will be answered each year.

A branch circulating 250,000 or more books a year should have about 8,000 square feet of floor space, all on one main floor, at sidewalk level, with about 75 seats for adults and young adults and 50 for children, and a book stock of 25,000 with active discarding and 1,500 books added annually. Currently, the trend is toward large regional centers or area libraries that combine reference and circulation services.*

A full-service branch would be open about eight hours a day, at least five days a week, and would have a staff of five or six full-time employees, exclusive of custodians, and including two or three librarians. The cost of constructing a branch building can hardly be estimated in these times of inflation; some estimate may be gained by consulting the annual reviews of building costs compiled and published in *Library Journal* (architectural issue)

---

* See Greenaway, "Trends in Public Library Service," cited earlier.

each December. These data are for the fiscal year ending the previous June 30, so they will not be current, but they may be projected to take account of probable changes. Branch buildings are not listed separately but are identified in the total list. When a national compilation of this kind is used, it is well to take account of regional differences in costs of construction. In going through the list of new buildings constructed during a recent year, it was observed that there is no typical size of branch library building. A total of 106 new branch buildings was listed. Of these, 48 were under 5,000 square feet in size; 21 were in a range of 5,000 to 8,000 square feet; 20 were in the range of 8,000 to 12,000 square feet; 14 were more than 12,000 square feet, but less than 20,000 square feet; and 3 were more than 20,000 square feet. However, it should be noted that 28 of the branches of less than 5,000 square feet were in one state (Mississippi), and several of these were less than 1,000 square feet in size, hardly qualifying as capable of full service. Judging from this one sample, the bulk of branch buildings appears to fall in the 8,000–12,000-square-foot category.

There has been very little research into the optimum conditions and characteristics pertaining to branch public libraries. The first question to be decided is whether a branch is required and whether it can be justified from a management standpoint. Often the situation will arise where a local organization will press for a branch library for a particular section or neighborhood, without any notion of the initial capital costs and the continuing operating expense that would be involved. The board of trustees and library administration should bear it clearly in mind that once a branch library is put into operation, it usually becomes very difficult to withdraw the service, even if the use does not justify the operation on a cost-benefit basis. So it will be wise to plan carefully and to be assured by sound market research that the venture will work out. This is not to say that the circulation of books is to be the only guidepost for measurement of benefits. Many branches in inner-city areas can be justified in terms of other measures, to be discussed later in this chapter under "The Branch as Library Neighborhood Center."

If the idea of a branch has been raised, or has presented itself, Brown suggests several steps that can be taken:

1. Test the area with bookmobile service (assuming the availability of a bookmobile on a temporary basis, of course).

2. Calculate the potential service area; it should have a one-and-a-half-mile radius of maximum attraction and a two-to-three mile radius of influence. (This would not be true in densely settled urban areas, where population to be served should be the criterion rather than geographic area.)

3. Secure all possible information about the area being considered: density of population, age, educational and economic levels, and other demographic data.

4. Check sources of books and book service already available in the area.

5. Consult with neighborhood representatives, political officials, city planning officers, and organized groups.[7]

The planning process, described in Chapter 2, should be applied rigorously with respect to the decision to open a new branch or to continue existing ones. The objectives of the branch operation should be specifically stated and understood, and there should be an effort to establish and maintain some regular kinds of measures of effectiveness that will be acceptable to all concerned, including the budgetary authorities.

A branch library should offer a full range of services and materials. There ought to be a wide selection of books, vertical file materials, current and back issues of periodicals, phonograph records with listening facilities, other audiovisual materials as these are developed and refined, and other nonprint materials.[8] As automated circulation and cataloging processes become more widespread, the neighborhood user will be able to locate any wanted item through a branch terminal in the system. This will be dealt with in more detail in Chapter 18, "Technical Processes." The branch should have a reference collection of several hundred to a thousand volumes or more, depending upon the service area and local needs. Regular educational and cultural programs for children and adults will be a part of the service program; and there should be active cooperation with schools, social agencies, and organizations in the community. The concept of the branch as a community center is discussed below in a separate section in this chapter.

To whatever extent money is being spent on branches too small to give a wide and useful range of services, to that extent the citywide distribution of funds is inefficient. There ought to be tangible and measurable returns on the investment in order to justify the continued operation of small branches. The cost of staff and building upkeep will rise and the investment will further decline. A good rule of thumb is fewer and stronger branches, supported by ready and convenient access to the resources of the central library. All too often, small branches are poorly housed, in converted city buildings, in a school building that is no longer used, or near parks or cemeteries. The branch library is basically consumer-oriented, and it will suffer from poor and unattractive quarters and unsatisfactory location in terms of potential uses.

*Location of Branches*

This brings up a key factor: the branch must be located in a center of pedestrian traffic—for instance, the neighborhood shopping center. Sheer size of building or of book stock can be negated by an unfavorable location, and branches smaller than indicated above can reach and exceed 75,000 circulation a year if well located. In the latter case, however, the small size of quarters, book stock, and staff will hinder the development of the branch as a library service agency. The investment in service branches will be justified only if the agency is located at a point where thousands of people tend to congregate. A library service branch should be at an intersection where an alert and aggressive businessman would want to place a store. By these standards such a branch could be expected to serve 30,000 people or more and in general could afford to be three or four miles away from any other library service agency.

The location of a library service branch is important; so in time is its relocation. Population shifts will inevitably occur and sometimes very quickly. The library must respond to these changes as well as it can, certainly by establishing new agencies in areas that are growing to 30,000 population or more, and at newly developing centers of pedestrian traffic. Conversely branches with declining population and service may well be closed if they are not profitable and the building sold, rented, or used for storage. Undoubtedly, not enough public library branches are sold or closed, especially those built long ago. The resistance of most communities to the threatened loss of a branch library may reflect the popular estimate of the library's value, but more likely only neighborhood pride. It is hard to use an old branch library building; some libraries are therefore designing and constructing new branches so the buildings can be easily converted to commerical use if the library were moved.

## Organization of a Branch System

When a city is large enough to have six or more branches, they involve enough cost and personnel and traffic to be considered in terms of a system, and they then need a branch or extension division head. Two main questions are involved in the organization of a branch system. One concerns the relationship between the branch librarians on the one hand and the director and other supervisory personnel on the other. The second question deals with the extent to which branches shall function on their own, or follow uniform practices set down for the whole system. Both questions need to be considered in the light of the distinction made between book distribution agencies and library service branches.

In any library with no more than five large branches, and that would include most libraries serving less than 300,000 population, a branch supervisor is not needed. The branch heads should report to the director, or at least to the assistant director. In turn the head of a service branch could be administratively responsible for any small branches, deposit collections, school service, or even whole bookmobiles in his general section of the city. This regional branch pattern has some advantages in large urban areas and in far-spread county and multicounty library units. In cities of 300,000 and upward, or in systems that extend for some miles, it could apply to general supervision of the work of the smaller units and perhaps also to the filling of their more elementary book needs as well as to the loan of staff from the large branch to cover emergency periods, vacations, and so forth. It is argued by some that unity and closer feeling are engendered among staff members working in the same geographic region, giving better operating results than does central control from one point for all extension agencies, or all branches, or even all small branches.

The validity and economy of this decentralization is questioned by others. They hold that the regional or intermediary branch is a sensible device only in metropolitan cities of over 700,000 population and with twenty or more branches. With the easy transportation of today it would ordinarily save substantially on book purchases and on paperwork and take no longer for requests to be made directly to central and for deliveries to be made direct from central to the customer's distributing point. In any good system, reference inquiries that cannot be filled at one agency should be mailed or sent in overnight to be looked up at central the next morning and the answer sent out by noon or afternoon to the agency. Only at central can the best reference service and variety of books be found. To shunt these requests and materials to or through an intermediate point appears to gain little in economy or promptness, but on the contrary slows things down. If there are two or three such intermediary branches, the costs for materials and extra paperwork is excessive, for there will be some requests that still must be passed on to central.

Between the large branches and the central library, each with its own well-developed program of activities and with some if not substantial differences in clientele and community, the relationship needed is *not* that between a branch librarian who is a generalist and a head of branches who is also a generalist. Instead the branch librarians need to have ready access to the policy-setting level of the librarian, and to the technical and subject skills of the heads of the special departments at the main library—for example, audiovisual, cataloging, children's work, and subject-informational help— and to all their materials. A branch library large enough to circulate at least 75,000 books a year and to offer the range of services indicated above will need to have as its head a person of ability and intelligence. Such people should then be free and encouraged to use their own best thinking in the development of library service in the community, adapted to the differences between neighborhoods sure to be found in an area large enough to have regional branches. Big business has faced this sort of problem often, and the weight of experience is that branch units above a certain size should be given the necessary flexibility to meet local conditions and then be judged on results achieved. To secure such local flexibility and adaptation, the supervisors of the major system-wide departments in the library should develop and exercise a continual and genuine interest in and responsibility for advising and assisting the branches (for instance, in developing branch library reference service), in providing them what they need in special resources and personnel (such as a better-than-average children's storyteller to serve in this capacity on different days in different agencies), and in stimulating public awareness and use of the available services of the branches.

### What Shall Be Centralized?

The second organizational question is: which activities shall be centralized? Evidently many activities must be centralized to secure the advantages of economy and efficiency in handling a large volume of like units and when there is no obvious reason to decentralize them. Thus book ordering, cataloging, and overdues today are centralized for all agencies, in order to make use of automation. The purchasing of equipment and supplies, the preparation of booklists and other publications, and many other functions are obviously better centralized.

But it is equally clear that in some areas of operation the decision if not also the work should be handled at the branch level. Though the library system may make available only a limited range of choices, branch heads should be free to decide within those limits and in line with their own thinking what they want or need for the provision of library service in their communities, as in the selection of books, equipment, and supplies. Branch flexibility and autonomy are especially fruitful for reader services. Thus, it would be unwise to lay down for all branches a uniform pattern such as for book promotion or adult film showings; what might be a great success in one neighborhood would be a failure in another. Uniformity should not be sought for its own sake but only for other results clearly to be gained and more desirable than the results of decentralization. And where it doesn't matter to other agencies what is done in one branch, the latter should be free to make its own decision—for example, whether and just how to use reader interest classification. This allows and encourages experimentation on the part of the individual branches.

There is always a borderline zone of activities that do not obviously belong in the one group or the other, and usually the answer has to be a pragmatic one in the light of available resources and library development. The rebinding of books should clearly be centralized, but how about book repair? Circulation rules (such as length of loan period) should be standardized. Pamphlets and other vertical file material should certainly be selected by the branches, but should they not be ordered, or requested if free, and subject-headed by central to save all this work at several agencies? An argument often used to justify decentralizing such functions is that some "busy work" is needed for desk assistants. A busy, well-supervised branch will not lack work for each desk assistant, and an agency that needs such work to keep its staff busy should be critically reviewed. The two great advantages of centralization are (1) that specialization breeds competence; and (2) that sufficient volume will justify the use of machines. In general whatever can be done as well or better and in less time at a central location should be so handled, in order to release the branch personnel to serve patrons. In particular, with millions of Americans moving each year from one house to another within the same county, and with libraries trying to make it easier for people to use two or more branches or libraries interchangeably, readers should not be confronted with varying practices in several branches of the same system, especially in regard to registration, overdues, loan periods, renewal privileges, and so on.

Any branch system needs three simple administrative devices. One is frequent meetings of branch librarians to exchange views, seek assistance, receive information, and keep up-to-date. This should be supplemented by a staff bulletin or notices and a procedures manual. The second device is that of a fluid collection of books on which branches may draw for temporary or long-term use and to which they can easily transfer books no longer needed at a given agency but too valuable or useful to be discarded. Such as pool can be used to check requests for rebinding or for purchase of replacement copies, and it should include some provision for central assistance to all agencies in filling reserves. An alternative to such a branch book pool, and almost as often found, is branch use of the general central collection, perhaps with some extra copies of new books for branch use and with branch withdrawals going into a central pool of withdrawals and duplicate gifts. The third device is a truck pickup and delivery system or arrangement with a local delivery company, for making daily rounds if possible, or at least every other day, to each branch, large or small. This assumes that a reader's needs for materials will be taken seriously enough, especially for reference questions, to give him prompt service.

### Running a Branch

*The Mission of a Branch*

The mission of a branch library is to give as much and as good service to as many citizens in its area as possible. In small branches this is likely to consist mainly of lending books and a high proportion of fiction, with some elementary reference work and reading guidance. In the large branch, the service so given will almost certainly include the loan of a larger proportion of adult nonfiction and other special materials, reference help and reading guidance on the intermediate level of difficulty or even the advanced level, and an active program of school visiting, cooperation with community organizations, and activity programs within the branch for children, young people, and adults.

The branch librarian's first main job is to become a specialist in the community served by his or her agency. Just as subject departments at the central library need staff members who are specialists in the literature of those subjects, so the branches need librarians informed on the nature of their particular community and aware of its social relationships and developments, be it rural, suburban, or urban. It is important for the branch librarian to attend PTA meetings and to know what the businesspeople's association is doing, without sacrificing management and supervising functions. Routine processes in the branch should be left to an assistant. A branch librarian may profitably spend a third of the time out in the community and half of the time on real administrative functions including supervision.

A second role of the librarian of a large branch is to plan, direct, receive reports, supervise colleagues, and make evaluations. Others on the staff, down to and including part-time pages, can do the work that needs to be done, but the branch librarian has to make the decisions and keep in touch with the library director and other supervisory personnel, with the other branches and the housekeeping agencies of the system, and with assistants. Not only are all the usual administrative functions involved, such as those of personnel administration, public relations, supervision, and development, but there is responsibility for the library building and for the public service program. The physical separation from the rest of the library inevitably throws on the branch librarian a greater responsibility than is borne by a department head at the central library, to meet emergencies, to make decisions, and to interpret established policies.

## The Administration of a Branch

Two main facets of the administration of a branch library warrant special mention here. One is the organization of assignments and the responsibility for staff supervision and development; the other is the handling of routine work and of special activities. Part of the challenge of branch librarianship is that in none of these areas is there a firmly established or satisfactory pattern. As in all of library work, intelligent people with outgoing personalities will be most effective. Handling a crowd of children or high school students in a branch is no job for a person who does not like the work.

In a branch of five or six staff members, including two or three professionals, the usual division is that one librarian is made responsible for children's work and another for adult work, with special attention to informational service. The librarians so assigned will usually select the new books for the branch in their fields, review the present collection from time to time, advise readers of the age level they serve, develop their skills and materials to answer reference questions, and probably plan special activities for patrons, subject to the approval of the branch librarian. One constant danger is for too few to try to cover too many activities. The librarians in the branches who specialize in these aspects of the work will meet with the library system supervisor or coordinator of work with children, young people, or adults, to benefit by their technical advice and assistance. Where the branch librarian is especially active outside the library, the responsibility for internal supervision of the branch staff and of the services given in the branch to its public may be assigned to the assistant branch librarian, who would plan work schedules and vacation schedules, sign requisitions for supplies, assist any other staff member in need of help, see that the necessary routine work is done correctly and on time, train new assistants, and so forth.

In a branch lending each year 100,000 books or more, three trained and three untrained assistants, even aided by a modern mechanical or simplified charging system, can hardly keep up with the volume of business. This calls for considerable skill in supervision. The branch librarian needs ability in selecting new assistants, in assessing their capabilities and shortcomings, and in finding appropriate methods of employee motivation. Supervision in a small branch, where only two people work and side by side, is different from supervision in a large branch, where contacts are less frequent and relations more formal. In addition, the trained assistants need to be developed and supervised to give elementary reference service and reading guidance for each of the three main age groups, as when they are on duty alone at mealtime or in case of illness or other emergency. Experienced but untrained library assistants should be able to file branch catalog cards and do preliminary weeding of pamphlets and books. In a branch so small as to have only one or two staff members, there is not likely to be a professional librarian, and each person has to be instructed as well as possible to attempt all the jobs at the agency.

## Attention to Major Functions

The branch librarian has to assign someone to be responsible in juvenile, young adult, and adult readers' service and material and to see that each aspect is being adequately covered. A branch librarian needs to develop adult reference services (which will be used also by school students) and to insist on enough trained reference workers to meet reader demands. The reference collection should be strong and up-to-date, including plentiful vertical file material.

The routine work of any branch, as in the whole system, needs to be done well. A procedure manual, good introductory training and systematic followup are all indicated. Specializing as it does in service, a branch library has numerous repetitive operations, resulting from reader request. Returned books must be shelved promptly, new magazines will be wanted the day received, borrower registrations must be ready for the next branch delivery. Routines should be regularly scrutinized to find simplifications; possibly something more can be transferred to the large branch or to central.

Just as its community changes and becomes interested in new subjects, so the branch library staff must try to identify the topics of major concern as they appear, and have books and appropriate library services ready to meet them. Activity programs, booklists, special exhibits, publicity, deposit collections to go to locations outside the branch, reserve bookshelves, better service to inquirers, more books on certain subjects—all these must be thought through, adapted, and completed in whatever staff time can be found, only to be succeeded by new programs and new activities, as the seasons change, the school assignments come and go, the developments on the national and international front find repercussions on the local scene, the forces and agencies in the local community make themselves felt, and the branch library itself asserts a role of leadership.

## The Branch as Library Neighborhood Center

Branch libraries had often served their communities to some extent as meeting places and to some degree as community centers, but the War on Poverty and community action programs of the 1960s, aided by large-scale private and federal funding, provided signal impetus and new scope and directions. Considerable interest in the neighborhood library as an agency for helping the disadvantaged deal with their problems was exhibited by officials of the Office of Economic Opportunity, one of the federal agencies charged with carrying out the War on Poverty. The OEO engaged the National Book Committee to study and report on some of the public libraries "in a few cities and rural places where public libraries have established multi-media neighborhood centers and undertaken new, special educational services."[9]

The term *library neighborhood center* was initially applied to a remodeled storefront library in New Haven, opened in August, 1964, with a three-year demonstration grant of $180,000 that had been made available from Ford Foundation funds through that city's community action agency. Meredith Bloss, then New Haven city librarian, described the idea:

New Haven's Library Neighborhood Centers are based on a simple idea. Take a branch library, with books selected for the people who live in the neighborhood. Have a friendly, inviting, attractive, accessible place. Have a friendly, ingenious, innovative, dedicated staff. Books and other materials, a place and staff . . . these are the ingredients.

The idea—the library as an agent for change. Facilitating the removal of barriers through *communication*. . . . The staff is not to say, "How can we get these people involved in *our* programs?" but how can staff get involved in these people's programs.

The *idea* is to make the library a center of neighborhood activity. It provides a place for meetings, and for individuals to take part in sponsored programs in education, recreation and community affairs. The library is the focal point, the center, the place where people can meet, learn, communicate.

The concept is based on the premise that the library is an agency for informal education, and *that* education takes place when there is free, purposeful communication among persons.[10]

The New Haven center was described by Drennan as an "offbeat library using a fresh mix of people and programs to produce surprising results."

He reported that because of federal interest, "the Office of Economic Opportunity (in charge of federal anti-poverty programs) has just appropriated funds to study the possibility of developing New Haven type library programs throughout the United States" (report published in 1967 and cited above). Drennan described New Haven librarian Meredith Bloss as the "father . . . of the innovative library center," and said he had expressed the view that "libraries must be aggressive agencies for social change. A library should be a force, not an institution." Drennan also observed:

And force is exactly what this community library is. Created by moving a 40-year-old branch library from dreary basement quarters in the old Scranton School to rented store-front space in a former supermarket, administratively the neighborhood library center is still a branch library. Actually, it seems to have a life of its own.

With street corner storytellers, puppet shows, art exhibits, music classes, drop-in tutoring services, political meetings, babysitters, and a doorbell-ringing staff determined to bring some library activity into every home in the neighborhood, this militant superlibrary is quietly smashing conservative library tradition.

"Not so," says Bloss. "There is plenty of precedent for what we are doing." He cites the New York City public libraries and their street corner lecturers who talked on subjects ranging from socialism to housing early in this century. He quotes the original Massachusetts library law that called for libraries to become "agencies to diffuse knowledge among all the people"—not buildings to store books. "Our library," says Bloss, "is kin to the Danish Folk School and to our own wartime USO library centers."[11]

In New Haven, three other library neighborhood centers were put into operation, initially with federal funding, then continued with municipal support as a part of the regular library budget. The National Book Committee study, cited above, contains a report on the New Haven centers and those in eleven other cities around the country, and includes a suggested plan for a model library neighborhood center:

This is a neighborhood center, a friendly gathering place for broadly-defined educational and cultural purposes, as parks and playgrounds are gathering places for recreational purposes. It is located near or in conjunction with other community services to make it a place where people will congregate. It may be mobile or fixed, in storefront or other accessible quarters; and it may be urban or rural.

The center is designed to provide a bridge to the mainstream culture of American society by meeting individual and community needs for communication, information, and life enrichment.

PLANNING

The first step in the establishment of a center is selection of an area for its location. This involves study of census figures for a statistical picture of the dominant economic, racial, housing and educational factors. Existing CAP agencies should be consulted in this process. It also involves meetings with local groups and with the personnel of public agencies active in the area in order to get a picture of the strengths of the community and neighborhood. A community without strong local organization will have people with strength who can participate in planning and operating a center.

The next step is the formation of a small advisory committee made up of the most effective community residents and agency personnel to develop a cooperative study of local needs and resources and a cooperative plan for the use of the center. This plan would include a study of the various sources of funding currently available, both private and public.

The report recommended massive funding by the Office of Economic Opportunity for library neighborhood centers on a broad scale, but when the War on Poverty program ended, the impetus from federal quarters was lost.

However, the points suggested for consideration in planning a library neighborhood center retain validity. As to location and quarters:

A center can be created in a storefront or other structure so long as it is convenient and accessible. . . .

The inside space should be flexible, capable of being rearranged to meet developing needs . . . open, inviting, accessible . . . there should be adjacent to the main center area, two or three smaller rooms for games, handicrafts, and studying. . . . [Also] office, staff and committee rooms . . . each about 300 square feet. Adequate space for the center means about one-half square foot per capita based upon the total population to be served. . . . Six to eight blocks is the effective service radius, although a three to five block radius is desirable in densely populated areas.

As to staff, the report recommended that "the first requirement . . . is that they have interest in, and proven ability to respond to, people of all ages." (In New Haven's first library neighborhood center, many of the most successful staff members were returned members of the Peace Corps with an obvious interest in people, which was fortunately supplemented by a desire to apply the media of communication in helping ways.)

There should be at least five to six full-time workers, with a ratio of one per 500 population. These include librarians, group workers, story-tellers, program workers, neighborhood workers, and volunteers to assist with programs or to carry them on.[12]

Two aspects of the library-neighborhood-center concept troubled many librarians and library directors: the (mistaken) view that the library was entering into the problem-solving area of the social work agencies; and the programs and activities. The point, however, was not that the library neighborhood staff was to be there to tell people what to do, or to solve their problems for them, but to provide the information, the communications media, the resources, by which they themselves might come to grips with their problems and deal with them, either individually or as organized groups. Major Owens dealt with this issue in the paper quoted in the chapter on reference services: "Information is power, and it is advocacy, itself." But that is not to say that the librarians in the branch library are there to advocate. Theirs is a service role, to help bridge the gap between the people's need for information and the informational resources.

As to the programs and activities, the library-neighborhood-center concept sees these as an integral part of the communications process. Information, knowledge, insights, and understanding are not conveyed solely by the printed word, or by the solitary reader consulting a book, periodical, or government report. Many people learn by visual means, or in groups stimulated by either structured or informal discussion. The branch library is not to be an alternative for the all-purpose community center but to be a different kind of community center, built around the printed and nonprinted record. Many neighborhoods support clubs and gathering places for entertainment, sports, and games; the library can be a place where the mind is encouraged to develop. Finally, the purpose of programs and activities is not to entice people into the library so that they may be encouraged to draw out books. The library's avowed goal is the "diffusion of knowledge" (information) and that can be done by various means.

The branch library as an agency that all persons, including the disadvantaged, can use to improve their own situations, has received considerable attention during the past ten or fifteen years, and there have been many reports, studies, and books on the subject, only a few of which can be cited here. In recent years, the information and referral function has been advanced as a way of serving the needs of people, and this has been discussed at length in the reference chapter. The points made there should be reviewed in considering the branch library operation, as the branch should be the information and referral point for the neighborhood being served. This should be in coordination with the other units in the system, since most of the information and referral resources will be city or regional in scope. Presumably, as this function of the library becomes automated, the branch library will have a CRT terminal connected into the main computer, which may be housed in the central library or elsewhere in the city and which will be updated as frequently as need be. The Cambridge, Massachusetts, Public Library developed such a system in 1979, with a substantial grant from the Health, Education and Welfare Department and the technical assistance of the Massachusetts Institute of Technology. It may serve as a model for other similar installations throughout the country.

Of special concern to the branch librarian, who is usually closer to the needs of the citizens than the central library staff, are the comments of Seymour and Layne (quoting a study by Childers) that

while most people—educated and non-educated alike—need essentially the same kind of information to survive, the disadvantaged person needs larger remedial doses in order to bring him to "information par" with the rest of society. More than the average, Childers reports, the disadvantaged individual needs such basic information as to how to obtain subsidized housing, welfare benefits, free school lunch, medical care, and so on. Closely allied to this are needs in the area of individual rights: What am I entitled to? How do I go about getting it? How do I protect myself legally? There are also needs associated with remedial adult education and day care for children. While they are hardly unique to disadvantaged Americans, says Childers, these needs pervade their lives out of all proportion.

The disadvantaged American, more than his counterpart in general society, does not know which formal channels to tap in order to solve his problems, or what specific programs exist to respond to his needs. He watches many hours of television daily, seldom reads newspapers and magazines, and never reads books. He usually does not recognize his problems as information needs, and even when he does, is not a very active information seeker. He is locked into an informal information network of friends, neighbors, and relatives that is itself deficient in the information ordinarily available to the rest of society.

Clearly there is a widespread discrepancy between what society requires of these many millions of isolated Americans and what they are able to achieve. For them there is special meaning to the biblical injunction "The truth shall make you free."[13]

## Bookmobiles and Other Extension Agencies

### Construction of Bookmobiles

Bringing books to people by bookmobile is the most dramatic and colorful and evidently the most efficient and economical type of everyday public library service. Its history goes back to horse-drawn book wagons around 1900. Rapid development of the automobile resulted by the 1920s in a number of motor vehicles converted from other uses for library purposes, usually in rural areas. Specially designed and commercially produced bookmobiles did not come into use in any large number until after World War II. Occasionally boats, railroad cars, streetcars, and other vehicles have been used for book transportation.

Bookmobiles are self-propelled and equipped with shelves built into the sides of the body. A few are of the house trailer type, or of the van type, pulled by a semiattached tractor. Though trailers have their own special advantages, the self-contained unit has greater flexibility and ease of operation. Bookmobiles range in size from a panel truck of a ton or less, capable of carrying only several hundred books, to larger vehicles built on a bus chassis, carrying 4,000 books or more. There are several companies in the country that now sell finished bookmobiles. Local firms that construct specialized truck bodies can also turn out an acceptable bookmobile. In all cases, a truck or bus chassis is purchased, a body of special design is added, and shelves, heater, and other equipment are added separately.

Bookmobile shelves are desirably slanted a few degrees, and with book-ends; this is usually enough to keep the books from falling, although for rough roads, a center strip of rubber can be added. The usual pattern today is to build the shelves on the inside of the vehicle, and to provide heat, artificial light, and air conditioning. Some vehicles carry their own electric generators (500- to 10,000-watt capacity) to provide heat and power for these uses and for book charging, a loudspeaker system, and other devices. Other vehicles get the necessary power by connecting a cable to a prearranged power outlet at station stops. Many of these new bookmobiles are tailored for use as media centers and are equipped to carry records, films, magazines, players, tapes and tape recorders, record players, projection devices, and portable TVs. Such vehicles are being used in rural areas and in the cities to serve the disadvantaged.[14]

## Policies of Bookmobile Operation

We have no firm factual basis for a "breaking point" of demonstrated economy or wastefulness as to bookmobile service, but sufficient experience is available to permit generalizing on the more usual policies of bookmobile operation. The same principles of operating economy are applied to bookmobiles and branches. The unit must be large enough to provide an adequate return on capital investment and current operating costs. Viewed strictly as a facility for the distribution of books, with perhaps some limited quick reference services, and given an adequate density of potential users, the bookmobile can be more economical than the branch in a fixed location. The bookmobile returns to headquarters each day and can bring out a changing stock. The turnover of books is high in contrast to costly stocks of books standing comparatively idle on the shelves of small branches. The per-circulation book and salary cost is cut to a third or a fourth of that in the typical small branch. Skyrocketing costs and unpredictable availability of fuel will surely affect our concepts of basic mobile services as we enter the 1980s.

The economics of bookmobiles suggest

1. that they should have a capacity of 3,000 to 4,000 volumes, and that none have space for less than 2,500;

2. that they be planned and operated to serve as many adults as children and to lend as many adult books as children's;

3. that school stops and the mass movement of children through the bus at the rate of one a minute no longer be acceptable bookmobile service;

4. that the investment in equipment, stock, and salaries be capitalized on by an all-afternoon and evening schedule of stops, at fortnightly intervals, at points where adults can and will visit the bookmobile;

5. that a trained person be present at all bookmobile stops, and staff schedules adjusted for this 1–9 P.M. duty;

6. that every bookmobile carry materials to render quick everyday reference service, for example, encyclopedias for adults and children, an almanac, a *Reader's Guide,* a few handbooks, and two vertical file trays of informational pamphlets; and

7. that the substantial type of library service be emphasized and publicized.

With these shifts in emphasis, the worth of our bookmobiles to society would be greatly enhanced.

To date the bookmobile has proved it can be an effective and economical book-distributing agency. Few bookmobiles answer many reference questions or carry more than a half dozen elementary reference tools. Typically bookmobiles carry only books, with perhaps a few pamphlets, current magazines, or phonograph records. In most cases there is no card catalog on the vehicle, and probably none is needed. Patrons can register for library cards and get started on borrowing. In most cases at present the bookmobile staff consists of a bookmobile librarian (who is likely not to be a professional librarian) and a clerk-driver; often the librarian works alone and drives the vehicle too. A large bookmobile carries a staff of three to five people, including one or two professionals, and two crews can operate it sixty to seventy-five hours a week.

If bookmobile service is to be given at schools, a separate vehicle should be used for this purpose alone, and it seems logical that it be purchased by the school system. Community stops are likely to be most worthwhile in the afternoons and evenings and on Saturdays; this calls for readjustment of staff schedules to ensure that there will be enough professionals to cover five or six evenings a week. Adherence to a regular schedule is a prime necessity, and the current schedule should be changed as seldom as possible, at most only twice a year, for the summer months and for the school year. For adult or community stops, favored locations are in residential areas of average to high density, neighborhood store areas, and in some cases the giant shopping centers, housing projects, or other pedestrian centers.

Like branches, bookmobiles too have a point of optimum economic operation. Briefly it is that no stop should be continued if after reasonable trial it fails to result in a rate of circulation of about a book a minute. Assuming the bookmobile is open for use around thirty hours a week, this will result in an annual circulation of about 90,000 books a year, and about half of this should be adult books. At this rate, the cost of a bookmobile's operation per circulation compares with that of a branch library with a circulation of, say, 60,000 books a year. This is so because the useful life of a bookmobile is not much more than twelve to fifteen years, and both its depreciation and variable costs (gasoline, repairs, and so on) tend to be higher than for a fixed branch. Many bookmobiles have total annual circulations well above 100,000 books a year and as much as 200,000 or more, and without emphasizing service to schools. Just as small independent libraries tend to be uneconomic and inefficient, and as small branches tend not to be worthwhile, so small bookmobiles are often operated at a high unit cost.[15]

The great flexibility of the bookmobile should be utilized always by seeking service stops located most conveniently for the largest number of people. Stops that fail to generate the necessary volume of circulation might be reduced in length or visited less often.

One of the great advantages of the bookmobile is that it can be used to give service quickly, as in the case of annexed territory or a mushrooming suburb; by the same token it can be used to estimate the likelihood of success of a branch in alternative possible locations. If a bookmobile is used to give service for more than one day at a given stop (very unusual), a trailer-type unit would be preferable to a self-contained mobile one. Some libraries exclude bookmobile stops from the service area of any branch, but other libraries have found that the book-distributing service of bookmobiles can be used to advantage in supplementing a branch in areas cut off from it by heavy traffic or natural barriers, and especially in service to children and general reading for adults.

### Administrative Considerations of Bookmobile Operation

The use of a bookmobile introduces a whole new set of administrative considerations, different from those usually met in other aspects of public library operation. The maintenance and repair of a bookmobile, for example, is not only a technical matter but one that brooks no delay. Should the city or county handle this service, not an uncommon arrangement today, the library should be certain that the bookmobile's repair and maintenance be given equal importance with the repair of other top-priority items like police cars. A disrupted schedule can kill public relations and service. If possible, financial provision should be made for accumulating money to replace a given vehicle, since its relatively short life requires some such depreciation allowance. Adequate housing of the vehicle at a desirable location can do much to help the efficient operation of the unit. The desirable volume of book circulation on a bookmobile makes it necessary to perform centrally as much of the technical and routine work as possible, as reserves and overdues. And selecting the bookmobile librarian poses special problems, in finding someone with the necessary physical stamina, the ability to meet patrons easily, and sufficient knowledge of books to operate without a card catalog. For each bookmobile librarian or driver, there should be another staff member trained and available in case of need. Working out the exact schedule is a minor art, involving travel time, allowance for meals for the staff, prevailing weather conditions, the most desirable route to follow (in view of hairpin turns, weight loads, and height limits), parking facilities at each stop, time for mechanical servicing of the vehicle, and so on.

The bookmobile is in itself a natural medium of library publicity, but it poses some special problems. In some cities, bookmobile stops are marked by a metal sign on a pole or by a poster. When weather or other conditions interrupt the schedule, there should be some way of getting word to the area so that people do not wait in vain, and bookmobile books due that day should be accepted at any library agency, be automatically renewed, or be able to be left at some store or home near the stop and be picked up later. A printed or mimeographed schedule of bookmobile stops is necessary and should be given wide distribution, perhaps via radio, television, and the newspapers.

Some libraries have created a special book collection for the bookmobile; though this is perhaps several times larger than the capacity of the vehicle, it still tends to set narrower limitations than are possible and desirable. The bookmobile should get new books currently, but it should also be able to draw on as large a basic book stock as possible, so as to be able to change its collection gradually but continuously with a minimum of paperwork. This is especially important if a serious bid is to be made for adult use of nonfiction books. In such a case, a bookmobile should have at any one time no more than one-fourth of its books juvenile and no more than another fourth adult fiction. These ratios, plus an ever-changing book collection, and provision for supplying any desired title on special request, make bookmobile service a truly stimulating and effective book-distributing agency. Crowded conditions and limited book capacity make it desirable that the charging system be one that eliminates slipping and makes returned books readily available for reuse. On-line systems have now been developed to allow portable units for bookmobiles.

### Other Extension Agencies

Stations constitute the group of extension agencies most often found, and they are usually defined as small collections of books made available in quarters not the property of the library, and either self-serviced or cared for by volunteers or by occasional visits of a staff member.

Stations are found in and are useful to both large and small libraries, and constitute the oldest and still the least expensive form of public library extension, partly because so little staff time is involved. In the first quarter of this century especially, public libraries experimented with stations in a variety of locations, as in factories, and with forms, as delivery stations where specifically requested titles were left for a reader. The depression of the 1930s wiped out many, and the bookmobiles have displaced others in more recent years. The basic difficulties with the idea of stations are that typically only a small number of books are available at any one location (up to about two hundred or so) and that there is little or no staff assistance. The bookmobile corrects both of these limitations, with only one main counterlimitation— the limited period of time it is available at any one stop. However, stations too are not always open to readers for any great length of time; some industrial stations, for example, have been open as little as an hour a week. Within these limitations, stations still have a role to play—for example, as storefront libraries, helping to provide a network of book-distributing points where the turnover per book justifies investing the price per book.

Stations have often been used in hospitals, and stations or small branches in housing projects. This sort of extension service to special groups is not usually profitable or desirable for a public library. A bookmobile stop would be preferable; if the housing project and its neighborhood could produce a circulation of 75,000, a branch would be justified. Library service to patients is often given by Red Cross Gray Ladies or other volunteer groups; it is as much a responsibility of the hospital administration as are other patient services and as is library service for the medical staff.

Updated versions of the station concept are the prefabricated and portable library units also known as the Port-a-Kiosk, Outpost Library, Port-a-Structure, and Instant Library. These units offer a quick affordable solution to extending library services to a large number of people. The portable structures can be assembled in just a few weeks and require minimum staffing. The kiosks operating in Washington, D.C., have been highly successful in providing a basic level of service. In West Virginia, Outpost and Instant libraries are widely used to meet the state's library obligations to its citizens. Numerous outpost libraries with seating for twelve readers, housing 4,500 to 5,000 volumes, were constructed in the late 1970s. Individual units were erected in less than four hours at a cost of $13,000. Earlier in the decade the state erected many somewhat larger outpost libraries, which have continued to serve a wide population.[16]

The main lesson to be learned from almost a century of public library extension service is the desirability of limiting the number of agencies or devices to those able to display many books, handle a large volume of circulation and a high turnover per book, develop a strong reference service, and provide a variety of other services, all at a low unit cost.

## Notes

1. Lowell A. Martin, *The Purpose and Administrative Organization of Branch Systems in Large Urban Libraries* (Chicago: University of Chicago Library, 1940) and by the same author, *Branch Library Service for Dallas* (Dallas: Dallas Public Library, 1958).
2. Harry N. Peterson, *Survey of the Fort Worth Public Library Branch Requirements* (Fort Worth, Tex.: Forth Worth Public Library, 1959). See also Andrew Geddes, "Current Trends in Branch Libraries," *Library Trends* 14 (April 1966).
3. Robert E. Coughlin et al., *Urban Analysis for Branch Library System Planning* (Westport, Conn.: Greenwood Press, 1972). See, by the American Library Association, *Public Library Systems in the United States* (Chicago: American Library Association, 1969), and *Minimum Standards for Public Library Systems, 1966* (Chicago: American Library Association, 1966).
4. Emerson Greenaway, "New Trends in Branch Public Library Service," *Library Trends* 14 (April 1966): 453.
5. *The American Library Directory*, 23d ed. (New York: R. R. Bowker, 1962).
6. *The American Library Directory*, 31st ed. (New York: R. R. Bowker, 1978).
7. Eleanor Frances Brown, *Modern Branch Libraries and Libraries in Systems* (Metuchen, N.J.: Scarecrow Press, 1970), pp. 87–89.
8. See guidelines for branches set down for Chicago Public Library by Lowell A. Martin in *Library Response to Urban Change* (Chicago: American Library Association, 1969).
9. *Neighborhood Library Centers and Services* (New York: National Book Committee, 1967), p. 1.
10. Meredith Bloss, "Take a Giant Step," *Library Journal* 91 (Jan. 15, 1966): 323–26.
11. Henry Drennan, "Little Miracle on Chapel Street," *American Education* 2 (July–August 1966): 1–5.

12. *Neighborhood Library Centers and Services,* pp. 30–35.
13. Whitney North Seymour, Jr., and Elizabeth N. Layne, *For the People: Fighting for Public Libraries* (New York: Doubleday, 1979), pp. 77–78, and Thomas Childers, *The Information Poor in America* (Metuchen, N.J.: Scarecrow Press, 1975).
14. Eleanor Frances Brown, *Bookmobiles and Bookmobile Service* (Metuchen, N.J.: Scarecrow Press, 1967), p. 39.
15. For an extended study of operating costs see Teh-wei, *A Benefit-Cost Analysis of Alternative Library Delivery Systems* (Westport, Greenwood Press, 1975).
16. Arlan G. Bushman, "Prefabricated and Portable Library Units Offer Quick and Easy Extension of Services," *American Libraries* 8 (November 1977): 546–48.

# 14  Running a Small Library

The present volume gives less attention than many would wish to special problems of the very large libraries, in order to be more useful to workers in libraries in cities of from 10,000 to 350,000 population. Libraries with less than 10,000 population may feel that various topics have not been discussed specifically enough in their terms. This population size has been chosen arbitrarily; to many people a small library may mean one that serves as many as 25,000 or 30,000 citizens.

This chapter is a summary of administrative aspects of operating small libraries. The ALA's Small Libraries Project, initiated by Joseph L. Wheeler in 1958 and financed by a grant from the Council on Library Resources, has produced a series of detailed informational leaflets, of 250 to 300 pages, for libraries serving populations of less than 10,000.[1]

Much of the material in those leaflets was summarized in an excellent general guide by Dorothy Sinclair, *Administration of the Small Public Library* (1965). A newly revised second edition of this volume was published in 1979, and it will be valuable particularly for directors and trustees of small libraries. Noting that "management of libraries in the United States, at all levels, has become more sophisticated," the author points out that the revised volume gives "relatively more attention to governance, finance, and planning in general." Chapter topics indicate the scope of contents: the small community; library objectives and community study; library governance; policies; finance; personnel administration; from objectives to service; operations in support of service; interlibrary cooperation and library systems; and buildings, other outlets, furniture, and equipment.[2]

Two facts have become clear. The small independent library can never afford the efficient and economical services to the public that they can secure by joining larger regional units. As integral parts of a large system they can have closer access to materials far beyond their own potential means; many processes can be centrally managed more economically and efficiently,

## The Administrative Function in the One-Person Library

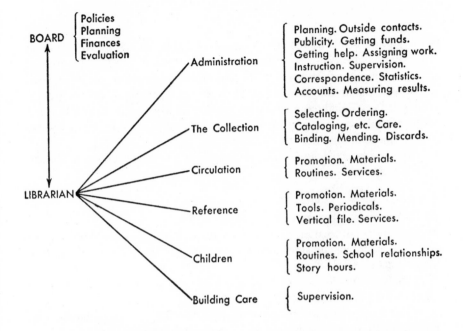

BOARD { Policies / Planning / Finances / Evaluation

LIBRARIAN

Administration { Planning. Outside contacts. Publicity. Getting funds. Getting help. Assigning work. Instruction. Supervision. Correspondence. Statistics. Accounts. Measuring results.

The Collection { Selecting. Ordering. Cataloging, etc. Care. Binding. Mending. Discards.

Circulation { Promotion. Materials. Routines. Services.

Reference { Promotion. Materials. Tools. Periodicals. Vertical file. Services.

Children { Promotion. Materials. Routines. School relationships. Story hours.

Building Care { Supervision.

releasing valuable time for direct local service to readers; each small library can draw more frequently and fully than at present on the strength that comes only from a corps of full-time trained specialists. By frequent visits, these specialists can pay attention to administration, organization, supervision, book selection, preparation, reference work, work with children, work with young people and adults, and the whole array of techniques. Each aspect of each small-town and village library would greatly benefit. Such regional or cooperative systems are now in successful operation in states throughout the country, in part stimulated by supplementary funds from the states and under Title III of the Federal Library Services and Construction Act.[3]

The other clear point: responsibility for internal good management has always to continue inside the small local library, as in the branches of a large city system. The small library cannot profitably go it alone, but it may constantly grow more efficient. There is great satisfaction in working with a small clientele in a small community or neighborhood; acquaintance and understanding between staff and readers can be close indeed. The ineffectiveness of small libraries stems largely from failure to search for and appoint competent people, as local budgets may not permit a full-time trained librarian unless the time and salary can be divided among two or three towns. Good appointments are more likely under central direction from a regional head.

## Policies

Librarian and board in a small community have to conceive of their library as a dynamic agency for spreading the use of print into every home, making all citizens aware of the ways in which printed information can serve them. The library should lead and not be led in interpreting its role in the community, as an agent of enlightenment and a counterinfluence against social, racial, religious, and economic prejudices and intolerance. More small libraries need to draw more adults into the circle of users.

Among suggested goals and objectives for the heads of small libraries are the following:

1. Attaining adequate fiscal support.
2. A staff of at least one full-time person (or equivalent) per 2,000 population, plus maintenance staff, which should be kept at not over one-sixth of total personnel.
3. Salaries and wages, such as per-hour pay, in line with those paid in other outstanding libraries.
4. At least one-third of the staff, not counting janitorial, having been professionally trained or having had some college education.
5. Resourcefulness in getting and training student, volunteer, and other part-time help for clerical work in numerous activities.
6. A circulation of eight or nine per capita, more than half of which are adult, with adult nonfiction at least 50 percent of adult circulation.
7. At least 30 to 35 percent of total budget spent on books and materials, and not less than one-third of the book budget to be spent on adult nonfiction and one-third on juvenile books.
8. Informational materials and services given prime attention to attain at least one-half informational and reference questions per capita per year (not counting directional questions or finding titles asked by readers).
9. Prompt local response and followup on informational requests; requests promptly transmitted to county, regional, or state headquarters for materials not in the local library, and readers notified or handed their material within five or six days of requesting it.
10. Continuing program of public relations and publicity to keep the library story always in the public mind and to encourage greater use by individuals.
11. Constant attention to economy: (a) not starting new activities unless they are essential and profitable to the library's main purpose; (b) omitting, reducing or simplifying all possible routines and paperwork; making every hour count in each person's daily work.

## The Library Board

The librarian in a small town will want the board to be as effective as possible. Working through the chairperson, the librarian should keep the group promptly informed, at monthly meetings, about developments in all aspects of the library, including staff, collection, services, expenditures, problems, trends, and public reactions.

The librarian should encourage full attendance at board meetings. Many libraries would profit by decreasing the number of trustees, from unwieldy groups such as fifteen or more to a workable active five or seven, and then capitalizing on the special interests and abilities of each trustee to further some aspect of library progress.

Trustees and librarian will formulate a statement of library policies, covering as many aspects of the work as possible, the question of joining a regional system, and any points on which public misunderstanding may be foreseen. Because many small libraries cannot afford a full-time trained librarian, some trustees may, as volunteers, be drawn into the internal routines and services; their responsibilities as related to the librarian's should be discussed and defined in memoranda prepared periodically.

Officially responsible for financing, trustees should be continually devising means to secure increasing public support. They should promote circulation and reference service. They have to evaluate the year's progress and the effectiveness of the librarian. They will support the librarian in seeing that staff members are developing and the staff strengthened each year. This means dropping ineffectual workers. The ALA guidelines are a great help in evaluating library operations.[4] These guidelines reflect the profession's movement from a quantitative viewpoint to a qualitative perspective.

## The Librarian's Varied Work

Planning what shall be attempted for the coming year, the coming month, the day ahead puts the librarian in control of library developments.

Citizens are glad to cooperate in publicity—for example, lending store window space for exhibits that can be prepared by high school students or volunteers. News stories can often be delegated to others to prepare if the librarian will choose the subject, outline the story, and have the data ready. The librarian's contacts with trustees and leading citizens should, among other things, lead to their active help in getting better library financing.

The librarian, in consultation with the trustees, will see that each employee is chosen for merit only, choosing among promising candidates. Resourceful librarians can attract intelligent, interested part-time students and volunteers to help on a variety of clerical routines and special tasks—arranging magazines and books; gathering, clipping, and arranging news items, articles, and pamphlets on local history; telling stories. The librarian has to give instructions to each worker, as teacher and supervisor.

Statistics and accounts should be kept at a minimum: juvenile, adult fiction, adult nonfiction circulation; number of reference questions answered successfully; and number of books added, withdrawn, and in the collection.

## The Collection of Materials

The director of the small public library will be responsible for the quality and character of the collection of books and other materials. The principles and policies that have been discussed in the chapters on adult service, children's service, and reference and information will all apply equally to the small library. The book selection aids have been treated in those chapters and need not be repeated here. It is critical that new book orders be placed at least once a month, and in advance of publication in the case of titles that are apt to be popular. Book-leasing systems may be found useful in the small library, as these bring in shelf-ready titles that can be replaced by others within a stated period. Simplified cataloging and classifying is recommended, and one of the commercial processing and jobber facilities may be found suitable for the small library that is plagued by a shortage of clerical staff. Centralized acquisition and processing is one of the benefits to be obtained by regional cooperative systems, and many small libraries are able to avail themselves of these services.

The small library should have a book selection policy; it should follow the goals and objectives that have been developed and agreed upon, as described in Chapter 2. There is inevitably some pressure to select and stock only the most popular titles, leaving the borrower to seek other resources for the standard, classic research materials and serious fiction and nonfiction. The policy will be for the local library director, staff, and trustees to decide and may depend somewhat on whether other resources are available and the willingness of the larger, urban library to support the needs of the small library users without adequate reimbursement. However, the problem is being cared for more and more by the regional approach, and by reciprocal borrowing arrangements, with county, regional, or state support.

## Reference Service

Even the small library needs to update its high school and its adult encyclopedias every four or five years, alternating their purchase among standard works of known strength. At least the *Abridged Reader's Guide* should be available, the key to forty or fifty magazines subscribed to in a town of 2,000. In towns of 7,500 to 10,000, the library will take 100 to 125 magazines (using the full *Reader's Guide*). A file of pamphlets, bulletins, clippings on topics in demand, including local history, activities, and services should be kept up; an intelligent volunteer with some instruction and occasional newspaper recognition may find this a worthwhile and interesting community activity. Each reference question should be followed through; sometimes a local citizen can give help or clues to the information, otherwise a larger library or the state library. This aspect of local and regional or state cooperation has undergone great improvement in recent years.

### Service to Children

Someone on the staff needs to have special interest in and knowledge of children's books. Perhaps someone, such as a mother who has reared a family of readers, may be discovered who can lead in this or serve as storyteller. Somehow any library has to find the way to develop understanding competent help for this important age group. Numerous printed aids and selected book lists are available. Other people are much concerned that similar special attention be given young adults—the fourteen- to twenty-year group—who use adult books primarily, and unfortunately are left to their own devices in most small libraries. Most of all, small libraries need to develop their services to adult readers.

### Building Care

In many libraries, the janitor is paid as much as the librarian. Trustees should realize that the building is of less importance than the services given in it. In a one-person library, maintenance should be cut to an hour or two a day for the days open by use of a rapid, conscientious part-time worker.

### Debatable Activities

Because many small libraries do not receive adequate support, it is held by some that more can be accomplished with the available workers by having fewer hours open to the public than with a longer schedule of hours. Some think audiovisual programs possible in a large library can be offered in the small library only by diverting time and money from reading and informational needs. It is true the small public library cannot offer audiovisual services in depth; however, it can provide the facilities and equipment for the use of materials borrowed from a system or other agency. It should be able to offer as well some less expensive materials of its own.

### Notes

1. These leaflets, issued by ALA in a series called Small Libraries Project, are too numerous to list by title. They cover all aspects of the administration of a small library, including book selection, weeding, staff, the setting up of a local history collection, and community relations.

2. Dorothy Sinclair, *Administration of the Small Public Library,* 2d ed. (Chicago: American Library Association, 1979).

3. Kathleen Molz's volume, *Federal Policy and Library Support* (Cambridge, Mass.: The M.I.T. Press, 1976), contains a discussion of the federal government's role in the growth of networks and systems. Robert R. McClarren, "State Legislation Relating to Library Systems," *Library Trends* 19 (October 1970): 235–49, examines the state role.

4. American Library Association, *The Public Library Mission Statement and Its Imperatives for Service* (Chicago: American Library Association, 1979).

# 15 Community Relations and Public Awareness

One of the major concerns expressed in the 1978 state conferences in preparation for the White House Conference on Libraries and Information Services was the pressing and continuing need to increase public awareness of the services that libraries have to offer. This need is particularly critical for the public library, as its potential clientele is so diverse and multifaceted. Many of the people who could benefit from the vast informational and cultural resources displayed in their public libraries are simply not aware that the resources exist, are there to be used, and that books and other media of communication could be of daily, practical value to them. Survey after survey reveals that the majority of the people do not think of the public library as an agency to which they might turn for answers to their coping questions, for cultural enrichment, for profitable entertainment. This point was brought out again and again in the conferences, by both laypeople and librarians.

The condition is not surprising. For one reason or another, or for many reasons, the public library is seen by many, if at all, as not so very relevant, as forbidding and aloof, as principally for women and children to obtain entertaining novels and picture books, and so on. Then the people who do "discover" the public library's resources are amazed (or so they say!) to find out what is there, and ask somewhat petulantly sometimes, "Why wasn't I told about this treasure house?" Making citizens aware of library resources requires constant and imaginative effort. In an era of massive communications campaigns, much that is mailed out, exhibited, announced, printed, and displayed on television simply goes unnoticed and unremarked. For the library to obtain some productive results in this glut of advertising and publicity is a formidable and challenging task but eminently worth the effort, in order to fulfill avowed goals and objectives.

The public library's program of community relations and public awareness will require the concern of trustees, the library director and department heads, and all staff. Upon their efforts will depend the average citizen's image of the library, the extent of the community's good will toward the library, and

271

its understanding of what the library is trying to do. Good relations with the community must begin with the goals and objectives, and the plan, as described in Chapters 1 and 2. If the library has worked out a set of goals and objectives with the active participation and assistance of a good segment of the community, the community relations program will have a firm foundation. If people have had a solid part in forming the library's service program, they obviously will be in a position to understand and support it. This is not to say that the library staff, as the technical experts, are to abdicate their responsibilities or leave the running of the library to citizens. It is a team relationship; the library is owned by the people, they must share in planning for its development; the library staff must provide the technical and professional advice and counsel, and management expertise, to provide what is wanted and needed.

Key phrases in good community relations, heard over and over again, are *relevance; courteous, efficient service; responsiveness to felt needs; anticipating community concerns.* The public library that is perceived as being well run, on top of its job, able to produce the needed materials quickly and with a minimum of red tape, will have taken the first major step toward a successful community relations program.

The public library is a service facility and exists to extend services as prescribed in its goals and objectives. The personnel in the support services have an equally important role to play, in seeing that the entire effort goes along smoothly. It is critical, for example, for books and other materials to reach the shelves without delay and to be cataloged and classified so that they can be easily retrieved. An aggressive publicity campaign cannot cover up for a sloppy or inefficient library delivery system. The major part of the library's public service transactions are one-to-one; for example, the user borrowing a book that he or she has selected from the open shelves and seeking to take out a library card for the first time. How is that transaction handled? With courtesy, tact, care? Does the new borrower receive the information necessary about library services and resources, as well as rules and limitations, hours of service? This is the initial opportunity for a favorable impression. A brusque, short registration interview will not enhance the impression, and will leave the new borrower somewhat cool toward the library. It is true that sometimes desk staff are harassed by many queries at once; ways must be studied for dealing courteously with this problem. Private businesses have similar problems; the fact that the library is tax-supported and hence cannot "go broke" does not make it unnecessary to give good service.

Therefore, satisfactory community relations must commence with the necessary training in service attitudes and procedures. Library employees are generally among the more helpful in public agencies, fortunately, but desire to serve must be fortified by continuing instruction in dealing with situations as they develop. It is not too much to expect that care be given to manner of speaking, answering the telephone, responding to the endless questions that flow in. In short, the community relations job begins in the library itself, with the staff, and the job will consist of a regularly planned and structured course of in-service training. It is not enough to leave this matter to chance, or to casual supervisory comments and observation. This point is made again and again, but library directors are prone to respond that they and the staff are too busy. That cannot be accepted as an excuse. The library's most powerful avenue for good community relations is the word-of-mouth advertising given by the satisfied client; it is also the least expensive!

## Public Relations as an Essential Part of Administration

Increasingly, the library finds itself competing with other community agencies for tax monies. An informed, interested, and involved public, the result of a successful public relations program, is the best guarantee of financial well-being. Yet, most libraries do not have a department or even a staff member assigned to public relations. Occasional large metropolitan libraries will have a public relations department, but in most suburban libraries, in almost all school, public, college, and special libraries, public relations is a disorganized, half-hearted effort, the duty of a staff member whose major responsibilities lie elsewhere. According to Allan Angoff, editor of *Public Relations for Libraries,* "This is surely one reason for the neglect of libraries by communities, students, political figures, university administrators and trustees. The library is accepted, of course, but all too often as one of the less aggressive and less troublesome candidates for the urban, university or corporate dollar."[1]

In the last five years, there have been a number of events designed to turn this situation around. The Council on Library Resources granted a fellowship for 1974–1975 to examine the state of public relations in some twenty-six libraries. The project resulted in a thirty-minute slide/tape production called *PR Tick/Click.*[2] In 1975 the Pennsylvania Library Association based its entire conference on public relations. That same year, ALA began a public service advertising program for libraries. During 1976 the association placed fifteen national wire service stories, thirteen national magazine articles and ten television interviews, and recently issued a series of pamphlets on public relations. A newsletter on public relations is also published by its Public Information Office. Catholic University, the University of Denver, and the University of Oklahoma recently offered PR seminars for credit in their graduate library schools.[3]

### Some General Factors

1. Community relations is a two-way process, requiring that trustees, administration, and staff acquire and maintain an awareness of the community being served, and further that the community be kept informed of library

services and resources—input from the community, and output to the commuity, in brief.

2. Librarians may sometimes tend to mingle with their own colleagues, and this is inevitable, but an effort must be made to see that lines are established with the various social, cultural, religious, economic, ethnic, and business circles in the community. The library board of trustees, if properly selected, should provide at least some of this mix of lines into the community; active Friends of the Library can also serve a useful purpose in this regard. But both trustees and Friends sometimes tend not to be fully representative of the area. If this condition is frankly recognized, it can be overcome by considering the establishment of citizen's advisory committees or groups; in a larger system there can be one for each branch or community library.

3. Frequent and regular contacts with the community's elected officials should be maintained; it is not enough for them to hear from the library only at budget appropriation time. The library director, and the appropriate branch librarians and department heads, should know the wards or areas served by the alderpeople or council members, and should keep them apprised of conditions or developments in the various libraries that might have an effect upon their constituents. Elected officials should be actively encouraged to use the meeting room facilities of the library buildings for committee meetings, hearings, and gatherings of the neighborhood. This is all a part of active community relations and making the library useful to the people.

4. Publicity about the library is not to be viewed as "blowing one's own horn." The library is there to be used; the people are paying for it; the director and staff are expected to let people know what they have paid for, what they can get, where the services are and where the money went. The users want to know about the library.

5. Community relations will emphasize that the library is a shared resource, that the books are to be used by a wide clientele, and that obviously sharing sometimes will mean waiting in line for one's turn. That does not obviate the need to make people aware of the resources; it is not a matter of being afraid of creating demands that cannot be filled.

6. A planned, continuous program is essential, not an erratic approach.

7. The public awareness program is not only to describe resources and materials that are available, it should also explain library objectives, problems, plans, projects, and accomplishments.

8. One of the specific topics about which users often inquire is the book and material selection process—how titles are selected, how decisions are made to retain and discard—and this is directly related to the goals and objectives of the library. People can be made aware of the vast publishing output and of the fraction that the library can select. This can lead into informing users about interlibrary loan arrangements and reciprocal borrowing with other libraries, for example.

## Organizing the Community Relations Program

*Planning*

It cannot be emphasized strongly enough that there must be a community relations and public awareness *plan*. This should be drafted and reviewed, by a staff committee, a joint committee of the staff and board, by citizen volunteers, or by a staff member especially skilled in this area. But it is critical that the plan be written, be discussed and reviewed, and then be refined and adjusted as necessary before being put into effect. There is so much that *can* be done, so much that doubtless *ought* to be done, that rigorous selection of tasks and priorities must precede the start of the execution. All the options and possibilities must be examined in the light of payoff: how much tangible return can be expected, the target areas, costs in relation to probable or certain benefits. Questions of skills and talents available to carry out the plan or program should be considered; who will do the work; how much time will be required; and so on.

As a guiding rule, it might be considered that one or two excellent publications or community relations activities, well executed, are much to be preferred to a multitude of hastily contrived and poorly carried out enterprises. Often one may observe that library public relations efforts do not compare favorably with those of the experts; they seem to have been put together in a hurry, without much thought or production skills. It might be better to rely on good service and word-of-mouth advertising to get the message across than to create a negative impression with an amateur effort.

*Budgeting*

No statistical or cost studies were found to justify any given percentage of the total budget for public relations. There are too many uncertain, informal, part-time, unreported factors, and most librarians seem agreed that results cannot be definitely measured in increased circulation. Results become evident enough when a bond issue is approved by the voters by a margin of five to one, or when circulation doubles in two years. Friend[4] and Cundiff[5] evidently studied, by questionnaires, approximately the same forty-three or thirty-two libraries, in cities of over 250,000 population, and found such varied activities, organization, and staffing that no cost figures or pattern could be arrived at. While nineteen of Friend's forty-three libraries reported "a full time director, one had in addition, two assistants for display and lettering, one for writing, one photographer, one secretary and two part-time pages." But department heads and staff who initiate, guide, or share in varied aspects of PR give much additional time. It comes down to two contending factors: how strongly the librarian believes in PR, and how much he or she feels can be spent from a never adequate budget. For a rule of thumb, we suggest 1 or 2 percent of the budget, for total staff, materials, printing, and outside costs.

## In Large Libraries

In cities of over 150,000, a full-time qualified person should be employed. Chief qualifications are a keen understanding of library objectives, a belief in the usefulness of books and printed information, a public relations background with writing experience, and the ability to work with people, including those who don't use the library. It takes also resourcefulness, a flexible outgoing mind, a solid educational background, and imagination and initiative to see, week after week, how books can tie into the stream of community activities.

Yet another qualification is the ability to plan the publicity work and to get through it without demanding too much expenditure of funds and staff help and without absorbing too much time in overhead motion. A rapid worker is an asset, especially one who can handle many contacts by phone in a cordial way. If such a person can be found within the staff, well and good. But an enthusiasm, for example, for making posters, lists, and exhibits is one of the least important qualifications needed. Often someone is brought in from a newspaper or an advertising agency. Unless such an "outsider" is a reader, and a library user, interested in library functions, there is considerable risk that the efforts will be superficial and only partly effective. In some instances, an "outsider" in the form of a public opinion research firm can be vital. The firm will aid in estimating whether special goals, such as a new building, can be attained, how they may be attained, the attitude of the public, and the probable public response to projected appeals.

## In Medium-Sized and Small Libraries

Although several cities of less than 150,000 population have a full-time publicity director, most cities smaller than that will have to designate an able staff member to handle PR work part-time, unless someone is available to come in from other employment for two or three hours a day. This person's chief practical problem is to persuade numerous other people inside and outside the library to help on definite assignments.[6] The smaller the library, the more resourceful it needs to be in getting citizen cooperation to help carry on community relations activities.

## Committee Work

It may be profitable to ask several staff members to thresh out and plan several projects. An Evansville staff committee session came up in ten minutes with twenty-eight suggestions on how to bring to people's attention the existence and location of the library—spot radio and TV announcements, street signs, staff talks to clubs, letters to new residents, marquee advertising, bookmarks, picture postcards, and so on. Another ten minutes produced nineteen ideas to meet the statement, "I don't have time to read." Calling a group of citizens together to plan and carry out publicity for the library is a successful method for finance or building campaigns. It would be an all-year device to get more publicity without great cost; for instance, a storeowner may be willing to run a series of store window exhibits, as well as have his show card writer do the lettering on posters and show cards.

### Drawing Ideas from Departments

The person in charge of PR should be informed about everything interesting and significant that goes on in the library, especially by the library director and each department and branch head. All of them are busy; they often forget news that should be played up, such as the arrival of important new reference service tools. They should have publicity-minded assistants to remind them of promising items. The PR officer should also encourage these sources and can use much of their information, news, exhibits, and circulars. A library may run in a seeming routine, but in most libraries there is something newsworthy happening every week or month; in large libraries there is something new every day.

### Public Relations Inside the Library

Current library design capitalizes on the part played by the building itself. Adequate directional signs and explanatory placards, which tell how to use the card catalog, how the building, department, and bookcases are arranged—everything that will make it easier for the public to use the library—will increase good will. Library users should enjoy their visits to the library, and the whole staff should be called on for suggestions as to how this can be assured. Several libraries encourage friends with gardens to bring in beautiful plants and flowers, to be placed on service desks, along with thank-you cards.

Board actions affect the public's concept of the library. Trustees should not be inhibited by public opinion but should take action for the public good and then inform the public, rather than assuming that what they do had better be kept quiet. Many libraries have a reporter attend board meetings. In fact, current "Sunshine Laws" should encourage the library to post its schedule of meetings with the news media. If the library has a PR officer, publicity from the board should be cleared through him or her, for it is that person's job to know how best to communicate with the public. On possibly controversial subjects, board and library director should work out with the PR director the wording of news releases.

## Public Relations Outside the Library

Having given attention to improving services and impressions inside the library, a library is better prepared to undertake varied outside publicity. The present chapter can be only an outline, not a handbook of publicity methods.

The essence of public relations is communication. Communication includes the media—newspapers, radio, television—and it includes as well door-to-door campaigns, talks by staff members to local clubs and student groups, and other efforts. Baeckler and Larson in their compendium of ideas urge getting out of the library and into the community and state that it "is absolutely essential for lively libraries. The greater the influx of new ideas and new people, the greater the stimulus for innovation and service, the greater the possibility that we will remember who we are and why we are in the library."[7]

### Door-to-Door Campaigns

Only a few libraries have assigned time for selected staff members to do intensive promotion, door to door, taking a few books, lists, or circulars and talking directly with householders—finding out their interests, projects, and problems and describing the materials and services they could get. This could give the staff, for the first time, a closeup of adult reactions to the idea of reading and reference help, a realistic understanding of why so many adults don't read, and what it is, if anything, that can appeal to them. This canvassing is time-consuming and involves careful preparation, but it may be rewarding.

### Talks by Staff Members

Whole groups of adults can be reached in far less time by arranging for library talks at meetings of organizations. This provides an opportunity to explain library objectives, methods, and problems. Arrangements can be made over the telephone, but the talk should be well planned and lively.

### Friends of the Library

Organizing and enlisting the help of a large organized auxiliary group of friendly and influential men and women has had notable results in spreading public knowledge of the library, enlisting support, getting funds, and passing bond issues. One wonders why it is not universal. Some trustees fear that the "Friends" will get so influential and active that they will tell the trustees how to run the library. A good board should be confident enough to welcome ideas from outside. True and fortunately, Friends in some cities have boldly intervened in library situations needing correction and have insisted on and financed critical surveys. They deserve credit for getting a great number of moribund, politics-ridden, and thoroughly bad library situations straightened out. A good Friends organization is considered by many progressive library directors of both small and large libraries to be their greatest public relations asset. But care should be taken, through the library director, that the officers chosen each year be not only strong, courageous leaders determined to push the library ahead, but tactful and discreet as well. They should neither antagonize library and public officials nor seek office for themselves but should help the library in ways that the community will be likely to approve.

*Newspapers*

From the standpoint of the amount of time required from the library, the variety of topics covered, and the wide diffusion of the library's message, top priority goes to the local newspaper. If there are several papers, the library should treat them all the same. It is vital that the library staff learn to distinguish between news and library propaganda.[8] The most frequent failure, however, is in not putting the point of the story into a short opening sentence and paragraph; as a result, the editor must do a large-scale rewrite that takes more time than the story is worth. The story should simply inform the reader what the library is doing for citizens as well as what it hopes to do.

*Radio and TV*

Radio offers an effective channel of communication in many areas. Because stations must devote a certain percentage of their time to public service announcements in order to retain their licenses, libraries should have a good chance at getting some air time. An initial one-to-one contact between the library director and the station manager should take place. This can be followed up by a conversation between the program director and the library's public relations person on practical details.

A creative public relations person should be able to suggest to the program director ways in which the library can fit into the radio's format, which includes news, sports, special events, interviews, music, announcements, and theater reviews. A weekly five-minute book review program might interest the station. Or it might welcome a storytelling program organized by the children's department.

The Public Library of Nashville and Davidson County, Tennessee, has for a number of years operated a radio station in the library, as a part of the library's regular service program, supported with funds from the library budget, and broadcasting classical music and other material of a cultural nature.

Television requires much more in the way of production capability than radio, but the potential rewards are substantial if a way can be found to design and mount a program or series.[9] The Milwaukee Public Library has sponsored for more than twenty years a weekly half-hour discussion program on a local television station, entitled "Public Conference." It covers a wide range of topics, from local current affairs and world politics, with visiting authorities, to practical subjects—for example, "Great Possibilities for Your Home" with an interior decorator, a consumer education specialist, and a builder. A branch librarian was moderator of this particular program; library staff usually arrange and moderate them. Often the programs have news value, when visiting dignitaries debate a controversial topic, and this redounds to the library's benefit as an effective communications agency. The Milwaukee Public Library also sponsors a regular series, "Critique," on another channel, with reviews of outstanding books, often by authors or critics, and with library staff participation. The library also carries on two children's programs, "Library Playhouse" and "Your Library Story," presented Saturday mornings on one station. There is another series on Saturday afternoons on another station, making a total of six television programs a week sponsored by the library.

*TV Production Studio*

Some larger public library systems, such as Columbus (Ohio), have TV production studios in the audiovisual or the public relations department for the production of spots or short subjects. These studios may be made available free or for a fee to groups in the community. Some of the items produced are for release to TV stations or cable networks, some for cassette utilization in the library's videocassette viewers and for home lending to those with videocassette viewing equipment. Not only can short subjects about the library and its services be produced, but subjects about the local community may be recorded, used, and preserved as well.

Cable television offers much promise for the enterprising local library. Public interest channels are usually required to be made available, and the library may wish to investigate the possibility of using one of these, perhaps in cooperation with other local agencies, municipal departments, or libraries in the area. This can be an excellent area for interlibrary cooperation, sharing the costs and work of arrangement and production, which may be considerable if a high level of performance is desired. But the results will generally be shared by more than one community; therefore, cooperation in production is quite realistic. And cable television can provide an excellent means of showcasing the library's resources and conveying information to an increasingly visually oriented clientele. If the television programming results in increased use of the library's print and nonprint resources, so much the better, but if a few thousand viewers can be informed, for example, about money management, buying information, housing, careers, and any of the other questions that people are concerned about, the library will have made a significant contribution. It will take some effort to arrange presentation by local experts, but many will be willing to have an opportunity to share their knowledge with the general viewer.

*Lists of New Books*

The weekly list of the library's new books published in the local paper is perhaps the most profitable and least expensive device to acquaint the whole community with each new title, omitting the less important ones, and giving two- or three-line newsy annotations. Large city papers are reluctant to give this space; few do. But most smaller city papers will. Some, even in very large cities, are willing to run short special lists in news-story form—for example, on the business or sports pages, or with a news heading tying up a few new books and bulletins with current events. Printed lists of new accessions are costly, but many libraries issue mimeographed unannotated monthly lists to be picked up by present borrowers at the service desks. If to be annotated, keep the ads, blurbs, reviews, or other descriptions attached to the original order card, inserting them in the book when it arrives, to remain with it until books and catalog cards are released. By bracketing and crossing out or adding words, one can prepare effective ready-made annotations in a few minutes, in contrast with undertaking to prepare careful original annotations. Selected phrases from what the author, publisher, reviewer say about a book may be more accurate and effective. Omit every word that does not describe; do not repeat what is implied by the title.

The foregoing is not intended to favor new books over worthy older ones. It is a library function to winnow out the superior books of not-so-recent days and to publicize and emphasize them as most worth reading. This is one of the objectives of selected book lists and displays.

*Selected Book Lists*

The preparation of selected short lists (10 or 15 to 25 titles) on various subjects calls for judgment and familiarity with the books, to have each title a superior one. Annotations will evaluate and compare books, their purpose, coverage, and type of treatment, packing facts and viewpoints into three or four interesting lines. Book lists go out of date in two or three years, on current events and current problems in three or four months; book lists on most subjects should be distributed promptly, be considered short-term affairs, and be revised and updated. Distribution should be mainly outside the library—for example, at garden club meetings and at civic, public affairs, cultural, and hobby group meetings. It is better for a library to use a first-class list prepared by another library and buy a few missing titles to back it up than to issue no lists, for it cannot often afford the time and printing cost to get out its own. Such lists are primarily to invite and need not be loaded with local call numbers. The value to the staff in building up its closer knowledge of important books, by the process of selecting and annotating, cannot be overestimated.

### Book Displays

Displays can reach a widely spread audience, informing users and potential users of what is available in the library, stimulating or motivating them to read in general or to seek out specific books, and guiding them in their choice of reading.

Book arrangement on the open shelves is a form of book display. New books are more often called for than old ones, cleaner and more attractive ones than those dirty and worn, books in colorful bindings than those in dull and solid colors, and books on shelves that are uncrowded and not too high or low than those that are jammed and not easily seen or reached. Most libraries have a special place for such groups of books as the newest acquisitions and collections on appropriate seasonal topics. A more systematic application of this practice is the idea of reader interest classification, cutting across but not replacing the Dewey decimal classification, in semipermanent but not inflexible groupings, and designed to express, by topic and by choice of books thereunder, dominant themes of current interest. Assigning the topic headings is a task for the professional staff, and there are technical problems in coding these headings on the books and on their catalog cards. The results are of value only to the reader who is not looking for a specific title, but there has been enough successful experience with this type of book classification, notably in the Detroit Public Library, to warrant consideration for its use in branch libraries and in general collections of not over 10,000 adult books.

### Exhibits Inside and Outside

If the library building is located in the midst of the crowd, its front can be remodeled and opened up to exhibit inside activities. Or it can have a large exhibit window facing the sidewalk. Or if it stands too far back, an exhibit case can be built close to the sidewalk, lighted and equipped with screened plexiglass to protect the contents. Some outside cases have not been designed to be weatherproof or to be easily accessible for changing exhibits. Increasingly, the design of new library buildings incorporates an exhibit area within the library. Any library can also get permission to use window space in vacant stores, or even in occupied, busy stores.

The range of subjects for exhibits is boundless, with pictures, collections, mementos, working models, and a variety of possible materials to supplement books on the subjects. Explanatory signs are essential. Some libraries that are adept in managing volunteer help get art classes, store decorators, and other outsiders to prepare and set up window exhibits, in order to reduce expense and staff time. Whatever time the library can give to exhibits should go into effective exhibits used outside the library as a promotion device, where crowds of people can see them, and they should be so eye-catching that people will stop and study them. The same is true of bulletin boards, especially outside the library, to display lists, posters, announcements, and book jackets.

*Library Visits*

The best exhibit of all is the display of the library in operation. As mentioned before, a look through the sidewalk windows into the library's busy interior can be inviting. Tours, however, with skilled explanation of the library's materials and services, are an excellent way for groups of visitors, especially adult groups, to become better acquainted with the library. Such tours need careful planning and scheduling. What are the most important things to be seen in thirty or sixty minutes? A staff conference with a representative of the tour group will help to sift out the essentials and arrive at priorities, then arrange a schedule in which the most can be seen and explained in the least time. There is the question also as to what has curiosity or sentimental appeal and what will really be of most service to the visitors. The choice of the guide means much; the most effective staff members for this duty should be made available for it.

*Book Talks*

Many organizations at all age levels welcome having a few appropriate books reviewed or commented on by selected staff members or by a volunteer authority. Reviewing books for readers of high school age calls for tact, perception, humor, and personality, for these young people are critical and exacting. Adult book talks, including book review clubs, deserve greater development; on history, travel, philosophy, biography, and "man, know thyself," they are comparatively infrequent, despite the sustenance such books could give the hearers. Current events, art and music, recent fiction, interpretations of foreign affairs and society today—these are the favorite themes and contribute to adult education. Radio and TV stations will run book talks if they are well enough presented. Indeed, book talk shows, like "Book Beat" and the book focus of the "Today" show, have become familiar elements in national network programming.

## Vacation Reading

An effective device bringing large-scale reading of books whose high quality can be guided by knowledgeable library workers is the planned program to encourage reading when children and young people are released from the pressure of school schedules. An incentive is often offered in the form of games, clubs, prizes, or other recognition. Details of many such programs are given in issues of *Wilson Library Bulletin* and *Top of the News,* and less frequently in state bulletins. To date, programs for grade school pupils predominate and possibilities are largely undeveloped for high school student and adult summer programs.

## Annual Report

Whether the library issues to public officials and to other libraries a somewhat detailed report of its affairs and progress, including those of individual departments and branches, some brief attractive summary report including its receipts and expenditures should also be issued and widely distributed to the public. A six- or eight-page leaflet with a few graphs and pictures, sent out with store bills, bank statements, and so forth, will help to bring a much clearer concept of the library to a wide circle of citizens than almost any other device, and in cities of 15,000 and upward it well justifies its cost. Most important is a summary, maybe one column, in the local paper. A graph showing increased use is profitable. The ALA can lend an assortment of samples for ideas and layout.

## Recognition of Cultural Accomplishments

Many libraries have an exhibit and news story whenever a local resident has a book, play, or musical piece published. This builds community recognition that the library is a cultural force in our society. The exhibit should contain photos and materials used by the author. One library has had exhibits of books that *should* be written about its city and state, showing large cellophane dummies of these nonexistent books, suitably titled and decorated, and surrounded by actual books from other cities and states.

## News About the Staff

Appointments, promotions, and transfers of staff are important news stories. The event will provide an opportunity to display staff educational and experience qualifications, subject interests, and views on library service in the community. Also, any outside activities in the library professional world should be reported in the local press: committee appointments, honors received, talks given, conferences attended, and so forth. The educational background of each staff member should be accented. Sometimes it is felt in some quarters that almost anyone can be a librarian—that all you have to do is to know how to stamp out books. This burden, fortunately, is decreasing as library employees become more militant and part of the "mainstream" of the community.

### Branch Library Publicity

Much of the publicity for the entire system must be produced centrally as a matter of economy and division of labor. Branch libraries ought not to be encouraged or allowed to mount separate publicity efforts if the work can be centralized profitably. But the branch personnel must have a role in planning and deciding what is to be carried out for the benefit of all units in the system. And the branch staff will need to be responsible for making neighborhood contacts, arranging for talks and discussions at local meetings, and conferring with leaders and elected officials in the area.

### Surveys

Libraries that have been critically and objectively surveyed can profitably capitalize on the survey as a public relations device. Citizens should be told why it has been undertaken; for example, to improve services and find economies; what the surveyor finds; and how much the library could do under better conditions. A surveyor for a tax-supported library will not indulge in theoretical discussion that larger budgets do not assure better service, but will comprehend the difficulties any library faces in getting adequate support and will aim for better personnel and methods that will produce a better library.

Some of the most fruitful surveys have been initiated by Friends of the Library and by local citizen organizations. These groups often are aware that the library board, or the library director, is out of touch, and wish to see the library brought up to today's concept of modern public service.

### Campaigns

When for any reason, generally for a bond issue for a new building, the voters have to approve some library project involving public expenditures, a large-scale concentrated campaign is essential.[10] The whole community has not only to be thoroughly informed as to facts and reasons but has to be made enthusiastic to rectify library conditions that in most cases have existed too long. Such factors as crowding, inconvenience to readers, obsolescence, the right of library patrons to have modern facilities, and the careful planning and attention to economy and efficiency involved in the enterprise have to be played up to enlist the support and cooperation of the voters. During such an enterprise, it is imperative to discover incipient objections and opposition and the causes and reasoning behind them and to issue carefully documented and argued explanations to combat them *before* the opposition can get organized. Good administration foresees trouble and heads off hostile pressures. Because some campaigns have not been carefully planned, with citizen committees and staff members working actively in every precinct and at every level of the population, they have failed, even for the second or third time. In other cases, bond issues for branches and for central improvement carried by two, or three, even five to one, because they were planned and managed as citizen enterprises with many people working in the library's behalf.

## Instruction in the Use of Books and Libraries

Few of even the best readers—college professors, for example—are sufficiently informed about reference services and tools, how to look up a subject, and how to be sure they have found all that might help them. As a result, if they use books and libraries at all they flounder, waste time, overlook items, and get only a part of the potential values.

Devices to instruct have been aimed mostly at school pupils, not adults, perhaps in the hope that if young people learn to use books the know-how will carry into adulthood, a doubtful theory. For even grade and high school pupils need to have some fundamental skills taught them several times as they become more mature and adept. Millions of adult readers need to know how they can use library materials for practical self-help, aided by the printed tools and indexes already available.[11]

### *Instruction of School Pupils*

Cooperation among local libraries could mean that a representative committee such as many cities now have would sit down and plan the coverage of an adequate instruction course from grades one to twelve. Such a course would preferably be given by and in the school, headed by the school librarian and particularized by each teacher, but would be shared in by the public library because these pupils will use their public library also, to get the fullest service.

A course in library use would cover:

1. Introduction to the library; location and arrangement; nature—a depository of a variety of recorded information; function—to acquire and lend materials for curriculum use and personal pleasure.

2. Printed parts of a book and their use: title page, copyright, preface, table of contents, introduction, body of the book, appendix, index.

3. Care of books: opening new books, avoiding dampness, always storing books upright, rough handling, soiling, heat; using proper bookmarks.

4. Arrangement of materials in the library; books—reference, fiction, non-

fiction, easy; pamphlets, pictures, clippings, etc.; periodicals—current and filed; videocassettes, films, filmstrips, and slides; framed prints; recordings.

5. Use of the card catalog: definition and arrangement; kinds of cards; information found on the card; uses: to locate a specific item of material, to determine what material the library has by an author or on a subject.

6. Reference books—characteristics and uses of: dictionaries, encyclopedias, atlases, almanacs and yearbooks, biographical dictionaries, periodical indexes, quotation books, miscellaneous reference books in subject fields.

7. Bibliography and note taking.

8. Choosing books for one's own library. Effective placement for each new topic of instruction is a matter of opinion, and the numerous instruction pamphlets and course outlines to date show great variation.[12]

### Notes

1. Allan Angoff, ed., *Public Relations for Libraries* (Westport, Conn.: Greenwood Press, 1973), p. viii.

2. Sue Fontaine, *Public Relations—Tick/Click* (Chicago: American Library Association, 1976). This provides an examination of PR problems and possibilities through case studies and personal commentary.

3. American Library Association, *The ALA Yearbook, 1977* (Chicago: American Library Association, 1977) p. 260.

4. David S. Friend, "Public Relations in Public Libraries: A Survey of Organization and Administration . . ." (Master's thesis, Florida State University, 1959).

5. Dorothy Cundiff, "Public Relations in Public Libraries . . . in Metropolitan Areas of Over 250,000 . . ." (Master's thesis, University of Mississippi, 1957). These two theses duplicate each other in many respects, especially enumeration and description of activities, Friend's covering more aspects.

6. American Library Association, "Publicity with a Purpose . . . for Libraries on a Shoestring," *Library Journal* 99 (March 1974): 862–63. This article contains many helpful ideas that cost little or nothing to develop.

7. Virginia Baeckler and Linda Larson, *GO, PEP, and POP!: 250 Tested Ideas for Lively Libraries, or GO (Getting Outside), PEP (Programs, Exhibits, Projects), and POP (Positive Operating Procedures)* (New York: U*N*A*B*A*S*H*E*D Librarian, 1976), p. 11.

8. Karol McNeely, "Public Relations in the Library," *Idaho Librarian* 27 (January 1975): 10–14. This article also offers hints on how to develop a news story and write a press release. See also American Library Association, *Get It into Print: The Library News Release* (Chicago: Library Administration Division, American Library Association, 1977).

9. American Library Association, *Broadcast Publicity* (Chicago: Library Administration Division, American Library Association, 1977).

10. Carlton C. Rochell, "Money: Secrets of Successful Seekers; Call the Shots Yourself," *American Libraries* 8 (1977): 574–75. Discusses successful Atlanta referendum for a new central library. Entire issue devoted to fund-raising activities.

11. Shirley Lois Hopkinson, *Instructional Materials for Teaching the Use of the Library: A Selected, Annotated Bibliography of Films, Filmstrips, Books, Pamphlets, Tests, and Other Aids* (San Jose, Cal.: Claremont House, 1975). See also John Lubans, Jr., ed., *Educating the Library User* (New York: R. R. Bowker, 1974), and Violet E. Peterson, *Library Instruction Guide* (Hamden, Conn.: Shoestring Press, 1965).

12. Carla J. Stoffle and Gabriella Bonn, "An Inventory of Library Orientation and Instruction Methods," *RQ* (Winter 1973): 129–33.

# 16 Nonprint Materials

Librarianship has been directly involved with the communications revolution that began with the invention of printing and that is now developing in radically new and different forms. There are those who say that the new technology will have as great an impact on the means of communication and information transfer as did the invention of printing. Although some contend that the printed forms will remain as the most efficient means for storing and disseminating information, automation, the computer, telecommunication, video discs, and tapes are opening a whole new range of possibilities and challenges for the public library of the future. Media other than print have for many years included films, phonograph records or audio discs, art reproductions, slides, and pictures. Now the library's stock will have to include, significantly, videodiscs or tapes and electronic media forms. This entire portion of the library stock is collectively known as "nonprint materials" or "the new media," for lack of a more exact description.[1]

The question is not whether the public library is to stock materials other than books; that question is academic. The materials are here; they must be dealt with; they have the potential for making a significant contribution in the field of disseminating information. People are increasingly oriented toward visual and audio information-transfer methods. The question therefore is what and how much and how to incorporate the new media, or the vast world of nonprint, into the collection and service program. Books are basic, and the book and print collection ought not to be sacrificed to the nonprint resources. But that is a matter of policy for each library board and administration to decide. Perhaps an investment in nonprint materials can focus attention on the need to maintain the bulwark of the library's print collections, since audio and video transmission of information is transitory and often fragmentary; it does not permit reflection, and referral and study, as easily as print. The point is that all media are to be used as the situation requires, with each supplementing the other in a productive manner. The total expenditure in 1978 by 7,635 public libraries in the United States for audiovisual materials

was $11,270,918, of a total expenditure for all library materials of
$336,291,461.

There is a substantial and growing body of literature on the communications revolution as it affects public libraries and other libraries. And the revolution itself is moving along quite rapidly, so that a general, brief discussion can only touch on the highlights, cite some recent and current books and articles, and perhaps suggest some general guidelines and principles. The library director and staff will need to keep abreast of the nonprint field by reading current articles, attending conferences, and visiting other libraries to see what is going on. A useful source of current information will continue to be the vendors' representatives, either as they visit the local library or as they display new products at library conferences.

## Sound Recordings (Audio Records)

Because phonograph records offered for many years almost exclusively music, they were usually placed with the collection of music scores and with the books about art and music. If there is no art and music department, the records are usually handled by the adult services department, and in the children's department for children's records. In some libraries, for example, the Carter G. Woodson Regional Library of the Chicago Public Library, all multimedia materials—including films, records, cassettes, and slides—are an integral part of the library's collection and are indexed in the library's main catalog.

Most public libraries have some phonograph records in their collections. The $33\frac{1}{3}$ rpm stereophonic records are preferred for general circulation. The 78 rpm and $33\frac{1}{3}$ rpm long-play are of interest for reference use. The 45 rpm record is produced by a few companies, but is less desirable for library use than the $33\frac{1}{3}$ rpm pressings. Quadraphonic records require a special amplifier and four speakers; these are perhaps not justifiable in public library collections unless a comprehensive collection of stereophonic records has already been assembled. Stereophonic tapes are being used increasingly for music and speech.

The Public Library Association 1975 standards for audiovisual materials and services for small and medium-sized public libraries recommended minimums for records: 1,000 to 1,500 recordings in all audio formats; 10 percent of recordings to be nonmusical; 500 discs; and 500 tapes are the minimum for a beginning collection.[2]

Selection periodical media for recordings recommended by Cyr include *The Booklist* (American Library Association); *Previews* (R. R. Bowker—includes reviews of nonmusical recordings, disc and cassette); *Hi Fidelity/Musical America* (Billboard Publications—includes reviews of musical recordings, discs, and audio tapes); *Hi Fi/Stereo Review* (Ziff-Davis Publishing—reviews stereophonic musical discs and audio tapes).

*Notes,* published quarterly by the Music Library Association (Research Library of the Performing Arts, 111 Amsterdam Avenue, New York, New York 10023), indexes reviews of recordings found in many periodicals, with symbol indication of favorable or unfavorable reviews.

*NICEM Index to Educational Audio Tapes,* published by the National Information Center for Educational Media, University of Southern California, University Park, Los Angeles, California 90007, is a guide to commercially produced educational audio tapes. It has a subject guide and a title section with complete descriptive data and list of distributors.

*Schwann Record and Tape Guide,* published by W. W. Schwann, 137 Newbury Street, Boston, Massachusetts 02116, a monthly, lists stereo recordings (discs and audiotapes) currently available. Mostly musical but some nonmusical.[3,4]

Stevenson recommends Richard S. Halsey, *Classical Music Recordings for Home and Library* (ALA, 1976), which "fills a long-standing and serious gap in the library literature, and should be quickly accepted as the standard guide to the recorded repertory. In addition to an extensive discography of in-print items, Halsey includes much information on selection, acquisition and organization."[5]

Sound recordings, or audio records, are available in two formats—disc and cassette—and cover a range of subject matter which are enumerated and defined by Sinclair:

Music: Classical, semi-popular, current popular, jazz, religious music, marches, children's music, well-known performers both vocal and instrumental, a few operas and operettas and musical comedies.

Language records: Albums to assist people to learn foreign languages, to be used with books or separately. These sets are expensive but extremely useful to many people.

Drama: Shakespearean plays, other drama, sound effects for the use of local drama groups.

Poetry: Readings by poets of their own work, or other poetry readings.

Documentary records: Real-life speeches and events of importance, or reconstructions of historic events.

Business: Shorthand dictation at different speeds for the beginner or expert.

Nature: Bird calls, for example, cannot be adequately represented in any other form.

Cassettes of texts: Now available for the blind, the semi-literate, for use in automobiles, or merely for the busy person . . . are a variety of stories of educational texts on cassettes.[6]

The audiodisc is the most commonly used audiovisual software among the public generally; most homes have one or more phonograph record players. However, many now also have tape cassette players. These are in the home and in automobiles as well. Stevenson observed that the audiences which provide the economic base for the recording industry consist of young people between the ages of fourteen and twenty-four. Within the industry there has been much concern about the decline in the size of this age group and its economic impact on the industry. Manufacturers were urged to begin to cultivate audiences (i.e., markets) of people who have passed the ripe old age of twenty-four. The modest increases in the sales of jazz recordings (a genre now largely supported by adults) and recordings of classical music seem to indicate beginnings of a change in patterns of production and sales that had been stable for more than a decade. . . . The cultural elitism, which for many decades limited most library collections to forms of classical music, was a thing of the past. Public libraries acquired large quantities of popular recordings.[7]

The cataloging of records usually and desirably involves subject cards for the type of music as well as entries for composer and by distinctive title. The first guide to such cataloging of records was issued in 1942, and a comprehensive code is now available from the Music Library Association, but small public libraries will probably use simple headings and brief descriptions. One good reason for doing so is that records wear out in the normal course of use, as do books, but cannot be "rebound" and are likely to be replaced by a more recent recording of the same composition. The card catalog of phonograph records is usually kept separate from the library's general catalog of books and near the records themselves, but a good argument can be made for filing cards for records in the general catalog.

Phonograph records require shelves a little deeper and a little taller than those used for books. Vertical dividers every five or six inches are also necessary to keep records upright, and browsing bins at counter-height level are desirable to permit easy scanning. A record collection is obviously incomplete without a record player, preferably with earphones for patrons to listen and decide whether to borrow a disc, and so that record concerts can be held if desired. Such an instrument can be purchased for less than $250, but a console model or one with two or more sets of earphones will cost substantially more. Large libraries need listening booths or a separate room, especially if the library maintains a reference collection of phonograph records.

Drolet has a summary of audio hardware available for libraries, and notes that *The Audio-Visual Equipment Directory* "is the 'yellow pages' of industrial/educational grade audiovisual hardware."[8] Drolet discusses phonograph record players, eight-track audio cartridge players, audiocassette players, reel-to-reel tape recorder/playback units, cassette tape recorder/playback units, cassette recorder/player with built-in synchronizer, and audio high-speed duplicators. He observes that

when a library begins to establish an audio-visual service, since it is most familiar with those product lines . . . it tends to select consumer products . . . to satisfy the library's audio-visual needs. Unfortunately, most consumer products are not designed to withstand the heavy use and the abuse experienced in a library setting. As a result, equipment failure and rapid depreciation are common occurrences. A complete audio-visual product line has, however, been designed to satisfy the heavy demands placed on hardware used in industry, schools and public libraries.[9]

## Motion Pictures (Film) and Filmstrips

"Film services in many public libraries have had a long and honorable history," it is reported by Miller.

Public librarians regard films as legitimate works of art, history, or literature, worthy of inclusion in the collection along with books, periodicals and records. In too many libraries, however, films are regarded as supplemental materials to be used as "book bait," i.e., to entice children, the uneducated, or the elderly to read. Although the term *book bait* has disappeared from library jargon, the underlying attitude that films are second-class library materials is still evident in some public libraries. This unfortunate attitude is now giving way to the more enlightened one that the film, as a unique form of literary or artistic expression, is worthy of representation in library collections. A wave of media-minded librarians is finding new ways to include films in library collections and services. Under their capable leadership, the future of film services in public libraries seems promising.[10]

Sigler reports that

the Madison [Wisconsin] Public Library provided the first recorded use of film in a public library. A film was used in connection with a children's story hour to illustrate the tale, and thus promote the reading of the book. Only four or five years later, the South Side Library in Milwaukee, Wisconsin, had "one of the most modern motion picture machines of the day" installed in its auditorium for the purpose of showing films "to interest people in library books."

He reports also that films were used in Seattle, in California, and in New Jersey in that decade.

In 1929, the Kalamazoo (Michigan) Public Library became the first public library on record to lend films. . . . The first significant study dealing with films and library service was Gerald McDonald's *Educational Motion Pictures and Libraries,* published in 1942. . . . McDonald's rationale was . . . that if the public library can bring books and people together, it could bring films and people together with equal success. Among the services he mentioned [were] film information and sources, assistance in borrowing films, a film collection which meets community needs, projection equipment and operator, and viewing facilities.

During the period 1947–51, Sigler reports,

the great strides that were made in public library film service development . . . were directly related to the degree and variety of support provided by the Carnegie Corporation. . . . When the Carnegie grant began in June 1947, there were about 12 public libraries in the United States circulating films. . . . In 1951, 114 libraries were circulating films. . . . Of these, 58 were individual libraries, the remainder belonging to one of the film circuits. Thirty-two libraries were located in cities of over 100,000 population.

Tracing the further growth and extension of the film movement in public libraries, Sigler observes that the role of the American Library Association, "although supportive, remained minimal and sparse with scattered publications, basic lists and meetings."

Sigler calls attention to the importance of films in the public library.

Among the conclusions of a recently published survey of current practice and case studies in public library media services were an increase in the library use of films, greater interest by the public in serious film study, film as an art form, the social documentary and interest from all ages in the improvement of cinema literacy, and the ability to interpret the film, the language of the present.

Credit has been duly awarded to the public library for its support over the years of continued distribution of the short film, classic documentary and independent film. Tom Brandon, former president of Brandon Films, was reported to have said in 1967 that "it has been the public libraries, with their high standards in taste and quality, that have kept the short film alive in the United States." Five years later, Brandon commented, "I cannot refrain from offering the view—not fully recognized by the library people, generally, themselves—that the public library is one of the most important resources on this continent for the growth of film culture." Leo Dratfield, then president of Contemporary/McGraw-Hill remarked that "great encouragement and support for growth over the years has come from the public library." Finally, Barbara Bryant, former public librarian and present vice-president of Phoenix Films, recently commented: "The public library is one of the few places where the independent film-maker can showcase his wares."[11]

## Film Selection and Processing

The selection of films, Cureton reports, is not an easy task, especially for a librarian who is familiar with the comprehensive array of selection and biographical apparatus available to the selector of print media. She notes that

a conservative estimate of the educational and short film features available in 16mm at the present time might be made at approximately 75,000. This figure does not include the many feature or entertainment films which have also been reduced to the 16mm format for home and library use.

. . . There are no accepted lists or recommended basic collections, no selection tools similar to the reference works which assist the librarian in acquiring print materials. Furthermore, there are no "jobbers" to whom one can send a list of titles with the assurance that the order can be filled. Even the terms are entirely foreign to someone familiar only with print materials.

In essence, the available selection tools are, in reality, "identification" tools, which may give sufficient information for making decisions on which films to preview. One of the best known is NICEM's *Index to 16mm Educational Films*[12] which lists all films submitted to the Library of Congress for copyright, giving release date, physical description, producer and distributor. This is probably the most complete listing of educational or short films available. A publication now in preparation is the CUFC/Bowker *Educational Film Locator.*[13] This work will list all the film holdings of the

Consortium of University Film Centers (approximately fifty university film rental libraries), with a complete annotation, rental and purchase information, and addresses. While this reference will be invaluable to schools and universities, it should also be helpful to public libraries which find an increasing number of patrons requesting this type of information. Another valuable reference is *Feature Films on 8mm and 16mm*, compiled and edited by James L. Limbacher. This is a directory of feature films available for rental, sale and lease in the United States. This book is in its fourth edition, with supplements printed annually by the Educational Film Library Association.

There is any number of professional journals and publications which include film reviews and filmographies for specific fields, as well as a few review services which list and review a wide range of materials. Among these are *Sightlines, Landers Film Reviews, Preview,* and *Media and Methods.* The Educational Film Library Association also publishes an excellent bibliography of periodicals, journals and books called *Film Library Administration.*[14]

Once the references have been acquired, the next step is to compile a list of film distributors or producers and write for their catalogs. In some cases, the film distributor produces no films but represents a number of producers in marketing their products, while in others, the producer and distributor are one and the same. Keeping up to date on what is available is difficult. . . . One method of handling this is with a double filing system. The first file should contain catalogs arranged alphabetically by source. The second is a subject file into which brochures or circulars on new releases can be placed for reference at the time of selection. The subject file is also a convenient place to store filmographies on specific subject areas.

Previewing is a practice seldom used in the selection of print material, but absolutely essential to film selection. The high cost of 16mm films ($7–$8 per minute for black and white and sound, $14–$16 per minute for color and sound) makes it mandatory that they be previewed before purchasing. Most reputable film distributors provide free film preview service for a period of one to two weeks. However, this privilege places a responsibility on the previewer to keep records of what films have been previewed, what evaluations were given and when the films were returned. A good evaluation system is essential. Some of the factors which should be considered are the audience to which the film is directed, the accuracy and effectiveness of the presentation, and the technical quality. Samples of evaluation tools are available in *Developing Multi-Media Libraries, Administering Educational Media,* and *AV Instruction: Technology, Media and Methods.* Another useful publication, at least in identifying the kinds of problems which may have to be dealt with is *Guidelines for Producers and Distributors of Educational Films,* published by the Consortium of University Film Centers. . . .

Once a film has been purchased and accessioned into the collection, the problems are only beginning. Unlike print materials, film is fragile. It should be inspected after each use, and repaired if necessary before the next circulation period. This requires adequate equipment for inspection, and personnel trained to provide this service. Too often, these basic facts of film life are ignored until the need for care and maintenance has reached a critical point. In planning a budget for a film collection, one must include funds for replacement footage, duplicate prints, inspection equipment, supplies, and required personnel in order to assure successful utilization.[15]

Peltier notes that

Although it may not be possible to formulate rigid definitions for the public library film, one can still define broad distinctions and general categories so that up-to-date definitions may be used as guidelines for public librarians responsible for building new film collections or for expanding existing ones. . . .

1. The teaching or classroom film—[This] has . . . no place in most public library collections, with the exception of public libraries specifically budgeted to service schools with films designed for the curriculum.

2. The information or idea film—These are nonfictional films produced for all audiences on any subject concerning humanity, the environment and the universe. . . .

3. The entertainment or recreational film—These are fictional films produced for all audiences, from children through adult, and created primarily to entertain, enrich or amuse. . . .

Peltier concludes:

The public library film—like the public library book—remains, as it has been, a basic educational and communicating tool. Its future form may be altered by magnetic tape, video disc, laser, or holograph, but the film librarian will remain responsible for guarding this visual record of the past, keeping it free from censorship, honest in content, and blessed with creative cinematic techniques.[16]

## Motion Picture Projectors

Drolet reports that the basic design of the 16mm projector has not changed in the past thirty years. Recent refinements, such as self-threading and slot-threading, eliminate some of the preparatory steps, but he observes that "a manually threaded projector, in the opinion of many audio-visual librarians, is still the best machine for projecting without danger of damage to the film."

He describes the various brands of 16mm and 8mm projectors that are currently available and offers some comments on each. He also reports on filmstrip and slide projectors.[17]

## Organization of the Film Collection

In simplest form, classification need be only alphabetical arrangement by film title. And instead of cataloging films, most public libraries issue a periodically revised list of films in the collection. Films are typically lent free of charge, though there may be a small charge for insurance. The circulation period is twenty-four to forty-eight hours, since usually there is only one print available of a given title, and it is lent for a specific showing. Reserves are necessary, and overdue fines tend to be high. Most libraries require special registration for the use of their films, including an assurance of the availability of proper equipment and an experienced operator. Typically, the library requires a report of the estimated number of people in the audience.

Because of the high cost of films, film cooperatives or film circuits are now common. A film circuit consists of several public libraries that band together to pool their funds and secure a group of films, which are then routed in blocks to each member library in turn, usually for a month at a time. Given advance notice of the films to be available in a given month, the local library can publicize these and accept reservations. Often the local market for the films in question has been exhausted by the end of the month, but over the year the same films will have had tremendous use in all the member libraries. As the years go by, the total number of films in the circuit increases, as does the size of each monthly block. It is an ingenious answer to a purely financial obstacle.

There are services that public libraries can render in regard to films. One is simply to provide film information; even if a public library has no films to lend, it can provide some of the printed tools and lists. A second area is that of lending films and providing related services—for example, preview facilities, union lists of films physically available in the community, and advice on the choice of films for particular programs. The third main type of service encompasses all that can be done to develop and improve film utilization in the community, such as free film showings at the library on a regular schedule, publicizing the films available and their potential uses, coordination with the school system and other local film libraries, creation of a film council, systematic showings of foreign films or art films or oldtime films, as from the Museum of Modern Art in New York City, development of a film festival, encouraging the use of films as a springboard for discussion, and relating books to films and vice versa.

Filmstrips (or slide films) consist of still pictures on 35mm film and are usually handled together with motion pictures. Filmstrips are useful for teaching purposes and story hours and in some ways are more effective than motion pictures. Some filmstrips are made for adult audiences, though most are for elementary and preschool grades; many deal with religious subjects. For most libraries, an alphabetical arrangement by title and a periodically revised list of titles will suffice for classification and cataloging. Some filmstrips have a sound track in the form of a phonograph record or cassette, which is keyed to the series of pictures on the film. Filmstrips come in color or in black-and-white. They are relatively inexpensive but require a special projector. Projectors for individual viewing are also available.

### Videodiscs and/or Tapes and/or Cassettes

Rohlf sees that

One of the most momentous things on the horizon (with respect to the future of libraries) is the whole question of video: cassettes, tape or disc. When the industry gets itself sorted out, we should end up with a single, compatible format for video players, rather than the problem we now have with one enormous corporation pushing discs and another pushing tapes; and they aren't compatible with each other's machinery. When that problem is resolved we are going to have a new format on the market that will have a greater impact on the use of leisure time and the transfer of information, than any other single thing since the invention of printing. . . . I think that video is the material of the future for libraries, and I think that those libraries that are not making plans about how they are going to add those materials are going to be left completely out of it, in the next decade. When the vendors get their compatibility problems resolved there will be a major explosion of materials available to be played on a home machine.[18]

Linford writes:

The video-disc will become a new medium in its own right. It will work just as printed matter: as a universal medium; because you have color, black and white, direct access, page by page; or you can go sequentially. The book is portable, the video-disc is not; that is, you need a reproduction facility; that is the only difference. But the disc will store visual as well as audio information; so it is more universal than the book. You can have text in digital form; sound, a half-hour of "My Fair Lady." Color, black and white, moving; the equivalent of film-strips of microfilms, or any kinds of media. So, the video-disc, as life wears on, will become a universal medium just as print is. None other than print has that universality.

Linford predicts that while there will be home libraries of videodiscs, they can be stocked in public libraries too. In fact, he points out,

The minute you have a portable medium like the video-disc, and if you have bought everything that will be available, it would exceed the budget of the average household. So there will have to be some place where people are going to try to borrow the medium. So libraries will have a very distinct role to play. . . . The cable TV companies will be much like libraries in that they will be programming computer games downline to homes. They are already doing this in Columbus, Ohio, in the cube system. Libraries could get into that act. . . . They could put full texts of materials up and have them accessible from a central information store, so that people could read them at home without having to go to the library and borrow a book. . . . That technology offends a lot of people right now. People don't like to sit and read from a TV set. Most of the TVs are not of a high enough resolution. But in 20 years, more or less, the next leap up will be a 1,000 or 2,000 line resolution on what is now a 500-line screen. That will make it possible to have high-quality reading material on a TV screen.[19]

Lipetz also observes that the

video-disc is going to pretty clearly change information supply in the home. It will make it possible, one, for people to have very, very visual libraries in the home where you can read the material on the screen which can be both pictorial and text. It will also make it possible for people, if they have the equipment, to receive the images from their local library as well as from more distant ones. . . . It is really cable television. There might be arrangements whereby people could call up the library and ask them to put on a certain disc; perhaps for a fee, perhaps without charge.[20]

In the federal government, according to the 1975 summary in the *Bowker Annual,*

the Lister Hill National Center for Biomedical Communication is exploring the uses of videodisc technology for biomedical communication. Videodisc equipment offers great potential for high-density storage, rapid random access, full video bandwidth, long life expectancy, and low reproduction costs. The National Library of Medicine is experimenting with videodisc technology for both mass storage of digital data and for storage and playback of library audiovisuals.[21]

In view of the fluid character of video technology, it would perhaps be better for a general work of this nature to refrain from any comments on the policies that ought to be adopted by the local public library, or the methods of organization, or the equipment to be used. It seems evident that there will be a public library role; it is perhaps too soon to see clearly what that role will be for the wide range of libraries. It will be for library directors and staff to become aware of the changing developments as they occur and to add video technology to the list of opportunities and challenges.

## Electronic Media

Another developing form—one that might more properly be considered under the library's information and reference function, although it is technically a "nonprint" medium—is the "paperless information system," as described by Lancaster[22] and others. The impact of the computer on the information retrieval process will probably be more significantly experienced by the larger research-type public libraries, although as more and more small and medium-sized libraries are able to receive the benefits of system and cooperative organization, they will be participating more and more in the use of electronic media, as many already are doing for the transfer of information from data storage banks.

What Lancaster foresees is that

at some date in the near future, there will begin a natural crossover from electronic production of print to electronic publication and dissemination (i.e., to the paperless mode of operation). . . . Before the paperless system can be implemented on a large scale, however, a rather substantial change in the market for information services must occur. . . . At the present time, most of the cost of creating a machine-readable data base is borne by the subscribers to the printed version. . . . This situation will change and we can expect to see the market for electronic services growing at a very rapid rate while, at the same time, the market for the printed services will steadily decline. To take an obvious example, it seems highly unlikely that a great untapped market exists for *Chemical Abstracts* in printed form. It is certain, however, that a large potential market still exists for on-line access to this data base on a pay-as-you-go basis. The demand for electronic access to this and other secondary data bases, then, can be expected to increase very substantially over the next decade, while the demand for the printed analogs will decline. It is only a matter of time before the size of the "electronic user" market, when coupled with realistic pricing strategies, is adequate to support the costs of building and maintaining the data base. At this point, the electronic version becomes the main product. Thereafter we can expect the rather rapid demise of the printed version. . . . The paperless society is rapidly approaching, whether we like it or not. Everyone reading this book will be affected by it in one way or another. . . . We may choose to ignore the electronic world, but this will not make it go away.[23]

What Lancaster is writing about has to do with scientific and technical information. Lipetz, however, is somewhat sanguine about the immediate effect of the electronic revolution upon the information needs and wants of the average citizen. He notes that

the cost of storing information, and of delivering large amounts of it over long lines, make it rather prohibitive to try to print out documents on demand. The quality is rotten, the costs are still bad, so the documents themselves that answer questions will have to come from depositories or libraries and the question of the best configuration is really an open question, still. . . . The finding systems are the networks and the commercial enterprises; they undertake to let you know whether something exists, sometimes they can give you abstracts, too. But the delivery systems tend to be public library systems or state library networks or academic consortia. . . . There may be a lot of growth in wide geographic linking of delivery systems. . . . And what may get lost in the shuffle is the whole question of local access for local citizens who don't have high-paying jobs or rich employers. The whole problem of citizen information is likely to be put in the wings for a while. There isn't much public money for information services for the common citizen.[24]

Goldstein reported in 1977 that

by year-end 1976, the number of public libraries committing time, money and effort to any and all aspects of video was small, probably not more than 400 to 500 out of a total of 11,000 such institutions in the United States. [But] video is one aspect of modern technology accessible to libraries of all sizes. Public libraries equipped with video equipment, such as a video cassette player, range in size from circulations of several thousand to several million and cover all regions of the country.

Goldstein's report drew much of its information from a mail and telephone survey of public libraries. He noted that other sources, "in particular, *The North American Film and Video Directory,* published in 1976 by R. R. Bowker Company, make much the same point: Video and its applications are tangible, accessible, and to a large degree affordable." He warns against the danger of video becoming modish, with libraries purchasing equipment, using it for a while, and then watching it collect dust as the novelty wears off. "The problem is more acute for video than for other forms of audiovisual media . . . because the development of video equipment has outstripped the availability of materials produced for that format."

Goldstein suggests three basic approaches for public library involvement in video: (1) As a collector of videotape and videocassette recordings and as a buyer of playback equipment. (2) As a producer of videotaped shows of community events for viewing in the library and as the basis for a separate library collection. (3) As a producer of programs for a local cable television channel to transmit programming to the homes of cable subscribers.

He discusses each of these approaches in some detail, and also provides practical information on video equipment; acquiring programming; collections, budgets, and sources; a model for the library programming center, with examples from various libraries around the country; and conclusions. In the latter, he notes:

For librarians video remains promising as a means of information dissemination, exciting as a format to attract and hold patrons but disappointing in terms of present accomplishments. Certainly one of the lessons learned from this report is that without clearly defined goals for their video programs, and a realistic assessment of the resources needed to achieve those goals, librarians run the risk of over promising and, ultimately, disillusioning their patrons and staff.

He summarizes by listing some of the issues and problems: what libraries have accomplished and the tasks that remain in the field of video application by libraries. He concludes:

Provided that libraries lay the proper groundwork—knowledge of the equipment and programming sources, their own capabilities, and financial and community support—there's every reason to believe that video collections will grow in importance, adding another dimension to the library's role as a repository and disseminator of information.[25]

As a result of a comprehensive survey carried out in 1975–1976, Brown "identified state libraries, selected local public libraries, and library systems that provide innovative new media services and activities; determined and reported on the general nature of these involvements and activities, and elaborated on some of these libraries for further description of ideas of potential worth to other libraries." Brown concludes, as a result of his review of the situation with respect to the new media, that "additional new responsibilities thrust upon [public libraries] will require applications of films, video, audio and other new media resources—along with or in combination with printed media which libraries have always provided." Among the trends mentioned are

increased independent study by adults; increased need for librarians of all types to meet clients on their own ground; increased knowledge of special contributions to learning to be made by each type of media; increased recognition of the fact that communications and information technologies are far from being fully exploited; and increased acceptance of the systematic, behavioral approach to the solution of community information problems.[26]

*Cable Television*

Cable television, of course, is not a medium in the same sense that films, recordings, and video are but rather the means by which libraries may transmit nonprint media into the homes of the community they serve, or at least into those homes that are connected into the cable network. This facility, formerly referred to as CATV, or community antenna television, simply carries signals by wire or coaxial cable (from the community antenna to the home), unlike broadcast television, which transmits signals through the air. The promise of public library participation in cable television

gained momentum in 1972 when the Federal Communications Commission promulgated regulations which obligated cable operators to provide services for educational and community organizations. Shortly thereafter, however, cable companies found themselves overextended and undercapitalized and were forced to cancel or curtail wiring plans for many communities.

Goldstein further notes that the FCC regulations concerning the allotment of channels to community organizations has been revised to lessen the requirements for the number of free channels. He considers a number of experiences of libraries with cable, "ranging from a few that are deemed successful to a larger number that have been somewhat disappointing."[27]

## Other Audiovisual Materials

Besides records, film, filmstrips, and video recordings, public libraries have collected and utilized in varying degrees other types of audiovisual aids, such as slides and stereographs, framed reproductions of art, posters, sculpture reproductions, and projected books. Of these, slides are by far the most numerous. They have a long history too. The older slides were 3¼ by 4 inches and the newer ones are 2 by 2 inches, the size of a 35mm film camera exposure. Slides may be purchased,[28] and they can be made locally. This latter feature enables any library to develop a graphic record of local history. Slides are often used in school teaching, but they are also valuable to adults for showing to a group or on television. Relatively few libraries collect slides, but there are a number of large collections.

Reproductions of art, on the other hand, constitute a relatively recent type of material for public libraries to handle on a loan basis and represent a phase of the great upsurge of interest in art in this country. Since the end of World War II, libraries across the country have purchased or rented some of the many excellent reproductions of art that are available in color, with all main schools of art represented. The pictures are without glass, are framed or mounted so as to be hung on the wall, and usually are lent to the patron, sometimes for a monthly fee.[29]

## Organization of Audiovisual Materials

In the smaller libraries, presumably the simplest form of bibliographic control will suffice, although there would be those who would disagree even about that. There is certainly a range of opinion on the subject, with many urging that nonprint be incorporated into the total bibliographic control system of the library and not be treated solely by format, as an adjunct. The theory is that the library exists to transfer information and that the transfer may be effected in some cases by print and in some cases more effectively by nonprint. In any event, the searcher should be able to view all the options available in pursuing a particular line of inquiry or research. Often, the nonprint, visual, or audio medium will supplement the printed resources; in other instances, the nonprint medium will be superior for a particular purpose.

Massonneau reports that the problem has been a lack of agreement about how to describe nonbook materials in a uniform way.

The early codes and manuals . . . were prepared for local application, but they are now prepared [for] universal adoption. The forms of nonbook materials have multiplied during this period and, as the report of the National Commission on Libraries and Information Science (NCLIS) observed, audio and visual materials have become an important part of our national knowledge resources; however, "like many natural resources, knowledge resources, uncoordinated in growth and usage, are in danger of being wasted and inefficiently utilized." This growing diversity of forms and the potential informational value contribute to the urgent need for control through rational and consistent cataloging codes, and through coordination of input to various data bases.

While some librarians have yet to comprehend the impact of nonbook materials on the knowledge resource system, others have embraced them enthusiastically, but have restrictive ideas about their management. The conclusions reached by Wesley Doak in a recent article have interesting implications: "(1) if you do not have an audiovisual or separate instructional resources department, do not start one; (2) if you have such a department now, get rid of it as soon as possible; (3) make everyone in your organization equally responsible for all information resources; (4) make familiarity and utilization of skill with media part of the rating and reviewing system for personal advancement; and (5) incorporate all library resources into one access vehicle." The last stipulation has the most pointed meaning for bibliographic control, but failure to understand the other four conditions has, in some instances, contributed to relegation of the newer media to an underutilized second-class status.[30]

Massonneau discusses in detail the impact of the new cataloging code (AACRII) upon the bibliographic control of audiovisual materials. She also draws attention to the work of the Library of Congress and others to standardize bibliographic input about nonbook materials into the various data bases. She reports that

subject cataloging of nonbook materials is also gaining new attention in the 1970s. At the ALA Midwinter Meeting in January 1975, David Remington, then of LC's

Subject Cataloging Division, presented a report to the Resources and Technical Services Division (RTSD) Nonbook Committee. He drew attention to the need for guidelines for the subject analysis of nonbook materials, which would aid in "interpreting nonbook materials in terms of the *primary uses* they may receive and applying the headings we have.". . .

There is at present no particularly dominant system of integrated shelving and housing of audiovisual materials. Elaborate and expensive equipment designed to integrate materials in single or adjacent sequences can be found in some facilities. The integration may be achieved through assignment of a bibliographic classification, through various sequential numbers, or through fixed location numbers assigned to drawers or trays. Nonbook materials are most often grouped together, while books remain in a separate location. In other cases, there is no effort to integrate nonbook forms with each other or with books. Generally, the equipment manufacturers see a definite move toward integration, while media managers and librarians have a variety of opinions.

This discussion of the present condition of nonbook materials management shows an encouraging spurt of forward motion, particularly since 1970. However, lucid codes may be written and grand agreements reached only to be disregarded by the practitioners.[31]

## Summary

We have taken brief looks at the major forms of nonprint materials in public libraries: sound recordings, films, slides and art reproductions, videodiscs, videotapes, videocassettes, and electronic media. The first four media listed are firmly established as integral elements in most library collections. The latter four are beginning to make an impact, in various ways, most of which have yet to be fully understood. It seems clear that printed materials will remain as the major stock in trade of most libraries for some time to come, but as the cost of print and paper continue to rise, the marketplace will continue to have its way, and alternative nonpaper forms of storing and disseminating some types of information will become more acceptable and necessary. The developments in computer technology may make it feasible for many libraries, and homes, to have access to information files with greater convenience and reliability than the present manual forms can provide. The example of the *New York Times Information Bank* is probably known to most reference librarians in public libraries, who have compared it with the exhausting and time-consuming task of manual searching in the printed counterpart, the *New York Times Index,* although this probably remains as the only recourse for many libraries today, because of the cost of the computer approach. But the *Information Bank* also provides access to a broader range of current information than the *Times Index.* The personnel cost of manual searching ought to be taken into account, whether by library staff or user. That time is worth something, too. It follows that administration may need to examine cost-benefit alternatives when considering the use of nonprint materials and methods, particularly in information transfer.

## Notes

1. See Lester Asheim and Sara I. Fenwick, eds., *Differentiating the Media* (Chicago: University of Chicago Press, 1975); David R. Olson, ed., *Media and Symbols: The Forms of Expression Communication and Education,* Seventy-third Yearbook of the National Society for the Study of Education, part 1 (Chicago: University of Chicago Press, 1974); and Tony Schwartz, *The Responsive Chord* (Garden City, N.Y.: Anchor Books, 1974).
2. Public Library Association, *Recommendations for Audio-Visual Services for Small and Medium-Sized Public Libraries* (Chicago: American Library Association, 1975), p. 14.
3. Helen W. Cyr, "The Basic Audiovisual Materials Collection: Selection, Evaluation, Organization" in Myra Nadler, ed., *How to Start an Audiovisual Collection* (Metuchen, N.J.: Scarecrow Press, 1978), pp. 9–14.
4. A somewhat dated yet definitive overview of music and recorded sound is Ruth T. Watanabe's *Introduction to Music Research* (Englewood Cliffs, N.J.: Prentice-Hall, 1967). See also Mary Pearson's *Recordings in the Public Library* (Chicago: American Library Association, 1963). A primary bibliographical aid is the *Library of Congress Catalog: Music and Records.* See also the July 1972 issue of *Library Trends.*
5. Gordon Stevenson, "Sound Recordings," in *ALA Yearbook,* 1977 ed. (Chicago: American Library Association, 1977), p. 275.
6. Dorothy Sinclair, *Administration of the Small Public Library,* 2d ed. (Chicago: American Library Association, 1979), p. 104.
7. Stevenson, op. cit., p. 276.
8. Sally Hericks, ed., *The Audio-Visual Equipment Directory* (Fairfax, Va.: National Audio-Visual Association, 1976–1977).
9. Leon L. Drolet, Jr., "Audiovisual Hardware," in Nadler, op. cit., pp. 26–39.
10. Jerome K. Miller, "Films in Public Libraries," *Library Trends* 27 (Summer 1978): 4.
11. Ronald F. Sigler, "Film as Public Library Resource," *Library Trends* 27 (Summer 1978): 9–23.
12. National Information Center for Educational Media, *Index to 16mm Educational Films,* 6th ed. (Los Angeles, Cal.: National Information Center for Educational Media, 1977).
13. CUFC/Bowker, *Educational Film Locator* (New York: R. R. Bowker, in progress).
14. Educational Film Library Association, *Film Library Administration: Selected Bibliography* (New York: Educational Film Library Association, 1977).
15. Jan W. Cureton, "Perspective on Establishing a Film Collection," *Library Trends* 27 (Summer 1978): 96–98.
16. Euclid Peltier, "The Public Library Film Redefined," *Library Trends* 27 (Summer 1978): 27, 34–35.
17. Leon L. Drolet, Jr., "Audiovisual Hardware" in Nadler, op. cit., pp. 39–51.
18. Robert H. Rohlf in *LJ Special Report* no. 12 (New York: R. R. Bowker, 1979), pp. 78–79.
19. John Linford in ibid., p. 82.
20. Ben-Ami Lipetz in ibid., p. 50.
21. *The Bowker Annual of Library and Book Trade Information,* 24th ed. (New York: R. R. Bowker, 1979), pp. 74–75.
22. F. W. Lancaster, *Toward Paperless Information Systems* (New York: Academic Press, 1978).
23. Ibid., pp. 163, 166.
24. Lipitz, op. cit.
25. Seth Goldstein, *Video in Libraries: A Status Report, 1977–78* (White Plains, N.Y.: Knowledge Industry Publications, 1977), pp. 1, 2, 57, 62.
26. James W. Brown, *New Media in Public Libraries: A Survey of Current Practices* (Syracuse, N.Y.: Gaylord Bros., 1976), pp. 6, 202–3.

27. Goldstein, op. cit., pp. 38–56.

28. See Metropolitan Museum of Art, *Sources of Slides: The History of Art* (New York: Metropolitan Museum of Art, 1970), and Art History Slide Curators and Librarians Association, *Sources for Art History Slides* (New York: Art History Slide Curators and Librarians Association, 1968). Also, Tom Lennox, "Slides Acquisitions," *Previews* (November 1972).

29. Charles D. DeYoung, "Art Collections for Public Libraries," *Illinois Libraries* 42 (April 1960): 246–50.

30. Suzanne Massonneau, "Organization of Audiovisual Materials," *Library Trends* 25 (January 1977): 666, and Wesley Doak, "Administrative Problems and Their Solutions," *Library Quarterly* 45 (January 1975): 66.

31. Ibid., 679–81.

# 17 Public Libraries in Systems and Networks

In this chapter, we intend to explore the movement among all types of libraries away from the independence that has characterized the growth of the American library movement and toward interlibrary cooperation. This phenomenon will be examined particularly from the standpoint of its effect upon public libraries of all sizes. The topics to be considered will include background of the concept, definitions of the various types of cooperating organizations, the nature of the problem, major current needs, factors that encourage and inhibit cooperation, statewide and county and multicounty systems, primary functions and services provided by cooperating organizations, the national plan, some suggested criteria and guidelines for cooperation among public libraries, and probable future trends.

The movement in the past decade or so among all kinds of libraries is toward a definite realization that only by means of sharing resources can libraries even begin to meet the burgeoning needs of the populations they are intended to serve. The rhetoric about "service to all" has never been even remotely realistic; only a small minority of the potential market has ever been tapped. The fact is coming clear now that only through joint effort can libraries hope to try to satisfy a reasonable proportion of the total information needs with which they might be confronted. Cooperation has long been stated as an ideal; it now is operative in many areas, on many levels, and among various types of libraries.

## Background

Public libraries in this country began as local circulating collections of books to serve the people of a particular village, town, or city. The libraries were organized and developed either as private institutions to serve subscribing members or as agencies of the local government. The simple conceptual basis was to provide books to read—a shared collection to add to, or to serve in place of, the home library. As time went on, other services and functions

306

were added: reading guidance, reference services (answering people's questions), services to children, and, in recent years, group activities and cultural programs.

But the size of the public library has always been related directly to the size of the population being served, at least until fairly recently. Public library standards, reports, budgetary recommendations, comparisons among libraries—all are expressed in per capita terms. The practical effect of this approach, as far as the citizen is concerned, is that the reader living in a town of 5,000 population would have direct access to a collection of perhaps 15,000 to 20,000 volumes (at most) according to the standards and to an input of perhaps 800 to 900 new books a year, for both adults and children. Of course, these meager resources might be extended by recourse to the sometimes effective interlibrary loan process, if the user was in no particular hurry and if the wanted book could be spared from some larger collection. But the fallacy of the concept of library services and collections related to size of population served has not become clear until fairly recent times. The thought that the villager might need to have access to more of a representation of the world's literature than that allowed by the standard of two to four books per capita has led to the development of cooperation and resource sharing among libraries. In fact, at the other end of the spectrum, the nation's largest libraries have also determined that they cannot ever hope to collect and maintain an adequate proportion of the publishing output *solo,* and have entered into cooperative acquisitions and resource-sharing arrangements.

Going back into the history of the development of the change in the local unit concept of public libraries, it may be worth noting that Kolb, in 1925, considered the minimum size of three service institutions that in his opinion were essential to the social and intellectual welfare of citizens: the hospital, the high school, and the public library. He arrived at a minimum number of service units that he thought was desirable for each of the three institutions: for the library, this was a book collection that would permit an annual circulation of 30,000. He further estimated that the minimum population required to meet his minimum conditions was about 4,000 for the library.[1]

Martin, in 1944, in his doctoral study, looked at the matter of minimum size in terms of services rendered, noting that these included provisions of "the basic and important current books of our time about common personal and social problems; personal assistance by experienced librarians in such specialized areas as children's reading, adult reading, and information service; and an organization of materials that facilitates and guides their use for popular educational purposes." Martin concluded that although it would be difficult to designate any single level as a desirable minimum, it seemed from the study that "the provision of even modest essential elements of service were not attained with any regularity until the 50,000 population or $40,000 income group."[2]

A major goal of American public librarianship has been to provide every citizen with access to adequate library service. That theme has constantly run through statements of library standards and plans for many years. The early presumption about the public library was the colonial one that the only purpose of the collection was to provide "something to read." The effectiveness of the library is measured, even to this day, principally in terms of the numbers of books "circulated." The notion, previously held, that reader needs for information and knowledge are less complex, varied, or extensive in small centers of population is obviously not valid. The library community and planners have begun in recent years to consider the advisability of larger units of library service; larger, that is, than the previously existing ones. In this account, it is hardly practical to trace the full history of these developments, but a number of factors may be mentioned. The increasing interest of the federal government that began with the Library Services Act of 1956 and its subsequent enlargement and extension (the Library Services and Construction Act of 1965) has had a positive effect on the development of larger units—or rather, to be precise about it, on the willingness of local public libraries to consider cooperation as a means for securing the benefits of increased resources and services. Title III of the LSCA specifically encouraged cooperation among public libraries and provided funds by which this could be carried forward. The 1956 revision of the Public Library Association Standards document *(Public Library Service)* said: "Libraries working together, sharing their services and materials, can meet the full needs of their users. This cooperative approach on the part of libraries is the single most important recommendation of this document."

Quoting this, the 1966 revision of the PLA standards, entitled *Minimum Standards for Public Library Systems,* noted that "the concept of library systems . . . is a method for meeting the needs of people for information, enlightenment, and recreation based on the philosophy that people need similar resources whether they live in cities, in suburbs or in rural areas."

The association's official position thus became one in support of systems, and stated that local, community libraries should join together into systems, and that "these suggestions assume that the system is designed to serve a minimum population of 150,000 people, which appears to ensure the most economical and effective use of staff, collections, and funds."[3]

The growth of "larger units of service" has been steady, and has been accelerated by a number of positive factors that will be noted later; it also has been impeded by some constraints. The subject is complex; there is a very considerable body of literature; this chapter can only sketch the outline of the problem, report in summary on status and probable trends, and on the experience with some of the main solutions. A few of the books and articles are cited here; others will be mentioned in the text.[4,5,6,7]

The matter is complicated by the wide variations in the geographic size of local government units, in the distribution of population and of wealth, in the legal structure for public libraries in the different states, and in the traditional role of cities and counties in various parts of the country. These variations explain why it is that one pattern, such as county libraries, may be acceptable and successful in California, where counties are large, populous, and wealthy, and be unknown in New England, where the county unit of government is weak and little used. The southeastern states have more multi-county libraries than any other part of the country, precisely because there were so few independent local libraries whose interests had to be considered. The result is that there has evolved no one national pattern of library service for a larger-than-local unit.

### The Nature of the Problem

Variations in two main factors make difficult the provision to all Americans of access to local public library service of at least reasonable quality: one is sparseness of population and the other is the cost of library operation. With few people scattered over a wide territory, in rural areas, the assessed valuation is low, and so is the tax support of the library. There will be few patrons of the library and insufficient use of its resources and services to justify more than a bare minimum of development. A library has a certain cost for physical quarters and book stock, and there will be a minimum operating cost to provide service of reasonable quality. Such overhead and operating costs are justified as the volume of use goes up and as the total expenditures of the library increase, until the unit cost of library service becomes less, per unit of use or per person served or per dollar of assessed valuation.

Public libraries were started first in cities, and they still have their main strength there. In the late nineteenth and early twentieth centuries, the state library extension agencies systematically developed and helped organize libraries in every municipality of any size. In many cases, libraries were started in communities too small and too poor to support them at all or to support them at a level to produce reasonably good service. The laws permitting libraries in every community are still on the books; they set no minimum standards in regard to population or financial support. It soon became evident to librarians that rural areas could never organize municipal-type libraries and that many towns were too small to secure adequate library service by independent action. The next obvious step then was to secure laws authorizing county public libraries, and for the last seventy years efforts have continued to organize such libraries. In 1935 there were 225 county libraries with incomes of more than $1,000; in 1944, 651 were recorded, and by 1960, there were 1,000.[8] While more people have access to libraries today, service outside of metropolitan centers is often inadequate.[9]

One approach, dating roughly from about 1935, has been the creation of multicounty libraries. Though theoretically able to include enough people and enough taxable wealth to justify a public library, a multicounty unit by the same token has to cope with the problems of giving service over a large area and to many small groups of people. Furthermore, because the county and multicounty library are one step removed from the local community, it has been difficult to persuade voters to approve the organization of such libraries or to provide anything more than minimum tax support.

## Major Current Needs

With the use of multicounty libraries and with other approaches to be described later, it is possible to see how local access to public library service can be provided to all people. But how to secure reasonably good library service to all is more difficult and will take longer. A third problem, and one increasing in scope and complexity, is that of the need for greater planning and communication among the libraries in metropolitan centers.[10] For some years, the great growth of population has been not in the cities themselves but in their suburbs, which typically resist consolidation with each other or with the central city. While this is a large problem for government generally to solve, and for other functions of government as well as for libraries, it brings out the need for public library service to be planned and coordinated, if not also administered, at a level above that of the smallest political unit. Approaches to such planning and coordination are being undertaken by various agencies in the country—for example, the Urban Libraries Council and the Reference, Research Resources Councils (3R's) of New York State, of which the New York Metropolitan Reference and Research Library Agency (METRO) is the one representing New York City.[11]

A national plan is needed that will suggest approaches by which to cope with the problems of providing all citizens with library coverage within a reasonable distance, of upgrading the quality of library service where it is now below standard, and of securing effective coordination of public library service in metropolitan areas.

Those concerned with library development and support must think of library service in terms of getting materials into the hands of individuals and not in terms of little library buildings in communities too small to warrant them, whether these are independent local libraries or too-small branches of a larger system.

Wight advances the thought that as governments are servants of society, the functions of government should be "assigned to the levels where they can contribute most effectively to what is loosely described as the 'good society.' " He observes that "this broad principle must recognize that, in our current complicated, technological socioeconomic society, functions of government have tremendously expanded over those of 1787 and now constitute a sort of web of interweaving threads rather than a series of independent functions." On this point, he notes:

The public libraries of small resources—whether they be municipal, county, regional or state—can effectively serve more limited specific functions than can those of tremendous resources. Libraries must objectify and specify their goals and state them in terms that can be met or approximated or exceeded. Distinction must be made in types of objectives—between membership in a network and operation of one. The hope of the future seems to me to lie in the local public library establishing high levels of service, using whatever size of unit is appropriate, and moving in the direction that Library Service and Construction Act Title III points—the cooperation of libraries to provide regional and national networks linking together those with different and specialized objectives and eventually with adequate resources for meeting them. The notion that each level of government has a completely unique set of library functions to perform has worked reasonably well for a hundred or so years. As applied to public library resources and services it is now unacceptable and is rapidly becoming completely inadequate. . . . Public library services should be assigned to those levels of government that are most competent to render them effectively and efficiently. . . . I should define competence as the attainment of the indicated level of quality of each type of service at the least cost per unit.[12]

## Some Definitions

The word *system* has been used to describe cooperative activity among libraries, but the word has so many meanings that it is necessary to look at the context in which it is being employed in order to derive a close meaning. As *system* is applied here, we are thinking of a library system that consists of at least two, and usually many more, *independent* libraries that have agreed to cooperate in order to achieve certain goals or to perform certain functions. More will be said about these goals and functions later in the chapter. But this definition of a system, if it can in fact be called that, does not include the library units of a large library, operated by a municipality or county, for example; that may also in fact be called a system. The difference lies in the fact that these independent, autonomous libraries (or systems) have agreed to cooperate. Hence, the thrust of this chapter will have to do with the problems, implications, trends, cost-benefit advantages, and other aspects that face the *independent* public library in the larger-area system—that is, *larger* (in this context) than its own territory or boundaries, or clientele. This goes somewhat beyond the thinking in the 1966 Public Library Association Standards, that a public library can provide adequate service if it is of a certain minimum size—for example, with a collection of 100,000 titles and serving a minimum population of 150,000. Most library planners now tend to discount that rather simplistic notion and to agree that nothing less than access to the nation's *full range* of library and information resources will be adequate.

The 1966 Public Library Association Standards document, setting forth the idea that adequate library service could only be provided by the library system, tended to steer away from a very precise definition of a system in that context, noting that "so diverse has been the development that it is difficult to define a system exactly. Reduced to its basic elements, however, a system may be said to provide accessibility of service, through branches, cooperating libraries, and bookmobile stops, plus a pool of resources in depth and variety, used in common by all the outlets."[13]

It is not clear from this statement whether the authors intended to speak of a grouping of *independent* libraries or of the units in a multiagency library, as in a large city or a county. Perhaps the key phrase is "cooperating libraries," which does seem to imply the concept voiced recently in a terse definition: "By federated system or cooperative, we mean a voluntary association of independent libraries for the purposes of mutual benefit."[14] In this definition, several key words and phrases emerge for review. The first is "voluntary association," the second is "independent libraries"—and this we take, again, to mean an autonomous library of whatever size, large or small, that may itself be designated as a system in the context of its own service area. And, of course, the "purposes of mutual benefit" concept is clear enough, and the underlying motive.

It is perhaps more productive to think in terms of interlibrary cooperation, rather than systems, in order to have a clearer concept of what is being considered. In his Maine report of 1961, Keyes Metcalf classified interlibrary cooperation into four types: "(1) joint storage; (2) cooperation in various aspects of what is sometimes known as bibliographical control; (3) joint acquisition programs; and (4) inter-library use."[15]

Defining networks and systems, Rohlf said:

The term *network* refers to "a single purpose or very limited purpose organization, OCLC or BALLOTS as an example." And the term *system* refers to "a library agency, federated or consolidated, which serves a number of independent or separate political jurisdictions and which provides, in varying degrees, a wide range of services or financial aids with integrated planning and direction for common goals." As examples, consider the Central Kansas Library System and the Suburban Library System in Illinois. . . . A public library can belong to a system that performs multiple functions and, at the same time, either directly or through the system belong to a network created to carry out a single function.

He went on to trace the reasons for the development of systems:

In 1956 the Public Library Association Standards stated that there ". . . should be a community library easily accessible to every reader and it should connect him with the total resources of his region and state." This, in effect, was a statement by PLA saying that one should either join a system or else become a statewide library (such as that which exists in Hawaii). The standards also said that the central library and the community libraries in a natural district (what's a "natural district"?) should function together in a system or affiliation for library service. In most states, systems were formed either out of fright, political pressure, economic despair, greed, or, in a few instances, farsighted idealism.

What were some of the accepted reasons that systems were originally formed?

1. State aid to public libraries became increasingly common, and, for a multitude of reasons, state aid was granted more often to *systems than to single libraries.*

2. Larger libraries were straining under an information load and were trying to share limited resources.

3. Smaller libraries were often passing on the more challenging information problems to the larger ones, particularly in urban areas.

4. In some areas, changes brought about in schools by consolidation or boundary reformation, changed relationships between the local public library and the local school district. This was particularly true in the late 1950s and early 1960s when there were the growing pressures of nonresident students going to the best (not necessarily their own local) libraries.

There were, of course, other reasons, among them growing financial concerns. But if one takes a historical perspective one can see that in public library activity there has always been growing financial concern.

The primary or basic objective of a system should be to provide "better" service to the users of the libraries which are a part of that system. *Better* in this sense can be defined in different ways. Quantitatively it might mean the same as better service for lower cost, or easier access to more materials or larger collections. *Better* can also be defined in qualitative terms such as greater convenience, or more rapid availability of material.[16]

An official statement of the Public Library Association (1979) expands on the 1966 PLA position, now recommending formation of *multitype* systems:

*Minimum Standards for Public Library Systems, 1966* recommended the creation of regional public library systems; *Imperatives for Services* proposes multitype library structures to coordinate public libraries and public library systems with all school, academic, and special libraries in a region. These regional multitype systems must be affiliated with state, multistate, and national networks.

At the local and regional level the public library has the responsibility, in cooperation with the state library agency, to coordinate access to all library and information resources in its community. The public library is the only agency in the spectrum of public and private library agencies which has, as its mission, service and accountability to its total community, although primary responsibility for developing statewide multitype library systems is vested in state library agencies. In the establishment of multitype library systems, a clear consensus should be reached on the role of each library and type of library within the system. The public library should assume, with the state library agency, leadership in negotiating this consensus.

Funding for the multitype systems should be based on the principle that no member library can be expected to support the total cost of cooperative services solely from its local budget.[17]

### Patterns of System Development

Five kinds of systems have emerged in the development of larger systems, as reported by Nelson Associates in a study for the Public Library Association. These are:

the county library, the multicounty or regional library, the special district library, the state supplementary, and the statewide, state-governed system. Each of these may be governed in one or a combination of the following structural patterns: the consolidated unitary form, contractual consolidation, federation of whole library units, cooperatives of individual libraries, and government by the state library.

The *county library* is the most common library unit after the municipal or city libraries. The basic aim of the county library, historically, has been the extension of adequate library service to all residents, whether rural or urban. The county library is almost always governed in a consolidated fashion. A characteristic weakness has been the unwillingness of the better established municipal libraries to become part of the system for fear of dissipating their resources. To add the strength of the larger libraries to the county, service has often been provided by contract, calling for the municipality either to administer all library service for the county, or merely to extend particular services, such as reference or centralized processing, or to join in a general pooling of resources. In addition, the county may contract for specific services with library units and centers outside its own boundaries. . . .

The *multicounty, or regional, system* is usually a response to the realization that the resources of one or more of the counties are inadequate by themselves. One of the first instances of the multicounty system is the contractual agreement in 1926 between Sierra County and Plumas County in California for the provision of library service. During the 1930s several early multi-county systems were established in the South. . . .

The *library district* usually is formed for the purpose of achieving structural consolidation. It generally consists of areas that are weak in resources and have difficulty uniting for library service because they are politically fragmented. . . .

The library district is a legal entity and customarily can raise its own revenues. Usually the amount that can be raised is strictly limited by law, and there appears to be great difficulty in lifting these restrictions to any degree. . . .

*State supplementary* systems have served specialized purposes. Early examples include Vermont and New Hampshire, where the states established regional centers to provide services to both libraries and patrons. The services to libraries include centralized purchasing and cataloging, the development of a union catalog, and borrowing from the state collection. The services to patrons include direct library services to citizens in areas not served by a local library.

Those states establishing supplementary services have tried to escape the charge of encroachment on local authority. Tennessee has set up state-supported regional centers, which serve as central resource libraries and provide both bookmobile service to libraries and professional help. They are administered under contract to the State Library, by a board appointed by the counties in the region being served. . . .

There are few *statewide, state-governed* systems. New Mexico operates a statewide service aimed at the otherwise unserved population, and does not usually provide service to libraries. In Hawaii all public library services are administered by the state librarian. Some other states provide statewide services to otherwise unserved areas, but New Mexico's and Hawaii's appear to be the most distinct cases of true statewide systems.

The state usually plays the critical role in system development. It establishes the legal framework which is often mandatory to the establishment of a system; it is the state which provides the legal measures granting the right to counties, parts of counties, or individual libraries to contract with one another and to unite in forming regional libraries and districts. . . .

State planning for libraries is not a new concept. County and regional libraries were a common feature in the plans of 45 states as far back as 1936. However, the state library then possessed little of either the coercive power or the stimulus of incentives needed to bring about system development. . . .

[Beginning in 1956] Library Service Act funds assisted in the development of systems in various ways, from surveying library conditions in the states to operating demonstration projects, and from founding state-operated systems headquarters to encouraging and supporting localities in the establishment of effective systems. Bookmobiles were bought, county libraries were founded, and multicounty libraries were encouraged, all to the end of trying to reach those who were not receiving library service.

The two major objectives of larger-unit systems were to provide increased quality of services and resources and increased accessibility. Sometimes there was more emphasis upon accessibility than upon quality; it was pointed out by critics that simply making the existing resources available to more people, or sharing paucity, was not a substantial gain. Inevitably, by the very nature of things, there were strong central libraries, with collections and staffs in depth, and branches and bookmobiles to bring a part of the services and resources to outlying districts that may not have had any service at all before the inauguration of some kind of system. In the early days of federal aid, one-third of the federal and state money produced by the Library Services Act went into the provision of bookmobiles. As it became clear that extending less-than-adequate library services to more people was not satisfactory, there was

a shift in emphasis in library thinking, and the shift was translated into federal legislation and state programs as well. A much heavier stress was laid on providing accessibility to a major resource collection. The chief pioneering effort in this activity was the New York State program for systems, a component part of which is that each system contain at least one central library with a minimum of 100,000 nonfiction books. The state took upon itself the major responsibility for bringing up the collection to the recommended level, but at the same time, built strong local incentives into its aid program.

While the Library Services Act had been aimed mostly at the rural population and used mostly to extend services to those who were receiving little or none, the Library Services and Construction Act of 1964 expanded the federal program to include cities.[18]

The 1969 study found that systems showed tangible evidences of service achievements, in access, collection, circulation, and services.

Access to library service is probably the greatest gain from systems experienced by patrons. *Many systems provide access to library service to large numbers of people for the first time. This access is probably the most fundamental accomplishment of public library systems.* In no less than 30 of the 58 selected systems, such access was provided to a substantial population for the first time. . . .

Library service to large numbers of unserved and greater access to better resources are evidence that *systems are fulfilling their most basic purposes.*

In the systems studied there has been a *substantial rise in volumes per capita.* Median per capita volumes rose from 0.7 in the first system year to 1.1 in the midyear and to 1.2 in 1966. Since the median first year for the 58 systems is 1957, and the median midyear is 1961, a rough comparison can be made with national statistics for public libraries for the years 1956 and 1962, during which time volumes per capita rose from 1.47 to 1.55. The overall national increase was thus about 5.4 percent, as compared to an increase of 57.1 percent for the 58 systems. . . .

In the 58 selected systems a substantial rise in per capita circulation has taken place. Median per capita circulation rose from 2.5 in the first system year to 3.8 in the midyear and to 4.7 in 1966. During the years 1956 and 1962 national statistics for all public libraries show circulation per capita rose from 4.18 to 4.68, an increase of 12 percent, as compared to an increase of 52 percent for the systems of this study between their median first year of 1957 and the median midyear, 1961. . . .

Perhaps the best indication of the extent to which services have improved under system operations is the judgments of the heads of affiliated libraries. While the data are thereby restricted to systems having affiliates, as distinct from branches, the source is both well informed and objective. . . . According to the responding librarians *the chief benefits to affiliates are more and better holdings, access to reference and other materials, and improved reference service.*[19]

Commenting on the Nelson Associates study in 1979, Rohlf observed:

Some of the questions the study asked were:

1. Do systems really produce more for the money?
2. Do local communities shirk their financial responsibilities and let the systems carry the load?
3. Do larger or stronger libraries become weaker as the smaller system members drain them?
4. Do smaller libraries actually drain the resources of the larger libraries?

In virtually all of the systems studied, finances loomed large, but on the other hand finances are a large problem in any library whether it is a member of a system or not. Some of the other things that the study discovered were, on the surface, obvious in some instances, and, in others, quite surprising. A combination of weak libraries did not necessarily make a strong system. . . .

Federated systems have had difficulty developing systemwide acquisition policies; and, while federation with a group of other libraries would appear to provide the opportunity for more systematic collection growth and planning, that opportunity does not appear to be exploited except in exceptional cases. The study also discovered that incentives alone, without a mandated local effort, do not attract all communities equally, and that some communities benefit without contributing their share. . . . [Other conclusions:] a strong headquarters staff was considered essential to a productive system; that basing tax support on the largest possible political unit tended to simplify many political problems of equalization, planning, the crossing of service boundaries, and the equity of local financial contributions; . . . personalities, particularly those of the top administration, were the single most important factor in the success, growth, development, or failure of a library system.[20]

### Networks

One of the terms that has come into recent use is *library networking,* although this is scarcely more precise than *systems.* Various definitions have been given for the concepts of library networking and resource sharing. Kent writes: "Resource sharing denotes a mode of operation whereby functions are shared in common by a number of libraries. . . . Consortium, network, and cooperation are terms used to label the organizational arrangements for achieving a variety of source sharing objectives."[21]

Markuson has distinguished three levels of library cooperative activities as follows:

*Library Cooperation*—any activity between two or more libraries to facilitate, promote, and enhance library operations, use of resources, or service to users.

*Library Consortia*—a specialized type of cooperative library activity usually restricted to a limited geographical area, number of libraries, type of library, or subject interest and having some degree of formalization of administration and procedures.

*Library Network*—a specialized type of library operation for centralizing development of cooperative programs and services, including the use of computers and telecommunication, and requiring the establishment of a central office and a staff to accomplish network programs rather than merely coordinate them.[22]

Butler observes that as library networking is a rapidly changing area, the first task is network definition and description. He sets out a "normative list" of "essential characteristics" of networks:

1. A network's function is to marshal resources . . . to accomplish results beyond the ability of any one of its members.
2. A network has developed an organizational design and structure that allows it to establish an identifiable domain. . . .
3. It has a base in communications technology.

A library network is defined by four characteristics: it is a *d*ependent organization and system providing *d*uplex *d*igital *d*istribution. To expand on the alliteration:

1. A *d*ependent system is one which is operated multilaterally "in concert" in response to the common desires of a group of member libraries, as opposed to various shared or cooperative services which are offered unilaterally to libraries of all types of vendors or other libraries.
2. The *d*uplex element is a way to avoid the much-overused phrase "feedback"; it describes a two-way communication which separates a network from a publication or one-way dissemination such as an information service.
3. *D*igital defines the exclusion of various multilibrary functions which fulfill the other characteristics, but do not involve some use of computer, telecommunications, or digital data manipulation (specifically excluding cooperatives and consortia which operate manually).

4. The distribution of information or materials may take many forms (catalog cards, printed information, CRT screen images) but is the essential service of the network.

The definition of a dependent system also implies an important complementary point: the network must be an *in*dependent organization separate from the administrative, political, and fiscal bounds of its several members.

Butler adds another definition: "network" is to

describe only that dependent system which is providing some type of interactive computer-based service. A "network resource" is a computer system, data base, or service which is available for use by that organization. The former is the multilibrary organization, the latter the production system *used by* the library network. We tend to talk of the wide variety of network resources as if *they* were the network. . . . The Ohio College Library Center can be described as one of a number of network resources. What we call "OCLC" can then be seen as an on-line bibliographic reference, cataloging, and card production service which is used by a number of regional library networks. . . . In sum, a *network* entity *need not create and operate all its resources—* and in fact, none of them do or are likely to do so.[23]

Two other definitions have been suggested in order to be somewhat more precise about networks:

*Bibliographic Utility*—an organization that maintains large online bibliographic data bases enabling it to provide processes and products to libraries and library patrons and whose purpose includes reducing the rate of increase of per unit costs in libraries and making resources widely available to library patrons. Examples of utilities include the Bibliographic Automation of Large Library Operations using a Time-sharing System such as RLG (BALLOTS), OCLC, and Washington Library Network (WLN).

*Service Center*—an organization acting as a broker or distributor of computer-based services from one or more bibliographic utilities in a particular region; or operating other bibliographic services such as a union file of location information, or a photocopy center; or offering computer-based information retrieval services. Examples of service centers include the New England Library Information Network(NEL-INET), Southeastern Library Network (SOLINET), AMIGOS Bibliographic Council, Midwest Region Library Network (MIDLNET), Bibliographic Center for Research (BCR), Pacific Northwest Bibliographic Center (PNBC), Pennsylvania Area Library Network (PALINET), New York State Interlibrary Loan Network (NYSILL), and the Illinois Library and Information Network (ILLINET).[24]

Martin reports that in the decade since the 1970 Conference in Warrenton, Virginia, on library cooperation,

more than 2,000 libraries in North America have become involved in on-line bibliographic processing as a means to streamline such internal tasks as cataloging. Yet in 1978, the goal of a comprehensive bibliographic network was beyond the resources of the library community. Such a network would provide every library with access to first quality cataloging information as well as to information on the holdings of member libraries in order to facilitate a free exchange of both bibliographic information, and of books, journals and other materials.

Defining networks, she suggests that

in modern usage, a network can be defined as a group of individuals or organizations that are interconnected. The linking must include a communications channel, and many networks exist for the express purpose of fostering a certain type of communication among their members. In the library world, institutions form networks primarily to achieve better sharing of resources—resources consisting both of bibliographic information and of collections—and better service to patrons. . . . A distinction must be made between networks used only for information retrieval and those used for input and modification of data as well as for retrieval.[25]

There is a considerable variety of network activity at all levels throughout the country, including a broad array of services. At the state level, there is some type of cooperative or network activity in all fifty states.

New York, Illinois, California, and Washington are often cited as models among the states, as each has a considerable history of network development. New York has one of the longest traditions of library systems, and there is now a new focus on multitype library cooperation, emphasizing activity rather than type of library. In Illinois, the statewide library network, first established in 1965 with the creation of library systems, is now known as ILLINET, or the Illinois Library and Information Network. This is a multitype network, with local public, academic, special, and school libraries; eighteen library systems; four research and reference centers; and two special resource centers of last resort. The basic services are interlibrary loan and reference, although the network is a vehicle through which many cooperative projects are funded. The California Library Authority for Systems and Services (CLASS) was established in 1976. CLASS is a public agency, designed to "govern, direct, set policies, establish computerized network standards, and handle all related business required." Its services will be made available to all California libraries of all types.

In Washington State there has been considerable emphasis since 1973 on the conversion of the Washington Library Network's computer system to an on-line mode. In 1973 the state legislature created a data-processing authority under whose auspices a library automation committee was formed with representatives from universities, colleges, public libraries, and the state library. This committee is charged with overseeing the development of an integrated computer system to assist the operations of all libraries. First priorities are cataloging and acquisitions subsystems, followed by circulation and serials control subsystems. On-line services are now provided and the entire software package is being offered to states and regions for adaptation to their needs. WLN has also joined forces with RLG/RLIN for enhancing and enriching services to users.

Networking activities of some type can be found in most of the other states, and new developments occur frequently. The Indiana Cooperative Library Services Authority (INCOLSA) has been established in Indiana. INCOLSA is an independent organization formed under state legislation enabling libraries to create cooperatives. There are also multicounty cooperatives: Area Library Service Authorities (ALSAs) was formed under the same legislation. All types of libraries may be members of ALSAs and INCOLSA (provided that there is a majority of public members), and can contract with both ALSAs and INCOLSA for service support.

Local cooperation may be among libraries of the same type, libraries of two types, or all types of libraries. Under some definitions, the public library systems found in many states could be considered networks. Examples of local "multitype" networks are the Total Information Exchange (TIE) program in southern California and the Illinois Regional Library Council. The Illinois Regional Library Council (IRLC) is the "multitype," multipurpose, multicounty library cooperative serving the Chicago area.[26]

### Cooperative Functions

A tally of the networks, consortia, and other cooperative organizations listed in *American Library Directory, 1978* shows a total of seventy-six in which public libraries are named as participating (the networks are for public libraries either by themselves or with other types of libraries). Of these, ten organizations are listed as having public library membership only; sixty-five are multitype organizations; and one is a public library–public school consortium.

In the preface to the *Directory,* the terms of inclusion are stated: "Included in this section are book processing and purchasing centers, statewide networking systems and other cooperating organizations."

In each of the entries there is a list of the primary functions as described by that cooperating organization. Some notion of the diversity and wide range of primary functions engaging the interest of cooperating libraries may be seen; among the total of seventy-six organizations, a total of thirty-eight primary functions is listed. Most numerous is interlibrary loan, offered by forty-five of the organizations. (This list, it should be noted, does not include the library systems of New York State, Washington, California, Illinois, and other states. These systems are, of course, also cooperating organizations in a real sense, in that they provide services and functions to member independent libraries.)

Other primary functions, and the number of cooperating organizations that offer them are: reference and referral, data base search services,* forty-two; staff development, continuing education, workshops, and job placement, thirty-four; cataloging, processing, bibliographic assistance, and access to bibliographic utilities, twenty-five; publications, directories, and newsletters, sixteen; delivery service, fourteen; cooperative (and) coordinated acquisitions, fourteen; professional assistance, consultant service, six; supply 16mm films, five; interlibrary center, three; resource development, three; and sharing resources, three.

---

* Not all these functions are offered by the number of organizations listed; like functions have been grouped together for convenience.

The following primary functions were listed as offered by two organizations: cooperative purchasing of library supplies; public relations program; resource development; sharing resources. The following primary functions were offered by one cooperative (it should be noted that this tally does not go into the number of functions listed by the various cooperatives; most listed more than one): film selection; automation in individual libraries; cooperative holdings for members; children's and young people's programs; translation service; retrospective microfilming; slide/tape package development; developmental studies; investigative studies; delivery and exchange of materials in microform; central resource center; interlibrary cooperation; sharing of A-V equipment; operation of public information station; books by mail; cassette tapebank; bookmobiles; area planning and coordination; collection development; duplicate materials exchange; multimedia exchange; and government documents depository.[27]

This listing can only offer a kind of shopping list of activities that a number of public libraries have selected for cooperative action. It obviously does not consider the depth, extent, or emphasis placed upon each in the specific situations; also, the functions are shown as listed; some may be similar in nature although described in different words. A 1967 study of systems in New York State adds to the list.[28]

As further examples of the development of systems, it may be noted that Illinois had in 1978 a total of eighteen regional systems, of which seventeen were cooperative and one was consolidated. The total library system income was $9,447,318; funded by the state according to a formula of $1 per capita and $35 per square mile of area served. Massachusetts has three regional library systems, serving the entire state; California has fifty-one county libraries, serving all fifty-eight counties.[29]

(The above is far from a complete listing of county and regional library systems but is included to give a sampling of the development that has occurred.)

### The National Plan

The National Commission on Libraries and Information Science was established July 20, 1970, by Public Law 91-3454, as an independent, permanent federal agency in the executive branch of the government. Under the law,

The commission is responsible for advising the president and the Congress on the development and implementation of national policy, for developing overall plans for meeting national library and information needs, and for coordinating activities at the federal, state and local levels in meeting those needs. Its overall goal is to ensure equal opportunity of access to information to every individual in this country, without regard to his location, economic condition, or nature of need. This is a broad charge and a heavy responsibility and we expect that it will take many years to effect such a service in anywhere near a satisfactory manner.

The National Commission's executive director, Alphonse F. Trezza, has proposed a "full-service network" that would not be restricted to being computer-based, but

refers to a rational, coherent pattern of integrated activity among information suppliers and information seekers. Within that framework, then, there is no mandate that all activity must be computer-based, nor do we see any need to issue such a mandate. Information is, and can be, transmitted in many ways; via computer is but one option. On the other hand, that framework does assume a coherent framework of communication. . . . Logical channels must be identified and utilized; the direction and flow of bibliographic data, of documents themselves, of information concerning bibliographic data, and of information itself must be structured if adequate service to the user is to be provided with optimal economy and efficiency through the network. This requirement for rationality applies equally to the transaction between information-seeker (e.g. the individual library patron) and information provider; between one library and another, laterally or hierarchically between library and vendor or publishers; or between a periodical access center, for example, and its users. And it applies equally whether the transaction is document delivery, or an interlibrary loan request, or an inquiry concerning an acquisitions decision.

A full-service network, in the NCLIS view, would have very practical implications for the local library user. Examples of how it would work when in operation are cited: One, a request for an accurate, current local weather forecast in a far-off city would be placed at a local library, would go to the weather service in the far-off city, perhaps via the state library in that state, and thence back to the inquirer. Second, a request is made for the full text of an article in a medical journal, mentioned in a local newspaper. The medical journal article is about a new medicine for an illness that a relative has. The full-service network would permit that request to go from the local public library to a medical library through established channels and be filled. Third, a commercial drug manufacturer has heard that a tropical research laboratory in Hawaii has issued an unfavorable report on a medicinal ingredient being tested by the commercial firm. The commercial firm should be able to make its request through its library, which would then relay the request via satellite, and would receive the report in a matter of days.[30]

The National Commission's recommended national program sets out eight major objectives, from which the following are excerpts:

*Objective 1.* Ensure that basic minimums of library and information services adequate to meet the needs of all local communities are satisfied.

Local libraries and information centers, whether large, medium, or small, and whether public, academic, or school, are vital links with the people. Local libraries are the first place in the community where most people generally go to find information. . . . It is . . . imperative that the National Program provide that local communities attain certain basic levels of service and materials and that their human resources are also strengthened. Only when local resources have been strengthened can resource sharing and other joint efforts lead to successful networking arrangements at state and national levels. . . .

*Objective 2.* Provide adequate special services to special constituencies, including the unserved.

There are large user constituencies which require services and materials of a specialized sort. Such groups include the poor, the illiterate, the blind, the visually and physically handicapped, the ethnic minorities, American Indians on reservations, the very young, senior citizens, inner-city youths, migrant workers, the institutionalized, and many other parts of our society. . . .

*Objective 3.* Strengthen existing statewide resources and systems.

. . . Some states have well-developed programs; others function at less-well developed levels; and still others have no statewide programs at all. Because the states are the essential building blocks in any national information system, it is important that they attain minimum levels of proficiency and strength as parts of a nationwide program. . . .

It is the view of the National Commission that any new National Program should rest on the understanding that the Federal Government would fund those aspects of the National Program that are of common concern nationally, in return for a commitment on the part of the states to accept, in cooperation with the local governments, a fair share of the responsibility for funding libraries within their own jurisdictions. . . .

*Objective 4.* Ensure basic and continuing education of personnel essential to the implementation of a National Program.

The development of adequate human resources for library and information service has been one of the Commission's concerns since its inception. . . .

*Objective 5.* Coordinate existing Federal programs of library and information service.

The Commission recognizes that existing library and information service programs in operation by the Federal Government—such as those in the Library of Congress, the National Library of Medicine, the National Agricultural Library, and the 2,300 or more Federal libraries and information centers—constitute invaluable operating programs that are of great significance to the proposed National Program. Many of these programs are already performing centralized bibliographical, reference, and other services that are of benefit to all libraries in the country. The National Program will make use of these national services and must ensure that they are well coordinated and continued at levels strong enough to fully satisfy the national need. . . .

*Objective 6.* Encourage the private sector (comprising organizations which are not directly tax-supported) to become an active partner in the development of the National Program.

The private sector has long been involved in using and providing information, and has built up a large body of expertise in handling information. In recent years it has initiated many new types of information services. Two distinct components of this sector can be identified as having the capacity to make special contributions to the National Program; the special libraries and information centers (in both for-profit and not-for-profit organizations); and various service organizations. . . .

*Objective 7.* Establish a locus of Federal responsibility charged with implementing the national network and coordinating the National Program under the policy guidance of the National Commission. . . .

One of the most important issues to be resolved in pursuing a National Program of Library and Information Services is deciding what kind of permanent operating agency is required at a Federal level for this purpose and recommending where the agency should be located in the government. . . .

. . . Three existing national agencies have been mentioned as possibilities: 1. The Library of Congress; 2. The Office of Libraries and Learning Resources, U.S. Office of Education. 3. The National Commission on Libraries and Information Science. . . .

*Objective 8.* Plan, develop, and implement a nationwide network of library and information service.

The National Commission believes that only by interrelating the pluralistic cooperative programs of the past and providing a national frame of reference for future development will the nation be able to achieve optimum exploitation of the rich information and knowledge resources in the United States. . . . [The purpose] of the proposed nationwide network . . . is to tie together information systems at all levels; Federal, multistate, individual state, and local, as well as compatible systems found in the private sector. The aim is to permit rapid delivery of needed services and materials to people in all jurisdictions without artificial institutional or geographic constraints.[31]

## Networks and Systems: The Future

Martin has summarized some of the elements of the library network of the future; they are excerpted below:

The technical characteristics of networks may not be suitable for all applications or library functions. Such procedures as cataloging, acquisitions or interlibrary loan represent a relatively small workload in a library's transactions; they also incorporate data which can or must be shared among libraries. These characteristics make these functions adaptable to shared network processing. Functions such as circulation, serials check-in and fiscal accounting rely upon local idiosyncrasies or a large proportion of local data. An attempt to incorporate these applications into a network system would be hampered by less efficient use of telecommunications links and of shared data.

Bibliographic and performance standards must be identified and agreed upon before a rational networking scheme can become operational. Work is ongoing in some of these areas; many standards have been developed and implemented in the past decade, including the MARC format, Anglo-American Cataloging Rules, international standard book and serial numbers, and the international standard bibliographic descriptions. More difficult to come to grips with are the less tangible issues such as performance standards, pricing algorithms and administrative structures. In 1978, very little work of a wide-ranging or satisfactory nature has been done in these areas, but the efforts of NCLIS and the Library of Congress are beginning to explore this difficult territory. Only through greater experience will vendors arrive at logical pricing and network managers at rational management structures.

Technological developments continue to provide expanded alternatives for network development. New techniques for allowing user access to on-line systems are being developed, e.g., Bibliographic Retrieval Services has made it easier for users to express queries in simple language, rather than learning and conforming to a variety of specially constructed syntaxes for retrieving data from each individual data base. In addition, minicomputers are being used increasingly, both in individual libraries and as components of library network configurations. Although equipment compatibility is less than universal, enough standards exist to allow minicomputers to communicate with each other or with larger computers. . . .

The economic and social climate in the late 1970s has made it apparent that the general retrenchment of the economy and of public services is affecting libraries. A climate of skepticism toward large-scale public expenditures is likely to continue for some time. The taxpayers' revolt, as manifested by the passage of Proposition 13 in California, raises serious questions about the place of libraries in the hierarchy of social priorities. If society intends to decrease its support of social services, it is not likely that libraries will be within the group of services labelled as "essential," such as police or fire. Two trends, diametrically opposed, may be discerned: 1) social conservatism is giving rise to an emphasis on local services, local systems, local autonomy and a de-emphasis on multi-institutional cooperation, but 2) diminishing funds may encourage certain kinds of shared resources, centralized processing and cooperation of institutions to mutual economic benefit. . . .

## NETWORK OF THE 1980s

Given these indicators, one may construct a possible network for the 1980s. Network resources will be housed in large computers in several regions of the nation, as repositories of large bibliographic data bases and as communications concentrators for messages among libraries. These resources will also be directly available service centers for libraries which do not have access to computer facilities or are not members of a local consortium. Regions will be interconnected by telecommunications links which will be a combination of regular telephone lines, value-added network utilities such as Tymnet and Telenet, microwave and satellite transmission. The Library of Congress will be a node in this nationwide network, and its bibliographic system will serve as the backbone of the national network and as the liaison with networks and information systems of other nations.

Minicomputers and/or terminals in libraries will either gain access to the data directly as is presently done with on-line networks, or will request that data be copied in machine-readable form from a network center to a local computer, to be processed locally for circulation, production of microform catalogs, etc.

With the above configuration, the reference and processing functions can gradually be linked. Even now, public service units in some libraries are able to tap the on-line processing systems in order to provide information to their users. This use of on-line bibliographic data bases will expand rapidly as the data bases themselves expand. A "giant leap" for the information profession will come when the bibliographic data bases with holdings information can be easily linked on-line to the reference data bases created by the abstracting and indexing services. With this increased access, librarians and users will experience a significantly different approach to our stored knowledge than has been possible in the past. Although the links between the files generated by libraries and abstracting and indexing services will be complex to develop both bibliographically and economically, procedures can be established to allow each data base to retain its own authority controls, while providing user access to files generated by a variety of institutions.

Martin comments that

until now, libraries have implemented automated or networking systems without radically changing the tools used by staffs and patrons. . . . The new systems are used, for the most part, to assist in maintaining the manual systems or to replace the manual systems without philosophical or intellectual change in approach. However, efficient and economic implementation of networks and other computer technology must force libraries to reconsider the traditional patterns of bibliographic control and access. In a few libraries, already the organizational structure has changed fundamentally, and this trend will undoubtedly increase. With on-line files, the traditional organization of technical service units may no longer be defensible.

Concluding her look into the future, Martin observes:

Libraries and library networks are dynamic. . . . It is almost impossible to describe the state of the art at any one moment: as soon as the words are spoken or written, the circumstances have changed, and technology has moved onto another step. . . . The network in 1978 is definitely here to stay, but its form and function may not be of the all-pervasive centralizing nature envisioned a decade ago. Networks are means rather than ends; they are tools to assist each library in meeting the service goals appropriate for its clientele. The national—and international—network would be structured to reflect this function.[32]

## Practical Implications

It is manifestly evident that larger units of service are here and will increase in complexity—in the kinds and levels of services and resources offered. As the availability of system affiliation becomes more and more feasible, it will be difficult if not impossible for even the smallest public libraries to remain unaffected. The national and state plans and the library leadership will speak to the urgent need for sharing of resources on a larger scale. And as the advantages become apparent, even the patient library patron, whose expectations of quality in library service have not generally been very high, will realize that it would be a fine idea to be able to tap into the books, films, reference data bases, and other sophisticated components of the nation's libraries, from wherever he or she might be. There are tugs of war among the various library interests in the library community for slices of the action and control of the operations. It will be very unfortunate if these activities get in the way of the major goal: to make the resources of the country available equally to all citizens.

The administrator, staff, and trustees of the local, independent public library may look at interlibrary cooperation with a number of criteria in mind.

A cooperative project should benefit all the library users of the region more or less equally. It should be able to be accomplished with the funds available or in sight. Also, the cooperative activity should:

Meet the most pressing needs of the library users of the region.

Be capable of being carried out with a reasonably good (75–100 percent) chance of success, on the basis of the known evidence.

Be financially supported by member libraries and/or other sources on a continuing basis if successful.

Be agreed to by the majority of participating units as meeting these criteria.

Not duplicate or conflict with services already being provided or to be provided by the state.

The basic premises of cooperation, in concrete terms, are simple:

1. Cooperation will permit member libraries to save on:
   acquisition of costly books and materials,
   storage space,
   specialized personnel.

As to books and materials, no library can afford, and should not afford, the acquisition and storage of every book its clientele might need.

As to personnel, the same principle applies: no library except the very largest can afford to employ all the various kinds of skills and experience that a modern library operation needs to have.

2. Cooperation, at least at the onset, need not require change in the government of a library that utilizes the services of the cooperative.

3. The main idea is that each library is to provide those services that it can provide best and to look to the cooperative for those services that can more economically be provided jointly.

4. The cooperative enterprise ought to build on the strength of the autonomous library units and to exist solely to serve the interests of the members and through them the library and information needs of the people being served.

In conclusion, it may be observed that the combined phenomena of hitherto undreamt-of advances in technology, just now available on a broad scale to the provision of library services, may bring about a considerable increase in the status and significance of library service as a social utility.

There can be little doubt that every adult person has a pressing and increasing personal need for information and enlightenment as he or she tries to make his way through the complexities of the modern world. A distinction must be made, however, between the *existence* of the need and the individual's *awareness* of the need. In short, needing information is universal, at least among people above the age of five in a literate society. Knowing that they need to know is not universal.

The significance, or perhaps the remedy, as far as public library service is concerned, lies not in surveys that result in conclusions deploring the small proportion of citizens who look first to the public library as a source of information, enlightenment, and recreational reading. Nor does it lie in trying to convince nonusers of the library service that they will be better, happier, and greater if they will just come to the library and partake of its benefits.

The hard fact is that getting services out of a public library, as it has always been organized, is not a simple task but is on the contrary somewhat forbidding for many people in all walks of life and at all levels. Successful usage often requires a considerable degree of ingenuity and patience. This does not reflect on the quality and character of effort of the library staff, who are uniformly among the most dedicated and helpful of public service personnel in the community. The difficulties facing many members of the community, who have information and recreation and cultural needs that might be satisfied by the library service, stem from the public library's inherent organizational pattern: the community's sharing a limited and set collection of materials and staff abilities and specializations, which cannot be expanded or revised to meet the needs as they are presented.

The promise and the challenge of library cooperation—via systems, networks, and perhaps forms of organization not yet seen—are that the total universe of information, broadly defined to incorporate the record of all kinds of materials, could now be tapped by every citizen as he or she might choose, through the local library outlet as a node in the system. There still exist many organizational, political, structural, and attitudinal obstacles to the achievement of that condition, but the technology is, or can be, in place to accomplish it. The problems are mainly human ones.

This is not to say that even in the future, with a model information network available, every last citizen might choose to make use of it. There will undoubtedly be many people who would still elect to go through life information-poor, or rather, perhaps, information-oblivious. But if people *could* walk into their local public library and get answers to questions, copies of materials needed, or resources for independent study with approximately the same degree of success that they can now learn about the balance in their checking account or withdraw money from it, there might well be a substantial increase in the number of people using the library.

Cooperation among libraries as they now exist, or as they may have to become, taking advantage of the tremendous advances in communication and technical methods of information sharing and retrieval, provides the possibility for almost unlimited increases in public service.

## Problems Facing Development of Cooperative Efforts

Robert H. Rohlf, director of the Hennepin County (Minnesota) Library, and author of the Illinois state plan that resulted in the library systems there, has summarized some of the problems and concerns that occur when libraries attempt to come together for cooperation in order to improve service. The first problem that usually arises is that of money.

When one deals with systems, one normally deals with multiple political jurisdictions, and . . . there is a problem of money . . . [mainly] of securing money equitably. How does one achieve uniform tax efforts from various taxing jurisdictions without getting involved in a significant amount of politicking over what is—or should be—an adequate tax effort. Libraries or systems that have to deal with more than one appropriating body find that their problems are geometrically, not arithmetically, increased. Often the problem of achieving equity in financing is not so much a reflection of a library program as a reflection of some other political dispute that may or may not have anything to do with the library itself, as road construction or improvement, stadium locations, swimming pools, golf courses, or who supported whom at the last political convention.

The second more significant concern, Rohlf observed, is that of governance.

There is an opportunity for constant conflict between authority at the system level—defined as authoritarian by many members, and (as described by system staff) a lack of understanding by member libraries as to what the system itself is attempting to do. This conflict can express itself as a local instance of the historic question of federalism versus centralism. Whenever you have funds coming from one location to another, or service to library patrons of one area paid for from funds secured somewhere else, you are going to have questions that are often emotional, sometimes legal, and, rarely, professional.

. . . Librarians with turf or status to protect can be as big a block (or even bigger) to library development, service and system success, as uncooperative politicians.

There are many barriers to system formation and system success. Some are based on personal characteristics, some are based on geography, and some are based on history or tradition. Most of us can probably name some of the other barriers . . . personalities, mistrust, the fear of the loss of local decision making, the fear of the unknown, the fear of the larger libraries that they will be overused by the smaller libraries, the fear of the smaller libraries that the larger libraries will take over the entire operation, local political jealousies or competitions that exist between differing local jurisdictions, the distances between libraries, the differences in quality and size of the library collections, and local historical or geographical barriers.

Rohlf urged librarians and library trustees to lay aside their fears of change and of cooperation.

The increasing stress being placed on the creation of a national library information system, the need for access to information or materials, and for processing of bibliographic data on other than a strictly local level, the increasing interests of academic libraries and or large foundations to fund national efforts relating to resource sharing and to bibliographic data is making it increasingly important for librarians to belong not just to local systems but also to regional systems and to networks.

He recommended that systems should exist whether there is outside financial aid or not; that it is better to manage change than to change plans, noting that change and growth result from deliberate choices; libraries must evaluate their own systems, and must develop better ways of explaining and delivering services. "Systems," he concluded, "require change and change requires innovation and risk, and whenever we have any kind of change or development we run into conflict.[33]

## Notes

1. J. H. Kolb, *Service Institutions for Town and Country* (Madison, Wis.: Agricultural Experiment Station of the University of Wisconsin, 1925).
2. Lowell A. Martin, "The Optimum Size of the Public Library Unit," in Carleton B. Joeckel, ed., *Library Extension Problems and Solutions* (Chicago: University of Chicago Press, 1946), pp. 38–39.
3. American Library Association, *Minimum Standards for Public Library Systems* (Chicago: American Library Association, 1967), pp. 10, 41.
4. Ruth W. Gregory and Lester L. Stoffel, *Public Libraries in Cooperative Systems* (Chicago: American Library Association, 1971).
5. Nelson Associates, *Public Library Systems in the United States: A Survey of Multijurisdictional Systems* (Chicago: American Library Association, 1969).
6. Charles H. Stevens, "Governance of Library Networks," *Library Trends* 26 (Fall 1977): 219–40.
7. National Commission of Libraries and Information Science, *Toward a National Program for Library and Information Services: Goals for Action* (Washington, D.C.: Government Printing Office, 1975).
8. Nelson Associates, op cit., p. 13.
9. National Commission of Libraries and Information Science, op. cit., p. 23.
10. See Lowell A. Martin's analysis of problems confronting the Chicago Public Library in *Library Response to Urban Change* (Chicago: American Library Association, 1969).
11. "Expansion Keynotes Metro Tenth Anniversary," *NYLA Bulletin*, April 1974, p. 6.
12. Edward A. Wright, "Precursors of Current Public Library Systems," *Library Quarterly* 39 (January 1969): 39–40.
13. American Library Association, op. cit., pp. 10–11.
14. Maurice J. Freedman, "Thoughts on Public Libraries," *Journal of Library Automation* 10 (June 1977): 123.
15. Keyes D. Metcalf, *Cooperation Among Maine Libraries*, a report prepared for the larger libraries of Maine (Belmont, Mass.: Keyes Metcalf, 1961), p. 7.
16. Robert H. Rohlf, "System Change by Choice," *Public Libraries* 18 (Fall 1979): 47–48.
17. Goals, Guidelines, and Standards Committee, Public Library Association, *The Public Library Mission Statement and Its Imperatives for Service* (Chicago: American Library Association, 1979), pp. 11–12.
18. Nelson Associates, op cit., pp. 15–20.
19. Ibid., pp. 242–43.
20. Robert H. Rohlf, op cit., p. 48.
21. Allan Kent, "The Goals of Resource Sharing in Libraries," in Allen Kent and Thomas J. Galvin, eds., *Library Resource Sharing* (New York: Marcel Dekker, 1977), pp. 15–32.
22. Barbara Evans Markuson, "Library Networks: Progress and Problems," in Donald P. Hammer, ed., *The Information Age: Its Development, Its Impact* (Metuchen, N.J.: Scarecrow Press, 1976), pp. 35–54.
23. Brett Butler, "State of the Nation in Networking," *Journal of Library Automation* 8 (September 1975): 200–201.
24. *Library Networking in the West: The Next Three Years* (Boulder, Colo.: Western Interstate Commission for Higher Education, 1976).
25. Susan K. Martin, *Library Networks, 1978–79* (White Plains, N.Y.: Knowledge Industries Publications, 1978), p. 5.

26. Vernon E. Palmour and Nancy K. Roderer, "Library Resource-Sharing Through Networks," in *Annual Review of Information Science and Technology*, vol. 13 (1978), pp. 156–57.
27. Jacques Cattell Press, *American Library Director*, 31st ed. (New York: R. R. Bowker, 1978), pp. viii, 1529–44.
28. *Emerging Library Systems: The 1963–66 Evaluation of the New York State Public Library Systems* (Albany, N.Y.: The University of the State of New York, 1967), 3:1–8.
29. Jacques Cattell Press, op cit.
30. Alphonse F. Trezza, "The NCLIS View—A Full-Service Network," *Journal of Library Automation* 10 (June 1977): 170–72.
31. *A National Program for Library and Information Services* (Washington, D.C.: National Commission on Library and Information Services, 1975), pp. 66–83.
32. Susan K. Martin, op cit., pp. 106–10.
33. Robert H. Rohlf, op cit., pp. 48–49.

# PART III

## ADMINISTRATION
## OF SUPPORT
## SERVICES

# 18 Technical Services

This chapter incorporates the various processes involved in acquiring, arranging, and controlling the library's stock in trade: the materials of the collection. These processes are defined in library parlance as order work or acquisition, cataloging and classification, book preparation, inventory, and circulation control, including borrower registration. It is true that circulation is still handled separately, as an operation, from order work and cataloging, but the advance of technology will doubtless make it feasible for at least the larger libraries and systems to treat the entire materials-handling procedure as one integrated process, using elements of the same data base for all steps, with the machines performing the work linked together.

## Order Work and Cataloging

This section is concerned with the ways in which the ordering, cataloging, classifying, and processing of materials are managed and with certain aspects and viewpoints that affect size of staff and operating costs.

To evaluate a book and its author's purpose—that is, to catalog and classify it in its strategic place in the library's collection so that it may be most useful to the user—are tasks requiring a high degree of skill, intelligence, imagination, and judgment. Such tasks were once integral to the operation of every library. With the growth of networks and computers, however, shared cataloging has become a fact of life. Computer-based networks such as the Ohio College Library Center (OCLC), the Research Libraries Information Network (RLG/RLIN), the Washington Library Network (WLN), and the University of Toronto Library Automation System (UTLAS) supply member libraries with complete bibliographical data on nearly all materials acquired, thus making cataloging too costly to pursue at the local level. Today, original cataloging in public libraries with few exceptions is a matter of intelligently managing machines and people.[1,2,3,4,5]

335

### The Technical Services Division

Although the technical services division is organized differently from library to library, the general basic pattern combines the order or acquisitions department with the cataloging department. In some libraries, the technical services division also includes the binding and photography departments. Some of the functions performed by these departments, particularly cataloging, lend themselves to network operation and shared on-line cataloging procedures, producing savings and/or added services. The key to the success of such an undertaking, however, is the use of standard cataloging rules.[6] For this reason, it is suggested that libraries follow the Anglo-American Cataloging Rules and accept without alteration LC cataloging data, to the extent that this is possible.

There is no reason for the small library to operate a technical services division if the state library or a library system provides central processing services. However, a large library may have separate departments for ordering, cataloging, and processing with someone heading each of the three and possibly a coordinator, or a technical services division head, to oversee all these services. This arrangement joins closely related activities, eliminates duplication of efforts, and permits a broad overview of the total operation. As automation and on-line systems continue to develop, more and more services are being added to the technical services division. Notably, these services include circulation control, information retrieval by subject, serials control, and remote catalog access.[7]

Where a decision to reorganize is based on having the cataloging head oversee technical services rather than appointing a separate overall head, steps should be taken to develop the chief cataloger's management ability, while relieving him or her of enough cataloging detail so that the span of control over the other services can be extended. If the head cataloger cannot handle this larger responsibility, someone else should be appointed who can serve adequately in this administrative capacity.

The processing (making the materials shelf-ready) should be handled in one central department, except in a few special situations in very large cities. The head of the technical service division constantly assesses the appropriateness of its procedures and devises improved methods. Finally, these procedures are not ends in themselves; they should be planned and measured in terms of meeting the needs of the public service departments and ultimately the library's users.

### Simplifying Methods in Technical Processes

A library can improve the functioning of its technical services by studying, simplifying, and saving time in its routines, thus reducing the unit cost, and improving quality. Improving quality in itself may not necessarily lower costs. Physical conditions are especially important to the functioning of technical processes because the staff works intensively without much moving about. Unless technical processes are on the same floor with the main catalog, an official catalog is almost a necessity. This is seldom possible except in larger libraries. However, the trend today is toward distributed or portable public catalogs in various forms, book, computer output microform (COM), or on-line, depending on patron needs, so that the location of the department no longer poses a problem. It could even be located outside the main building.

Practices may be kept long after they are useful. A systematic examination of each procedure can usually eliminate costly steps, permitting much greater output per person and reduction of cost. For example, most libraries no longer record the dealer, price, and so on inside the book, for in replacing they have to look up the current price anyway. Books should be moved the fewest times, the shortest possible distance, with the fewest possible handlings. All cards and records should be made simultaneously wherever possible, instead of in a series of steps. Simplifying routines applies equally to libraries of all sizes.

### Division of Work

Each step in a technical services operation should be specifically assigned to an individual employee. Most steps are clerical. In the past many were performed by professionals, but now almost all work, when properly supervised, can be done by clerical personnel. This assumes that the intellectual elements of acquisition are, as they should be, either associated with public services or directed by a separate department head equal in rank to the other department heads.

The use of machines in the technical processes applies primarily to the large library and to the duplication of cards. There is no point in using a machine unless it reduces costs, speeds up the operation, or improves the quality of work.

### Acquisitions

*Order Routines*

The major concerns of ordering are (1) to secure the maximum discount consistent with other costs and services; (2) to prepare and place orders promptly;[8, 9, 10] and (3) to establish and maintain appropriate financial controls.

Acquisition is closely tied to the interests of all public service departments, the branches, and the business office. The mechanics, though not the intellectual side, of book selection should be centralized at the order desk or department. The order section will check titles considered for purchase to prevent duplication. It will also consolidate all orders from departments and branches. While it may be necessary to order separately the first or main library copies of important titles, to make them promptly available to users, the branch copies should, if possible, be ordered at one time and be processed together.

Library patrons are keenly aware of delay in obtaining new books after they have seen the titles advertised or reviewed. An efficient library orders books promptly and at least once a week if the book budget is over $20,000 a year (an average of 200 to 250 books a week). A prime objective is to have new books in hand, cataloged, and on the shelves by publication date. Special "rush" orders and "rush" cataloging, special orders for replacement copies of older titles, pamphlets, paperbacks, prebound juveniles, records, tapes, films, and other media may also be necessary. Periodicals are usually ordered by a blanket subscription, as noted later.

The main record in an order section is its order file, a record of books on order and not yet received. Larger libraries may keep a file or record of books received and not yet processed, but as every such record is a burden, it should not be needed if the books are processed promptly. If the library uses multi-copy order forms, one may be kept in the order file until the catalog cards are ready and will thus serve as an automatic record of books in process. Efficiency comes not from such records but from prompt processing within two or three days after receipt. In the absence of an accession record, the order department may keep the file of paid invoices, filed chronologically, and often with the first item given its respective accession number. Some libraries have given up the use of accession numbers to identify duplicate copies of books and now use copy numbers instead. As automated systems develop, the unique aspects of the accession number are more valued.

A want list of titles desired but out of print or "can't afford yet" should be kept by the appropriate public service departments to be checked against dealers' catalogs and gift books, or orders for out-of-print titles can be placed in the hands of a dealer. A special central desiderata list is probably not worth its time cost in cities of under 500,000 population.

Most order departments keep the record of book expenditure by agency, by month or quarter, and perhaps by type of material or even type of book. These categories should be kept at a minimum unless other records, such as gift copies versus bought books, can be proved essential. Because of varying discounts and "shorts," invoices and orders never completely agree, and it will save much time if expenditures for book allotment accounts are recorded by totaling the bills received rather than orders placed. Each month or two the order department should prepare a statement showing each agency's annual allotment for materials and how much has been spent to date. More detailed expenditure figures are unnecessary if each agency roughly estimates its outstanding orders and the free balance available. The order department checks books received from dealers against the invoices and order records.

Invoices when cleared are passed to the business office for payment and accounting.

The classic order routines described here are handled differently when libraries are part of a system or network. In this situation, which small libraries may choose in order to take advantage of greater discounts on purchases, much of the order work is carried out by a central library agency. Order routines are modified too when automation enters the picture. Increasingly, larger libraries are automating many acquisition routines, either by participating in commercial automated systems offered by vendors or by creating their own automated systems. The latter approach seems to be gaining in popularity as minicomputers grow more cost-efficient and the services offered by systems become more available to member libraries.

An automated system has certain advantages. It eliminates duplication in recordkeeping, ensures accurate reporting, and institutes financial controls. The system can be programmed to maintain files, such as the on-order file and books-received file, as well as to record agency expenditure reports, gifts, and special funds.

*Relations with Dealers*

Libraries sometimes buy books from a local bookstore, and a number of publishers are willing to sell direct. Almost universally, however, public libraries buy books from a jobber or wholesaler. One jobber alone, for example, supplies over 2,600 library customers and carries 150,000 titles in stock. Jobbers offer high discounts and attractive but monopolistic services such as prepackaged, automated systems for acquisitions, which obviously make it advantageous for libraries to buy all their books through one jobber. There are those who view this situation with concern, because it makes libraries too dependent on very large jobbers. A local bookstore can usually supply rush or special orders, but it cannot be expected to give high discounts or special services. A public library is under no obligation to buy its books locally, for local dealers cannot carry the stock, or give the discount or service, of a jobber. On the other hand, every library must deal directly with some publishers, who sell their books direct and in no other way. In other cases the publisher offers no discount or no greater discount to a jobber than to a library, and the jobber will not usually bother with such orders. Very large libraries might find it to their advantage to buy a large proportion of books direct from publishers if they can obtain full discounts. But for most libraries the substantial saving on paperwork and the greater convenience of dealing with one efficient, experienced jobber outweigh any possible higher discount that may be received from some individual publishers when ordering direct. In fact, most publishers prefer not to deal with public libraries, especially for single copy orders, and will refer them to a jobber.

At 1979 prices a book jobber would, in general, give public libraries a minimum of 33 percent discount on trade books (zero to 25 percent on technical and textbooks), on a volume of up to $10,000 a year. At $50,000 a year, the discount might be 36 to 38 percent, with greater discounts for a larger volume of business, though a few jobbers go above 38 percent.

The increase in book prices has been well documented elsewhere.[11] Competitive bids on discounts should be asked every two or three years, from several jobbers, before making a contract specifying services expected, such as prompt and prepaid delivery at least weekly or semimonthly (with reports on titles not delivered in thirty or sixty days), as well as any exceptions to be observed, such as the library's right to subscribe to book clubs. There should also be provision for cancellation of the contract for stated reasons. Librarians and trustees often overlook the fact that prompt, accurate, intelligent service and billing save so much staff paperwork time that they are more important than a 1 or 2 percent difference in discount. Unless exclusion by ordinance is sought, the competitive bidding process is the method that most librarians must take to select a jobber. The danger is that the process will result in unrealistically high discount quotes followed by poor service.[12]

Soliciting competitive bids for periodicals usually results in little difference between the net prices; far more advantageous (if permitted in public contracts) is the inclusion of three-year subscriptions and of the "till forbid" system of periodical subscriptions, which saves money and reduces paperwork to a minimum. Ordering priced pamphlets is best done from a pamphlet agency such as the Bacon Pamphlet Service, East Chatham, New York, and Beverly Books in Linden, New Jersey, because the costs of locating, writing direct, and paying separately for each pamphlet will exceed the list price of many of them.

### Relations with Municipal Offices

Individual libraries vary in their freedom to order books, from complete independence of action to total dependence on the purchasing office of the city, county, or school board. Centralized purchasing of municipal supplies that are standard and used by several agencies is undoubtedly desirable and economical and can be made to work efficiently, including their stockpiling. But library books involve a continual stream of individual items, each different, each of comparatively small cost, with probable changes in the status of each book—not yet published, out of print, out of stock, will be available again in a month or two, and so on. Buying library books, with all their individual peculiarities, special discounts, and billings, through a city purchasing office wastes time in useless paperwork and delays service. Library books and related materials should be exempted from the general pattern of centralized purchasing. In fact, they should be excluded by ordinance from purchasing department procedures and rules. Requests for payment should go directly to the finance department certified for payment by the library. If possible, the library should also be allowed to carry forward book funds from one fiscal year to the next. It can be reasonably argued that no other segment of local government is subject to the circumstances of book ordering, which demands the carryover of encumbered funds, as described below.

In several cities with central purchasing, officials have modified the rules so that the library prepares and mails the book orders and clears the invoices, sending carbons to the city officer to file with the warrant or voucher copy. In some cities they have set up blanket annual or quarterly requisitions to jobbers, by lump-sum warrants and by other devices, especially when there is an annual contract based on competitive discount bids. All this paperwork should not be duplicated at taxpayers' expense.

The problem of closing out the book fund, and not overspending at the fiscal year's end, arises from the fact that purchase orders for books are certain to be outstanding, in order to keep constant the inflow of new books. Titles ordered may not show up for several months. Outstanding orders represent commitments of current funds. Nevertheless, in some cities it is not permissible to carry over into the next fiscal year the encumbered funds so represented. It is no solution to suggest that all book purchases be completed early enough in the fiscal year so that there are no such outstanding and unfilled orders; this disregards the rights of users to an uninterrupted flow of new books. Such unfilled and outstanding book orders are an inevitable factor (for active book flow and good service) and do not vary appreciably from year to year as a percentage of total purchases (about 10 percent at any one time). If these orders are figured as an obligation or a carryover at the year's end and, together with any bills received in excess of available funds in the current budget, are carried into the next fiscal year, the library can avoid (1) overspending; (2) carrying forward any substantial obligations; and (3) slowing down the inflow of new books for which the public is waiting. The librarian should seek the advice and assistance of the appropriate officials, explain these problems, and develop methods to meet the operating needs of the library within the spirit of the law.

## Relations with the Catalog Department

Obviously the order and cataloging operations should proceed in adjoining space with no barrier between. If the catalog department head has general oversight of the order work, the relationship will be simple and flexible; for example, he or she can decide without involved discussion what data shall be put in the books before they move from the order work stations to the catalogers' shelves or desks.

If the order department is responsible for securing the bibliographical information needed for completing the order cards, it must use the card catalog, *The Weekly Record,* publishers' announcements, MARC tapes, and other tools, most of which are also used by the catalogers. All these tools and the tables and stands to use them should be located between the order and the cataloging personnel to avoid unnecessary travel. The order department needs a large table on which to open, spread out, and compare the books against their invoices, and sufficient shelving for the usual flow of books. The placement of work stations deserves serious study. Most order departments handle incoming serials, documents, gifts, and other materials, and the head has to assign each of these added responsibilities.

## Original Cataloging

Original cataloging, a process by which a book or other material is evaluated and given a class number and catalog headings to make it accessible to library users, has been, except in special situations, abandoned by local public libraries. Some still perform original cataloging on "rush" materials because of their high priority rather than waiting for LC cataloging copy to be supplied by LC proof slips, their jobber, a network, or a central processor. For the most part, however, libraries capitalize on work executed by the Library of Congress or other libraries. Original cataloging is still a concern of large public libraries with special collections.

### Assigning Work

In large libraries, materials are assigned to different catalogers according to language or subject—or form, such as audiovisual materials. Indeed, in the Library of Congress, descriptive cataloging is separated from subject cataloging and classification. Processes of varying difficulty and responsibility are assigned to people according to the skill, training, experience, and ability required for each task. Usually one person catalogs and classifies nonfiction titles, because both steps involve an understanding of a book's subject and coverage.

Increasingly, professional librarians are assigned to duties requiring management experience in special training in computer systems as well as cataloging and classification expertise. All work that can be done by experienced nonprofessional and clerical assistants should be so assigned. These duties include filing, typing, reproducing cards, handling added copies, cataloging fiction books, keeping records, and all the marking, pasting, and other activities associated with the book preparation process. Where local systems subscribe directly to a bibliographic utility such as OCLC, the searching and editing via a computer terminal is carried out by clericals under the supervision of professionals.

Nonprofessionals need adequate in-service training, competent supervision, and encouragement to contribute to the improvement of the order and cataloging process. Each clerical assistant should be acquainted with several different parts of the department's work, to permit shifts in assignments.

This instruction and supervision of the nonprofessionals may well be assigned to an able assistant, thus relieving the head of the department of the job.

All clerical assistants, or at least all part-time clerical employees, might be supervised by one person, to ensure that their time is spent where most needed. Care should be taken not to divide authority over the same person between two or more departments. Alert nonprofessional employees are often able to suggest improvements in the work process, and should be encouraged to do so, for this makes them feel more a part of the team. Other things being equal, typists should work near the catalogers; books and cards can then be easily passed across, and this encourages the catalogers to release more duties to the nonprofessionals.

The use of temporary cataloging should be avoided, especially if a typed card will later be replaced by a printed card simply to have uniform and elaborate cards from Library of Congress or some card supplier. This does not mean that a copy of the order slip could not be filed in the public catalog to show library users whether and when the book was ordered. However, it should be removed when the book is actually cataloged. To the proposal that a sort of preliminary cataloging be done and then scrapped when the ultimate card is ready, the answer is prompt cataloging when the books arrive. The catalogers can work directly from them and make final cards that meet the library's standards.

## Cataloging from Outside Sources

Questions bearing on costs, promptness in getting new books into users' hands, and the possibilities of avoiding duplicated effort by various forms of cooperative, centralized, or commercial cataloging are a set of administrative problems for every individual library. There is a trend in the library world to confront these problems jointly with the institution of a national network of bibliographic services. Certainly, the breakthrough established by the OCLC network and the subsequent growth of other networks—RLG/RLIN, WLN, and UTLAS being the most important examples—coupled with the activities of the Library of Congress and with a host of special purpose networks and programs, have demonstrated that large-scale networks can be successful.[13] Further discussion of networks and services from bibliographic utilities is contained in Chapter 17.

### Regional and Cooperative Cataloging

Obviously it is more efficient for a large library to catalog a number of copies of a title than to have catalogers in a number of nearby libraries all work on their copies of the same title at about the same time and with about the same results. To be sure, these copies must be done in the same way, and individual libraries must accept certain minor departures from what they have been doing. This is the basic principle behind regional and other centralized cooperative cataloging networks. The commercial cataloging services that have sprung up will make some adjustments in their procedures to meet the wishes of individual libraries, but at an extra cost.

In this book we can do little justice to the organization and operation of processing centers in which library materials for several independent libraries, either by contract or informal agreement, are ordered, cataloged, and physically prepared for use by library patrons at some central point. The rapid changes, the diversity, and the complexity of local solutions call for an extended analysis and comparison not feasible here. Such analysis, to be useful, would need to break down the libraries studied into size categories, for objectives and costs vary greatly according to the volume of accessions. Detailed discussion of processing centers is available elsewhere.[14,15] Each local library should investigate the pros and cons of joining such a system.[16]

### Use of Printed Cards

Wholesale and nationwide duplication of cataloging of the same title is greatly reduced by the use of Library of Congress, or OCLC, printed cards.

The great bottleneck is the wait for the cards after ordering them, especially in libraries that rightly attempt to order important new books in time to receive and catalog them before the publishers' release date. Though LC has reduced this delay considerably, it is still great. For an individual library to give prompt service, which is its obligation, it has to (1) scan publishers' announcements and advertisements and other sources of advance information; (2) order its books before publication date; (3) order LC or OCLC cards from source copy by LC card number, ISBN, or author and title; and hope that by the time the book arrives the cards will have arrived.

Through several commercial firms, libraries can now order their books and have them arrive accompanied by LC cataloging, obviating the separate local ordering, filing, and unfiling of LC records as well as the major jobs of cataloging and classifying.

In many libraries, a clerical assistant now receives the proofs of LC or other records, checks new book orders against the proof-slip file, and indicates on the order of a title if a proof exists. A professional worker has to scan and eliminate the proofs that evidently won't be needed. Obviously, a great deal of time is involved in this routine.

### The Cataloging Process

The work to be done by a cataloger for new books, each title having a copy of the order slip and an LC or OCLC proof slip, is to prepare a record, such as a copy slip or worksheet for computer input, the classification number, the correct author entry, the bibliographic description of the title, the relevant subject headings, and added entries.

Most public libraries still use the Dewey decimal classification; since it is up to date and so nearly universal, centralized classification is possible. Changes in successive editions of the Dewey classification schedules should be considered carefully before being adopted, and they should be applied only to new books until it is clearly desirable (and possible) that the older books be reclassified, for redoing of older books is costly and probably not required. If reader interest classification is used, it should be not in place of but in addition to Dewey.

Use of the Dewey system of LC or OCLC source copy should not be allowed to result in classification numbers of formidable length. The Cutter number, designed to arrange alphabetically by authors' names all books under a given class number, is being replaced by the first initial of the last name of the author and in some libraries has been abandoned altogether, as the author's surname appears on the back of most books. This saves a step in the cataloging process and is no handicap in small or medium-sized public libraries or in most branches of large systems, which would have relatively few books on any one subject.

In the past, bibliographic description of a book in the average public library was far less detailed than that used in a large university library or for a rare book.[17] Today most public libraries, however, cannot afford to create new, individualized copy for their collections. It is more cost-effective to use the more elaborate LC cataloging, OCLC, or other ready copy. When such copy does not exist for a particular item, then the library must create its own record. Unfortunately, the cataloging of nonprint materials—records, cassettes, films, instructional media kits, toys, and the like—is not being handled very well at LC, and no other single, well-coordinated national effort exists. If libraries do want to provide some sort of cataloging for nonprint materials, they may have no choice but to produce some of it themselves. This is particularly true if speed is important. In general it can be stated that the newer the format, the slower the cataloging copy from LC.

## Subject Cataloging

The careful assignment of subject headings, class numbers, and other details of entries is important indeed. The usual catalog for the public library has authors, titles, and subjects in one alphabet. Deciding on subject headings is difficult, and it is made more so by the changing nature of words and subject phrases, by the unforeseeable developments of subject knowledge, by the vagaries of patrons' interests, all complicated by the time dimension.

There is no easy answer to keeping all subject entries continuously current in terminology, internally consistent, and correctly descriptive of the contents of books, but much time can be saved by using the Library of Congress list and thus utilizing the immense effort involved in their successive revisions. This also avoids maintaining a costly local authority file of headings. Perfection in subject cataloging is probably more of a librarian's ideal than the typical user's concern; practically speaking, from a cost-effective standpoint, it is better to take the subject headings as they come than to try to alter them, in the hope of possible improvement. "See" references are more profitable than "see also" references; a copy of the subject headings list at the public catalog may serve as substitute for both. Few books in a public library need more than one or two supplementary subject headings, but these do help recover more of the investment in the book and its cataloging, by leading to it readers who have an interest in each field but no knowledge of the specific title. The question of updating subject headings after twenty years (for instance to replace "domestic economy" with "home economics") should prompt a review of the books themselves when they are that old and to the withdrawal of many of them and of their catalog cards.

The common tendency to use the same set of headings for a given book at the main library and at the smallest branch has two aspects. In a very large city library, simpler cards may be needed for small agencies and perhaps also for juvenile books—with fewer subdivisions—and more detailed ones for the main catalog and for adult books. On the other hand, two treatments for the same book make extra costs. Is it justified? Updated mimeographed lists for periodical holdings, placed at the catalog and at the reference desks, are more effective than catalog records, which must be kept current. Subject headings may be as desirable for fiction as for nonfiction, but a copy of the Wilson *Fiction Catalog* may make these unnecessary. Annotations used on the cards are appreciated by patrons, but it is rather costly even to clip and paste on the notes from *Publishers Weekly* or *Library Journal* or to file the annotated cards available from the latter.

From force of habit, a class number or a subject heading may be overused. This creates formidable blocks of cards, or other records, and baffles patrons and staff alike in many libraries today, though the use of printed cards makes this less frequent. When noticed, these blocks need to be broken up, by an extra digit, a date heading (to divide books before or after a given year of publication), or in some other manner to bypass the older material.

*Card Duplication*

There are so many different procedures being followed by local libraries that it is difficult to describe a card duplication procedure that will be widely applicable. The following assumes that books are cataloged locally, perhaps from LC proof slips or Marc-fiche. It obviously does not apply where cards are supplied from an outside source.

When the cataloger has completed the copy slip, a clerical assistant can perform most remaining operations. These steps are all done according to a formula worked out in advance, incorporated in instruction sheets, that can be thoroughly mastered by a clerical assistant in a few months of continuous performance of the same tasks.

Normally, if there is only one copy of a book, it is more economical to type the three or four cards needed than to prepare them by any other process, in the absence of a photoduplication machine through which a few standard catalog cards can be passed. At five or more duplicate copies of the same card (without changes on the top line), it is profitable to use some mechanical reproduction.

Some of these methods have the advantage that they can turn out all necessary catalog and shelf-list cards (with subject headings produced in advance in quantity, or added later by hand) and also book cards and book pockets; all needed repetitions of the same information are done at one time, in one way, with one revision of the master copy. But space and cost are involved for filing and storing the master copy device or extra copies of the card so created, or for recreating it upon need if it is not kept. Count also the time lost, by some methods, in getting the books and/or cards to and from the copier and together again for revision.

Membership in a network like OCLC might be the ultimate advantage. OCLC produces computer line-printed cards for members. In addition, some libraries are locally producing catalog cards by means of a commercially produced device that will print cards when attached to a computer terminal in the library.

### How Many Catalogs Need Be Maintained?

Duplicating cards is influenced also by the number and types of card catalogs maintained. In a small library, there will be one dictionary catalog of author, title, subject, and other entries for adult and juvenile books. A larger library, with its service departments on the main floor and its catalogers upstairs, may have to take on the burden of a public and an official catalog. This may be avoided if the catalogers' travel route to the public catalog is shortened. The children's catalog will be the next to be separated, especially if the children's room is on the second floor or in the basement. Branch libraries usually combine juvenile and adult catalogs. A shelf list is almost universal except in small libraries, though for branches it is increasingly considered unessential; the fiction section, at least, duplicates the fiction cards in the catalog in the same order. More and more, branch catalogs reflect the holdings of the entire system. The state-of-the-art indicates that the computer output microform (COM) catalog is best suited for this purpose. The Public Library of Columbus and Franklin County (Ohio), with ten central library departments and twenty-one branches, is entirely on COM. Card catalogs have been removed and most of the cabinets sold. With the COM catalogs showing all holding locations of a title, the daily transfer of copies from library to library within the system to meet borrower requests has increased dramatically.

Saffady reports that "the number of library COM applications has increased dramatically" since 1975, following the publication of a number of studies and articles describing successful applications both in this country and abroad. Saffady also says COM "denotes the product (computer-output-microfilm), the process (computer-output-microfilming), and the device (computer-output-microfilmer) that converts machine-readable, computer-processable digital data to human readable textual or graphic information in microform *without first creating* paper documents."

Saffady observes that the

current intense library interest in COM has been stimulated by several important developments, including the growing availability of library holdings data in machine-readable form made possible by the Library of Congress' MARC program, combined with increased awareness of the high cost of maintaining conventional book and card-form catalogs. . . . One of the most important factors in the increased availability of machine-readable data for COM recording is the wide-spread use of the Ohio College Library Center system and the consequent availability of individual library holding in archival tapes.[18]

Several commercial organizations have developed the capability of converting machine-readable tapes to COM catalogs. Surprisingly, or perhaps not so in this age of increasing reliance upon the TV screen as a means of communication, public reaction, as reported in public and academic library installations of COM catalogs, has been favorable. People do not seem to mind, in fact may even prefer, searching for library holdings on a screen similar in size and appearance to an average TV screen, and they seem to have mastered the mechanical details of operation. It is true and has been noted often that the average public library card catalog is not the easiest device to use for finding out whether the library has a book, especially when the search is for books on a subject. The display on the screen of a number of entries in sequence seems not to offer an impediment to consultation. Updating the microform catalog is not as costly as it might seem it would be, but it does involve reproducing the entire film. This may be done at intervals of every three months, with weekly or monthly supplements issued in the meantime. There are variants in this procedure, which are discussed in detail by Saffady in the report cited, and to which the interested reader should refer. It should be noted that the library may elect to convert the card catalog records to 16mm roll microform or standard 105-by-148mm (approximately 4-by-6-inch) microfiche. Roll microform is produced on reels, cartridges, or cassettes. It is the simplest and least expensive microform to create, consisting of processed microfilm wound onto a plastic holder. Films are various lengths, 100 and 215 feet being the most common. The reel microform offers the two main advantages that the contents of the catalog can be kept together on one reel and that the sequence is fixed and cannot be altered by the user. A disadvantage of the reel format would occur when the entire catalog would not fit on a single reel. This can be overcome, if need be, by dividing the catalog by subject, author, and title, for example. Several readers for the use of the public will be needed in any case, so this does not really present a problem. The reel stays in the reader and is not touched by the user at all.

Microfiche has the advantage that the readers are less costly than those for microfilm rolls, and also the advantage of semirandom retrieval. However, a roll microfilm reader with a motorized film advance and an index feature can overcome the seeming disadvantage of the user having to pass through all preceding microimages in order to reach the desired entry. In any event, in a public library with a variety of users, it would doubtless not be at all practical to use a microfiche catalog, with users responsible for retrieving and inserting the fiche.

The library administration and technical services department, at this stage of the development of technology available for bibliographic control, do in fact have to make several decisions. There are significant options. Without delving into the subject as much as one might be tempted to do, because it is a fascinating one in many ways, the choices may be summarized. The closing of the Library of Congress catalog, now scheduled for January, 1981, and the adoption of the AACRII rules, will have some impact upon public libraries, although the extent of this impact is still not clear. Estimates of the number of subject headings that will be affected range from 11 to 17 percent. On reflection, this does not seem to be a threatening number. It would seem that most public libraries, if not all, could afford to live with a few broken files (with subject cards noting "new subject introduced") rather than to attempt to "purify" the catalog, revising all entries by bringing them into line with the new rules. In any event, this will be one decision to make. Another may be to decide whether to close the local catalog. This might be considered when and if the library is to convert to a machine-readable format.

There are some experts who contend that the COM catalog is only a temporary and intermediate step, on the way to the on-line catalog. That will be another decision to consider. The on-line catalog is a system whereby the user or catalog searcher has access by CRT terminal to the library's bibliographic data base on magnetic tape or disc. Libraries that subscribe to a bibliographic utility have an on-line catalog at this time, of course, but the present inquiry methods are too complicated for the general reader to employ. It is undoubtedly true that the on-line catalog is down the road, in the future, but when it will be practical for the average public library is hard to say. One factor that may keep it impractical for the multibranched system simply involves the ongoing costs of line charges that must be paid to the telephone company. This cost could be prohibitive as distances and numbers of branches increase.

So the question arises of whether it will be better to stay with the card catalog until the on-line catalog is feasible for general use or to consider the COM catalog as an intermediate step—or, of course, to stay with the card catalog indefinitely. It would be a good idea to think of the COM catalog as a backup facility, however, even if the library were to go to an on-line catalog in the future. If the computer feeding the on-line catalog were to be out of service, access to the data would be impossible for both readers and staff. The COM catalog is essentially mechanical in nature once the microform has been produced, and since the public library would have several microform readers in service, if one or more were to be in disrepair, access would not be denied to the bibliographic record.

This discussion suggests, however, that the library director, technical services staff, and public services staff would do well to prepare a plan of action, after considering the various alternatives, costs, and requirements. Whatever plan is adopted, there will be far-reaching implications affecting budgetary allotments, staff workloads, and public use and satisfaction. An example of such a study is the one done by the Library, University of California at Berkeley. It is perhaps more comprehensive than would be required by most public libraries, but it does provide an excellent model of the problems to be considered and the conclusions that might be drawn by a staff study group. The California report, "Future of the General Library Catalogs of the University of California at Berkeley, Phase 3," and dated August 6, 1976, was published in 1977 by the library.*

*Identifying Duplicate Copies*

Good public service calls for knowing the present location, within the system, of all copies of each title. In larger libraries, there seems to be no practical alternative to keeping this information on the shelf list or on the official catalog card. In both cases, patrons and staff must await a telephoned report from (or personal visit to) the catalog department for this information. In small and medium-sized libraries, copy locations can be shown on the cards in the public catalog, but this slows down the transfer of books and results in a sizable workload in correcting locations on all catalog entries for transferred books—a good example of the extra duties that absorb catalog department time. To avoid repeated changes in the location of mobile books, as for deposit loans or for use in small branches, it is possible to show them on the catalog cards as in a certain collection or pool, and with the exact present location of each book recorded only in the charge-out file, but this again requires reference to a second file. The data bases in automated circulation control and/or computer output microfilm catalogs will provide the means for identifying current locations and availability of all duplicate copies. This is a substantial advantage of automation and eliminates a great deal of manual recordkeeping.

* Available with prepayment of $3 from Librarian's Office, University of California General Library, Berkeley, California 94720, check payable to Regents of the University of California.

*Filing Cards in the Catalogs*

Normally, the catalog department files cards into the public catalogs at the main building. Sometimes it also is responsible for filing in branch catalogs, but more often branch personnel do their own filing. Branch catalogs in many libraries are revised every two or three years by an experienced fast filer. New catalog cards should be distributed and filed promptly, desirably through a supplement drawer to avoid handling individual drawers of the complete catalog every day. But a portion of the supplement is filed into the complete catalog daily so cards will not be delayed over a week.

Filing rules of most American public libraries, based on the official ALA code,[19] are too complicated for most patrons and even many library staff members to understand or remember. In small and medium-sized libraries, at least, cards should be arranged in as nearly a straight alphabetical sequence as possible, ignoring punctuation and differing types of entry. Simplified filing rules usually make it possible for card filing to be done by intelligent, interested nonprofessional assistants.

As the state-of-the-art progresses, and libraries move to on-line, COM, or book catalogs, card filing will be unnecessary. Cards will be "filed" by the computer and catalogs updated. The new edition of the Anglo-American Cataloging Rules, scheduled to be operational in January 1981, will cause many research libraries to go on-line with catalogs earlier than intended and may affect large public library decisions in this regard.

*Assisting Patrons in Using the Catalogs*

It is desirable to issue to library users a reasonably brief and current statement on the organization of the catalog. This sort of publication is common in academic libraries but is needed even more in public libraries, which typically serve patrons less well prepared and less motivated to use a catalog. In addition to a pamphlet publication, signs and graphics are useful. An assistant should be scheduled near the catalog, whatever its form. At the outset patrons will require more assistance with the newer forms of catalogs—for example, the COM catalog. Much of the work and effort that goes into preparing an excellent catalog comes to nothing if patrons don't understand how to use it. A library can improve catalog effectiveness by recurrent studies of patron use.

*Other Departmental Activities*

The typical catalog department spends time on other essential jobs, such as the processing of maps, records, and other nonbook materials, or updating records for withdrawn or transferred books. Few catalog departments escape revision of various aspects of the catalog in the name of better public service—

for example, reclassification of individual books or groups of books, cataloging documents or other materials not previously cataloged, or recataloging older books to bring them into line with newer practices. Desirable as these projects may be, they should be regarded critically; often the situation will be resolved in time by the withdrawal of the materials. One library proposed to charge a department's book fund fifty cents for reclassifying each old book into the present system; that ended the idea of embarking on the costly enterprise. Older books cataloged and in closed stacks need not be reclassified. These various duties outside the main flow of new books consume time that often is included in "the cost of cataloging"—one reason why it is so hard to calculate fairly.

## The Book Preparation Processes

While the unit or master catalog card is being reproduced, the books themselves are being made ready for circulation—pasting, marking, jacketing, counting—by other assistants. Sometimes in large libraries only one copy of each title goes to the cataloger and the other copies go directly to be processed for use. If so, one of these copies should have an instruction slip or copy of the order slip, showing the destination of each copy. As an aspect of method study, a library needs to determine whether it will save time to keep all cards and their books together, or at what point to type or duplicate their cards, pockets, and so forth before pasting and labeling and then to reassemble books and records to make them ready for the public service departments. Also, the book number has to be placed on the spine of the book. The number can be written, marked with an appliance, or affixed via a label. Gaylord markets a device called Se-Lin Labeler, which attaches to a typewriter, permitting the typing of labels in a neat and consistent manner. Se-Lin-produced labels also permanently adhere to the spines of books, having originally been created to meet the archival needs of research libraries. It is possible, through attachments, to print labels in connection with securing products through bibliographic utilities such as OCLC.

Each book must be marked also as library property, preferably by rubber-stamping the edges of the book. Embossing or perforating takes longer and is less effective. An accession or serial number is used in many libraries large enough to have numerous copies of a book, to distinguish the copies, so this is also needed on the book pocket, book cards, and at one place in the book, as well as on the shelf list or official catalog card. A good idea is to stamp these all at one time, using a numbering machine with the last two digits of the current year and then a serial number. Other libraries ignore serial numbering and write in the copy number when needed. Plastic covers have made a vast improvement in the appearance of library books, allowing the retention and use of the publisher's book jacket, usually colorful as well as valuable for its commentary and biographical notes. These preparatory processes should be done promptly and swiftly and the books dispatched to the public service agencies as soon as possible. If each worker visualizes the patron awaiting the book, things will move faster and the day's work will be more interesting.

## Statistics

Smaller libraries may be content with one figure of total "books added," which can be taken from the inclusive monthly accession numbers, if any are used. Larger libraries can save time and not delay books if they record their book statistics just before the books leave the technical services department, when all processes are finished and books and cards are together. This need not include more than the number of adult fiction, adult nonfiction, and juvenile books, and in cities of over 40,000 or 50,000 the number of new books, titles, and cards. Withdrawals have to be recorded also, but is it necessary to record the number of gift volumes added each year? The question as to whether more or as many statistics as those just noted are worthwhile should be discussed by those concerned and the decision incorporated in the instruction book. A simple monthly statistics sheet may be copied, with a cross line per day; thirteen sheets give the year's record and totals. As the on-line environment develops, careful thought needs to be given to statistics relating to production and library holdings, as they are as simple to gather and circulate as a program change.

A copy of the order slip that accompanied the books from their receipt by the order section may now be used to secure removal of another copy of the order slip from the order file, where it had been serving as an in-process record *if* such record seemed essential. In libraries of up to 100,000 population it seldom is, for books should go through so promptly that it will not be needed. Once ready for use, new books should be delivered immediately to the public service agencies, daily in the case of central library departments and as often as possible (and no less than weekly) in the case of the branches.

## A Few Tests for Evaluating Technical Processes

It is desirable to summarize here three objective tests of the department's performance: (1) the elapsed time needed to order, catalog, and prepare a book for use and place it on reader shelves; (2) the workload standards, (the number of department staff members needed to do the work); and (3) the cost in salary time. Wide variations in individual libraries will affect the validity of these tests—for example, the volume of books added, staff ability, the number of catalogs maintained, and the degree of bibliographical completeness desired. But the following tests are offered as fair for the average American public library of medium size. Increased skill and use of processing centers will improve these standards. But quality of the work is a separate consideration, hard to measure.

"Publication date" of American trade books, formerly two or three weeks after the new books are actually delivered to dealers, seems increasingly only a reference point and not a firm commitment. So it is not easy to specify a desirable total elapsed time for the technical processes. Assuming some advance notice of a new book and that copies will arrive from the jobber before publication date, it should generally take no more than an average of five weeks from the initial selection of the title to its availability to readers. Where the jobber is within overnight mail distance, this might be cut to four weeks. By tightening up on any possible delay, it may be cut to three weeks for many titles. In the book selection system for a city of 150,000, it may take about two weeks to gather orders for the title from all branches, combine them on one multiple-copy order slip, and forward the order to the jobber. The library without branches should be able to get off its orders inside the week. Assuming that copies of the book are on the shelves of the jobber, as is usual for 90 percent of the titles, delivery should be made to the library within two weeks. The process of checking in the books, cataloging them, preparing them for use, and delivering the books to the public service agency should take on the average no more than another two weeks. There will be numerous causes of delay: the jobber may have to be prodded, but paperwork in excess of that recommended here is a major cause of delay.

Cost figures are even more difficult to measure. There are several layers of costs of varying degrees relating to processing. Costs are affected by the degree to which, if at all, for example, the library performs original cataloging, and the extent to which its processing is carried out by exterior agencies. In general, it is best to use figures for direct costs only (salaries and materials) and not to try to allocate indirect and overhead expenses. Secondly, total *elapsed* time does not vary much for a single copy of a new title, or for a new title with multiple copies going through at the same time, but cost figures are greatly affected by these factors. It is therefore always desirable, in reporting cataloging cost figures, to specify the ratio of volumes to titles. It is more accurate to conduct a time study of several batches of books (and at least two hundred volumes in all) and to convert the time figures into dollars according to the salaries actually paid to the people who did the work.

Elapsed time and average unit cost figures are valuable indexes but are necessarily based on samples and influenced by other considerations. More meaningful and more immediately useful would be workload standards that specify the number of staff members needed for a given total number of books added.

### Inventory

For some years, it was common practice to inventory the entire book collection every two or three years by comparing the shelf list with the books on the shelves and with the "out" book cards in circulation trays. Books found missing in two inventories were considered lost and the catalog cards removed. Today, few public libraries take regular, complete inventories, because experience has shown that loss rates are low—less than 1 percent of the book stock per year—and the cost of a complete inventory of a large or medium-sized library is high. With some of the modern circulation methods, it is possible to check books that are on loan. Present on-line circulation systems also allow inventory control and tracking not possible a few years ago. Normally, individual titles sought and not found over several months may be considered lost. Either they should be replaced or the catalog cards should be withdrawn. Books in greatest demand disappear soonest. The routine of reserving books affords the promptest way to discover that a book is missing, and it should be replaced promptly.

Inventory taking is a joint enterprise and the responsibility of the cataloging and circulation departments of the technical services division.

### Circulation Control

As has been previously noted in this book, the American public library began as a shared collection of books to be borrowed for home reading and returned for others in the community to use. Hence, the term *circulation*—books going out and coming back—was viewed as the library's primary function. This notion has carried on, so much so that in many quarters still the popular image of the "librarian" is the person who "stamps out" the books being borrowed, accepts the books returned, sends out overdue notices, and does the other work associated with the "circulation" function.

The fact is that circulation control, including the registration of borrowers, is basically a current inventory activity, requiring only clerical and technical skills and training. The circulation control process is not, and should not be considered as, appropriate to the duties of a librarian, whose job is to select, organize, and interpret the library's collection. The control of the collection—lending the books and other materials, maintaining records of loans, keeping the stock in order—is of course of critical importance in support of the librarian's work, and the public service and cataloging and classification librarians must be generally and closely aware of the circulation control procedures and activities. Doubtless, a librarian will be in charge of the technical services department, in libraries large enough to require or permit that kind of specialization. It is true that the circulation activity is physically located in the public service rooms of the library, and that therefore the technical services head will supervise it from a distance; a circulation section head (a management employee) will be directly in charge of circulation and responsible to the technical services head.

It is also true that in smaller libraries and branches there will be occasions when it will be desirable or necessary for a librarian to work at the loan desk. It is not intended to recommend such a finely tuned division of labor that a professional employee cannot be allowed to perform some clerical or technical work as the situation dictates. The public service must be carried out with dispatch and efficiency at all times. The main point is to ensure that skills and training of staff are employed at a reasonable degree of efficiency, with appropriate attention to return on salary paid.

In addition to the fact that the circulation control function is clerical and technical in nature, there are two other reasons for including it with technical services organizationally. One is the obvious one that the *data base*—the bibliographical information about the items being circulated—is originated during the cataloging process. The data will include author, title, call number, copy number, and accession number, if used, or whatever distinguishing symbol is used to set that item apart from all others, both on the shelf and in storage. The second reason is that, because the circulation control activity does in fact use some (though not all) of the bibliographic data base that has been originated in cataloging and classifying, it becomes possible, as the entire materials-handling process is automated via computer, to have an integrated approach to that process. The unfortunate condition is that library automation has developed based on things as they are presently organized, rather than as they might be with a total look from a scientific management point of view.

The result has been that one set of suppliers has tackled the cataloging problem and another the circulation control problem and still another the acquisitions problem. Progress is being made toward achieving the desired compatibility so that an integrated, single approach can be realized. Doubtless, it will be some time before the benefits of these advances can be realized generally, but as more independent libraries are persuaded, or find it possible, to take part in systems or other cooperative organizations, it will be possible to handle most if not all of the problems of stock and borrower recordkeeping in a more businesslike and efficient manner, so that the librarian staff can devote full time to selecting, organizing, and interpreting the library's contents to the citizens of the community.

*Planning for Circulation Control*

It would be worthwhile to review briefly the main elements of the circulation control function: what it is intended to accomplish, with what results, and by what means. Rohlf and Pennington, in an article discussing plans for automated circulation control, have drawn up a list of functional criteria to be considered. The list could be used by any library in reviewing the circulation process. Boss, in another report, has described an "idealized circulation system" that also treats this subject. Portions of these two reports are reproduced here as handy checklists for the heads of the technical services department and the circulation section to use in reviewing the circulation process in the local library, whether considering an automated system or simply looking toward making the present system as efficient as possible.

The first step in a systematic approach to the automation of circulation activities is the setting of functional criteria for the automated system. This requires a thorough investigation of the statistics related to circulation activities and specification of the requirements and capabilities of the system desired. It is at this point in the functional analysis that a list should emerge of those activities that are absolute requirements of the automated system and of those capabilities that are desired but not absolutely essential during the initial installation of the system. The following, used by Hennepin County Library in discussing its plans with other libraries, is a menu of functions of an automated circulation system, designed as a main course and á la carte items. The main course consists of activities considered absolutely necessary, while the á la carte items are capabilities that may be desirable but, depending on individual requirements, are not necessary during the initial phase of the system.

### Menu of Functions of an Automated Circulation System

MAIN COURSE

1. Charging of materials rapidly
2. Discharging of materials rapidly
3. Renewals
4. Identification of delinquent patrons
5. Fines, amounts due calculations, receipts
6. Damaged or lost materials handling
7. Registration of patrons—efficiently and rapidly
8. Reserve holds—add, delete, & trapping of materials (system-wide and local)
9. Location and status of each item
   a. on shelf of which agency
   b. at bindery
   c. missing
   d. in circulation
   e. in transit
   f. in preparation
10. Overdue notices
11. Invoices for non-returned materials
12. Data entry and updating
13. New materials processing
14. Processing of withdrawals
15. Operations statistics and summarization
16. Error messages and system prompts

À LA CARTE

1. Variant patron identification (from outside service area)
2. Variant materials identification (ill)
3. Acquisition support (lists of materials which are heavily borrowed or have more than x number reserves per copy owned)
4. Withdrawal support (lists of circulating copies which are not borrowed)
5. Circulation statistics reports
   a. circulation by agency
   b. by hour of day (for staff scheduling?)
   c. by broad subject area (based on call numbers)
   d. by book
   e. by patron
6. Patron statistics reports
   a. by area (based on zip code)
   b. percent of registered borrowers usage
7. Status inquiries by staff
   a. where item is
   b. who has item
   c. when item is due to be returned
   d. number of reserves against item
8. Recall notices
9. Overdue statistics
   a. usual date of return so notices can be sent at the optimum time
10. Listing of materials held by a given borrower (for overdues staff)
11. Loan period modification based on type of material or borrower
12. Diverse types of charging (pamphlets, framed prints, rent-a-best-seller)
13. Handling ambiguities in system
    a. item not at location where being checked out
    b. item already charged out (at charging out)
    c. item not charged out (at discharge)
14. Extensive back-up system with data file protection against system failure.
15. Waiving of fines or other charges (to what amount and by whom)
16. Printed notices to patrons of reserves which are awaiting pick up
17. Statistics on agency holdings (for distribution of materials)
18. Printing out patron cards
19. Registration statistics
20. Recording number of times each item has circulated
21. Keeping track of all interlibrary loan requests
22. Reporting when library has borrowed a title on ill repetitively
23. Recording items on order, in cataloging, received, en route to an agency
24. Performing an inventory
25. Responding to ill requests from other library systems
26. Printing date-due slips
27. Printing routing slips for materials to be sent to other agencies/library systems
28. Keeping a log of materials unable to supply.[20]

## An Idealized Circulation System

A library should not choose a new circulation system by merely eliminating the deficiencies of its existing system but should begin with the ideal system and work back to the level of its budget. An ideal system should be able to do the following:

1. Permit the library staff to quickly determine that a patron is eligible for service, what his or her privileges are, and at what address he or she can be reached.
2. Permit the library's patrons and staff to quickly determine what titles are in the library's collection and where they are located.
3. Enable the staff to quickly and efficiently charge and discharge library materials, and to keep accurate and current records of these transactions.
4. Permit the library patrons or staff to quickly determine what is currently in circulation and when it is or was due back.
5. Produce overdue and recall notices, and permit the library staff to quickly determine what notices have been sent to patrons with materials charged out and what action is next to be taken.
6. Place holds on items, and permit library staff to quickly determine what titles are being held for patrons, for whom they are being held and after what date the materials are no longer wanted.
7. Provide management information on the utilization of the collection to aid in staff scheduling, collection weeding and storage, and acquisitions.
8. Accommodate dramatic increases in collection size, number of users, number of transactions, or number of locations without major system redesign.[21]

In the quoted report, Boss goes on to list a number of desirable features that can be used to compare available systems. He notes that not all libraries will require all these features; they have been compiled from more than a dozen specifications that were developed by academic and public libraries during the past three years. Features are grouped under the following headings: circulation, reserve, management information, training program, and flexibility of system.[22]

Markuson, in her report on automated circulation systems, discusses a broad view of circulation control that suggests additional functions for circulation systems. She states that these activities might include,

assistance to users of a quasi-catalog-reference nature, and the recording, analysis, and dissemination of statistical data relevant to the weeding and development of the book collection. In this view, the objective of circulation is not only to regulate the loan of material in such a way that the borrower can be held responsible for returning the material to the library, but also to provide services that make these materials available under as favorable conditions as possible. . . .

The proponents of the broad view of circulation control believe that circulation should be concerned with maximizing the investment that the library has expended in acquiring and organizing its collections, and that therefore circulation should provide every assistance feasible to both the library and the user.[23]

Steady progress has been made in circulation systems technology, thus simplifying circulation routines. This has resulted in improved service to the public. Generally, libraries that have introduced automated circulation services have not reduced personnel costs, however, since they have retained existing personnel to perform additional functions.[24] It is worth noting also that the broad view of circulation described by Markuson should not cause libraries to retreat from the position that the activities can and should be performed by nonprofessional clerical and technical personnel.

*Borrower Registration*

The history of the registration of public library borrowers is an example of the steady pressure to reduce the complexity and the importance of routines. Only a generation or so ago, an applicant for a library card was expected to give a good deal of personal information and one or two references who were in either the current telephone or city directories, and to reregister every three years or so. These requirements were steadily whittled down, in part because they did not succeed in eliminating all losses of unreturned books and in part because newer systems of charging books made formal registration unnecessary. Modern charging systems usually result in a record that contains the name and address of the borrower of each book lent. The record is more likely to be of current value if based not on a library card issued three years ago but on a document in the possession of the patron that establishes identity and current place of residence.

Various simplifications of borrower registration have been devised,[25] and some libraries have eliminated registration. Only an alphabetical record is kept of those who owe the library books or fines above a certain amount; with copies of this list at every service point, unreturned books have not increased significantly as a percentage of total circulation and economies have been realized in supplies and in elimination of paperwork. In addition, there has been a favorable public reaction. The value of borrower registration in analyzing public library use is minimal, because an unknown number borrow books on other people's cards or read those borrowed by other people, and many of those registered make little or no use of the library. With automated charging on the increase, borrower registration is evidently on the way out except in small libraries. As a matter of principle, readers should be finding it easier to qualify for borrowing books once circulation routines are modernized.

Some public libraries give service to nonresidents at little or no charge. Generally, though, the trend has been to charge the nonresident at least as much as the local per capita tax support and perhaps twice that much, since borrowing books is probably for the whole family. Many states have counteracted this trend, however, by funding reciprocal borrowing agreements where nonresidents may use services without a fee across local jurisdictional lines.

## Circulation Control Systems

In the last thirty-five years or so, new systems have been developed to replace the traditional hand charging and discharging methods. These are well described in the literature.[26] An improved manual system pioneered by Shaw at Gary about 1940 and still used in larger libraries is the serially numbered transaction card (T-card) method. Since its inception, this method has been applied to a variety of photographic devices, audio recording machines, handwritten charges, edge-punched and machine-punched cards, and numbered slips for one-time use. The great advantage of the T-card system is that it eliminates the slipping or discharging process, probably the greatest shortcoming and most time-consuming part of the traditional hand charging systems. The T-card system is flexible, allowing for many different possible combinations, such as once-a-week due dates, one loan period or more, and formal borrowers' cards or none; it is relatively easy and economical to convert to and from; it is applicable to both small and large libraries; and it may be mechanized or used as a hand system.

Growing out of the T-card system is the punched-card system. When books are returned, their punched cards are removed and sent to a central computer center. Periodically, the computer center forwards to the circulation control department a list of numbers representing missing cards. These constitute overdues.

## Automation of Circulation Control

A major problem about making the decision to automate is that the body of experience is relatively limited. Although the basic assumption is that the library seeks to replace manual operations by machine, there appears to be little clear evidence of a substantial reduction in costs. Several good reasons for this should be noted. For one, the automated systems now in use are new and also are being frequently revised and made more efficient, so that it is next to impossible, it appears, to set a time period against which to amortize the initial capital outlay. Whereas a typewriter will wear out in a predictable period, a computer and its software, of which critical components are replaced and reprogrammed as new developments take place, may last for many years. Other reasons are related to increased effectiveness. For example, the automated system, if properly programmed and intelligently applied, will allow substantial savings in stock control and use and the elimination of continued withdrawals by delinquent borrowers. Moreover, a more "rational" book selection process (in which materials expenditures can be closely related to real needs) may result from the detailed data generated on materials demand and use. The materials collection could thus be more tightly controlled and money put to better use. This more "rational" process can then replace the present "educated guesses" concerning both anticipated needs and actual uses of book stock. Futhermore, automation may result in the collection turning over more quickly and being located more readily, saving both staff and user time. If the circulation system is linked with a number of libraries, interlibrary loan or referral can be expedited as well. The automated system can inform the patron at the desk whether a wanted book is owned by a neighboring library and whether it is currently on the shelf. It can also take a "hold" order. The patron can then decide whether to go to that library and get the book or to ask that it be sent to the library where he or she is, or some other library, if there is a delivery procedure in place.

This brief summary of some of the benefits may point out the difficulties of attributing cost-performance-savings factors in this area. How much is it worth to have a more efficiently utilized materials collection—a higher proportion of costly stock actually in use? Obviously, there is a money value here, but it would also be costly to find out what it is.

### Selecting the Automated System

Conferences with librarians and visits to libraries with successful installations are first-priority methods for the library director and staff to use to find out both whether to automate and, if so, what system to select. The technology is changing rapidly, and there is very little that can be said now that would be useful in the future about specific systems. The prudent library director and staff will explore all avenues, gather as many facts as possible, talk with vendors, and above all, review critically and in detail what it is that the library seeks to accomplish.

Boss suggests that there are several elements in the process of selecting an automated circulation system. He mentions that the most up-to-date, useful sources are handbooks and manuals supplied by vendors to clients, which may usually be borrowed. "Another excellent source for information is a vendor's response to a bid specification by a library much like one's own. Contact the library to borrow or examine such a document on-site when visiting another library."

Boss recommends that the library develop its own specifications instead of having them written by a consultant or copying those of another library. He points out that this is a good way to ensure that the library gets what is wanted and is also a way of "getting the interest and commitment of those who will have to manage the system after it is installed."[27]

Whatever system is selected, the library will have to convert present bibliographic and borrower records to machine-readable format. If the conversion can be linked with existing machine-readable cataloging records, so much the better. If the library is considering a machine-based, automated catalog, it would be eminently worthwhile to consider the idea of automating the catalog prior to the development of the circulation system, as such activities as circulation and acquisitions may more efficiently become subsystems of an overall integrated approach.

Various methods of conversion of records are available, and these may be discussed with potential vendors and with the automation consultant if one is retained. The cost of conversion for discreet circulation purposes may equal or exceed the cost of the initial system, so that this is a major decision to be made. Obviously, once done, it does not have to be repeated. Further, it is not always necessary to convert all the library's holdings at the outset. Some libraries follow the method of converting those items that are returned from circulation over a period of four to six months. Others both input returns and convert items as they are charged out. In due course, as the opportunity is presented, the backlog of unconverted materials can be entered, or the library may continue indefinitely to enter only the items brought to the desk to be charged out. The library will wish to consult with staffs of libraries that have converted their records to get an idea about the best method to use. The same process will apply to the borrower files.

Preparation and installation, once the decisions have been made for the purchase of the equipment, will be another major step. Boss discusses this in a very helpful section, including the site preparation, preliminary staff training, and file conversion. The various methods of file conversion are summarized.[28] Conversion of manual catalogs is also treated in Butler et al., and this will have some pertinence to the process of converting the circulation control system, particularly if the decision is made to embark on an overall integrated approach of catalog, circulation acquisitions, and so forth.[29]

### Rules for the Loan of Books

Under this heading fall a number of specific points that need to be decided, explained to patrons and staff alike, and reviewed from time to time. The recent trend has been to set no limit on the number of books a patron may borrow, or any ratio of fiction and nonfiction. The usual length of loan period in public libraries is two weeks, subject to renewal, with new and popular books lent for only one week and nonrenewable. The others, mostly large libraries, lend books for up to four weeks and do not renew them, partly as a convenience to borrowers, partly in the hope of reducing the number of overdues, and partly to simplify the operation of the charging system. One efficient method is a variable loan period of three to four weeks, making all material due on Friday, which is, traditionally, a light day and thus gives the staff time to discharge items and get them back on the shelf. It seems logical that the longer the loan period, the more the turnover of books is reduced. Book budgets have steadily decreased in proportion to total library budgets, and nearly every library feels the need for more books. There are few libraries that do not have too many "reserves" backed up—one of the best measures of book demand. If the objective of all charging systems is, as it should be, to bring books to the most people at the least cost, it appears more than inconsistent to lend more books to a reader and let him or her keep them longer than need be, when other people are waiting to use them. Researchers are showing interest in variable loan policies. M. K. Buckland reports on a study of such a loan policy at the University of Lancaster. There the loan period is determined by demand for the book.[30] The length of loan should not be solely dictated by some mechanical device in order to save clerical time and money, while losing book money from unnecessarily slower turnover. The four-week reader may be pleased but may be depriving another reader.

*Circulation Rules Manual*

The circulation control department will make frequent studies of the rules and initiate recommendations for their improvement, subject to review by other staff members and the library director. Major rules should be formally adopted by the trustees after they have heard the pros and cons of points on which there may be reader objections. There should also be some recognition of the director's authority to make exceptions. The rules should then be printed for distribution to patrons, especially when they register for a library card, and to all library employees. Staff members who serve the public should have systematic and periodic instruction and review of these rules, together with an explanation of why the rules are the way they are and amplified directions on how to apply them to various types of cases. Even if a general staff manual is not feasible, the circulation rules and their interpretation should be available in typed or mimeographed form for staff members to consult. Any such set of rules will probably need modification every three or four years; they should be reviewed by a staff committee and some of them tested by collecting appropriate new data to see if they are still functioning as expected. Another principle of modern circulation control is that rules for the loan of materials should be made to justify themselves in imposing no more controls than are clearly necessary to secure the desired results.

*Overdues and Thefts* [31]

The matter of overdues illustrates the value of rethinking a technical problem in the light of accumulated experience and modern conditions. It appears that the number of overdue materials can be reduced but not eliminated. Some libraries have tried charging no overdue fine, and some have levied a heavier than usual fine; either way a few items are always kept overdue (about four to five for every hundred borrowed) and some are never recovered (about two to three out of every ten thousand lent). This low figure deserves publicizing as evidence that public libraries are not wrapped in red tape but are effective guardians of public property, to see that each item is kept in uninterrupted use. Overdue notices are a service to patrons, not a right to which they are entitled; and one or two notices per overdue book or other material are as effective and less expensive than more would be.

In manual circulation systems, overdue notices can be sent as a form postcard that does not specify author or title. They can be mailed third class at a bulk rate and request return information. Prompt followup should be made within a week or two. Final penalties, such as refusing the patron any further loans or even taking extreme cases to court, can deter others and publicize the library's concern for the interests of other users. Commercial concerns, doing the volume of business that public libraries do, expect a certain rate of loss from items stolen, purchased on credit and never paid for, or bought on the installment plan and repossessed but not for full value. Such losses are part of the cost of doing business, and they are probably less in libraries than in retail business.

Most modern circulation control systems will automatically print overdue notices and recall notices. Renewals are not so easily handled, at least by telephone; and when the book is presented for renewal by the borrower in person, it amounts in effect to a new charge or loan. However, the new computer-based systems excel with the reserve process. Automated systems maintain "flags" on files and a list of those patrons waiting for a particular book. When the book is returned, it is automatically checked for a reserve.

"Unauthorized loans"—that is, thefts—have become a matter of increasing concern to librarians in recent years. Many have successfully met the problem with the installation of theft detection systems. The purpose of theft detection systems is to identify books or others materials that have not been properly checked out as they are being removed from the library. All systems insert into library materials some specially treated device or element. When the library materials are not properly charged out, and the patron attempts to pass through a detection point with the materials, these treated elements trigger an alarm in the form of a buzzer or chime, a locked exit or turnstile, or a flashing light or lighted sign.

Theft detection systems operate in two ways—by the full-circulating method and by the bypass method. With the full-circulating method, the treated elements in library materials are desensitized during the charging process. This is carried out in one of two ways. The elements are deactivated or they are "shielded" by cards, tags, or slips. The patron then passes through the detection point with the library materials. With the bypass method, the patron gives the library materials to a staff member stationed near the detection point. The patron next passes through the detection point. The library assistant then checks to see if the library materials are correctly charged out and returns the materials on the other side of the detection point. In this method the treated elements are never deactivated because the library materials bypass the detection point.

There are advantages and disadvantages to each method. The bypass method is generally less costly than the full-circulating method. It also requires fewer steps in the charging process. However, it takes up more staff time, since a patron must pass the library materials to a library attendant each time he or she leaves the library even though these materials have been previously charged out. The full-circulating method offers the convenience of having to check books out only once. However, it usually adds an additional step to the charging process: the desensitizing operation. Most systems can be converted to either the bypass or full-circulating modes.

Expense is an important consideration for most libraries. Tables 4 and 5 provide basic cost data for the major systems. These figures represent the cost of detection equipment—and activating/deactivating equipment where needed—for a one-exit installation. The cost of entrance and exit gates, or turnstiles, is not included. Exhaustive analysis of various installations are contained in LTP reports cited with Table 4.

### Circulation Statistics and Records

For many years, it was the practice to have circulation reports show daily, monthly, and annual circulation by the ten main divisions of the Dewey decimal classification system. Now, libraries with automated charging systems are able to make complex cross analyses of data on books borrowed. These new systems also handle file maintenance and the statistical figures described in this section.

The most elementary figures, and the most valuable, are of total circulation. There is still a diversity of practice with regard to counting renewals, nonbook items, loans of books for classroom use, and so forth. Add to this the use of estimates by some libraries, and the result is a serious limitation to the comparison of circulation in one library with that of another. A group of libraries, especially if selected as representative, constitutes a more reliable basis of comparison.[32] Comparing one library's circulation in a given year with that of earlier years is valid, if no major changes in procedure of counting were made. Adult fiction, adult nonfiction, juvenile, and total loans are the only circulation data that every library should have to report regularly, for the library as a whole and for each agency separately. Transaction-card charging systems do not usually allow for the automatic cumulation of these subtotals (as they do for the grand total), but analysis of the circulation for one day a month under any system (with annual cumulation and derivation of total percentages of these categories) gives results very close to what complete counting of the year's circulation would give, and at much lower cost.

Spot checks or analysis of circulation for a day or a week will in most

**Table 4.** Cost Data for Each System

| Name | Detection Equipment | Activate/ Deactivate Equipment | Rental Price (per month) | Lease Price (per month) | Service Contract (per year) | Installation |
|---|---|---|---|---|---|---|
| Checkpoint Mark II and Mark III | $4,400 | None required | $123.75 (for 36 months) | $202.50 (for 36 months) | $378* | $75–150† |
| Gaylord/Magnavox | 5,710 | $ 515 | 253‡§ 239 | 253‡§ 239 | 333* | 750 |
| Knogo Mark II | | | | | | |
| Single corridor | 5,500 | | 190 | ** | 250 | 350 |
| Double corridor | 7,500 | | 280 | ** | 350 | 600 |
| Standard, with verifier | | 1,400 | 55 | ** | 50 | |
| Standard, without verifier | | 900 | 45 | ** | | |
| Universal with verifier | | 1,500 | 55 | ** | 50 | |
| Universal without verifier | | 1,000 | 45 | ** | | |
| 3M Tattle-Tape, Model 1850— single corridor | 4,800 | | ** | ** | 390 | 250–500 |
| 3M Tattle-Tape, Model 1850— double corridor | 6,100 | | ** | ** | 510 | 250–500 |
| 3M Tattle-Tape, Model 1250 | 3,100 | | ** | ** | 250 | 250–500 |
| 3M Tattle-Tape, Model 940 | | 525 | ** | ** | | |
| 3M Tattle-Tape, Model 950 | | 1,200 | ** | ** | | |
| Sentronic/Book-Mark | 4,750 | | 200 | 185 (for 5 years) | 400– 900 | 250–750 |
| Deactivator mounted beneath counter | | 875 | | | | |
| Activator in book return chute | | 875 | | | | |
| Activator mounted on wheeled table | | 895 | | | | |

\* None for first year.
† Depending on complexity of installation; no charge if library maintenance people perform the work under Checkpoint supervision.
‡ Full-circulation system.
§ Bypass system.
** Varies depending on length (years) of agreement.
*Source: Adapted from* Library Technology Reports *15 (May–June 1979): 224–25.*

**Table 5.** Cost of Targets

| System | Cost (depending on quantity) |
|---|---|
| Checkpoint | |
| CHECKlabels, plain | 10.5 to 19¢ |
| CHECKlabels, printed | 11.5 to 21¢ |
| "Teeny Beepers," plain | 6 to 15¢ |
| "Teeny Beepers," printed | 7 to 17¢ |
| CHECKcards (shields), plain | $30 per 1,000 |
| CHECKcards (shields), printed | $35 per 1,000 |
| CHECKtabs (shields) | $ 8 per 1,000 |
| Gaylord/Magnavox | |
| Detector tags | 10 to 12¢ |
| Bypass strip | 6¢ |
| Full-circulation strip | 7¢ |
| Knogo | |
| Book Detection Strip | 7½ to 10¢ |
| Record and Cassette Strip | 20 to 30¢ |
| 3M Tattle-Tape | |
| Tattle-Tape Book Detection Strips | 14¢ maximum |
| Tattle-Tape Cassette Markers | 30¢ maximum |
| Sentronic | |
| S75 Targets for books | 10¢ |
| S74 Target Strips | 10¢ |
| ST73 label for tape cassettes | 25¢ |
| ST72 label for 33⅓ rpm records | 25¢ |
| ST71 label for 45 rpm records | 25¢ |
| ST70 label for magnetic tape decks | 25¢ |

*Source: From* Library Technology Reports *15 (May–June 1979): 224–25.*

cases be enough for any specific purpose—for example, to ascertain how many books are borrowed by patrons from an area served by contract. A principle of modern public library circulation routine is that the records and statistics kept regularly should be few, simple, and obviously justified by their meaning and use.

### Shelf Work

The most time-consuming circulation routine, and the one least affected so far by machines or modern thinking, is the work of replacing on the shelves the many books returned by borrowers or used in the library. Human error is inevitable in performing this task, and since readers often put books in the wrong place on open shelves, the books frequently must be individually examined to ensure accurate arrangement; this is called "reading the shelves." A third type of task is to find and bring from the stacks or open shelves the books and periodicals desired by patrons or by the professional librarians.

Because so much of this work involves lifting or carrying and being on one's feet, it is usually done by high school or college students working part-time or by other young people, typically called "pages." Usually they also serve at the loan desk, charging out books, discharging them, registering borrowers, handling reserves, and so on.

Because of the youth of most pages and resulting high turnover, it is important that their supervisor be particularly good in teaching how to do the jobs and able to maintain good relations with assistants while enforcing standards of service and of businesslike conduct.

In most libraries, more part-time employees will work in the circulation control department than any other, and all such employees in the central library might well be supervised by the circulation head or by a designated supervisor. This would allow shifting of pages when needed and would enable them to perform a wider variety of tasks. It would also be conducive to better training of these young people, and to the use of performance standards. Not a few professional librarians began by working as pages in public and college libraries; and superior supervision of shelf assistants is likely to have desirable indirect results in recruitment for the profession as well as in improving work production directly. This is in keeping with the principle of public library circulation routines, that the large volume of necessary work that cannot be mechanized or further simplified should be handled as efficiently, as economically and with as much imaginative supervision as possible. A library where books used by readers are not returned to the shelves in twenty-four hours is a poorly run library.

*Quarters*

Usually the circulation department occupies a sizable area on the main floor next to the main entrance, symbolic of its central importance. More people enter the library to borrow and return books than for any other purpose. Assistants who work at the loan desk need adequate lighting and nearby shelves for the sorting of returned books, for reserved books waiting to be picked up, for books needing repair, and for snags, which can be expected under any system. The old U-shaped loan desk is increasingly rare, especially in the case of libraries adopting automated systems of charging. Few will regret the change to the more compact sectional desk of today, usually placed at the side of the entrance to avoid creating a psychological barrier. Current study is needed in most libraries to improve the existing physical arrangement and equipment as well as work methods of circulation departments. Professional staff members no longer have the personal acquaintance with users and their reading that they had when they worked behind the loan desk; accordingly, loan desk clerical assistants should be chosen in part because they have some knowledge of books and concern for the users' needs.

### Conservation of Materials

With the rapidly increasing cost of purchasing and replacing library materials, and of the labor cost of preparing them for use, it is abundantly clear that conservation has become a significant concern for libraries. Many items in the library's collections are actually irreplaceable: publishers' printings tend to be more limited than they were formerly, and hence titles may go out of stock within a year or two after publication, thus becoming virtually irreplaceable.

The systematic and regular rebinding and repair of the library's general stock as volumes become shabby and loose-jointed through constant use will add to the attractiveness of the materials and make the books more attractive to the reader. Good rebinding makes a book last longer than it would in the original publisher's binding. But rebinding must be considered with caution, as noted below. Some books can be mended in the library's own technical services department, and this should be done when possible. A good mender with proper equipment can repair about 5,000 volumes a year. Rebinding can amount to about 2 percent of the library's current operating expenditures.

Conservation of library materials, while of concern for many years, has only recently been recognized as a serious enough problem to warrant study and research. The National Conservation Advisory Council (NCAC) was established in 1973 as a "national forum for cooperation and planning among institutions and programs concerned with the conservation of cultural property in the United States." A report by the Council's Study Committee on conservation needs in libraries was issued in 1978. Among the points made by the report: The first introductory course in conservation for librarians was offered in 1971. Studies by Barrow indicated that 90 percent of the books published in the first half of the present century would be unusable by the next century. The preservation of books, their bindings, and the other materials of the collection—microforms, photographs, maps, prints, and drawings—all involve climate control, storage methods, use policies, and preventive treatments for restoration.

The report takes note of the fact that "there is some question whether the two most popular techniques (for conservation) can really be said to serve the ends of conservation." Reference is made to the "Class A" library binding.

While [this process] has provided sturdy coverings for millions of books, it does not meet the conservation criteria of reversibility and non-destructiveness, and old and rare books butchered by this process are not uncommon. Libraries are beginning to call for improvement, and the library binding industry is showing interest in providing different types of bindings. . . .

The other major area of library conservation activity is in a sense administrative and bibliographic rather than technical: replacement of deteriorated materials with microforms or reprints. This type of activity tends to be concentrated in older and larger institutions. . . .

In archival institutions, the most common restoration process is "archival lamination"; that is, the lamination of previously deacidified documents with cellulose acetate and reinforcing tissue. Many of the larger archives have laminating machines, and it is probable that some smaller organizations utilize the facilities of the larger ones. . . .

One of the problems of the field is that cellulose acetate lamination is often assumed to be the only preservation choice available. This assumption creates, as also in the case of "Class A" library binding, a procrustean bed in which diverse problems are forced to conform to one preconceived solution, whether that solution is appropriate or not.

The report recommends regional or cooperative centers as one solution to the conservation problem.

The overwhelming obstacle to the desperately needed conservation treatment in libraries and archives is cost, particularly at this time when costs are escalating as financial resources may be shrinking. Regional or cooperative conservation centers, modeled on a well-established museum conservation center and a variety of cooperative efforts among libraries, have been discussed with increasing frequency as an efficient method for delivering conservation services.

There is much to commend regional or cooperative centers. They could reduce costs below those of profit-making work of comparable caliber; they could provide consistency and perhaps improve the level of standards; they could be particularly helpful to smaller institutions unable to afford their own facilities; they could offer services that may not appeal to qualified private practitioners; they could gather and disseminate information on conservation; and they could participate in some types of training. Moreover, the concept of regional centers appears to be consistent with the idea of regional and national cooperation among libraries as proposed by the National Commission on Libraries and Information Science and by the Library of Congress. . . .

Such centers would provide storage, consultant services, workshops, and protective enclosures for documents and would provide actual treatment of materials needing sophisticated handling.

The report has some cautions. Photocopy is not equivalent to preservations of the original; it does not permit the user to determine the authenticity of the material copied.

Insufficient information and deficient technology have combined to limit the usefulness of reproduction for conservation purposes. . . .

1. Librarians and archivists need to know the approximate range of total cost involved in a given kind of physical conservation treatment to permit comparison with the total filming cost, including film storage, for the same broad classes of material in quantity. . . .

2. Librarians and archivists need to understand more clearly what kinds of

materials, by reason of extreme deterioration, are likely to be beyond practical physical restoration. . . .

3. Improved filming equipment and techniques should be developed with conservation needs specifically in mind in order to reduce the filming time and to minimize damage to materials as they undergo the filming process. The Prismascope is one recent example of a specially developed camera accessory that can be employed to film tightly bound books without loss of text and without damage to the book. Further improvements in technology are badly needed to increase the usefulness of reproduction.[33]

*How to Choose a Binder*

Many of the commercial binderies of the country belong to the Library Binding Institute, which worked with ALA committees to prepare the current specifications for Class A library binding. The institute certifies binderies that can qualify, provides libraries with a free service of testing rebound books, issues various publications, and otherwise promotes good binding. Any LBI member bindery is likely to be reliable and satisfactory, but so also may be some binderies that are not members of the institute. The three main considerations in choice of a binder are (1) quality of work, regularly checked by a librarian who can recognize the difference between good and poor binding and by having LBI inspect and report critically on sample volumes; (2) services, which are quickly measured by experience; and (3) the price schedule, which should be reevaluated every other year or so by comparison with prices and work from other binderies. It is desirable to stay with one good binder as long as possible, if prices are close to the lowest bid. It takes months for library and bindery staffs to understand each other's problems. Reestablishing relationships and changing paperwork every year is a hardship and will cancel some differences in prices.

A public library should be able to choose its own binder, and it should do so on the basis of the written ALA-LBI specifications.[34] If the choice must be made by sealed bid, the award of the contract should not be based on price alone; service and quality of actual work are important too. Specifications should stipulate the use of Class A library binding and especially the use of oversewing by machine, which produces a chain of stitches, all in an even line and close to the back edges of the book. The individual sheaves of pages when so sewn to each other are flexible and easy to open, but every page is held securely in place. It is also essential that ease of opening be assured by only scraping and sanding off the old glue on the backs instead of trimming them by a cutter; even a tiny fraction of an inch taken off the inner margin makes the book harder to hold open for reading. If some modification is desired, such as the "economy binding" for periodicals, it should be described in reasonable detail. Some firms offer low prices but are unable to meet ALA specifications and should not be allowed to compete. Ask for samples of the binder's work, to see how carefully it is done.

Services from a good binder include prompt work—that is, most books returned to the library in no more than a month—and pickup and delivery service. Prices of magazine binding and book rebinding are usually quoted by the height of the book and will double from below 8 inches to above 12. Not all binders are equally efficient, and prices vary considerably, not always directly with the quality of work and adequacy of services. A library spending about $5,000 a year can expect a discount of at least 30 to 40 percent below the published price scale, especially if the binder has a contract for all the library's work.

### Finance and Organization in Conservation

Another question concerns the allotment of the binding funds to library agencies.[35] In small libraries, the binding fund needs only to be apportioned among juvenile rebinding, adult rebinding, and periodical binding. Hardly any library, even a large one, has sufficient binding budget to allow each agency to send in every book in need of rebinding. Quotas must be assigned by departments and branches, perhaps also by main types of books. Quotas by number of books are preferable to quotas by dollars, involving less figuring and paperwork. Quotas should be reviewed annually, based on key factors such as book stock and circulation.

An important question is where and how decisions are to be made to rebind, repair, or discard a book. Many, perhaps most, books can be repaired within the library and need not be rebound; others need to be rebound or replaced. Such decisions should be made by the person designated to be in charge of binding and repair, who can then learn to know best what should be done in each case.

A final policy question concerns the place of conservation in the organization. Conservation is one of the technical processes and ought to be combined and located with order work and cataloging in a technical services department; in smaller libraries, the head cataloger can be responsible for supervision of binding and repair. This is rather natural, for it combines the physical preparation of new books for circulation and use with the rebinding and repair of those already in use. The person responsible for preparing books for binding and for doing major repairs should be able to maintain good quality with high production levels and be provided with adequate work stations, supplies, and such equipment as a bindery press and paper cutter. A chief problem is the flow of work, not only to and from the outside bindery, but within the department, so that books will not stand idle for days and weeks awaiting action.

Simple mending should be done at the individual agency. It costs too much in time and paperwork to send to one central place every book needing pencil marks erased or a torn page repaired. This simple type of repair to be done in the agencies should be defined and limited and the methods and materials prescribed, and those who do the work should come together for instruction. An unskilled library staff member can do as bad a job of rebacking or recasing as any home amateur, and the time and materials may cost too much in view of the poor results achieved.

### Binding and Rebinding

Binding and rebinding are not simple. There are alternatives to binding, principally microfilm and other microforms—especially for bound newspapers with their great bulk, their rapid decay of paper stock, and their susceptibility to mutilation. Other alternatives include paperbacks and Vinabind. Many magazines are also available now in microform, but most readers find that regular printed issues are quicker to use.

Forms and records for routing books and magazines to and from the bindery should be minimized. The objective is to maintain a steady flow in both directions and prevent backups before the material is sent out and after it comes back. Periodical issues to be bound should be collected and checked for completeness at the periodical check-in unit, which would be the first to know of the completion of a volume and the number of volumes to be bound together.

Upon return of books from the bindery, the instruction slip and the invoice should be checked against the volume. Some books in every shipment should be checked for quality of binding. Collation of individual books or magazine volumes page by page, before or after binding, by either the library or the bindery, is unnecessary if pages are checked by flipping through the volume. Volumes are marked, plated, and pocketed and date slips pasted in (one reason why binding flow is often combined with new-book preparation).

### Repair and Related Work

The number of books mended and repaired in a typical public library is at least four or five times the number rebound. There is a wide range of possible repairs and related work, from relatively simple jobs such as tipping in loose plates or photo prints of missing pages to rebacking a book or even recasing it when the sewing is still sound but the hinge has torn loose, making slip cases, reinforcing magazine covers, mounting pictures, and so forth. One objective is to regulate the flow of books coming for repair in order always to have enough on hand but not more than enough for two or three weeks. Water-soaked books should be stood on end in a warm room, with the covers spread so the pages can dry. As preservation is increasingly emphasized, the body of practical literature on the subject grows. The director of the library should react to the importance of practical considerations by appointing a committee of knowledgeable professionals to recommend short- and long-term plans that will help to protect the only reason that the library can and should exist—its collections.

Preservation will receive greater attention in the immediate future as the profession comes to realize that dealing with deteriorating collections ("the time bomb in the stacks") must become a high priority. Already there is a rightly persistent call that the problem is so costly and so universal that it must be attacked by a program on the national level, such as the National Periodicals Center.[36]

## Notes

1. *Library of Congress Cataloging Service Bulletin,* a continuation of LC's *Cataloging Service;* irregular, 1978 to date; official information on changes in policy and practice. *Hennepin County Library Cataloging Bulletin,* bimonthly, 1950 to date; provides alternate subject headings and decimal classification numbers useful for public libraries. *Library Resources and Technical Services,* quarterly, 1957 to date; discusses in-field work.
2. Bohdan S. Wynar, *Introduction to Cataloging and Classification,* 5th ed. (Littleton, Colo.: Libraries Unlimited, 1976). Although this offers thorough coverage of cataloging and classification, the new cataloging rules put it out of date. See also Esther J. Piercy, *Commonsense Cataloging: A Manual for the Organization of Books and Other Materials in School and Small Public Libraries,* 2d ed. (New York: H. W. Wilson, 1974). Describes in detail how to organize library materials.
3. Edmond L. Applebaum, ed., *Reader in Technical Services* (Washington, D.C.: NCR Microcard Editions, 1973). Traces historical development of technical services and offers practical information. See also, Rose Mary Magrill and Constance Rinehart, *Library Technical Services: A Selected, Annotated Bibliography* (Westport, Conn.: Greenwood Press, 1977), and Helen Welch Tuttle, "Coordination of the Technical Services," in Melvin J. Voigt, ed., *Advances in Librarianship,* (New York: Academic Press, 1975), 5:123–46.
4. Steven Ford, *The Acquisition of Library Materials* (Chicago: American Library Association, 1973). The standard work in the field. Elizabeth Futas, ed., *Library Acquisition Policies and Procedures* (Phoenix: Oryx Press, 1977). Comprises a comprehensive collection of the acquisition policy statements of representative public and academic libraries. *Collection Building: Studies in the Development and Effective Use of Library Resources.* (Syracuse, N.Y.: Gaylord Professional Publications, in association with Neal-Schuman Publishers, three times yearly, 1978 to date).
5. Maurice J. Freedman and S. Michael Malinconico, eds., *The Nature of the Catalog and the Nature of Technological Change* (New York: Neal-Schuman Publishers, in progress). An important work in progress. Contains essays by Seymour Lubetzky, Frederick Kilgour, and others. See also Albert James Diaz, ed., *Microforms and Library Catalogs: A Reader* (Westport, Conn.: Microform Review, 1977), and Paul S. Dunkin, *Cataloging U.S.A.* (Chicago: American Library Association, 1969). The Dunkin work is a classic in the field. It outlines general principles of cataloging and catalog use.
6. Susan K. Martin, *Library Networks, 1976–77* (White Plains, N.Y.: Knowledge Industry Publications, 1976), p. 14. See also Kenneth F. Duchac, "Evaluation of Processing Centers," *Library Trends* 16 (July 1967): 21.
7. See Lewis B. Mayhew, *Computerized Networks Among Libraries and Universities: An Administrator's Overview* (Stanford, Cal.: ERIC, ED115220, 1975).
8. American Library Association, *Guidelines for Handling Library Orders for In-Print Monographic Publications* (Chicago: American Library Association, 1973).

9. American Library Association, *Guidelines for Handling Library Orders for Microforms* (Chicago: American Library Association, 1977).

10. American Library Association, *Guidelines for Handling Library Orders for Serials and Periodicals* (Chicago: American Library Association, 1974).

11. Nada Beth Glick and Filomena Simora, eds., *The Bowker Annual of Library and Book Trade Information,* 23d ed. (New York: R. R. Bowker, 1978). The *Annual* prints surveys of yearly book prices.

12. See Ung Chon Kim, "Purchasing Books from Publishers and Wholesalers," *Library Resources and Technical Services* 19 (Spring 1975): 133–47. Evaluates efficiency of suppliers—observations based on a study conducted at Indiana State University in 1973. Also useful is Evelyn Hensel and Peter Veillette, *Purchasing Library Materials in Public and School Libraries: A Study of Purchasing Procedures and the Relationships Between Libraries and Purchasing Agents and Dealers* (Chicago: American Library Association, 1969). Also, Harold L. Roth, ed., "An Analysis and Survey of Commercial Library Supply Houses," *Library Trends* 24 (April 1976). The complete issue is devoted to the evaluation of dealers in various fields, including serial subscriptions and audiovisual materials.

13. Henriette D. Avram and Lenore S. Maruyama, *Toward a National Library and Information Service Network: The Library Bibliographic Component* (Washington, D.C.: Library of Congress, 1977). Reports on work of LC in the field.

14. James R. Hunt, "The Historical Development of Processing Centers in the United States," *Library Resources and Technical Services* 19 (Spring 1975): 133–47. A good introduction to the field.

15. Automation and processing are treated in these key articles: Maurice J. Freedman, "Automated Network Catalog Products and Services," *Journal of Library Automation* 9 (June 1976): 145–55; Maurice J. Freeman, "Processing for the People," *Library Journal* 101 (Jan. 1, 1976): 189–97; S. Michael Malinconico, "The Library Catalog in a Computerized Environment," *Wilson Library Bulletin* 51 (September 1976): 53–64; and S. Michael Malinconico and James A. Rizzolo, "The New York Public Library Automated Book Catalog Subsystem," *Journal of Library Automation* 6 (March 1973): 3–36.

16. The following may be helpful in evaluating processing services: Ronny Markoe, "The Cooperative Information Network: A Report," *California Librarian* 35 (July 1974): 16–21. Also, Theodore C. Hines, "Commercial Cataloging Services," *Library Trends* 24 (April 1976): 775–83; American Library Association, Resources and Technical Services Division, Commercial Processing Services Committee, "Guidelines for Selecting a Commercial Processing Service," *Library Resources and Technical Services* 21 (Spring 1977): 170–73; and David G. Remington, "Issues in Commercial Processing Services," *Library Resources and Technical Services* 21 (Spring 1977): 174–75.

17. Paul S. Dunkin, *How to Catalog a Rare Book,* 2d ed. (Chicago: American Library Association, 1972). A practical guide.

18. William Saffady, *Computer-Output Microfilm: Its Library Applications* (Chicago: American Library Association, 1978).

19. American Library Association, *ALA Rules for Filing Catalog Cards,* 2d ed. (Chicago: American Library Association, 1968).

20. Robert H. Rohlf and Jerry Pennington, "Planning for Automated Circulation Control," in *Buying New Technology, LJ Special Report No. 4* (New York: R. R. Bowker, 1978), pp. 9–10.

21. Richard W. Boss, "Circulation Systems: The Options," *Library Technology Reports* 15 (January–February 1979): 19.

22. Ibid., pp. 20–22.

23. Barbara Evans Markuson, "Automated Circulation Control Systems: An Overview of Commercially Vended Systems," *Library Technology Reports* (July, September 1975): 6–7.

24. Lois M. Kershner, "User Services: 1973 Applications Status," in *Library Automation:*

*The State of the Art II,* Susan K. Martin and Brett Butler, eds. (Chicago: American Library Association, 1975), p. 45.

25. Glen Mallison, "Permanent Registration of Library Patrons," *Library Journal* 84 (Dec. 15, 1959): 3813–17. Also, Walter H. Kaiser, "Are Registration and Library Cards Musts?" *Library Journal* 82 (June 1, 1957): 1393–99.

26. Richard W. Boss, op. cit. See also Paula Dranov, *Automated Library Circulation Systems, 1977–78* (White Plains, N.Y.: Knowledge Industries, 1978), and William H. Scholz, "Computer-Based Systems—A Current Review and Evaluation," *Library Technology Reports* 13 (May 1977): 231–325. *LTR* surveys new developments in the field about every two years. It is the best source for up-to-date information, as the speed of evolving new technologies makes books on the subject passé even before they are printed. *LTR* is published by the American Library Association. See also Barbara Evans Markuson, op. cit.

27. Richard W. Boss, op. cit., pp. 77–82.

28. Ibid., pp. 86–88.

29. Brett Butler, Brian Aveney, and William Scholz, "The Conversion of Manual Catalogs to Collection Data Bases," *Library Technology Reports* 14 (March–April 1978): 109–206.

30. M. K. Buckland, "An Operation Research Study of a Variable Loan and Duplication Policy at the University of Lancaster," *Library Quarterly* 42 (1972). See also Abraham Bookstein, "Optimal Loan Periods," *Information Processing and Management,* 11 (1975).

31. Comments in this section on theft detection systems were adapted from an article by Nancy H. Knight, "Theft Detection Systems for Libraries," *Library Technology Reports* 12 (November 1976).

32. *Indices of American Public Library Circulation and Expenditures.* Compiled annually by Library Research Center, University of Illinois Library School, and published in *American Libraries*—see vol. 10 (September 1978): 487.

33. National Conservation Advisory Council, *Report of the Study Committee on Libraries and Archives: National Needs in Libraries and Archives Conservation* (Washington, D.C.: National Conservation Advisory Council, 1978), pp. 6–7, 26–28, 34–35.

34. Library Binding Institute, *Standard for Library Binding,* 5th ed. (Boston: Library Binding Institute, 1971). See also Tauber, *Manual,* chap. 4.

35. Alex Ladenson, "Budget Control of Book Purchases and Binding Expenditures in Large Public Libraries," *Library Resources and Technical Services* 4 (Winter 1960): 55–58. Allotment practices of six libraries.

36. Council on Library Resources, *A National Periodicals Center: Technical Development Plan* (Washington, D.C.: Council on Library Resources, 1978).

# 19 Office Procedures and Records

There is a tremendous growth in the creation, handling, analysis, and storage of paper records. A recent survey reports that this "paperwork explosion" costs more than $35 billion each year.[1] Despite office machines, or perhaps encouraged by them, the trend is still strong. Public libraries and other municipal agencies are not immune to pressure for increased clerical activities. In many cases, municipal agencies handle a portion of the library's office routines, thus freeing the library of much work. Nevertheless, every librarian should have a clear understanding of the work—if only to be able to evaluate the service. The subject is discussed here under four main headings: the library office, clerical functions, statistical records, and financial records and activities, including purchasing and the distribution of supplies.

## The Library Office

The larger the library, the more certain it is to have a central office to perform the various clerical activities for most of the system. In small libraries, these are handled by one person. In libraries large enough (about 20,000 population) to justify at least a part-time secretary for the librarian, he or she will perform many of these library office functions. The secretary should be able to manage dictation, statistical records, financial accounts, and typing of book orders.

### The Office Head and Staff

When a library has a staff of 20 to 25 (that is, for 40,000 to 50,000 population), the librarian will need a full-time secretary. This same 4 or 5 percent ratio of office staff to total staff seems applicable in large libraries also, but large libraries are not likely to provide sufficient clerical help to department heads for their correspondence and records. Many of the functions of the library office are outgrowths of the library director's activities; it is therefore natural that the library office is directly responsible to him or her.

But in the largest libraries, the extensive development and specialization of these clerical activities will require delegating their supervision to an office manager who may report to the assistant librarian.

When the volume of office work justifies more than one person, the question arises whether it is better to centralize such services in one office or to decentralize them in departments and branches. While circumstances in some cases, such as distance of an agency from the library office, may justify decentralization, clerical services should be centralized as far as possible, at least up to the point at which a department or branch has so much clerical work as to require its own full-time clerical assistant. Centralization makes possible the development of specialized functions and justifies the use of machines. Furthermore, five people on the staff of the library office (which would presuppose a total staff of at least 100 and a population served of about 200,000) can perform more as a team than the total of each working apart from the others. Office management has become a specialized occupation; with the right person in charge it can promote the whole library program, and department or branch heads will have little cause to desire decentralizing their part of the work. In a well-run library, the office clerical staff can find satisfaction in their work and be recognized by the staff and the community as a key factor in good service.[2]

It is not easy to get the right person as head of the office staff, trained and experienced in office management, with a flair for management detail and efficiency, and dedicated to helping the rest of the library achieve its goals. Because business firms can pay better salaries, the library often has to find someone on the nonprofessional staff who comes closer than anyone else to these standards, and then has to train him or her for this job. This adds another important position to the career opportunities open to nonprofessional employees. In general, all the office staff should be good typists (at least 40 to 45 words per minute). Typing can be tested when interviewing applicants. The office head, however, should be selected by actual observation of work performance, administrative and instructional ability, personality, and general intelligence.

A commercial course in high school or in a business college is important, but systematic in-service training for the office staff is also needed. This training should embrace the content, the methods of work, the attitudes of the office staff toward the rest of the library, and a constant search for better ways of doing things. Each should know enough about the work done by the others in the office to be able to substitute in an emergency and to understand the interrelationships of each job with the others. A procedures manual is highly useful for orientation and training.[3] Many office problems and their solutions are similar to those in other institutions and in business, and the office manager can get much continuing on-the-job training outside the library, at meetings of such organizations as the National Office Management Association, and from books[4] and journals on this subject.

*Working Quarters*

Efficiency and productivity are fostered by good physical quarters. Placement near the librarian's office will save considerable time. Space is needed for a desk for each person, for files, adding machine, duplicator, typewriters, shelves, and other equipment—100 square feet per person, if possible. Good lighting, adequate heat, air conditioning, and some measure of sound control are important. Arrangement of the room can save much time. If one person is to serve as receptionist, for example, that desk should be convenient to callers. Usually it is best to space desks a foot or two apart but close enough to share a phone, and with all equipment nearby that will be used in common. L-shaped desk units will make space count more, and 42 inch (counter-height) or 62 inch movable partitions will reduce distraction.

Usual equipment for the library office includes a typewriter for each person, if possible one electric typewriter and one wide-carriage machine, one or more outside telephones, plus inside phones or other intercommunication devices, and for cities of over 20,000 population a mimeograph and an office copier. Larger libraries will need in addition a tape calculating machine and an adding machine, a paper folder, metal file cases with hanging folders, and one or more metal movable typewriter tables.

The general objective of the library office is to draw together and handle at one point the large volume of paperwork that can be shifted without much time loss, from departments and branches and from the librarians. The work in the technical services department, for example, cannot economically be shifted, because it would involve moving the books and would break up the work flow, adding to costs. Office work in libraries needs searching analysis of present practice and a streamlined revision by specialists in the organization and layout of paperwork jobs.

*Specific Clerical Functions*

The physical layout of the building, the organization of the particular library, the abilities of the office and related staffs, and other factors vary so greatly that no list of clerical office activities will fit more than a few situations.

Usually someone in the library office serves as receptionist to business callers, including job applicants, salespeople, and patrons with complaints. He or she must know the library well enough to screen the callers who wish to see department heads and the library director and to handle each caller tactfully.

Typing is the major office work, such as minutes of trustees' and other meetings, purchase orders, correspondence, book orders and form requests for free material, payroll, news releases, monthly and annual reports, and statistical tables. The quality and quantity of typing may be raised in several ways.[5] A dictating machine used by the director and department heads will save the secretary's time. Prepared forms can be used for correspondence.

*Telephone Services*

External communications encompass the following: Tie lines reduce costs for toll charges if the volume of calls is high enough. The rule of thumb is that a tie line or leased circuit is justifiable if the total cost of toll calls between two points is 150 percent of what the cost would be for the tie line. Another outside system is the WATS (Wide Area Telephone Service), which makes it possible to place unlimited calls within specified areas for a flat monthly rate. Still another is Telpack, a point-to-point service that transmits telephone and teletype messages as well as facsimile and data information. PBX, the traditional telephone switchboard, has been in use for some time. A newer external communications system is Centrex. Centrex allows PBX stations Direct Inward Dialing (DID), which enables outsiders to call direct to any telephone in the office, and Direct Outward Dialing (DOD), which makes it possible for insiders to call out without going through the PBX operator. Another Centrex feature is its Intercom capacity, which permits calls within the organization without going through the PBX operator. It also has special Night Connections.[6]

*Office Records and Forms*

Costs for filing, keeping, and finding an item increase as the size of the total file expands. One idea is to hold new papers for six months; by then, most of them can be discarded. In another weeding, every five years, most can safely be thrown away, placing in storage units the papers that should still be kept but are not likely to be needed for current reference. A rough rule of thumb is to have no more than one file drawer of current office papers for each 20,000 people served. This file should be kept in one alphabet. Only office personnel should file and take out papers, and all papers to go into or come out of the file should be handled by the same person if possible, to minimize errors and to have a record of any papers borrowed.

Archivists and business firms are fairly well agreed on a few principles for discarding records. A records retirement schedule should be prepared for approval by the board, listing main classes of records and specifying length of time to be kept and manner of disposition. Some financial records, such as petty cash receipts, can be destroyed as soon as the financial audit has been completed for that year. Bids for library contracts should be kept for several years, and board meeting minutes and annual financial and departmental reports indefinitely. Microfilming the records to be kept will reduce the needed space and increase their life. Many states now regulate the disposition of all governmental papers.

The library office is normally the agency responsible for creating and distributing all needed forms. Some forms could be combined, some need review and simplifying, and possibly new ones are required. Every form should have a descriptive title and carry the name of the library, a serial number, and the date it was prepared or last revised. An up-to-date sample book or catalog of current forms is useful. A forms requisition is necessary in larger libraries so that those concerned can study the details and design of any new form before printing and each time it is revised. Directions for using a form should be built into it. The first question to ask of each existing form is whether it is really necessary at all.

The library office usually handles incoming and outgoing first-class mail, and that involving acquaintance with postal regulations. A library using direct mail advertising (in towns of over 25,000 population) may need a third-class mailing permit. Postage meters are helpful in larger libraries. If the library has a telephone switchboard, it is often in or under the control of the library office.

## Statistical Records

The library office is the logical unit usually involved in collecting, preparing and distributing statistical reports, tabulating the data, and filing and storing the papers. The tendency is for statistical records to increase in number and complexity.

The kinds of measurement and evaluation records to be maintained will be discussed in Chapter 21. The important consideration is to collect and maintain only those data that will have some practical application in library planning and operations. Collected statistics should be reviewed periodically to see that they fill the need. Most state library agencies require annual reports to be made on a specified form; perhaps this form can be used to provide the basis for the library's statistical recordkeeping. Also, the state library agency is required to collect data in a given form for reporting to the U.S. Office of Education for grant purposes in such programs as the Library Services and Construction Act.

## Business Procedures

### Purchasing

Much will depend on the degree of the library's inclusion in local government and its processes. Frequently, for example, the procedure for purchasing supplies and equipment will be specified and perhaps even handled by the city. Such a practice is increasing in large city and county libraries. The local government may even provide some materials or services to the library on requisition and not involve the library in any dealings directly with the vendor. However, some smaller libraries are independent of the city in their purchasing arrangements, though even then there may be state rulings to be observed.

The spirit of all legal requirements for purchasing by public bodies is that competitive sealed bids be sought from qualified vendors, to secure the best possible price for a given quality. This generally means written specifications and sealed bids for purchases above a certain dollar value, and the system usually works well. Thus sealed bids for the same model car of a given make, or for the newest models of two or three equally good typewriters, may vary by 20 percent from highest to lowest. If the public library can control the specifications issued for a given purchase, it can greatly benefit by this system. Even when the library handles its own purchases, it can usually get from vendors the same competitive low prices on fuel, light bulbs, typewriters, and so on that are offered to the city or school board. Since inevitably there are differences between bidders that are not subject to measurement in dollar terms, such as the promptness of service, it is well to award contracts not to the lowest bidder but to the best and lowest.

Bidding is not usually called for on purchases of below $1,000 or so. The library board may permit direct purchasing by the director for any single expenditure of no more than, say, $500 and may require that expenditures of more than that be submitted for advance approval, often with quotations from more than one vendor. By the same token, it is wise to decentralize to the individual branch or department the authority to purchase any item costing no more than about $10, and not available by requisition, with a report of these to be made to the business office.

For libraries of 75,000 population and up, some brief record of all purchases should be kept, with date, quantity, prices, and notes as to staff evaluations of the product and service and the trade names of what have been found to be the most satisfactory brands. Changes should not be made by the business office in catalog cards, letter paper, pencils, and other items without consulting the people who will use them. A list of brands preferred by the staff will also save the office staff from most of the time-consuming visits of manufacturers' representatives.

### Distribution of Supplies

Purchasing is tied to the distribution of supplies to the individual library agencies and staff members, and the two functions are usually handled by the same people. Supplies should be kept under lock and key and distributed from the office. A list of all the supplies currently available should be maintained, and in larger libraries it should be mimeographed for distribution to all agencies for use as a requisition list. In such cases, the head of each branch or department should sign the requisition, and it is then the authorization for disbursement of the supplies from the stockroom. There is no reason why an item of current and continued usefulness in a public library should be unavailable in the stockroom; a reserve supply should be set up of each such item, sufficient to meet all requests likely to be received in the time necessary for reordering.

Purchasing a reasonably large quantity of an item secures better discounts and avoids repeat orders, which sometimes cost $10–$20 for paperwork. But too large a supply of an item may result in spoilage. An agency's request for any approved item not currently available should result in placing an order for it, notifying the agency of this action, and marking the purchase order with instructions upon receipt to forward the needed quantity to that agency. Once a year the stockroom shelves need review to clear out items no longer used or useful.

*Insurance*[7]

Arrangements for insurance will also depend on the closeness of fiscal relationships to the city, county, or other local government. But though the matter may be completely handled by another body, even to payment of the premium, the director should be acquainted with the insurance arrangements, read the policies themselves, especially the fine print, and seek all necessary and desirable provisions. Typically, a public library will have insurance on its buildings and contents against damage by fire or certain other natural hazards (usually designated as "extended coverage"). The premium paid for this insurance will be greatly reduced if coinsurance is used. This means simply that the library agrees to maintain insurance protection for 80 or 90 percent of the full value of the property, and the company agrees to charge a lower premium. To maintain coinsurance, it is well to call for an engineering survey of the library buildings every five years or so; this may result in some rise in total valuation, but it will maintain the coinsurance clause and will serve to detect potential fire hazards.

Building contents may be included in the general fire insurance policies. But for about the same premium cost as for fire and extended coverage, an "all risk" policy will provide coverage against all hazards except those stated in the contract. According to the ALA, a model "all-risk" policy should include coverage for

the common risks of fire and extended coverage perils, vandalism, theft, water damage of any kind (including floor damage), collapse of the building or stacks, collision of carrying vehicles, explosion of a steam boiler (or other explosion), landslide, earthquake, sand storms and dust storms, damage caused by overheating of the building through faulty operation of heating equipment, and any other causes not expressly excluded.[8]

A card record of major equipment should be maintained in larger libraries, partly for insurance valuation purposes and partly as a record of identification, repairs, serviceability, and so on. Many possible kinds of insurance are often *not* needed. Insurance should be used to cover a possible loss that would be too large to be handled from current revenues. Thus, on automobile liability policies, use the maximum deductible amount that the library can afford to pay in case of damage. A liability policy for accidents to readers and staff is always desirable and is sometimes required, as in the case of an elevator.

Insurance is a matter complicated enough to require study. Ask a good agent to explain what coverage is needed and why and what items can be omitted. A three-year policy costs less per year than a one-year policy, a five-year policy less yet. Book coverage can be based on the average cost of books of different kinds, such as adult, juvenile, fiction, nonfiction, and reference, but for most public libraries this degree of detail is not necessary. In any case, review the library's insurance policies every few years to see what changes may be indicated. Self-insurance* is not recommended.

*Other Business Procedures*

The handling of gifts of money and of the resulting investments is usually done under the direction of the board of trustees, often calling on the community's best investment authority for free advice. But the director should know what is being done and should review it critically. Accounting systems to determine the cost of a given service or activity have an extensive literature as related to industry, business, and office work, and a few studies have been made in libraries. The difficulty of getting measurable units of operation and the consequent noncomparability of cost data in different libraries have been pointed out. A more practical approach is to keep a few simple records for year-to-year comparisons, involving only direct costs—that is, labor and supplies—without attempting to allocate indirect or overhead costs. Any attempt at cost accounting may produce figures higher than were expected and should lead the director to reevaluate the activity in question.

## Financial Records

Financial records, universally required by law to show how public funds are spent, are essential to assign and control expenditures. The temptation should be resisted to keep accounts in greater detail than is clearly required for either of these purposes. If the city or county government insists on maintaining full financial records of the library, and the library can secure adequate and prompt reports when it calls for them, there is no need for a duplicate set of records in the library. Most libraries of any size and all those whose finances are independent of local government have to keep their own records. Often the local or state government requires that financial re-

---

* Self-insurance is the periodic allocation into a special fund by the institution to cover any losses that might occur due to various designated risks.

cords be kept in specified form, and the library must conform. Often too, the library has such difficulty in getting data from account books at the city offices that it has to keep duplicate accounts itself. Sometimes official approval can be secured to modify a requirement that involves excessive paperwork or delays—or, better still, the account keeping can be delegated to the library.

In some cities, the preparation of voucher checks, drawing on the library's funds in the city treasury, is all done at the library. In such a case, the voucher checks can be prepared in triplicate; one copy is the check for payment, the second is sent to the city fiscal office, and the third stays at the library, with original bills and other documents attached. The city accounting office thus knows about every transaction and can make its annual audit of the library's accounts. The stub or back of the voucher check has a schedule according to budgetary items, and the total amount of the check is broken down into these parts. All the expenditures are thus ready to be posted in their proper columns, and no figure has been copied more than twice for disbursements or recordkeeping. The payee detaches the accounting half of the voucher check and then has a check in the usual form, plus a separate detailed record of the transaction in case he needs it.

## Bookkeeping and Revenues

A public library usually does not need double-entry bookkeeping or more than one book of financial records—a ledger account by date of all revenues and all expenditures. (It does need also a simple monthly sheet to record each day's overdue fines and other cash receipts, and petty cash expenditures.) Each such entry in the ledger should be given a separate line, with the date, the nature of the transaction, and the amount of money involved. It may carry a serial number for each check or voucher issued. To provide a cross check at the end of the month, the dollar amount should be entered both in the column headed "Total Revenues" (or "Total Expenditures") and in the column headed with the name of the budget item under which the transaction falls. It is desirable (and sometimes required by law) that all revenues and all expenditures of the library appear in its financial record book, whether or not the revenues are of tax funds, gifts, transfers from other government bodies, cash receipts, or from any other source, and the expenditures are for operating costs, capital outlay, debt retirement, or any other purpose. It may also be desirable to have separate groupings of some of these transactions in the monthly and annual financial reports, or in the daily record of petty cash, but all financial transactions should be shown in one place, and a monthly and annual fiscal report prepared therefrom.

Most revenues of a public library come from one source, the local government tax on property. In many cities the tax distribution is made twice a year, and will vary somewhat from announced or anticipated figures by the amount of unpaid taxes, unpaid taxes of previous years that have been collected, last-minute changes made in assessed valuation, and so on. Other sources of library revenues include state aid, payments from other libraries or other units of government for library service, and a miscellaneous grouping of fines for overdue or damaged books, payments for lost books, fees for various services, and the sale of old books or waste paper.

## Petty Cash

The record of receipts from these miscellaneous sources should be kept in no more detail than necessary, since altogether they seldom account for as much as 5 percent of library revenues. A simple mimeographed or printed sheet, with a line for each day and a column for each month, should suffice for record, unless budgetary rules require an estimate of expected revenues for each single, specific kind; even then, a one-month-a-year sample may be enough for an estimate. In any case, cash revenues should always be recorded when received and in the actual cash amounts, and not when due or in the amounts expected.

Technical questions arise in the handling of cash receipts. Most librarians consider a cash register at the circulation desk to be a nuisance, but it does provide a record of the amount received each day,[9] and it is often required by the parent governing authority. Most public libraries use a cash drawer, segregate unusual or large receipts, lock up the money every night, and deposit it in the bank each day or week, keeping in the drawer only enough to make change or for petty cash expenditures. The amount of cash received should be recorded in the daily petty cash account, and when the library office deposits it in the bank, the proper entry should be made in the ledger as "miscellaneous cash income" or under subordinate headings. Large libraries bond the person who receives and handles the library's cash revenue.

The phrase "petty cash" is sometimes misinterpreted as meaning a source of funds for expenditures. Petty cash is simply money in the form of cash, or small checks to the library, for fines and daily routine matters, and such cash may be used to pay for petty items, whereas other expenditures are usually made by check. But expenditures from the cash drawer at any agency must all be recorded on the daily cash account sheet and by the business office in the ledger and be debited to one or another of the various budget accounts, each of which has a total authorized amount for expenditure in a given year. The petty cash device permits making small purchases promptly and with a minimum of paperwork, but it cannot be used to avoid the limits of authorized expenditures.

At least once a month, the total spent from petty cash for any one type of purchase should be recorded as revenue ("miscellaneous cash income"), and again as an expenditure (for example, under "books and magazines" if these were payments for current local newspapers). Unless local auditing rules require it, the original petty cash records need not be kept on file. One modification in making purchases out of petty cash is to establish a petty cash checking account in the name of the director or business manager. This allows for purchases limited to, say, $10, paid by what amounts to a personal check, with periodic restoration of the bank balance by charging each expenditure account with its total of such checks and by issuing an official library warrant or check for the grand total to the credit of the checking account.

Somewhat akin to but separate from the petty cash fund is the idea of a revolving fund, as in the case of a library that rents duplicate copies of currently popular books. Any such fund should be established only by approval of the board of trustees, and usually requires an initial appropriation of money. Once established, however, a revolving fund secures its future revenue from specific sources allocated to it, as in this case the rental fees paid by patrons who choose to borrow the pay copies. The money so received can usually be spent only for a specified purpose—for example, to purchase more such rental books.

*Expenditures*

Some cities of over 50,000 population require three steps in the handling of an expenditure: the issuance of a purchase order, the receipt and validation of the bill, and the issuance of the check in payment of the bill. Unless the expenditure is being made out of petty cash (or under some similar arrangement), many cities require that there be a record available to the library of every commitment which it is making and for which it is promising to pay. In the case of salaries, the last payroll can be taken as a reasonably close approximation of the next; similarly, bills for light, water, and other utilities for one month can be used as a record of such necessary (and committed) expenditures for the next month. But for all those expenditures that are not so regular—for example, for supplies, equipment, books, repairs—a purchase order should be issued to the vendor or supplier in question and a copy of it kept in the business office of the library as a record of just what was ordered and of the funds committed.

If the total dollar amount of purchase orders issued in a given year exceeds the funds available or budgeted, it will not be possible to accept delivery or to pay for all the goods ordered. Perhaps in a one-person library, the details of all authorized purchases can be kept in mind, but delays in shipment, changes in the order, and other variables will surely cause trouble sooner or later. In any library with more than one staff member, a system of at least simple typewritten purchase orders should be used. In many cities it is required that the amount of the purchase order be entered in the official record of disbursements as an encumbrance or anticipated expenditure, so as to make certain that a financial report at any time will recognize the existence and amount of these outstanding orders. A simpler method to secure the same result is to keep in a separate file all outstanding purchase orders and to add the total amount so committed to the monthly report of actual cash transactions. This has the further advantage of making unnecessary a correction to the ledger entry of the original encumbrance resulting from a change in dollar amount of the actual purchase (as, for example, if the vendor cannot supply the whole quantity ordered, or if there has been a price change).

*Clearing Invoices*

When supplies or equipment are delivered, they are usually accompanied by an invoice. This should be checked by the appropriate person against what was delivered, to be sure that the quantity and quality of product are as ordered. If satisfied he or she will sign and date the invoice and give it to the business office assistant. This same procedure should be followed in the case of bills for which there is no invoice—for example, a bill for repair services should be reviewed by the superintendent of buildings and grounds, and approved in writing as correct. In the business office, the receipted invoice or bill should be matched with its appropriate purchase order (and the absence of a matching purchase order may indicate a duplicate bill), and these should be accumulated for review by the director and for submission to the board of trustees. Many libraries are required to secure an affidavit or claim form from each vendor certifying to the accuracy of the bill and witnessing that it has not already been paid. No bills should be presented to the board without critical scrutiny by the director if possible, or in large libraries by the business manager. Much can be learned of the daily operation of a library by reviewing current bills, especially as more and more authority is delegated to others. It is desirable, and sometimes it is required, that the director initial the bills, indicating approval that they are correct and should be paid.

Usually the board of trustees or its finance committee approves the bills submitted to it in a group or as a list. But almost always public libraries can pay bills only upon express approval of the governing body, though special provision should be made for early payment of bills that offer a discount for promptness. Occasional review of the bills by the board is healthy for critical evaluation of purchasing practices. Once the bills are approved, the checks are written, usually at the library but sometimes at the city offices, perhaps according to the procedures outlined above under the heading "Financial Records." A stub record or duplicate check is kept by the library, the expenditures are recorded in the financial ledger, and the bills are marked with the number of the check and filed, desirably by year and then alphabetically by name of vendor.

*Salary Payments*

Salary payments constitute by far the largest expenditure of any one type, and the bulk of the checks issued by the library. There must be some systematic provision, to the person who prepares the payroll, of such basic information as an accurate roster of those entitled to pay for a given payroll period, the gross amount of such pay, and the necessary or requested individual deductions and other changes.

In a library with a staff of even ten people or more, preparation of the payroll can be a task of no small magnitude and complexity, and its details will warrant periodic review. The present trend is for the parent governing authority, city or county government, to handle the actual payment and reports on salaries. In libraries where the activity remains independent, however, there should be a personnel or salary card set up for each member of the staff, with all necessary information on previous and present salary and deductions. In larger libraries, it may be useful to have an "adjustment in pay" form to secure in writing the details of any change in salary or in deductions, and its approval or authorization. These "adjustments in pay" forms are then arranged by payroll period, and the changes made on the salary cards at one time just prior to preparing the payroll. The actual payroll can then be made in one typing operation by combining a printed check (with space to show salary changes and deductions) and a payroll form that records all this information alphabetically by staff members' names and allows for totaling gross pay, each kind of deduction, and net pay. In effect, this is what an electric bookkeeping machine will do automatically. In small libraries, it may be reasonable to assume that each staff member is entitled to salary unless word is received to the contrary. In large libraries, it is necessary to have a time sheet or other certification by the employee or supervisor that he or she has been at work, especially in the case of part-time employees paid by the hour. Also in larger libraries, the entire financial record system including the payroll and check writing may be fully automated. This will include the rapid printing of the annual W-2 forms all libraries must supply to all employees early in the new year for their federal income tax filing.

*Financial Reports and Audits*

To utilize effectively the information contained in the many entries in the library's ledger, the trustees and director need a summary of them. Such a monthly financial report is usual, though in small libraries it may be quarterly. It should appear promptly and show a total of all revenues (and by each main source) and a total of all expenditures (and by each main budget expenditure account). In addition, to convey a picture of the library's current cash position, the report should begin with the library's bank balance at the beginning of the previous month, and show the total at the end of the month; this will serve as a cross check on the totals in the ledger and should also be reconciled with the statement of the library's bank account.

For each budget item of income or outgo, the monthly report should show in successive columns the total allowed for the year, the amount spent up to the end of the previous month, the amount spent during the month just completed, the amount of outstanding purchase orders in each expenditure category, then the percentage of the annual amount already spent or committed to date, and finally the balance for the remainder of the year. The last two columns of the report show the extent to which expenditures are proceeding too fast or too slow, in general and in each specific budget account. In the case of any important deviation, the director should be able to explain the reasons, and should plan to get the outflow under control, especially at the year's end. In libraries with automation, detailed monthly financial reports are a useful by-product of the automated system.

Many public libraries publish annual reports that lack any financial statement, though an annual financial report is almost always required by law of all government bodies, and the form and details are often specified. Such a report or a summary of it should desirably be presented to the board of trustees and made available to the public, including an accounting of any trust funds, gifts, grants, or special funds. As noted in Chapter 7, it is essential that the library lay all its financial cards on the table, at least in summary form. The annual financial report is usually used as the basis of an audit of the year's financial records, which may be made by a private accounting firm or more often by the city auditor or finance officer. The audit will review the accuracy of the entries in the financial books, the adequacy of the documents backing up those entries, and the library's conformity to applicable laws and regulations. For the director's protection, he or she should insist on an audit and work closely with those who make it.

The best library accounting system is the one that will give only the essential information as to money received and spent in the simplest form possible. The advice offered in this chapter is to set up no bookkeeping or transaction record that is not necessary and, where municipal regulations compel elaborate systems that may be essential for other municipal departments spending ten or fifty times as much as the library, to seek a simpler procedure, so that library paperwork and service delays will be minimized. Small libraries should not be disturbed if their records are simpler than those suggested above, provided they show what is going on financially.

### Notes

1. Dennis Zalden, "The Paperwork Explosion," in Robert S. Minor and Clark W. Fetridge, *Office Administration Handbook* (Chicago: Dartnell Corporation, 1975), p. 517.

2. Fred K. Foulkes, *Creating More Meaningful Work* (New York: American Management Association, 1969).
3. Morris Philip Wolf, *Effective Communication in Business* (Cincinnati: Southwestern, 1974).
4. Carl Heyel, ed., *Handbook of Office Management and Administrative Services* (New York: McGraw-Hill, 1972).
5. Doris Lillian and B. M. Miller, *Complete Secretary's Handbook*, 3d ed. (Englewood Cliffs, N.J.: Prentice-Hall, 1970).
6. H. B. Maynard, ed., *Handbook of Business Administration* (New York: McGraw-Hill, 1970), pp. 14–22.
7. Gerald E. Myers, *Insurance Manual for Libraries* (Chicago: American Library Association, 1977). The ALA calls this a valuable guide for libraries who want to set up an insurance program or evaluate a present one.
8. American Library Administration, *Protecting the Library and Its Resources: A Guide to Physical Protection and Insurance* (Chicago: American Library Association, 1963).
9. Arthur Yabroff, "Cash Registers in the Library," *Wilson Library Bulletin* 35 (May 1961): 711ff.

# 20 Building Planning and Care

The library director, or someone assigned to the matter, has to be keenly aware of the custody of the building, an important and expensive property. An attractive, well-equipped, efficient, clean building is a great asset in promoting library objectives. Keeping it in good running order, bright and inviting, may be assigned to the head of a competent janitorial staff. But the library director must pay attention to building condition, and care and cost, as an important aspect of administration. Poor maintenance of building and equipment will adversely affect staff and reader morale. Furthermore, when planning new buildings or alterations or enlargements, the people concerned and responsible for building custody and maintenance should participate.

## Care and Maintenance

The custodian, janitor, or part-time cleaning person has an important job that affects everyone in the library. He or she should be chosen with care, by tryout as well as by interview, and not only from those who may apply or answer an advertisement but also from a list of the most competent people who can be found. If the position is under civil service, the library person responsible for hiring should still exercise due care and concern about the selection. Sometimes, in a public employment situation, there will be some pressure to place a "deserving" resident on the payroll to handle the custodial duties, on the grounds that the duties are simple and can be performed by almost anyone without special training or knowledge. This is not the case; not only the building but its contents are of value and must be treated accordingly. Proven ability in the care and maintenance of floors, lighting, furniture, and all other elements of the property will be required. Like all other library employees, the building maintenance person must be energetic, healthy, intelligent, capable of learning new ways of doing things as required, and flexible about schedules and duties. The work will vary, seasonally and for other reasons. There will be certain daily jobs to be done; when the weather is inclement there will be added work. All this should be understood. A physical examination should be required. Good moral character is important. The custodian may be called upon to help maintain order in the building; a certain amount of ability in this area will be helpful.

In order to be assured that the appointment of the library custodial staff is not at the mercy of the political process, the library director ought to make clear to the trustees how important it is that they stand with him or her to resist this pressure. This is a library service requiring real ability, initiative, energy, and devotion. The part-time solution is increasingly common in smaller buildings and branches; a reliable man or woman living close may come in for two or three hours a day. Atlanta and other cities have used a pair or team of men who move from branch to branch, each taking care of a specialty. Some larger libraries contract for special services, such as high-up window cleaning or snow removal, especially if the janitor or building staff are part-time or have all they can do to keep up with regular work.[1]

### Training the Building Staff

The head janitor, building superintendent, or library director should see that all building workers receive training for their jobs. The new recruit's schedule should be arranged for instruction in a class for municipal or school caretakers, unless the supervisor can give it effectively. Methods and materials have changed much in the last few years. The library director should make clear to each new custodial worker that the work is considered important and worth doing well. There is instructional material for building personnel available.[2,3,4] In addition, there are guides issued by state education authorities and by the U.S. Department of Health, Education and Welfare. The library should have a list of typed instructions that set forth exactly what is to be done daily, weekly, monthly, and at other intervals; also, by whom, if there is more than one custodian. The custodial employees may well be members of a collective bargaining unit; if so, this factor has to be taken into account, and the agreement or contract should, of course, be observed meticulously. But the employer retains the right to lay out the work and to make certain that it is done. This is just as important, if not more so, in a situation of public employment; if private employers want to put up with low productivity or sloppy workmanship, that is their problem; the public employer is entrusted with public tax funds and is expected to expend them for the most good.

The manuals and books on the subject have given due attention to the most efficient way in which to sweep down a stairway or clean a workroom in order to get it done properly and in the least time. Handing out the instructions to the janitor is not sufficient; the supervisor should go over the material as often as is necessary, keep posted on progress, and encourage trial of new ideas. In libraries kept clean and fresh, it will be found that the building staff is given special attention and is appreciated.

*Management of Building Care*

The superintendent, head janitor, or in small libraries the library director has to divide and assign the work to the various workers and follow through, to see that all goes well and that things are done promptly, efficiently, economically. Despite all the money invested in library buildings and in their annual custodial care, we have few figures as to costs per square foot for their care. Obviously a building that is simple in design, open and with few interior walls, and devoid of expensive trim and moldings means great savings in construction and upkeep compared with buildings of the Carnegie era. On the other hand, heavier patronage and more glass areas in proportion than before create new building care problems, but they do give the feeling that library buildings are far more useful than ever and better deserve the investment in good care.

Data on public libraries acquired by the National Center for Educational Statistics (NCES) in a 1974 survey show that total expenditures for public libraries were $1.1 billion. Of this amount, $107 million, or slightly less than 10 percent, was for plant operation and maintenance. Of the total full-time public library staff, amounting to 86,003 people, 7.4 percent were plant operation and maintenance staff.[5]

In larger libraries, the building superintendent normally deals with contractors, often writing specifications and soliciting sealed bids. He or she should be present when bids are opened, to advise the board and the library director on the choice of the best and lowest bid. If sealed bids are not required, he or she will solicit quotations from two or three firms judged to be competent and reliable, and either decide who is to do the job or recommend a choice to the library director. The superintendent should see that details are studied in advance (to avoid changes during the work), watch its progress, consult with the contractor on essential variations, see that the contractor has the cooperation needed, and be sure that the work is well done. The superintendent should learn how new equipment is installed and how it is to be serviced and maintained. He or she and the library director should review and inspect the finished job in order to recommend its acceptance by the board.

The management of maintenance breaks down into four parts: assigning responsibility for each aspect; cleaning and straightening-up operations; care and operation of heating and other mechanical equipment; and repair and maintenance. It includes general safety, health, comfort, and convenience of staff and public; condition, appearance, and cleanness of grounds, approaches, and exterior; cleanness and orderliness of the interior, its equipment, and furnishings; sanitation throughout, especially floors,[6] washrooms, and plumbing; fire safety; effective operation of heating, ventilating, lighting, sewage, water, and other service; proper storage of all materials; prevention of damage by water or by wear and abuse—all with a minimum of paperwork and records, none in smaller libraries. These management areas call for careful definite scheduling, even though unforeseen interruptions can upset any exact schedule.

### Some Reminders on Building Care

*Floor cleaning.* Machines for cleaning and polishing floors were once important purchases for libraries. Today most floors are carpeted. Moreover, cleaning is often done by contract with an outside business concern, which can be held responsible for cleaning standards set up by bid specifications.

*Heating.* Today only very large buildings can justify any heat system or fuel use that involves more than a few minutes a day to operate.

*Washroom problems.* These often involve disagreeable personal situations. A janitor with backbone can help in policing, tactfully drive out undesirables, and save time and embarrassment for the staff in smaller buildings. One way to reduce abuse of toilets is to require that patrons ask for a key and to post a sign "Washroom Available Only to Library Users." The question of moving or completely renovating old unsanitary washrooms in many buildings deserves study and some expense. In most older buildings, the needs of the handicapped were ignored in washroom design. Today, most states have provisions in the building code for making washrooms usable by the handicapped, and the American National Standards Institute has specifications.[7] Use metal waste containers. Open electric bulbs and removable fixtures are a temptation to vandalism.

*Basements.* The chief fire cause in libraries is failure to clean out completely each week the basement accumulation of waste paper, cartons, cleaning rags, and discarded materials. A staff member should be made responsible for checking safety matters. Check burnt-out lights, decrepit chairs, splinters on table legs, misplaced ladders, and so on. The library director should accompany the head janitor once a month in at least a short inspection of all buildings.

### Repairs

Libraries should handle minor repairs—simple woodwork, like shelving and alterations in counters and furniture, and small painting jobs.

If there is a superintendent in a library serving up to 100,000 population, he or she should be a head janitor. The superintendent should have some mechanical aptitude and be able to mend and refinish furniture and make simple repairs. Larger libraries will have their own full-time all-round mechanic and, in cities of 500,000 and up with many branches, a carpenter, a plumber, an electrician, and so on. Some sort of shop space with a bench and tools is essential in libraries of 20,000 and up. Branches should send in an annual priority list and a monthly memo requesting repairs or alterations, so work can be planned, materials delivered to the job, and time lag prevented. The library should keep ready and in good condition a set of the building blueprints; they show where plumbing, telephone lines, electric outlets, and other service points are located, and they often save time, mistakes, and false starts. Labels painted on the walls should show water cutoffs and other service points and danger spots.

### Remodeling

A library building consultant can show how in old, and even in fairly recent buildings, staff time can be saved and readers given more convenient service, more economically organized, by properly relating functions and service points. Prized main floor space can often be gained by (1) cutting into halls to recover wasted space; (2) getting less important things upstairs or to the basement, and rearranging the main floor, even cutting through walls; and (3) if the ceiling is fifteen feet high or more, installing mezzanine or balcony reading and book space, which is the best supplement to main floor space. Many buildings have central halls open to the roof and even to a dome. A suspended membrane, perhaps ten feet from the floor, to completely ceil this central space, will save great loss of heat escaping upward, and under the new surface an entirely new efficient lighting system can be installed.

### Lighting

The quality of library lighting is more important than the maintained intensity. (Maintained intensity is about 70 percent of the initially installed intensity, or the minimum light output before the light sources are cleaned or replaced.) Keyes Metcalf notes a steady increase in recommended intensities from 1900 to 1965. They doubled every ten years in the earlier decades, and it was not unusual later for programs presented to architects to call for 125 footcandles.[8]

Since Dr. Metcalf's 1970 study of library lighting, the energy crisis has been widely recognized, and lower intensities are being endorsed by architects. The higher intensities of light require more energy initially, and they create more heat, requiring more energy when buildings are air conditioned. Anyone contemplating library lighting problems for new or remodeled buildings should read the Metcalf study.

The Metcalf recommendations of 30 to 35 footcandles as sufficient for 70 to 80 percent of a general reading area at the working surfaces, and 60 to 70 footcandles for most remaining areas, should meet reader needs and save energy.

Fluorescent lights emit ultraviolet rays, which are damaging to paper. These same rays cause a newspaper left in the sun to turn brown and brittle. The intensity of the rays in fluorescent light is much less and is not too serious for libraries except in book storage areas, where material such as local history and rare books should be retained for many, many years. Where the damaging rays need to be filtered out, sleeves are available made of UF-3 or Acrylite OP-2, which slip over standard fluorescent tubes.[9]

Good lighting is not easily attained. The basic aim is even diffusion and absence of glare from spots of light. One room equipped with ingeniously designed desk and table lamps, which nevertheless prevented good diffusion, was transformed by the installation of softly diffused light from fixtures close to the ceiling. Advertisements of some fixtures show the light source so placed that the reflection from reading matter, paper, and table or desk top bounces directly into the worker's eyes, such as carrels with a fluorescent light tube under the shelf in front of the reader. Electric lighting should come from nearly white ceilings or high surfaces and be diffused over the work surface. All-over translucent ceilings, with the outlets, lamps, and service piping installed above the corrugated suspended ceiling, are highly satisfactory. Large diffusing grids, or large, shallow plastic bowls, maybe five or six feet square, shielding fluorescent tubes, are efficient and less costly. Some ingenious and otherwise beautiful fixture designs directly conflict with good lighting. In most workrooms, the single central ceiling outlet or fixture provides little diffusion and leaves the corners dark. Inexpensive upward-aimed lights can be set on bookcases or attached to the walls, to throw the light at ceiling corners, hence on work surfaces.

There are many areas of activity in a library. Besides the usual reading, reference, technical processing, and bookstack areas, many libraries contain meeting rooms, conference rooms, seminar rooms, display areas, exhibition areas, rare book rooms, audiovisual rooms, individual study areas and carrels, microform viewing spaces, data-processing facilities, lounge and office places, entranceways, and lobbies. Each of these may present special lighting problems. A key consideration is the level of illumination required to perform a particular task, as Table 6 shows. Other considerations include surface reflection, color, glare, and the supply of daylight.[10]

Enthusiasts for various wall colors may overlook significant differences in color reflection; some tints and shades that seem to be fairly reflective may kill off 15 to 25 percent of the light. The nearer to white, especially in ceilings, the better is the reflection of daylight and electric light. Floors should reflect 20 to 30 percent, ceilings 80 to 90 percent—that is, be as nearly white as possible—walls 70 to 80 percent. Dark desk tops and work surfaces cause eye fatigue from too great contrast. Architects and decorators working up impressive dark and light wall contrasts should be told that lighter tints of all colors are preferable.

**Table 6.** Levels of Illumination Currently Recommended for Libraries (in footcandles and dekalux)*

| Area | Equivalent Sphere Illumination Unless Otherwise Indicated | |
| --- | --- | --- |
| | Footcandles on Tasks† | Dekalux on Tasks† |
| Reading Areas | | |
|     Reading printed material | 30 | 32 |
|     Study and note taking | 70 | 75 |
| Conference areas | 30 | 32 |
| Seminar rooms | 70 | 75 |
| Bookstacks (30 in [76 cm] above floor) | | |
|   Active stacks | 30§,‡‡ | 32§,‡‡ |
|   Inactive stacks | 5§,‡‡ | 5.4§,‡‡ |
| Book repair and binding | 70‡‡ | 75‡‡ |
| Cataloging | 70 | 75 |
| Card files | 100 | 110 |
| Carrels, individual study areas | 70 | 75 |
| Circulation desks | 70 | 75 |
| Rare book rooms—archives | | |
|     Storage areas | 30‡‡ | 32‡‡ |
|     Reading areas | 100 | 100 |
| Map, picture, and print rooms | | |
|     Storage areas | 30‡‡ | 32‡‡ |
|     Use areas | 100 | 110 |
| Audiovisual areas | | |
|     Preparation rooms | 70‡‡ | 75‡‡ |
|     Viewing rooms (variable) | 70‡‡ | 75‡‡ |
|     Television receiving room (shield viewing screen) | 70‡‡ | 75‡‡ |
| Audio listening areas | | |
|     General | 30‡‡ | 32‡‡ |
|     For note taking | 70 | 75 |
|     Record inspection table | 100**,‡‡ | 110**,‡‡ |
| Microform areas | | |
|     Files | 70 | 75 |
|     Viewing areas | 30 | 32‡‡ g |
| Office Areas | | |
|     Detailed drafting and designing cartography | 200 | 220 |
|     Rough layout drafting | 150 | 160 |
|     Accounting, auditing, tabulating, bookkeeping, business machine operation, computer operation | 150 | 160 |
|     Reading poor reproductions, business machine operation, computer operation | 150 | 160 |
|     Reading handwriting in hard pencil or on poor paper, reading fair reproductions, active filing, mail sorting | 100 | 110 |
|     Reading handwriting in ink or medium pencil on good quality paper, intermittent filing | 70 | 75 |

**Table 6.** *Continued*

| Area | Equivalent Sphere Illumination Unless Otherwise Indicated | |
| --- | --- | --- |
| | Footcandles on Tasks† | Dekalux on Tasks† |
| Reading high contrast or well-printed materials | 30 | 32 |
| Corridors | 20††,‡‡ | 22††,‡‡ |
| Toilets and washrooms | 30‡‡ | 32‡‡ |

\* Dekalux is an SI unit equal to 0.93 footcandles. 1 dekalux = 10 lux.

† Minimum on the task at any time for young adults with normal and better than 20/30 corrected vision.

‡ Equivalent sphere illumination: the level of sphere illumination which would produce task visibility equivalent to that produced by a specific lighting environment (see Appendix C). As of this printing, methods to predict this value during the design procedure have been or are being established. A device to measure it directly is still under development. Although methods have been established for predicting values of equivalent sphere illumination, the designer should carefully consider the guidelines for reducing veiling reflections as outlined in Appendix D.

§ Vertical.

\*\* Obtained with a combination of general lighting plus specialized supplementary lighting. Care should be taken to keep within the recommended luminance ratios. These seeing tasks generally involve the discrimination of fine detail for long periods of time and under conditions of poor contrast. The design and installation of the combination system must not only provide a sufficient amount of light, but also the proper direction of light, diffusion, color, and eye protection. As far as possible it should eliminate direct and reflected glare as well as objectionable shadows.

†† Or not less than 1/5 the level in adjacent areas.

‡‡ Footcandles or dekalux as measured with a light meter (rather than ESI).

*Source: Adapted from* Library Technology Reports *(July 1974), p. 3.*

## Enlargement

The preservation of historic buildings gained in national interest during the 1970s. Also, the steadily increasing square-foot cost of new construction has caused library administrators and trustees to look first at the existing building's potential for enlargement and remodeling before embarking on a new building project. Care, however, must be taken in evaluating the cost of the remodeling phase, for it may exceed the cost of new construction, and the remodeled portion may never succeed in being functionally effective as a public library building.

Hoyt Galvin itemized concerns to be evaluated before undertaking a project of remodeling, addition, and renovation, and he emphasized that a building program should be written as a measure for the potential.[11]

Joseph L. Wheeler, coauthor of the initial edition of this volume and eminent public library building consultant during his lifetime, urged consideration of additions to the front of existing buildings, bringing the buildings forward to the sidewalk for ease of access and merchandising. In the 1970s much deserved concern evolved for making buildings accessible to handicapped people. Many of the older buildings had a long flight of steps at the front entry, and any addition to the front should provide easy access for the handicapped.

Although it is sometimes feasible to add an elevator to the interior of a building, it is much easier and less expensive to add an elevator to the exterior, perhaps at the point where a new addition adjoins the existing building. It is presumed the new addition would be at sidewalk level.

Library building consultants are a bargain, even when the library director has building experience. A new look by an experienced consultant will reveal potentials overlooked by the board, staff, and architect. The consultant, or the library director and consultant, should write a building program before the architect is engaged and before a decision is made for remodeling and enlargement. Having the comprehensive word picture of the needed facilities, the architect can assist in evaluating the existing building for an addition, remodeling, and/or renovation.

### The New Building Project

The decision that more space in the form of a new building, or an addition, is needed will be the primary responsibility of the library director and staff, with concurrent advice and counsel of the board of trustees. Often, if there appears to be some question of community acceptance of the need, or if the director has no prior experience in the matter of determining the need for modern, functional library space requirements, it would be a good idea to call in an outside person with such experience, to prepare a feasibility study—that is, to look at the feasibility of providing additional space for the library service program. Sometimes this outside counsel can be provided by the state library's extension service or by a library system headquarters unit. The feasibility study, typically, will take into account the library's service plan as described in Chapter 2, or if that document has not been prepared, it will be necessary to prepare one, incorporating all the essential points. The questions will have to be faced: What is the additional space needed for? Why is it needed? Answers are basic to the library building program statement, to be discussed later, and to arranging for the capital expenditure, whether from public or private sources. The feasibility study will contain an objective statement of total space required, in both descriptive and statistical terms (square feet needed for the specific functions), and an appraisal of the present space. This appraisal should be both in terms of the quality of the present space and in the square foot shortages as compared with the requirements. Finally, there should be a suggested course of action to guide the library director and trustees to the next steps.

The feasibility study will be reviewed in draft form by library director, staff, and trustees to ensure that it represents the situation as it exists. In this connection, it should be observed that a competent library building consultant will expect to be able to render an expert appraisal of the situation, based on the facts. The director, staff, and trustees should not expect to have the consultant deliver a "directed verdict" that will tell them what they may feel they want to know regarding the need for space. The facts may support the need; on the other hand, the trustees may really feel that there is no need for the added space and will expect the consultant to "prove" that. This is not to say that the feasibility study, whether carried out by the director and staff or by an outside consultant, should not be subjected to exacting scrutiny by the trustees, public officials, and others. It should be. The facts should be checked out in every regard; only in that way can the groundwork be laid for a successful fund-raising effort, first, and the development of an adequate new addition or building, finally.

### The Decision to Build

The feasibility study will provide the factual basis for the decision to provide more space; also, how much and what kind. Once this decision has been made, and often it does take some time for review and consideration by everyone concerned, it is then possible to go to the next step: the preparation of the library building program statement. This document is an extension in detailed form of the space requirements as laid out in the feasibility study, plus any refinements that may have been brought forward during the review of that study.

If the decision to build has already been made, it is then possible to omit this step; in this case, the community analysis and other planning data will form the introductory portion of the building program statement.

### The Library Building Consultant

At this point, it will be very wise for the trustees to consider the employment of a library building consultant who will serve as the library's adviser throughout the planning and building process. Even if the library director, or someone on the staff, has had extensive experience in planning for library buildings, it will be a prudent investment to have an outside source of advice, review, and counsel. If the consultant for the feasibility study was an outside person—that is, not from the state library or system headquarters—it would obviously be best to continue that relationship, assuming that it was a satisfactory one. Lists of consultants are available from the American Library Association and usually from state library extension agencies. It may be noted that there are no standards or requirements in this field; therefore, in selecting a consultant, it will be best both to interview two or three candidates and to inquire from their clients as to their performance before making a selection.

The cost of a consultant in relation to the total project cost is relatively low, and the expense for a consultant will be likely to be the best buy of the project. Either the client (trustees and library director) or the consultant will describe in writing what services the consultant is to perform within what time frame; or the consultant, after discussion with the client and review of the problem, will draw up a suggested scope of services. Either of these documents will form the basis for a contract between the client and the consultant that will include the fee, the time schedule, and other details, such as number of copies of any written material to be provided by the consultant and site visits to be made. Lushington describes the consultant selection process and lists items to be included in the contract, in a planning handbook written especially for building projects in communities serving populations of 30,000 or less, but much of the information given can be applied in other situations.[12]

The consultant may be engaged on a per diem basis, or on a flat fee basis, which may be a specified amount or a fractional percentage of the project cost. The percentage approach is of doubtful value, as the consulting tasks required may vary with the specific job. The important consideration is the importance of the consultation to the project. In any event, there should be an agreed-upon upset fee (the maximum for the complete job), with the possibility of further work if and as required, and as specified by the client.

Sometimes it will occur that a board of trustees, or public officials, will decide that the library has a space problem and will bring in an architect to advise them. The architect, at this point, will be somewhat at a loss, practically speaking, since he will need to know what functions and requirements are contemplated in order to render a useful opinion. Therefore, it is never practical for the client to talk with architects until the feasibility study and building program statement have been completed and agreed upon by all members of the client group: library director and staff, board of trustees, and any other public groups that ought to be involved.

*Determining Building Size*

Space requirements are clearly a product of library goals, objectives, the library's community role—the entire library plan as described in Chapter 2. The experience formula shown below may be used for comparative purposes, but it would not be advisable to apply it in any given situation as a hard and fast statement of space needed. Many factors will enter into the computation in a particular community: the nature and extent of other library facilities in the area to be served, whether the library is a member of a system that will provide some services and resources, and all of the other factors that will have been incorporated in the library's plan of action.

Rather than apply a fixed formula related to the population to be served, it will be advisable to arrive at the size requirements by applying space equivalents to the library's action plan. In this way, the building size is determined by a series of blocks, or functional elements: number of books to be displayed on open shelves and stored, now and in the future; number of reader seats to be provided; other rooms or facilities called for in the library plan or feasibility study. Each of these elements will be in detail as to services for adults, for young adults, and for children. In addition, there will be space provided for a community room or multipurpose area, and the size of this clearly will be determined by local needs. How many and what kinds of programs and activities are to be carried out by the library? If there are no other community meeting room facilities available in the community, it may be desirable for the library to meet some or all of that need, but the library ought not to go into the community meeting business to a great extent. The main purpose of the library community room is to support and extend the library's service program. The space for administrative and supportive services will form another element in the requirements; these will be based on the number of staff needed now and in the future. Planning handbooks spell out exactly how much and what kind of space ought to be provided. (See also "Workrooms," on page 411.)

All of the foregoing will be added up to constitute what is known as the "library net assignable space," or the space that will be devoted to the library functions. Finally, there will need to be space for nonlibrary functions: mechanicals, corridors, custodial storage, stairs (as required), restrooms. In a reasonably efficient building, the library net assignable space should be at least 80 percent of the gross area. The size elements will have formed a critical portion of the feasibility study if that has been prepared, and in any event they will be incorporated in the library building program statement.

The field/performance theory of library space planning has been proposed by Meredith Bloss. This, he suggests,

will require a new approach to space planning. Factors that bear upon space requirements will be derived from examination both of the field in which the library exists, and the level of performance to be supported.

Determination of factors defining the library in the field: This includes inventory of present space resources in the array of library and information services in the community being served, and a review of missions of the other units in the array; what part and what kind of the total load is each unit carrying?

Determination of future intentions of other units regarding space, mission, or program: Before planning space requirements for *any one* of the library service units in the community's array of libraries, one would first look to the others to find out where they are, what they are doing, and where they plan to go, both as to space and as to program.

This will require more information, and perhaps more analytical know-how, than many communities have been willing to devote to planning a library information program.

As to library performance, the steps outlined in Chapter 2 under the library program will be carried out: "The field/performance theory can be applied to library space planning. It should yield a program that would be more amenable to accountability than the present factors based on input standards and the myth of isolated clienteles."[13]

*Experience Formulas for Library Size*

A variety of formulas have been devised over the years for estimating the size of a needed library building.[14,15] Formulas were omitted in the chapter on physical facilities in the book *Minimum Standards for Public Library Systems.*[16] Since the mid 1960s, there seems to be general recognition that a formula will not meet the needs of a given community. What is too small for one community may be too large for another.

Table 7 was included in the initial 1962 edition of this volume, and it is still about as useful as a formula can be.

Since 1968 the December 1 issues of *Library Journal* have included cost tables, prepared by building consultant Hoyt Galvin, on library buildings completed during the fiscal year ending June 30 of the year. The tables show summary square-foot cost for construction, furnishings and equipment, and other costs, plus detailed tables arranged by state of the costs for all the buildings reported. Even these up-to-date tables during this period of rapid inflation must be inflated by 10 to 15 percent annually, but the tables provide the best data available on public library building costs.

*The Library Building Program Statement*

A detailed, clear, specific written statement of what kinds of space are wanted, for what purpose, and of what quality is an absolute essential for the project to be successful. The building program is the client's statement to the architect, telling him what the client expectations are. The building

**Table 7.** Formula for Library Size

| Population Size | Book Stock Vols. per Capita | No. of Seats per 1,000 Popula. | Circulation Vols. per Capita | Total Sq. Ft. Per Capita | Desirable 1st Floor Sq. Ft. per Capita |
|---|---|---|---|---|---|
| Under 10,000 | 3½–5 | 10 | 10 | .7–.8 | .5–.7 |
| 10,000 35,000 | 2¾–3 | 5 | 9.5 | .6–.65 | .4–.45 |
| 35,000 100,000 | 2½–2¾ | 3 | 9 | .5–.6 | .25–.3 |
| 100,000 200,000 | 1¾–2 | 2 | 8 | .4–.5 | .15–.2 |
| 200,000 500,000 | 1½ | 1¼ | 7 | .35–.4 | .1–.125 |
| 500,000 and up | 1–1¼ | 1 | 6.5 | .3 | .06–.08 |

program states the functional requirements. It will not go into the design, unless the trustees or the community wish to specify a certain quality of building or lay down other givens; for example, in some communities there will be a desire not to have flat-roofed public buildings. There may be other requirements, but it is better not to tie the architect's hands with too many restrictions but simply to state what it is that the building is to do. The building program, in addition to the feasibility study elements previously described, will first list general considerations as to exterior and interior and will then go through every public and nonpublic room or space in detail. For example, the section on the children's room will describe the numbers and kinds of books to be shelved; will specify numbers of shelves, heights, and widths; and will list number of chairs and tables to be allowed for (although will not specify design) and everything else to be included in the space.

It is not possible in this chapter to outline all that will need to be covered in a library building program. If there is no consultant and the library director and staff are required to prepare the program, they may wish to borrow copies from other libraries that have had successful building projects, or they may obtain copies from the professional library of the American Library Association. If there is a consultant, the library director and the consultant should study the existing building. They should then have a conference with staff leaders and board members to think out the services to be rendered and the facilities needed to render the services properly. The consultant, or the director and consultant jointly, should write a program that will be a detailed word picture of the needed building, describing the areas within the needed building, the relationship of these areas to one another, and their size requirements, materials capacity, and seating and the nature of the furnishings and equipment.[17]

Raymond Holt included tables of space measurements, as well as a list of suggested topics for a library building program, in the Wisconsin Library Building Handbook.[18]

With all these valuable tips and leads, the library building consultant will more than earn his fee in the formulation of the library building program. If there are forgotten items and areas in the program, they will probably be forgotten in the building plans. The building program is the key that the architect uses in developing the graphic expressions of floor plans and elevations. The interior designer also uses the program to lay out the furniture and equipment.

*Site Selection*

An existing site may be used, but often a new site must be selected and purchased. It may seem as if every citizen in the community has become an expert in library building site selection. The site should be where the largest possible percentage of the people to be served will pass the site frequently in the daily pursuit of their normal activities. The site's surrounding land use should be compatible with a library, and the size of the site should allow parking and future expansion of the building.

Much has been written on site selection and space does not permit repeating it here, but the selection committee should prepare themselves for the task by extensive reading.[19,20]

It should be noted that much of the literature about library site selection tends to be somewhat simplistic, based on observation and opinion rather than research. Robinson commented on the general failure of public libraries to make use of market research techniques and findings, in respect to the advantageous placement of library buildings even though the public library has all of the characteristics of a retailing operation. His major theme is a demonstration of how one particular aspect of market research (retail site selection) can be related to public library location. He discusses the theory and principles of retail site selection. There is an apparent need for a piece of thorough research that would support similar principles on library site location. Robinson concludes that "it is bad enough to have no theories of library site selection, but it is even worse to remain ignorant of the theoretical work in a related discipline."

Robinson reviews the principles of retail site selection to suggest ways in which they might be used by public librarians. He contends that the patterns of retail site location have changed so appreciably in recent years, affecting the commercial structure of cities, that relying on previously held basic assumptions about library sites—pedestrian density, parking, closeness to retail outlets—"is reckless." He looks at the growth of suburban shopping centers and the decline of the central business district in many cities and suggests that library site planners may need to consider these factors as well. There may be some hesitation on the part of librarians to extend the principles of site selection from the profit sector to the nonprofit sector, but it must be considered that library users are, in a sense, consumers. The central point is that the assumptions that have been advanced by consultants and library directors about the placement of library buildings for maximum effectiveness need to be reviewed from time to time.[21]

### Next Steps in the Building Project

Once the building program has been prepared, the site has been chosen, and the architect has been selected, the project is under way. In some instances, the funds are secured or assured prior to the selection of the architect and his preparation of plans; in other cases, the funds are voted only for the preparation of plans and not for the construction cost. These funds will then be voted, or not, based on estimated costs, and (regrettably) in some cases on whether the community approves of the plans. It cannot be too strongly emphasized that the need for additional space or a new building should be considered on the facts and the merits of the case, rather than on design factors or costs. The space will cost a certain amount; the board of trustees, as the public body entrusted with the responsibility, should be allowed to build if that is the decision. It may be assumed that they will not spend the taxpayers' money recklessly; in any event, they will be accountable. The question, in short, is whether the community can afford a functional library building; that should be determined on the evidence.[22,23]

With the building size determined by the building program, the funds needed to construct and equip the building must be secured. County or municipal officers usually have to approve the project and the amount of money requested. Legal rights and procedures have to be considered. For some years, it has been usual to submit the building project to the voters for bond issue approval, accompanied by an active campaign to inform them about the project if success is to be assured.

With the program document, the librarian, board, and Friends must proceed to sell the appropriate authorities on the need for the building. The librarian must serve as the behind-the-scenes liaison for any fund-raising or bond issue campaign. When funds are in hand, the architect and interior designer should be added to the planning team. Raymond Holt's *Wisconsin Handbook* cited below contains nine useful pages of tips on the architect selection process.

### The Planning Team

The planning team for a library building project consists of the (1) governmental authority representative(s), (2) library director, (3) architect, (4) interior designer, and (5) library building consultant. The functions of the members of this team have been touched upon here, but writings by others are being cited so that those to be involved as members of the team can have an opportunity to inform themselves thoroughly about their respective responsibilities and opportunities as members of the planning team.[24,25]

An interior designer is an important, and oft forgotten, member of the planning team. Occasionally, the architect will have experience and talent or even an interior design department in the firm, but library experience is most important. A few interior design firms specialize in library interior work, and these firms should be considered. When engaged, the interior designer should be active as soon as the architect begins the development of floor plans. The following advice to a consulting client on furniture and equipment is included with the permission of consultant Hoyt R. Galvin:

#### FURNITURE AND EQUIPMENT

The furniture and equipment for a library should harmonize with the architecture and contribute to the efficiency of the library service program, and provide a comfortable, inviting environment. The furnishings should be selected or designed with appropriate beauty, durability and ease of maintenance. Special aspects of durability for libraries include the following:

1. High pressure laminates provide the only reading table surface capable of withstanding the wear and tear of public library usage.

2. Upholstered chair arms should be avoided since library use will soon create worn arm upholstery with the remainder of the chair's upholstery in good condition. Library budgets seldom allow frequent re-upholstery.

The interior planner to be responsible for planning the furniture and equipment should be designated as soon as the architect begins preliminary plans. The interior planner will test initial floor plans with preliminary layouts of furniture. At this early stage, the floor plans can be easily adjusted to accommodate efficient furniture arrangements. Ceiling lighting plans, electric convenience outlets, and telephone outlets must not be planned until the furniture and shelving layouts have been approved.

The responsibilities of the interior planner include the following:

1. Preparation of furniture and equipment layouts on early floor plans as a test of the floor plan efficiency, and consultation with the planning team to adjust the plans.

2. Preparation of final furniture and equipment layouts on the approved floor plan, and consultation with the architect and electrical engineer on ceiling lighting plans, electric convenience outlet and telephone outlet plans.

3. Upon approval of furniture layouts, actual furniture and equipment selections are made and illustrations of these selections are presented to official bodies for approval.

4. Upon approval of selections, biddable specifications are prepared; bids are taken; and recommendations are made to the owner on bid acceptance.

5. Inspection is made of furniture and equipment delivered and installed by the successful bidders.

Bids for furniture and equipment should be taken and contracts awarded some six months before the building is occupied. Some items such as steel bookstacks may require more than six months to fabricate and erect depending upon the number of back orders accumulated by the manufacturer. In 1979, furnishings and equipment including bookstacks but not floor coverings can be expected to cost $6.50 per gross square feet. These square foot costs have been increasing at approximately 50¢ annually.

## Preparation of Building Plans

The three basic phases of the process of preparing the plans should be clearly understood by all members of the client group, as there are decision times involved in all three phases, and these must be made at the appropriate time. After the architect has been selected and the contract for his work has been signed, it is desirable for the client group to have a preliminary design conference with him. At this time, the building program should again be reviewed in detail, and in discussion, in order to clear up any misconceptions about exactly what is wanted. The architect is professionally responsible for meeting the needs as stated, but these must be reasonable and well understood.

*Phase One,* plans preparation, is schematic design. The detail in this phase may vary from one architect to another, but basically what is to be shown will be area relationships, elevations, and exterior and interior design—in brief, a general, graphic representation of the building program in architectural terms. The architect is saying to the client: this is what the building, and the spaces in it, will look like. At this time, the client group will go over the schematics in detail and make any comments or criticisms necessary. It may be necessary for the schematics to go through two or more stages before consensus is reached. While the library's comments ought to be written, for the record, much of the exchange at this stage ought to be via conference between the architect and the library group.

*Phase Two,* preparation of preliminary drawings (or design development). Once the schematics have been agreed upon, the architect will proceed to the next step. These drawings will be as complete and specific as possible, showing furniture placement, windows, doors, lighting, heating, ventilating and air conditioning, floor covering, electrical outlets, materials for exterior and interior, and all other details. The client will spend a considerable amount of time reviewing the design development plans and will have as many conferences with the architect as are needed in order to be assured that everything is clearly understood. Any subsequent changes will be costly or, in some cases, impossible.

*Phase Three,* preparation of bid documents, also known as working drawings. This step follows approval of the design development plans. The working drawings will form the basis for the construction of the building. The client, by agreeing to the design development phase, has authorized the final plans to be prepared. That is why changes must be made in phases one and two and not in phase three.

### *Thoughts on Specifications*

In the past, specifications for library shelving, furniture, and equipment have been of the so-called "nuts and bolts" variety; for example, as to shelving, the specifications would spell out the gauge of steel to be used and other construction details. These were generally taken from manufacturer's specifications, sometimes verbatim. It is more practical from the library's standpoint to write performance, or functional specifications, for items to be purchased, that will state what the item is to be used for and what performance standards are to be met. For example, as to shelving, it might be stated that the shelving must be capable of supporting 60 pounds of books on the top shelf of a free-standing unit without tipping over; as to carpeting, it might be stated that it should be capable of handling a traffic load of X thousand persons over a stated time period. In short, the buyer should state the requirements, and the supplier should decide how to meet them.

### Workrooms

Adequate work quarters are quiet, orderly, well lighted, and attractive. Recent studies show that excessive noise and conversation cut production among clerical workers and executives. Noiseless typewriters, muffled phones, sound-absorbent ceilings and walls, including folded wall drapes, screening noisy equipment by absorbent end and back panels—these all help. Some extra-noisy equipment may have to be placed in an adjoining space. Plastic foam absorbent tile and rolls are now available.

#### Furniture Arrangement

To lay out a workroom, do not limit the thinking to the department head but have all the staff, especially newer workers, study not the present arrangement but what should be the logical sequence, to minimize steps and the movement of materials and to group related operations as closely as possible. Make a dotted line for the steps that each worker will take and another for the movement of materials. Try diagrams of various layouts to attain continuous streamlined progression of work and avoid backtracking. Keep each stage of the work close to the next stage, and related operations near one another, preferring a strip along the windows but usually leaving an aisle between desks and windows. Place storage shelving and files against inside walls, if that will not increase travel. Keep the whole space open and undivided; even low screens are seldom needed around desks. Confidential interviews can be held somewhere else in the building. Forgo barriers that create an obstruction in free flow of work. To cut travel time, each workroom, unless it adjoins a washroom, should have a one-piece washbowl, with a four- or five-inch flat flange on both ends on which to lay materials (not an expensive sink recessed in a bench of other material).

### The Work Station

This term refers to the desk, counter space, or other surface at which each worker generally sits and carries on assigned work. The most common work station is the office desk, partly because it is purchasable ready-made with needed accessories included. The former usual depth, 34 inches or more, with the desks set up in groups, generally wastes floor space, and the 30-inch depth is now in favor, with 48 or 54 inches instead of 60 inches of length. This depth permits spacing desks 32 to 36 inches apart for easier access. But desks can now be had in almost any size. A 30-by-40-inch desk and a chair take 18.2 square feet, but if the desk is 60 inches long they take 27.5 square feet. Most modern desks are adjustable from 29 inches (usual) to 30½ inches in height. Desks should not face each other but should face in one direction. They should not face the light; preferably, daylight should come from the left.

One person may do two quite different jobs, such as charging books at the loan desk, then moving to a terminal to process overdues, or to the catalog, where the operation requires an array of books and "tools." It is often better to leave the work spread out to save time in picking up and then laying it out again; several work stations need to be provided, each suitably laid out and reached with few steps. Conflicting formulas could be cited for space needs: secretaries, 100 square feet; department heads, 150 square feet. Most library departments need at least 100 square feet per station because so much material has to be laid out, especially in catalog and reference rooms. In mechanical work like marking, pasting, rubber stamping, and so on, arrange materials in pickup sequence in a half circle close to the worker.

The "Techniplan" or "modular" L-shaped combination of smaller desk plus work counter or machine platform, generally 18 inches deep, at right angles to the left end of the desk, and usually 26½ inches for a typewriter, doubles the work surface with a quarter turn of the chair. New low movable screens can be set up to give privacy, if needed. Consider simple work counters 24 to 30 inches deep, built in against walls and cut to fit odd lengths and irregular spaces around piping and posts. They utilize space otherwise lost and cost half as much as desks. Wood pedestals with three or four drawers are also inexpensive, can be placed to suit, and can support the work tops. Long work counters with 3- or 4-foot space allotments and pedestals, with a shelf on the wall above, are especially good for mending and so on, but also for constricted public departmental workrooms. A short work counter or table on wheels is useful; the setup for some operations can be moved to suit. Place materials and accessories most often used closest to the point of use, to be reached without rising. Building planning and interior design require technical knowledge and broad appreciation for function and aesthetics. Most librarians are not trained or experienced to undertake such projects without the advice and assistance of consultants. Whatever the investment it usually works out to be an economy in terms of flexibility, good utilization, and satisfaction with the work environment by employees.

### Notes

1. Edwin B. Feldman, *Industrial Housekeeping, Its Technology and Technique* (New York: Macmillan, 1963); also by Feldman, *Housekeeping Handbook for Institutions, Business and Industry* (New York: Frederick Fell, 1969).
2. Thomas Sack, *Complete Guide to Building and Plant Maintenance,* 2d ed. (Englewood Cliffs, N.J.: Prentice-Hall, 1971).
3. Bill Clark, *Professional Cleaning and Building Maintenance: How to Organize a Money*

*Saving Service Business or a Department for Floor and Building Cleaning* (Hicksville, N.Y.: Exposition Press, 1960).

4. Philip K. Piele, *Building Maintenance,* Educational Facilities Review Service no. 3, January 1972, ED 058 623 (Washington, D.C.: Educational Resources Information Center, 1972).

5. Marie D. Eldridge, "NCES 1974 Survey of Public Libraries," in *The Bowker Annual of Library and Book Trade Information, 1976,* 21st ed. (New York: R. R. Bowker, 1976), p. 252.

6. Bernard Berkeley, *Floors: Selection and Maintenance, Library Technology Reports* no. 13 (Chicago: American Library Association, 1968).

7. American National Standards Institute, *ANSI A117.1: Specifications for Making Buildings and Facilities Accessible to and Useable by the Physically Handicapped* (New York: American National Standards Institute, 1961).

8. Keyes D. Metcalf, *Library Lighting* (Washington, D.C.: Association of Research Libraries, 1970).

9. Library of Congress, *Environmental Protection of Books and Related Materials,* Preservation Leaflet no. 2 (Washington, D.C.: Government Printing Office, 1975).

10. "Recommended Practice of Library Lighting," *Journal of Illuminating Engineering Society* 3 (1974): 253–81, reprinted in *Library Technology Reports* (July 1974). For other discussion see Keyes Metcalf, *Library Lighting.*

11. Hoyt R. Galvin, *Addition/Remodeling/Renovation Projects, Library Journal Special Report* no. 1 (New York: Library Journal, 1976), pp. 61–62.

12. Nolan Lushington, *Libraries Designed for Users* (Syracuse, N.Y.: Gaylord Professional Publications, 1979), pp. 60–62.

13. Meredith Bloss, *The Field/Performance Theory of Library Space Planning, Library Journal Special Report* no. 1 (New York: Library Journal, 1976), pp. 52–54.

14. Public Library Association, *Interim Standards for Small Public Libraries* (Chicago: American Library Association, 1962).

15. Joseph L. Wheeler, *The Small Library Building* (Chicago: American Library Association, 1963).

16. American Library Association, *Minimum Standards for Public Library Systems, 1966* (Chicago: American Library Association, 1967).

17. Hoyt R. Galvin and Martin Van Buren, "The Programme for a Library Building," in *The Small Public Library* (Paris: UNESCO, 1959), chap. 5.

18. Raymond M. Holt, "The Library Building Program Statement," in *Wisconsin Library Building Handbook* (Madison, Wis.: Wisconsin Department of Public Instruction, Division of Library Services, 1978), chap. 4. Tables of space measurements: pp. 80–83. List of suggested topics for a library building program: pp. 219–229.

19. Hoyt R. Galvin, ed., *A Public Library Site Symposium, Library Journal Special Report* no. 1 (New York: Library Journal, 1976), pp. 15–29.

20. Joseph L. Wheeler, *A Reconsideration of the Strategic Location for Public Library Buildings, Occasional Paper* no. 85 (Urbana, Ill.: University of Illinois School of Library Science, July 1967).

21. William C. Robinson, *The Utility of Retail Site Selection for the Public Library, Occasional Paper* no. 122 (Champaign, Ill.: University of Illinois School of Library Science, 1976).

22. See Carlton C. Rochell, "Money: Secrets of Successful Seekers: Call the Shots Yourself," *American Libraries* (November 1977): 574–75.

23. Hoyt R. Galvin and Martin Van Buren, "The Publicity Campaign," in *The Small Public Library Building* (Paris: UNESCO, 1959), pp. 38–41.

24. Hoyt R. Galvin, *The Planning Team, Library Journal Special Report,* no. 1 (New York: Library Journal, 1976), pp. 74–77.

25. Holt, op. cit., pp. 127–32.

# 21 Measurement and Evaluation

Evaluation of the public library's effectiveness in achieving stated goals and objectives is a critical element in the administrative process. First and most significant, the board of trustees and the appropriating bodies wish to know what results are being realized from the funds allotted. The library's accounting of these results is the major basis on which the library's budget estimates will be reviewed. As has been noted in Chapter 7, there is an increasing interest on the part of budget review bodies to consider performance as a criterion.

Five aspects of evaluation of public library effectiveness will be considered in this chapter: the compilation of statistics, the measurement of performance (these two being closely related to each other), standards, surveys, and research. These aspects are at various levels of development, as will be seen. Much of what has been done in these areas until fairly recently has been of a relatively unplanned and uncoordinated nature, making it somewhat difficult to draw useful data for conclusions. Public library evaluation and measurement has been to a large extent the result of empirical judgments, based on considered opinions of leaders in the library profession and on reports on what were thought to be the more exemplary library operations in the country. This approach to evaluation has been moderately successful in the past, when competition for the use of public funds was perhaps less keen and when a budget could be argued on the grounds that a public library is a good and necessary community facility and that to be against it would be inappropriate and anti-intellectual. As the citizenry moves into the information age, and as the public library is presented with both the opportunity and the challenge of becoming an important and significant information resource for a wider spectrum of the population, it also becomes necessary for the administration, staff, and trustees to attend more carefully to measurement and evaluation of institutional effectiveness. And this can hardly be done in a realistic way without first being clear about the institution's goals and objectives—what it is supposed to be doing for the community, what *kind* of a library it is.

## The Significance of Goals and Objectives

This subject has been discussed at some length in Chapter 1, and we won't repeat except to emphasize again the need to have a clearly stated and understood statement of what the library is intending to do and to have this spelled out in terms that can be measured in some tangible way. The generalized public library goals of education, information, and recreation seemed to suffice in the past, but only because they were never scrutinized very closely, if at all, by reviewing authorities. More will be said about the matter of goals and objectives in the sections that follow, as they apply to the particular aspects of evaluation.

### Statistics

Practically every library in the country collects and compiles a statistical record of operations, of one kind or another. Counting the number of books lent, and sometimes the other materials lent, is probably universal among all libraries, large and small. This record of library circulation has been frequently attacked as a less-than-useful measure of effectiveness and has been defended as well, sometimes on the grounds that there is no other equally useful record and that in any case the public library is basically a collection of circulating books for community use, so therefore it is desirable to be able to report on how many books were circulated. It is not the purpose of this discussion to argue the point one way or the other, except to observe that when circulation statistics rise, the library operation is pointed out as successful; but when they fall, the problem is said to be due to external factors over which the library has no control! One is reminded of the comment of a crusty municipal board-of-finance chairman, who said when presented with a glowing report of a substantial increase in public library circulation over the preceding year, "What am I supposed to make of this? How many books *should* the library be lending?"

But statistics about the library's operation are important and do have some definite application in the process of measurement and evaluation. Childers has noted:

The term descriptive statistics can mean a variety of things. It can mean total counts of a recurrent phenomenon, such as number of registered users. It can mean nominal descriptors, which do not involve counting a recurrent phenomenon but merely describe a simple condition, such as hours of operation. It can mean statistics as the statistician defines them: data collected from a sample in such a way that they represent the whole population. . . . *[Statistics]* is one of the adjectives that is intended to describe how big, how fast, how often, how many, how costly, etc.

The adjectives through which a given field chooses to describe itself are at least partly a function of how that field sees itself. Librarianship's "self-perception" necessarily helps determine the kind of data it chooses to report. For instance, it is probably significant that book-related statistics are commonly reported in a variety of ways (total volumes, volumes added, volumes weeded, books per capita), while audiovisual software is often ignored or reported collectively as a single figure.

The adjectives by which a field describes itself incorporate the limitations inherent in measurement. First, a field can report only what it can measure. Second, there is a natural tendency to measure those phenomena that can be measured *easily;* and perhaps for this reason circulation is often the exclusive descriptor of library use, even though it is widely condemned as inadequate.

Descriptive statistics are supposed to aid in the decision-making process. They provide data to which judgment can be applied. They can be used at the microlevel—inside a single library outlet—to decide things about internal operations. They provide information at the macrolevel, for decisions in the national and international arenas. And they are used everywhere in between—by agencies, associations, and administrative units at the state, county, regional, and local levels.[1]

## *Statistics as a Factor in Administration*

What purpose is served by the time and effort required to collect and compile statistics at the local level? If the library has definite objectives and purposes, is concerned about how it is progressing toward avowed goals, and feels responsible toward its constituents, then it is under as much obligation as any competitive business to keep major statistics, to measure itself against others, to see what quality of library service is being returned for the taxpayers' dollars. The library should be in a continuing posture of accountability. Only by the systematic recording of performance data can the library know where it is headed and how far it is along the road to stated goals.

At one time, the American Library Association recommended a standard form for the reporting of local library statistics, but this is no longer in use. State library agencies, in connection with state aid to local library programs, usually require submission of statistics from each library on an annual basis.

It is important to note the difference between statistical records of *library* performance and work or job analysis of employees. Sometimes the staff will tend to view the collecting of statistics as a check on their productivity. That is a different but perhaps related matter.

Childers has commented on statistics as they are kept, and their validity:

The classical statistics reported by library units are characterized by a striking sameness over the years. They most frequently include the categories of:

materials owned
materials recently acquired
materials circulated
interlibrary loans
    (infrequent)
questions answered (rare)
materials processed (for example,
    volumes bound)
income, by source

expenditure for materials
expenditure for personnel
operating expenditure
capital expenditure
square feet of physical plant
seating capacity
clients registered
total client population
hours of operation

With the exception of "materials circulated" and the relatively rare figure "questions answered," there is no statistic above that suggests impact on the client. While certain kinds of special libraries—especially those hosted by profit-making organizations—are inclined to seek quantitative descriptors of impact, those descriptors are maintained for the purposes of managing internal operations and thus are not generally reported outside the host organization. The statistics reported by most libraries are related to input rather than to output (impact). They describe the resources through which services may be provided. They do not describe service per se; they say virtually nothing about the library/client interface, the point at which the user comes in contact with the resources of the library.[2]

## National Statistics About Public Libraries

Little progress has been made recently in gathering statistics at the national level on the state of the country's public libraries. Since the 1960s only one national survey of public libraries has been carried out. That survey was conducted in 1974 by the National Center for Education Statistics (NCES), an arm of the U.S. Office of Education, as part of the *Survey* series, *Libraries General Information System* (LIBGIS).[3]

The *Survey* revealed that the total number of public library service outlets in the fall of 1974 was 89,142. The results showed that there were 8,307 central libraries, 5,852 branch libraries, 56,276 bookmobile and other mobile unit stops, and 8,707 other outlets. Information was also collected for staffing, income and expenditures, collections, library loan transactions, physical facilities, and hours of operation. The method used in the *Survey* was to use data from all libraries serving 100,000 or more and a sample of 1,148 of the remaining libraries. The sample libraries were stratified by regions. Responses were received from 98 percent of the sampled libraries.

The *Survey* has been analyzed in an article by Little and in publications by others.[4,5]

## National Inventory—1975

The 1974 *Libgis Survey* was used as the data base for the *National Inventory of Library Needs, 1975.* Applying six standards, of "indicators" which will be explained in the section on standards in this chapter, the *Inventory* collected and compared data by state, region, and nation related to adequacy of service, professional and nonprofessional personnel, holdings of print and nonprint, acquisition rates, facilities, hours, and funding levels and needs. Data comparing libraries in urban, suburban, and nonmetropolitan areas show how such libraries differ.

*Other National Statistics*

The *American Library Directory,* published annually by R. R. Bowker and edited by the Jacques Cattell Press, is a source of statistical information about public libraries of all sizes throughout the United States, its possessions, and Canada. The information is collected by means of questionnaires sent to every public library listed in the *Directory.* Where the library did not respond to the questionnaire and to followup requests, information is used from other sources as available. The *Directory* has been collecting and publishing this information for a number of years and has enough status in the field to warrant general cooperation by libraries; practically all larger libraries, it would appear from a cursory examination, do indeed comply with the requests and supply the requested data. In addition to the usual kinds of directory and personnel information, the statistics included are:

Income total, and by source, when reported.

Expenditures total; by status, for personnel when given (professional and clerical). Also, for books, periodicals, audiovisual materials, microforms, and binding.

Library holdings: number of book titles and volumes, periodical subscriptions, bound volumes, documents, microform, audiovisual holdings, document depositories; also, special interests and special collections (descriptive). Also, consortia in which the library participates.

Population served; circulation; number of bound volumes in branches; number of bookmobiles. (The directory information requests the number and names of branches.)

The *Directory* for 1978 listed a total of 8,455 public libraries, including 1,162 public libraries with branches. The number of branches was 5,963. The total number of public libraries including branches was 14,418.

The significance of this statistical source for the local library director who is statistically oriented or motivated is that a reasonably accurate comparative table for libraries of a certain population class may be drawn up, by region or for the country, from which there may be drawn off per capita figures for support, staffing, expenditures (by purpose), circulation, and so forth.

For the listing by states, there is a statistical summary that lists: date of the statistics for the libraries in that state, the state's population according to the 1970 census, the population served by public libraries, the population unserved, total volumes in public libraries, total volumes per capita (and, in some cases, total volumes per capita served), total circulation, per capita circulation, total public library income, sources of income, expenditures per capita, the number of county or multicounty (regional) libraries in the state, the number of counties served, the number of counties unserved, and the amounts of grants-in-aid to public libraries from federal and state sources. (There are some variations, it may be noted, in the state summaries.)

The *Urban-Suburban Public Library Statistics,* compiled by Joseph Green, of the Montgomery County (Maryland) Public Library, was begun in 1969 and is published annually in the *Bowker Annual of Library and Book Trade Information.* This compilation notes that "pertinent data about comparative use between urban libraries and the suburban libraries around those urban agencies is our primary goal." Incidentally, Green offers another definition of a library system, as "one that is centrally funded and uses a common policy for controlling the basic operation of public libraries within a particular jurisdiction." (As has been noted at other points in this book, agreement on nomenclature is a goal much to be desired in the library profession; several definitions of *system* were put forth in the chapter on larger-area units of service, as having been suggested by writers and commentators in the field.) Green continues:

The purpose of our survey has been to develop comparative information between urban and suburban libraries; primarily an indication of relative use between the city and suburban libraries near a particular city was sought.

He reported in the 1978 compilation that fifty libraries were questioned and forty-four replied.[6] There is a problem about this, he observed.

All library systems that participated in the survey collect data, for whatever reason, to meet their own local needs and priorities, thus making it impossible to draw anything greater than informal comparisons between library systems. Until universally accepted and more precise information exists . . . for circulation, reference, and staff members, the lack of extremely meaningful comparable library data will continue to remain a problem.[7]

The Green statistical summary contains five tables: Tables 1–4 are arranged by reported population. Table 1 has total operating expenditures, state aid, and federal aid. Table 2 includes expenditures for library materials, salaries, other expenses, and number of service outlets. Table 3: circulation, reference questions, total staff, and professional staff in full-time equivalents. Table 4: per capita support, library materials support per capita, circulation per capita, and workload per staff member. In Table 4, the systems are ranked by volume in the following four separate categories: per capita support, library materials support (both in dollars), per capita circulation, and workload per staff member. There are, incidentally, some interesting correlations to be observed in this approach. High support does not necessarily yield high productivity or returns, judging from the measures employed, which are admittedly primitive.

A more inclusive statistical report is that which has been compiled biennially for a number of years by the Public Library of Fort Wayne and Allen County, Indiana. (The most recent edition was issued in June, 1979.) The universe considered is all public library agencies whose entries in the *American Library Directory* indicate populations served of more than 100,000. As noted in the preface,

in many cases we could not determine whether an agency was a library performing direct service to the public or the headquarters of a cooperative. Rather than miss any library unintentionally, we included many doubtful cases in the survey. This produced a list of 519 agencies to which we sent our questionnaires. 317 libraries returned usable responses. 49 disqualified themselves from consideration.

The survey published in June, 1979, was conducted in February and March, 1979, and responding libraries were asked to provide data as of January 1, 1979. Arrangement is alphabetical by name of city; statistical information listed is: population served, total budget, expenditure per capita, total appropriations for materials (books, periodicals, pamphlets, binding, audiovisual), appropriation for salaries other than maintenance and building, and salaries of director, assistant director, and beginning professional librarian.[8]

Various kinds of statistical reports are issued from time to time by state libraries and state library extension agencies, reflecting the data that have been collected by those agencies from local libraries. A notable example is the *California Library Statistics and Directory,* issued as an annual supplement to *New Notes of California Libraries,* official journal of the California State Library. The 1979 edition contained forty-seven pages of statistics about the public libraries of the state, including: population, area served in square miles, total number of service outlets, service hours of the main library, total weekly service hours, total number of staff, total number of staff paid from library budget and broken down by class (librarian, library technical assistant, clerical, and other), total income from local sources (also broken down into various categories), expenditures (books, periodicals, microforms, audiovisual materials, all materials), library staff, salaries and benefits, operations, contracts, transfers within jurisdiction and reimbursing other jurisdictions, capital outlay expenditures, percentage of operating expenditures for materials and salaries, and expenditure per capita and equivalent tax rate per $100 of assessed valuation.

The data also include a salary survey for thirteen classes of positions, figures on additions to the collections and total holdings in eleven categories, and, finally, data on total circulation, circulation by types of material, requests, interlibrary loans, and reference and reading aid.

*Interpretation of Library Statistics*

Since libraries began to keep statistics, the figures and their interpretation have been sharply criticized. In the 1920s, rapid circulation gains and decreased per-circulation costs in many libraries were actively publicized and brought a barrage of deprecatory phrases: "quality versus quantity," assuming one inconsistent with the other; and "large numbers are not necessarily better than small ones," implying that greater circulation must mean more and poorer fiction and less and poorer nonfiction lent, due to "publicity methods . . . which have undergone little change from their use in commercial fields."

It is hazardous to draw many conclusions from statistics. There is a lack of continuity, changes of bases and in methods of reporting, frequent gaps and errors. There is also the influence of general economic conditions on such major factors as total budgets, total circulations, and resulting per capita and unit circulation costs. Data arising from library operations have to be interpreted in the light of cost index changes, of salaries in parallel fields, of time-saving studies and devices in business and public administration, of paperback and periodical sales and the growth of school libraries, and of the library's access to another library, a branch, or networks. To identify such factors seems essential to research for planning.

## Standards

Standards are employed in various activities, and they have potential use in the evaluation of public library service. In practice, public library standards are somewhat different from those used in industry—for example, industrial and engineering standards. Library standards are usually viewed as models to be achieved or followed rather than codes to be enforced. Public library standards have been drawn up on the national level by the American Library Association, and hence can be applied only in an advisory way; those prepared by the state library agencies, and sometimes modeled on the national standards, are often used as the basis for distributing state aid and therefore do have force in that regard. The first statement of public library standards was a two-page document issued by the ALA in 1933. The second statement, in 1943, covered ninety-two pages of qualitative and quantitative measures. The 1956 revision moved somewhat away from quantitative standards and emphasized principles of service. The 1966 document, which has been cited from time to time in this work, was a comparatively minor revision of the 1956 statement, except that it declared that only by means of systems serving at least 150,000 persons could a reasonable level of library service be maintained. The standards documents through the years were prepared by committees of librarian members of the Public Library Association. The 1956 and 1966 statements both drew attention to the limitations of this method and suggested the need for research "to validate the conclusions that had been presented."

One of the problems about library standards is that there is not any agreement about what they are and about what they are supposed to accomplish. The South African Library Association, for example, has pointed out that there are many interpretations of the purpose of such standards: "Standards may be interpreted variously as the pattern of an ideal, a model procedure, a measure for appraisal, a stimulus for future development and improvement, and as an instrument to assist decision and action, not only by librarians themselves but by laymen concerned indirectly with the institution, planning and administration of public library services."[9]

Public library directors, staffs, and trustees probably use standards for all or most of these purposes from time to time in support of budget estimates, for example, or in connection with requests for capital outlays for additional space or new buildings. Problems have arisen when critical budget review authorities seek to examine the base of the standards and the library is required to admit that they are empirically generated and represent no more than considered opinions about what "ought to be" and an amalgam of experience drawn from the records of "exemplary" libraries. Other critics have observed that some library standards are descriptive, making it difficult to apply them for evaluation, that standards are mostly related to inputs to the library rather than outcomes for the users, and that standards tend to discourage progress in that meeting the standards implies that the library has an adequate service program. A major problem also is that the standards have tended to be stated for *libraries* rather than for services to the community, and also that they assume there is a model public library pattern that can be applied and put into practice in any town, city, or jurisdiction, regardless of local conditions, needs, other resources, and other local factors. While there are common elements among the public library concept, the fact is that public libraries necessarily must differ from one setting to another, and that the kind and character of the independent public library must be shaped by the role, the goals and objectives, and the priorities and action plan for that library, as described in Chapters 1 and 2. But there ought to be some common denominators and elements of public library service that would apply across the board, in *all* local situations, and on which there would be consensus.

In discussing the subject of standards as a tool for measurement and evaluation of library services, Lancaster has suggested that "there are definite requirements that must be met when formulating standards. Without these, standards have little real value or meaning. Some requirements for meaningful standards include:

1. *Research* and the compilation of statistics in the areas being standardized, perhaps the most urgent and basic of all needs in the development of standards.
2. *Measurability,* to provide a basis for evaluation and evaluative judgment. A service or other activity must be measurable in order to determine if the function in question "meets the standard."
3. The standard must be clearly defined and *definable* so that it conveys the same meaning to all who read it.
4. *Appropriateness* to the institution or service to be evaluated is essential.
5. *Authoritativeness,* which bases the standard on practices and research, not on assumptions or prejudices.
6. In order to be effective, the standard must be *realistic.* Otherwise, it will be ignored and result in wasted effort.[10]

## National Standards

Six "indicators of needs by public libraries" were used in preparing the *National Inventory of Library Needs, 1975.* These indicators were based on review of then existing state and national association standards, and were stated as in Table 8.

## State Standards

Ladd, in the *National Inventory of Library Needs, 1975,* observed that:

Using the methods of experimental research to identify community information needs and measure the library's performance in meeting them is a fairly new concept in the library field. The proponents of such studies recognize and emphasize that getting definitive results will take a long time. In the meantime, how are librarians, and library-users, to evaluate their institutions? Standards have been under fire for being subjectively established, not taking local conditions and needs into account, and not reflecting growth in interlibrary cooperation. It is said that they are based on an outmoded conception of library services and penalize small struggling libraries while encouraging flourishing libraries to become self-satisfied. Some responsible leaders advocate abandoning the whole idea of "standards" in favor of a set of goals and guidelines. . . .

Although standards continue to have an important role, for measuring overall progress and establishing eligibility for state aid, many professionals also want other kinds of yardsticks for planning and evaluation. Librarians have always known that having books on the shelf and a person on duty behind the desk does not guarantee adequate service.[12]

Ladd reported that there were "striking differences among the levels and types of standards currently applied to public library service in the states" in that some have the force of state statutory authority, some were statements

**Table 8.** Indicators of Needs by Public Libraries, 1975

---

**Staff**

| | |
|---|---|
| a. Professional | One full-time equivalent (FTE) per 6,000 persons in the population of the area served. |
| b. Support* | Two per professional, or per professional expected, whichever is greater. |

**Collection**

| | |
|---|---|
| a. Print materials: Books, journal periodicals, and microform equivalents | 10,000 volumes, or three per capita, whichever is greater, up to 500,000 population; above 500,000 population, 1.5 million volumes plus two per capita in excess of 500,000. |
| b. Audiovisual and other materials | Up to 25,000 population, 1,000 titles, or one per ten persons, whichever is greater (based on audio recordings); |
| | 25,000 to 50,000, 2,500 titles plus one per nine persons in excess of 25,000 (based on audio recordings plus at least 8mm films); |
| | 50,000 to 150,000, 5,300 titles plus one per 17 persons in excess of 50,000 (based on audio recordings, 8mm and 16mm films, framed prints, slides . . .); |
| | 150,000 and up, 17,500 titles plus 21 per thousand persons above 150,000 (based on full range of materials, dominated by 16mm films and audio recordings). |

**Acquisitions during the year**

| | |
|---|---|
| a. Print materials | One per 6 people up to 500,000 population, plus one per 8 people above 500,000 population. |
| b. Audiovisual materials | 10% of collection expected for population up to one million; |
| | 7% of collection expected for population exceeding one million. |

| | |
|---|---|
| **Net assignable space** | 0.6 sq.ft. per capita in the main library† |
| Operating expenditures | $9 per capita for up to 150,000 population; $10 per capita for libraries serving 150 to 500,000; $12 per capita for libraries serving more than 500,000. |
| Hours of service, main library | 45 hours per week for population up to 25,000; 66 hours per week for population of 25,000 and more. |

---

* Technical, clerical, secretarial . . . ; does not include plant operation and maintenance staff.

† Actual space in main library can be compared with the indicator of space needed for more than half of the public libraries in 1975—those with only a main library; for the larger libraries, the space in main library is not separable from the LIBGIS reports, which called for total "net area, in square feet, assigned for library purposes."[11]

*Adapted from the* National Inventory of Library Needs, 1975.

of the state professional association, others included long-range programs and goals for development, while still others simply stated that they subscribe to the standards of the American Library Association.[13]

## International Standards

The first compilation of standards for all kinds of libraries operative in twenty-two countries was prepared by Withers and published in 1974. Standards for public libraries are listed for twenty countries and cover some 200 pages. Withers observed, in respect to public library standards, that "there is no shortage of standards documents" because there is "greater uniformity of needs and perhaps a greater opportunity to work on common lines." Withers found that for the most part the standards are quantitative in terms of total expenditure, book stocks, and so on. There was general agreement on the purposes of the public library, on the disadvantages of the small unit, and on the need for cooperation.[14]

## Practical Implications of Standards

The hard fact is that standards for public library service, as they now exist, have very little if any value for the public library planner and administration; in fact, they have not been valid or used widely for a number of years in most jurisdictions. In order for the standards to become useful, several steps would have to be taken in order. (1) There would have to be a consensus among a sufficiently large number of libraries to constitute a valid statistical universe, as to goals, objectives, priorities, and action plans for public library service: a more or less uniform *definition* of public library service. (2) This definition would have to be followed by agreed-upon, acceptable, and applicable *measures* of performance, or output: what the defined library service has accomplished. (3) There would have to be a planned, coordinated, systematic collection of output data over a period of time—that is, performance measures as reported by the public libraries that had a consensus on the definition of public library service and that had agreed upon the measures of performance to be employed. (4) The participating libraries would also have to have recorded the input elements that had been required in order to achieve the stated levels of performance: how many books (per capita, of what level of quality and relevance) were required in order to meet a measurement level as stated. This assumes, for example, that a performance measure would in some way or in some degree be related to effectiveness as reflected in patron inquiries. The same process would apply to numbers and kinds of staff, hours of service, reader seats, and so forth. After a substantial body of this kind of data had been collected over a period of time, from a wide representation of similarly defined libraries, scientifically derived standards would be available. It could then be said, for example, that in order to achieve or maintain a certain desired level of performance, it has been determined by research that so many books of a certain relevance or character are required, based upon the experience of a number of operating and participating libraries.

Obviously, that state of affairs is a long way into the future, if indeed it is even in the future. In the meantime, the position of the American Library Association in respect to public library standards is that

future standards for public libraries must flow from the needs of the institution. This means that goals and specific quantifiable, measurable objectives must be determined by each public library and system in terms of local community concerns and needs. . . . Library performance must be measured by its outputs or services rendered, rather than by its inputs (budgets, materials added, personnel positions, buildings). In measuring performance, continuous effort must be made to clarify relationships between output and input.[15]

In respect to the existing 1966 public library standards, a Public Library Association committee in 1979

recommended [to the PLA executive board] the adoption of the position statement: "In the past PLA has prepared and endorsed national quantitative standards stipulating what the 'input' to library service ought to be. The latest edition of such a document is the *Minimum Standards for Public Library Systems, 1966* published in 1967. PLA does not intend to revise this document and believes that because of the local orientation of public libraries, standards of this nature are not valid on a national basis at this time. PLA does believe, however, that standards developed by and for an individual state may be valid within that state. In the spring of 1980, PLA will publish *A Planning Process for Public Libraries,* which outlines procedures which a public library can use to develop a program suited to the conditions and needs of a local community. This planning process may be useful to states as they develop standards. Once a sizeable group of public libraries have used this process, PLA intends to examine the results and assess the need to produce guidelines which would assist local libraries in planning."[16]

### Surveys

When librarians initiate a survey, it is usually because they either wish to have a frank evaluation to stimulate the library's progress or have become discouraged by trustee, municipal, or community indifference and realize that an experienced evaluation from outside may command enough official and public attention to produce remedies. The desire to be surveyed is usually a sign of a good library, though frequently library affairs reach such a low point in administration that the trustees realize a drastic change is due. They look to a surveyor to be frank and realistic and to discover facts and situations that an outsider can see with a fresh eye and interpret from a fresh viewpoint. The surveyor can lay his conclusions before the library director, board, and community, whereas the library director or trustees may find it difficult or embarrassing to do so, and their conclusions may be discounted. As one board president said: "We have found out more about our library from this first day of objective study by an outsider, than I ever knew about it in ten years as a trustee."

Surveys are becoming a common device. They have shown the trend is to simplify cataloging and technical services, circulation, reference, personnel, organization, book collections, branch systems, buildings, promotion, and so on. A consultant can hardly be effective without substantial administrative experience, familiarity with methods and operating costs, knowledge of books, familiarity with budget preparation, experience with public relations, and knowledge of the techniques to deal with the political consequences of such findings and recommendations as may come out of a survey.

The value of a survey is in its improvement of the library. In some instances, an outside surveyor can produce the best result. Lowell A. Martin points out that there are

several proper roles for the surveyor. He may have specialized knowledge neither possessed nor expected to be possessed by the administering librarian or the local staff. Examples are the building expert, when a new structure is in prospect, or the cataloging expert, when a change in a classification system is under consideration. Or the surveyor may be called in as a friend of the court to help make the case for a line of action that the librarian wants and may already have proposed. Thus, the campaign of the chief librarian for a more competitive salary scale or for faculty status for the professional staff of a university library may need outside support. The surveyor brings his prestige to the cause or his power of convincing, or both. The expert as a witness for the prosecution has its place, so long as this downright function is clearly recognized as such, but I question this type of survey when the so-called expert is used essentially as a rubber stamp.

The survey and the surveyor seem to me most useful when they are called upon to analyze a genuinely complex situation, with disparate factors and hard alternatives ahead. The most challenging of such situations often involve more than one library: the public or university libraries throughout a state, all libraries in a metropolitan region, or the several libraries serving students in a community.[17]

A surveyor usually makes an evaluation of the library service potential of the community, gathering facts and figures about the library, some of it by advance request, including a careful definition of what the library director considers major problems. The surveyor has to be sensitive to many intangibles—background, recent developments, personalities, relationships, viewpoints, and morale. This has to be repeated in each department and for each aspect—finances, book collection, organization, personnel, objectives, administrative abilities and ideals, methods, services, and public opinion.

The report (requiring twice or thrice as much time as the on-the-scene study) will be more than a summary of facts and an impressive array of figures. Its value lies in its program for improving the local situation. It must envision a possibly revamped organization, usually calling for better supervision. Unless a situation is so bad that only complete frankness can rectify it, a survey, both in its scrutiny and general development, should avoid embarrassing the present personnel.

## Surveys by Nonlibrarians

Efficiency experts and public administration analysts who know little about library services or operations (they may never have used a public library's reference tools and services) have to guard against the following as they make surveys: unwillingness to take time to study all the problems; preconceptions; failure to study, comprehend, and weigh vital against unessential objectives and procedures; and impatience with suggestions from staff members, who are often conservative and sensitive. Some surveys by outside consultants have included recommendations that librarians consider extravagant, such as proliferating small branches and elaborate overhead. Yet such surveys can be useful, and the number of commercial research firms specializing in library study is steadily growing.

## Self-Surveys

It may be argued that if a committee of perceptive executives in a staff can survey their own library, much good will result and the cost of an "outside survey" can be saved. Such a self-survey should and often does turn up unnoticed facts, but the participants in a self-survey will have to spend as much or more time to gather the facts as would an outside surveyor. It is also difficult to be objective about the intangibles of management and supervision. Staff members are often inhibited in their approach, hesitating to criticize or make drastic suggestions that might offend their colleagues. They may lack the fresh, challenging viewpoint that comes from wide experience in scrutinizing other libraries. Such self-surveys and evaluation, frankly and objectively made, stimulate improvement and should be encouraged, though they do not meet the need for critical intensive review by experienced surveyors.

The self-survey of user satisfaction, by carefully prepared questionnaire, is an effective device but rarely attempted. Do users get what they have taken the trouble to visit the library for? If so, to what extent, in what categories are they most or least successful, and why? Perhaps libraries need more of the competitive urge.

Surveys by door-to-door interviews, the outgrowth of new outreach services, might discover why families read no books at all and whether they have an idea of the personal help they could get at the library. Only the edges of this problem have been touched.

In short, research within the library on each department and activity is indispensable for good administration. Measuring and evaluating are not, of course, ends in themselves; they are a means to improve operations. They have to be aimed at a definite result; the data gathered have to be carefully planned to produce significant facts.

## Criteria for Measurement

For the most part, measurement and evaluation have been carried out with respect to the public library as an institution, as though all libraries were identical in purpose and context—as though any given library could be set up against a model set of requirements or criteria and it could be stated unequivocally whether that library was above, below, or at the requirement level for adequate service. For example, a typical "standard" or requirement is for a certain number of books per capita, without regard to the quality, relevance, up-to-dateness, or other characteristics of the collection so measured. This simplistic approach to measurement has come increasingly under critical review, and, as noted above, the Public Library Association is looking toward the development of performance measures that will focus upon outputs, in terms of the library user, rather than inputs.

Following is a summary statement, taken from Goldhor's contribution to Lancaster's authoritative treatment, of the importance of evaluating the library service program:

Evaluation is one of the important steps in the administrative process. In brief, it consists of the comparison of performance with the objectives of the agency, in order to determine (a) whether there has been any change in performance for a given time period, (b) if so, whether the change is in the desired direction, and (c) if so, to what extent. The theory of evaluation is quite simple; you need to have specific and clear objectives, and you need to have measurement tools which are easy to apply and are adequate for the purpose.

In practice, the process of evaluating library services is usually difficult and often completely lacking, precisely because the requirements in the theory are almost never met. Most libraries, as well as many other institutions, have no clearly defined, up-to-date, and well-thought-out objectives to govern their policies and determine their practices. . . .

When concrete and meaningful objectives are adopted and implemented, evaluation of the resulting services and products becomes critical. In such a situation, evaluation closes the loop and provides feedback on whether or how well the system is working. . . .

The second major element needed for the evaluative process consists of measures of performance which, ideally, are easy to apply, relevant, and reliable. . . .

Difficult though it may be to devise valid measures of library service, it is heartening to observe the great activity and progress in this regard during the last decade or two. . . .

Heightened awareness of the adequacies and inadequacies of the present performance of libraries will inevitably hasten reevaluation of the scope and mission of libraries, and will enable earlier decisions to be reached concerning proposed or possible services. In short, improved measurement of library service will surely increase the tempo of change in the profession on a sound basis.[18]

Lancaster has suggested:

It is feasible to evaluate any type of service at three possible levels: effectiveness, cost-effectiveness, and cost-benefit.

*Effectiveness* must be measured in terms of how well a service satisfies the demands placed upon it by its users. Such an evaluation can be subjective (e.g., conducted by gathering opinions via questionnaires or interviews), objective (e.g., the measurement of success in quantitative terms), or a combination of the two.

An evaluation of a system's *cost-effectiveness* is concerned with its internal operating efficiency. Such a study measures how efficiently (in terms of costs) the system is satisfying its objectives; that is, meeting the needs of its users.

A *cost-benefit* evaluation is usually the most difficult to conduct. It is concerned with whether the value (worth) of the service is more or less than the cost of providing it. In other words, a *cost-benefit* study attempts to determine whether the expense of providing a service is justified by the benefits derived from it.

The expression *cost-performance-benefit* refers to the interrelationships among costs, performance (level of effectiveness), and benefits. These interrelationships cannot be completely separated. In practice, it is difficult to differentiate between cost-effectiveness and cost-benefit studies; a particular change in a system may increase its effectiveness, its cost-effectiveness, and its benefits. . . .

Another distinction worth making is the difference between *macroevaluation* and *microevaluation.* The effectiveness of a system or service may be evaluated by either method. Macroevaluation measures *how well* a system operates, and the results usually can be expressed in quantitative terms (e.g., percentage of success in satisfying requests for interlibrary loans). It reveals that a particular system operates at a particular level, but does not, in itself, indicate why the system operates at this level or what might be done to improve performance in the future. Microevaluation, on the other hand, investigates *how* a system operates and *why* it operates at a particular level. Because it deals with factors affecting the performance of the system, microevaluation is necessary if the results of the investigation will, in some way, be used to improve performance.[19]

Lancaster has commented that many writers over the years have considered public library concepts and goals for the purposes of evaluating effectiveness. Most simply stated, the entire concept of the library may be seen as an interface between users and resources. Other related functions include accessibility (services on demand), exposure (making resources known to users), and making resources available in ways that will be convenient to users. Another way of putting library goals: to satisfy user needs with a minimum of the user's time. Most libraries also recognize another goal: to increase the number of library users.

Lancaster summarized a group of user requirements, which he noted

may be considered as criteria for evaluating information retrieval systems:

1. *Coverage* of the collection. The scope of the collection in terms of the extent to which it is complete in various subject areas.

2. *Recall.* The ability to retrieve literature relevant to a particular subject when a request for such literature is made to the system.

3. *Precision.* The ability not to retrieve irrelevant literature in response to a request to the system. Jointly, *recall* and *precision* measure filtering capacity: the ability to let through what the user wants and not let through what he does not want.

4. The amount of *effort* the user must spend in exploiting the system. If the effort required is excessive, the system will not be used. Some people may even prefer to do without needed information, if the task of locating such information is particularly burdensome to them. This point was well explicated by Calvin Mooers in 1960 as "Mooers' Law": "An information retrieval system will tend *not* to be used whenever it is more painful and troublesome for a customer to have information than for him not to have it!"

5. The *response time* of the system. How long the user has to wait to obtain needed literature or references to such literature.

6. The *form of output* provided by the system.

. . . . Coverage and recall relate directly to the accessibility/exposure objectives of information services; the other four criteria relate directly to the additional objective of providing this accessibility/exposure as efficiently as possible. . . .

These six criteria are applicable to the evaluation of library service in general. . . . Unfortunately, many of these requirements are in conflict. There tends, for example, to be an inverse relationship between recall and precision. What one does to improve one aspect may well cause a decrease in the other. . . .

The objective of the library is to maximize the accessibility of these resources to the user or to maximize the exposure of the users to the resources. In addition, the library should be organized to minimize the amount of effort required to obtain access to needed bibliographic materials, and to supply such materials as soon as possible when the need for them arises. The effectiveness of any library can be evaluated in terms of how well it satisfies these objectives. Cost-effectiveness can be evaluated in terms of how efficiently it makes use of available funds in the satisfaction of these objectives.[20]

## Methods of Measuring Library Effectiveness

The development of measuring library effectiveness by other methods than counting the number of books lent and reference questions asked (or answered) is fairly recent in the history of public library operations. There is still no measurement system that has been widely adopted and put into use by regulation.

Hamburg and associates have presented a complete discussion of procedures for measuring user exposure to library materials, assuming that in order for the library service to have some effect on the user, there must have been some kind or degree of such exposure. They recognized three possible measures of exposure:

1. counts of exposure: circulations, direct-in-library use, interlibrary loan, and indirect exposure (use by a library staff member in behalf of a user)

2. item-use days: an estimate of the number of days of actual use per circulation, to be obtained by questioning the user upon return of the material

3. exposure time: again, for circulated items, by questioning the user; for in-library use, by observing and recording the time spent by the user.

The Hamburg theory of measurement, as the authors make clear, is based solely on the view that the "library is to serve the social function of bringing together individuals and recorded experience."[21]

A study sponsored by the Public Library Association, and authorized for the first three of five proposed phases by the U.S. Office of Education, was conducted by the Bureau of Library and Information Science at Rutgers University. The research team sought to offer new alternatives for gathering statistics in order to measure the performance of public libraries, and in that process sought to identify certain library activities that can be quantified, such as availability of materials and staff and use of facilities. Six statistical measures were proposed: description of the collection (probability of user obtaining materials); building usage; circulation (in-library, outside library); patterns of reference usage; facilities usage (seating, copiers, meeting room, microfilm reader, record player); and profile of the public service personnel (median age, average length of employment in that library, average number of hours at public library service, average number of hours at other duties, highest degree earned, and average number of people assigned to public service by hour).[22]

The *Instructional Manual* for the Rutgers proposal, published three years later, listed eleven types of information to be collected, tabulated, and summarized:

1. The ownership and shelf availability of a random sample of recently-published books.

2. The ownership and availability of a random sample of periodicals selected from eight commonly-held indexes.

3. The shelf availability of materials listed in the library's shelf-list.

4. The number and type of materials borrowed for use outside the library.

5. The number, type and time-of-day use of facilities and materials within the library building.

6. The characteristics of persons using the library: occupational or student status, sex, contact with the staff, length of stay and general satisfaction with the library.

7. The number, type and time-of-day use of equipment, seating space and special facilities in the library.

8. The availability of staff to assist patrons.

9. The number of contacts and types of assistance rendered by public service staff.

10. Materials circulated for outside use.

11. The types of requests for assistance that patrons make of staff members.

The measurement process is to be done primarily on a given day, or a series of days, excepting that activities 1 through 4 can be done at any time, and activities 5 and 6 are preferably done on the monitored day.[23]

Another research project sponsored by the Public Library Association is expected to produce a proposal for measurement of library effectiveness, as part of a planning manual to be published in 1980. The draft of the publication proposes fifteen measures. These have been based on the measures developed and tested by DeProspo and others, and described above, and also other measures for testing the effectiveness of municipal agencies and services. The proposal would use a variety of methods for particular measures: patron observation, staff tallies, user surveys, citizen surveys, and staff surveys.

In summary, the future of measurement as a means of evaluation still remains somewhat clouded, and will probably continue to be so until there is a reasonable degree of consensus among most libraries about goals, objectives, and priorities. Stated measurements of performance imply such consensus, but it does not in fact exist except in the most general terms. In fact, the Public Library Association's official stance, as expressed in the 1980 planning process manual is that each library is to establish its own role, goals, objectives, priorities, and so forth. Hence, it seems unlikely that a uniform set of measures can be devised that will be applicable to all libraries.

One early critic of measurement, Wight, observed that

most measures of library services are not what they say they are; that is, most of our measures are of resources, not services. Library service takes place when a resource of the library supplies something that one or more persons (normally patrons) want. Books and information stored on shelves, in the memories of computers or of librarians, or elsewhere do not constitute services until they reach a person.[24]

Finally, as to measurement, some friendly advice was offered by Seymour and Layne, from the layperson's point of view:

For many years, one of the basic mistakes public-library administrators have made is to attempt to measure the value of their services in terms of "circulation" and "numbers of users," as if they were running a grocery store. Slowly we have come to realize that a library is not a profit-making business whose success or failure depends on turnover of inventory. It is an *essential community resource* like the hospital and fire department. Eighty-eight percent of all Americans give the public library top billing as the number-one cultural resource they want in their own community. That is not because they want to go into the library every day and take out a book. . . . Most people in the community want a public library available so it is there when they need it. One does not measure the success or failure of a hospital by the number of people who become sick or need an operation, or of a fire department by the number of homes or businesses that have conflagrations. It is the size of the community served, the number of people in the general population, which is the proper measure of the need for a public library and the size of its staff and budget.

Where measurement of library users becomes important is in the field of special library services necessitated because of the special characteristics of the community the library serves. It is significant for supplemental budget allocations to know how many disadvantaged users are given special literacy training or social-service counseling in a public library located in a low-income community; or how many blind or institutional users are served by a public library in a community with an especially high proportion of senior citizens. Here the numbers provide a measurement of the effectiveness of special programs and an indication of additional funding requirements.[25]

## Research

Statistics and their study are only one of numerous types of research. There are also the gathering and study of opinion and details of methods followed in other libraries and in other fields. Concern about what is being done in other libraries is a mark of sound public library administration. Most libraries that consistently gather data and report progress are the ones whose planning and decisions put them out in front, as leaders. They like to know what they are doing and why. The research on which to base policies and plans will include all pertinent information, including the study of intangibles that may often be pinned down by definite instructions and procedures. Many factors in planning cannot be measured by statistics. Well-planned, intensive publicity, or a change in the administration of a department or agency, may drastically improve both morale and effectiveness. The statistics will indicate what happened but will not explain why. Psychological factors will have entered into the equation.

It is readily apparent that the total amount of well-planned, coordinated research that has been carried on in the public library field is not at all adequate to the need, although there has been some increase in the past couple of decades. Libraries are required to adapt services and programs to the changing requirements of the communities they serve, but they lack the sound data on which to make intelligent planning decisions. Most operational policies are perforce dictated by the "conventional wisdom," by what seems to have worked out well in other libraries, and by empirical methods. The lack of substantial research in public library operation and administration has been laid to various factors. Public librarians are necessarily concerned with the day-to-day business of the library. They are often hard put to keep up with the daily demands upon their time, without the leisure to sit back and plan and then carry out research plans and proposals. The irony is that well-planned and well-completed research into many areas would result in much saving of time all around. But library science is taught as an applied rather than a theoretical science, for the most part, with the result that librarians are not trained to be sensitive to research needs and possibilities. Library schools have not trained students in research procedures or encouraged them to be critical of accepted techniques. There is very little funding for support of research, although the federal government has recently made grants available for research, much of which has been carried out for the benefit of academic and research libraries.

Ennis has characterized library research in the United States as "non-cumulative, fragmentary, generally weak, and relentlessly oriented to immediate practice." He further pointed out that what good research has been done is often ignored rather than being used as a basis for further research; in the absence of continuing work on major problems, it is impossible to build up a body of knowledge in any area. He expressed the view that the fragmentary nature of current research is illustrated by library surveys, each of which is carried out in isolation. Since these surveys differ in content and method, there can be no comparisons among libraries and no understanding of how and why libraries differ in resources and services.[26]

Some progress has been made. The Office of Research and Development was established at the ALA headquarters in 1965; it has since become the Office of Research, with a full-time director. At the outset, the role of the office was understood to be instigative and catalytic rather than operational in the sense of actually carrying out research projects. The ALA Office of Research, as described by the ALA, "focuses on the research needs of the profession, surveys existing activity and, in cooperation with the units of the Association, universities, and other agencies engaged in library research, translates unmet needs into active programs. The Association's Committee on Research is advisory to the Office with responsibility for recommending general programs, policy and priority."[27]

The first of nine stated goals of the Public Library Association is: "Conducting and sponsoring research about how the public library can respond to changing social needs and technological developments." The PLA Research Committee is

to coordinate activities of the PLA division in the field of research, receiving input from committees as research projects emerge as a result of committee business; to be aware of new research applicable to public libraries and make it known to members; to identify needed research in the field by whatever method may prove workable . . . to facilitate mounting and progress of research so identified through appropriate means, such as preparation of proposals, obtaining funds, finding investigators, and so on; and to communicate with the ALA Office of Research and utilize its expertise and assistance as needed and available.[28]

The PLA official publication, *Public Libraries,* now includes a department: *Research in Action,* containing reports on research of interest to public libraries.

There has long been a strong realization of the need for more research to assist public library administrators. The first edition of this book stated the case over and over again and listed eleven specific topics for study (many of which still need to be looked into).

Some additional impetus to the official concern in the library profession for more organized attention to research was provided by the publication of the much-quoted *Goals Study* by Allie Beth Martin in 1972. The *Study* concluded that a "program of extensive research and investigation will be required to provide needed knowledge for effective performance." Specifically the study encourages further research into characteristics of users and non-users; pros and cons of user fees; social and political environment of the library in the community; library education; operating constraints and advantages in terms of factors such as systems, costs, civil service, and unionization; and evaluation.[29]

Some additional subjects that need careful research, the results of which would help to achieve more scientific and responsive administration of public libraries, may be summarized:

1. The appropriate distribution of staff among professional, technical, and clerical functions; analysis and testing of the present rule of thumb, empirically derived formula of two-thirds clerical to one-third professional; study of the impact of automation on professional and clerical personnel requirements.

2. Cost-benefit-performance analysis of automation on technical and other services; amortization period for equipment, conversion investment, other costs. Does automation result in reduction of personnel costs; what increases in services result and can these be assigned a cost-benefit factor?

3. Is a single, monolithic national bibliographic system that will be applicable to the academic and research libraries going to be able to meet the several and often differing requirements of the wide range of public libraries? Or will a more simplified, more people-oriented bibliographic system be required for most medium-sized and smaller public libraries?

4. What factors are apt to produce high circulation per capita? Is there a desirable minimum? Is there a desirable proportion of circulation, among adult fiction, adult nonfiction, juvenile?

5. How should allocations for materials be apportioned among subjects, fiction, juvenile materials, books, audiovisual, and so forth? In the absence of standards, what should guide the library administration in the preparation of budget estimates for materials: circulation costs, other factors?

6. Consideration of the feasibility of a single generally accepted role and goals statement for public library service.

7. Analysis of performance measures currently in use and proposed. Study of the feasibility of uniform measures among libraries of similar purpose, identity, and community role.

8. Definition of reference work; measurement procedures for this activity; study of the relationship of information and referral; is this an extension of the regular library reference function or an added activity for a special segment of the population?

9. What are the functional elements of library supervision? Which of these present the most difficulties? Which of these elements satisfy executives least, and assistants least?

10. Do children who use library services when they are young tend to be library users when they grow up?

11. Is there any correlation between library programs for children (story

hours, films, puppet shows) and the children's use of library resources to satisfy informational needs?

12. Do children move from reading low-quality books to those that have greater information and cultural value and impact?

13. Both as to children's and adults' materials, what is the real meaning of the so-called "quality versus demand" issue in materials selection? Is there a dilemma? Does demand always imply low quality? Does high quality necessarily mean little or no demand? What is the public library's function as to content, level, character of the collection? Can this be determined by research, or is it entirely a matter of local policy arrived at by the value judgments of the staff, trustees, and community?

14. What is the correlation between well-developed school library facilities and the need for public library services for children? Are the two types of services actually used in different ways, serving different purposes?

15. Should there be salary recognition and reward for exceptional staff ability and effectiveness?

16. Reevaluation of library tasks, in terms of professional, clerical, and technical functions and activities.

17. Field analysis of library education: Do library school graduates really learn what they need to know in order to be innovative and effective in the day-to-day operation of public library services and programs? What procedures are there at present, if any, for exploring this area? What regular methods of communication should be established in order for this exploration to take place and become useful?

Doubtless, most public library directors and staffs could add to the above two lists several more issues and topics that they find of concern in the day-to-day management of the library. It is one thing to propose and urge the need for research; it is another thing to see that it comes about and that the research is planned, structured, and carried out in such a way as to be useful, and not just a report to be cataloged and shelved and forgotten about. Perhaps it would be a good idea to suggest *first* a priority research project: to explore the feasibility of public library action research: by whom should it be done, under what auspices, with what fiscal resources, and for what purpose?

There is not any question but that the administration of public library services could benefit immensely by facts to replace the "conventional wisdom" and experimentation that now guides most administrative decisions. The question is when and how the research will be performed.

### Public Library Administration: Challenge and Prospect

It is and will be an exciting time in which to be, and to look forward to becoming, a manager of public library services. There are challenges and problems to be overcome, but there are prospects for new solutions that have not heretofore existed to the degree that they do now. There is a current diagnosis which states that "the nation's public libraries are in serious trouble. For the most part, the public library of today is geared to the social needs of the nineteenth century which created it." In a way, that view may be a correct analysis. But it is not the public library *concept* that is in trouble. The need and rationale for an active agency that will collect, organize, and disseminate the resources for information have never been greater or more urgent.

It is repeatedly observed that this is an information age, and there can be little doubt of that. Information is *needed* by every person from earliest childhood throughout life, just to get through the complexities of daily living, to say nothing of adding some degree of enjoyment and cultural enrichment to life. According to the current Public Library Association definition of information (which regards it as "the sum total of recorded human experience—factual, imaginative, scientific, and humanistic—and the unrecorded experience which is available only from human resources"), is information made available by public libraries on a broad and generous scale? This is a problem, or challenge, of management. It is a problem of the people who work in and operate the agencies of the public library. The *idea* of the public library itself is as sound and firm as it was when the citizens of this country formulated it a century and a half ago.

It is imperative that public librarians remember who they are and what they are for: the concept of librarianship. Public librarians are uniquely the community's *specialists* in books and other informational materials; there are no others who are charged with this responsibility. People of all ages, from all walks of life, from various levels of information readiness have a right to expect that the public librarians will bring to the community a *mastery* of books and other materials that is based on intelligent choice and taste and that flows from reading, judgment, and belief in the social utility of the product. Librarianship is in fact a cultural profession. It assembles and organizes and mediates for use the best, most appropriate, most practical, and most inspiring of mankind's cultural heritage in recorded form.

The public library has been criticized for the vagueness of its purposes and has been urged again and again to declare itself. This admonition has to mean that public librarians must declare themselves, to say what they are for, in a positive way. The need for a social contribution is paramount. Librarianship has the potential for cutting across all the intellectual specialties, of bringing them together in ways that will permit and encourage the creation of new ideas, new thoughts, new inventions, and dreams. The public library is free, not so much because it is without cost (to the immediate user) as because its use is voluntary, without compulsion, individual, leisurely, as useful or as useless as the seeker wishes to make it. In the *free* public library, the individual may consort with the knowledge of the ages; in the mass medium, he or she is at the mercy of the single speaker. The library is indeed one of the last refuges of the individual.

The responsibility of those who plan and direct the public library services for general users is clear and profound. A couple of centuries or so ago, the libraries were largely the private domain of the upper classes. Now this concept of the intellectual elite has been broadened to include any person, from any background, who chooses to enter it. In that broadening process, it is of the utmost importance that public librarians maintain and uphold the high standards of selection and service that have characterized the public library concept. Public librarians should not be swerved from that high purpose by a false sense of "catering" to the new masses; people will be short-changed indeed if they now find their way to a library that has been watered down to what someone in charge has mistakenly considered to be a contemporary level of quality.

It should be stated again that the purpose of the public library is to foster, promote, and initiate the reading of books and the use of other related materials—materials that not only serve the community but also stretch the minds and imaginations of the people to heights of ability that they never dreamed of.

It is said by some that the public librarian's duty is to give the people what they want. This is construed by them to mean that the librarian has no right to intervene or to build a library based upon judgment and taste. Giving the people what they want, in that context, is the goal of the tradesman; it is successfully followed in the mass media, with great profit. People have a right to expect more than that from their professionals; and they do. They do not go to the physician to be given what they want but to be healed; they do not engage an architect and then tell him how to design the building. They have a right to come to a public library that has been created by experts; to a library that has value; that aggressively by its contents attacks the mediocre, the slick, the sentimental, the commercial.

It has been the purpose of this book to present some of the principles and practices of current public library management in the belief that they may be a contribution to the men and women who are directing and who will direct the nation's public library service programs. In public libraries, as in all other human enterprises, the differences among them are differences due to the quality, character, aggressiveness, and innovation of leadership. It is the administrative staff—the director most of all, plus the department heads and responsible assistants—who determine the kind of library service that is offered to the community. While there are, and should be, common elements and ingredients in all public library service programs, the ways in which these elements are planned and offered, the levels of excellence sought for and achieved, the results in user terms are determined by the people on the library staff. Beginning with the essential content of the materials collection—whether it is a good library or a mediocre one, whether it is entirely oriented toward the lowest common denominator of public taste or whether it conveys some sense of and regard for the permanence and the greatness of the record of human experience—will be for the director and the planning and administrative staff to determine. They will set the tone of the library, by decisions and by action.

The administrative policies and actions will also influence the quality and character of the other two major elements of the library's service program: (1) the personal mediation of the library's information specialists on behalf of the client-user and the supportive functions provided by staff, and (2) the display, storage, consultation, study space, and equipment that the library provides for the community.

Administration, in all its facets and contents, is the key: the difference between a successful and a mediocre public library service program. The wise and prudent public library director and administrative personnel will study and apply the principles and practice of sound management and will provide the leadership needed to give the entire staff, supportive and public service, the sense of participation and commitment that will be satisfying. They will yield an appreciated and necessary product to the people who are being served.

## Notes

1. Thomas Childers, "Statistics That Describe Libraries and Library Service," *Advances in Librarianship* (New York: Academic Press, 1975), pp. 5, 107–8.
2. Ibid., pp. 110–11.
3. Helen M. Eckard, *Survey of Public Libraries, LIBGIS I, 1944* (Washington, D.C.: U.S. Department of Health, Education and Welfare, 1977).
4. Robert David Little, "Public Library Statistics: Analysis of NCES Survey," in *The Bowker Annual of Library and Book Trade Information,* 23d ed. (New York: R. R. Bowker, 1978), pp. 248–54.
5. Analyses of the 1974 survey data have also been done by the research firm Government Studies and Systems, Inc.: *Improving State Aid to Public Libraries, Evaluation of Effectiveness of Federal Funding of Public Libraries,* and *Alternatives for Financing the Public Library.*
6. Joseph Green, "Urban-Suburban Public Library Statistics," in *The Bowker Annual of Library and Book Trade Information,* 24th ed. (New York: R. R. Bowker, 1979).
7. Ibid. in *The Bowker Annual of Library and Book Trade Information,* 21st ed. (New York: R. R. Bowker, 1976), p. 239.
8. *Statistics of Public Libraries in the United States and Canada Serving 100,000 Population or More* (Ft. Wayne, Ind.: The Public Library of Ft. Wayne and Allen County, 1979).
9. *Revised Standards for South African Public Libraries* (Cape Town, South Africa: South African Library Association, 1966).
10. F. W. Lancaster, *The Measurement and Evaluation of Library Services* (Washington, D.C.: Information Resources Press, 1977), p. 290.
11. Boyd Ladd, *National Inventory of Library Needs, 1975* (Washington, D.C.: U.S. Government Printing Office, 1977), p. 40.
12. Ibid., pp. 251–52.
13. Ibid., pp. 263–65.

14. F. N. Withers, *Standards for Library Service: An International Survey* (Paris: The UNESCO Press, 1974), pp. 10, 127–338.

15. *The Public Library Mission Statement and Its Imperatives for Service* (Chicago: American Library Association, 1979), p. 10.

16. Shirley C. Mills, "Report on the 1979 Annual Conference in Dallas," *Public Libraries* 18 (Fall 1979): 61.

17. Lowell A. Martin, "Personnel in Library Surveys," in Maurice F. Tauber and Irlene Roemer Stephens, eds., *Library Surveys* (New York: Columbia University Press, 1967), pp. 124–25.

18. Herbert Goldhor in Lancaster, op. cit., pp. vii–viii.

19. Lancaster, op. cit., pp. 1–2.

20. Ibid., pp. 7–8.

21. Morris Hamburg, Richard C. Clelland, Michael R. W. Bommer, Leonard E. Ramist, and Ronald M. Whitfield, *Library Planning and Decision-Making Systems* (Cambridge, Mass.: MIT Press, 1974), pp. 20–23.

22. Ernest R. DeProspo, Ellen Altman, and Kenneth E. Beasley, *Performance Measures for Public Libraries* (Chicago: American Library Association, 1973), pp. 46–57.

23. Ellen Altman, Ernest R. DeProspo, Philip M. Clark, and Ellen Connor Clark, *A Data Gathering and Instructional Manual for Performance Measures in Public Libraries* (Chicago: Celadon Press, 1976), pp. 1–1 to 1–3.

24. Edward A. Wight, "Precursors of Current Public Library Systems," *Library Quarterly* 39 (January 1969): 37–38.

25. Whitney North Seymour, Jr., and Elizabeth Layne, *Fighting for Public Libraries* (New York: Doubleday, 1979), pp. 154–55.

26. Philip Ennis, "Commitment to Research," *Wilson Library Bulletin* 41 (May 1967): 899–901.

27. *ALA Handbook of Organization, 1978–1979* (Chicago: American Library Association, 1978), p. 70.

28. Ibid., pp. 43–45.

29. Allie Beth Martin, *A Strategy for Public Library Change: Proposed Public Library Goals-Feasibility Study* (Chicago: American Library Association, 1972), pp. 50–52.

# For Further Reading

## 1: Goals, Objectives, and Functions of the Public Library

Carnovsky, Leon, and Howard Winger. *The Medium-Sized Public Library: Its Status and Future.* Chicago: University of Chicago Press, 1963.

Henry, Nelson B., ed. *Adult Reading.* Chicago: University of Chicago Press, 1956. 55th Yearbook, National Society for the Study of Education, part 2.

> Ten interesting chapters by nationally known specialists such as Asheim, Gray, Schramm, Dale, Houle, Witty. Priority reading for those intending to promote greater library use by adults.

Knight, Douglas M., and E. Shepley Nourse, eds. *Libraries at Large: Tradition, Innovation, and the National Interest.* New York: R. R. Bowker, 1969.

> The resource book based on the materials of the National Advisory Commission on Libraries.

Learned, William S. *The American Public Library and the Diffusion of Knowledge.* New York: Harcourt, 1924.

> Still valid as an educator's stimulating interpretation of his careful inquiry into the operating and services of many libraries. Emphasizes their potential value in constructive cultural and social progress.

Leigh, Robert D., ed. *The Public Library in the United States.* New York: Columbia University Press, 1950.

> This is the summary report of "The Public Library Inquiry," a three-year objective study of all aspects of the subject, made by a group of social scientists. Its conclusions have been influential.

Matthews, Virginia. *Libraries for Today and Tomorrow.* New York: Doubleday, 1976.

> A popular survey by an acknowledged authority and friend of libraries.

Price, Paxton P., ed. *Future of the Main Urban Library: Report of a Conference in Chicago.* Las Cruces, N.M.: Urban Libraries Council, 1978.

> Contains three thoughtful considerations of the main urban library: its historical role and function by R. Kathleen Molz; its future by Lowell Martin; and its interface with the National and International Network by Henriette Avram. In addition, there is a benign "humanistic" summary of the whole prepared by Lester Asheim, who was evidently a careful listener. These major papers are impeccably professional and purposely provocative.

Shera, Jesse H. *Foundations of the Public Library: A Social History of the Public Library Movement in New England from 1629 to 1855.* Chicago: University of Chicago Press, 1949.

A classic account that puts the modern public library in perspective.

————. *Introduction to Library Science: Basic Elements of Library Service.* Littleton, Colo.: Libraries Unlimited, 1976.

Wellisch, Jean B., Ruth J. Patrick, Donald V. Black, and Carlos A. Cuadra. *The Public Library and Federal Policy.* Westport, Conn.: Greenwood Press, 1974.

Report of a study by the System Development Corporation. History and current status of the public library, organization, financing, staffing, services, evaluation, systems, and recommendations.

## 2: A Program to Serve the Whole Community

Berelson, Bernard, and Lester Asheim. *The Library's Public: A Report of the Public Library Inquiry.* Westport, Conn.: Greenwood Press, 1976. Reprint of 1949 ed.

Survey and evaluation of characteristics of users and patterns of use in American public libraries; claims to show that libraries were founded to serve a small minority of the population: the better educated and the decision makers.

Columbia University School of Library Service. *Knowing the Community: A Manual for Investigating and Identifying Information Needs in Neighborhoods.* New York: Columbia University Library School, 1975.

Conant, Ralph W., and R. Kathleen Molz, eds. *The Metropolitan Library.* Cambridge, Mass.: MIT Press, 1972.

Collection of papers presented at a symposium; combines the views of specialists from the disciplines of both social and library science.

Guthman, Judith Domma. *Metropolitan Libraries: The Challenge and the Promise.* Public Library Reporter, no. 15. Chicago: American Library Association, 1969.

A section on "The Urban Ghetto Resident," which emphasizes the role of the public as an agent of urban change, is of special interest.

Martin, Lowell A. *Library Response to Urban Change: A Study of the Chicago Public Library.* Chicago: American Library Association, 1969.

A major study by an eminent student of library principles and policies that covers all phases of the library operations. Recommends clear-cut goals. Stimulating and provocative; should be read by all library directors and planners.

Palmour, Vernon E., and Marcia C. Bellassai. *A Planning Process for Public Libraries.* Chicago: American Library Association, 1980.

A manual that provides practical guidance for local libraries to use in drawing up goals, objectives, priorities, and standards for library service.

## 3: The Library Board

Batchelder, Mildred. *Public Library Trustees in the Nineteen Sixties.* Chicago: American Library Association, 1969.

Garceau, Oliver. *The Public Library in the Political Process.* New York: Boston Gregg Press, 1972. Reprint of 1949 ed.

A report of the Public Library Inquiry, this evaluates the political world of the public library. Of special interest are chapters dealing with the library's political potential and the unit of government for library service.

Joeckel, Carleton B. *Government of the American Public Library*. Chicago: University of Chicago Press, 1935. o.p.

This classic in library literature describes, analyzes and evaluates the position of the public library in the community.

Ladenson, Alex, ed. *American Library Laws*. 3d ed. Chicago: American Library Association, 1973.

"Basic general laws for all types of libraries and a wide variety of other statutory provisions." Federal government, the states and territories. Original texts of the laws are reproduced. Index.

1st supplement, 1973–1974. 1975.

2nd supplement, 1975–1976. 1977.

Robbins, Jane. *Citizen Participation and Public Library Policy*. Metuchen, N.J.: Scarecrow Press, 1975.

Young, Virginia, ed. *The Library Trustee: A Practical Guidebook*. 3d ed. New York: R. R. Bowker, 1978.

Appendixes. Index. The standard guide for trustees, edited by a former president of the American Library Trustee Association and a national leader in public library trustee circles.

## 4: Administrative Policies and Techniques

Likert, Rensis. *The Human Organization: Its Management and Value*. New York: McGraw-Hill, 1967.

Application of group dynamics techniques to management.

McConkey, Dale D. *MBO for Non-Profit Organizations*. New York: Amacom, 1975.

A thorough study of management by objective principles and practices by a business executive.

Mercer, James L., and Edwin H. Koester. *Public Management Systems: An Administrator's Guide*. New York: Amacom, 1978. 309 pp. Index.

Discussion of practical applications of management systems and procedures to public organizations.

## 5: Personnel Policies and Procedures

*A. Personnel in General*

Chaplan, Margaret A., ed. "Employee Organizations and Collective Bargaining in Libraries." *Library Trends* 25 (October 1976).

Guyton, Theodore Lewis. *Unionization: The Viewpoint of Librarians*. Chicago: American Library Association, 1975.

A historical and theoretical study; research and writing done apparently in 1970–1971. Investigates the causes and factors for the development of unions in libraries.

Ricking, Myrl, and Robert E. Booth. *Personnel Utilization in Public Libraries*. Chicago: American Library Association, 1974.

The result of a study in the late 1960s of the deployment of professional staff libraries; intended to aid administrators in using professional help. Useful as a tool to help in restructuring and eliminating professional positions by a systems approach to task analysis. The target group of the study: small to medium-sized public libraries and school libraries.

Schlipf, F. A., ed. *Collective Bargaining in Libraries.* Urbana, Ill.: Graduate School of Library Science, University of Illinois, 1975.

Stebbins, Kathleen B. *Personnel Administration in Libraries.* 2d ed. Revised and largely rewritten by Foster E. Mohrhardt. Metuchen, N.J.: Scarecrow Press, 1966.

Covers all phases of personnel; includes many examples of forms and policies used by libraries. Somewhat out of date, however.

### B. Supervision

Black, James Menzies. *The Basics of Supervisory Management.* New York: McGraw-Hill, 1975.

Cummings, L. L., and Donald P. Schwab. *Performance in Organizations: Determinants and Appraisal.* Glenview, Ill.: Scott, Foresman, 1973.

Gordon, Francine, and Myra Strober. *Bringing Women into Management.* New York: McGraw-Hill, 1975.

See also S. L. and D. J. Bem, "Case Study of a Nonconscious Ideology: Training the Woman to Know Her Place," in D. J. Bem. *Beliefs, Attitudes and Human Affairs.* Monterey, Cal.: Wadsworth, 1970.

Hereman, Herbert, and Donald Schwab. *Perspectives on Personnel Human Resource Management.* Homewood, Ill.: Irwin-Dorsey, 1978.

Kafka, Vincent W., and John H. Schaefer. *Open Management.* New York: Peter H. Wyden, 1975.

Levin, Selman. *You're in Charge: A Practical List of Books on the Significance of Management and Supervision.* Baltimore: Enoch Pratt Free Library, 1971.

Pigors, Paul, and Charles A. Myers. *Personnel Administration.* New York: McGraw-Hill, 1977.

Singer, Edwin J., and John Ramsden. *Human Resources.* London: McGraw-Hill, 1972.

U.S. Civil Service Commission. *Introduction to Supervision.* Washington, D.C.: Government Printing Office, 1970.

### 6: Public Library Organization

Bone, Larry Earl, ed. "Current Trends in Urban Main Libraries." *Library Trends* 20 (April 1972): 595–800.

Examines the main library as an entity in itself; eleven articles.

Kent, Allen, Jacob Cohen, and K. Leon Montgomery, eds. "The Economics of Academic Libraries." *Library Trends* 28 (Summer 1979): 3–120.

Some valuable points of view and facts for public library administrators in this issue.

White, Lawrence J. *Is Productivity Stagnant in Public Services? Some Evidence for Public Libraries.* New York: New York University, 1978.

Points to decreased productivity as measured by book circulation in public libraries; concludes that public libraries "operate at a low level of absolute efficiency in the use of resources."

### 7: Budgeting and Finance

Government Studies and Systems. *Alternatives for Financing the Public Library.* Washington, D.C.: Superintendent of Documents, 1974.

A study prepared for the National Commission on Libraries and Information Science.

_____. *Evaluation of the Effectiveness of Federal Funding of Public Libraries.* Washington, D.C.: Superintendent of Documents, 1976.

Reviews the twenty-year history of federal legislation and funding, in terms of the stated purposes and their impact on state and local funding.

_____. *Improving State Aid to Public Libraries.* Washington, D.C.: National Commission on Libraries and Information Science, 1977.

A report prepared for the Urban Libraries Council; "objective is to demonstrate that public library development should be an integral part of the state's mandate to provide public educational services."

Prentice, Ann E. *Public Library Finance.* Chicago: American Library Association, 1977.

Covers the entire range of financial issues faced by public libraries; offers procedures for accountability.

_____. *Strategies for Survival: Library Financial Management Today.* LJ Special Report no. 7. New York: R. R. Bowker, 1978.

A summary of current trends and practices: budgeting methods, cost of personnel, library services, resource sharing. Bibliography.

Steiss, Alan Walter. *Public Budgeting and Management.* Lexington, Mass.: Lexington Books, D. C. Heath, 1972.

Bibliography. Index. Covers public budgeting, effectiveness measures, strategic planning, operations planning and control, and other subjects.

White, Lawrence J. *The Dilemmas of the Public Library.* New York: New York University, 1978.

Examines the funding problems and the clientele (largely middle-class) and concludes in favor of a modest fee-for-service approach to public library support.

### 8: Adult Services

Broadus, Robert N. *Selecting Materials for Libraries.* New York: H. W. Wilson, 1973.

Covers the broad field of materials selection: principles of selection, background, types of printed materials, nonprint, selection by subject field.

Brown, Eleanor Frances. *Library Service to the Disadvantaged.* Metuchen, N.J.: Scarecrow Press, 1971.

A review of practice in libraries throughout the country.

Bundy, Mary Lee. *Metropolitan Public Library Users: A Report of a Survey of Adult Library Use in the Maryland-Baltimore-Washington Metropolitan Area.* College Park, Md.: University of Maryland, School of Library and Information Services, 1968.

Carter, Mary Duncan, Wallace John Bonk, and Rose Mary Magrill. *Building Library Collections.* 4th ed. Metuchen, N.J.: Scarecrow Press, 1974.

Principles and practice of book selection for public libraries; lists and describes book selection aids and national and trade bibliographies. Appendixes and index.

Cole, John Y., and Carol S. Gold, eds. *Reading in America, 1978.* Library of Congress, 1979.

Ennis, Philip H. *Adult Book Reading in the United States: A Preliminary Report.* National Opinion Research Center Report no. 105. Chicago: University of Chicago, National Opinion Research Center, 1965.

Futas, Elizabeth, ed. *Library Acquisition Policies and Procedures.* Phoenix: Oryx Press, 1977.

Includes twelve public library acquisition policies and excerpts from others. "Intended as a cross-section of the current thinking that governs librarians in selection and acquisition."

Gallup Organization. *Survey on Libraries and Reading.* Chicago, Ill.: American Library Association, 1978.

Haines, Helen E. *Living with Books: The Art of Book Selection.* 2d ed. New York: Columbia University Press, 1950.

The traditional view of book selection for libraries; emphasizes the need for librarians to consider the quality of their choices for the collection.

Kahn, Alfred, et al. *Neighborhood Information Centers: A Study and Some Proposals.* New York: Columbia University School of Social Work, 1966.

This seminal work laid the groundwork for the recent growth of information and referral services in the health and welfare field.

Kronus, Carol L., and Linda Crowe, eds. *Libraries and Neighborhood Information Centers.* Urbana, Ill.: University of Illinois, Graduate School of Library Science, 1972.

Papers presented at a conference in Illinois.

*Library Service for the Undereducated.* Report of a Conference Directed by Dorothy Bendix. Drexel Library School Series no. 15. Philadelphia: Drexel Press, 1966.

Martin, Lowell A. *Adults and the Pratt Library: A Question of the Quality of Life.* Baltimore, Md.: Enoch Pratt Free Library, 1974.

An analysis of adult use and recommended directions for development.

*Neighborhood Library Centers and Services.* New York: National Book Committee, 1967.

Describes programs for the disadvantaged offered by eleven public libraries and proposes a national program of centers.

Peterson, Richard E., and Associates. *Lifelong Learning in America.* San Francisco, Cal.: Jossey-Bass, 1979.

An overview of current practices, available resources, and future prospects from the Jossey-Bass Series in Higher Education.

*Public Library Service to the Disadvantaged: Proceedings* [of an Institute]. Atlanta, Ga.: Division of Librarianship, Emory University, 1969.

Talks by social workers Gloria S. Gross and Hugh Saussy, Jr., and librarians Meredith Bloss, Pauline Winnick, and Mildred L. Hennessy.

Savage, Ernest A. "Book Force." *The Library Association Record* (September 1956): 327–31.

Turick, Dorothy. *Community Information Services in Libraries.* LJ Special Report no. 5. New York: R. R. Bowker, 1978.

A review of current developments and operations.

Selected findings of the Book Industry Study Group's 1978 study of American book-reading and book-buying habits and discussions of those findings at the Library of Congress on October 25 and 26, 1978.

Warner, Edward S., et al. *Information Needs of Urban Residents.* Baltimore, Md.: Regional Planning Council, 1973.

A report of research conducted by Westat, Inc. under a grant from the U.S. Office of Education.

Yankelovich, Skelly and White. *Consumer Research Study on Reading and Book Purchasing.* Darien, Conn.: Book Industry Study Group, 1978.

### 9: Reference Services

Brooks, Jean S., and David L. Reich. *The Public Library in Non-Traditional Education.* Homewood, Ill.: ETC Publications, 1974.

A detailed account of a Dallas Public Library project in the early 1970s, in which the library acted "as agent to help interested individuals in the Dallas area to gain the knowledge needed to take CLEP exams successfully."

Bundy, Mary L. *Reference Service in American Public Libraries Serving Populations of 10,000 or More: Report of a Nationwide Survey by . . .* [a Committee of] *The Reference Services Division of ALA.* University of Illinois Graduate Library School, Occasional Papers no. 61 (March 1961).

Butler, Pierce, ed. *The Reference Function of the Library.* Chicago: University of Chicago Press, 1943.

Papers at the 1942 Chicago Summer Institute on large public and university library situations.

Childers, Thomas. "The Neighborhood Information Center Project." *Library Quarterly* 46 (July 1976): 271–89.

An article based on the author's evaluation of the project in which five major urban public libraries experimented with information and referral services from 1972 to 1975. Lists implications of the study and elements that contribute to the success of a public library's I & R enterprise.

Galvin, Thomas J. *Current Problems in Reference Service.* New York: R. R. Bowker, 1971.

Gotsick, Priscilla. *Community Survey Guide for Assessment of Community Information and Service Needs.* Morehead, Ky.: Appalachian Adult Education Center, 1974.

Hutchins, Margaret. *Introduction to Reference Work.* Chicago: American Library Association, 1944.

A well-organized, thorough treatise with much essential hard-to-find material. Worth careful study and frequent review. (One hopes that updating will mean adding and not deleting.)

Jones, Clara S., ed. *Public Library Information and Referral Service.* Syracuse, N.Y.: Gaylord Professional Publications, 1978.

A guide for libraries planning to introduce information and referral service.

Katz, William A. *An Introduction to Reference Work.* 2d ed. New York: McGraw-Hill, 1973–74. 2 vols.

Kochen, Manfred, and Joseph C. Donohue, eds. *Information for the Community.* Chicago: American Library Association, 1976.

Articles on information needs and the provision of information and referral services.

Phelps, Rose B., and Janet Phillips, eds. *The Library as a Community Information Center.* Champaign, Ill.: Illini Union Book Store, 1959.

Papers on major reference administrative topics, from twelve large college and public libraries.

Rothstein, Samuel. *The Development of Reference Services Through Academic Traditions, Public Library Practice and Special Librarianship.* Chicago: American Library Association, Association of College and Reference Libraries, Boston Gregg 1972 reprint of 1955 ed.

Valuable background for understanding current theories and policies.

Sheehy, Eugene P., comp. (with assistance of Rita G. Keckeissen and Eileen McIlvaine). *Guide to Reference Books.* 9th ed. Chicago: American Library Association, 1976.

This is the revision of the standard reference books guide, and lives up to the Kroeger-Mudge-Winchell tradition. It is designed as "a reference manual . . . a selection aid for the librarian . . . and a textbook for the student pursuing a systematic study of reference books." Has comprehensive, up-to-date coverage, effective organization and presentation, and accurate descriptions.

Shores, Louis, *Basic Reference Sources: An Introduction to Materials and Methods.* Chicago: American Library Association, 1954.

Primarily a valuable annotated list of reference materials, but chapter 1, "The Practice of Reference," is the best fairly recent statement of activities. It includes summaries of several important studies, such as those by Florence Van Hoesen, Dorothy Cole, and Helen C. Carpenter, which analyze categories of readers' questions in order to be prepared for them by knowing the type of materials found effective.

Spigai, Frances G. *The Invisible Medium: The State of the Art of Microform and a Guide to the Literature.* Stanford, Cal.: ERIC Clearinghouse, 1974.

An annotated guide that covers the history and technology of microforms.

Walford, Albert John, ed. *Guide to Reference Material.* 3d ed. London: Library Association, 1973.

Wyer, James I., Jr. *Reference Work.* Chicago: American Library Association, 1930.

This older book has a wealth of practical, stimulating ideas that are still valid. Reflects a dynamic personality and philosophy.


### 12: Children's Services

American Association of School Librarians. *Media Programs: District and School.* Chicago: American Library Association, 1975.

Standards for school media centers.

Bonn, George S., ed. "Science Materials for Children and Young People." *Library Trends* 22 (April 1974).

Fenwick, Sara Innis. "Library Service to Children and Young People." *Library Trends* 25 (July 1976).

Ladley, Winifred, ed. "Current Trends in Public Library Service to Children." *Library Trends* 12 (July 1963).

Eleven articles and an introduction on the collection, standards, and other aspects of children's work, by practitioners.

McColvin, Lionel R. *Libraries for Children.* London: Phoenix House, 1961.

An overview of current British practice as interpreted by an administrative leader with lifelong interest in children's work.

Spain, Frances L., ed. *Reading Without Boundaries: Essays Presented to Anne Carroll Moore on . . . the Fiftieth Anniversary of Service to Children at the New York Public Library.* New York: New York Public Library, 1956.

Describes early developments in work with children and the contributions of one of the leaders.

## 13: Branch and Extension Work

Brown, Eleanor Frances. *Modern Branch Libraries.* Metuchen, N.J.: Scarecrow Press, 1970.

A review of principles and practices; includes standards, space requirements, materials selection.

Coughlin, Robert E., Francoise Taieb, and Benjamin H. Stevens. *Urban Analysis for Branch Library System Planning.* Westport, Conn.: Greenwood Press, 1972.

One of the few systematic studies; considers factors of system structure, theory, and people or market areas served by libraries.

Geddes, Andrew, ed. "Current Trends in Branch Libraries." *Library Trends* 14 (April 1966): 365–471.

The history, organization, establishment, role, staffing, and materials collection of branch libraries.

## 15: Community Relations and Public Awareness

American Library Association. *Public Relations: What It Is—Who Does It.* Chicago: American Library Association, 1977.

Angoff, Allan, ed. *Public Relations for Libraries.* Westport, Conn.: Greenwood Press, 1973.

Carey, R. *Library Guiding: A Program for Exploiting Library Resources.* Hamden, Conn.: Linnet, 1974.

Center, Allen H. *Public Relations Practices.* Englewood Cliffs, N.J.: Prentice-Hall, 1975.

Edsall, Marian S. *The Harried Librarian's Guide to Public Relations Resources.* Madison, Wis.: Coordinated Library Information Program, 1976.

Kies, Cosette. *Problems in Library Public Relations.* New York: R. R. Bowker, 1974.

Covers all kinds of libraries and all kinds of relations—staff, patrons, trustees, students, and so forth. Each chapter contains a case history of a given situation, in both narrative and dialogue form, followed by the author's comments on how the case was handled and sometimes how it might have been done.

*Public Relations News.* Weekly. $89 per year. 127 East 80th Street, New York, N.Y. 10021.

For large libraries, this will provide stimulating ideas and accounts of projects, lists of materials, and so on. Many of these large-scale projects can be modified for small library use. Other materials, including bibliographies, are issued by

Public Relations Society of America, 845 Third Avenue, New York, N.Y. 10022. Its annual Public Relations Register lists 8,500 members, many connected with welfare, educational, and governmental agencies; no doubt their local affiliates could be enlisted to help on library promotion.

Rice, Betty. *Public Relations for Public Libraries: Creative Problem Solving.* New York: H. W. Wilson, 1972.

Deals with libraries in general; has some worthwhile thoughts on the philosophy and techniques of public relations.

Sherman, Stephen. *ABC's of Library Promotion.* Metuchen, N.J.: Scarecrow Press, 1971.

On the philosophy of library public relations and the practicalities of publicity and public relations: how to deal with newspapers, how to prepare materials for radio and television, even how to make one's own films and slides.

## 16: Nonprint Materials

"Films in Public Libraries." *Library Trends* 27 (Summer 1978).

Contains an introduction, eleven signed articles, and a list of acronymns. Subjects: a rationale for the film as a public library resource and service, the public library film redefined, the contemporary avant-garde film, film service to the elderly, captioned and nonverbal films for the hearing-impaired, the core film collection, 8mm film, bibliographic control of films, establishing a film collection, and licenses to videotape films.

Halsey, Richard S. *Classical Music Recordings for Home and Library.* Chicago: American Library Association, 1976.

An excellent guide to selection.

Murray, Michael. *The Videotape Book: A Basic Guide to Portable TV Production.* New York: Taplinger, 1975.

A handbook that explores the "video phenomenon" and explains each phase of video production, including portapak, the portable TV camera and recording deck.

Nadler, Myra, ed. *How to Start an Audio-Visual Collection.* Metuchen, N.J.: Scarecrow Press, 1978.

Bibliography. A handy brief guide covering the essentials.

Rufsvold, Margaret I. *Guide to Educational Media: Films, Filmstrips, Multimedia Kits, Programmed Instruction Materials, Recordings of Discs and Tapes, Slides.* 4th ed. Chicago: American Library Association, 1977.

## 17: Public Libraries in Systems and Networks

"Library Networks: Promise and Performance." *Library Quarterly* 39 (January 1969): 1–108.

Proceedings of the thirty-third annual conference of the Graduate Library School, University of Chicago, 1969.

Martin, Susan K. *Library Networks, 1978–79.* White Plains, N.Y.: Knowledge Industry Publications, 1978.

Nelson Associates. *Public Library Systems in the United States: A Survey of Multijurisdictional Systems.* Chicago: American Library Association, 1969.

## 18. Technical Services

*A. General References*

Atherton, Pauline, and Roger W. Christian. *Librarians and Online Services.* White Plains, N.Y.: Knowledge Industry Publications, 1977.

Butler, Brett, and Susan K. Martin, eds. *Library Automation: The State of the Art II.* Chicago: American Library Association, 1975.

Ford, Stephen. *The Acquisition of Library Materials.* Chicago: American Library Association, 1973.

Textbook for library science courses and a reference book for practitioners. Covers books and other forms of materials. Appendixes and index.

Kent, Allen, and Thomas J. Galvin, eds. *The On-Line Revolution in Libraries.* New York: Marcel Dekker, 1978.

Nyren, Karl, ed. *Buying New Technology.* LJ Special Report no. 4. New York: R. R. Bowker, 1978.

Sixteen articles by authorities on various aspects of automated circulation control and other computer-based systems for libraries.

Saffady, William. *Computer Output Microfilm: Its Library Application.* Chicago: American Library Association, 1978.

A technical guide to the use of this new approach; very useful.

*B. Conservation*

Cunha, George. *Conservation of Library Materials.* Metuchen, N.J.: Scarecrow Press, 1971.

Horten, Carolyn. *Cleaning and Preserving Bindings and Related Materials.* Chicago: American Library Association, 1969.

Tauber, Maurice F., ed. *Library Binding Manual.* Boston: Library Binding Institute, 1972.

Wessel, Carl J. "Deterioration of Library Materials." In *Encyclopedia of Library and Information Science.* Vol. 7. New York: Marcel Decker, 1972. Pp. 64–120.

## 20: Building Planning and Care

Cohen, Aaron, and Elaine Cohen. *Designing and Space Planning for Libraries.* New York: R. R. Bowker, 1979.

Lushington, Nolan, and Willis N. Mills, Jr. *Libraries Designed for Users: A Planning Handbook.* Syracuse, N.Y.: Gaylord Professional Publications, 1979.

"For those planning medium-sized libraries serving 200 to 2,000 people a day in communities of 10,000 to 100,000."

Metcalf, Keyes D. *Planning Academic and Research Library Buildings.* New York: McGraw-Hill, 1965.

Much of the detailed and practical information in this major work will be useful to public library building planners: the modular system, problems relating to height, housing the collection, lighting and ventilating, the planning process. Contains program examples, formulas, and tables; a wealth of material.

## 21: Measurement and Evaluation

Beeler, M. G. Fancher, et al. *Measuring the Quality of Library Service: A Handbook.* Metuchen, N.J.: Scarecrow Press, 1974.

A compilation of methods and techniques from many sources.

Hamburg, Morris, et al. *Library Planning and Decision-Making Systems.* Cambridge, Mass.: MIT Press, 1974.

"The result of a research project to design and develop a model for a library . . . management system, for university and large public libraries."

International Federation of Library Associations: Section of Public Libraries. *Standards for Public Libraries.* Munich: Verlag Documentation, 1973.

"Guidance as to the levels of provision needed to maintain efficient public library services."

Lancaster, F. W. *The Measurement and Evaluation of Library Services.* Washington, D.C.: Information Resources Press, 1977.

"A survey and synthesis of, as well as a guide to, published literature in the field." Developed as a textbook for library school courses in "the evaluative attitude. . . . Concentrates primarily on techniques that can be used to evaluate the public service of a library."

Line, Maurice B. *Library Surveys: An Introduction to Their Use, Planning Procedure and Presentation.* Hamden, Conn.: Shoestring Press, 1967.

"An elementary and highly derivative introduction to the subject, for the librarian who may be interested in conducting his own survey or who wishes to gain a critical if superficial understanding of the surveys of others."

Morse, Philip M. *Library Effectiveness: A Systems Approach.* Cambridge, Mass.: MIT Press, 1968.

Treatment of general mathematical models with which to analyze the use of library materials.

Withers, F. N. *Standards for Library Service: An International Survey.* Paris: The UNESCO Press, 1974.

A compilation of standards in effect in twenty-two countries, including standards for public libraries in twenty countries.

# Index